Measurement Theory and Applications
for the Social Sciences

Methodology in the Social Sciences

David A. Kenny, Founding Editor
Todd D. Little, Series Editor
www.guilford.com/MSS

This series provides applied researchers and students with analysis and research design books that emphasize the use of methods to answer research questions. Rather than emphasizing statistical theory, each volume in the series illustrates when a technique should (and should not) be used and how the output from available software programs should (and should not) be interpreted. Common pitfalls as well as areas of further development are clearly articulated.

RECENT VOLUMES

DOING STATISTICAL MEDIATION AND MODERATION
  Paul E. Jose

LONGITUDINAL STRUCTURAL EQUATION MODELING
  Todd D. Little

BAYESIAN STATISTICS FOR THE SOCIAL SCIENCES
  David Kaplan

CONFIRMATORY FACTOR ANALYSIS FOR APPLIED RESEARCH, SECOND EDITION
  Timothy A. Brown

PRINCIPLES AND PRACTICE OF STRUCTURAL EQUATION MODELING, FOURTH EDITION
  Rex B. Kline

HYPOTHESIS TESTING AND MODEL SELECTION IN THE SOCIAL SCIENCES
  David L. Weakliem

REGRESSION ANALYSIS AND LINEAR MODELS: CONCEPTS, APPLICATIONS, AND IMPLEMENTATION
  Richard B. Darlington and Andrew F. Hayes

GROWTH MODELING: STRUCTURAL EQUATION AND MULTILEVEL MODELING APPROACHES
  Kevin J. Grimm, Nilam Ram, and Ryne Estabrook

PSYCHOMETRIC METHODS: THEORY INTO PRACTICE
  Larry R. Price

INTRODUCTION TO MEDIATION, MODERATION, AND CONDITIONAL PROCESS ANALYSIS: A REGRESSION-BASED APPROACH, SECOND EDITION
  Andrew F. Hayes

MEASUREMENT THEORY AND APPLICATIONS FOR THE SOCIAL SCIENCES
  Deborah L. Bandalos

Measurement Theory and Applications for the Social Sciences

Deborah L. Bandalos

Series Editor's Note by Todd D. Little

THE GUILFORD PRESS
New York   London

Library of Congress Cataloging-in-Publication Data

Names: Bandalos, Deborah L., author.
Title: Measurement theory and applications for the social sciences / Deborah
  L. Bandalos.
Description: New York: Guilford Press, [2018] | Series: Methodology in the
  social sciences | Includes bibliographical references and index.
Identifiers: LCCN 2017007303 | ISBN 9781462532131 (hardcover)
Subjects: LCSH: Social sciences—Statistical methods. | Social
  sciences—Methodology.
Classification: LCC HA29 .B356 2018 | DDC 300.72/7—dc23
LC record available at *https://lccn.loc.gov/2017007303*

In memory of my mother, father, sister, and brother, who all would have been so proud of this book

Series Editor's Note

Measurement, measurement, measurement: It is such a critical part of quality research, yet it is too often neglected or assumed to be relatively unimportant compared to the design or analysis phases. The phrase "garbage in, garbage out" encapsulates what happens when measurement is neglected. The theory and craft of measurement is, in my view, more important than the analysis phase and perhaps even the design phase. High-quality measurement yields high-quality data, which makes the analysis phase almost pro forma. Creating reliable and valid indicators of constructs is underemphasized in many graduate training programs. The vestiges of neglecting the measurement phase degrade whole programs of research in a compounding manner. Thank goodness we now have Deborah Bandalos's book, *Measurement Theory and Applications for the Social Sciences*.

Bandalos is the quintessential person to author this comprehensive book on measurement theory. She brings a wealth of experience and acumen to the topics covered and she's reached out to a couple of top-notch colleagues (Christine DeMars and Laine Bradshaw) to bring their particular expertise to two chapters (on item response theory and diagnostic classification models, respectively). All chapters emphasize a conceptual understanding from ground-floor principles to the pinnacle of current knowledge and understanding on any given topic. Bandalos also adds extensive exercises at the end of each chapter that, when combined with the articulate and clear presentation of each topic, promote deep learning and critical thinking. Because the book is flexibly organized, instructors can easily assemble a curriculum and syllabus that fit the needs of any course, whether for undergraduates or graduates or at the introductory, intermediate, or advanced level.

Bandalos is a natural communicator. With a balance of humor and lilting exposition, she presents clear explanations accompanied by useful real-world examples from a variety of social and behavioral science disciplines. She's methodical and thorough in taking us through each topic, decision by decision, and each equation, step by step. This level of clarity and depth yields a comprehensive textbook for students as well as a reference volume for experienced researchers. The breadth of topics spans all the essential topics in the field of measurement, including scale development, item writing and analysis, and reliability and validity. She also covers more advanced topics such as exploratory and confirmatory factor analysis, item response theory, diagnostic classification models, standard setting, generalizability theory, and equating, as well as test bias, fairness, and legal issues.

As a fellow disciple of the need for valid and reliable measurement practices, I laud Debbi Bandalos for adding this valuable jewel to the collection of works in my *Methodology in the Social Sciences* series. I see this book as one of her crowning achievements in a remarkable and illustrious career.

With gratitude and, as always, enjoy!

TODD D. LITTLE
Wit's End
Lakeside, Montana

Preface

Whether we like it or not, testing is pervasive in the modern world. It is difficult to imagine any aspect of life in which testing is not involved. Of course, testing is widely used in education, psychology, employment settings, and certification for various professions. And during even a brief encounter with news or social media outlets, readers are bombarded with information obtained from opinion and attitude surveys. Add to these the many informal "tests" designed to answer such weighty questions as "What kind of tree are you?" or "Do you party like a true rock star?" and one begins to wonder whether there is any issue that does not involve testing of some sort. Given this, I could make (and have made; see Bandalos & Kopp, 2012) the argument that some knowledge of the theory and practice of testing is essential for an informed citizenry.

Unfortunately, even in professions such as teaching, in which knowledge of testing is clearly essential, the majority of training programs provide little instruction in this area (Plake, Impara, & Fagan, 1993; Schaefer & Lissitz, 1987; Wise & Conoley, 1993). Aiken, West, and Millsap (2008) reported that fewer than half of the professors teaching in graduate-level psychology departments felt their students had adequate knowledge of even the most basic measurement concepts. Although many excellent textbooks on measurement theory exist, they are too often outdated, overly technical or otherwise inaccessible, or not sufficiently comprehensive.

My goal in writing this book was therefore to provide a user-friendly and up-to-date text to introduce readers to the field of measurement theory and its applications. It is true that many measurement theory concepts are somewhat technical, but I have made every attempt to make these concepts accessible through the use of clear explanations and illustrative examples. When equations are presented, they are accompanied by verbal descriptions of the underlying concepts. Exercises focused on conceptual understanding as well as computational ability are included for each chapter.

THE AUDIENCE FOR THIS BOOK

I have written this book for those who will in some way be involved in testing. Such involvement can take a variety of forms and includes those who develop tests and study their properties, those who select and administer tests and interpret their results, and those who use tests in research or evaluation studies. These audiences differ considerably in what they need to know about measurement theory and the depth at which they need to know it, so my goal in writing this book has been to provide treatments of measurement topics that are accessible to a variety of readers. To this end, I present most material conceptually, rather than mathematically, making liberal use of examples. Some topics, however, are inherently mathematical, and some readers will want at least some of the mathematical underpinnings of the measurement concepts. I have therefore tried to adopt a middle ground, presenting mathematical details for topics that require them but accompanying these with conceptual descriptions and examples. Of course, in trying to please everyone, I run the risk of pleasing no one, and I am sure there will be times you wish I had provided more or less detail, more or fewer examples, or more or less mathematical background. With the permission of your instructor, please feel free to skip through details, mathematical underpinnings, or examples that do not enhance your understanding of the material and concentrate on those that do.

With regard to the background required to read and understand this book, I assume that you are at least somewhat familiar with algebra. On the rare occasions I use matrix operations, I accompany them with explanations that should allow you to follow the discussion. I also assume you are familiar with correlation and regression, preferably multiple regression. If you are not, you may want to read through the relevant sections of one of the many introductory statistics or multiple regression textbooks available.

Given my belief in the public's need for measurement knowledge, I would like to think that this book would be read by every member of society. But as much as I would like to think this, I am compelled by rationality to admit it is unlikely. I have, however, tried to make the book accessible to as wide a variety of students in the social sciences as possible. The primary audience for the book is graduate students and advanced undergraduate students in the social sciences. Students in disciplines such as education, psychology, business, social work, and the health sciences who are training for careers in which they will use tests in some way will benefit from this book. Specifically, this book is targeted to those whose future (or current) career involves selecting, administering, interpreting, or developing tests. Because of its comprehensiveness, this book can also serve as a reference for those who are currently involved in testing activities. In addition to the essential measurement topics of reliability and validity, I include chapters on item writing and analysis, scale development, exploratory and confirmatory factor analysis, item response theory, bias and fairness in testing, equating, standard setting, and cognitive diagnostic models. I assume readers will have some knowledge of introductory and intermediate statistical concepts, including analysis of variance (ANOVA) and multiple regression. As much as possible, I have steered clear of matrix algebra and calculus, but in the few instances in which these are used I provide explanations in plain English.

ORGANIZATION OF THE BOOK

The chapters in the book can be broken down into three sections. The first section covers guidelines for writing both cognitive and affective items, and conducting an item analysis. This section also includes an introductory chapter in which I define terminology and present a brief history of testing and a chapter on test score interpretation in which I discuss types of scores that are commonly used, such as z- and T-scores, percentiles, stanines, normal curve equivalents, and grade equivalents. The chapters in the first section could be used as the basis for a course in scale development, as well as the first part of a broader course in measurement theory or psychometrics.

In the second section of the book, I cover the basic psychometric properties of reliability and validity. I break the material on reliability into four chapters. In the first of these chapters, I provide an introduction to reliability and the classical test theory model. In the second, I discuss commonly used methods of assessing reliability, including coefficients of internal consistency, equivalence, and test–retest consistency. In this chapter, I also discuss the standard error of measurement and the reliability of difference scores. The third reliability chapter is devoted to interrater agreement and reliability. I chose to devote a separate chapter to these topics because they are often given short shrift in measurement texts. In the fourth chapter, I cover generalizability theory (G theory). In the chapter on validity theory, I first discuss the historical origins of this concept and its earlier manifestations in the form of the "three C's": content, criterion-related, and construct validity. I then present newer conceptualizations of measurement validity and sources of validity evidence, and connect these with the latest recommendations from the *Standards for Educational and Psychological Testing* (American Educational Research Association, American Psychological Association, & National Council on Measurement in Education, 2014). The chapters in the first and second sections could form the basis for an introductory course in measurement theory for graduate or advanced undergraduate students.

The third section of the book is devoted to advanced topics in measurement theory. Here I include chapters on exploratory factor analysis (EFA), confirmatory factor analysis (CFA), item response theory (IRT; cowritten with Christine E. DeMars), cognitive diagnostic models (CDMs; cowritten with Laine P. Bradshaw), test bias and fairness, standard setting, and test equating. These chapters could be used as the basis for an advanced course in measurement theory, or instructors could choose some of the chapters to serve as advanced material at the end of an introductory measurement theory course.

As I have implied above, the chapters do not necessarily have to be read in the sequence presented in the table of contents. Instructors may choose to omit certain chapters, and in some cases I have indicated chapter sections that can be omitted, depending on the instructor's goals for the course and the level of the students. These sections typically contain more technical material than may be needed. Instructors who wish to include material on advanced topics at the end of an introductory course can pick and choose from among the chapters at the end of the book. Although I have tried to connect concepts that are similar across chapters by referencing other chapters where appropriate, most chapters can also be read as independent units.

Many useful computer packages are available to perform the analyses described in this book, but I have elected not to include information or instruction on a particular package. I know that this will disappoint some readers, but given the rate at which computer packages change and new packages emerge, I felt that keeping this material current would be an impossible task. In addition, many packages are now so user friendly that detailed instruction is often not needed. The one exception to my decision to stay away from particular software packages was to include code from the M*plus* program in Chapter 13. Because methods of assessing measurement properties using such software are not well known, I thought a specific example was needed.

PEDAGOGICAL FEATURES

The book's pedagogical features include:

- Clear conceptual explanations.
- Examples illustrating key concepts and procedures.
- End-of-chapter summaries covering key points.
- End-of-chapter exercises focused on conceptual understanding.
- Suggested answers to exercises at the end of the book.

ACKNOWLEDGMENTS

First and foremost, I would like to thank my students, both present and past, for inspiring me with their love of learning in general and their love of measurement in particular. I have had so many wonderful students, and I hope the others won't mind if I single out two who continue to inspire me. Craig Enders's (2010) amazingly clear and well-written text on missing data methods inspired and challenged me to write something that would even come close to its quality. Sara Finney, teacher and research mentor extraordinaire, by far surpasses me in these areas and serves as my constant example. Craig and Sara, your friendship and support mean a lot to me. To paraphrase the well-known quotation about dogs and their owners, I wish I could be as good a mentor as you seem to think I am.

I have tried to include the names of many of my students in the examples and exercises used in the book, and I apologize in advance for any whose names I have inadvertently omitted. In particular, my thanks to the students in my 2015 and 2016 measurement theory classes and the students in Keith Markus's 2016 psychometrics class for their useful feedback on earlier versions of the book chapters.

Second, I am deeply indebted to Keith Markus and Dena Pastor, whose comments and suggestions on draft chapters were invaluable. Dena has been the very model of patience and helpfulness during the past years, during which I have unceremoniously barged into her office with endless requests for advice, and Keith's penetrating wisdom, which he so generously shared with me, has made sections of this book much more lucid than they would have been without his comments. In addition, I owe a debt of gratitude to the following Guilford reviewers: Jeri Benson, Education, University of Florida; Marcus Boccaccini, Clinical Psychology, Sam Houston State University; Theresa Canada, Educational Psychology, Western Connecticut State University; John Donohue, Psychology, University of Ottawa; Scott Graves, Education and Counseling Psychology, Duquesne University; George Johanson, Education, Ohio University; Daniel Jurich, National Board of Medical Examiners; Insu Paek, Education, Florida State University; Dena Pastor, Education, James Madison University; John Wallace, Psychology, Ball State University; and Leigh Wang, Education, University of Cincinnati. Most importantly, I am indebted to my editor, C. Deborah Laughton, who is truly "the best in the business," as I was assured by a colleague. C. Deborah showed incredible patience as I slowly made my way through the writing of this book, and her feedback and encouragement are what kept me going.

Third, I would like to thank Laine Bradshaw and Christine DeMars, who are rock stars in their fields and whom I was fortunate to have as coauthors of, respectively, Chapter 15 (on diagnostic cognitive classification models) and Chapter 14 (on item response theory). Laine and Christine displayed endless fortitude throughout the many rewrites it took for me to understand their topics.

The fourth group of people I would like to thank are my colleagues. My academic career has spanned three institutions, beginning at the University of Nebraska, where I was privileged to work with and learn from Barbara Plake, Jim Impara, Steve Wise, Ellen Weissinger, and John Creswell. From Nebraska, I moved to the University of Georgia, where I was fortunate enough to have Al Cohen, Seock-Ho Kim, Karen Samuelsen, and Jon Templin as colleagues. In 2010, I moved to James Madison University to join the wonderful faculty in the Assessment and Measurement program, including Allison Ames, Christine DeMars, Sara Finney, Keston Fulcher, John Hathcoat, Jeanne Horst, and Dena Pastor. My heartfelt thanks to all of you for your exceptional support and collegiality, which means so much to me.

Fifth, I would like to thank my mentors at the University of Maryland, where my education in measurement theory began. Many thanks to Chan Dayton, George MacCready, Charlie Johnson, and especially Bob Lissitz, who recruited me into the field of measurement and quantitative methods. I have learned so much from all of you. In particular, I would like to thank my advisor, Jeri Benson, who convinced this first-generation college student that she was indeed qualified for an academic career and thus made this book possible. Jeri's steadfast support and encouragement have meant the world to me. I would also like to thank my "academic grandmother," Linda Crocker, whose authorship of a classic text in measurement theory inspired the writing of this book. Special thanks also go out to Paul Levy and my colleagues on the Examination Committee of the Association of State and Provincial Psychology Boards, whose steadfast encouragement kept me going over the years. More special thanks to artist and longtime friend Pamela C. Day, who provided the publicity photo for this book; to Heather Harris, who created many of the figures; and to Chi Au, who worked through and corrected the answers to all of the exercises.

Finally, I would like to dedicate this book to my sister, Kathy Meman, and my brother, Chip Brown. Kathy and Chip both died, of separate illnesses, during the writing of this book, Chip in 2008 and Kathy in 2016. I miss them every day.

Contents

6 • Item Analysis for Cognitive and Noncognitive Items   120

PART II. RELIABILITY AND VALIDITY

7 • Introduction to Reliability and the   155
Classical Test Theory Model

Part I

Instrument Development and Analysis

1

Introduction

When I told my relatives and friends I was writing a book about measurement, the most common reaction was confusion. How hard can measurement be, they asked, that you need to write an entire book about it? Just take a ruler or thermometer and measure whatever it is you want to measure. For many physical measurements, it is indeed this simple, although the measurement devices we now take for granted, such as rulers and thermometers, took some time to develop and become accepted. In the social sciences, however, measurement is not so simple. This is because most of the things social scientists want to measure are not physical but mental attributes. That is, social scientists are interested in such things as people's intellectual abilities, attitudes, personality characteristics, and values. Such attributes do not lend themselves easily (or at all) to physical measurement. We cannot look at a person and discern his or her attitudes or values, nor is there any ruler- or thermometer-like device we can use to measure them. Instead, we hypothesize the existence of theoretical entities known as *constructs* (also called *latent constructs, factors,* or *unobserved variables*) to account for certain characteristics or behaviors. For example, a researcher might recognize, based on long experience working with people, that some seem to learn faster and adapt more quickly to new situations than others. The researcher hypothesizes a construct now known as intelligence to account for this difference. Note that the researcher cannot directly observe people's intelligence, but must infer the existence of intelligence from observations of their behavior. Other examples of constructs include creativity, anxiety, attitudes toward gun control, altruism, propensity to buy a product, and aptitude for learning. All of these are latent in the sense that we cannot measure them directly but must devise some way of getting at them indirectly.

Measurement of constructs is therefore indirect, relying on samples of behavior such as responses to test items or observations of behavior. A *test* is a way of eliciting such behaviors. Here, and throughout this book, I use the term *test* to refer to a procedure for obtaining a sample of behavior that can be used to infer a person's level or status on a construct of interest. The terms *measure, instrument,* and *scale* are often used in the same way as "test," and although some authors make distinctions among them, the terms are generally used somewhat interchangeably, a practice I follow in this book. As an example of a test, suppose a researcher theorizes that the ability to apply knowledge learned in one context to a new context is one aspect of intelligence. To measure this ability, the researcher would have to devise a series of tasks requiring test takers to apply knowledge learned in one subject area to other subject areas. These tasks could make up a test of the ability to apply knowledge to new contexts, which could then be administered to test takers.

I note several things about this procedure. First, the researcher would likely be able to think up many tasks that could elicit the desired ability. In fact, there may be limitless tasks that can measure many constructs (consider, as an example, the ability to add two-digit numbers). This implies that the tasks included on a test are typically a sample of all the possible tasks that might have been used. Second, the researcher would have to put some limitations on the manner in which test takers are allowed to complete the tasks. For example, the researcher might stipulate that test takers cannot consult outside resources, such as websites or friends, to help them complete the tasks. The researcher might also impose a time limit so that some test takers do not have more time than others to complete the tasks. Thus, the test would likely be administered under controlled, or standardized conditions. Third, although the researcher would like to assume that correct completion of the tasks was an indication of the ability to apply knowledge in new contexts, this may not be the case. Suppose some test takers are able to complete the task in a new subject area by some other means than generalizing knowledge from the original subject area. For example, suppose some test takers are completely unable to generalize their knowledge to the new subject area but know a great deal about the new subject area and are able to answer correctly based on that knowledge. Would the test still measure the ability to apply knowledge learned in one context to another? Probably not, because the test takers did not use that ability to answer the questions. This example points to a persistent problem in the measurement of constructs: it is always possible that the tasks used do not actually elicit the construct of interest.

PROBLEMS IN SOCIAL SCIENCE MEASUREMENT

In the previous section, I discussed some of the issues inherent in measurement in the social sciences. One issue is that tests are usually based on limited samples of behavior; we cannot ask every possible question or observe every instance of behavior. A related issue is that there is no one "correct" method of measuring a construct. In the previous example, the ability to apply knowledge in new contexts could have been measured by performance assessments in which test takers are given problems to solve in different subject areas, by multiple-choice tests asking test takers to choose the most likely outcome of a theory if applied in a new context, or by interviewing test takers about how they would solve the problem in a new context, just to name a few. Use of the different measurement methods would get at somewhat different aspects of the ability, and each method would have its own advantages and disadvantages. The researcher developing the test would therefore have to carefully consider which type of test would be best aligned with the purpose(s) of testing. For example, different methods might be appropriate for testing theories about the ability than for selecting students for an advanced educational program.

Another testing issue is that many things can (and likely will) interfere with our measurement of the construct of interest. As indicated in the previous section, test takers may be able to complete the tasks using skills or abilities other than those the test was designed to measure. Or some test takers may have the requisite abilities but may be so anxious about the test that they fail to complete any of the tasks correctly. Other test takers may have the ability to complete the tasks but have limited English proficiency, causing them to misinterpret the tasks or instructions. Other types of interference are more relevant to attitude measurement. For example, respondents to attitude items may not answer truthfully because they know their attitudes are not politically correct and they do not want to draw attention to this; this tendency is known as *socially desirable responding*. Some respondents may have a tendency to choose a "neutral" or middle response option, whereas others may tend to choose more extreme response options. Such *response styles* are ubiquitous in the measurement of attitudes, personality characteristics, and psychological disorders. Those measuring psychological disorders must also contend with *malingering*—the tendency to exaggerate one's symptoms in an effort to obtain a particular diagnosis.

All of these issues in the measurement of constructs come under the broad heading of *errors of measurement*. It is important to understand that such measurement errors are part and parcel of most social science measurement. As a result, our measures are not perfect, but they should instead be thought of as approximations. Although some tests may provide quite good approximations, none are error-free. One of the tasks of those developing and using tests is therefore to be aware of the possibilities for error in test scores and to interpret and use test results with these possibilities in mind.

WHAT IS MEASUREMENT THEORY?

Another important task for those involved in social science measurement is to investigate the impact of measurement error on test results and to use the findings from these investigations to improve the tests and testing procedures. Such investigations are part of the broad field of *measurement* or *test theory*, known in psychology as *psychometrics*. These terms refer broadly to the study of methods for measuring constructs, and of their attendant problems. Measurement theory is therefore the study of how to develop tests that are as free as possible of measurement error and that yield the most appropriate measures of the desired constructs. Without good tests, social scientists would be unable to diagnose many learning disabilities and personality disorders, to study individual differences in constructs of interest, or to test theories involving these constructs. Our measurements are the basis of our diagnoses and of our ability to test theories, which are therefore only as good as the measures underlying them. Good tests are thus crucial to both practical applications and to theory development in the social sciences.

MEASUREMENT DEFINED

So what do I mean by *measurement*? Stanley S. Stevens's (1946) definition of measurement as the "assignment of numerals to objects or events according to rules" (p. 677) is commonly cited. This definition was later amended to clarify that it is the properties of objects (usually people), such as the strength of their attitudes or their levels of altruism, and not the objects themselves that are measured. Note that, according to Stevens's definition, coding responses on a questionnaire with a "1" for male and a "2" for female constitutes measurement because this process involves assigning numerals (1 and 2) to properties of objects (male and female), according to the rule that 1 means male and 2 means female. Stevens defined four levels of measurement: nominal, ordinal, interval, and ratio. These levels are distinguished by the properties they include and are hierarchical in the sense that a higher level of measurement includes the properties of those lower in the hierarchy. In the sections that follow I describe the four levels and their properties. I also indicate the statistical operations for which Stevens felt each level was appropriate.

The Nominal Level of Measurement

Nominal measures are those for which the numbers serve only to distinguish different categories and do not have any real numerical meaning. The previous example of coding males as 1 and females as 2 exemplifies the nominal level of measurement. The only property of this type of measurement is that of distinctiveness. That is, the numbers distinguish the two categories of male and female but have no quantitative meaning. The coding of most demographic variables, such as political party or hair or eye color, constitute nominal measurement. Such measures can be transformed by applying any one-to-one substitution. In other words, we could substitute any other pairs of numbers, such as 3 and 4, or 65 and 83, for 1 and 2 because they serve to distinguish the categories equally well. The only transformation we cannot use is one in which the same number is used to represent both male and female categories because this would destroy the property of distinctiveness. Because the numbers used in nominal measurement have no numeric meaning, it is not appropriate to add, subtract, or otherwise manipulate them numerically. The only statistical indices appropriate at this level are those based on counts, such as the mode or the chi-square tests of independence and goodness of fit.

The Ordinal Level of Measurement

At the ordinal level of measurement the numbers represent a rank order of the properties of objects. The rank order could be based on size, speed, importance, correctness, or any other property capable of being ranked. Common examples of ordinal measures are the outcomes of a race (first place, second place, etc.), military ranks, and class rank. To the property of distinctiveness, ordinal measures therefore add the property of order. Although the numbers used in ordinal measurement imply rank order, the intervals between adjacent scale points are not assumed to be equal. Taking the outcomes of a race as an example, we know that the person finishing first is faster than the person finishing second, but we do not know how much faster because ordinal measurement does not tell us anything about the amounts by which scale points differ. We also do not know whether the time difference between those finishing first and second is the same as that between those finishing second and third because for ordinal measurement these intervals are not assumed to be equal. Ordinal measures can be transformed in any way that preserves the original order. Thus, we could substitute the numbers 3, 18, and 21 for the numbers 1, 2, and 3 without losing the properties of distinctiveness and order. Because ordinal measures cannot be assumed to have equal intervals, it is not meaningful or appropriate to perform arithmetic operations such as addition or subtraction on them. Statistical indices such as the mode, median or interquartile range are appropriate because these do not assume equal intervals.

Items measured on the commonly used "strongly disagree" to "strongly agree" Likert-type scale (see Chapter 5) are, strictly speaking, at the ordinal level of measurement. This is because we do not know whether respondents consider the psychological distance between "strongly agree" and "agree" to be the same as that between "strongly disagree" and "disagree," or any other adjacent scale points. Having said this, researchers differ in their willingness to treat data from Likert scales as having equal intervals. Some argue that such data probably have equal or nearly equal intervals and that little is lost, statistically speaking, by treating these data as interval. Others argue that this does not make sense unless we know that respondents do treat the intervals as equal and we generally do not have such knowledge.

The Interval Level of Measurement

In addition to the properties of distinctiveness and order, interval measures have the property of equal intervals. This means that the intervals between adjacent scale points are assumed to be the same across the entire scale continuum. A common example of interval level measurement is temperature as measured by the Fahrenheit or Centigrade scales, in which the difference in heat between scale points of 50° and 51° is the same as the difference between 90° and 91°. Interval measures can be transformed through any linear transformation of the form $y = a + bX$. Because of their equal-interval property, it is appropriate to calculate nearly all parametric statistics, such as the mean, standard deviation, and correlation from interval level data.

The Ratio Level of Measurement

The ratio level is the highest of Stevens's (1946) levels of measurement. In addition to the properties of distinctiveness, order, and equal intervals, ratio-level measurement has the property of a true zero point. A true zero point is one that represents the absolute lack of the property being measured. For example, $0 indicates the absolute lack of any money. The Kelvin temperature scale is on a ratio scale because, on that scale, zero degrees indicates a complete lack of heat. This is not the case for the Fahrenheit and Centigrade scales, which is why they are relegated to the interval level of measurement. Many physical scales, such as height, weight, and time, as well as things that can be counted, such as the number of test items correct or the number of students in a classroom, are at the ratio level of measurement. Numbers on a ratio scale can be legitimately transformed only through multiplication of scale points by a constant. Adding a constant, as is permissible at the interval level of measurement, is not permissible at the ratio level because this would change the value of the zero point, rendering it nonabsolute. All parametric statistical operations are permissible for variables at the ratio level of measurement.

It may seem that test scores are at the ratio level of measurement. This depends, however, on how we want to interpret the scores. If we are content to interpret a test score as the number of points obtained on the test, the scores can be considered as ratio level. This is because the zero point can be appropriately interpreted as the absolute absence of any points obtained. However, if we want to interpret the test score as an indication of a particular level of knowledge or achievement, achieving the ratio level of measurement becomes much more problematic. This is because it is difficult to argue that a test score of zero means the absolute absence of any knowledge or achievement. A more likely interpretation is that a student earning a score of zero has some knowledge but does not have knowledge of the particular questions included on the test. It may be that if different questions had been asked, the student would have obtained a higher score. Or the student may have suffered from test anxiety, may have been unable to correctly interpret the test questions, or may have marked the answers incorrectly on the bubble sheet. As you can see, it is much more difficult to make ratio-level interpretations for abstract constructs such as achievement than for more concrete entities such as the number of points earned.

Criticisms of Stevens's Levels of Measurement

Although Stevens's (1946) levels of measurement are widely used in the social sciences, it is important to point out that not all experts agree with his conceptualizations. In particular, Joel Michell (1986, 1997) has argued forcefully that Stevens's definition of measurement does not adhere to the rules of quantitative structure. In other words,

Michell contends that Stevens's levels of measurement are not truly quantitative and that, even if they were, Stevens has provided no method for determining their quantitative properties. According to Michell (1997), measurement is defined as the "estimation or ratio of some magnitude of a quantitative attribute to a unit of the same attribute" (p. 358). Measurement, in Michell's definition, requires a quantitative structure in which the numeric relations (additivity or ratios) between points on the scale can be verified. Stevens's definition of measurement does not qualify because it is based on what Michell calls operationalism. This means that in Stevens's system a measure defined as being at a particular level of measurement is simply assumed to have the properties of that level of measurement. Stevens did not propose any methods for determining whether, for example, the equal-interval property of interval measures actually holds. Michell argues that measurement theories such as those advanced by Luce and his colleagues (Luce, Krantz, Suppes, & Tversky, 1990; Luce & Tukey, 1964), in which it is possible to test such quantitative properties of measures, are preferable because they allow for empirical verification of measurement properties.

Debates about the quantitative structure of social science measurement (or lack thereof) will likely continue in the coming years. Although I cannot predict the outcome of these debates, the history of testing may offer some insight about their origins. It is to this history that I now turn.

A BRIEF HISTORY OF TESTING

By any account, testing has had a long and storied history. Dubois (1970) traces so-called "modern" testing back to three major influences: Chinese (and, later, European and American) civil service examinations, assessment of individual differences in the early European and American psychological laboratories of the 19th and early 20th centuries, and the assessment of achievement in early European schools and universities. While it is true that educational and psychological testing as we know it today had its origins in these early testing efforts, other early societies also made use of various testing methods. For example, as we shall see, testing in early Greek society could be quite a harrowing experience. In this chapter, I will trace the history of testing from its early origins in China to the early educational and psychological tests developed in the United States, with a brief detour into the somewhat different procedures employed by the Greeks.

The Chinese Civil Service Examinations

Dubois (1970) dates the Chinese civil service examinations back to as early as 2200 B.C.E. Initially, examinations were conducted only for the purpose of evaluating civil servants to determine whether they should continue in office, a practice that took place every three years. At some point, however, Chinese rulers decided that examinations should also be used to choose candidates for civil service positions. The examinations were continued until 1905, at which time they were superseded by university credentialing.

Although the date of 2200 B.C.E. is commonly cited as the approximate origin of the Chinese examinations, there is some controversy about this date. For example, Bowman (1989) disputes Dubois's claim that these date back to 2200 B.C.E. stating that "[t]he attribution of examinations to dates of 2200 B.C.E. and 1115 B.C.E. is unsupported by evidence and at variance with what we now know about the societies of those times" (p. 577). Bowman dates these exams to between 200 and 100 B.C.E. However, Kim and Cohen (2007) defend Dubois's claim, stating that the earliest examinations were developed during the reign of Emperor Shun, which they date at 2255 B.C.E.–2205 B.C.E. (p. 5). Whatever the date, it seems safe to say that these examinations represent the earliest documented use of testing for widespread selection or evaluation purposes.

The major problem in dating the earliest civil service examinations is related to the fact that these were oral rather than written examinations. As Bowman (1989) points out, there are no written records about testing from the period covering the disputed date of 2200 B.C.E., for the very good reason that writing had not yet been developed (although some symbolic forms of communication had been used; see Kim & Cohen, 2007). The development of the Chinese character system is commonly ascribed to the Shang dynasty (c. 1500 B.C.E.). Dubois (1970) and Kim and Cohen state that during the later Chou dynasty candidates were examined in the "six arts" of music, archery, horsemanship, writing, arithmetic, and ceremonial protocol. Although some of these examinations may have been written, we can infer from the subject matter that most were oral or performance based. Dubois puts the date for these examinations at around 1115 B.C.E.

In contrast to the divergences of opinion regarding the beginnings of the early oral examination system, the advent of the largely written literary examinations is ascribed by most scholars (including Bowman) to the time of the Han dynasty (c. 206–220 B.C.E.). Many historical accounts from this period describe the use of examinations for the selection of civil service officials. Candidates were examined on the "five studies": civil law, military affairs, agriculture, revenue, and geography. These examinations were held at the district, provincial, and national levels, with candidates succeeding at a lower level going on to test at the higher levels. Students today who find the day-long procedures for the SAT tests grueling may be interested to know that the Chinese civil service examinations lasted three days and three nights!

China had no formal university or public school systems during this time. However, the civil service examinations served as a means of implementing a national curriculum. Because candidates had to be familiar with the "five studies" and, later in the period, with the Confucian classics, aspiring civil service employees from around the country were compelled to study these subjects in order to succeed. Thus, the examination system contributed to the stability of the Chinese empire both by ensuring a steady supply of qualified government administrators and by effecting a common knowledge base. Despite its success, the civil service examination system in China was abolished in 1905, superseded by university degrees and qualifications.

By this time, however, the Chinese system of civil service examinations had made its mark in Western countries, having been introduced by British diplomats and missionaries who were so impressed with the system that they suggested it be implemented in England. Their recommendations led to the first such examination, introduced in 1833 to select trainees for the Indian Civil Service. The success of this venture led in turn to interest in the United States, where the Civil Service Act of 1883 established competitive tests for entry into government service.

Testing in Ancient Greece

In contrast to the Chinese civil service examinations, tests in ancient Greek societies were not written but were typically oral or performance based. Examinations were conducted for the purpose of determining whether men (and of course then it was only men) were qualified for various aspects of Greek life and citizenship; examinations were not, as far as we know, used to select citizens for government positions. Tests in physical skills, such as running, jumping, wrestling, and discus and javelin throwing, were very common and highly standardized in both execution and scoring. Examinations of mental achievements were also carried out but were generally less highly standardized than those in the physical arena. As an example, Doyle (1974) described a test of oral reading in which each student began reading where the last student left off, presenting the possibility for differences in text difficulty from one reader to the next. Overall, however, the Greeks were cognizant of the need for what we would now call standardization in testing.

Testing in ancient Greece was generally utilitarian and, in the mental sphere, focused on skills in the areas of rhetoric and recitation, which were considered the foundations of good citizenship. For the same reasons, tests of mental achievement tended to emphasize morality to a greater extent than intellectual prowess. Thus, students in Athens were expected to be able to speak extemporaneously on the issues of the day and were tested in this regard both formally and informally. Similarly, Spartan students were routinely asked questions such as "Who is the best man in the city" and expected to provide not only a ready answer but sound reasoning for their choice. One cannot help but think that such a requirement might serve us well in current democratic states. Students today who feel disappointed at receiving a low grade may take comfort in the following quotation from Plutarch (quoted in Doyle, 1974) regarding the assessment of Athenian students who, if "answered not to the purpose, had his thumb bit by the master" (p. 209).

For most of these tests, scoring was somewhat subjective and was typically based on the judgments of either the teacher or a larger audience of older citizens. Scoring does not appear to have been formalized and consisted mainly of either praise for good performance or punishment, usually physical, for poor performance. Although tests in early Greek societies were not systematically used for selection of civil servants as in China, testing did play a part in such selections. For example, Plato, in the *Republic*, discusses the importance of assessments of character as well as of knowledge and the ability to connect the various branches of knowledge in determining suitability for state offices. Thus, as in China, testing helped to both form and reinforce the national character.

Early European Testing

As in early Greece, the earliest testing in Europe was concerned with what today would be called student assessment. University exams are known to have been used in Europe as early as 1219 (at the University of Bologna) for determining eligibility for degrees. These exams were exclusively oral; written tests were not used until much later when the Jesuits pioneered the use of this format beginning in the sixteenth century. The parallels between the rules for these examinations, established in 1599, with those used today are striking. For example, examinees were enjoined to "be present in the classroom in good time," "come supplied with books and writing materials," "diligently look over what he has written, correct and improve it as much as he may wish," and "clearly know how much time is granted for writing, rewriting, and revision" (McGucken, 1932, quoted in DuBois, 1970, pp. 9–10).

At Oxford University, oral examinations for both the BA and MA degrees were introduced in 1636, and written exams can be dated back to at least 1803. The success of such an examination system has been credited with leading, at least in part, to easier acceptance of later civil service exams based on the Chinese model.

Beginnings of Psychological Measurement

As noted by Goodenough (1949), early research in experimental psychology was focused on the study of physical sensation. German psychophysical laboratories of the early 1800s, such as that of Wilhelm Wundt, were concerned with obtaining precise estimates of reaction time, visual and auditory perception, and other physical sensations under various conditions. Because many early students of psychology were also trained in such "hard" sciences as biology and physiology, it is not surprising that these researchers turned to such physical measures in their attempts to understand mental functioning. Unlike today's testing efforts, however, individual differences were not the focus of these studies. On the contrary, such differences were generally considered to be the result of imperfect control of experimental conditions, and every effort was made to design studies in which such differences were minimized.

Another influence on psychological research at this time was the publication of Darwin's *Origin of Species* in 1859. The possibility of an evolutionary basis for variation in mental abilities, suggested by Darwin's theories, was not lost on psychologists. Indeed, Francis Galton, a cousin of Darwin, wrote several works on the heritability of scientific aptitude. Galton is well known for the establishment of laboratories for the collection of physical measurements such as height, weight, strength of pull, and discrimination of colors. The first of these laboratories was established at the 1884 International Health Exhibition in London, where over 9000 people paid three pence each to have their measurements taken and immortalized in the form of normal curves, the idea for which Galton adopted from the Belgian scientist Quetelet. In fact, it is Galton's development of the ideas for many of the statistical techniques used today for which he is best known. From his studies of variation in physical measurements, Galton realized the power of the normal curve for organizing the vast amounts of data he had collected. He went on to develop the concept of correlation, although the actual mathematics was worked out by his protegé and friend Karl Pearson.

Galton's interests were wide ranging, and he soon became interested in expanding his anthropometric measures to include measures of a more psychological nature. He became aware of the work of James McKeen Cattell, who was in Germany at the time, studying psychology in Wundt's laboratory. According to Sokal (1987), Galton contacted Cattell to find out more about his apparatus for measuring reaction time. Sokal reports that it was through this contact with Galton (whom Cattell later called "the greatest man I have ever known") that Cattell became interested in the measurement of individual differences, which, as noted previously, were not of much interest to European psychologists at that time. After receiving his doctorate, Cattell served as an assistant in Galton's Anthropometric Laboratory, where he developed further tests of perception and memory. He continued his work in this area at the University of Pennsylvania, where he was appointed to a professorship in psychology, and later at Columbia University. It is in the series of tests he developed in the United States that we begin to see precursors of those commonly used today to study mental functioning. In 1890, these included tests of strength of squeeze, rate of arm movement, acuity of sensation, amount of pressure causing pain, least noticeable difference in weight, reaction time for sound, time taken to name colors, accuracy in bisecting a line, accuracy of judging time elapsed, and number of letters that could be repeated on one hearing. Although many of these tasks were clearly influenced by the psychophysical measures common at the time, some movement toward the measurement of mental processes can be detected.

The tension between the use of anthropometric measures and tests focused on the measurement of mental processes became more evident as psychologists continued their studies in the United States. In 1895, the American Psychological Association appointed a committee to study the feasibility of combining efforts across the different psychological laboratories in collecting data on mental and physical characteristics. While most members of the committee favored an emphasis on anthropometric measures, this view was not unanimous. James Baldwin of Princeton University argued that anthropometric tests were given too much weight and that tests of the higher mental processes were also necessary to more fully understand mental functioning. The proponents of anthropometric measures, however, prevailed. Arguments for the use of such measures, as put forth by Cattell, were largely utilitarian, emphasizing that psychological traits were simply too difficult to measure.

Unfortunately for their proponents, however, the utilitarianism of the anthropometric approach to measuring mental processes did not carry over into the applications envisioned for these measures. For example, Cattell felt that his tests could be used to evaluate academic abilities, and to this end he administered these tests to his students at Columbia. He also collected data on the course grades of these students and had his student Clark Wissler use the newly developed formula for the correlation coefficient to determine the degree of relationship of the tests with each other as well as with course grades. The results were disappointing, to say the least. Wissler reported a correlation of −.05 between tests of reaction time and the ability to identify occurrences of the letter A in a grid of randomly arranged letters—two tasks that had been thought to be fairly similar. Similarly small correlations were found between scores on Cattell's tests and his students' course grades. After other researchers across the country found similar results, interest in the use of anthropometric measures began to wane.

Binet's Contributions to Intelligence Testing

Meanwhile, Alfred Binet was pursuing his well-known work in France with a focus that was much more in sympathy with those favoring an emphasis on higher mental abilities. Binet believed that differences in abilities to think and reason, to adapt to new conditions, and to solve problems were critical to mental functioning. The problem was to find suitable tasks to elicit these abilities, a problem to which Binet devoted much of the remainder of his short life. As early as 1896, Binet published an article in which he described tests of memory, mental imagery, imagination, attention, comprehension, suggestibility, aesthetic appreciation, force of will (operationalized as amount of effort in muscular tasks), moral sentiments, motor skill, and judgment of visual space; many of these survive in some form in today's "modern" aptitude tests.

During the period in which he was developing these tests, Binet served as a member and later president of a subgroup of the Société Libre pour l'Étude de l'Enfant (or the Free Society for the Study of the Education of Children, loosely translated). As part of his involvement with this group, he organized a working group concerned with the best way to educate what were then called "mentally retarded" children. This group recommended that such children should not be sent to special schools for the retarded unless an examination showed that the child would be unable to profit from regular education. The obvious problem was that no such examinations were then available. Although both medical and educational examinations were proposed as possibilities, Binet developed a new procedure, based on his ideas about measuring mental capacity, which he referred to as the psychological method. This became the first intelligence scale, developed by Binet and his colleague Theodore Simon in 1905. They argued that this was a better diagnostic tool than either medical tests for mental capacity, which were not diagnostic for all cases, or the educational tests of the time, which were primarily tests of memory.

Binet and Simon administered their early tests to both "normal" and retarded children in order to determine whether the tests would distinguish between these groups, as well as among children of different ages and levels of retardation. Tests were evaluated by giving them to children of different ages, based on the idea that the ability to answer more difficult questions should increase with age. Items were chosen systematically to cover different difficulty levels and, foreshadowing today's standardized ability and achievement tests, had highly standardized instructions for administration. The 1905 test contained many item formats still in use today, such as identifying parts of the body, obeying simple commands, identifying objects in pictures, repeating sentences and digit sequences, and identifying similarities.

The next version of Binet and Simon's scale, published in 1908, featured several new tests, including those requiring children to name as many words as possible in a given timeframe, naming the days of week, unscrambling sentences, executing three verbal commands sequentially, and detecting absurdities. Instead of being ordered by overall difficulty level, as in the previous version, these tests were ordered by age, based on the results obtained from administration to 303 Parisian school children ages 3–12. Age levels were determined by placing each test into levels based on the age at which the majority of students were able to pass it. For example, if the majority of 4-year-old children passed a test, it was assigned to level 4. This allowed for children's scores to be expressed as "mental levels" or, later, as "mental ages." Although Binet himself disliked the latter term, its use of a familiar reference point may have helped to sell the concept of ability testing to the general public (Anastasi & Urbina, 1997).

The third revision of the Binet–Simon Scale was published in 1911. The main revision at this point was the extension of the scale to the adult level. During this year, Binet also reported on a great many extensions of his scales, including plans for group in addition to individual testing, testing of military applicants and criminals, and studies of the relations between the Binet–Simon scales and school success. Unfortunately, he died in 1911 before these applications could be fully developed.

Testing in the United States

The Stanford–Binet Scale

Binet published his work widely, and soon psychologists in other countries began to adapt his work for their own use. Among these psychologists was Robert Yerkes, who would later go on to direct the development of the Army Alpha test for military recruits during World War I. However, the most successful American version of Binet's scale, still in use today, was developed by Lewis Terman of Stanford University; this is the well-known Stanford–Binet scale. Although over half of the tests on Terman's scale were based on the 1911 Binet–Simon scale, others were developed as part of his doctoral dissertation. These tests were administered to over 2,500 children and adults of various levels of ability. Terman put a heavy emphasis on clear and consistent instructions for administering his scale, spending six months in training the examiners. Students who have scored the current version of the Stanford–Binet will be impressed by the fact that Terman scored every one of the over 2,500 tests himself to assure reliability. Goodenough (1949) tells us that Terman's devotion to training and scoring seems to have paid off, as higher correlations with school success and other indicators of ability were found in Terman's study than in the earlier unsuccessful studies by Cattell and Wissler.

Another of Terman's contributions was the development of the intelligence quotient. Although the concept was originally developed by William Stern, Terman was the first to fully develop this type of scoring in his 1916 scale. To implement the idea, he moved tests from one age level to another until the median mental age at each age level was equal to its corresponding chronological age level. Thus, children at each age would have an average intelligence quotient of 1, or 100%.

Group Testing

The Army Alpha

The Stanford–Binet was then, as it is now, individually administered. Group testing was not unknown at the time that scale was developed, but it was not commonly used. However, one of Terman's students, Arthur Otis, was interested in the idea and worked with Terman to develop a group intelligence test. Otis developed what was then the first intelligence test that could be objectively scored, relying heavily on use of an early form of the multiple-choice item. The development of this test proved to be serendipitous because at about the same time Robert Yerkes, as president of the American Psychological Association, had focused his attention on determining how that organization could best help the country in its prepara-tions for World War I. Yerkes organized several committees to study this issue, and because of his previous work in ability testing, he chaired the committee concerned with psychologi-cal examinations for military recruits. Terman, among other testing pioneers in the United States, was asked to be on the committee and brought with him the group testing materials developed by his student Otis. The committee quickly decided that the development of psy-chological tests would provide the most benefit to the war effort and that all recruits should be tested. Given the decision to test all, a group test was deemed most practical, and many of the materials developed by Otis were either used outright or adapted for use in the new test.

The speed with which the committee developed the resulting test has probably not been equaled since and is surely the envy of those working in today's testing companies. In a brief seven days, the committee reviewed different types of items, chose 10 of these types for development of subtests, wrote enough items to create 10 different forms of the test, and prepared one operational test for tryout. The operational test was tried out on a variety of groups, including inmates in a reformatory, high school students, and avia-tion recruits. Eight months after the initial meeting of the committee, the Army Alpha, as it was called, was ready for military service. Only 8 of the original 10 subtests sur-vived the tryouts: oral directions, arithmetical reasoning, practical judgment, synonym/ antonym, disarranged sentences, number series completion, analogies, and informa-tion. The Army Alpha represented the first wide-scale use of the multiple-choice item. Although difficult to imagine today, such items were not in common usage at that time. An example, as reported by DuBois (1970), was the following:

> Why ought a grocer to own an automobile? Because:
>
> _____ it looks pretty.
>
> _____ it is useful in his business.
>
> _____ it uses rubber tires.
>
> _____ it saves railroad fare.

Overall, at least 1,250,000 recruits were tested with Army Alpha. For recruits who were unable to read and write in English, the Army Beta, a nonverbal version of the test, was developed and used. As with Terman's Stanford–Binet, strict attention was paid to the clarity and consistency of instructions.

The development and use of the Army Alpha (and Beta) is widely recognized today as the impetus for the development of a wide variety of group tests, as well as for greater involvement of psychologists and psychological testing in areas ranging from education to industry. After World War I, group testing became all the rage, and group ability and achievement tests, as well as interest inventories, occupational aptitude tests, and personality inventories, began to proliferate.

Group Achievement Tests

Joseph Rice was an early proponent of using scientific means to improve learning in schools. He reasoned that before determining whether students were learning at an adequate rate, he must first know how much students could be expected to learn in a given time period. To this end, Rice administered standardized tests of spelling and arithmetic to thousands of children. He used the results to determine the average level of achievement that could be expected at different grades. Although Rice was not involved in test development per se, the development of these early normative data paved the way for their use in later standardized achievement tests. Rice's work caught the interest of E. L. Thorndike who, along with his students at Columbia University's Teachers College, developed many of the early educational achievement tests. Based on this early work, the first achievement battery, which included tests in several school subjects, was developed by Thorndike's student Truman Kelley, along with Terman and Giles Ruch. This was the Stanford Achievement Test, still in use today in its 10th edition.

Occupational Interest Inventories

Thorndike did not confine his interests to measures of achievement. He was involved in a wide variety of testing applications, one of which was the Thorndike Intelligence Examination for High School Graduates (1919), an early college admissions test. Thorndike also began work on the measurement of academic interests, work that was followed up by Truman Kelley. Kelley's interest inventory expanded on Thorndike's by asking students to rate their level of interest in various magazines, books, and activities. K. M. Cowdery, in his doctoral dissertation under Kelley, made further refinements in this area, including items measuring interest in sports and amusements, types of pets, reading material, and types of people. Cowdery was among the first to use an empirical keying system in which items were selected on the basis of their ability to discriminate between members of different professions and demonstrated for the first time that people in different professions have different patterns of interests. Edward Strong further refined Cowdery's scale, publishing the first version of the Strong Vocational Interest Blank in 1927. He continued to work on this scale until his death 36 years later, developing new items and conducting studies of the scale's reliability and validity. Finally, G. Frederic Küder (1934) developed a new form of item in which test takers were forced to choose among three alternatives rather than simply indicating whether or not they liked something.

This is the so-called forced-choice item that remains popular today in scales such as the Myers–Briggs Type Indicator.

Testing in Business and Industry

In addition to the Army Alpha, psychologists involved in test development for the armed forces created and evaluated tests of specific aptitudes for jobs ranging from stenography to piloting an airplane. Those involved in the development of these tests included Yerkes and Thorndike, as well as such notables as L. L. Thurstone. Thurstone developed a test for telegraphers and in so doing demonstrated the basic procedures, still in use today, for validating a test against an external criterion (which, for the telegrapher's test, was the highest receiving speed). Thurstone also developed a test for selecting office workers for nonmilitary occupations, which included tests of such abilities as checking errors in arithmetic, finding misspelled words, and alphabetizing. The tests developed during and after World War I were not the first to be developed, however. DuBois (1970) notes that as early as the 1880s the U.S. Civil Service Commission had begun development of a series of tests for applicants for government jobs, an idea borrowed from the successful use of such procedures in Great Britain (which, in turn, as already noted, got the idea from the Chinese civil service examinations). After World War I, the Civil Service Commission contacted some of the psychologists involved with the Army Alpha and arranged for an experimental administration of that test to clerical workers. This was followed up with the development and validation of various occupational aptitude tests by researchers at the Commission.

Personality Assessment

As Anastasi and Urbina (1997) note, the term *personality testing* is typically used to refer to nonintellectual facets of human behavior, such as attitudes, values, beliefs, emotional states, and relationships with others. Test development in this area paralleled that in the area of intelligence testing, to some extent, beginning with early work with free association tests by Galton and the early German psychophysical laboratories, and later developing into more standardized measures due to the impetus of World War I. Although Galton experimented with free association techniques by trying them out on himself, the most systematic early attempts at using these methods were made in the early German psychophysical laboratories of Wundt by his student Emil Kraepelin, who experimented with a type of free association technique in which examinees were instructed to reply to word prompts with the first word that came to mind. Kraepelin's interest was in determining the effects of physical factors such as fatigue and hunger on mental processes, but the technique was seized upon as a way to study mental illness by such notables as Carl Jung. In 1921, Jung's student Hermann Rorschach famously adapted the procedures by substituting inkblots for the words that had previously been used as a stimulus. (Interestingly, this technique had earlier been proposed by Alfred Binet and Theodore Simon.)

Robert Woodworth is generally credited with being one of the first to develop a group, self-report test for personality. His measure, later known as the Woodworth Personal Data Sheet, was motivated by the need to assess the susceptibility of military recruits to shell shock, or what might now be called posttraumatic stress disorder. Although the war ended before Woodworth could thoroughly test his instrument, its development set the stage for the use of group testing of personality.

SUMMARY

A construct is a theoretical entity hypothesized to account for particular behaviors or characteristics of people. Examples of constructs abound in the social sciences and include creativity, intelligence, various abilities and attitudes, personality characteristics, and value systems. Such constructs are latent in the sense that they are not directly observable but must be measured indirectly, relying on samples of behavior that are thought to characterize them. These samples of behavior can take the form of responses to test items or other questions, performances on physical or other tasks, behavioral observations, or any other methods thought to elicit the construct. A test is a method for eliciting these samples of behavior, such as paper and pencil (or, increasingly, computerized) questions to which test takers respond, physical tasks test takers perform, or behaviors that are elicited through overt or covert means and observed and coded by others. The fact that measurement of constructs is necessarily indirect leads to problems with their measurement. Perhaps most important among these problems is that the behavior sample thought to elicit the construct does not do so. This can happen for a variety of reasons, but perhaps the most common one is that the behavior sample was based on insufficient knowledge of the construct, of the method of measurement, or of the match between the two. Measurement of constructs is also based, in most cases, on a limited sample of the possible test questions, performances, or behaviors that are possible. As a result, our measurement of constructs is, to some extent, incomplete. In addition to these issues, test anxiety, inability to understand test questions or instructions, malingering, and response styles such as socially desirable responding can result in inaccurate measurement of the intended construct. Such errors of measurement are endemic in social science measurement, rendering the jobs of those who develop, administer, and interpret tests difficult. One purpose of this book is therefore to raise awareness of the potential pitfalls in testing and to provide those involved in testing with the background necessary to develop, use, and interpret test results appropriately.

This chapter also reviewed the history of testing, pointing out that testing developments in areas as widely varied as employment, intelligence, achievement, and personality have developed in much the same way. In many cases, the same researchers were involved in work in all of these areas, and improvements were freely shared across both substantive and geographical areas. Given this fact, it is not surprising that the procedures for test development in different areas share many of the same procedures for item development and evaluation. It is on these procedures that we will focus in the remaining chapters.

EXERCISES

1. Define the following terms:

   a. *Test*

   b. *Construct*

2. Discuss two problems inherent in social science measurement.

3. According to Stevens's definitions, what are the levels of measurement of the following measurements? Justify your answers.

   a. Recycling behavior as measured by the following scale:

      1 = "never recycle"
      2 = "sometimes recycle"
      3 = "usually recycle"
      4 = "always recycle"

   b. Assigning the numbers 1, 2, and 3 to survey respondents living in houses, apartments, and condominiums, respectively.

   c. Distance traveled to work.

4. A researcher assigns the numbers 1, 2, and 3 to distinguish urban, suburban, and rural areas, respectively.

   a. Does this constitute measurement according to Stevens's definition? Why or why not?

   b. Does this constitute measurement according to Michell's definition? Why or why not?

5. In what ways did testing in ancient Greece differ from testing in ancient China?

6. Many early psychological tests were based on anthropometric measures such as reaction time and ability to perceive differences in weights. Why did early tests rely so much on this type of measurement? What is one reason that such measures were eventually abandoned?

7. What was the impetus behind Binet's development of the first intelligence test in 1905?

8. How did multiple-choice items come to be used on the Army Alpha test?

2

Norms and Standardized Scores

Measurement, like nature, abhors a vacuum. By this I mean that scores obtained from measurement instruments cannot be interpreted in isolation but must instead be related to a referencing system to make them meaningful. For example, when a friend tells you she has received a score of 20 on a recent math test, you are likely to ask one of two questions: "How did everyone else do?" or "How many questions were there?" These two questions are examples of the two referencing systems most commonly used in the social sciences to put scores into context, known respectively as *norm* and *criterion referencing*. Norm referencing creates a context for scores by comparing an individual's performance to that of a reference group, known as the *norm group*. For instance, your interpretation of your friend's score might be enhanced by knowing that her math score of 20 was higher than the scores of 90% of the students in the class. Here, the class members serve as the norm group, and your interpretation of how your friend fared on the test is put into context by comparing her performance to that of the group.

Note, however, that, even though your friend may be heartened by the fact that she scored higher than 90% of the other students, this does not necessarily mean that she has answered most of the questions correctly. It may be that she has only answered two questions correctly but has still done better than the 90% of the students who were unable to answer any of the questions correctly. This illustrates the fact that norm-referenced scores only indicate how well one has done relative to the norm group; not how well one has done in a more absolute sense. To make the latter type of interpretation, we must use criterion referencing. Criterion referencing relates scores to some predetermined criteria. For example, interpreting scores of 90–100% correct as "A" work, 80–89% as "B" work, and so on, provides a criterion-referenced interpretation in which it has been decided that a student must get at least 90% of the questions right to qualify for an "A". Note that these percentages are not percentages of students, as in norm referencing but percentages of correct answers.

Common examples of criterion-referenced measures are determinations of passing or failing on driving examinations or on qualifying examinations for doctors, airline pilots, and other professionals. In these situations, we are not so much interested in whether our doctor or airline pilot outscored other doctors or airline pilots; rather, we are interested in how much of the relevant content they have mastered. We are unlikely to feel confidence in a doctor or airline pilot who has obtained a higher score than his or her colleagues unless we also know that the score represents an acceptable amount of knowledge mastery.

WHICH TO USE?

By now, you may be wondering which should be used: norm- or criterion-referenced scores? In addressing this question, it should first be pointed out that there is no reason both types of scores could not be used in a complementary manner. For example, you could interpret your friend's score of 20 as being both higher than the scores of 90% of the class *and* as representing 20 out of 40 questions, or 50% correct (assuming these interpretations are correct). Many widely used educational achievement tests report both norm- and criterion-referenced information, the former by relating students' performance to that of a national norm group and the latter by reporting on the number of questions students answered correctly for various content domains. Having made this statement, however, I should point out that most commonly used measures in the social sciences are associated primarily with one or the other type of referencing. In general, the purpose of criterion referencing is to make judgments regarding the respondent's amount of the construct being measured, usually with the object of classification, diagnosis, or credentialing. As mentioned earlier, for example, qualification examinations for those in medical and other professions fall into this category. Similarly, medical and psychological measurements sometimes take the form of symptom checklists. In order to be classified as clinically depressed, on nonambulatory, for instance, a respondent would have to exhibit a specified number of symptoms on the checklist.

In contrast, the explicit objective of norm-referenced testing is to compare respondents to each other in terms of the construct being measured. Most parents will be familiar with height and weight norms for babies, which tell them how their baby compares in these areas to other babies of the same age; this is an example of norm referencing. Many achievement, ability, and personality tests are also norm-referenced. Perhaps the most well known of these tests are the so-called IQ or intelligence tests, such as the Weschler and Stanford–Binet series. Scores on such tests are based on the respondent's relative performance compared to that of others who took the test. Norm-referenced tests are often used for selection purposes. This is the case with college admissions tests, such as the SAT and GRE. However, not all norm-referenced tests are used for selection; the purpose of norm referencing may simply be to see where the respondent stands in relation to the norm group, as in height and weight norms.

The type of referencing system that should be used therefore depends on the purpose(s) of testing. If scores are to be used to determine how an individual compares to others, norm-referenced scores are most appropriate, whereas if the object of testing is to determine how much of the construct an individual possesses, criterion-referenced scores are most relevant. Because most of the commonly used types of scores in the social sciences are norm-referenced, the following sections will focus on this type of score. Let us begin by discussing what a norm group is and the characteristics of a norm group that are important to consider.

NORM GROUPS

As explained in the previous section, scores in norm-referenced systems are obtained by comparison of an individual's score to the scores of a group. Such a group is known as a *norm group*, and the scores obtained from that group are sometimes referred to as the *norms* for that test. A norm group is therefore simply a reference group that provides a context for interpreting scores. Norm groups for widely used tests are often quite large, such as those for large-scale standardized achievement or ability tests. However, norm groups do not have to be extremely large; the size and nature of the norm group should be chosen with regard to the types of comparisons that are desired. Because standardized achievement tests such as the Iowa Test of Basic Skills are used across the United States, the norm group for that test should be representative of all school students in the country. Infant weight data, on which norms developed by the Centers for Disease Control and Prevention are based, were obtained from the birth records of over 83 million babies across the United States! At the other extreme, a classroom teacher may want to compare the scores of each of her students to the class average. In this case, a large national norm group is neither necessary nor desirable. Thus, norms can be national, as with infant weights; state, as with state standardized achievement tests used to measure student progress; or local, as when individual schools or classrooms develop norms for "in-house" comparisons. Age- and grade-level norms are also common. For example, weights of infants are compared to the weights of other infants of the same age (in months). Grade norms are often used for achievement tests, with students' scores being compared to those of other students in the same grade. For some tests, a fixed norm group is used. This is the case with SAT scores, for which all scores are compared to those of the group of over one million students who took the test in 1990.

Important Characteristics of the Norm Group: The "Three R's"

In evaluating whether a norm-referenced test is appropriate to use with a particular group or individual, we should consider several characteristics of the norm group. These are the "three R's": recency, representativeness, and relevance. A norm group that is recently obtained is important for any situation in which it is likely that the characteristic being measured has changed in the years since the norm group was obtained. Infant weight norms obtained in 1920 may not yield an appropriate basis of comparison for today's babies, owing to improvements in health care and nutrition and concomitant increases in weight. As another example, the original norm group for the SAT was obtained in 1941, and you would not need too much imagination to think of a variety of ways in which characteristics of that norm group differ from those of today's students.

Representativeness is an important consideration for any situation in which we would like to compare scores to those of a more general populace. In our example of infant weight norms, for instance, it is important that the babies in the norm group are representative of all babies in the United States because that is the population to which we are interested in comparing. Although not all norm groups will be as comprehensive as that for infant weights, the norm group should reflect what are thought to be the most important characteristics of the population to which we want to make inferences. The phrase "most important characteristics" means those that are most likely to influence the attribute being measured. For example, research suggests that school achievement can vary across urban, suburban, and rural areas, as well as across private and public schools. If, on the one hand, a measure of school achievement were to be used in all of these types of schools, we would want the norm group to include schools in each category. On the other hand, assuming achievement is not affected by students' shoe size, the fact that those with small shoe sizes are not well represented would not be an issue.

The criterion of relevance is closely related to that of representativeness. However, relevance has more to do with the similarity of the norm group's characteristics to those of the specific group with which one is working. To further belabor the infant weight example, if one is interested in the weights of prematurely born infants, comparison to the national infant weight norms may not be appropriate—not because those norms are not nationally representative, but because they are not as relevant for infants born prematurely. Such infants represent a subpopulation for which the general weight norms do not hold. To summarize, comparisons to a norm group can be useful in interpreting scores, but those using such scores should be cognizant of the degree to which the norms are recent, representative of the population of interest, and relevant to that population in terms of characteristics that might affect interpretations.

TYPES OF NORM-REFERENCED SCORES

The popularity of norm referencing has resulted in the development of many types of norm-referenced scores that are commonly used. This section presents a discussion of several of these types, including percentile ranks, z- and T-scores, normalized z- and T-scores, stanines, normal curve equivalents, and grade- and age-equivalent scores. These scores represent various ways of transforming raw scores to make them more interpretable. By raw score, I mean a simple sum score, as in the number of correct responses on a math test, the number of symptoms checked on a checklist, or the sum of the point values for a set of Likert items. As discussed previously, such values are difficult to interpret in isolation. The scores presented in the next sections were developed to render raw scores more meaningful.

TABLE 2.1. Frequency Distribution of Raw Scores

Score	f	cf	%	$c\%^a$	PR^a
36	2	52	4	100	98
35	2	50	4	96	94
34	6	48	12	92	87
33	2	42	4	81	79
32	2	40	4	76	75
31	3	38	6	73	70
30	7	35	13	67	61
29	5	28	10	54	49
28	5	23	10	44	39
27	7	18	13	35	28
26	8	11	15	21	13
25	3	3	6	6	3

[a] Rounded to the nearest whole number.

Percentile Ranks

Percentile ranks indicate the percentage of people who scored below a given score. For example, if 50% of those in a particular norm group obtained scores below a raw score of 73, we would say that a score of 73 is at the 50th percentile rank. Percentile ranks have the advantages of being easy to understand and being applicable to any norm-referenced test. Commonly used percentile ranks such as $P25$, $P50$, and $P75$ are referred to as *quartiles*. $P10$, $P20$, $P30$, and so on, are referred to as *deciles*. Table 2.1 shows a cumulative frequency distribution of 52 scores. The frequency (f) of each score is shown in the second column, followed by the cumulative frequency (cf), the frequency expressed as a percentage of the total number of scores (%), the cumulative percentage (%), and the percentile rank (PR) for each score. The cumulative frequency is obtained by adding the frequency of each score to the cumulative frequency of the score below it (for the lowest score, the frequency and cumulative frequency are the same). The cumulative frequencies are the number of people who obtained a score at least that high. For example, 18 people obtained a score of 27 or lower. The cumulative percentage is obtained by dividing the cumulative frequency by the total number of scores and multiplying by 100. These represent the percentage of people in the sample who obtained scores in that score interval or lower.

You may wonder why the percentile ranks are not the same as the values in the cumulative percentage column, given that both quantities are supposed to represent the percentage of people with scores that fall below a given score interval. The reason is that the cumulative percentage represents the percentage of people in a given score interval or below, whereas a percentile rank represents the percentage of people below a given score interval. For this reason, the cumulative percentage includes all of the scores falling into the given interval, but the percentile rank includes only half of those scores. For example, to compute the percentile rank of a score of 27, formally expressed as PR_{27}, we take the number of scores *below* a score of 27 (11, from the cumulative frequency column) and add half of the scores in the interval 27 (½ of 7, or 3.5), for a total of 14.5. We then divide this total by the total number of scores, 52, and multiply by 100 to obtain the percentile rank of 28 (rounding to the nearest whole number). Expressed as an equation, the process is

$$PR = \frac{cf_l + 0.5f}{n} * 100 \qquad (2.1)$$

where cf_l is the cumulative frequency in the interval directly below the interval containing the desired score, f is the frequency in the interval of interest, and n is the sample size. This formula assumes that the interval width is always 1.0; that is, each interval spans only one score, as in Table 2.1. Percentile ranks can be calculated from distributions in which more than one score is grouped into an interval (aptly named *grouped frequency distributions*) with a slight change in the formulation of Equation 2.1. However, use of grouped frequency distributions introduces more error into the calculations, so it is not generally recommended.

Why do we include only half of the scores in a given interval when calculating percentile ranks? To answer this question, I introduce two assumptions that underlie the computation of percentile ranks. First, even though raw scores are typically discrete values such as 27 or 28, it is assumed that the underlying trait is continuous, such that scores of 27.3356 or 28.5925 could theoretically be obtained. It is only the limitations of our relatively crude measurement process that prevents us from obtaining more precise values. Under this conceptualization, a seemingly simple score of 27 actually represents an entire range of scores from just above 26.5 to just below 27.5. The observed score of 27 is the midpoint of this interval. This brings us to the second assumption. Because we do not actually know each person's exact score on this theoretically continuous range of scores, we assume that scores are spread out evenly throughout the interval. In our example, this would mean that the seven scores of 27 are evenly spread out between 26.5 and 27.5, so that only half the scores in the interval would actually fall below 27. Strictly speaking, therefore, the number of scores below a score of 27 is equal to the sum of the eleven scores of 26 or below plus half of the seven scores in the interval for the score of 27.

Of course, like many statistical assumptions, the latter assumption is somewhat untenable, if not downright silly. For example, if there were only one score of 27, we would have to assume that half of that person's score was below 27 and half was above 27, which stretches the bounds of credibility. In reality, the underlying continuous scores are probably not evenly distributed throughout the interval, although we have no way of knowing for sure (which is why we have to assume). However, the important point is that, to the extent that this assumption is not met, some error is introduced into the calculation.

Although percentile ranks are easy to interpret, they are subject to some misunderstanding. One such misunderstanding is the fact that percentile ranks have equal intervals and can therefore be averaged or otherwise manipulated mathematically. However, because conversion to percentile ranks is not a linear transformation of the scores, PRs do not have equal intervals for most score distributions. If the distribution of scores approximates a normal distribution, the differences in PRs for scores in the middle of the distribution will be larger than those for scores at the ends of the distribution. This is because PRs are based on the frequency of scores, and in a normal distribution there are more scores in the middle of the distribution than at the ends. Thus, PRs for scores in the middle increase more quickly from one score to another than do PRs for scores in the tails. This can be seen in Table 2.1, in which the difference in PRs between the scores of 30 and 31, in the center of the distribution, is 9 while the PRs of the scores 35 and 36, at the high end of the distribution, differ by only 4. To take another example, if Bonnie obtains a score at PR_{87} on the test represented in Table 2.1, an appropriate interpretation is that she scored higher than 87% of the norm group. However, suppose that Bonnie scored at PR_{94} on a later administration of the same test, while Neil obtained PRs of 39 and 49, respectively, on two similar administrations. It would not be appropriate to conclude that Neil gained more than Bonnie because we can see from Table 2.1 that both gains correspond to exactly one score point. Thus, PRs represent each person's relative standing within the norm group but not the amount of difference between the associated scale scores. Similarly, if Neil obtained a PR of 80 on one test and 90 on another test, it is not necessarily the case that he obtained a higher raw score on the second test. We can only say that he obtained a higher score *relative to the norm group* on the second test than the first. Unless we know that the norm group and the score distribution are the same for both tests, it is not appropriate to assume that his raw score is higher on the second test than on the first.

In addition to these problems in comparing differences between percentile ranks, it is also *not appropriate* to average or otherwise mathematically manipulate percentile ranks, even though this is often done. This again is due to the inequality of units across the percentile rank scale. Finally, it should be noted that PRs in the middle of the distribution are typically more stable than those in either tail. This is because there are more scores in the middle of the distribution (assuming it is approximately normal), so PRs in that part of the distribution are based on more information than those in the tails.

Percentile points are sometimes confused with percentile ranks, but these two quantities are actually the converse of each other. Whereas percentile ranks are percentages, percentile points are score points associated with given percentile ranks. For example, Table 2.1 shows that the PR of a score of 35 is 94, indicating that 94% of scores fall below 35. This can be written as $PR_{35} = 94$. Conversely, we could say that the 94th percentile is 35, or that $P_{94} = 35$. To obtain percentile points, the following formula is used:

$$P = x_{ll} + \frac{\text{Width}}{\text{Interval\%}}(P - CP\%) \qquad (2.2)$$

To calculate a percentile point, we must first determine the interval in which the percentile of interest will fall. For example, in Table 2.1, P_{94}, the score corresponding to the

94th percentile, would fall in the interval containing the score of 35. Having made this determination, we can now use Equation 2.2, in which x_{ll} is the lower score limit, typically taken as 0.5 less than the score, or 34.5, for reasons explained previously. *Width* is the interval width, or number of scores spanned by the interval. In this example, as in any ungrouped frequency distribution, this is 1. *Interval%* is the percentage in the interval, in this case, 4%. *P* is the percentile of interest, in this case 94, and *CP%* is the cumulative percentage of scores in the next lower interval: 92 in this example. Substituting these numbers into Equation 2.2 yields

$$P_{94} = 34.5 + \frac{1}{4}(94 - 92) = 34.5 + \frac{2}{4} = 35.0$$

Standardized and Normalized Scores

Although *PRs* are useful for determining the relative standing of individuals' scores within the norm group, they have the disadvantage of being on an ordinal scale with unequal intervals. This is due to the use of a nonlinear transformation in converting raw scores to *PRs* and makes it inappropriate to compare differences in *PRs* or to average or otherwise manipulate these scores mathematically. In this section, several types of scores are discussed, known collectively as *standardized scores*. Procedures for obtaining standardized scores use linear transformations to convert scores, yielding scores with equal intervals. Standardized scores are those that use the standard deviation of the norm group to express an individual's distance from the mean. A common example is the z-score that is often learned in introductory statistics courses.

Use of linear transformations does not result in changes in the shape of the distribution or in one's relative position within that distribution. Thus, if the raw score distribution is normal, the distribution of standardized scores will also be normal. The same holds for non-normal distributions. For example, a positively skewed distribution of raw scores will result in a distribution of standardized scores with exactly the same positive skew. A common misconception is that standardizing scores will always result in a normal distribution of standardized scores, but this is not the case. The standardized scores will have exactly the same distributional shape as the raw scores, whatever that is. There are, however, methods that can be used to transform any distribution of scores into a distribution that is normally distributed. Such transformations are aptly called *normalizing functions,* and the resulting scores *normalized scores.* Such transformations are nonlinear, however, and will not necessarily preserve the original raw score differences. I first discuss standardized scores.

Standardized Scores

z-scores are the most basic type of standardized score. They are computed by subtracting the mean of the norm group from each raw score and dividing this difference by the standard deviation of the norm group. For example, suppose Javarro obtained raw

TABLE 2.2. Computation of z-Scores

English	Math
$x = 24$, mean $= 30$, $SD = 12$	$x = 14$, mean $= 10$, $SD = 2$
$z = \dfrac{24-30}{12} = -0.5$	$z = \dfrac{14-10}{2} = 2.0$

test scores of 24 in English and 14 in math. On the surface, he appears to have a better performance in English. However, with only raw scores to go by, we really know nothing about his relative performance on the two tests. The mean and standard deviation (*SD*) for both scores and the *z*-score computations are shown in Table 2.2. Based on the *z*-scores, we can see that Javarro actually scored higher on the math test, relative to the other students in the norm group.

z-scores are easy to interpret, because scores above the mean have positive values, while scores below the mean have negative values. Values of 0 indicate scores exactly at the mean, and the further from 0 (in either a positive or negative direction) a score is, the further it is from the mean. The unit in which *z*-scores are expressed is the *SD*; that is, a *z*-score of +1.0 indicates the score is exactly 1 *SD* from the mean. One important advantage of *z*-scores and other standardized scores is that they are on a common metric. For example, a *z*-score of 1.0 always indicates 1 *SD* above the mean, regardless of the metric of the raw scores. So, converting scores to *z* or other standardized scores allows us to make comparisons across different tests that may not originally have been in the same metric. Of course, this is appropriate only if the tests being compared share the same norm group. If different norm groups were used, the *SD*s would not typically be the same, resulting in unequal units even after standardization.

Although their properties do make *z*-scores easy to interpret, they also result in scores that some find objectionable. In particular, many children (and parents) may find it difficult to understand how a negative score could be obtained on a test with a positive number of questions. *z*-scores are typically expressed in fractions or decimals; another undesirable feature of these scores. For these reasons, *z*-scores are often further transformed to have a more appealing metric. This is done by using the formula

$$X_{new} = z(SD) + \bar{X} \tag{2.3}$$

where *z* is the *z*-score, *SD* is the desired standard deviation, and $\bar{X}$ is the desired mean. Because this is a linear transformation, the shape of the score distribution will not be changed, nor will individuals' relative standing in the distribution.

To apply Equation 2.3, a mean and *SD* for the new scores must be chosen. Although these choices are somewhat arbitrary, they are usually made such that the resulting scores will not be negative and there will be no need for fractional scores. One commonly used metric is the *T*-score scaling, attributed to McCall (1922, 1939), which has a mean of 50 and an *SD* of 10. *T*-scores are used on many scales, such as the Behavior

Assessment System for Children (BASC; Reynolds & Kamphaus, 1992–2004). To obtain T-scores, first obtain z-scores, and then apply Equation 2.3 as

$$T = z(10) + 50$$

where 10 is the desired *SD* and 50 is the desired mean. The SAT tests use a metric with an *SD* of 100 and a mean of 500, whereas the Weschler IQ scales have an *SD* of 15 and a mean of 100. As with *T*-scores, conversion to these scales begins by obtaining z-scores for each raw score in the distribution and then applying Equation 2.3 with the appropriate mean and standard deviation.

Normalized Scores

As you have seen, converting scores to z- or T-scores, or to other types of standardized scores, does not change the shape of the original score distribution. Because such transformations are linear, the standardized scores maintain the same shape and relative distances among scores as in the original distribution. There are at least three reasons, however, that we may want to use a transformation yielding scores that are normally distributed. First, comparison of standardized scores from tests with different distributions is not appropriate, strictly speaking. This is because differences in distributional shape result in differences in the relative distances between scores, depending on where the scores are located within the distribution. For example, a score 1 *SD* above the mean (i.e., a z-score of +1.0, or a T-score of 60) based on a normal distribution will be farther from the mean in absolute terms than the same score based on a leptokurtic (peaked) distribution. However, if the leptokurtic distribution could be converted to a normal distribution, or *normalized*, the comparison would be more valid.

The second reason that normal distributions are desirable is that these distributions have known percentages of cases falling above or below each score point that can be obtained from any standard normal z-score table. These percentages are useful in helping us to conceptualize peoples' relative positions within the distribution. Specifically, the normal distribution has the following properties:

- Approximately 68% of scores fall between 1 *SD* below and 1 *SD* above the mean.
- Approximately 95% of scores fall between 2 *SD*s below and 2 *SD*s above the mean.
- Approximately 99% of scores fall between 3 *SD*s below and 3 *SD*s above the mean.

In a normal distribution of Weschler IQ scores with a mean of 100 and an *SD* of 15, this would mean that 68% of all scores would fall between 85 and 115, 95% between 70 and 130, and 99% between 55 and 145. This is illustrated in Figure 2.1. It is therefore easy to see why IQ scores of 130 are considered to be high; only about 2.5% of scores would be above this value.

Third, normalized scores might be preferred because many commonly used statistical procedures are based on assumptions of normality. Because of advantages such

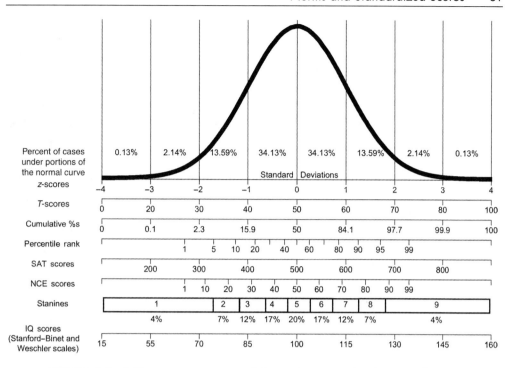

FIGURE 2.1. Different score types and their relations under the normal curve.

as ease of comparison for scores based on equivalent distributions, correspondence of scores to known percentages of the distribution, and the ability to satisfy normality assumptions, scores are sometimes *normalized*, or transformed, such that the resulting distribution is normal. Such transformations are nonlinear and therefore change the relative distances between scores to some extent. If the original distribution of scores is fairly normal to begin with, normalization will have little effect. However, to the extent that the original distribution deviates from normality, the differences between adjacent scores in the normalized distribution will differ somewhat from the original.

To create normalized scores, we first find the percentile rank for each of the original scores. The second step is to find the z-score corresponding to the percentile rank of each score based on the standard normal distribution, sometimes referred to as the normal z distribution. This distribution is typically tabled in introductory statistics texts and can also be accessed through statistical packages such as SPSS and SAS, or through Excel. Once the appropriate z-score is found, it is assigned to the corresponding original score. For example, someone who scored at a *PR* of 50 would be given a normalized score of 0 because 0 is the z-score corresponding to that *PR*. Someone with a score at a *PR* of 84 would be given a normalized score of 1.0 because 1.0 is the z-score that has 84% (50% + ½ of 68%) of the scores below it. This process is completed for each score in the distribution to create a new set of scores. Because these scores are obtained from the normal z distribution, they will be normally distributed z-scores. Such scores are referred to as normalized z-scores. If a distribution with a different metric is desired, Equation 2.3 could be applied to the z-scores.

The fact that normalizing transformations change the relative distances among scores in a distribution raises the question of whether such transformations are justifiable. The extent to which this type of transformation is justified depends on whether the population distribution of the attribute being measured is thought to be normal. You may well wonder why, if the population distribution is normal, a normal distribution is not obtained in the first place. There are at least two possible reasons for this. One reason is that the items used are flawed in some way. Thus, although the attribute being measured is normally distributed, our poor measurement method is not able to fully capture this. For example, if the measure consists of multiple-choice items that are poorly written, the resulting scores may be either too easy or too difficult, resulting in scores that are positively (for overly difficult) or negatively (for overly easy) skewed. However, in such a case one might argue that rewriting the items is a better solution than transforming the scores. The former practice fixes the problem, whereas the latter simply disguises it.

Another reason commonly given for the use of normalizing transformations is that although the population distribution is normal, such normality may not be obtained in a given sample owing to sampling fluctuations. This is especially true if the sample is one of convenience or is otherwise nonrandomly obtained. However, as Angoff (1971) has pointed out, normalizing transformations may not be appropriate if the sample to which they are applied has been obtained through prior selection. In such a case, it may well be that values of the attribute in the selected sample are not representative of those in the normally distributed population. For example, achievement scores from students in a gifted class will generally not be normally distributed because students in such classes are often selected on the basis of their higher than average achievement scores. In such cases, application of a normalizing function would therefore result in a distortion of the score distribution for the selected group. Given such problems, use of normalizing transformations should be used very cautiously. If the original distribution does not differ substantially from the normal, little distortion will be introduced by normalizing the scores. You may detect, however, that this implies normalized scores are most appropriate when they are least needed—that is, when the distribution of interest is fairly normal already. Be that as it may, you will undoubtedly encounter several types of normalized scores that are in common usage. The most common of these are normalized z- and T-scores, stanines, and normal curve equivalents (NCEs).

Stanines

The term *stanine* is shorthand for "standard nine." This type of score was developed in the early days of computers when computer memory was at a premium. Their popularity was due in part to the fact that, because they are limited to one digit, they only require one column of storage space. Another positive feature of stanines is that they represent fairly broad categories and thus mitigate against the tendency to overinterpret small differences in scores. This tendency toward overinterpretation can be problematic with scores such as *T*-scores or percentiles, for which a difference of one point may not be particularly meaningful. However, the downside of this feature is that stanines are relatively coarse measures that cannot be used to make fine differentiations among scores.

Stanines divide the distribution of raw scores into nine sections such that specific percentages of scores fall into each. Specifically, a score of 1 corresponds to the bottom 4% of the distribution, a score of 2 contains the next 7% of the distribution, a score of 3 the next 12%, a score of 4 the next 17%, a score of 5 the middle 20%, and scores of 6, 7, 8, and 9 contain the same percentages as scores of 4, 3, 2, and 1, respectively (see Figure 2.1). The resulting distribution of stanines is approximately normal, with a mean of 5 and a standard deviation of about 2. Thus, stanines are normalized scores. Because they are obtained from placing specific, and unequal, percentages of scores into the nine stanine categories, stanine scores do not have equal intervals and are best treated as ordinal in nature. As can be seen in Figure 2.1, for example, the distance between stanines of 1 and 2 is much greater than that between stanines of 4 and 5.

Normal Curve Equivalents

Normal curve equivalents are another type of normalized score. They are obtained by using the procedures described previously to obtain normalized *z*-scores and then transforming these to a special kind of *T*-score with a mean of 50 and an *SD* of 21.06. The reason for this seemingly odd choice of *SD* is that it results in NCEs of 1 and 99 that correspond exactly to the 1st and 99th percentile ranks, as can be seen in Figure 2.1. Note that although NCEs of 1, 50, and and 99 correspond exactly to the percentile ranks with the same values (i.e., the 1st, 50th, and 99th), this relationship does not hold for other NCEs and percentile ranks. This is because NCEs have equal intervals, whereas percentile ranks do not. Thus, for example, an NCE difference of 10 points represents the same score point distance at any point along the scale, as can be seen in Figure 2.1. You can verify that the same is not true for percentile ranks. This equal-interval property of NCEs is useful because it means that these scores can be used to compare score gains or losses across respondents and conduct other mathematical operations that are inappropriate with percentile ranks.

Developmental-Level Scores

The final types of scores discussed here are *grade-* and *age-equivalent scores*. These are sometimes called *developmental-level scores* because they reference scores to those obtained by others at a similar stage of development. Grade-equivalent (GE) scores are often used in educational achievement testing as a means of comparing a student's achievement to that of other students in the same grade. Similarly, age-equivalent (AE) scores are commonly used to describe age-related attributes of young children such as vocabulary or other language abilities, or physical attributes such as height or weight. Given that both school-related achievement and age-related cognitive, motor, and physical attributes tend to increase from one school grade or age level to the next, it seems reasonable to use grade or age as a basis for establishing normative scores. Because grade and age levels are widely understood metrics, such scores have become popular with consumers as an intuitive way to understand children's performance. Both GE scores and AE scores are derived in the same manner and share a common set of limitations, so the following discussion focuses only on grade equivalents. However, the discussion applies equally well to age equivalents.

Computation of GE and AE scores begins by administering a test containing sets of items that are the same across adjacent grade levels, known as *common* or *anchor items*, to students at several adjacent grade or age levels. The average (or median, if scores are not normally distributed) score for each grade or age level is then obtained. For example, suppose a test of math achievement is given to students in grades 3, 4, and 5 during the second month of the school year, and the following standardized scores are obtained.

Grade level	Average score
3.2	30
4.2	40
5.2	50

A grade level of 3.2 indicates the second month of third grade. Given that the average score at this point is 30, that score would be given a GE score of 3.2. A student obtaining this score would be said to be performing as well as the average student in the second month of the third grade. Similarly, scores of 40 and 50 would be given GE scores of 4.2 and 5.2, respectively. Although this takes care of those particular scores, we would also want GE scores for the scores in between. There are two ways of obtaining these scores. One is to administer the test to students in each month of each school year. However, you may see potential problems with this approach, as it would require an inordinate number of test administrations to obtain sufficient samples of students at each level. Another way to obtain intermediate GE scores is through linear interpolation. Using the example table, a student who obtained a score of 35 (halfway between 30 and 40) would be given a GE score of 3.7 (halfway between 3.2 and 4.2). Other intermediate GEs could be obtained in a similar fashion.

Suppose a fourth-grade student has obtained a GE score of 7.8 in math achievement. It is tempting to interpret this as meaning the student has the same math knowledge as a student in the eighth month of seventh grade. This is not the case, however, and such an interpretation would be misleading. Students can earn high GE scores by doing very well on the material they have learned to date. Thus, it is not the case that the fourth grader with a GE score of 7.8 knows what a seventh grader knows; she has simply done very well on the fourth-grade content on which she was tested. Typically, GE scores are not obtained by giving students in different grades exactly the same test. Instead, tests at different grade levels are *linked* by including sets of common items on tests at adjacent grade levels. For example, the third- and fourth-grade tests might consist of 50 items,

10 of which are the same for each grade and the remaining 40 of which differ across grades. Thus, the tests for each grade level will consist primarily of items specific to that grade level. So, students at different grade levels do not take the same test. This is another reason that it is misleading to interpret a GE score higher than a student's grade level as meaning the student knows the content taught in the higher grade.

Other limitations of GE (and AE) scores include the following:

1. The interpolation process used to obtain these scores is based on the assumption that knowledge increases linearly with time. That is, in using this process, we must assume that students gain exactly the same amount during each month of school. Anyone who has attended school is probably aware that this is not the case, however. To the extent that it is not, error is introduced into the calculations.

2. Whereas interpolation involves calculating scores *within* the range of those actually obtained, *extrapolation* involves calculating scores *beyond* the range of obtained scores. For example, it is possible to obtain a GE score of 11.8, even though no eleventh-grade students have been included on any of tests being scaled. Such scores are obtained by assuming that the increasing trend we observe for scores from lower grades continues in exactly the same way for all higher grades. Such an assumption is tenuous at best and typically introduces even more error into scores than is introduced by interpolation. This is because, although interpolation is error prone, it is at least based on observed data. Extrapolation, in contrast, is based on no real data at all. For this reason, the highest GE score for some achievement tests is simply reported as 10.0 + or 11.0 +.

3. Not all students in a given grade will obtain GE scores equivalent to their grade level. Because GE scores are based on the average (or median) score in each grade, half of the students in each grade will have a GE score below grade level. Although this is not necessarily a problem if consumers understand the reason for it, in many cases they do not. Thus, students and parents can be caused unnecessary concern because of scores that indicate performance that appears to be "below grade level."

4. In order to be useful, GE scores must be based on content that can be considered to be more or less the same across grade levels. Subjects such as basic reading and math skills lend themselves to expression in terms of GE scores because these subjects are taught to all students in more or less the same format across several grade levels. Once students reach middle and high school, however, they become more heterogeneous in terms of the classes they take. For example, some middle school students take basic math while others take algebra. Given such heterogeneity, it no longer makes sense to think of math achievement as falling on a single continuum on which students can be compared. Consequently, GE scores are not particularly useful past the sixth or seventh grades.

5. GE scores are not on an interval scale. For example, the differences between GE scores of 1 and 1.9 and 6 and 6.9 are not necessarily the same. This is because children

often develop more quickly when they are younger, with the result that one month of growth in the first grade is not equivalent to one month of growth in the sixth grade. Also, GE scores in different grades depend on the amount of content covered as well as the homogeneity of content, and these also differ across grades and subject areas.

6. Although GE scores are sometimes used to compare students' scores across subjects, it is not good practice to do so because growth does not occur at the same rate in different content areas. In fact, there is increasing evidence that patterns of growth are different across subjects.

7. A related issue is that students do not all gain at the same rate. In general, research has shown that students at high achievement levels tend to gain more than 1.0 GE score in a year, while students at lower achievement levels tend to gain less. Thus, the use of GE scores for indicating "normative" growth may be somewhat misleading.

Score Profiles

Consider our earlier example in which Javarro obtained z-scores of −0.5 in English and 2.0 in math. Converting Javarro's scores in this way allowed us to compare his performance in the two areas. Comparisons of this type are common when using large-scale achievement tests, such as the *Stanford 10*. Such tests, sometimes referred to as *test batteries*, typically assess student performance in several different subject areas. The advantage of such test batteries is that, if tests of different subjects are all administered to the same norm group, scores can be compared across subject areas. Such comparisons yield a *score profile* that can be useful in determining students' strengths and weaknesses across subject areas. However, it is important to note that, if scores in different subjects are not normed on the same group, score differences will be due, at least in part, to differences in the norm groups. If separate but comparable norm groups are used, scores can still be compared as long as the user keeps in mind the possibility of distortion due to norm group differences.

Even when all the subject area tests have been normed on the same sample, it is still possible that the amount of variation in the scores from different subject areas will not be the same. This is because students' knowledge or abilities may be more homogeneous in some areas than in others. As a result of this variability across subject areas, the same difference in raw score points may not correspond to the same difference in standard score points. Recall that standard score units are based on the *SD* of the norm group, so if these *SD*s differ across subjects, so will the standard score units. For example, if we change our earlier z-score example such that the *SD*s of the English and math tests were both 4, we can see that Javarro's scores on the two tests would be much closer together. Differences in scores should be interpreted with this in mind, even if they are based on the same norm group. One common way of doing so is to place confidence intervals around each score, as is discussed in later chapters on reliability. These confidence intervals take into account possible differences in test *SD*s as well as differences in test reliabilities.

CRITERION-REFERENCED TESTING

The types of scores discussed thus far are all norm-referenced approaches. As noted in the introductory sections of this chapter, however, criterion-referenced approaches are also possible. Although such approaches have not been as popular as norm referencing in the past, criterion-referenced testing has been gaining in popularity in educational contexts. This is due at least in part to the fact that educators have increasing interest in assessing what students know and can do, as opposed to how students compare to their peers. As with any measurement system, however, criterion-referenced measurement comes with its own set of issues. Among these issues is the need for careful articulation of the content domain of the test. Because of this need for clear definitions of the content domain, criterion-referenced tests tend to cover a narrower range of material than norm-referenced tests, but to cover this material in more detail. Because of space limitations, I do not cover criterion-referenced tests in detail in this chapter, but you can refer to the books by Berk (1980) and Popham (1978) or the review by Haertel (1985) for more information. For now simply note that most of the indices for assessing item and test quality discussed in this book were developed for use with norm-referenced rather than criterion-referenced tests. One implication of this is that these indices usually reach their optimum values for norm-referenced scores and will not necessarily provide useful information for criterion-referenced measures. In the upcoming chapters on reliability, validity, and item analysis, this issue is discussed in the specific contexts of these topics.

SUMMARY

Raw scores can be transformed to make them more meaningful. The two basic approaches to the task of imparting meaning to test scores are norm referencing and criterion referencing. In the norm-referencing system, an individual's score is compared to the average score of others taking the same test, known as the norm group. In the criterion-referencing system, an individual's score is given meaning by relating it to a specific amount of the attribute, such as 70% of the questions being answered correctly. This chapter focused primarily on norm-referenced scores. When such scores are used, it is important that the norm group is recent, representative, and relevant to the population of interest.

There are many types of norm-referenced scores, all of which have their attendant strengths and weaknesses. Percentile ranks are easily understood, but they are on an ordinal scale, which limits their use in mathematical operations. Standardized scores such as z- and T-scores are easily calculated and represent an interval level of measurement. These scores preserve the distributional form of the raw scores from which they were computed. If obtaining a normal distribution of scores is of interest, normalized scores such as stanines and NCEs can be obtained. Finally, GE and AE scores are commonly used for scaling attributes that increase developmentally. Although the fact that they are linked to well-known metrics such as grade or age level makes the use of GE scores and AE scores attractive, their seemingly straightforward interpretation often results in misconceptions about their meaning.

EXERCISES

1. What is the difference between *standardized* and *normalized* scores?

2. Why are raw scores (RS) not the best scores to use for interpreting student performance?

3. Your neighbor has received the information below from her fourth-grade son's school regarding his recent performance on a standardized achievement test (No. of items is the total number of items on each test; *RS* is number of correct responses; *SS* is standardized score; *PR* is national percentile rank):

Subject	No. of items	RS	SS	PR	GE
Vocabulary	22	10	380	26.4	3.5
Reading	60	33	395	30.4	3.0
Math	30	13	290	14.3	2.5
Science	45	42	744	96.9	9.8

Your neighbor is concerned that her son has GE scores in vocabulary, reading comprehension, and math that are lower than his grade level (he is in the fourth grade). What two issues with GE scores would help your neighbor understand that this is not necessarily a problem?

4. Your neighbor has noticed that her son obtained a GE score of 9.8 in science. She decides he should be placed in a ninth-grade science class because this score shows that he already knows the ninth-grade science content. Is your neighbor correct? Why or why not?

5. Are the following types of tests most likely norm or criterion referenced?

   a. The GMAT (Graduate Management Admissions Test)

   b. Tests to obtain a driver's license

   c. Master's or doctoral comprehensive exam scores

   d. Standardized achievement tests

   e. Nursing licensure examination

Table 2.3 shows scores for 50 students along with the frequency (*f*), cumulative frequency (*cf*), interval percentage (%), and cumulative percentage (%). Use this information to answer Questions 6–9.

TABLE 2.3. Score Information for Questions 6–9

Score	f	cf	%	$c\%$
18	4	50	8	100
17	5	46	10	92
16	6	41	12	82
15	9	35	18	70
14	8	26	16	52
13	7	18	14	36
12	4	11	8	22
10	3	7	6	14
9	2	4	4	8
8	2	2	4	4

6. Calculate the percentile ranks for scores of 10, 15, and 18.

7. Why are the percentile ranks for these three scores not the same as their cumulative percentage values?

8. The mean and *SD* of the scores in Table 2.3 are 14 and 2.6, respectively. Calculate the z-score values for scores of 9, 13, and 16.

9. Calculate the *T*-score values for the same scores (9, 13, and 16).

10. A state education administrator is quoted in the local paper as saying, "We plan to compare the average percentile ranks for test scores across a 5-year period for each school district to determine which district has made the most gains." What, if anything, is wrong with this idea?

11. A human resources director analyzed job aptitude scores from employees with the highest supervisor ratings and found that the scores were negatively skewed. The director decided to apply a normalizing function to obtain a more normal distribution.

    a. What are two score-normalizing functions that could be used?

    b. Is it appropriate to apply a normalizing function in this situation? Why or why not?

12. Consider a highly skewed distribution of scores. If these scores were transformed into the following score types, would the resulting distribution be highly skewed or normal? Why?

    a. z-score

    b. *T*-score

    c. Stanine

    d. Normal curve equivalent

13. Liz and Heather are participating in an intervention to improve short-term memory. Their percentile ranks on a standardized test of short-term memory before and after the intervention are shown in Table 2.4.

TABLE 2.4. Percentile Rank Information for Question 13

	PR before intervention	PR after intervention
Liz	50	57
Heather	90	97

a. The percentile ranks for both Liz and Heather increased by 7. Would the increases in their raw scores have been equal as well? Why or why not?

b. Did Liz and Heather show equal gains in short-term memory? Why or why not?

3

The Test Development Process

Imagine that you have been asked to evaluate a program designed to change participants' attitudes about smoking. How would you go about it? One aspect of such an
evaluation that might immediately come to mind is that you would need some way of
determining whether attitudes had, in fact, changed, and this would necessitate some
way of measuring these attitudes. This is just one of many examples of situations in
which researchers would be faced with the task of developing a scale. Other examples
include those in which a teacher wants to evaluate the degree to which students have
learned the material being taught, a medical professional is interested in the degree to
which medication lessens patients' levels of pain, a human resources professional wants
to determine whether job applicants have the skills needed for the job, or a psychologist
is tasked with determining whether clients should be diagnosed as having a particular
psychopathology.

In each of these situations, some type of measurement is required. Note, however,
that the purposes of these measurements are quite different. The psychologist is interested in making a diagnosis—that is, a yes/no decision about whether the client should
be classified as having a specific psychopathology. The teacher is interested in the
amount of learning that has taken place to determine the next step in the educational
sequence. The human resources professional wants to select the applicants that are most
likely to succeed on the job. And the medical professional is interested in changes in the
levels of pain felt by patients to evaluate the effectiveness of their medication. The fact
that these measurements are expected to fulfill different purposes implies that the ways
in which they are developed and evaluated would also be somewhat different. In the
following sections, I discuss the basic steps involved in developing scales. As you read
these sections, keep in mind that, although the basic steps of the scale development process are fairly similar for different types of scales, the way in which the steps are carried
out may differ. In this chapter, the focus is on the commonalities of scale development
across different types and purposes of testing, and, as appropriate, note is made of situations in which procedures would differ.

STEPS IN SCALE DEVELOPMENT

Many authors have outlined the steps involved in the scale development process (Benson & Clark, 1982; Clark & Watson, 1995; Crocker & Algina, 1986; DeVellis, 2003). The process described in this chapter draws from these sources and from my own experience. Briefly, these steps are:

1. State the purpose of the scale.
2. Identify and define the domain of the construct to be measured.
3. Determine whether a measure already exists.
4. Determine the item format.
5. Develop a test blueprint or test objectives.
6. Create the initial item pool.
7. Conduct the initial item review (and revisions).
8. Conduct a large-scale field test of items.
9. Analyze items.
10. Revise items.
11. Calculate reliability.
12. Conduct a second field test of items.
13. Repeat steps 8–11 as necessary.
14. Conduct validation studies.
15. Prepare guidelines for administration.

After reading through all of these steps, you may well be wondering how anyone would ever have the time and/or resources to develop a scale. Certainly, scale development is a resource-intensive and time-consuming process. However, keep in mind that the outcomes of one's research study, program evaluation, or client diagnosis are completely dependent on the quality of the measures used. If the measurement scales used do not accurately reflect the constructs of interest, any inferences made on the basis of these measures are suspect. In fact, I would argue that many of the issues with questionable and nonreplicable results in the social sciences can be traced back to poor measurement development. Accordingly, the time and resources devoted to developing quality measurement scales are time and resources well spent. In particular, if the scale being developed has the potential to be used in "high-stakes" situations, such as diagnosing learning disabilities or psychopathologies, determining whether students should be promoted to the next grade or graduated from high school, selecting applicants for higher education or for employment, or granting certification or licensure, it is crucial that the process of scale development be as thorough as possible. Although adherence to the steps outlined earlier will result in a better product, in some situations a less comprehensive process will still yield an adequate scale. For example, if a researcher is developing a scale to use in his or her own research and does not anticipate that the scale will be used in any other context, it may not be necessary to conduct multiple field tests of the items.

Another caveat about these 15 steps is that the order in which they are carried out is not set in stone. Logically, of course, some steps must be carried out before others. One cannot review or analyze the items before they have been written, for example. And, as is discussed in the following sections, it is not a good idea to write items before carrying out steps 1 and 2. However, there is nothing wrong with carrying out reliability or validity studies earlier in the process, if sufficient data are available. In addition, the steps need not be carried out in a linear fashion. Instead, researchers may decide to revisit an earlier step, such as deciding on an item format, after writing items.

In the following sections, most of the 15 steps are discussed in more detail. In some cases, the operations involved are sufficiently complex as to merit a separate chapter. So, for example, topics such as determining the item format, writing items, and conducting analyses of the items' performance and of the reliability and validity of the scores obtained from these are discussed thoroughly in Chapters 3–11.

State the Purpose of the Scale

You may think it goes without saying that one would state the purpose of the scale being developed. After all, why would a scale be developed for which there was no stated purpose? However, having a purpose in mind and communicating this purpose clearly in publications are not synonymous. In a recent review of the scale development literature, my coauthors and I found that very few researchers clearly stated the purposes for which their scales were intended (Fisher, Gerstner, & Bandalos, 2013). This is unfortunate because scales intended for different purposes should be developed and validated in different ways. And, scales developed for one purpose are not necessarily useful for other purposes. As one example, scales that are designed to diagnose math disabilities are not particularly good at measuring general math knowledge. Because scales are most useful in measuring the outcomes for which they were designed, it is crucial that the uses for which the scale is intended be clearly specified.

Identify and Define the Domain

This aspect of scale development is concerned with the delineation of the construct to be measured. It is at this point that the researcher develops a detailed definition of the construct. It is crucial that sufficient attention be paid to this definition, as it will influence other aspects of scale development. As with step 1, many researchers gloss over this step, feeling, perhaps, that the definition of the construct being measured is self-evident. Nothing could be further from the truth, however. To demonstrate this point, you need look no further than that quintessential psychological construct, intelligence. You may wish, as an exercise, to ask several different people to write down their definitions of intelligence, emphasizing what intelligence does and does not encompass. I have done this as a class exercise and can assure you that views on the nature of intelligence vary widely. Researchers should therefore not assume that others share their definition of a particular construct but should instead take pains to explicate their view of the construct as thoroughly as possible. Such a definition should include explanations of how this view differs from those of other theorists or of how the construct differs from other, similar constructs. As part of this process, researchers should also pay attention to the construct continuum. That is, researchers should define the meaning of low and high levels of the construct and indicate the ways in which those at different levels of the construct continuum would differ.

What else should be included in definitions of the construct? I suggest that researchers first write out a brief one- or two-sentence description. This can later be elaborated but will serve as a useful starting point. Researchers should also think about the degree of breadth or generality of the construct. For example, in the area of self-concept, one can envisage a broad, general self-concept as well as more specific aspects of self-concept, such as social, intellectual, and physical self-concepts. One could focus on measuring only one of these, or all of them. In their review of scale development research published in the journal *Psychological Assessment*, Clark and Watson (1995) found that the majority of scale developers focused on fairly narrow constructs.

Related to the breadth of a construct is its generality. In measuring patients' perceptions of pain, for example, would one scale apply to patients of all ages, or would separate scales be needed for children or other subgroups? In many cases, there is good reason to think that the content of measurement scales may not generalize to all populations. Items, and even constructs themselves, can be culture and gender specific. Finally, the definition of the construct may specify whether it is common to most contexts or whether it is restricted to particular contexts. As one example, it has been shown that individuals who are scrupulously honest in a work context may not necessarily be so in other contexts, such as that of paying taxes. So, a researcher developing a scale to measure honesty would need to delineate the contexts to which the scale items apply.

Another aspect of construct definition involves differentiating the construct of interest from other, similar constructs. To go back to the self-concept example, how does self-concept differ from self-efficacy or self-confidence? Researchers should also consider what other constructs might be related, either positively or negatively, to the construct being measured. As discussed by DeVellis (2003) and Clark and Watson (1995), such determinations are difficult, if not impossible, in the absence of theory. Thus, it is critical that those who are developing scales be thoroughly familiar with theories about the construct of interest as well as those of related constructs.

Determine Whether a Measure Already Exists

By now you may have an inkling of the idea that scale development is not for sissies, to paraphrase actor Bette Davis's well-known quotation about growing old. Done well, scale development is a time-consuming, though fascinating, endeavor. Thus, if a scale that measures the construct of interest already exists, why reinvent the wheel? Instead of doing so, once researchers have determined, through following steps 1 and 2, what it is they want to measure, they should investigate whether a scale to measure it already exists. Several resources are available to help in this search. The *Mental Measurements Yearbook* (MMY) and *Tests in Print* (TIP) are multivolume resources published by the Buros Center for Testing. Now available electronically through many libraries, the MMY contains reviews of commonly used commercially available educational and psychological tests. Most tests are reviewed by two unbiased experts, making the MMY a sort of *Consumer Reports* for tests. TIP contains brief descriptions of these tests and serves as an index of sorts for the MMY. Another resource in the area of psychology is the online database *PsycTESTS* maintained by the American Psychological Association (*http://www. apa.org/pubs/databases/psyctests/index.aspx*). In contrast to the MMY and TIP, *PsycTESTS* focuses on unpublished, noncommercially available tests. In addition to providing information about the tests, which often include the test items, *PsycTESTS* provides links to publications related to the development and use of the tests.

For attitude measures, the somewhat outdated *Scales for the Measurement of Attitudes* (Shaw & Wright, 1967) includes scales measuring a plethora of attitudes in areas including (but not limited to) politics, religion, social and family life, and international affairs. The more recent volume *Measures of Personality and Social Psychological Attitudes* (Robinson, Shaver, & Wrightsman, 1991) provides scale items as well as information on the measurement quality (e.g., reliability and validity information) for a wide variety of personality and attitude constructs. The related volume *Measures of Political Attitudes* (Robinson, Shaver, & Wrightsman, 1999) has a similar format but focuses, as you may have guessed, on measures of attitudes specific to various aspects of politics. More recent volumes in this vein focus on the areas of marketing (*Handbook of Marketing Scales: Multi-Item Measures for Marketing and Consumer Behavior Research*; Bearden, Netemeyer, & Haws, 2010) and communication (*Communication Research Measures: A Sourcebook*; Rubin, Palmgreen, & Sypher, 2009; *Communication Research Measures II: A Sourcebook*; Rubin et al., 2009). For health-related measures, the online Health and Psychological Instruments (HaPI) database, available through many libraries, contains information on instruments used in health-related research. The database is searchable and provides an abstract to the article in which the instrument was first published, as well as references to articles in which the instrument was used. There are also volumes specific to measures of depression (*Practitioner's Guide to Empirically Based Measures of Depression*; Nezu, Ronan, Meadows, & McClure, 2000) and anxiety (*Practitioner's Guide to Empirically Based Measures of Anxiety*; Anthony, Orsillo, & Roemer, 2001). As their names imply, these resources are targeted to clinicians. Sections on the instruments' clinical utility, time requirements, costs, and administration in addition to psychometric properties are included. Finally, the International Personality Item Pool (IPIP; *http://ipip.ori.org*) provides a wide variety of personality and individual differences measures that are available free of charge.

Determine the Item Format

In Chapters 4 and 5, I discuss many item types used to measure cognitive and non-cognitive constructs. For cognitive items, these include multiple-choice, true–false, matching, short-answer or completion, essay, and performance tasks. For noncognitive items, I discuss Thurstone, Guttman, and Likert item types. The most basic consideration in choosing an item type is its match to the type of response desired. If, for example, a teacher wants to determine whether students can explain concepts in a way that indicates deep understanding, some type of essay item would probably be best. In this situation, true–false items are unlikely to provide the desired information because they are not capable of measuring the ability to explain concepts. Another consideration in choosing an item format is the degree to which it is susceptible to contamination from extraneous influences such as guessing (for cognitive items) or responding in a socially desirable manner that does not reflect the respondent's true attitudes (for noncognitive items). These issues are discussed in Chapters 4 and 5.

Write Out the Testing Objectives

Once the construct has been thoroughly defined and its domain delineated, it is good practice to write out the cognitive or noncognitive objectives the associated scale is intended to measure. Although this step is most commonly associated with cognitive measurement, it can be quite useful for noncognitive assessments as well.

Objectives for Cognitive Measurement

Who among us has not taken a classroom test for which we thought we were perfectly prepared, only to discover that the material on the test was completely alien? Such tests represent poor practice because classroom assessments give important messages to students about the material the instructor thinks is most important to know. If instructors base tests on tangential or irrelevant information, students will be understandably confused about what they are meant to learn in the course. A good assessment is therefore one that reflects the most important cognitive goals and content areas of the instruction that has taken place. Thus, it is *de rigueur* in the cognitive realm to specify clear, measurable learning objectives. Linn and Gronlund's (2000) text on educational measurement, for example, devotes an entire chapter to the topic of writing instructional objectives.

Such objectives are typically represented in a *test blueprint* or *table of specifications* that delineates the content areas to be tested, along with the cognitive levels at which test items are to be targeted. Specification of the content areas to be covered for a course exam can be determined fairly easily from the course outline or syllabus. The number or percentage of items to be devoted to each content area is typically determined by the importance of the topic, which should be in alignment with the amount of class time spent on it. Specification of the cognitive levels of the items is somewhat more complex. However, several taxonomies of educational objectives are available to assist in this task. These taxonomies delineate various levels of cognitive outcomes arranged in hierarchical order from least to most complex. The classic example of such a taxonomy is Bloom's *Taxonomy of Educational Objectives* (1956). This work specifies six levels, each of which can be broken down into numerous sublevels.

1. *Knowledge*: This, the most basic level of the taxonomy, focuses on simple memorization and recall of factual information. Examples include knowledge of names, dates, common terms, and basic principles

2. *Comprehension*: This level goes beyond simple recall to require some basic understanding of information. Examples include providing examples, distinguishing terms, and providing basic explanations.

3. *Application*: As its name implies, operations at this level require students to use knowledge to solve problems, construct graphs or charts, or apply concepts or principles in new situations.

4. *Analysis*: Tasks at this level require students to break a concept, text, or other material down into its component parts. Examples include distinguishing facts from inferences, analyzing organizational structures (such as in music, art, or written material), and creating flow charts.

5. *Synthesis*: Tasks at this level require students to combine material, ideas, or skills to form a new product. Examples include giving a presentation, writing a short story, arguing a position, or solving a novel problem.

6. *Evaluation*: At this level, students are required to make judgments about the appropriateness, adequacy, value, correctness, or other qualities of a product or process. Examples include evaluating an argument, justifying a position, or critiquing an essay.

Although Bloom's taxonomy is still in use, recent researchers have provided taxonomies that, it is argued, are more useful for educators. One such taxonomy is that of Quellmalz (1985), which consists of five levels: recall, analysis, comparison, inference, and evaluation. These map onto Bloom's levels. For example, "recall" subsumes Bloom's levels of knowledge and comprehension. In my experience, these levels are often quite difficult to differentiate, so combining them seems reasonable. Quellmalz's "analysis" and "evaluation" levels are basically the same as Bloom's levels of the same names. Both the "comparison" and "inference" levels in Quellmalz's taxonomy map onto Bloom's "synthesis" level, but "inference" also maps onto Bloom's "application" level. Table 3.1 shows the correspondence between the two taxonomies.

A table of specifications typically lists the content to be covered along one side and the cognitive levels to be targeted on the other. An example table of specifications based on Bloom's cognitive levels and part of the content in Chapter 2 is shown in Table 3.2.

TABLE 3.1. Alignment of Bloom's and Quellmalz's Taxonomies for Cognitive Levels

	Quellmalz				
Bloom	Recall	Analysis	Comparison	Inference	Evaluation
Knowledge	X				
Comprehension	X				
Application				X	
Analysis		X			
Synthesis			X	X	
Evaluation					X

TABLE 3.2. Example of a Table of Specifications

	Cognitive level						
Content area	Knowledge	Comprehension	Application	Analysis	Synthesis	Evaluation	% of test
Standardized scores	5%	10%	10%	5%			30%
Transformed scores	5%	15%	5%				25%
Norm and criterion referencing	5%	5%				15%	25%
Developmental-level scores	5%	5%				10%	20%

The number or percentage of items desired in each cell is entered in the body of the table. It is also common to include a column indicating the overall percentage of items on the test that should be written for each content area, as has been done here. It is best to establish this *before* items are written. If items are written without the benefit of a table of specifications, items often tend to cluster in one part of the table. This is because items in certain content areas or at certain levels of cognitive complexity are easier to write. Note that it is not necessary to fill in every cell in the table. The cells for which items are written should reflect the overall goals of instruction. The entries in Table 3.2 suggest that the test will concentrate on the fairly basic cognitive levels of knowledge, comprehension, and application, with only a few items at higher levels. However, for the last two content areas, students should be able to evaluate whether a situation calls for norm- or criterion-referenced testing, or whether developmental level scores are being appropriately interpreted—operations that call for the higher levels of cognition associated with Bloom's evaluation level.

Objectives for Noncognitive Measurement

In the noncognitive domain, it is much less common to create a formal table of specifications. However, development of some form of such a table can be a useful way to delineate the specific content to be included on the scale. Often noncognitive scales are designed to measure several related, but somewhat different, subdimensions of a construct. These subdimensions are frequently developed into formal subscales that are scored separately. It is therefore expedient to use a table of specifications to delineate the number or percentage of items that should be devoted to each subdimension. It is also possible to specify different levels of affect, using taxonomies such as that of Krathwohl, Bloom, and Masia (1964). Unlike cognitive taxonomies, which are arranged according to cognitive complexity, affective taxonomies are arranged in order of increasing affective intensity. Such taxonomies are most often used for classifying intensity levels of attitudes, but they can be applied to any noncognitive target. Krathwohl's taxonomy has five levels, described here in the context of a scale designed to measure attitudes toward vegetarianism:

1. *Receiving*: At this level, respondents are simply willing to pay attention to the object of the attitude. For example, a person may be willing to listen to arguments for vegetarianism.

2. *Responding*: Respondents at this level begin to express some opinion (positive or negative) about the object. With regard to the vegetarianism example, a person at the responding level may begin to express tentative opinions that it could be wrong to consume animals.

3. *Commitment*: At this level, the respondent expresses a strong opinion regarding the object and is willing to commit time and energy to it. The respondent might change her diet to a vegetarian one and possibly commit time or money to vegetarian organizations.

4. *Organization*: Respondents at this level begin to change their other beliefs to be more compatible with their attitude toward the object. For example, a person may stop wearing leather or buying things containing animal by-products.

5. *Characterization*: At this highest level, respondents develop their attitude about the referent into a life philosophy that guides their actions and other beliefs. Thus, a person may devote more and more time and money to the vegetarian movement or even join a community organized around this belief.

In most cases, peoples' attitudes do not go beyond level 3; therefore, most items on attitude scales are written to target levels 2 or 3. However, if the population of interest is likely to include many people with more intense attitudes, items targeted at level 4 or even level 5 will be needed.

Create the Initial Item Pool

It is at this point in the scale construction process that the proverbial rubber hits the road. Based on the previous steps in the process, the researcher should now have a clear idea of the purpose of the scale, the item format to be used, the content to be included (and not to be included), and the cognitive or affective levels at which items should be targeted. In addition, the researcher has delineated the domain of the construct to be measured and has determined that no preexisting scale is available to measure the construct of interest. It is now time to create a pool of items. How many items should be in the pool? The table of specifications can provide some idea of the number of items needed, but most experts recommend writing many more items than will be included on the final scale. This is because items do not always function as well as one would hope. In fact, items have an annoying tendency to completely ignore the purpose for which they were developed and to function in ways that are utterly at odds with the scale developer's intentions. For this reason, DeVellis (2003) recommends writing three to four times the number of items that will ultimately be needed. Clark and Watson (1995) suggest including items that are broader in scope than one's original delineation of the construct domain. Although this suggestion may appear to contradict the suggestion to carefully delineate the construct domain, it is actually a good one. This is because, although irrelevant items will be revealed through subsequent item analyses, such analyses cannot suggest content that has been omitted. So, it is better to err on the side of inclusiveness than exclusiveness in initial item writing.

How do researchers think up these items? Many sources are available. One's knowledge of the theory underlying the construct to be measured is one obvious source. A related source is the literature review that has been done to develop this knowledge, which will often suggest ideas for items. Another popular method of generating items is to examine existing instruments that measure similar constructs. Although I am not suggesting that researchers plagiarize other instruments, seeing the types of items others have written can be an excellent source of ideas. Once ideas from such sources are fresh in one's mind, DeVellis (2003) recommends conducting a brainstorming session in which researchers think about their definition of the construct and write statements that paraphrase aspects of that definition. Then, the researcher can try to think of other ways to state the same ideas, or they can add statements corresponding to other aspects of the construct. At this point, one need not worry too much about redundancy or construct coverage. Once a sufficient pool of items is generated, the researcher can critique the items for clarity, redundancy, and content coverage (see Chapters 4 and 5 for item-writing guidelines).

Many researchers conduct focus groups with people like those to whom the scale will eventually be administered. Focus group members are asked to talk about their conceptualizations of the construct, and these conceptualizations can be used as the basis for items. The advantage of this method of generating items is that, because the items are based on the language used by focus group members, they are more likely to be clear to those who will eventually answer them. Individual interviews can be used in the same way. A related method involves the use of a think-aloud procedure in which respondents are given a definition of the construct and asked to verbally report any thoughts it conjures up. Or respondents can be asked to write down the ideas that are brought to mind. A variation on this method is to pose written open-ended questions related to the construct and ask respondents to write down their reactions. For example, if a researcher is developing a measure of depression, answers to open-ended prompts such as "What behaviors would you expect a person to exhibit if they were depressed?" or "Describe how you feel when you are depressed" might be useful in generating items.

Focus group and interview participants should be chosen to represent the population with whom the instrument will eventually be used. However, another group of people who can provide useful suggestions consists of those who are experts on the construct of interest. Although such experts may not be willing or able to write items, they may be willing to review the table of specifications or domain definition and suggest aspects of the construct that may have been overlooked. The methods described in this section are also very useful in the item review and revision process. For example, focus group participants and interviewees could be administered the items that have been written and asked to comment on the items' clarity and reading level. Subject matter experts could be asked to provide feedback on the degree to which the items match the table of specifications, as well as whether the items fully represent the construct of interest. I discuss item review procedures in more detail in a later section of this chapter.

In some cases, the scale being developed is based on symptomatology classifications for mental disorders, such as are found in the *Diagnostic and Statistical Manual of Mental Disorders* (DSM), or more broadly, for epidemiology, such as are found in the *International Classification of Diseases* (ICD). In such cases, the appropriate manual is often used to determine the content of items to be included on the instrument. Depending on the nature of the instrument, more general clinical observations may also be used to develop additional items.

Behavioral observations are an obvious candidate for items to be included on behavior checklists, such as those used to assess level of functioning for those with disabilities or for young children. For achievement tests, reviews of instructional objectives, curricular goals, or the "scope-and-sequence" documents used in many school districts to delineate the instructional targets for each grade are invaluable for determining the content and cognitive level to be targeted. Scale developers also often review commonly used textbooks in the content area to be measured. For college-level content, course syllabi could be used to determine appropriate content to include.

Finally, many tests that are designed for purposes of personnel selection use job samples or analyses of job activities to determine the content to be included. Job samples are, as the name implies, tasks that are part of the everyday duties required for a job (see Anastasi & Urbina, 1997). The most well-known examples are tests of typing or keyboarding skills or of ability to operate machinery or drive a car. Although the tasks included on tests for personnel selection are often the same as those an employee in that job would actually do, the time allowed and the setting in which the task is completed are typically standardized. Such standardization is necessary to ensure that no candidate has an unfair advantage in terms of time or working conditions. In some cases, having applicants carry out the actual job task is either unethical, unfeasible, or both, as in tests for such jobs as airline pilots or demolition experts. In such cases, simulations can be used.

A job analysis requires researchers to obtain a thorough description of the job duties an employee carries out on a typical day, focusing on what tasks or knowledge differentiate the job from other jobs. In addition, job analysts must focus on the knowledge, skills, and dispositions that distinguish experts or highly proficient workers from those who are less proficient. This procedure is sometimes referred to as the *critical incident technique* and was originally developed by Flanagan (1949, 1954). The *job element method* (McCormick, 1979, 1983; Primoff & Eyde, 1988) is a more modern take on this technique in which job elements are broken down into specific behavioral elements, which are then used to create items.

Conduct the Initial Item Review

Once items are written, the scale developer will want to obtain some basic feedback on item clarity, match to the test specifications, any violations of item-writing or grammatical principles, readability, possibility of offensiveness or unfairness, and readability level. This review process often involves two parts: review by experts and preliminary item tryouts. Expert review is useful for determining the degree to which items match the original test specifications, violate item-writing or grammatical principles, are at the appropriate reading level, or have the potential to offend any respondents. Given the variety of these criteria, it is unlikely that one group of experts will be able to judge them all. For example, judges who are expert in item-writing guidelines will often not be experts in the subject matter being measured. Similarly, those with item-writing or content expertise may not be capable of judging the offensiveness of items. As a result, several review panels are usually needed. If experts were asked to suggest ideas for items during the item development phase, or if they were consulted about item-writing guidelines, these same experts might be willing to review the items again. Although it may be possible for the same review panels to make judgments regarding offensiveness or fairness, this is not typically the case. Offensiveness is often in the eye of the beholder, and what offends one group may not offend another. If those writing items are members of a majority group, for example, they may not be aware that the terminology or subject matter being used is offensive to members of other groups. It may also be the case that words or phraseology have different meanings across different ethnic, cultural, or regional groupings. In the context of achievement testing, items should be reviewed to determine whether some aspect of an item's wording or subject matter makes it more difficult for some respondents than others. For example, the item "What color is an emerald?" is likely to be more easily answered by children who have actually seen such gems. Items should therefore be reviewed by representatives of all subgroups with whom the instrument will ultimately be used, with instructions to flag any items that are likely to be offensive or unfamiliar to members of that group.

If items are intended to be administered to children or adolescents, it is important to make sure that the vocabulary and sentence structure are appropriate. This can be accomplished by asking children to read the items and mark any words with which they are unfamiliar and any sentences they do not understand. A more time-consuming but possibly more revealing approach would be to ask children to read the items aloud and explain what they mean. Although such analyses are most important for scales that are intended to be used with children, readability should be considered for respondents of all ages.

A recent study by McHugh and Behar (2009) illustrates the need to consider the reading level of both the items and directions included on a scale. In this study, the authors note that the average reading level among adults in the United States is at approximately the eighth grade. Given that this is the average, however, many respondents will have a lower reading level. Thus, a common recommendation is to target instruments to the fifth- or sixth-grade reading level to accommodate the greatest number of respondents. In their study of 105 self-report instruments measuring either anxiety or depression, McHugh and Behar found that the average reading level of depression items was 7.6 (i.e, the sixth month of seventh grade), and for anxiety items the average was an even higher 8.7. Reading levels for scale instructions were even higher, at 8.4 and 10.1, respectively, for depression and anxiety measures. One consequence of this mismatch between the reading levels required by commonly used instruments and the reading levels characteristic of those responding to them is the introduction of response inaccuracy, which may be substantial. The authors recommend (as do I) that careful attention be paid to the reading level of both items and directions. One source that can assist in creating easy-to-read instruments is available from the National Cancer Institute (*www.cancer. gov/cancertopics/cancerlibrary/clear-and-simple*).

Conduct Preliminary Item Tryouts

Another source of item information can be obtained from preliminary item tryouts. At this stage of the game, it is probably not necessary to worry about obtaining a large, randomly selected group of respondents, unless unlimited resources are available. Because items are likely to be changed, sometimes considerably, at this stage, it is probably best to save one's resources to obtain a larger sample for later item tryouts. Johanson and Brooks (2010) recommend a sample size of approximately 30 respondents, whereas Hertzog (2008) is somewhat more conservative, recommending sample sizes of 70–80 respondents. As respondents answer the items, the test developer should observe them for signs of confusion or frustration, such as long pauses, changing answers, heavy sighs, or repeatedly banging their heads against the wall (the last-named, in particular, is not a good sign). Respondents can be invited to provide written comments on items they find confusing, irrelevant, or otherwise problematic. The scale developer may also wish to conduct a focus group after the administration of items, in which respondents can provide feedback on any confusion or other difficulties encountered while answering the items. Finally, although most tryout samples will be insufficient to obtain stable statistics, it is useful to examine the spread of responses (see Chapter 6). If respondents choose only one or two response options, the item may be too easy or difficult (for cognitive items) or too extreme (for noncognitive items).

Based on the results of these tryouts, items are often revised or even completely rewritten. However, unless an item appears to be beyond hope, it is better to defer decisions to eliminate items until a full field test can be done. Because preliminary item tryouts typically involve a small sample of respondents who may not be representative of the ultimate population of interest, it is best not to make consequential decisions such as eliminating items until after a large-scale field test is completed. It is to this field testing that I now turn.

Conduct a Large-Scale Field Test of Items

At this point, the scale developer has some initial information about item performance based on the reviews of expert panels and focus groups and on the information gleaned from preliminary item tryouts. Now is the time to obtain a large sample of respondents and calculate the first set of item statistics. How large is large? Nunnally and Bernstein (1994) suggest that the sample be at least twice the size of the number of items, or at least 200, whichever is greater (p. 333). Both DeVellis (2003) and Watson and Clark (1995) recommend a sample size of 300, although DeVellis notes that fewer respondents might be used if the number of items is fewer than 20.

Need for a Large Sample Size

There are two primary reasons a large sample size is needed. First, a small sample may not adequately represent the population of interest. This is particularly true if that population consists of subgroups that might be expected to respond somewhat differently to the items. In this situation, it is important to obtain responses from all subgroups of interest so that the entire gamut of possible responses can be observed. Similarly, it is important to obtain responses that span the entire range of the construct of interest. For achievement tests, this means that those expected to have little knowledge, those expected to do well, and those at all levels in between should be included. For psychological constructs, respondents with the entire range of affect from positive to negative or from low to high should be represented. If only those with high or low levels of the construct are sampled, it will not be possible to determine whether the items can differentiate between these levels.

The second reason a large sample is needed has to do with stability of the statistical indices. Most indices used in item analyses and in assessment of scale reliability and validity are based on correlations. Correlation coefficients are notoriously unstable in small samples, as can be seen from the accompanying figures. Figure 3.1 shows a plot of

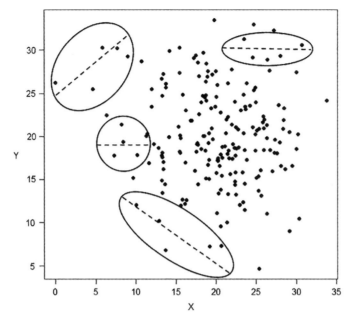

FIGURE 3.1. Scatterplot corresponding to a zero correlation.

two variables with a correlation of zero, based on a sample size of 200. This scatterplot is characteristic of a zero correlation, as there is no discernible trend indicated by the points. Rather, the points are scattered around in a haphazard pattern. However, suppose I randomly sample five cases from this "population" of 200. The ellipses surrounding various sets of points in the figure represent four such samples. I have drawn in approximate regression lines for each ellipse. From these you can see that, even though the population correlation is zero, correlations based on samples of only five cases could range from strongly negative to strongly positive. This is what is meant by sampling instability. Clearly, we would not like to think that the values we obtain from our item tryouts are subject to this type of instability. If they were, it would be difficult to have any faith in the generalizability of our results to another sample. Suppose, however, that I had taken samples of 100 instead of five? An inspection of Figure 3.1 should show you that this would result in correlations that are much more similar from sample to sample. Thus, it can be seen that larger samples will result in greater sampling stability.

Aside from sample size, there is an additional influence on the sampling stability of correlation (and correlational-related) indices. This is the magnitude of the correlation itself. The relationship of correlation magnitude to sampling stability can be seen by considering Figure 3.2. As in Figure 3.1, this figure is based on 200 cases. However, the correlation between X and Y in Figure 3.2 is quite high at .87. If I were to repeat my demonstration of sampling stability by sampling cases from the points in Figure 3.2, you can see that many more of the samples than in Figure 3.1 would result in correlations of similar magnitude and direction. This is because most of the points follow a similar pattern—that of a strong positive correlation.

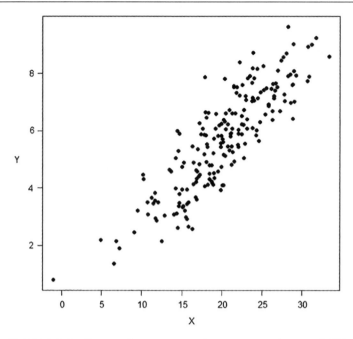

FIGURE 3.2. Scatterplot corresponding to a correlation of .87.

Restriction of Range

Another issue to consider in selecting a sample for item tryouts is *restriction of range*. Restriction of range occurs when respondents with values above or below a certain point on the X or Y scale are not included in the sample. This issue was discussed previously in the context of obtaining a sample that represents the entire range of the construct. In addition to being nonrepresentative, failure to include those with high or low scores can adversely affect the values of correlation-based statistics. To illustrate, I have restricted the range of the X variable in the plot shown in Figure 3.2. A graph of the remaining points is shown in Figure 3.3, in which only those with X values to the right of the vertical line have been selected. The result is that only those points shown in the ellipse are available for calculating the correlation, and as can be seen from Figure 3.3, these points exhibit a much weaker correlational pattern, which would result in a much lower value of the correlation coefficient. Restriction of range can occur as a result of sampling from a selective group, such as a class of honors students, a group of elite athletes, or a sample of Fortune 500 executives. Such samples are appropriate only if these are the groups for whom the scale is intended to be used.

Inclusion of Validation Items

Field testing of items is often the most resource-intensive part of the scale development process. Thus, scale developers will want to make the most of the data collection process. This often involves including variables that can be used in later validation studies.

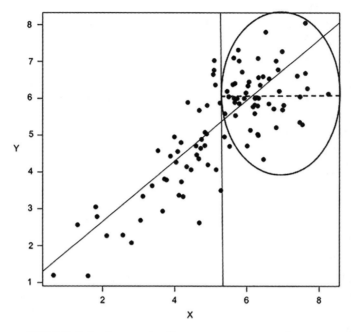

FIGURE 3.3. Scatterplot illustrating restriction of range.

Measurement validity is discussed at length in Chapter 11, but for now suffice it to say that validation is concerned with investigating the degree to which scores on a scale can reasonably be interpreted as intended. For example, if scale developers intend that scores be used to predict a criterion, it is incumbent on them to provide evidence that the scores do provide a reasonable prediction. If scores are intended to be interpreted as indications of respondents' levels of creativity, evidence that the items do measure creativity, and not something else, should be provided. Obtaining evidence of validity is an ongoing process, but one good place to start is by including variables in the field test that can be used in later investigations of scale validity. For example, if the scale developer hypothesizes that women should have higher scores on the scale than men or that scores should increase with age or be related in particular ways to scores on other scales, these variables should be included in the field test. Although I discuss many other forms of validity evidence in Chapter 11, some basic evidence for measurement validity can be obtained by the relatively simple studies suggested here.

Prepare Guidelines for Administration

Determining Time Limits

This last step in the scale development process typically occurs after items have been field tested and item analyses have been conducted. However, this should not be taken to imply that the development of guidelines for administration and scoring should be an afterthought. On the contrary, scale developers should collect data to inform these guidelines throughout the scale development process. For example, scale developers should closely monitor the amount of time respondents take to complete the scale. This information can then be used to develop appropriate time limits for scale administration. Determination of appropriate time limits will depend on the type of scale being developed. For most attitude and personality scales, it is desirable to allow respondents plenty of time to complete the scale. Imposition of strict time limits will cause respondents to rush through the items without reading them carefully, introducing error into the resulting scores.

Speed and Power Tests

In the measurement of achievement or aptitude, determination of an appropriate time limit for a test depends on whether it is a *speed* or *power* test. A *pure speed* test is one on which the time limit is so short that no examinee is expected to complete all the items. Speeded tests typically consist of items that are fairly easy, such as marking a certain letter in a series of letters or words. It is therefore expected that respondents will be able to answer the items, so the main interest is in *how quickly* respondents can answer. Such tests are often used to estimate the extent to which respondents have automatized the response process(es) involved. In contrast, *pure power* tests are those on which respondents are given as much time as needed to answer, but items are much more difficult than those on speeded tests. Note that simply imposing a time limit on a test does not necessarily make it a speeded test. In a pure speed test, virtually none of the respondents are expected to finish. In contrast, most achievement and aptitude tests have timelines of some sort, but these timelines are not so strict that the majority of respondents would not be able to finish. Pure speed and power tests are somewhat rare in practice, although they do exist. In general, however, most achievement and aptitude tests are combinations of speed and power tests. Such tests do have time limits, but these are usually imposed more for practical reasons (e.g., limited available time for testing) than to assess the automaticity of responses.

Determination of Time Limits for Speed and Power Tests

As stated previously, it is desirable to allow generous time limits for attitude and personality tests because strict time limits tend to result in careless answers that do not reflect respondents' true levels of the construct. In achievement and aptitude testing, however, the process of setting time limits is somewhat more complicated. For power tests, Nunnally and Bernstein (1994) state that setting time limits such that at least 90% of respondents can finish without feeling rushed will not adversely affect scores by introducing large amounts of error. For speeded tests, these authors recommend determining the time limit that results in the largest possible amount of variation in scores. This approach will yield a test that best discriminates among respondents. Some experimentation will be necessary to determine this time limit. For example, the researcher can administer the test to groups of respondents under varying time limits and record the standard deviations of the resulting sets of scores. Because items on pure speed tests are fairly easy, nearly all respondents will obtain perfect scores under generous time limits. As time limits become more stringent, respondents will differ in the number of items reached. With a very stringent time limit, most respondents will complete only a few items, and the variability in scores will decrease. The ideal time limit is therefore somewhere between the generous and the very stringent points but must usually be determined through experimentation.

Test Administration Guidelines

The stringency and complexity of test administration guidelines vary widely across situations. A researcher or program evaluator administering an attitude questionnaire may stick to a simple paragraph such as the following:

> Below is a list of statements about your attitudes toward X. Please respond by indicating how much you agree or disagree with each statement using the response options 1 ("strongly disagree") to 6 ("strongly agree"). There are no right or wrong answers; just answer thoughtfully and honestly.

Aptitude or employee selection tests, in contrast, may include elaborate instructions specifying strict timelines, carefully scripted directions, and instructions about how the test administrator should reply to any questions. Some tests require materials such as blocks or other manipulatives that must be uniform across all testing situations, and these must be obtained prior to testing. The term *standardized test* refers to tests with this type of standardized administration conditions. Strict standardization is necessary for so-called *high-stakes tests*, on which highly consequential outcomes such as graduation, certification, selection for employment, or admission to college depend. In these situations, it is important that respondents are not advantaged by having extra time, hints about answers, or directions that may lead them to correct answers. In some testing situations, computers are required. If this is the case, consideration should be given to issues such as how respondents' work will be saved and how test security will be maintained.

SUMMARY

Development of a sound measurement instrument is not a job to be taken on lightly. Thus, before beginning any scale development project, researchers are advised to determine whether a preexisting instrument would provide adequate measurement. Several resources for locating such instruments have been provided in this chapter, and these represent only the tip of the iceberg. Researchers should scour the literature in the appropriate content area to locate resources appropriate to their interests. However, if no acceptable instrument can be located, those who are developing instruments should pay careful attention to scale development guidelines such as those discussed in this chapter. Before item writing can begin, careful consideration should be given to defining the construct to be measured, determining the levels of breadth and generality of the instrument, explicating the cognitive or noncognitive objectives to be measured, and choosing an item format. Once these tasks are completed, the scale developer can begin writing items. Item writing is typically based on a thorough review of the literature.

Often, instruments designed to measure the same or a similar construct can be reviewed to obtain ideas for items. Focus groups, individual interviews, think-aloud protocols, and expert panel suggestions are also often used during the item development process. Many more items than will be needed in the final scale should be written, as items do not always perform as anticipated. Some shortcomings of items will be revealed during the initial item tryouts. During this phase, the items are administered to a small sample of respondents, chosen to be representative of those to whom the instrument will ultimately be administered. These respondents can provide useful feedback on item clarity, match to the test specifications, readability, and possible offensiveness. It is best to use several panels, as any one panel of respondents may not be able to provide adequate feedback in all of these areas.

Finally, guidelines for administration of the scale, such as instructions, time limits, and level of standardization should be developed. Once items are written, the scale developer will want to obtain some basic feedback on item clarity, match to the test specifications, any violations of item-writing and grammatical principles, readability, and the possibility of offensiveness or unfairness. However, the fact that these considerations are discussed last is not meant to suggest that they should be an afterthought. On the contrary, researchers should keep these considerations in mind throughout the scale development process and should make note of any information that might be relevant to them.

EXERCISES

1. A researcher wants to develop a scale to measure understanding of number concepts among first-grade children. What type of item format would be most appropriate?

2. What, if any, problems do you see with the table of specifications in Table 3.3, designed to test first graders' knowledge of how to make a peanut butter and jelly sandwich? (Numbers in each cell refer to numbers of items.)

TABLE 3.3. Table of Specifications for Question 2

Cognitive goal	Choosing ingredients	Methods of sandwich making	Accompanying beverages
Knowledge	1	1	1
Comprehension	2	2	
Application			
Analysis			
Synthesis	4		4
Evaluation	4	4	

3. For the following test items, indicate the level of Bloom's taxonomy at which the item most likely falls (you do not have to answer the questions themselves, although this may be a useful exercise).

   a. The mean and standard deviation of a set of raw scores are 20 and 3. If Kelly receives a raw score of 25, what is her z-score?

   b. What is the name of the type of standardized score that ranges from 1 to 9 and has a mean of about 5?

   c. What is the difference between a percentile rank and a percentile point?

   d. Table 3.4 was written to guide item writing for a graduate-level test on the material in Chapter 2. Is this an appropriate table of specifications for this group? Defend your answer.

TABLE 3.4. Table of Specifications for Question 3d

	Norm and criterion referencing	Standardized and normalized scores	Types of standardized scores	Types of normalized scores	Proper interpretation of grade equivalents
Knowledge	3				
Comprehension	3	4	5	3	3
Application		3		2	2
Analysis		1	1		1
Synthesis					
Evaluation		1	1	1	1

4. For the same items as in Question 4, indicate the levels of Quellmalz's taxonomy at which each item would fall.

5. For the following items on attitudes toward gun control, indicate the level of Krathwohl's affective taxonomy at which each item would fall.

   a. I regularly call on my representatives in Congress to support gun control.

   b. I can understand the arguments of those on both sides of the gun control debate.

   c. It seems to me that some control over guns might be a good idea.

   d. I plan to quit my job so I can devote all my time to gun control.

6. Rochelle wants to develop a scale of attitudes toward bullying for use in middle schools. What are three strategies she could use in developing the items? What are the advantages and disadvantages of each strategy for this situation?

7. What is the effect of sample size on:

   a. The stability of sample estimates.

   b. The representativeness of a sample.

8. What is the difference between a speed test and a power test? What are some disadvantages of speed tests?

4

Writing Cognitive Items

It is axiomatic in educational settings that "what you test is what you get." That is, students tend to focus their attention on the types of skills or knowledge on which they are tested. The question "Is this going to be on the test?", though annoying to teachers, is nevertheless understandable when you consider that tests provide important signals to students about what teachers consider important. Through their choices of what to include on tests, teachers give the strongest possible messages about what they think is important for students to learn, and there is growing evidence that students pay close attention to such messages. The same is true in employment settings: employees pay attention to aspects of the job on which they are likely to be assessed. It therefore behooves those who develop tests to consider carefully what message they are giving when they prepare an assessment for a classroom or other setting. If, on one hand, we test students on facts taken verbatim from their textbook, we give the message that the learning outcome we most value is memorization. If, on the other hand, we require students to use what they have learned to solve novel problems, we encourage the development of the type of higher-order thinking skills needed to do so. Of course, determinations of the type of outcome we value depend on many factors, including the age and cognitive level of the students and the type of knowledge being taught. Very young students cannot be expected to master higher-level thinking skills, and there are many knowledge areas in which memorization is important, such as learning math facts or foreign language vocabulary. The important thing therefore is to match the test items to the desired learning outcomes and appropriate cognitive level.

In this chapter, I consider item types that can be used to measure cognitive outcomes, with an eye toward choosing those that are most appropriate for a given learning outcome. Most readers will be familiar with item types such as multiple-choice and essay questions from long experience with classroom and standardized achievement tests. Few, however, are actually exposed to the details of constructing such items. Although you may never need to develop a cognitive test, some knowledge of the principles involved is necessary for understanding how such tests function (and may even help you on your next test.)

Cognitive items come in many shapes and sizes, such as essay, multiple-choice, and performance items. These items are sometimes broadly categorized into *objective* items and *performance assessments*. The objective items are more structured and typically have only one correct answer. These items can be scored objectively, as their designation implies, usually as correct or incorrect. Performance assessments, as again implied by the name, require the respondent to engage in a performance or create a product that is then rated in some way. These assessments are typically less structured than objective item types, allowing the student more flexibility and choice. There is usually no single correct response; instead, the product or performance is rated by experts on whatever dimensions are considered to be most important. The product or performance can take a wide array of forms, from a short essay question to a performance for which students practice an entire year. In the following sections, I discuss objective item types and performance assessments, focusing on their advantages and disadvantages, types of material for which they are best suited, and suggestions for item writing.

OBJECTIVE ITEM TYPES

Within the broad category of objective test items, a distinction is often made between *selection-* or *recognition-type items* and *supply-type items*. Examples of the selection type include multiple-choice, true–false, and matching items, in which the respondent is required to recognize the correct answer from among those provided. In contrast, supply-type items such as sentence completion or short-answer items require the respondent to generate the correct answer. In the following sections, I briefly discuss guidelines for writing multiple-choice, true–false, matching, sentence completion, and short-answer items.

Multiple-Choice Items

Multiple-choice items are considered by some to be the most versatile of all item types. Although it is often argued that such items can measure only rote recall of information, multiple-choice items, when cleverly constructed, are capable of tapping into higher-level cognitive processes such as analysis and synthesis of information. Items that require respondents to detect similarities or differences, interpret graphs or tables, make comparisons, or items that cast previously learned material into a new context all focus on such higher-level cognitive processes and are appropriate for a wide variety of subject matter.

Another advantage of multiple-choice items is that they can provide useful diagnostic information about respondents' misunderstandings. To do so, the incorrect options (known as *foils* or *distractors*) must be based on common misconceptions or errors. One way of obtaining such distractors is to administer the item in a short-answer format and then rewrite the item in multiple-choice form, using the most frequently given incorrect answers from the short-answer question as distractors. The main disadvantage of multiple-choice items is their difficulty of construction. If you have never tried to write such items, you need only try to realize that it is a much more difficult task than you would have thought.

Writing Multiple-Choice Items

The following is a list of common guidelines for writing multiple-choice items.

1. Use the item stem to present the problem or question as clearly as possible. For example, the stem "Multiple-choice items," followed by a list of options, does not guide the respondent toward the specific knowledge about multiple-choice items needed to answer. A better stem would be "The main disadvantage of multiple-choice items is . . . " This stem provides the impetus for the respondent to start thinking in the right direction.

2. Include as much of the necessary wording as possible in the stem (but try not to make the stem overly wordy). Consider the following example:

> In objective testing, the term *objective*:
> - A. refers to the method of identifying the learning outcomes.
> - B. refers to the method of selecting the test content.
> - C. refers to the method of presenting the problem.
> - D. refers to the method of scoring the answers.

Clearly, the wording *refers to the method of* could be included in the stem. Note that doing so would also be more satisfactory in terms of the previous criterion.

3. State the items in positive form whenever possible. Some respondents have a tendency to overlook negative words such as *not* or *no* when they appear in the stem of an item. If such words must be used, they should be bolded or otherwise emphasized.

4. Make all alternatives the same length. Savvy test takers are aware that the longest option is most often the correct answer. This is because qualifying phrases or additional explanation is often necessary to ensure that the option is clearly correct.

5. Make sure that all alternatives are grammatically consistent with the stem. In the following example, option D can easily be ruled out even by a respondent with no knowledge of the subject matter.

> The recall of factual information can best be measured with a:
> - A. matching item.
> - B. multiple-choice item.

C. short-answer item.

D. essay item.

6. Avoid verbal clues that might enable students to select the correct answer or to eliminate an incorrect alternative. In the next example, respondents could take advantage of the verbal clue in option B to answer correctly.

An advantage of objective item types is that they can be:

A. written easily.

B. scored objectively.

C. used to assess performances.

D. good conversation starters at cocktail parties.

Option D violates another guideline, which is that all options should be plausible. Other verbal clues to be avoided include the use of so-called specific determiners such as "all," "always," "never," or "none," and "usually," "sometimes," or "may," which often suggest the correct answer. The former set of words tends to clue the test-wise respondent that the answer is incorrect because it is difficult to write an absolute answer that is clearly correct. The latter set often signals the correct answer because such qualifiers are often needed to ensure that the answer is clearly correct.

7. Alphabetize the alternatives or arrange them randomly. By using these methods, the test developer can ensure that one option does not appear as the correct answer more often than the others.

8. Make sure that one item does not give away the answer to another. This often occurs in longer tests in which the same content is represented in more than one item.

True–False Items

True–false items have two big advantages: they are fairly easy to construct, and they are very easy to score. Use of this item format also allows for coverage of a wide range of content because respondents can answer a large number of questions in a fairly short period of time. However, true–false items are very susceptible to guessing. In addition, this type of item provides very little diagnostic information. With multiple-choice items, a careful examination of how many students chose each distractor can yield valuable information about the extent to which students have various misconceptions. True–false items cannot yield such information; if a student answers incorrectly, there is no way to tell why beyond the fairly obvious fact that the student does not know the correct answer. One way to increase the diagnostic value of true–false items is to have students revise the false items to be true and the true items to be false. For this practice to be effective, however, items must be written in such a way that it is not possible to make the revisions by simply including or removing a word such as "not." The true–false format is most useful for measuring content such as definitions, the ability to identify the correctness of statements, and the ability to distinguish fact versus opinion, cause and effect, or similar dichotomous outcomes. True–false items are not well suited to measuring higher-level learning outcomes, such as the synthesis or analysis of information, or in content areas in which absolute statements cannot be made.

Writing True–False Items

Suggestions for constructing true–false items include the following:

1. Avoid taking statements verbatim from the text. Doing so communicates to students that the desired learning outcome is memorization of the text. Unless this is the type of learning that is desired, this method of constructing true–false items should be avoided.

2. Avoid the use of negative phrasing, especially double negatives. Such phrasing is easily misread and/or misunderstood. If words such as "no" or "not" must be included, these should be emphasized by bolding or italicizing.

3. Make sure that all items are entirely true or false. Avoid broad general statements, which are rarely clearly true or false.

4. Avoid the use of specific determiners such as "never," "always," "all," "none," or "sometimes" and "usually." The reasoning behind this is the same as that for multiple-choice items.

5. Use precise terms such as 50% rather than more general words such as "several," "seldom," or "frequently." The latter phrasing is ambiguous because such terms are subject to a wide range of interpretations.

6. Use approximately equal numbers of true and false items. Because false items tend to discriminate better between students with high and low levels of knowledge than true items, some researchers recommend using more false items.

7. To measure the ability to analyze information, base true–false questions on tables or graphs.

8. Do not write items that are based on opinion unless the opinion is attributed to a particular source with which students are expected to be familiar.

Matching Items

Matching items are those in which respondents must match the words in one column, sometimes referred to as the "stimuli," to those in a second column of possible options.

This type of item is most suitable for content involving "who, what, when, and where" questions. For content areas in which large numbers of such factual associations are to be tested, the matching format is quite efficient. Matching items are fairly easy to construct and very easy to score; they are also less susceptible to guessing than true–false or multiple-choice items. However, they are not as useful as multiple-choice items for diagnosing student strengths and weaknesses and are appropriate in only a limited number of situations. In those situations for which they are appropriate, however, matching items are much more efficient than a series of multiple-choice items because they can measure the same knowledge in a much more compact format.

Although not impossible, it is difficult to write matching items that measure levels of cognitive processing beyond simple factual recall. Thorndike (2005) gives a useful suggestion for using matching items to measure application, comprehension, or interpretation of information, which he calls the master or classification list. In this formulation, the stimuli consist of statements that can be classified in different ways and the options represent these different classifications. For example, the stimuli might be a series of statements that could be classified as being based on factual evidence, opinion, logical reasoning, or emotional appeal, and the options would be these four types of persuasion. The task would then be to match each statement with the type of appeal it represents. Basically, this item type is similar to a true–false type item for which there are more than two possible answers.

Writing Matching Items

Suggestions for constructing matching items include the following.

1. Make sure the stimuli used represent homogeneous material. For example, stimuli and options might consist of the names of famous inventors and their inventions, or the names of famous historical events and their dates, but they should not be drawn from both sets of information.

2. Have more options than stimuli. This will prevent respondents from being able to discern the correct answer through the process of elimination, and thus make the items more informative.

3. As a variation on the previous suggestion, respondents can be allowed to use an option more than once. If this variation is chosen, respondents should be clearly informed that this is the case.

4. Clearly specify the basis on which matches are to be made. In many cases, as with famous inventors and their inventions, this will be obvious, but it is always best to give clear directions.

5. Arrange the lists in alphabetical or chronological order to guard against unintentionally arranging the lists in such a way as to give away some answers. This type of arrangement also makes it easier for those who know the correct answer to find it.

6. Make sure the two lists can fit on one page, as having to flip back and forth between two pages is unnecessarily distracting to respondents.

7. Keep lists relatively short; most measurement specialists recommend between five and eight entries in each column. This makes it easier to keep content homogeneous and keeps the cognitive burden on respondents at a reasonable level.

Short-Answer or Completion Items

Short answer and completion are *supply-type* items in which the respondent must provide an answer in the form of a word, number, or short phrase. The main difference between short-answer and completion-type items is that the short-answer type is posed as a question with the answer to be provided at the end, while the completion type contains a complete sentence with one (or more) words missing that are to be filled in by the respondent. Advantages of these items types are that they are relatively easy to construct and, unlike the recognition-type items discussed previously, are less susceptible to guessing. This type of item is somewhat more difficult to score than are recognition-type items because responses are not limited to a carefully controlled set. The result is that respondents can, and often do, provide answers that are outside the range of what the test developer expected but are not really incorrect. For example, I might ask the question, "This is an example of what type of question?" expecting the respondent to say "short answer." However, many other responses, such as "a measurement question" or even "a dumb question" might legitimately be considered correct. Although careful attention to the item-writing suggestions that follow will help to alleviate such problems, short-answer and completion items, by their very nature, will always pose more of a scoring challenge than their recognition-type cousins.

Another commonly cited disadvantage of these item types is that they tend to concentrate on lower-level cognitive outcomes such as knowledge of facts or definitions. They may also be difficult to write in such a way that only one answer is clearly correct. Short-answer and completion items tend to be most useful for measuring knowledge of definitions or terminology, specific facts or principles, methods or procedures, interpretations of graphs or tables, or the ability to solve numerical problems. In the last-named context, short-answer items are particularly useful for problem-solving items in which it is of interest to see how the steps involved were carried out.

From a cognitive point of view, there is a big difference between *recognizing* and *generating* an answer. Generating an answer requires the respondent to search long-term memory for a specific fact, procedure, or definition, whereas recognizing an answer simply requires the respondent to read through the answers provided, searching for one that triggers the necessary association. In some cases, the process involved in providing an answer may be the same, but if not, the distinction between the two cognitive processes may be important. For example, a question that requires the respondent to carry out a series of mathematical operations could be written in either a multiple-choice or short-answer format. In both cases, the respondent would likely carry out the required operation in the same way and either supply it, in the case of a short-answer item or, for a multiple-choice item, search the options for the one matching the obtained result. In this example, the cognitive processes used to obtain the answer are basically the same for the two types of items. In contrast, a short-answer question about the dates of the Second World War would require the respondent to dredge this information from memory, whereas the same question written in multiple-choice format would only require the respondent to recognize the correct dates. These differences should be borne in mind when choosing among item formats.

Writing Short-Answer and Completion Items

Here are some suggestions for writing short-answer and completion items:

1. Make the task as clear as possible. I have already provided one example in which the task was not made clear. A better wording of that question might be: "This is an example of which of the item types discussed in class?" This wording sets up the question such that it is clear to the respondent that an answer in the form of an item type is expected. Clarity is especially important for completion items. For example, in the item "George Washington was president in _____," the item writer may have expected the answer to be in the form of a date, but an answer such as "the United States" is not really wrong. A better wording would be "George Washington was president in the years _____."

2. Do not take statements directly from the text. As discussed in the previous section, doing so gives the (hopefully unintended) message that the goal of learning is to memorize the textbook.

3. Avoid grammatical clues. These include specific determiners, such as the use of "an" when the expected answer begins with a vowel. Specific determiners were discussed previously in the context of multiple-choice items.

4. Avoid the use of excessive blanks in one question. An item such as "Multiple-choice questions are _____ for _____ except when measuring _____" is more a test of reasoning than of factual knowledge.

5. Put the blanks at the end rather than the beginning of a sentence or use a direct question instead of a blank. Putting the blank at the end sets up the question so that by the end of the question the respondent (one hopes) knows what type of answer is expected.

6. For numerical answers, indicate the units in which the answer should be expressed and the number of decimal places desired (if applicable).

PERFORMANCE ASSESSMENTS

In the previous sections of this chapter, I have focused on objective item types. Although it is widely believed that such items can only be used to measure relatively simple cognitive processes such as knowledge of facts, principles, and definitions, I have pointed out some ways in which objective items can be written to tap into higher-level processes. However, there are many important learning outcomes for which objective item types may not be appropriate. In many occupations, it is important to learn not only content knowledge, but also skills and procedures that would be difficult to assess using objective item types. For example, those in the health professions must be able to carry out medical procedures such as giving injections and operating medical equipment. Most of us would not feel confident in the skills of nurses or technicians who had not passed practical examinations showing they could actually carry out such procedures, regardless of how well they may have scored on a multiple-choice examination on the same information. Assessments of such skills are known as *performance assessments* and have long been used to assess abilities in areas such as public speaking, sports, writing, artistic performance, and many vocational arenas.

Some critics of traditional educational testing strategies have called into question the heavy reliance on objective item types which has characterized K–12 testing programs. Opponents of such programs argue that reliance on objective item types has resulted in a focus on the lower-level learning objectives which such items are best suited to measure, with the result that higher-level cognitive and critical thinking skills have been largely ignored. Because the latter types of skills are arguably more important in an information-based society, the fear that students are not developing these skills is well founded. Many educational reformers have therefore called for more focus on the teaching of higher-level skills and the concomitant use of assessments that can measure these skills, such as performance assessments. Reformers have also argued that, because both students and teachers are more likely to direct their attention to knowledge and skills on which they are tested, changing the focus of tests can be a powerful way of changing the focus of instruction and student learning. Thus, use of performance assessments is seen as both a driver and an outcome of educational reform. The success of such reform efforts remains to be seen. Regardless of their role in educational reform, however, such assessments are invaluable in measuring outcomes that take the form of performances or products. In addition, they are very well suited for measuring the ability to organize and synthesize ideas, analyze and critique material, express oneself clearly in written or oral form, and gather and integrate information; all of which are clearly important learning outcomes that would be difficult (if not impossible) to measure using objective item types.

In contrast to objective item types, performance assessments are less structured in terms of both the task to be carried out and the scoring procedures. This does not mean that performance assessments lack structure; rather, it signals that the very nature of the tasks being measured necessarily precludes the type of highly structured questions and scoring that are characteristic of objective item types. As an example, in an assessment of a musical performance, students maybe allowed to choose which piece they will play, rather than having the same piece assigned to everyone. Scoring of the performance would also be different than with an objective item type because there is clearly no single right or wrong "answer." On the other hand, the conditions under which the performance is to be rendered might be the same for all students, and the same method of scoring would be used for all students. Use of performance assessments thus provides much greater latitude than use of objective item types for choosing the type of performance or product, the conditions under which it is produced, and the way in which it is scored. This latitude allows for these characteristics to be tailored to the specific conditions thought to be most appropriate for a particular situation.

Another commonly cited feature of performance assessments is their authenticity. Such assessments are thought to be more authentic than objective item types because they are more direct measures of the outcomes of interest and are more likely to be cast in a form that mimics a real-life situation. To go back to the earlier medical example, nurses are routinely assessed on their ability to carry out procedures such as giving injections, beginning on inanimate objects and working their way up to actual clinical situations. This type of assessment contrasts starkly with objective item types, which rarely, if ever, resemble real-life tasks. The authenticity of performance tasks is widely held to result in assessments that are more interesting, and thus more motivating, to students.

Moreover, it is arguably important to assess performance on authentic tasks because these are the tasks that will form the basis of future performance in work environments. Such tasks are complicated and are becoming more so. As simple tasks become ever more automated, those in the workforce must continually update their skills, be able to process large amounts of information, and adapt to constantly changing work requirements—competencies that require the types of higher-level thinking thought to be measured by performance assessments. Relatedly, it has been argued that the most important problems in today's world, such as global warming, poverty, and illiteracy are *ill structured* (Simon, 1978); that is, they do not have clear-cut solutions. Instead, potential solutions must be defended on the basis of complex combinations of available (but imperfect) evidence, logical reasoning, and extant theory. It therefore seems clear that the skills required to solve important problems are often not of the type that can be assessed using objective item types.

Essay Questions

Despite the movement within educational circles for greater use of all forms of performance assessments, the most widely used assessment in this category is still the fairly traditional essay question. This is probably due to its long history, which has resulted in an overall familiarity with and acceptance of this type of question for assessing cognitive outcomes. As you saw in Chapter 1, use of the essay question began with the Chinese civil service examination at least 2,000 years ago (and possibly longer). Essay items have many advantages. They allow respondents to develop and demonstrate their skills in written expression, higher-level and critical thinking, and organization and integration of ideas. They can also encourage originality, creativity, and divergent thinking. Essay questions provide useful diagnostic information about students' strengths and weaknesses and about their misconceptions, making them an excellent teaching tool.

On the downside, essay items are not well suited for assessing knowledge of basic facts. This is not because they are unable to assess such knowledge, but because more objective items can assess this type of knowledge much more efficiently. Thus, essay questions should not be "wasted" on the assessment of factual knowledge but should be reserved for assessment of more complex learning outcomes. Although essay items appear easy to write, it is somewhat more difficult to write a good essay question than it may appear at first blush. This is because a great deal of thought must be given to defining the parameters of the desired answer and to communicating these to respondents. The main disadvantage of essay questions, as with all performance assessments, is that they are much more time consuming to score than are objective item types. They are also more time consuming to answer, so tests involving essay items will not generally cover as wide a range of content as those consisting only of objective item types.

Essay questions are sometimes classified as either *restricted response* or *extended response*. *Restricted response* essay questions limit the content and type of response, or both, by stating in specific terms what type of answer is desired and what should be included (and not included) in the answer. This type of essay question is especially well suited to measuring students' ability to apply or interpret data or information. However, it may be less valuable than extended response essays for measuring outcomes involving integration, organization, and/or originality. The *extended response* essay allows students more freedom in choosing what information to include in their answer, how to organize it, and how to integrate and evaluate ideas. As a result, extended response essay questions are valuable for assessing students' ability to develop arguments, analyze problems, and sequence ideas in a logical manner.

Writing Essay Questions

Suggestions for writing essay questions include the following.

1. Use essay questions only for learning outcomes that cannot be measured with more objective item types.

2. Be sure the question will actually elicit the desired learning outcomes. (Note that this requires the test developer to think about the desired outcomes *before* writing the questions.) In many cases, essay questions that were intended to measure the ability to integrate or analyze information can be answered by simply recalling information from memory. For example, a question such as "What are the advantages and disadvantages of objective items and performance assessments?" could be answered by generating lists

of facts from memory. If the interest is in students' ability to analyze this information, a better question would be "Your colleague is interested in assessing whether her fourth-grade students understand how to construct and interpret a pie chart. What type of test items would you recommend she use? In your answer, explain the relative advantages and disadvantages of the different item types as they relate to your recommendation."

3. Use of words such as *compare, contrast, explain, predict,* and *evaluate* are useful in essay questions, as they tend to get at the types of learning outcomes for which such questions are most useful.

4. Provide the scaffolding respondents will need to complete the task successfully. Too often, test developers assume that once students have a certain level of subject mat-ter knowledge they will be able to answer higher-level questions. This is unfair because it is not the case that students spontaneously develop the ability to answer complex questions just because they have high levels of content knowledge. The ability to answer complex questions must be developed, just as content knowledge is developed. This means that instruction and practice in answering higher-level questions must be pro-vided if students are expected to answer them. This help can be provided in a classroom setting, through homework problems, or as part of a preassessment in which students are exposed to such problems and are given opportunities to practice them.

5. Set up the problem clearly. The purpose of essay questions is to measure respon-dents' ability to answer the question, not their ability to determine what is being asked. Be as specific as possible with regard to what is expected and how the question will be scored. A clearly written essay question should establish a framework for the type of response desired. Keep in mind that the more clearly written the question is, the easier it will be to score because clear instructions will mitigate against unintended interpre-tations of the questions. Of course, one advantage of essay questions is that they allow respondents some freedom in formulating their answers. Thus, instructions should be tailored to the level of such freedom that is deemed appropriate.

6. Some measurement specialists recommend specifying an approximate length for each answer. This has at least three advantages. One is that it helps respondents to bud-get the time they spend on each question, which is especially useful if there are several questions to be answered in a relatively short timeframe. It also provides for more equity in scoring, as it standardizes this aspect of the responses. Finally, specifying an answer length requires respondents to plan and organize their responses carefully to provide the best answer in the allotted timeframe. If these skills are considered to be important, use of this strategy should be considered.

Scoring Essay Questions

One disadvantage of essay questions, discussed in the previous section, is that they are much more difficult to score than objective item types. Careful attention must be paid to the scoring process to ensure that scoring is done in the same way for all respondents, and that the scoring system is faithful to the learning outcomes that were intended. Scoring suggestions that will help to achieve these goals include the following:

1. Use a masked scoring method in which respondents' names are not shown. This can be accomplished by having respondents use an ID number instead of their name to identify their paper. In the usual situation in which the scorer is familiar with the respondents, as with a classroom teacher scoring students, scorers tend to give the benefit of the doubt to respondents who are known to be good performers and to be more dubious of answers provided by respondents who are not. This is often done unconsciously and so is difficult to guard against in the absence of a masked scoring method.

2. Have an answer key that outlines an ideal answer that addresses all the features thought to be important in a good answer, and award points according to these criteria. This practice has two advantages. One is that such a practice forces the test developer to think carefully about what knowledge and/or cognitive skills the question is meant to tap into. Is the ability to organize, critique, and/or apply information an important learning outcome? If so, this should be included in the answer key. The second advantage of this practice is that it focuses the scorer's attention on the important aspects of the answer and mitigates against giving credit for features of the response that may be admirable but do not demonstrate the intended learning outcomes. For example, it has been argued that respondents often receive credit for well-written responses even though they do not really demonstrate the intended knowledge or cognitive skills. If the question was intended to measure writing or organizational ability, this is appropriate, but if not, scorers should not be swayed by elegant writing. If the question has been used before, scorers might want to select an anchor or exemplary response from among the previous responses that best meets the scoring criteria and use this as the "ideal answer."

3. Be sure that respondents know the scoring criteria. In particular, if aspects of the response such as spelling, grammar, organization, or creativity are part of the scoring criteria, respondents should be so informed. In some cases, it may make sense to provide separate scores for content, mechanics, or other characteristics. Many educators recommend sharing the scoring criteria with respondents. To some, this may seem like "giving away the answer." However, others have likened the attempt to answer a question without knowing the scoring criteria to trying to hit a target without knowing where it is. Those of you who have been penalized because your answer to a test question lacked a criterion you did not know was required can attest to the fact that it is a very frustrating experience.

4. If there are several essay questions on a test, score one question at a time; that is, score all the answers to question 1, then move on to question 2, and so on. The reasoning behind this suggestion is similar to that for suggestion 1. Even if respondents are not identifiable by name, scorers are more likely to perceive an answer favorably if the respondent's previous answer was a good one. This is known as the *halo effect* and, as

with the similar tendency involving name recognition, it is usually done unconsciously. Scoring one question at a time mitigates against this tendency. An additional advantage of this practice is that it makes it easier to keep the scoring criteria in mind.

5. Scorers of essay questions are often confronted with irrelevant responses, which typically occur when the respondent does not really know the answer but attempts to provide a response anyway, drawing on the theory that some answer is better than no answer. This is the essay question equivalent of guessing and is problematic because it wastes time that the scorer could otherwise use in more productive ways. Perhaps more importantly, rewarding respondents for such behavior by awarding score points sends the message that irrelevant responses are acceptable. Although this may be true for politicians, it should not be in learning situations. One way of subverting such responses is to penalize respondents for irrelevant responses. Although this approach may seem harsh, it has the distinct advantage of being very effective.

6. Reread all responses before assigning final scores. Even when careful attention has been paid to designing and applying scoring criteria, scorers have a tendency to "drift," becoming more or less lenient with changes in mood or energy level. In some cases, scorers might change the scoring criteria midway through the scoring process without realizing it. It may be that new criteria or unanticipated but correct answers are discovered, or that one or more criteria prove to be untenable. If so, it is better to change the scoring criteria than to use flawed criteria. However, if this happens, all responses must be rescored.

7. One advantage of essay questions is that they reveal respondents' misconceptions and areas of weakness. They give the scorer the opportunity to provide feedback designed to correct misconceptions, provide suggestions for improving organization or other characteristics, and otherwise help the respondent to improve. Feedback should also be provided on things respondents have done well. Research has shown that such formative feedback has positive effects on student learning (Black & Wiliam, 1998; Crooks, 1988).

Performance Tasks

As discussed previously, performance tasks have a long history of use in the measurement of skills in areas such as public speaking, athletics, writing, the arts, speaking a foreign language, counseling, and medicine. Performance tasks are also necessary for measuring "hands-on" vocational or practical abilities such as those involved in mechanics, computer programming or repair, cooking, woodworking, and driving. You can likely think of many other possible uses of this type of assessment in your own area of study. As with essay questions, performance tasks vary along a continuum from more to less restricted. Restricted performances generally involve more narrowly focused tasks or skills, and respondents are given more structured directions about how to go about the task and/or what to include in their answers. In contrast, less restricted tasks, sometimes referred to as *extended performance tasks*, are less struc-tured, allowing for more freedom and creativity in responses. Extended performance tasks typically require respondents to gather and integrate information from a variety of sources and to create a unique product based on this information. For example, in a restricted performance task, respondents might be required to write five multiple-choice questions on the subject of the history of testing, whereas an extended perfor-mance might involve the development of a classroom test in students' own areas of study, with respondents determining the appropriate types and numbers of items to use based on the nature of the material to be taught and the age and characteristics of the students.

Restricted performance tasks are useful for situations in which there is a need to determine whether students have mastered individual skills or concepts before they are required to put them together into a more extended performance. In the context of the previous example, an instructor may wish to assess whether students can successfully develop the different types of items before requiring them to develop a complete test. Because of their more focused nature, restricted performance tasks generally require less time to complete than extended performance tasks and therefore allow for more content coverage. The greater level of structure typically found in restricted perfor-mance tasks also results in products that are easier to grade than are those from extended performances.

In addition to determining the degree to which responses are restricted, those developing performance tasks must also decide whether the performance is to be observed in a naturalistic or simulated setting. For many school-based tasks, simu-lated settings can be quite adequate to measure the intended skills as long as care is taken to make them as realistic as possible. For example, students in a business class may create business plans based on hypothesized rather than actual companies. In more naturalistic settings, actual musical or dramatic performances in front of live audiences are typically observed. If job performance is to be evaluated, observation of actual on-the-job performance is usually the preferred target of assessment, unless such performances are difficult to observe. This could occur if the performance of interest occurs only rarely or if it might be dangerous or intrusive to observe. For example, opportunities to conduct a live observation of a psychologist counseling a suicidal client would, one hopes, be infrequent. In any case, such observations would clearly be unethical. It might therefore be best to use role play instead of actual clients in such situations.

Both restricted and extended performance tasks require careful attention to the creation of the tasks as well as to the scoring criteria used to ensure that these tasks are focused on the desired learning outcomes. However, careful use of the prescribed scoring criteria is particularly important for extended performance tasks, as these permit greater latitude of responses. The following sections provide some suggestions for developing and scoring performance tasks. Because essay items are a form of restricted performance task, most, if not all, of the suggestions made previously in the context of that item type are also relevant to performance tasks.

Creating Performance Tasks

Following are some suggestions for creating performance tasks.

1. Recognize that performance tasks typically require a greater amount of time, both for respondents to develop their answers and for scoring. These tasks should therefore be used only for learning outcomes that cannot be measured in any other way.

2. Minimize task dependence on skills or knowledge that are not relevant to the intended learning outcomes. A common example of such an irrelevant skill is reading ability. In many cases, reading ability is an important learning outcome. However, if the purpose of the performance task is to assess respondents' ability to correctly carry out the steps in a scientific experiment, those with poorer reading ability should not be disadvantaged. Thus, instructions and other materials should be written in such a way as to minimize the reading requirements. Similarly, respondents should not be able to complete the tasks by using task-irrelevant skills or knowledge. For example, suppose the purpose of a performance tasks was to assess students' ability to choose an appropriate graphical display, given the characteristics of a set of data. Students with good computer skills may be able to read the data into a computer package, quickly create multiple graphs, and choose from among them. However, this is not the same as carefully examining the data characteristics and determining the graph that would best display these characteristics.

3. Determine the appropriate level of authenticity. As noted previously, one advantage of performance assessments is that they require respondents to complete tasks that are similar to those in real life. However, the level of authenticity needed varies across learning outcomes and skill levels, and is affected by such considerations as safety and ethics, as well as by more practical concerns such as feasibility. Certainly the most authentic task for assessing counseling skills would be to have students conduct sessions with real-life clients, but most training programs would not recommend this approach for beginning students because of ethical concerns. Airline pilots practice on simulators before moving on to jumbo jets full of passengers. And although students' ability to speak French might be best assessed by letting them loose in France, it would likely be cost prohibitive for most students. Thus, compromises are often needed between authenticity and safety, practicality, and ethics. Often, simulated tasks can be used to assess the intended learning outcomes, especially at beginning skill levels.

4. Set up the task as clearly as possible. Although this suggestion was made in the context of essay questions, it is even more crucial in developing performance tasks because of the greater complexity of such tasks. Performance tasks provide some degree of latitude in carrying out the task(s) and developing a response. However, for such assessments to be fair, all respondents must be aware of the parameters within which the work is to be carried out, so that everyone will have the same opportunities to

demonstrate their knowledge. For example, if computers or other equipment can be used, be sure that all respondents know this and have access to these aids.

5. Determine whether the product, process, or both, should be the focus of the assessment. In many cases, performance tasks require an end product, such as a report, a painting, a poem, or a model of some sort, and it is this product that is assessed. In these situations, it may not be necessary to observe the process by which the product was produced. In other cases, however, the process is as important as the product itself. For example, in woodworking, it is important that tools be used properly, both to prevent injuries and to ensure an optimal product. In such cases, the process is often the focus of assessment in the early stages of learning when the correct procedures are being taught. Once procedures have been learned, the focus may switch to the product being created. Or both the process and product may be of interest, so the task must be developed so that both can be observed. This is often the case in teaching athletic skills, such as hitting a baseball or a golf ball. Although gifted athletes may obtain amazing outcomes using unorthodox form, most instructors emphasize proper form for beginning students. In such situations, it is important to assess both the product, in the form of the trajectory and speed of the ball, and the process or form used. Finally, there are situations in which the product *is* the process, such as in a dramatic performance or dance.

6. As with essay questions, respondents should be aware of the scoring criteria. This awareness on the part of respondents is more crucial with performance tasks because often, as you will see, scoring criteria for performance tasks are quite complex and may combine elements such as process and product criteria in specific ways. Knowing the scoring criteria ahead of time helps respondents to focus their efforts on those aspects deemed most important.

A primary disadvantage of performance tasks is that they are time consuming for both the respondents and the scorers. Development of a good set of scoring guidelines that specifies what aspects of the performance and/or product will be taken into account can reduce both the time needed for scoring and the inherent subjectivity of the scoring process. A set of such scoring guidelines is known as a *rubric* and can be as simple or complex as the task requires. Regardless of the level of complexity, however, rubrics should direct raters' focus to the most important aspects of the performance. For example, in rating oral presentation skills, should raters focus on the organization of the presentation, the correctness of the material being presented, the mechanics of the presentation, such as the clarity and pitch of the presenter's voice, or on all of these? Development of a good rubric requires that sufficient time be spent up front on determining what, exactly, is most important to score.

Most rubrics involve some type of rating scale, which can be either numerical or descriptive, or they might combine these two methods of identifying the meaning to be assigned to each scale point. The simplest form of rubric is the checklist, in which the features of the performance are checked off as being either present or absent. Checklists are most appropriate for performances that follow a logical sequence, such as science experiments or safety procedures. Performances that are sequenced in this way allow for the features to be listed in the order in which they would occur, so that the rater can simply go down the list and check them off sequentially. A slight variation on this theme is to include common errors on the checklist, allowing the rater to check whether or not these were made. Checklists can also be used with nonsequential performances; in this case, the desired aspects of a product or performance can be checked as either absent or present.

Rating scales are similar to checklists but use a scale rather than a dichotomous present/absent format. Either numeric or verbal labels can be used, although it is best to use both (e.g., 1 = "below average"). Common formats for verbal labels are those in which raters judge the frequency (e.g., "never," "sometimes," "often," "always"), quality (e.g., "below average," "average," "above average") or proficiency (e.g., "below basic," "basic," "proficient," "expert") of the product or performance. A common recommendation is to provide short descriptions of the performance or product qualities expected at each scale point. This allows for more precise definitions of each category and more clearly communicates the desired criteria to those being rated. In addition, descriptive labels can improve consistency across raters by clarifying the meaning of each category.

Performance tasks can be scored either *analytically* or *holistically*. Analytical scoring requires raters to provide a judgment on each of several criteria considered important for evaluating the product or performance. For example, in rating a verbal presentation, the features of interest might include organization, accuracy of the material, and mechanics of the presentation. Within each of these features, there may be several subcategories, such as clarity, loudness, pace, and expressiveness. Once the rating criteria are determined, separate rating scales must be created for each, although these are typically combined into one overall rubric form. Raters would then be provided with rubric forms on which they would indicate scores for each criterion. This type of scoring system is useful for situations in which separate judgments on the various scoring criteria are desirable. An advantage of this type of scoring system is that it focuses respondents' attention on specific criteria of interest and clarifies the performance expectations for each criterion.

In holistic scoring, products or performances are classified into broad groupings based on the rater's overall impression. Raters often find it difficult to reliably classify performances or products into more than three or four holistic categories, and in most cases this will be sufficient. Rubrics for this type of scoring provide broad, overall descriptions of expected characteristics for each rating category rather than separate rating scales for specific characteristics as in analytic scoring. Another way to do this type of scale *anchoring* is to use actual examples of the product being rated that exemplify performance at that point on the scale. For instance, examples of student essays considered to be typical of those categorized as "inadequate," "acceptable," "good," and "excellent" could be used to illustrate the four performance levels, and each essay being rated could be compared to the four exemplars. Holistic scoring is used for situations in which it is not necessary to provide ratings at the level of detail used in analytic scoring. Instead, only an overall score is needed, although raters can always provide additional written feedback as appropriate.

Scoring Performance Tasks

Suggestions for scoring performance tasks or products include the following.

1. Clearly identify the learning or performance outcomes that the performance task is intended to measure. This will help to focus the rating scale on the desired characteristics of the performance or product and reduce the contamination of ratings from extraneous factors.

2. Be sure the characteristics to be rated are observable. Characteristics such as attitudes or effort are rarely overt and are therefore not appropriate targets for performance tasks.

3. Clearly define all characteristics to be rated. Vague or incomplete descriptions of the characteristics to be rated and their related scale points are leading causes of inaccurate and unreliable ratings. To the extent possible, characteristics and scale points should be defined in such a way that everyone involved has a similar understanding of their meaning.

4. Use three to seven scale points for rating criteria. The exact number will depend on the situation and on the degree of differentiation needed. As noted previously, however, raters can seldom make discriminations beyond three or four scale points, unless performances or products vary widely in quality.

5. If multiple tasks are to be rated, rate all performances on one task before moving on to the next. As with scoring essay questions, this will help to prevent the intrusion of halo effects into the scoring process.

6. If the results of the performance task will have important consequences on respondents' future education or careers, ensure that ratings are as accurate as possible. In such situations, it is common to use several independent raters and to pool or average the results across them to obtain a final score. By doing so, it is more likely that individual idiosyncrasies in rating, such as personal biases or tendencies to be overly lenient or severe, can be averaged out.

SUMMARY

In this chapter I have considered various ways of measuring cognitive outcomes, with an emphasis on matching the type of item to the learning outcome desired. The so-called objective item types, which include true–false, matching, multiple choice, and short answer or completion, are relatively easy to score objectively but can be extremely difficult to write well. With the exception of short-answer and completion items, they are also susceptible to guessing. Objective-type items have been criticized because they are thought to elicit only lower-level cognitive outcomes such as memorization or knowledge of facts. Although this may be true overall, it does not have to be the case.

The cognitive demand of such items can be increased by, for example, casting the material into a novel context.

Performance assessments are appropriate for measuring products or performances that would be difficult, if not impossible, to assess adequately using objective item types. Such assessments are more time consuming for the respondent to answer as well as for the instructor to score, and so should be reserved for outcomes such as products or performances, or for measurement of tasks requiring extended time and/ or the incorporation of outside resources. Examples of such tasks include performing science experiments, conducting conversations in a foreign language, organizing and analyzing materials or resources, as in writing a term paper, and gathering and integrating information for a research paper. Such tasks are thought to be more "authentic" in the sense that they are more closely aligned with tasks respondents might do in real life. Accordingly, performance assessments are generally held to be more interesting and motivational for respondents. Performance assessments vary along a continuum from less restricted to more restricted, and the level of restriction should be matched to both the purpose of the assessment and the capabilities and cognitive level of the respondents. The traditional essay question is perhaps the most well-known form of performance assessment and is typically fairly restricted in format. At the other end of the continuum are tasks such as oral presentations and research papers in which respondents are often given a great deal of latitude in the format and topic of the product.

No one item type is "better," in some sense, than another. Instead, different item types are appropriate for different types of learning outcomes and cognitive levels. In choosing an appropriate item type, therefore, you should think carefully about the most important aspects of the learning target and design assessments that will measure them. In addition, the age and cognitive level of respondents should be taken into account. Although higher-level cognitive processes such as analysis of information are undeniably important, they may not be appropriate learning targets for very young students or for those who are beginning learners. As in the specification of learning targets, therefore, it is important to think judiciously about the cognitive level that can reasonably be expected of respondents.

EXERCISES

1. Approximately 1 week before a test is to begin, a professor goes though the textbook carefully and constructs true–false items based on the material in her book. She always uses the exact wording of the textbook for the correct answer so that there will be no question about whether it's correct. After the test is scored, she creates a frequency distribution of scores and determines each student's letter grade based on how well they did compared to the other students.

   Based on this scenario alone, determine whether the following statements are more likely true or false, and explain your choice.

a. The professor's students spend most of their study time memorizing facts from the textbook.

b. The professor is helping her students to develop critical thinking skills.

c. The professor learns a lot about her students' misconceptions and errors in thinking from the results of her tests.

2. What is the difference between *selection-* and *supply*-type items? Give an example of each.

3. An instructor is creating a test for a large amount of material that consists of composers and their most famous works. What item format would be most efficient for the test items?

4. Identify the flaws in the following multiple-choice items (there may be more than one flaw for each item):

a. Essay items:

   A. are easy to score.

   B. are good for measuring higher-level thinking skills, creativity, and problem-solving ability.

   C. are difficult to construct.

   D. have been shown to increase IQ by 15 points when used regularly.

b. One advantage of a table of specifications is that it:

   A. reduces the amount of time needed to write test items.

   B. specifies the content and cognitive level to be covered in a table.

   C. makes it easier to construct test items and reduces time spent scoring.

   D. increases test objectivity.

5. Identify the flaws in the following true–false items:

a. True–false items are not one of the objective item types.

b. Some have argued that essay items can be useful.

c. True–false items should never be used on tests.

6. Identify the flaws in the following short-answer/fill-in-the-blank items:

a. Short-answer items _____.

b. What is the best way to score essay questions?

7. A professor is teaching a graduate-level class and is interested in assessing students' ability to defend a position by carefully choosing supporting materials and

integrating them into their response. Would a restricted or extended essay question be most appropriate? Explain.

8. A nursing instructor is developing a performance task to assess students' ability to explain medical procedures to patients.

   a. Would a naturalistic or simulated task be most appropriate for this type of assessment? Explain.

   b. Give examples of three scoring criteria that should be included on the rubric for this task.

5

Writing Noncognitive Items

Who among us does not take an interest in the attitudes, values, and beliefs of others? Very few, I would argue, based on the public's interest in the results of opinion surveys, political polls, and the endless tests provided by popular magazines urging us to "rate your relationship" or measure our "healthy eating habits." In addition to these contributions from popular culture, measures of such *noncognitive* characteristics are often of interest to researchers in the social sciences. From the graduate student interested in attitudes toward students with disabilities to the social psychologist assessing the degree to which beliefs are affected by one's peer group, measures of affect are often at the heart of social science research. In this chapter, I discuss measures of attitudes, beliefs, and values. Also included in the category of such noncognitive measures are instruments designed to measure personality characteristics such as extraversion, depression, and conscientiousness.

Noncognitive measures differ from the cognitive measures discussed in the previous chapter in a number of ways. Whereas cognitive items are measures of *maximum or optimal performance*, noncognitive items are measures of *typical performance*. It almost goes without saying that on cognitive tests we should put forth our best effort, or maximum performance, in selecting the correct answers. In the context of noncognitive measurement, however, the concept of maximum performance does not make sense. We would not ask someone to respond to a set of items measuring conscientiousness in terms of their all-time maximal level of conscientiousness. Instead, we would be interested in how conscientious they *usually* are, that is, their *typical* performance. Respondents might claim to be more conscientious than they actually are, leading us to another difference between cognitive and noncognitive measures. Although guessing and test anxiety are common problems encountered in cognitive measurement, they are not relevant to measures of affect. Instead, noncognitive measures can be distorted by various forms of faking, or dissembling. For example, respondents may not wish, for various reasons, to report their true levels of anxiety but may instead report more or less anxiety than they really feel. And because noncognitive measures are typically *self-reports*, in which respondents relate their own levels of such characteristics, we often have no way of knowing whether such responses are accurate. Another issue in measuring affect, especially in personality assessment, is that respondents may have imperfect insight into their own nature. This may be particularly true for individuals with various psychopathologies. Finally, responses to noncognitive measures can be affected by seemingly minor changes in item wording. For example, Langer (1989) examined the percentages of respondents who agreed with the following three statements regarding affirmative action that were included on separate attitude surveys:

1. "All in all, do you favor or oppose affirmative action programs in employment for blacks, provided there are no rigid quotas?" (Harris poll)

2. "Do you think blacks and other minorities should receive preference in hiring to make up for past inequities, or not?" (Associated Press poll)

3. "Do you favor or oppose affirmative action programs for blacks and other minorities, which do not have rigid quotas?" (Harris poll)

The percentages of "agree" responses to the three questions varied dramatically, with 74% agreeing to the first, 21% to the second, and 56% to the third. These differences in agreement are quite substantial and may be at the extreme end of what would be expected on the basis of wording changes alone. However, they are indicative of the sensitivity of such questions to choice of language.

In the following sections, I explore some of the theories that have been advanced for such sensitivities. First, however, I discuss three common formats for noncognitive items and their uses. I then consider theories that attempt to explain how people respond to noncognitive questions. I close this chapter by considering issues in noncognitive measurement. Some of these relate to so-called *response sets*, such as the tendency of respondents to provide responses they feel are socially desirable rather than honestly reporting their affective states. Others have to do with more practical issues, such as how many response categories should be included and how to label them.

NONCOGNITIVE ITEM TYPES

This section presents three commonly used noncognitive item types: Thurstone scaling, Likert scaling, and Guttman scaling. Although these methods were all developed in the context of measuring attitudes, they are also widely used in the measurement of personality characteristics, interests, values, and beliefs.

Thurstone Scaling

Thurstone scaling bears the name of its developer, L. L. Thurstone, who originally described it in a 1929 monograph. Thurstone was influenced by psychophysical measures used to study perception that were popular at the time. In these measurement methods, respondents were asked to answer questions comparing stimuli, such as determining which of two weights was heavier. Pairs of such weights were repeatedly presented to respondents with the goal of obtaining a range of weights for which the perceived differences between all adjacent pairs were equal. In other words, the goal was to create an equal-interval scale. Such experiments were common in psychophysics and were applied to many types of stimuli, such as lengths of lines and loudness of sounds. Motivated by such methods, Thurstone briefly considered scaling attitude statements by asking respondents to indicate which of a pair of statements was more favorable to a particular attitude. He soon realized that such a task would be tedious in the extreme, given that he had developed 130 items that would require respondents to make a total of (130 * 129)/2, or 8,385 such judgments. Realizing that such dedication was unlikely to be forthcoming from his respondents (mainly undergraduate students), he developed the idea of asking respondents to instead *sort* the statements into 11 categories from most to least favorable, with the middle category indicating a neutral attitude. Thurstone was careful to point out that respondents, or judges, as they are sometimes called, were not supposed to indicate their own attitudes but rather their judgments of how favorable or unfavorable the statements were to the referent ("Attitude Toward the Church," in Thurstone's original scale). After all the items had been judged, the average ranking of each item across all judges was calculated and taken as the scale value of that item. For example, if item 1 received 100 rankings of 1 and 100 rankings of 2, its scale value would be 1.5. Thurstone then chose 45 of his original 130 items, in such a way that "they constitute a more or less uniformly graduated series of scale values" (p. 59). Thus, items with scale values across the entire rating continuum from 1 to 11 were chosen, with approximately equal numbers of items from each range of scale values. In this way, Thurstone was able to create a scale with what he called "equal-appearing" intervals. Interestingly, Thurstone took pains to point out that intervals on such a scale were not truly equal, but that they were "probably as close as is necessary" (p. 59). Thurstone also based his choice of items on item wording, eliminating those that lacked clarity or otherwise violated guidelines for good item writing (The next section provides more information on such guidelines). In addition, he recommended examining the dispersion of the rankings for each item and eliminating those for which the rankings were most disparate.

Developing Thurstone Scales

Thurstone used 130 statements and 300 judges in his original study, but such numbers would likely be difficult to obtain in practice and so are not typically recommended in measurement texts (although see Nunnally & Bernstein, 1994, who recommend 100 judges). As so picturesquely stated by Rice (1930, quoted in Likert, 1932), it is one thing to ask undergraduate students to make such rankings, but "it is difficult to imagine securing comparable judgments . . . from bricklayers, business men, Italian-Americans, nuns, stevedores, or seamstresses" (pp. 190–191), or, for that matter, anyone at all. Instead, common recommendations are to develop a series of 20–25 items and recruit as many judges as possible to rank these into 11 categories. Note that the judges should *not* be the same people as those to whom the scale will eventually be administered. Judges should be individuals with sufficient knowledge about the construct being measured that they can reasonably be expected to differentiate degrees of favorableness. Although the mean rank value across the judges is still often used as the scale value for each item, it is probably more defensible to use the median value, given the ordinal nature of the rankings. A measure of dispersion, such as the interquartile range (if the median is used as the scale value), or the standard deviation (if the mean is used) should also be calculated, and items with high levels of dispersion should be eliminated because such items indicate a high level of disagreement among judges. The final set of items is then assembled in random order (not in order by scale value), and respondents are asked to check those with which they agree. Scores are calculated as the mean or median value of all items a respondent checks.

As an example, consider the fictitious scale of attitudes toward assisted suicide shown here. Hypothetical scale values are included in parentheses after each item. Recall that these values would be obtained from judges' rankings of the items from 1 ("least favorable") to 11 ("most favorable").

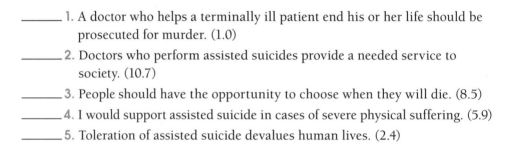

_____ 1. A doctor who helps a terminally ill patient end his or her life should be prosecuted for murder. (1.0)

_____ 2. Doctors who perform assisted suicides provide a needed service to society. (10.7)

_____ 3. People should have the opportunity to choose when they will die. (8.5)

_____ 4. I would support assisted suicide in cases of severe physical suffering. (5.9)

_____ 5. Toleration of assisted suicide devalues human lives. (2.4)

Of course, a real application would use more items, spread across the entire noncognitive continuum. However, for the purposes of illustration, let us say that Dena checked items 1 and 5, while Craig checked items 2, 3, and 4. Dena would be given a score of 1.6 (using either the mean or median of the scale values), and Craig's score would be 11.9 (using the mean) or 8.5 (using the median). Based on these results, Craig is clearly more favorable toward assisted suicide than is Dena.

As you can see from this explanation, Thurstone scales are somewhat time consuming to construct because judges must be recruited to rank items and scale values must be calculated before the scale can be administered. There is, however, at least one situation in which developing a Thurstone scale is worth the extra effort. Suppose a researcher wants to develop two or more equivalent versions of a scale. As an example, the researcher may want to conduct pre- and posttests but may not want to use the same measure because of possible memory effects. This could be done by obtaining Thurstone scale values for a large number of items and then assigning items with the same scale values to each of the two or more scales. Balancing the scale values across versions in this way can help to enhance (though not to guarantee) equivalence. Aside from the situation in which equivalent scale versions are required, however, Thurstone scaling is not often used in the social sciences, probably because of the time-consuming process of constructing them. Instead, many researchers rely on *Likert scaling*.

Likert Scaling

Recognizing what he called the "exceedingly laborious" methods involved in Thurstone scaling, Likert (1932) proposed a much simpler method in which, instead of using judges to rate items, a common response scale (Likert originally proposed the use of "strongly approve," "approve," "undecided," "disapprove," and "strongly disapprove") is used for all items with numeric values (in this example, 1–5) assigned to the scale points. This method has become so popular in the social sciences that you are likely already familiar with it, even though you may not know it by name. As with all attitude scales, the idea is to develop a measure that would allow researchers to differentiate respondents along a range of affect. In a typical application, not only would researchers like to distinguish those with positive attitudes from those with negative attitudes, but also those with stronger positive or negative attitudes from those who feel less strongly. To make such differentiations, items should be written to assess the entire range of affect from strongly negative to strongly positive. In contrast to Thurstone scaling, neutral items are usually not included because such items do not help to spread respondents out along the underlying attitude continuum. Typically, between 10 and 20 items are included. Once items have been written, they are assembled on the page (or increasingly, a computer) in random order. Respondents are then asked to indicate an answer to each item using a set of response options. The familiar "strongly disagree" to "strongly agree" format in the following example has superseded Likert's original suggestion. However, other formats, such as "not like me" to "very much like me" or frequency scales such as "never" to "always" are also common.

1	2	3	4	5
Strongly disagree	Disagree	Neither agree nor disagree	Agree	Strongly agree

Scoring Likert Scales

Scores for each respondent are obtained by summing their responses to each item. For this reason, Likert scales are sometimes referred to as a *summative* technique. However, care must be taken to *reverse-code* items that are negatively oriented. To illustrate why, consider the following two-item example (of course, more than two items would typically be used, as noted previously):

_____ 1. Measurement theory is fun.
_____ 2. Measurement theory is boring.

Leaving aside for the moment the issue of whether these are good items for assessing attitudes toward measurement theory, let us suppose that Keston, who loves measurement theory, answers as follows, using the scale above:

__5__ 1. Measurement theory is fun.

__1__ 2. Measurement theory is boring.

Sara, who hates measurement theory, provides the following answers:

__1__ 1. Measurement theory is fun.

__5__ 2. Measurement theory is boring.

Perhaps you have anticipated where I am going with this example. In summing their answers to obtain scores, both Keston and Sara receive scores of 6. Without reverse coding the negatively oriented item (e.g., "Measurement theory is boring"), it is not possible to differentiate positive from negative attitudes.

Reverse scoring simply means that the researcher "reverses" scores for the negatively oriented items so that, if the respondent answers "5" it is switched to "1," if he or she answers "4" it is switched to "2," and so on. A general rule is to add one to the highest response category (5, in our example) and subtract the original response. This is done for each of the negatively oriented items. So, Keston's response to the second item would be reversed to $(5 + 1) - 1$ or 5, and Sara's response to $(5 + 1) - 5$, or 1. (Such operations are easily done in statistical software packages such as SPSS and SAS or in spreadsheets such as Excel.) After reverse coding, Keston's score would be 10 and Sara's 2, scores that more accurately reflect the attitudes of these two respondents. Note that there is no reason I could not have reverse coded the positively oriented items and left the negatively oriented items alone. If this had been done instead, Sara would have received a score of 10 and Keston a score of 2. Thus, a higher score would reflect a more negative attitude. So, the choice of which type of item to reverse score just depends on the meaning desired for a high score. If positively oriented items are reverse coded, a high score will indicate a more negative attitude; if negatively oriented items are reverse coded, a high score will indicate a more positive attitude. Of course, all of this assumes that the "strongly disagree" option is coded as 1 and the "strongly agree" option as 5.

Writing Likert Items

Some of the suggestions from the previous chapter on cognitive items also apply to writing noncognitive items. Items should be short, use simple language, and contain only one complete thought. However, because the nature of cognitive items is quite different from that of noncognitive items, additional suggestions apply to them. Thorndike (2005) credits Edwards (1957) with the following suggestions for writing

Likert items, although many of these suggestions appeared in Likert's and Thurstone's original monographs.

1. Avoid statements that refer to the past rather than the future. Many younger respondents would be hard pressed to provide an answer to the following item:

> There is more support for same-sex marriage in today's society than there was 30 years ago.

Even those of us who were alive at that time and therefore in a position to remember may not be able to do so. In addition, this item violates the next suggestion in that the amount of past support for same-sex marriage is really not a matter of opinion.

2. Avoid statements that are factual or capable of being interpreted as such. I often see items such as the following on attitude scales.

> Nonmedical marijuana use is illegal in West Virgina.

The answer to this item is not a matter of opinion; it has a clear-cut right or wrong answer. Nevertheless, I routinely observe that respondents will disagree with such an item. Does this mean that they disagree with the fact that marijuana use is illegal? Or are they not aware of this fact? Or have they simply misread the item? The problem, of course, is that we have no way of knowing.

3. Avoid statements that can have more than one interpretation.

4. Avoid statements that are irrelevant to the attitude being measured. This may seem obvious, but I often find that in an effort to develop a sufficient number of items, scale developers strike out into territory that is not clearly within the definition of the construct.

5. Avoid statements that are likely to be endorsed by almost everyone or almost no one. Most respondents, one would hope, are likely to disagree with the next item.

> Use of marijuana should be punishable by death.

Recall that the purpose of creating an attitude scale is to spread respondents along a continuum from positive to negative attitudes. This item is not likely to accomplish that purpose. However, an important caveat should be noted. If the purpose of one's study is to identify those with extreme attitudes or personality characteristics, extreme items are necessary. For example, the majority of respondents will not endorse questions about suicide attempts, but without including items on this topic we would be unable to identify suicidal individuals.

Another reason for avoiding extreme statements can be illustrated by going back to the example used to explain reverse coding. Suppose that instead of items reading "Measurement theory is fun" and "Measurement theory is boring," I used the items "I love measurement theory" and "I hate measurement theory." On the surface, these items may seem reasonable, but what if someone thinks measurement theory is okay but doesn't love it. Should this person agree or disagree with the item "I love measurement theory"? Technically, he should disagree because he does not love measurement theory. But because he is somewhat positive (or at least lukewarm) about measurement theory, his answer should really be on the positive or agree side. Similar logic applies to the item "I hate measurement theory." A person who dislikes measurement theory, but whose sentiments do not extend to actual hatred, would be in a quandary about how to answer. Use of extreme statements can thus sometimes backfire, as these examples show.

6. Select statements that cover the entire range of the noncognitive scale of interest. As noted previously, the entire range of affect from negative to positive should be represented. However, neutral statements should not be included.

7. Keep the language clear, simple, and direct.

8. Statements should be short, rarely exceeding 20 words.

9. Each statement should contain only *one* complete thought. Items violating this suggestion are referred to as "double-barreled." For example:

I believe in God and country.

If one believes in one but not the other, what is the appropriate response?

10. Statements containing universals such as "all, always, none, and never" should be avoided. Such wording tends to bias respondents toward thinking of exceptions, resulting in less agreement than would otherwise be the case. Consider the following item:

No one is immune to the effects of alcohol.

One's natural reaction is to think of examples of those who may be immune (such as oneself).

11. Words such as "only, just, merely" are leading and should be used with care.

12. Whenever possible, statements should be in simple sentences rather than compound or complex sentences. Attempting to respond to the following item should demonstrate why you should follow this suggestion.

I believe that having sex before marriage may be detrimental to a couple's relationship but that there may not be negative consequences if the couple has a stable, committed relationship.

13. Avoid use of vocabulary that respondents may not understand. In general, keeping vocabulary to about a sixth-grade reading level is recommended.

14. Include equal numbers of positively and negatively oriented statements. Including both positively and negatively oriented items, such as "I love measurement theory" and "I hate measurement theory," is sometimes erroneously thought to prevent respondents from engaging in acquiescent responding—that is, agreeing (or disagreeing) with all statements. However, respondents who answer in this way typically do so because they are not reading the questions carefully in the first place, so changing the orientation of the items will not prevent this type of responding. The real reason for this suggestion is that it allows the researcher to *identify* acquiescent responders through their illogical pattern of responses. Patterns in which respondents agree (or disagree) with both positively and negatively oriented items can be flagged as being of dubious accuracy and possibly discarded from the analysis.

15. Avoid the use of negatively phrased statements. Although this appears to contradict the previous suggestion, there is a difference between *negatively phrased* and *negatively oriented items.* The former includes a negative particle, such as "no" or "not," while the latter indicates a negative attitude toward the concept of interest. For example, "I do not like measurement theory" is a negatively phrased item; "I hate measurement theory" is negatively oriented. The reason for the prohibition against negatively worded items is that it is difficult for many respondents to disagree with a negatively phrased item in order to indicate agreement. For our previous example, a respondent who liked measurement theory would have to answer "I disagree that I do not like measurement theory," clearly a confusing construction. I return to this issue in a later section of this chapter.

16. Statements should be clearly negatively or positively oriented. In addition to indicating that neutral items should not be included, this suggestion is also intended to guard against items such as the following, which was intended to measure attitudes toward sex before marriage.

> It is okay for two people to have sex before marriage if they have dated for at least a year.

The problem with this item is that both respondents who favor sex before marriage and those who oppose it could respond negatively. Those in favor could disagree because they feel that no conditions should be placed on a couple's decision, while those opposing sex before marriage could disagree because they feel it is not permissible regardless of the timeframe. As an aside, I often find that items such as this, in which the item writer attempts to qualify or put conditions on the statement, are problematic.

Guttman Scaling

Guttman scaling (1941, 1950), or, to use the author's terminology, *scalogram* analysis, was developed in an attempt to create scales in which persons' attitudes could be pinpointed simply by asking them to check the most favorable statement with which they agree. Thus, in contrast to so-called *summative methods* such as Likert scaling, in which respondents' scores are simply the sum (or average) of the scale values for the items chosen, Guttman scaling is an example of a *deterministic method*. With deterministic methods, respondents' scores are determined on the basis of the most extreme attitude statement with which they agree. Perhaps an example is the easiest way to understand these methods. Consider these four statements:

1. Assisted suicide should be available to anyone who wants it.
2. Assisted suicide should be available to any severely ill person who wants it.
3. Assisted suicide should be available to any terminally ill person who is in extreme pain.
4. Assisted suicide should be available to those with incurable medical conditions.

These four items were developed such that they represent a hierarchy of favorableness, with item 1 the most favorable. Presumably, a person who would agree to item 1 would also agree with all the items below it, a person who would agree to item 2 but not to item 1 would also agree with items 3 and 4, and so on. In Guttman scaling, therefore, a hierarchical series of items (typically four or five) is written and presented to respondents *in the hierarchical order*, with the most favorable item at the top. Respondents are then asked to check the item highest in the hierarchy with which they agree.

Although Guttman scaling is a reasonable method in theory, it is very difficult to construct a set of items that follow the rigid hierarchy it requires. In order to do so, the construct to be measured must be strictly *unidimensional*; that is, it must tap into only one attitude or idea. To do so, it is usually necessary for the construct to be defined very narrowly. If such a definition is undesirable, as it often is, Guttman scaling is probably not a good choice.

Instead of determining the item hierarchy a priori, it is possible to determine it empirically. The researcher could administer a set of items to a group of respondents, ask them to check all items with which they agree, and keep track of the patterns of agreement. If the pattern of responses supports a strong hierarchy of items then these items could be retained for a possible Guttman scale. Empirical methods can also be used to determine whether a set of items is "scalable" in a Guttman sense. To do this, responses to a Guttman scale are obtained, and an index known as the *coefficient of reproducibility* is calculated as

$$C = \frac{\text{Number of errors}}{\text{Total number of responses}}$$

Here, *number of errors* is the number of *inconsistent* response patterns, or response patterns in which a respondent fails to agree with an item meant to be lower in the hierarchy while agreeing with a higher item. For example, a response pattern in which the respondent agreed with items 2 and 3 in the previous example but did not agree with item 4 would be considered an error. The total number of responses is simply the total number of people who provided responses to the scale. According to Crocker and Algina (1986, p. 56), a coefficient of reproducibility less than .90 would be taken to indicate that the scale is not properly ordered.

THEORIES OF ITEM RESPONDING

Earlier in this chapter, I introduced an example in which three opinion polls, all measuring attitudes about affirmative action, resulted in very different percentages of favorable responses. Clearly, respondents had very different interpretations of the three items. Will it always be the case that subtle changes in wording affect response rates so dramatically? Or are there ways in which questions can be worded to avoid, or at least ameliorate, such effects? In this section, I begin to explore these issues. The vast majority of research on response processes has been conducted in the context of attitude or opinion surveys (e.g., see Schwarz & Sudman, 1996; Sudman, Bradburn, & Schwarz, 1996; Torangeau, Rips, & Rasinski, 2000, on which I draw heavily in this section). I will focus on two theoretical developments that have had considerable impact in this area. One of these is concerned with the cognitive processes that are involved in responding to questions about affect. In the second framework, researchers view the process of responding to noncognitive items as a form of social encounter in which people follow the same "rules of conversation" as in everyday interactions. Although these two theoretical frameworks are discussed separately for organizational purposes, the cognitive processes implied by each likely operate jointly to influence how a person will respond to a given question.

The Cognitive Process Model of Responding

Sudman and colleagues (1996) describe four components that underlie the response process: (1) interpreting the item, (2) generating a response, (3) formatting and reporting the response, and (4) editing the response. One of the primary issues in noncognitive measurement is that respondents vary considerably in the thoroughness with which they engage in these four processes. Krosnick (1991) attributes such differences to variations in respondents' propensity to *satisfice* rather than *optimize*. *Optimizers* are respondents who make a sincere effort to engage in the response process to the best of their ability. *Satisficers* either skip some of the necessary processes entirely ("strong satisficing") or put forth less than their best effort ("weak satisficing"). Krosnick views satisficing/optimizing levels as being on a continuum, rather than representing two distinct typologies of responders. In fact, while answering a single questionnaire, respondents may switch from optimizing to satisficing as they become fatigued or distracted. This is particularly likely if the questionnaire is lengthy and/or difficult to answer. Indeed, task difficulty is one of the conditions that increase the propensity to satisfice. Factors that decrease the propensity to satisfice include higher levels of motivation, which can be influenced by a personal interest in the topics being measured, or by a general *need for cognition* (Cacioppo & Petty, 1982, 1984). Need for cognition is a personality trait characterized by an individual's enjoyment of thinking and mental exercises, and preference for challenging cognitive tasks. Higher familiarity with the topic will also result in lower levels of satisficing. Krosnick, Narayan, and Smith (1996) have found that levels of satisficing are lower for those with more education. This is probably related to the fact that more highly educated respondents have a greater ability than those with less education to retrieve information from memory and integrate that information into a response. In the following sections, I discuss the four components of the response process with an eye toward how these might be affected by satisficing behavior.

Interpreting the Item

The first step in answering any question is to understand it. In responding to an item, therefore, the respondent must first parse out its meaning. Sudman and colleagues (1996) describe several pitfalls in this process. The most obvious of these is that the question may be unclear. This is why suggestions for item writing emphasize clarity. Lack of clarity is particularly problematic for satisficers. These respondents may not take the time to fully comprehend the question. Instead, satisficers are content with a vague or superficial understanding that allows them to provide an answer without putting forth too much effort. When responding to a set of items on a scale, satisficers may use the first few items to get a sense of the topic and may then answer the subsequent items on the basis of this understanding, without really processing them.

Other, more subtle problems in item interpretation have to do with the choice of words used in either the item itself or the answer choices. Use of terminology such as *big business* or *socialized medicine* conjures up different images for different people—a fact with which political ad writers are all too familiar. In addition, words such as *sometimes* and *a few* can have widely different meanings. On a whim, I once asked students in one of my classes to write down what they thought *several* meant and was shocked to find that answers ranged from 2 to 20! Terms such as these are best replaced with actual numbers when writing noncognitive items, as well as in response options. Similarly, words such as *youngster* or *middle-aged* can elicit very different meanings to different people. Numerous examples are provided in the interesting volume by Belson (1986). In one study, respondents were asked whether they thought that children "suffer any ill effects" from watching television programs containing violence (p. 13). When asked what was meant by the term *children*, respondents indicated ages ranging from babies to 20-year-olds. Some respondents even included qualifications about the type of children referred to, stating that these were meant to be "children who have been brought up properly." (Poorly brought up children, presumably, would be so used to violence that they would not be affected.) Therefore, if a particular age range is of interest, it is best to indicate what this is rather than use terms that might be loosely interpreted. Finally, context can play a role in respondents' interpretations. In a popular example quoted in Bradburn (1992, p. 317), researchers were surprised to learn that some respondents had 20 to 30 children, only to find that these respondents were teachers who thought the researchers were referring to their students. This example suggests that researchers should carefully consider the context when asking questions. It is possible that had this question been asked at the teachers' homes, they would have interpreted it in the intended manner.

Another way in which contextual effects may affect interpretation is through other items that are included on the same scale or questionnaire. If, for example, a researcher first asked several questions about respondents' grandparents, the respondents might provide more favorable answers to a subsequent set of questions about their attitudes toward Medicare. It has even been found that simply including demographic questions asking for respondents' sex or race can influence responses to other items if these demographic questions are asked first. This effect has been attributed to the fact that answering questions about respondents' sex or race causes the respondent to think about these when answering subsequent items. It may even be that respondents infer from the fact that they are being asked about sex or race that such characteristics are salient to later questions. For this reason, it is typically recommended that demographic questions be placed last in a questionnaire.

Finally, respondents may acquire context from the response options. An interesting example is provided in a study by Schwarz, Hippler, Deutsch, and Strack (1985) in which respondents were asked to report the average amount of television they watched per day. Half of the respondents were given an answer scale that ranged from "up to a half hour" to "more than two and a half hours" in half-hour increments. The answer scale for the other set of respondents ranged from "up to two and a half hours" to "more than four and a half hours." The percentages of respondents reporting they watched more than two and a half hours were 16.2 % for those who received the first (low frequency) scale, but 37.5% for those receiving the high frequency scale. This effect has been found in many other content domains (see Schwarz, 1990, for a review). One explanation for this phenomenon is that respondents, instead of trying to count up the number of hours they watched television, engage in a thought process that goes something like this: "Well, I don't know exactly how many hours I watch per day, but I don't think I watch any more or less than other people so I'm probably about average. I'll just choose the middle response." This is a form of what Krosnick (1991) refers to as weak satisficing. In Schwarz and colleagues' study, respondents did indeed choose the middle category most often, but only when using the low frequency scale. So, although there is some support for the hypothesis that respondents engage in this type of thinking, this is only one possibility. Another explanation is that respondents edit their responses after viewing the response scale. For example, respondents who watch more than two hours a day may report fewer hours once they see that this is the most extreme response category. One last example of the ways in which response scale characteristics can affect answers has to do with the labeling of numerical options. In another study by Schwarz and his colleagues (1991), numeric labels for ratings of "Success in Life" varied from –5 to 5 in one group and from 0 to 10 in another. When negative numbers were used in the response scale, most people chose responses labeled with a positive number, but when the scale ranged from 0 to 10, responses were much more evenly spread throughout the scale. Schwarz et al. conjectured that respondents were reluctant to choose negative values because they interpreted these as indicating failure rather than simply a lack of success. This was the case even though the lowest endpoint (either –5 or 0) was labeled as "not at all successful" in both scales.

Generating a Response

Once respondents have interpreted an item, their next task is to generate an answer. This, in turn, necessitates forming a judgment about the attitude or noncognitive state in question. If the item refers to a topic on which the respondent already has an opinion, or a noncognitive state of which he or she is well aware, this information is readily called into memory and used to provide an answer. Such information is said to be "chronically accessible" and is typically information on topics with which the respondents have had personal experience, information that is important to them because of their religious, political, or personal values, or personality characteristics that are particularly salient. For example, a respondent who is active in the anti-abortion movement will likely have easily accessible attitudes available on the subject of abortion. Respondents for whom the topic is not important may not have such a "readymade" attitude available to them and must instead generate an answer based on whatever information is accessible. Such respondents might, for example, draw on related information, such as their beliefs about when life begins, or they might consider experiences friends or family members may have had. Another source of information is the respondent's general impressions or stereotypes about the topic. A respondent who has been inconvenienced by anti-abortion protestors may access this information when asked about attitudes toward abortion. Or respondents who consider themselves to be generally liberal in political orientation may draw on negative stereotypes about the anti-abortion movement in generating an answer. All of these are strategies that optimizers might use in situations in which no readily accessible response is available. In contrast, satisficers might simply select the first answer that comes to mind or agree with any assertion presented to them (known as *acquiescence*). Strong satisficers may even skip step 2 entirely and instead simply choose a neutral or "no opinion" response, if offered, or engage in what Krosnick (1991) terms "mental coin-flipping"—choosing randomly among the options provided.

The degree to which relevant information is accessible affects both the ease with which a response can be reported and the *consistency* of responses. Those for whom information is chronically accessible and who have strong opinions on a subject tend to report more consistent attitudes than those for whom the topic is less important or accessible. Those in the latter category may access a variety of information, some of which is favorable and some unfavorable. Respondents cannot be expected to do an exhaustive search of memory (the average amount of time to respond to a typical survey question is about five seconds, according to Torangeau et al., 2000). Instead, even optimizing respondents will stop searching their memories once they feel they have sufficient information to provide a response. For satisficers, the search may stop as soon as a single piece of information is called to memory. In either case, some relevant information will be omitted from consideration. If, on another occasion, the previously omitted information is brought to mind, the response may well change. Such changes will be more likely for respondents who do not have strong feelings about the question being asked or for those who are satisficing (or both).

The need to search memory for response-related information is also why context can play an important role in shaping responses, as in the Medicare/grandparents example presented previously. Asking questions about a respondent's grandparents has a "priming" effect on memory that results in some information (in this case, presumably favorable information, unless the respondent has had negative grandparent experiences) becoming more salient than other, more negative information. Priming effects can also be invoked when a series of items such as those on a typical attitude survey or personality checklist are presented. Answers to items appearing earlier in the list may cause respondents to think more deeply about the topic, thus leading them to answer subsequent items differently than might have been the case had the items been presented in isolation. As evidence, it has been found that items adjacent to each other on the page are more highly correlated than those that are not (Knowles, 1988). However, the possibility of order effects is *not* a reason to include only one item about a topic. On the contrary, including multiple items with different phrasings is recommended as a way of "balancing out" idiosyncratic wording effects. This is one important reason that multi-item scales rather than single items are recommended.

As alluded to in the previous paragraph, information that is accessed to provide an answer must be combined in some way. If the weight of the favorable information is clearly greater than that of the unfavorable (or vice versa), this process is fairly simple. If not, optimizing respondents must use other methods to combine the information. Satisficers may not have much information to integrate, given that their memory search is likely to have been suboptimal to begin with. Instead, such respondents will tend to provide a response based on initial impressions of where the preponderance of the information lies, with an "agree" response being chosen if it is felt that most of the information is positive.

In some cases, however, even optimizers may be confused about what information should or should not be considered. For example, if a respondent were asked, "How often do you use research to inform your decisions," an obvious question might be what is meant by "research." Does this include personal research, such as the fact that I have personally tried both chocolate chip and oatmeal cookies and made a decision to buy the former? Or does "research" refer only to published, peer-reviewed research? If such a question were to be asked on a self-report scale where respondents were not able to ask for clarification, they might search for clues in other items on the questionnaire or in the context in which the questionnaire was administered. For example, if the questionnaire contained other questions related to published research, it would be reasonable for respondents to infer that this is what was meant by the term *research*.

What, then, are the implications for creating scales in practice? First, make the wording as clear as possible. Ask others to review items for clarity. Do not use vague terms such as "often" or "a few." If a numerical answer is required, ask for exact numbers whenever possible or provide numerical ranges. Do not use ambiguous phrases such as "big government" or emotionally charged terminology such as "military machine." Word items clearly so that respondents do not feel the need to clarify item meaning through reference to the response options. Carefully consider the possible effects of context. If demographic questions are to be included as part of a larger questionnaire, it is best to put these at the end. Encourage respondents to take their time in answering. Although some respondents will rush through their answers regardless of instructions to the contrary, providing plenty of time to answer will help some respondents to access a more complete set of relevant information with which to provide an answer. Finally, order items within a scale randomly. That is, do not include all of the positively oriented items or all of the negatively oriented items together. Even better, create different versions of the scale in which items are ordered in different ways. This will not prevent order effects, but if responses are combined across versions, such effects should balance out. If items are administered via computer, as is increasingly common, order can be randomized.

Formatting and Reporting the Response

After respondents have come up with a response, they must report it on the scale provided. Although in some cases open-ended questions are asked, the formats discussed in this chapter provide a set of response options from which respondents must choose. I have already discussed some of the ways in which the response options can affect responses. Respondents sometimes use the answer choices as a source of normative information that is used to generate or modify their answers, as in the television-watching example. Numeric response scales can be particularly tricky, with respondents showing a preference for positive rather than negative numbers, regardless of how these are labeled. And what happens if, after formulating an answer, the respondent cannot find a corresponding response option? In such cases, according to Sudman and colleagues (1996), respondents simply may not answer.

I often find that scale developers do not pay as much attention as they might to the choice of response scale options. In many cases, the response scale is simply not appropriate for the item, as in the following example:

The federal government should provide more support for education.

Never	Sometimes	Often	Always
1	2	3	4

Aside from the fact that it includes vague terms such as *sometimes*, which is not ideal, the response scale in general does not seem to be a good match to the item. If respondents' level of agreement with this statement is of interest, a "strongly disagree" to "strongly agree" scale would be more appropriate. If the interest is in frequency, what would an answer of "sometimes" imply? Does it mean that the respondent thinks this sometimes but not at other times? Or does it mean that the respondent thinks the government should only be supportive sometimes (and if so, when?)

Research in the area of psychophysics suggests that respondents use the extremes of response scales to "anchor" or contextualize their responses. For example, readers may be familiar with experiments in which people report that a weight is lighter if they have previously lifted a heavier weight, or that a sound is louder if they have previously heard one that is less loud. There is some evidence that similar anchoring is done with both numerically and verbally labeled rating scales. A commonly reported example is taken from the research of Schwarz and colleagues (1988) in which respondents were asked to report how many "irritating experiences" they had on an average day. When the response scale contained low frequencies, respondents assumed that major irritations were meant and reported fewer irritating experiences, whereas when the response scale contained high frequencies respondents assumed this phrase referred to minor irritations and therefore reported more events.

Results of studies in these areas suggest that those who are developing scales should be very careful in their choice of response options. First, be sure that the response options are appropriate for the items. In addition, the meaning of each response option should be as clear as possible. Each response option should be labeled. In some cases, researchers label only the endpoints of the scale, as in this example:

1	2	3	4	5
Strongly disagree				Strongly agree

The respondent is left to infer the meaning of options 2, 3, and 4. The problem with this, of course, is that respondents may infer very different meanings for these options. Is option 3 meant to be interpreted as being midway between "strongly disagree" and "strong agree," as "neutral," or as something else? It makes logical sense that scales for which the response options are not all labeled leave more room for error than scales for which options are all labeled. This is because the latter type of scale leaves less room for idiosyncratic interpretations. Research shows that fully labeled scales result in higher reliability than scales with unlabeled or partially labeled scales (Krosnick & Berent, 1993).

Editing the Response

In some cases, respondents may edit their response before reporting it. The most commonly discussed reason they do so is known as *social desirability*. Social desirability refers to a tendency for respondents to give overly favorable impressions of themselves. Of course, this presupposes that respondents know, or at least think they know, what the socially desirable response is. DiMaio (1984) describes two ways in which a socially desirable response could be defined. One way is through cultural values that respondents assume are shared by those who might see their responses. The other is through what respondents view as societal norms, even though the respondent may not share these norms. DiMaio provides the examples of happiness or satisfaction as values most people would share, and of not engaging in promiscuous sex as an example of a societal norm. Respondents might report higher levels of happiness or satisfaction because they do not want others to know they don't "measure up" in this area, and they might report lower levels of promiscuity because they are aware that such activity is considered immoral by many (even though they personally may not share this belief). In either case, the problem is that such respondents' true levels are not reported, which can bias results of studies in which such effects are operating.

Sudman and colleagues (1996) state that the size of social desirability effects is "usually modest" (p. 74) and is limited to situations that respondents might find threatening. Perhaps not surprisingly, these authors state that socially desirable responding has been found to be more prevalent in face-to-face interviews than on self-report surveys. DiMaio (1984) reports that levels of socially desirable responding vary across such demographics as sex, age, and ethnicity. Again, this is not surprising because what is considered to be desirable often varies across demographic groups. Suggestions about how to reduce socially desirable responding vary, but common recommendations are to put respondents at ease as much as possible and to ensure them of the confidentiality of their responses. Scales designed to measure one's propensity toward socially desirable responding, such as the Marlowe Crowne Social Desirability Scale (MCSD; Crowne & Marlowe, 1960) or the Balanced Inventory of Desirable Responding (BIDR; Paulhus, 1988) are available, and researchers concerned about bias due to such responses often administer one of these as part of a study. Those with high scores can then be flagged and possibly removed from the dataset. Another option is to partial out the effects of social desirability using statistical methods. Finally, researchers concerned about social desirability bias might consider using an *implicit attitude measure* (Fazio & Olson, 2003; Lane, Banaji, Nosek, & Greenwald, 2007).

Item Responses as Social Encounters

One way in which the response process can be understood is as a form of social encounter. Although responses to self-report items are written rather than verbal, they do constitute a form of communication. And, interestingly, researchers have found that respondents apply many of the guidelines used in everyday conversations to answering self-report questionnaires (e.g., Strack & Schwartz, 1992). Viewing the response process as a form of conversation can therefore help us to understand why people respond as they do. The starting point for such theories is a chapter by Grice (1975), in which he discusses four "conversational maxims" or tacit rules that those engaging in conversation are assumed to follow:

1. The maxim of quantity: Contributions to a conversation should contain as much information as necessary but not more.
2. The maxim of quality: Contributions to a conversation should be truthful and should be based on evidence.
3. The maxim of relation: Contributions should be relevant to the conversation.
4. The maxim of manner: Contributions should be clear and not overly wordy.

One way to understand how these maxims might affect the response process is to consider how they might relate to the four components of the response process discussed in the previous sections. With regard to the first component, comprehension of the question, the maxim of quantity suggests that respondents will assume that the question provides all the information they need to supply an answer. It is not surprising, then, that respondents turn to the response options or other contextual clues when questions seem unclear. They are assuming that if the necessary information is not given as part of the question, it will be given somewhere else. A similar effect results from the maxim of relation. Because respondents assume that all the information provided is relevant, they will attempt to use it all in understanding the question. This information includes the response options, which are brought into the "conversation" to help clarify the question. The maxim of manner implies that respondents have a right to expect that items will be clearly and succinctly written. In some cases, respondents take a lack of such clarity as license to omit the question, as I have often seen respondents do with confusing items.

The maxim of quantity also has implications for the second component of the response process—that of generating a response. According to this maxim, information should not be provided if it is not necessary. For example, if we ask someone how to get to the post office, we do not expect her to also tell us how to get to the bank. If she did so, we might assume that the post office is near the bank, making it necessary for us to know the location of the bank. In the same way, respondents to noncognitive items assume that all of the information provided, including the information in the response options and other context cues, is needed to provide an answer. This is another reason it is not surprising to find that respondents pay attention to such information. At the same time, the maxim of relation would prevent respondents from including irrelevant information in their responses. For example, when asked how many times they have been to the beach during the past summer, respondents understand that they should not also include the number of times they had been to the mountains. And the maxim of quality implies that respondents should not lie and state they have been to the beach if they have not.

With regard to the formatting and reporting of the response, respondents will assume, based on the maxim of relevance, that the response options provided are appropriate for the item. Thus, respondents will be justifiably confused when frequency-type response options are provided for items that require agreement or disagreement, as in the earlier example. They will also expect the response options to be sufficient to cover any response they might provide. By the same principle, respondents will assume that the entire range of response options is meant to be used (by someone, if not necessarily by them). This helps us to understand why respondents use the endpoints of the response scale to anchor their responses, assuming that those points represent the "low" and "high" end of reasonable responses.

Finally, the maxim of quantity has implications for the last response component, editing the response. This maxim implies that respondents should not provide more information than is requested. Going back to the beach and mountain example, suppose that respondents were first asked whether they had been on any out-of-town trips during the past summer. In a second question, they are asked whether they had been to the beach during the past summer. Respondents who had been to the beach *and* on other out-of-town trips may go back and edit their response to the first question, assuming that it referred to trips *other than* the beach. If not, why was a second question specific to beach trips included?

You may be wondering about the role of socially desirable responding in this context. After all, does socially desirable responding not violate the maxim of quality? Clearly it does, but Grice acknowledges that "a participant in a talk exchange may fail to fulfill a maxim in various ways" (1975, p. 49). Conversational maxims are obviously not legal requirements and are, in fact, violated frequently, as anyone who has carried on a conversation knows very well. Socially desirable responding is an example of a communication in which the respondent chooses to sacrifice what Grice refers to as the "cooperative principle" in order to maintain a positive impression.

PROBLEMS IN MEASURING NONCOGNITIVE OUTCOMES

In the discussion of the processes involved in answering noncognitive items, I have alluded to some of the problems involved in this type of measurement. These include issues of *response distortion*, such as socially desirable responding, faking, and malingering. This section addresses these issues, drawing on what we have learned about the response process where appropriate.

Response Distortion

Response distortion refers to a *systematic* tendency to respond to a *range of items* on some basis other than the intended content. Portions of this definition are italicized to emphasize two things. First, response distortion is *systematic*; that is, it is something that a respondent does routinely, not just on random occasions. If such responding were random, its effects would be expected to balance out across a large number of respondents, and average scores would not be biased. But the fact that response distortion is systematic means that this type of responding can result in biased estimates of overall levels of the construct being measured. Second, response distortion typically occurs on a *range of items*, not simply on one or two. If only one or two items on a multi-item scale were affected, overall scores would not be biased to any great extent. However, response distortion is characterized by its effect on multiple items. The problem, again, is that estimates of total scores for the scale are likely to be biased. The potential for such bias is the reason that response distortion is considered problematic.

The fact that response distortion is systematic does not mean that it will occur on every occasion or in every situation or context. Some researchers differentiate between respondents who habitually distort their responses in some way, such as those who exhibit consistent tendencies to respond in a socially desirable manner, and those who exhibit such response patterns only on certain occasions or in specific situations. The former type of distortion is referred to as a *response style*, whereas the latter is sometimes called a *response set*. As an example of a response set, a respondent who is fatigued may show a greater tendency to choose the neutral option on a Likert scale to avoid searching memory for a more accurate answer. In contrast, a respondent with a response style of choosing the neutral option would select that option whether or not he was fatigued. Thus, response styles are thought to be more trait-like and exhibit greater consistency across situations and time points, whereas response sets are conceived of as more state-like, occurring only in certain contexts.

Types of Response Distortion

Although socially desirable responding is perhaps the most widely studied type of response distortion, other types also bear mentioning, including *acquiescence, extremity and moderacy,* and *malingering.* (Although these types of responding are often discussed in the context of attitude scales, they can occur for any type of noncognitive characteristic, including measures of personality, values, and interests.) Acquiescence is the tendency to either agree (yea-saying) or disagree (nay-saying) with an item, regardless of its content. This tendency has been found to be relatively stable across different content areas and situations, and is therefore considered to be a response style. A commonly recommended antidote for acquiescent responding is to include roughly equal numbers of positively and negatively oriented items on a scale. However, as noted earlier in this chapter, doing so will not *prevent* respondents from yea- or nay-saying. But inclusion of positively as well as negatively oriented items will allow the researcher to identify such respondents through their aberrant response patterns (e.g., responding "strongly agree" to items that are both favorable and unfavorable to the referent). Some experts have also pointed out that if both positively and negatively oriented items are included, *and* both yea- and nay-sayers are present among respondents, acquiescent responses from the two types of respondents would cancel each other out.

Although this logic makes some sense, I am not aware of any research indicating that yea- and nay-sayers are likely to be present in equal numbers, which appears to be a necessary condition for the argument to hold. A more reasonable argument maintains that, if negatively (or positively) oriented items are reverse coded, both yea- and nay-sayers should receive scores near the midpoint of the scale because their positive and negative responses will balance out. Such responding will therefore not bias measures of central tendency.

Extremity is a tendency of respondents to (as the name implies) select the most extreme response option (e.g., "strongly agree" or "strongly disagree"). It could be argued that such respondents are simply very enthusiastic, or have very strong opinions, and that such responding should not be viewed as a response distortion. This is likely true in some cases. It is also true that one respondent's "agree" may be another's "strongly agree"; that is, we really have no way of knowing how much "agreement" such responses truly indicate. However, it is interesting to note that Price and Eriksen (1966; quoted in Nunnally & Bernstein, 1994) found that paranoid schizophrenics were more likely to be extreme responders than were controls. Moderacy bias is the opposite of extremity bias. Moderate responders tend to choose response options in the middle of the scale. Like extreme responding, moderate responding can result in bias (either positive or negative) in total scores as well as in decreased variability of scale scores. Moderacy response bias has not been studied as extensively as other types, but there is evidence suggesting that respondents from some Asian countries are more likely than their American counterparts to choose the middle response option (see Yang, Harkness, Chin, & Villar, 2010). In practice, it is difficult to eliminate or control for either extremity or moderacy bias. Although a researcher could flag those whose responses do not exhibit an expected amount of variability, there is no way of knowing whether such responses are simply valid indications of extremely strong or weak attitudes and personality characteristics, or truly represent response distortion.

Malingering refers to a tendency for respondents to portray themselves as more disturbed or pathological than is actually the case. It is unlikely that malingering will be problematic when measuring attitudes or opinions. However, in personality measurement, malingering can be an issue for situations in which respondents are undergoing evaluation for treatment or for criminal prosecution. Some popular scales such as the Minnesota Multiphasic Personality Inventory-2 (MMPI-2) include special scales designed to detect malingering. The MMPI-2 F (infrequency) scale was developed from a set of items to which fewer than 20% of a restandardization group agreed. Because the items for the F scale were chosen from scales associated with a variety of psychopathologies, it would be very unusual for a respondent to answer all of them in a positive direction. Instead, high scores on this scale are taken as indications that a respondent is either deliberately malingering or is very careless or eccentric, or that there are errors in scoring. Thus, high scores are generally flagged as invalid.

Socially Desirable Responding

As noted earlier in this section, socially desirable responding is probably the most widely studied type of response distortion. Some researchers in this area have described two (or more; see Paulhus, 2002) components of such responding (Paulhus, 1984). *Self-deceptive enhancement* refers to responses reflecting the fact that respondents truly view themselves in a more favorable light than is actually the case. Such respondents are simply not completely aware of their own shortcomings and honestly feel that they are providing honest and accurate self-reports. *Impression management* refers to a conscious attempt on the part of respondents to "fake good." Such respondents are aware of their shortcomings but are reluctant to reveal these flaws in self-reports or interviews. Paulhus and others view impression management as a response style that can bias self-report data and should therefore be controlled to the extent possible. Self-deceptive enhancement is more difficult to deal with because it does not represent a conscious effort on the part of the respondent but is instead part of the respondent's personality, related to self-image.

Not all researchers agree that socially desirable responding results in biased estimates of personality measures. Ones, Viswesvaran, and Reiss (1996) are among those who have argued that socially desirable responding is not necessarily a cause for concern. These researchers conducted a meta-analysis of the extant research relating socially desirable responding to measures of personality, as well as to outcomes such as school success and job performance. In addition, Ones and colleagues compared meta-analytically derived correlations of social desirability with personality characteristics, based on both self- and other-reports. The logic behind the latter analyses was as follows. Correlations between social desirability and personality variables could result from either a particular susceptibility of certain personality measures to socially desirable responding, or to the fact that social desirability is tapping into the same construct as the personality variable with which it correlates. If the former is the case, we would expect that personality variables as rated by others (such as a partner or family member) would *not* be related to socially desirable responding because others are unlikely to be aware of the individual's tendency toward socially desirable responding. And even if others were aware of this tendency, it would be unlikely to affect their ratings. In contrast, if other-rated personality is found to be related to social desirability, the implication is that social desirability is related to, or perhaps an aspect of, the personality characteristic being rated. In this case, social desirability is confounded, to some extent, with the personality characteristic being rated, such that the other person could not help but include both in the ratings.

Although Ones and colleagues (1996) found that the social desirability/personality correlations were much lower for other-ratings than for self-ratings, they attributed this to the lower reliabilities associated with other-ratings and concluded that social desirability is tapping into the same construct as some personality measures. In particular, they found social desirability to be positively related to emotional stability and conscientiousness. Although Ones et al. make a reasonable argument, their results are also consistent with the hypothesis that certain self-rated personality measures are simply more susceptible to social desirable responding. This latter view is supported by the fact that social desirability/*self*-rated personality correlations are substantially higher than social desirability/*other*-rated personality correlations.

In my view, another aspect of the Ones and colleagues (1996) study provides stronger support for the argument that social desirability is an individual-difference variable related to other personality constructs rather than a nuisance variable that biases measures of personality. In another part of their study, these researchers investigated the effect of partialing out social desirability from relationships between personality variables and job performance. If social desirability is, in fact, a response bias that distorts such relationships, we would expect these relationships to change when it is partialed out. However, the relationships did not change at all as a result of such partialing, indicating that social desirability does not have an adverse influence.

Managing Response Distortion

Overall, researchers continue to disagree about the extent to which response distortions such as socially desirable responding result in biased estimates of levels of personality characteristics or attitudes. In contrast, suggestions for managing such responding are fairly consistent. Dilchert, Ones, Viswesvaran, and Deller (2006) review such strategies, which include strategies to *discourage* response distortion, *hurdle* approaches that make it more difficult to engage in such responses, and methods to *detect* response distortion.

Recommendations for discouraging response distortion include encouraging respondents to provide honest and accurate answers through such means as ensuring anonymity and emphasizing the importance of accurate answers to the validity of the study. Of course, in some situations, such as admissions or hiring decisions, anonymity cannot be ensured. Another method of discouragement is to warn respondents that faking or other response distortions will have negative consequences. However, issuing such warnings when negative consequences will not really be forthcoming is unethical. In addition, Dilchert and colleagues (2006) point out that it is not clear whether such warnings result in scores that are closer to respondents' true levels of the construct. Such warnings may either miss the mark by annoying respondents, resulting in even more distortion, or cause respondents to correct responses too far in the opposite direction.

Hurdle Approaches

So-called *hurdle* approaches are those that attempt to make it more difficult to respond in a socially desirable or otherwise distorted manner. One approach commonly suggested is to include equal numbers of positively and negatively oriented items on Likert scales; this approach is designed to discourage respondents from yea- or nay-saying. The problem with this particular strategy is that some respondents have difficulty responding to negatively oriented items. In addition, yea- and nay-saying are forms of satisficing, and satisficers do not typically read the items carefully in the first place. Thus, there is no reason to think this approach would be effective.

One hurdle approach designed to foil socially desirable responding is to use measures that are so subtle respondents cannot guess what type of answer is desirable. These are sometimes termed "implicit measurement techniques." The Conditional Reasoning Test of Aggression (James & McIntyre, 2000) is one example of such a measure. This "reasoning test" does not actually measure reasoning at all. Instead, it presents items that purport to measure reasoning but actually assess respondents' levels of aggression by using items similar to the following:

> John was walking down the street and a man bumped into him, knocking his coffee out of his hand. Which is the most logical explanation?
>
> a. The street was crowded.
>
> b. The man did not like coffee.
>
> c. The man wanted to pick a fight with John.

The idea is that an aggressive individual may feel that c is the "correct" answer, even though a is more logical.

Implicit Association Tests

A more recent method for measuring constructs that are subject to socially desirable responding involves the use of so-called *implicit association tests* (IATs). IATs are typically administered via computer and are based on the idea that respondents will take longer to match words they consider to be incongruent than words considered congruent. The approach is most easily explained in the context of an example. Let us say that a researcher is interested in measuring possible biases against women having careers in mathematics or science. Respondents are presented with a series of gender-related words such as "sister" or "brother" and asked to type one letter if the word is associated with the referent "female" and another if the word is associated with the referent "male." Respondents are then asked to complete a similar task with words associated with the referents "math/ science" and "liberal arts" by presenting them with words such as "trigonometry" and "literature." One reason for administering these first two tasks is to obtain base rates for responding. The two content areas are then combined, with respondents asked to type one letter if the word is associated with either "male" or "math/science" and to type another letter if the word is associated with "female" or "liberal arts." These combinations are then switched, and the respondent is asked to indicate whether the word is associated with "male" or "liberal arts" or with "female" or "math/science." The idea is that response times for responding to the first set of pairings will be shorter than response times for the second set to the extent that a respondent feels men are more suited to math/science than are women. In other words, it should take less time to make pairings the respondent views as congruent than to make pairings viewed as incongruent. This will be the case even if such attitudes are implicit. Readers interested in this technique are encouraged to visit the fascinating website for this project at *https://implicit.harvard.edu/implicit/* to take a "demonstration" test. For introductions to IATs, see Fazio and Olson (2003) or Lane and colleagues (2007).

Do implicit measurement techniques work? It is probably too soon to tell, but during the relatively short time these methods have been used, they have generated a great deal of research. However, according to Fazio and Olson (2003), who have reviewed the research on implicit measurement techniques, this research has been "surprisingly atheoretical" (p. 301). These authors point out that recent implicit measurement techniques are no different from earlier projective or "unobtrusive" methods (see Webb et al., 1966, for a review of unobtrusive methods) in that it is not the attitude itself that is implicit, but the method being used to measure it. That is, respondents may not be unaware that they have certain attitudes; they may simply be reluctant to admit to them. With regard to how well implicit measures, well, measure, the answer is "it depends." According to Fazio and Olson, the correlations between implicit and explicit attitudes are typically quite low when the object of measurement involves possible prejudice or stereotypical views about the referent. However, when the referent is noncontroversial, implicit and explicit measures yield results that are more similar. The degree to which this similarity holds depends on how motivated a respondent is to edit her response in a socially desirable way and how much time she has to do so. So, as we know from crime novels, everything hinges on opportunity and motive.

Much of the research on IATs concerns the ability to differentiate between two groups of respondents who are either known or expected to differ in a particular way—so-called known groups studies. For example, males and females would be expected to have different attitudes toward women having careers in science/math. Known groups studies based on IATs have been quite successful in identifying such differences (see Lane et al., 2007). With regard to whether IATs can predict behavior, Fazio and Olson (2003) have reported mixed results. At the same time, Lane and colleagues (2007) discuss several studies in which IATs have been used with some success to predict behaviors thought to be related to the implicit attitude. Such studies tend to involve stereotype-related or undesirable behaviors, such as smoking or drinking. Finally, Lane and colleagues discuss research showing that IATs can be used to measure changes in attitudes as a result of new learning or interventions. In terms of other psychometric characteristics, test–retest reliability estimates for IATs, in which the same test is administered two or more times and the results are correlated, often reach values of .6, according to Fazio and Olson, and Lane and colleagues report test–retest values ranging from .25 to .69 for time periods of less than one day to one year. Lane and colleagues also report an average internal consistency value of .79 from a meta-analysis of IAT-based studies conducted by Hofman, Gawronski, Gschwender, Le, and Schmidt (2005).

Detecting Socially Desirable Responding

Although hurdle approaches such as the use of implicit measures are becoming more popular, the most commonly used methods for managing response distortion continue to be those that allow researchers to *detect* such responses. These methods have already been discussed briefly in the context of socially desirable responding. Typically, detection methods involve administering a social desirability measure such as the MCSD (Crowne & Marlowe, 1960) or the BIDR (Paulhus, 1988). Respondents with high scores on such measures can be flagged and possibly removed from the dataset. It is also possible to partial out social desirability when computing correlation or regression coefficients. However, as noted in a previous section, partialing out the effects of social desirability from relationships of personality variables to outcomes such as job performance was not found to have any effect on the coefficients in Ones and colleagues (1996) meta-analysis.

PRACTICAL ISSUES IN NONCOGNITIVE SCALE CONSTRUCTION

In addition to issues with response distortion, researchers constructing or using noncognitive scales should be aware of recommendations regarding the "nuts and bolts" of putting together such scales. Common questions concern the number of scale points that should be included and whether scale points should be labeled; whether negatively oriented items should be included; and whether to include a neutral or "no opinion" option.

Number of Scale Points

In deciding on the number of scale points to include, several things must be considered. Perhaps the most fundamental consideration is the degree to which respondents will be able to discriminate among the scale points. There appears to be somewhat of a consensus that the largest number of categories among which respondents can reasonably be expected to discriminate is about 11. Although this number represents the maximum, not all respondents will be able to differentiate this finely. In addition, the ability to do so will depend on the context. Research in which respondents use rating scales that range from 0 to 100 has revealed that most respondents choose common values such as 10, 25, or 60 rather than intermediate values such as 38. Thus, even when provided with a scale in which finer differentiations could be made, respondents do not tend to do so.

Some researchers recommend use of *visual analogue* scales in which respondents are presented with a continuous line that is anchored at each end, with adjectives describing opposite ends of a continuum. For example, respondents might be asked to describe their mood using the following visual analogue:

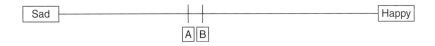

The idea is for respondents to place a mark on the line to indicate their level of whatever construct is being measured. However, does the level marked by respondent B really indicate more happiness than that marked by respondent A, or does the difference simply indicate idiosyncratic marking methods on the part of the two respondents? We generally have no way of knowing, but research on 0–100 scales suggests that such differentiations may not be reliable. As DeVellis (2003) points out, however, visual analogue scales do have the *potential* to be very sensitive to small differences.

Although researchers should not overwhelm respondents with too many scale points from which to choose, they should provide sufficient scale points that any variability among respondents will reveal itself. Use of only two response categories, for example, limits the variability of responses, and this in turn limits the *reliability* or consistency of the items on the scale. Research in this area indicates that reliability increases with the number of scale points up to about seven scale points, after which gains in reliability begin to level off (Bandalos & Enders, 1996; Lissitz & Green, 1975). Of course, the number of scale points will also depend on the age of those who will use the scale. For children in elementary school, three, or at most, four scale points is typically the most that can be differentiated.

A final consideration concerns the level of measurement of the scale. As we have discussed in a previous chapter, some theorists consider that social science measures can never be considered to be at the interval or ratio. At best, it is argued, such measures are at the ordinal level of measurement. Other theorists argue that even though ordered categorical data such as that obtained from Likert scales may not have equal intervals, such data yield reasonable approximations to true continua, provided a sufficient number of scale points is used. A corollary to this argument is that the difference in statistical results obtained from a continuous scale and from a Likert scale is minimal, given an adequate number of scale points. A number of simulation studies support this point (Bandalos, 2014; DiStefano, 2002; Dolan, 1994; Flora & Curran, 2004; Johnson & Creech, 1983; Rigdon & Ferguson, 1991), typically finding that with five or more scale points, continuous and ordered categorical data yield very similar statistical results. These findings, combined with the considerations discussed in the previous paragraph, indicate that at least five scale points should be used, unless the age or educational level of the intended respondents necessitates fewer.

Labeling of Response Options

Consider the item shown below:

I believe sex before marriage is wrong.

1   2   3   4   5

Clearly, at the very least the endpoints (1 and 5) must be labeled; otherwise respondents cannot determine which end of the scale indicates agreement or disagreement. But what about the other scale points? Is it necessary to label them all? In general, the answer is "yes." This is because, without labels, the numeric values of scale points are open to many different interpretations. For example, even if I know that a 1 corresponds to "strongly disagree" and a 5 to "strongly agree," the meaning of a 3 or 4 is not entirely clear. Labeling scale points provides the scale developer with an opportunity to clarify the meaning of each scale point. Another reason for labeling all scale points is that respondents may be drawn to the scale points that are labeled, with the result that unlabeled scale points will be chosen less often than they would be if they had been labeled. Krosnick and Berent (1993) have found that labeling all scale points as opposed to only labeling the endpoints resulted in increased reliability of the responses.

Of course, labeling is beneficial only if the labels are clear. As discussed earlier, the use of vague labels such as "seldom" and "several" should be avoided. Yet, labels should not be overly specific or lengthy, for such labels will be difficult for respondents to hold in memory. In addition, overly detailed labels may make the task of mapping one's response onto the response options more difficult because there will be more aspects of the label with which one's response must match. Finally, some evidence suggests that respondents tend to assume response options are equally spaced (Parducci, 1965), so labels that are consistent with this notion should be chosen.

Inclusion of Negatively Oriented Items

As noted previously, a common recommendation in scale development is to include both positively and negatively oriented items. This suggestion can be traced back at least as far as Likert's (1932) original paper, in which it was recommended as a way to reduce what Likert referred to as "a stereo-typed response" (p. 46), or what we might now call acquiescence. Although it is not clear that the practice is effective in this regard, including items with different orientations might allow researchers to detect acquiescent responding. However, more recent research strongly suggests that the inclusion of negatively oriented items alters the nature of the scale. For example, numerous studies have found that the inclusion of negatively oriented items changes the dimensionality of a scale because such items tend to cluster together to form so-called "method factors" (Barnette, 2000; Lai, 1994; Marsh, 1986; Motl, Conroy, & Horan, 2000; Pilotte & Gable, 1990; Schriesheim & Hill, 1981). The inclusion of negatively oriented items has also been shown to result in decreased reliability for the scale (Barnette, 2000; Schriesheim & Hill, 1981). And there is substantial anecdotal evidence that respondents find it difficult to respond to negatively oriented items, particularly when such items include words such as "no" or "not." This is exemplified by the following statement made by Adelson and McCoach (2011) in the context of the development of a scale to measure children's attitudes toward mathematics: "During survey administration, several of the students verbally expressed confusion in how to respond to these two items because they are negatively worded ('unable')" (p. 234). Although children are particularly susceptible to such confusion, there is considerable evidence that people of all ages have difficulty processing negative statements (Peterson & Peterson, 1976; Sherman, 1973, 1976; Wason, 1959, 1961). These studies have found that negative statements take longer to process than positive statements and engender more errors in comprehension and responding. These effects are strongest for statements that include overt negative wording, such as the word *not*.

Respondents with lower levels of cognitive ability, reading skill, and/or education have been found to demonstrate more difficulty in responding to negatively worded items. Marsh (1986) reported that younger children were more likely to have difficulty responding to negatively worded items on a self-concept measure than were older children. He also found that reading ability had a moderate, positive correlation (.42) with a method factor composed of negatively worded items, indicating that the ability to respond to negatively worded items was related to reading skill. Researchers have reported similar findings in studies of adults, in which responses to positively and negatively oriented items were found to be less congruent for those with lower educational levels (Cordery & Sevastos, 1993; Melnick & Gable, 1990). Finally, Krosnick (1991; Krosnick, Narayan, & Smith, 1996) has consistently found that respondents who engage in "satisficing" or nonoptimal responding have less education and less need for cognition than do nonsatisficers. Thus, respondents with less cognitive ability may be both less able and less willing to respond appropriately to negatively oriented items.

Aside from the linguistic explanations for problems with negatively oriented items, psychometricians have offered several other explanations as to why such items tend to result in the appearance of method factors. According to the "substantive" hypothesis, negatively and positively oriented items simply represent different constructs. That is, being sad is not just the opposite of being happy but, rather, represents a separate construct. Similarly, in the context of personality measurement, it can be argued that the presence of positive affect is not the same as the absence of negative affect. Some support for the substantive hypothesis is provided by studies in survey research methodology in which the percentage of respondents favoring issues such as freedom of speech was found to be much higher when the question, "Do you think the United States should allow public speeches against democracy?" was used than when the wording was "Do you think the United States should forbid public speeches against democracy?" Although many explanations have been offered for such differences, one is that "forbidding" is not the same as "not allowing."

An opposing view holds that method factors are simply artifactual, reflecting *method variance* that results from the different distributional characteristics of negatively and positively oriented items. Because items with different distributions have been shown to form separate, artifactual factors (Ahlawat, 1985) and because the distributions of positively and negatively oriented items do typically differ, this explanation makes some sense. If the method variance explanation is true, we would expect that such artifactual variance would not relate to substantive constructs of interest. The research in this area provides mixed results, however. Roberts, Lewinsohn, and Seeley (1993) found support for the method variance hypothesis in that scores on a scale measuring loneliness were found to relate in the same way to other constructs regardless of whether the loneliness scores were based on positively oriented, negatively oriented, or all items. This suggests that the variance due to wording was irrelevant to the construct. But other studies have found method factors to be related to personality constructs (e.g., DiStefano, Morgan, & Motl, 2012), suggesting that method variance is not artifactual but contains a substantive element. What this element represents, however, is not clear.

A more basic view is that method factors result from careless responding, in which respondents simply do not read the items carefully. Thus, method factors are the result of satisficing. Such respondents, it is argued, take the view that, because items on a scale all measure the same thing, the easiest thing to do is to answer them all in the same way. When both positively and negatively oriented items are included, this results in a method factor. This explanation has been offered by, among others, Schmitt and Stults (1985), who used computer-generated data to demonstrate that if at least 10% of respondents answered in this way, a method factor would emerge. More recently, Woods (2006) confirmed these results using an item response theory approach.

Finally, the view of method variance as reflecting differences in personality has a longstanding status in the literature. As early as 1946, Cronbach suggested that such variance resulted from individual response styles, such as acquiescence. Such individual differences were not thought to represent substantive aspects of the construct being measured, as in the substantive hypothesis. Instead, these differences were thought to be stable aspects of individual differences in response styles that may (or may not) be of substantive interest in their own right. This view is supported by findings that method factors are correlated across time (Horan, DiStefano, & Motl, 2003) and across different measures (DiStefano & Motl, 2006).

Including a Neutral Option

Researchers disagree about whether a neutral or "no opinion" response option should be included. Schuman and Presser (1996) describe three possible positions on the decision to include or exclude such an option. The argument for including such an option is that it allows respondents who really are neutral or who really have no opinion to indicate this. If the neutral option were not included, these respondents would be forced to either provide an inaccurate response or skip the item altogether. The counterargument holds that choosing a neutral alternative is a way of satisficing that respondents use to avoid the mental effort required to respond optimally. Such respondents find it easier to simply choose a neutral or "don't know" option.

The third position is that those who choose a neutral option actually have attitudes on the subject at hand, although these attitudes may be relatively weak. Such respondents will provide an opinion if the neutral option is not offered. Some evidence supports this position. Schuman and Presser (1996) report that when a middle or neutral option is offered, those with low-intensity attitudes are more likely to choose it than those with high-intensity attitudes. However, because such respondents choose the pro and con sides of the issue in proportions that are equal to those with more intense attitudes, the overall proportions of these two response options are not changed. Finally, Gilljam and Granberg (1993) found that the responses of those who were forced to take a stand rather than responding "don't know" were highly predictive of later voting behavior on the issue. In other words, the "forced" responses were consistent with later behavior, suggesting that the forced responses were accurate. One final consideration is related to the conversational maxim of quantity discussed previously, which indicates that respondents expect those asking questions to provide them with all the response alternatives that are necessary. Excluding a neutral option sends the implicit message that having no opinion is unacceptable.

In the end, decisions about whether or not to include a neutral response option depend on the degree to which the researcher feels it is reasonable to expect all respondents to have an attitude on the issue at hand. If on one hand, the issue is well known and highly topical, such an expectation is reasonable, and including a neutral option is probably not necessary. On the other hand, if it seems possible that some respondents will legitimately be neutral or unaware of the issue, inclusion of a neutral or "don't know" option allows them to express this. Researchers should keep in mind that although an interview situation allows respondents to simply volunteer a "don't know" response, this is not usually possible on a self-report instrument. With the self-report format, respondents will likely skip a question that asks them to supply an opinion they do not have.

SUMMARY

In this chapter, I have discussed measurement of noncognitive outcomes such as attitudes, values, and personality characteristics. Although Likert, Thurstone, and Guttman scales are all used for such measures, Likert scales are by far the most common, owing to their relative ease of construction and scoring. Developing Thurstone scales requires recruiting judges who provide ratings of the favorableness of items. The mean or median of these ratings across judges is taken as the scale value of the item. This approach is useful when the goal is to create equivalent versions of a scale, but given the additional effort needed to create Thurstone scales, they do not tend to be used widely. Guttman scales represent a form of deterministic measurement in which respondents' attitudes can be inferred from the strongest statement they are willing to endorse. Such scales are difficult to construct in practice because item responses must follow a strict hierarchy that can only be met if the construct to be measured is narrowly defined.

Responses to noncognitive items are influenced by characteristics of both the respondent and the item wording and context; understanding such influences is crucial in developing and using noncognitive measures effectively. Theories of response processing can help us to understand and anticipate these influences and to develop items that are as free as possible from idiosyncratic and biased responding. In this context, I discussed the four components of the response process—comprehension, generation of a response, formatting and reporting the response, and editing the response—and the implications these have for developing noncognitive scales. Because responding to items can be seen as a type of conversation, understanding Grice's (1975) conversational maxims can also help us to understand the response process. To this end, I have discussed these maxims and how they may come into play as individuals respond to questions.

Response distortion processes such as socially desirable responding, acquiescence, malingering, and extreme responding are thought by many to bias responses to noncognitive measures. I have discussed the degree to which response distortion has been found to contribute to biased assessments of affect, based on the extant research, and I have related these response patterns to processing models. Practical issues such as whether to include a neutral point or negatively oriented items, how many response options to include, and how to label them are also important to consider when developing and administering noncognitive measures. There is no clear-cut answer to many of these issues, which leads some to conclude that the development of noncognitive measures is more art than science. However, one unambiguous finding is that items should not be ambiguous (with the exception, of course, of cases in which they should be, such as with implicit measurement techniques). To paraphrase the slogan of realtors everywhere, there are three things that are sure to contribute to better noncognitive scales: clarity, clarity, clarity.

EXERCISES

1. A researcher is developing a scale to measure aesthetic appreciation, defined as the degree to which people appreciate beauty in any form. Should the researcher be interested in maximum or typical performance? Why?

2. In Thurstone scaling, each item has a scale value. How are these values obtained?

3. What was Likert's primary objection to Thurstone's method of creating scales? In what way(s) is Likert's method different from that of Thurstone?

4. Identify the flaws in the following Likert-type items developed to measure attitudes toward assisted suicide:

   a. Alternative medicine is a good alternative to assisted suicide.

   b. Fifteen percent of all deaths in the United States take place following the withdrawal of life-sustaining treatments.

   c. People in very bad physical health cannot be trusted to make judgments about whether to go on living because their mental health is often affected by their illness and they may not make good decisions.

   d. Ten years ago assisted suicide was a minor issue because medical technology was less advanced.

   e. It is never permissible for a doctor to end a patient's life.

5. The following items were written to assess attitudes toward diversity. Would these items be appropriate for forming a Guttman scale? Why or why not?

   a. I look for opportunities to interact with other cultures.

   b. It is important for me to know a language other than my own.

   c. I feel that anyone who lives in the United States should learn to speak English.

   d. I enjoy eating foreign foods.

6. The following options represent possible thought processes people might have when asked the question, "How many times have you been to the hospital in the past year?" For each option, indicate whether it represents satisficing or optimizing.

   a. I broke my arm 10 months ago and I know I haven't been since then, so I'll say once.

   b. The middle response option is three, so I'll choose that because I'm probably about average.

   c. I know I've been at least three times, but definitely not five times, so I'll say four.

   d. Most people go once a year, so I'll say once.

7. The following options represent people's possible thoughts while responding to the question, "How many alcoholic drinks do you have in an average week?" For each option, indicate whether it most likely occurred at the interpretation, response generation, response formatting and reporting, or response editing stage of Sudman, Bradburn, and Schwarz's (1996) model of the response process.

   a. To be honest it's about 30, but I'm not going to say that, so I'll just put 5.

   b. I wonder what counts as an "alcoholic drink"?

   c. I guess I have about 2, but that's not an option so I guess I'll check 3–5.

   d. Let's see; I only drink on weekends, and I never drink more than two drinks, so I'll say about four.

8. Those writing items for achievement tests often include irrelevant information in the items. This is typically done to determine if respondents are able to determine which piece(s) of information is (are) necessary in providing an answer. Respondents who are fooled into using irrelevant information in their responses are often judged less competent than those who correctly ignore this information. However, Grice's (1975) conversational maxims may suggest other explanations. Which maxim(s) might be relevant to this type of responding?

9. Define the following terms:

   a. *Acquiescence*

   b. *Extremity*

   c. *Moderacy*

   d. *Malingering*

10. What are two reasons that all scale points should be labeled?

11. Researchers at a commuter campus are developing a scale to measure students' attitudes toward the availability of parking on campus. Should the researchers include a neutral option on the response scale? Why or why not?

6

Item Analysis for Cognitive and Noncognitive Items

Once items have been written and administered, an obvious question is, "How well did the items work?" As I discuss in the chapters on reliability and validity, there are many ways to answer this question, depending on what we mean by "work." In this chapter, I discuss ways to determine such things as whether the items were confusing to respondents, whether they differentiated among respondents with different levels of the construct, and whether items designed to assess the same construct were appropriately related. Collectively, the procedures used to answer such questions fall under the heading of *item analysis*, a term that refers to a wide range of strategies, both quantitative and qualitative, that are used to assess the quality of a pool of items. These strategies are typically used during the scale development process to help select the best set of items from a pool of potential candidates. As such, item analysis procedures are fundamental to the scale development process and are a necessary precursor to the reliability and validity studies discussed in the chapters on those topics.

Indeed, proper attention to item development and analysis is the most effective way to ensure that scores from the resulting scale will pass muster when it comes time to investigate the reliability and validity of the resulting scores. Often, researchers give short shrift to the work involved in item development and analysis, only to find that later studies of the scores' reliability and validity yield weak evidence of these important psychometric properties. Thus, time spent in the development and analysis of items is, in the long run, time well spent. Through the use of proper item development and analysis procedures, researchers can build adequate levels of reliability and validity into their tests.

Because the type of outcomes assessed by cognitive and noncognitive items are somewhat different, the item analysis strategies for the two types of items also differ to some extent. Although the types of analyses that might be conducted for cognitive and noncognitive items overlap considerably, the focus and interpretation of the analyses are often quite different for the two types of items. Therefore, it is probably least confusing to discuss analyses for the two types of items separately. For cognitive items, I will discuss indices of item *difficulty* and *discrimination*, and for multiple-choice items, *distractor analyses*. For noncognitive items, the components of an item analysis include analysis of the frequency of response to each option, examination of the correlations among items, assessment of the contribution of each item to the *reliability*, or consistency of the total score, and comparison of the item means of those with high and low levels of the construct. For both item types, examination of item wording is an important component of an item analysis. Because the importance of item wording is discussed extensively in Chapters 4 and 5, the discussion will not be repeated here, except to point out that wording problems are often revealed during the item analysis phase. However, this does not mean that those developing scales should disregard good item-writing practice, with the idea that poorly worded items will be exposed by item analyses. On the contrary, if too many items are flawed, the ability of item analysis procedures to detect these problems will be impaired. This is because many item analysis procedures are based on use of the total scale score, and this score will be misleading if many of the items are poorly written. As a result, the item analysis procedures discussed in this chapter should be preceded by a thorough review of item wording, with an eye toward detecting the wording problems discussed in Chapters 4 and 5.

ITEM ANALYSIS FOR COGNITIVE ITEMS

Before beginning this section, I note that the item analysis procedures described here were designed for use with norm-referenced tests and may not be appropriate for use with criterion-referenced tests. This may be because many standardized tests, for which most item analysis procedures were developed, are meant to differentiate among respondents as much as possible; in other words, they are norm-referenced tests. Such tests are designed to yield scores that are spread across a wide continuum, often resulting in a normal distribution of scores. Consequently, norm-referenced tests tend not to include items that everyone gets right (or wrong), as might be the case on a criterion-referenced test. The indices typically used to assess the quality of items on norm-referenced tests are not necessarily relevant to the quality of items on a criterion-referenced test, owing to differences in the purposes of the two types of tests. In this section the focus is solely on analyses appropriate for norm-referenced tests.

As mentioned in the previous section, two indices of interest for cognitive items are those measuring levels of difficulty and those measuring levels of discrimination. The former is simply the proportion of respondents who get the item right, and the latter refers to how well the item was able to distinguish among respondents with different levels of knowledge. Both of these indices are discussed in the following sections. In addition to difficulty and discrimination, analyses for multiple-choice items often include an investigation of the performance of the distractors, and this, too, will be discussed.

Item Difficulty

Item difficulty is usually symbolized as *P* and is simply the proportion of those responding correctly. It is calculated as

$$P = \frac{\text{Number of correct responses}}{\text{Total number of responses}}$$

So, if 60 out of 100 respondents got the item correct, $P = 60/100$ or 0.6. Note that if items are scored by assigning 0 points for an incorrect answer and 1 point for a correct answer, as is typically done, the item difficulty is equal to the item mean. In this example, 40 respondents would receive 0 points, 60 respondents would receive 1 point, and the mean would be

$$\bar{X} = \frac{40(0) + 60(1)}{100} = \frac{60}{100} = 0.6$$

Thus, any computer program that can calculate the mean can be used to compute item difficulties.

Because they are proportions, item difficulties can range from 0 to 1.0. Readers may have already noticed that the term *item difficulty* is something of a misnomer, as this index really quantifies item easiness or the proportion of correct responses. Of course, the index could be changed to replace the numerator with the number of incorrect responses, but the current formula appears to be entrenched in the literature. Given this fact, one simply has to keep the contradictory name of the index in mind when providing interpretations.

Most items on large-scale standardized achievement tests, such as those to which you may have been subjected in elementary school, have difficulties in the range of about 0.3 to 0.7, with fewer items that are in the easier or more difficult ranges. The reason is twofold. First, if student achievement levels are assumed to be normally distributed, as is typically the case, most students would be in the middle range for achievement, with fewer students at the lower and higher ends of the continuum. Thus, items in the middle range of difficulty are most closely matched to the level at which most students are expected to perform. Second, items in the middle range of difficulty will have the greatest amounts of variance, which means that these items will yield the greatest spread of scores. For dichotomously scored (right/wrong) items, variance is calculated as

$$\sigma_i^2 = P_i(1 - P_i)$$

where P_i is the difficulty of item *i*. I leave it to you to verify that the highest value for an item variance is obtained when P_i is 0.5. The fact that item variance is at its highest when P_i is 0.5 means that test scores will differentiate maximally among students when half the students get the item right and half get it wrong. Although such a criterion may seem somewhat harsh, keep in mind that the purpose of a norm-referenced test is to reveal differences among respondents. If items were chosen such that all respondents answered correctly (or incorrectly), the item variances would be 0 (as you can verify), and everyone would obtain the same score. Thus, although a test with very easy items may be popular among respondents, it would not yield any information about differences in achievement levels.

Item Discrimination

In general, one would expect that respondents with a high level of knowledge or skill would be more likely to answer an achievement or aptitude item correctly than those with lower levels of knowledge, and vice versa. *Item discrimination* indices are measures of the degree to which an item can be used to make such distinctions. Patterns of high-knowledge students answering correctly and low-knowledge students answering incorrectly are so commonsensical that you may wonder how things could be otherwise. Why might those with less knowledge be more likely to answer correctly than those with more knowledge?   Several possibilities suggest themselves, none of them good. Perhaps the most obvious of these possibilities is that the item was *miskeyed*; that is, an incorrect answer was mistakenly keyed as being the correct answer. This problem can usually be easily remedied by reviewing the item content and answer key. Another possibility is that the item is ambiguous. That is, the "best" response is not clear. Consider the following example, the content of which you should remember from Chapter 2:

> A child in the third grade received a grade-equivalent score of 6.0.
> Which of the following statements is true?
> - a. He should be placed in the sixth grade.
> - b. He is in the 60th percentile for children his age.
> - c. His score is three standard deviations above the mean of his grade level.
> - d. His score is higher than the average score for third graders

An astute (or argumentative) respondent might answer that option a or c may be "true," even though it is not a correct interpretation of the meaning of a grade-equivalent score. Such a respondent may argue that it may very well be the case that the student is three standard deviations above the mean, and it may at least be possible that he should be placed in the sixth grade, even though neither of these is a correct interpretation of a grade-equivalent score. A less ambiguous wording of the item stem, as I have learned from long and painful experience, would be:

> A child in the third grade received a grade-equivalent score of 6.0. Which of the
> following statements *is an accurate interpretation of the grade-equivalent score?*

Another possible reason for an answer pattern in which those with more knowledge have less chance of a correct answer than those with less knowledge is that the item has two correct answers. If only one of these options is keyed as correct, and respondents with more knowledge favor the other option, such a pattern would occur, as in the following example (determination of the correct answers is left to you as an exercise):

An advantage of short-answer items is that they:

a. can be used to measure a variety of simple knowledge outcomes.

b. are good for measuring problem-solving ability.

c. can be constructed easily.

d. are relatively free from guessing.

Many ways of assessing item discrimination have been suggested (see Engelhart, 1965, for a brief overview). One common method that is often recommended in texts on educational assessment is to divide respondents into an upper and a lower group based on their total scores on a test. If the number of respondents is small, it is best to divide at the median. If there is a large enough group, some experts suggest that creating the upper and lower groups from the top and bottom 27% of respondents will provide a more sensitive index of discrimination. This guideline is based on an often-cited study by Kelley (1939), but more recent studies have found that when sample size is sufficiently large, use of the upper and lower 30% or 50% yields essentially the same results (Beuchert & Mendoza, 1979; Engelhart, 1965).

After dividing respondents into upper and lower groups, the proportion of those who obtain the correct answer in each group is assessed. Discrimination (D) for an item is calculated as the proportion of those in the upper group who respond correctly minus the proportion in the lower group who respond correctly, or

$$D_i = P_u - P_l$$

Note that P_u and P_l are *proportions*, not frequencies, for the upper and lower groups. Consider the following example, which shows responses to a fictitious multiple-choice item. The asterisk next to option C indicates that this is the correct answer.

	A	B	C^*	D	Total
Upper	3	2	12	3	20
Lower	6	5	2	7	20

There are 20 respondents in each of the two groups. So, the proportions of correct responses in the upper and lower groups are $P_u = 12/20$ and $P_l = 2/20$. Given this, D_i can be calculated as

$$D_i = \frac{12}{20} - \frac{2}{20} = 0.6 - 0.1 = 0.5$$

Maximum discrimination occurs when everyone in the upper group responds correctly and everyone in the lower group responds incorrectly. This will yield a D-value of 1.0, which indicates that the item was able to perfectly discriminate between those in the upper and lower groups. Note that a discrimination value of 1.0 implies that difficulty must be 0.5 (assuming that the upper and lower groups are of equal size). However, a P-value of 0.5 does not guarantee a D-value of 1.0 because a P-value of 0.5 could also result if everyone in the lower group scored correctly and everyone in the upper group scored incorrectly. This unsatisfactory state of affairs would result in an item that is *negatively discriminating* (with a D-value of -1.0), and would certainly be cause for concern because it would mean that those with more knowledge are much less likely to score correctly. Discrimination indices range from -1.0 to 1.0, with -1.0 indicating perfect negative discrimination and 1.0 indicating perfect positive discrimination. A value of 0 would indicate that the item is unable to discriminate between those in the upper and lower groups. Such a value could occur because the item is either very easy, with everyone scoring correctly, or very difficult, with no one scoring correctly.

The type of discrimination index just described relies on an *internal criterion*; that is, the upper and lower groups are formed on the basis of the same test for which the discrimination is being calculated. Although this is a very common method of calculating discrimination, it could be inaccurate if the overall test scores are flawed in some way. For example, if too many of the items are confusing, incorrectly keyed, or have low discrimination, test scores could be compromised. Another way to determine the upper and lower groups is to use an *external criterion*. This might be a score on another test of the same material, a teacher rating, or an external measure of performance. External criteria for determining item discrimination are often used in situations such as employment testing and assessment of psychiatric syndromes for which external criteria such as job performance, supervisor ratings, or clinical evaluations can be used to determine the upper and lower groups.

The advantage of using external criteria is that items that maximize such criteria should also maximize the level of discrimination or diagnostic accuracy for those criteria. This means that the ability of the test to predict those criteria or provide diagnostic information will also be maximized. As a result, external criteria are often used when the purpose of the test is to predict behavior or to make classification or diagnostic decisions. Although this is appropriate for tests used in making such decisions, it should be noted that maximization of external discrimination will often result in tests on which items are less homogeneous than items from tests developed using internal criteria. This is because external criteria are typically much more heterogeneous than internal criteria. Job performance, for example, requires many different skills including job-specific skills and abilities, as well as more global abilities such as time management and social skills. Hence, it seems clear that prediction of such a broad criterion may require a more wide-ranging predictive test. Use of an internal criterion, on the other hand, will maximize the *internal consistency* of the test (Anastasi & Urbina, 1997, p. 180).

Another class of discrimination indices is based on correlations of item scores with the total test score. One advantage of these methods is that they do not throw away information by using scores from only the upper and lower 27% or 30% of the distribution. On the other hand, it can be argued that use of the upper and lower groups results in a more clear-cut differentiation. Here I discuss two of the correlation-based discrimination indices. The first correlation index that may come to most peoples' minds is the Pearson correlation coefficient. However, recall that use of the Pearson correlation requires that both variables being correlated are continuous. This is usually assumed to be true for the total test score. For item types such as multiple choice or true–false, however, this is clearly not the case because responses are scored as either 0 or 1. Such items are referred to as *dichotomously scored*. Thus, what is needed is a correlation coefficient that can accommodate relationships between continuous and dichotomous values.

One such coefficient is the *point-biserial correlation*, which is a special case of the Pearson correlation for just such a situation (that in which one variable is dichotomous and one is continuous). The *biserial correlation* is a bit more complicated. In the biserial formulation, it is assumed that a continuum underlies the observed dichotomous responses. Because of the crudeness of our measurements, we are only able to observe the dichotomous response, but we assume that the "real" underlying response scale is continuous and normally distributed. The biserial correlation is an estimate of the correlation between the assumed continuous score underlying the dichotomous response and the continuous total test score (see Nunnally & Bernstein, 1994, pp. 120–130, for more discussion). Both the biserial and point-biserial correlation can be used as indices of item discrimination.

At this point, you may be wondering whether it is best to use the group differences method discussed in the previous section or one of the correlation indices to assess discrimination. Overall, studies conducted by Beuchert and Mendoza (1979) and by Oosterhof (1976) suggest that differences among these discrimination indices are minimal. Some researchers have found that the values of D obtained from the group differences method and the point-biserial correlation are highest for items of medium difficulty, whereas the biserial correlation is not influenced by item difficulty. However, results based on any of the D indices discussed should be essentially the same. So, researchers should feel free to use whichever index is available in the software they have available.

Evaluating the Distractors for Multiple-Choice Items

In addition to evaluating the item as a whole using the difficulty and discrimination indices, for multiple-choice items test developers should also evaluate the performance of the distractors. Discrimination indices can be calculated for each distractor to determine whether it is functioning appropriately. Unlike item-level discrimination, distractor discrimination should be *negative*, attracting more of those in the lower than the upper group. To be effective, a distractor should represent a plausible alternative or common misconception or error. When this is the case, an analysis of distractors can be a useful source of information about the number of people who have such misconceptions.

If a distractor does not attract any respondents, it may be implausible and therefore not a good distractor. As noted previously, such guidelines apply more to norm-referenced than criterion-referenced testing, although we may still want to identify common errors or misconceptions in criterion-referenced testing. However, in criterion-referenced testing, respondents are often expected to get most questions right, which means that distractors may not attract many respondents from either the upper or lower groups.

Following are some examples of response patterns that might result from different problems with multiple-choice items. (An asterisk is used to denote the correct answer in these examples.)

Item Ambiguity or Miskeying

	A	B	C*	D	Total
Group					
Upper	9	1	10	0	20
Lower	3	7	2	8	20
	$P = 0.3$	$D = 0.4$			

Option A may be ambiguous because almost as many students in the upper group chose it as chose the correct answer. Also, many more students in the upper than the lower group chose A, even though it is keyed as an incorrect answer. Given these facts, another possibility is that option A is a correct answer in addition to the keyed option C.

Miskeyed Item

	A	B	C	D*	Total
Group					
Upper	18	0	0	2	20
Lower	1	10	6	3	20
	$P = 0.125$	$D = -0.05$			

Most of those in the upper group chose option A rather than the keyed correct answer. Possibly option A is really the correct answer. Also note that item difficulty is very low (it is a very difficult item), and item discrimination is very low and *negative*, which is problematic.

Very Easy Item

	A*	B	C	D	Total
Group					
Upper	20	0	0	0	20
Lower	18	1	1	0	20
	$P = 0.95$	$D = 0.1$			

Almost everyone in both the upper and lower groups chose the correct answer. Note that this results in a very easy item, and also in a low level of discrimination. Although we would not want the bulk of most norm-referenced tests to be composed of such items, tests should include some easy and some difficult items. If all of the items were at medium levels of difficulty, we would not be able to discriminate levels of knowledge at the lower and upper ends of the continuum. Because most norm-referenced tests are designed to discriminate along a wide range of knowledge or ability levels, it is important that item difficulty levels span the entire continuum.

Guessing on an Item

	A	B	C	D*	Total
Group					
Upper	5	6	4	5	20
Lower	7	4	5	4	20
	$P = 0.225$	$D = 0.05$			

For this item, respondents in both the upper and lower groups chose the various distractors as often as the correct answer. No real pattern of responses is evident, which suggests random guessing. Note that the discrimination is low and the difficulty high. A pattern such as this is most likely to occur on very difficult, ambiguous, and/or tricky items.

Item with an Ineffective Distractor

	A	B*	C	D	Total
Group					
Upper	4	11	5	0	20
Lower	7	3	10	0	20
	$P = 0.35$	$D = 0.40$			

On this item, no one has chosen distractor D, which is therefore failing in its purpose of attracting respondents. It may be that this distractor represents a misconception that respondents have now understood, in which case the instructor(s) would be pleased with these results. However, it may also be that D is an implausible distractor. If this is the case, it should be replaced with a better distractor, if possible. Options A and C are both performing well, as evidenced by their negative discrimination.

Corrections for Guessing

You will probably not be surprised to learn that, when respondents do not know the answer to a multiple-choice, true–false, or other items on which it is possible to guess, they will often do so. However, respondents are not equally likely to guess, and therein lies the problem: two respondents with the same level of knowledge or ability could obtain different scores simply because one is more likely to guess than the other. Thus, scores will depend not only on the attribute being measured (knowledge) but on an attribute that is irrelevant to what is being measured (propensity to guess).

Corrections for guessing are one way in which test developers attempt to adjust scores for the possibility that some respondents can obtain higher scores through guessing. Frary (1988) points out that the term *correction for guessing* is somewhat of a misnomer because it implies that the "corrected" scores are approximations to those that would have been obtained if no guessing had occurred. This is not really the case, however, as will be seen. Instead, Frary recommends use of the term *formula scoring*. The most commonly used formula is as follows:

$$\text{Formula score} = R - \frac{W}{C-1}$$

In this formula, R and W represent the numbers of items answered correctly and incorrectly, respectively, and C is the number of response options. For example, on a multiple-choice item with four response options (one correct answer and three distractors), C would equal 4. The formula is based on two assumptions, neither of which is particularly plausible. The first assumption is that all incorrect answers are the result of (poor) guesses. This is the reason that respondents are penalized for wrong answers by subtracting a fraction of the incorrectly answered items from their number-correct score. The second assumption is that guessing is always completely random. This is operationalized in the formula by dividing the number of incorrect answers by the quantity $C-1$. The idea here is that if there are four response options ($C=4$), a respondent would obtain a correct answer one out of four times, on average, just by guessing at random. This means that for every four guesses, one would result in a correct answer and three would result in incorrect answers. Let us say that a respondent has answered 10 questions correctly and three questions incorrectly on a four-option multiple choice test. If random guessing is assumed, the three questions answered incorrectly actually represent *four* random guesses, of which three were incorrect and one was correct. Thus, one point $W/(C-1) = 3/(4-1)$ would be subtracted from the number-right score (10) to adjust for the one point gained by guessing. However, note that the assumption that guessing is random precludes the very real possibility that respondents may have sufficient knowledge to eliminate at least one option. In such cases, guessing would not be purely random, and respondents would have a greater-than-chance-level probability of obtaining correct answers through guessing.

Some authors have argued that the main reason for using formula scoring is to discourage test takers from guessing. This is because if such scoring is used, test takers must be informed of this and be advised that it is not to their advantage to guess randomly. However, test takers will not respond to such a message in the same way. Less risk-averse students will continue to guess, as will those students who feel confident about eliminating at least one option, giving themselves a better than chance probability of guessing correctly. Frary (1988) also points out that use of formula scoring can

increase the time taken to complete a test because some respondents will spend inordinate amounts of time trying to decide whether they should risk guessing on an item.

Given these arguments, you may wonder why formula scoring would ever be used.
The usual answer is that, because random guessing contributes to error in scores, the
use of formula scoring should reduce error and result in more accurate scores. However,
studies have not shown consistent evidence of this benefit, and in those that have the
gains in accuracy have been minimal. Thus, researchers such as Frary (1988) and Thorndike (2005, p. 467) recommend the use of formula scoring only for situations in which a
large amount of guessing is expected. These situations include those in which tests are
highly speeded, tests that are very susceptible to guessing (such as true–false tests), or
tests that are difficult but require a very low score to pass. Recall that speeded tests are
those on which respondents are not expected to reach all the questions. Thus, there may
well be a large amount of random guessing on items toward the end of the test as respondents hurriedly mark answers in the hope that some will be correct. For difficult tests
on which the passing score is sufficiently low, respondents may be able to pass simply by
guessing randomly. For example, on a 40-item multiple-choice test with a passing score
of 10 and four response options, random guessing should yield passing scores for about
one quarter of the respondents. In such situations, use of formula scoring may yield more
accurate assessments of respondents' "true" levels of knowledge.

Summary of Analyses for Cognitive Items

Up to this point, I have discussed commonly used indices for evaluating the quality of
cognitive test items. Item difficulty and discrimination are the two most important indices. Difficulty is defined as the proportion of respondents obtaining a correct answer on
an item and is therefore a measure of item easiness rather than difficulty. Even so, for
historical reasons the term *difficulty* is used. Item discrimination refers to the extent to
which an item results in differentiation between those with high and low levels of knowledge, with positive discrimination occurring when those with high levels of knowledge
respond correctly while those with low levels of knowledge respond incorrectly. The
determination of the high- and low-knowledge groups can be made on the basis of the
total test score—an internal criterion—or on the basis of an external criterion such as
teachers' ratings or scores on another test. Item discrimination can also be calculated by
correlating dichotomous (e.g., right/wrong) item scores with total test scores. Because
dichotomously scored items are not on a continuous scale, Pearson correlations are not
appropriate for this purpose. Instead, biserial or point-biserial correlations should be
used. Use of point-biserial correlations assumes the dichotomy is a "true" dichotomy,
such as that between two mutually exclusive groups (e.g., experimental/control). In using
biserials, the researcher assumes that a continuum underlies the dichotomy, but because
of the crudeness of our measurement (i.e., scoring items as correct/incorrect rather than
on a more continuous scale), we are only able to measure a dichotomous response.

For situations in which multiple-choice items are used, researchers may be interested in conducting an analysis of the distractors to determine how well these are functioning. I have discussed the use of distractor analyses to detect problems such as miskeyed items, items that are too easy or difficult, ineffective distractors, and random guessing. Finally, I have discussed formula scoring methods that are used to adjust test scores for the effects of random guessing. Such scoring is not widely used, but researchers in this area have suggested that formula scoring may be efficacious for situations in which guessing is expected to be widespread. Such situations include highly speeded tests and tests using a true–false format.

ITEM ANALYSIS FOR NONCOGNITIVE ITEMS

As noted previously, item analyses for noncognitive items include many of the same elements as analyses conducted for cognitive items. However, the focus of the analysis is somewhat different. For example, although calculating difficulty per se is not relevant for noncognitive items, scale developers may look at the item means to determine how extreme the item is. Discrimination is important for noncognitive items, as it is for cognitive items. For noncognitive items, information on item discrimination is provided through correlations of item scores with the total scale score and/or comparing the item means of groups expected to have high or low scores on the scale. Other common elements of an item analysis for noncognitive items include examination of the frequency distributions of responses to each item and the correlations among items.

Frequency Distributions and Descriptive Statistics

As a first step in a noncognitive item analysis, it is invaluable to look at frequency distributions for each item. This is similar to the distractor analysis for multiple-choice items discussed in the previous section. It can give one an idea of how spread out the responses were, whether there were some response options that were not chosen at all or some that were chosen exclusively. Items for which everyone chooses the same option do not allow for differentiation among respondents. This purpose is best achieved when there is a spread of responses across all the options. If a neutral option is provided on the response scale, it is usually of interest to see how many respondents have chosen it. A preponderance of neutral responses can be an indication that the item is confusing or poorly worded. Because of this, the wording of items on which many people choose the neutral response should be examined carefully.

Statistical packages that provide frequency distributions can provide descriptive statistics at the same time. In particular, statistics such as the item mean, standard deviation, skewness, and kurtosis can be useful. Very high or low item means usually indicate extreme items, whereas those with low standard deviations reveal items on which responses did not vary substantially. Such items cannot differentiate well among respondents. The *skewness* of an item indicates the degree to which the item's distribution deviates from symmetry. A symmetric item will have a skewness value of 0, whereas values outside the range of 2.0 (either positive or negative) are often taken to indicate high levels of skewness. *Kurtosis* is often thought of as a measure of the peakedness of a distribution, but also has to do with the area in the tails. Positive kurtosis is characterized by both a higher peak (sometimes referred to as "peakedness") and heavier tails ("tailedness") than those of a normal distribution. More generally, however, positive kurtosis can result from only peakedness, only tailedness, or a combination of the two (DeCarlo, 1997). Distributions with negative kurtosis values have the opposite pattern to those with positive kurtosis: lighter tails and a flatter shape. A rectangular histogram, in which each value on the horizontal axis is equally likely, is a common example. Most kurtosis values are scaled so that a value of 0 represents the kurtosis of a perfectly normal distribution. As with skewness values, kurtosis values greater than |2.0| are often considered to represent "large" departures from normality, although some researchers (Kline, 2005; West, Finch, & Curran, 1995) suggest a more liberal value of |7.0|. In terms of item analysis, items with high positive kurtosis tend to be those on which most people have chosen the same response option. From the scale development point of view, this may not be desirable because such an item would not have much discriminating power. On the other hand, negative kurtosis values usually indicate a wide spread of responses, which is generally desirable.

The accompanying distribution is from an item with a skewness value of .06, a kurtosis value of –1.0, and a mean of 3. This indicates that the average response was at about scale point 3, which for this scale indicates "neutral." However, most respondents chose response options 2 or 4, corresponding to "disagree" and "agree," respectively. It is easy to see the symmetric nature of the distribution from the frequency distribution.

Response	Frequency	Percent	Cumulative percent
1 "Strongly disagree"	5	6.8	6.8
2 "Agree"	25	33.8	40.5
3 "Neutral"	14	18.9	59.5
4 "Agree"	23	31.1	90.5
5 "Strongly agree"	7	9.5	100.0
Total	74	100.0	

Interestingly, this item was taken from a scale designed to measure attitudes toward assisted suicide and reads:

Each state should be allowed to choose whether or not to legalize assisted suicide.

Respondents are clearly divided on this issue, which makes this item a good one with which to differentiate among those with different opinions. However, in some cases, a symmetric item distribution can be the result of a neutral attitude on the part of most respondents, as in the following example.

Response	Frequency	Percent	Cumulative percent
1 "Strongly disagree"	2	2.2	2.2
2 "Disagree"	12	12.9	15.2
3 "Neutral"	52	55.9	71.7
4 "Agree"	22	23.7	95.7
5 "Strongly agree"	4	4.3	100.0
Total	92	98.9	
Missing	1	1.1	

This item has a skewness value of 0 and a kurtosis value of 0.7. As can be seen from the frequency distribution, however, the reason for the low skewness value is that most respondents chose option 3, which is "neutral." This item was taken from a scale of attitudes toward interracial marriage and reads:

> Interracial marriages are usually successful.

Most likely, the reason for the many neutral responses is not that respondents do not care whether such marriages are successful, but that they simply do not know, making it difficult to render an opinion. In such cases, respondents are likely to do exactly as they did here: choose the neutral option.

The next example shows an item distribution with a skewness value of –2.0 and a kurtosis value of 4.6. It is common for high levels of skewness and kurtosis to co-occur in this way because strong asymmetry (skewness) usually means that scores have piled up, resulting in peakedness (kurtosis).

Response	Frequency	Percent	Cumulative percent
1 "Strongly disagree"	1	1.1	1.1
2 "Disagree"	2	2.2	3.3
3 "Neutral"	6	6.5	10.0
4 "Agree"	20	21.5	32.2
5 "Strongly agree"	61	65.6	100.0
Total	90	96.8	
Missing	3	3.2	

As can be seen from the table, most respondents chose options 4 or 5 ("agree" or "strongly agree") for this item. The item was taken from the same interracial marriage scale and reads:

Interracial marriage is legal in the United States.

Although this is a factual statement, some respondents apparently were not aware of it, as evidenced by the three respondents on the "disagree" side of the scale. Three additional respondents simply did not answer (note the three "missing" responses), possibly because they were not sure how to provide an opinion to an item that is clearly factual. You may recall from a previous chapter that factual items should not be included on attitude scales, for the simple reason that they are not likely to evoke attitudinal responses. This example shows how poor item-writing practice can be detected through the use of item analysis information

Having discovered items with skewness and/or kurtosis values outside the normal range, what should be done? When making this decision, scale developers should attend to at least two important considerations: the reason for the non-normality and the purpose of the scale. As we have seen in the previous examples, non-normal item distributions can result from poor item-writing practice. If it can be determined that this is the case, the offending items should be rewritten or discarded. However, keep in mind that scales are often written such that the proportion of items across different content domains is balanced. The developer of the interracial marriage scale, for example, may have wanted approximately equal proportions of items dealing with different aspects of this issue. If most of the items dropped were concentrated on only one aspect of interracial marriage, content would no longer be balanced. Therefore, it is best to rewrite items rather than delete them, if possible. If not, deleted items should be replaced with other items from the same content domain.

The second important consideration is the purpose of the scale. In most situations, the reason for developing the scale is to be able to differentiate among respondents with a wide range of attitudes, values, or levels of personality attributes. For example, suppose a researcher is interested in studying attitudes toward dating violence. An item such as "Sometimes a man has no choice but to hit his girlfriend" would likely result in a very skewed distribution of responses, or so we would hope. However, if the researcher is interested in identifying those who have extreme attitudes, inclusion of extreme items is necessary as these are the very items that will allow such differentiation. Thus, it is important to think carefully about the levels of the construct of interest that will most likely be represented among those being studied. A researcher who is interested in assessing those with severe levels of depression may need a scale with more extreme items than one who is interested in depression in a nonclinical population. In other words, items should be matched to the population of interest. This also suggests that the sample from which item statistics are obtained should be representative of the population with whom the scale will ultimately be used. If the scale is intended to be used with a clinical population, samples of college students or from the general public will likely yield item distributions that are much more non-normal than those that would be obtained from a more appropriate sample. This could result in dropping items that may have been useful for clinical work.

The next example demonstrates how some problems with items can be detected from an inspection of the frequency distribution. The item associated with the following distribution appeared on a survey of attitudes toward sex before marriage.

Response	Frequency	Percent	Cumulative percent
1 "Strongly disagree"	3	3.8	3.8
2 "Disagree"	11	13.9	17.7
3 "Neutral"	31	39.2	57.0
4 "Agree"	30	38.0	94.9
5 "Strongly agree"	4	5.1	100.0
Total	79	100.0	

Note the large percentage of "neutral" responses to this item, which likely occurred because of its confusing wording:

> I believe that having sex before marriage may be detrimental to a
> couple's relationship but that there may not be negative consequences
> if the couple has a stable, committed relationship.

Although not the case here, confusing items such as this one often result in many missing responses.

Interitem Correlations

When constructing noncognitive scales, it is important that item content be homogeneous in the sense that items measure the same construct. If this is not the case, interpretation of the total scale score would be difficult, if not impossible. The implication here, however, is not that scales cannot be made up of two or more subdimensions, or subscales. For example, the well-known Test Anxiety Inventory (Spielberger, 1977–1980) has two subscales designated as Worry and Emotionality, which are theorized to represent two distinct but related aspects of test anxiety. Both subscales have strong theoretical and empirical relationships with the overall construct of test anxiety. In effect, the two dimensions of worry and emotionality are thought to jointly make up the overall test anxiety construct. This is clearly different from a scale containing items designed to measure, for example, two dimensions such as depression and altruism because these represent two seemingly unrelated constructs. Scores on such a scale would be difficult, if not impossible, to interpret.

Examining a table of the correlations among the items on a scale is a straightforward way to determine the degree to which items are related. Items that are not correlated with others on the scale are usually problematic in some way. The most obvious interpretation for a low correlation of an item with the other items is that it is measuring a different construct. This is not necessarily the case, however. Other reasons that an item can have low correlations with other items on its scale are that (1) it lacks variance or (2) its distribution is very different from that of the other items. Both of these possibilities should be investigated.

Table 6.1 shows the intercorrelations of some of the items on a scale designed to measure attitudes toward sex before marriage. Note that the last two items (items 16 and 17) have very low correlations with the other items. Item 16 reads:

Sex before marriage is one of the main factors contributing to teen pregnancy.

Although the content of this item does appear to be consistent with attitudes toward sex before marriage, it still does not relate to the other items. So what is wrong? The answer lies in the factual nature of the item. Certainly, it is a fact that sex is a main contributing factor to pregnancy; in fact, as far as I am aware, it is the *only* contributing factor. As we have seen, factual items have no place on attitude questionnaires. The main problem with such items is that they are unable to differentiate between those with positive and negative attitudes. Those with attitudes on either end of the continuum could agree with this item.

Another reason this item fails to correlate with other items on the scale is its distribution. Unlike the other items on the scale, which tend to be negatively skewed, this item is positively skewed. Such differences in distribution limit the degree to which items can intercorrelate. In general, items will correlate more highly with other items that are similarly distributed than with differently distributed items, and the difference is greatest for items of opposite skew (Bernstein & Teng, 1989).

Item 17 reads:

The government should do more to stop the spread of AIDS.

The reason for this item's low interitem correlation is obvious from its wording. The content of this item is tangential, at best, to the attitudes toward sex before marriage.

TABLE 6.1. Intercorrelations of Selected Attitudes toward Sex before Marriage Items

	Item 10	Item 11	Item 12	Item 13	Item 14	Item 15	Item 16	Item 17
Item 10	1.00							
Item 11	.44	1.00						
Item 12	.65	.75	1.00					
Item 13	.61	.64	.84	1.00				
Item 14	.59	.61	.79	.75	1.00			
Item 15	.51	.43	.55	.58	.59	1.00		
Item 16	.16	.22	.25	.37	.26	.18	1.00	
Item 17	−.03	.02	.08	−.02	.05	.11	.09	1.00

Item–Total Correlations and Information from Reliability Analyses

Although looking at tables of interitem correlations can be useful in detecting items that do not seem to fit on the scale, this process can be quite tedious, especially if there are many items. Instead, most statistical packages provide an index referred to as the *item–total correlation* as part of a reliability analysis. Although I have not yet discussed reliability analyses in detail, I refer here to two indices available from reliability output because they are useful in assessing the degree to which items are part of a homogeneous set.

An item that is highly correlated with the other items on a scale will also be correlated with their sum. Thus, the correlation of an item with the sum of all the items, known as the item–total correlation, can be used to assess the homogeneity of the items. Typically, the *corrected* item–total correlation is calculated. This index corrects for the fact that the item being correlated is also part of the total score. Because an item must be correlated perfectly with itself, inclusion of the item within the total would inflate the item–total correlation. To adjust for this, each item is correlated with the sum of all other items, *except* itself. The resulting index is referred to as the *corrected item–total correlation* or the *item–remainder correlation*. Higher values indicate, as usual, that the item is highly correlated with the sum and thus with the other items. Although it may not be obvious, the item–total correlation index described here is similar to the discrimination index described in the context of cognitive item analysis. Thus, the item–total correlation is a discrimination index.

Another useful index is a measure of the degree to which the scale's internal consistency, a measure based on interitem correlations, would decrease if an item were to be deleted. One index of internal consistency is *coefficient alpha*. Because coefficient alpha is an index of internal consistency based on interitem correlations, it can be useful in assessing interitem consistency. As with item–total correlations, high values of coefficient alpha are indicative of greater interitem consistency (although alpha is also affected by the number of items on the scale). Therefore, the degree to which an item contributes to high coefficient alpha values is an index of its consistency, or correlation, with the other items on the scale. This can be assessed by calculating coefficient alpha *without* a given item and determining the degree to which alpha decreases. If the item is strongly related to the other items, coefficient alpha should decrease because an item that contributes to consistency has been removed. If removal of an item were to result in an *increase* in alpha, this would indicate that the item is actually detrimental to interitem consistency because consistency is higher without the item. Such values are termed the *alpha-if-item-deleted* values and indicate what the value of alpha would be if a given item were removed from the scale.

To interpret these values, we must first know the value of coefficient alpha when all items are included. In the following example, the alpha value is .93. Any item that has an alpha-if-item-deleted value *higher* than this would be flagged as potentially problematic because consistency (alpha) would go up if the item were deleted from the scale. In other words, the item is *lowering* the reliability of the scale. In most cases, we would be better off, psychometrically speaking, if the item were removed from the scale. An item

TABLE 6.2. Corrected Item–total Correlations and Alpha-If-Item-Deleted Values for Attitudes toward Sex before Marriage Items

Item	Corrected item–total correlation	Alpha if item deleted
1	.70	.93
2	.75	.93
3	.75	.93
4	.85	.93
5	.82	.93
6	.59	.93
7	.75	.93
8	.67	.93
9	.63	.93
10	.62	.93
11	.69	.93
12	.85	.93
13	.80	.93
14	.86	.93
15	.64	.93
16	.18	.94
17	.04	.94
18	.15	.94
19	.85	.93
20	.35	.94
21	.43	.93
22	.26	.94
23	.27	.94

might be lowering the scale reliability for the same reasons as those discussed earlier in the context of interitem correlations: the item may not be measuring the same thing as the other items, it may be worded poorly, it may have distributional characteristics that are very different from the other items, or it may lack variance. All these possibilities should be investigated.[1]

Table 6.2 shows the corrected item–total and alpha-if-item-deleted values for items from the sex before marriage scale. Although alpha is quite high, several items are

---

[1]Some experts, such as Raykov and Marcoulides (2011; Raykov, 2007), argue against the use of alpha-if-item-deleted indices. These authors point out that alpha is an underestimate of the true reliability value in most cases and that use of alpha-if-item-deleted may therefore result in incorrect decisions regarding item retention or deletion. These issues are discussed in more detail in Chapter 8.

decreasing the reliability of the scale. These items are **bolded** in Table 6.2. Not surprisingly, these include items 16, 17 and 23, which we have already discussed.

Item 18 reads:

> The possibility of contracting sexually transmitted diseases is one good reason to refrain from sex before marriage.

The main problem with this item is that it will not necessarily differentiate among those who favor and those who oppose sex before marriage. Those in favor might agree, thinking something like "Well, yes; in fact this is the *only* good reason" while those who are opposed may agree even though they think this is not the *best* reason.

Item 20 states:

> The only reason for sex should be to reproduce.

Most readers, whether or not they hold this opinion, would probably agree that it is a fairly extreme view in most Western societies.

Finally, Item 22 reads:

> To ensure sexual compatibility and to strengthen the relationship, couples should be required to engage in sex before marriage.

This item is double-barreled because one might feel that, although such a requirement may ensure sexual compatibility, it would not necessarily strengthen the relationship. However, most readers would probably agree that this item is quite extreme, although in a different direction than Item 20. Of course, if the purpose of the scale was to detect those holding extreme attitudes, items such as 20 and 22 may be necessary.

Group Comparisons

In many cases, scales are designed to differentiate among groups or to make diagnoses. For example, personality scales such as the MMPI-2 (Butcher, Dahlstrom, Graham, Tellegen, & Kaemmer, 1989) are often used to distinguish among those with different types of personality disorders. In the field of education, diagnostic screening tests are often used to identify specific areas of math or reading in which students are struggling. Other examples include scales that have been designed to diagnose conditions such as autism spectrum disorder or attention-deficit/hyperactivity disorder (ADHD). In situations in which the intent is to make differentiations or diagnoses, scales are often developed by choosing the items on which the groups of interest show the greatest differences. Although scales developed using this procedure will not necessarily be the most internally consistent, they should provide more accurate diagnoses than those developed on the basis of item consistency alone. Such scales may not be internally consistent because a variety of things may distinguish those with a particular disorder from those without that disorder, and these things may not necessarily be strongly related. Consequently, the items needed to differentiate the two groups may be somewhat heterogeneous. A similar point was made earlier in this chapter in the discussion of item discrimination indices, where it was noted that prediction of external criteria such as job performance typically necessitates use of a relatively heterogeneous test. The same may be true for tests designed for classification and diagnostic decisions. This is not to say that item consistency is not important for such scales. Whenever total and/or subscale scores are to be interpreted and used, it is important that the items forming these be internally consistent. However, it may sometimes be necessary to trade off some internal consistency to obtain a scale with the best predictive power. The situation in which the need for a broad-based scale results in lower internal consistency is known as the *attenuation paradox* (Loevinger, 1954).

Determining which items best differentiate among the groups of interest is fairly straightforward. The items must be administered to respondents from the groups to be differentiated. Item means for each group are then computed and compared. Those items with the largest mean differences are selected for the scale. This method of developing scales is sometimes referred to as *empirical* or *criterion-based keying*. However, rarely do scale developers choose items based only on their ability to differentiate groups. If the scale is composed of different subscales, as is often the case, it would be necessary to ensure that there are sufficient items to measure each of these subscales. In some cases, scale developers may want a specific proportion of the items to reflect the content of each subscale. And, as noted previously, internal consistency is an important consideration for any scale, so the items chosen should not be so heterogeneous that they would not be considered measures of the same construct.

Finally, development of scales based solely on empirical keying has been criticized because such methods are often atheoretical and as such do not help to advance understanding of the underlying theory (e.g., Clark & Watson, 1995). A common example of empirical keying is that of interest inventories designed to guide students in the choice of a career or college major. Items for such inventories are often chosen on the basis of their ability to differentiate those who are successfully employed in a particular job from those who are not. So, for example, if engineers like jazz music more than those in other occupations, preference for jazz music might be used as an item on the "engineer" scale. However, knowing about this preference does little to further our understanding of *why* a person might be a good engineer. Although this example is admittedly oversimplified, it is intended to make the point that use of empirical keying *in isolation* may result in nonsensical and unreliable scales. At the same time, use of empirical keying in conjunction with other criteria can be very useful when the purpose of the scale is to provide diagnostic or predictive information.

The process of choosing items that best differentiate among groups can be illustrated with a hypothetical example based on the development of the ADHD Rating Scale–IV (DuPaul, Power, Anastopoulos, & Reid, 1998). Items on this scale were written to correspond to symptoms of ADHD specified in the fourth edition of the DSM (DSM-IV).

The scale is completed by a parent or teacher who indicates the frequency with which the child exhibits each symptom. The 18 items on the ADHD Rating Scale–IV were chosen from a larger pool of items based, in part, on the degree to which they could discriminate children who had been diagnosed with ADHD by a clinician from those who had not. Table 6.3 shows fictitious data consisting of the mean responses of groups with and without an ADHD diagnosis to a subset of the actual items on the ADHD Rating Scale–IV. Given these data, items 1, 4, 5, and 7 would be among those chosen for the final version of the scale because these items resulted in the greatest differences in ratings for children with and without an ADHD diagnosis.

Note that this process is basically the same as that discussed for calculating discrimination for cognitive items. Recall that one way of calculating a discrimination index for cognitive items is based on the difference in correct responses from upper and lower groups. The difference here is that the groups are formed on the basis of an external criterion rather than on the internal criterion of the total test score as in cognitive item analysis. In the fictitious example given in this section, the ADHD group was formed on the basis of a diagnosis from a clinician, and not on the basis of total scores on the ADHD rating scale. As noted in the earlier section on discrimination indices for cognitive items, use of an external criterion such as clinical diagnosis in the computation of item discrimination indices should result in more accurate diagnostic information with respect to that criterion.

Factor Analytic Methods

Although factor analytic methods are not discussed until Chapter 12, these methods should at least be mentioned here as they are widely used in scale development. Essentially, factor analysis is a method for determining the degree to which variables relate

TABLE 6.3. Fictitious Mean Responses to ADHD Rating Scale–IV Items by Group

Item	Item means		
	ADHD diagnosis	No ADHD diagnosis	Difference
1. Has difficulty sustaining attention in tasks and play activities.	3.5	1.5	2.0
2. Fidgets with hands or feet or squirms in seat.	3.3	2.9	0.4
3. Does not seem to listen when spoken to directly.	3.4	2.7	0.7
4. Interrupts or intrudes on others.	3.6	1.8	1.8
5. Leaves seat in classroom or in other situations in which remaining seated is expected.	3.8	2.0	1.8
6. Is forgetful in daily activities.	3.5	2.5	1.0
7. Does not follow through on instructions and fails to finish work.	3.6	2.1	1.5

Note. Response scale is 0 = "rarely or never"; 1 = "sometimes"; 2 = "often"; 3 = "very often."

to constructs in the hypothesized manner. In the context of scale development, the variables are the items designed to measure the construct of interest. Because the items have been developed to measure a specific construct, we would expect them to relate to each other and to the overall construct. For example, a researcher developing a scale to measure anxiety might include items reflecting both physical (e.g., feeling jittery) and cognitive (e.g., inability to concentrate) symptoms. It may be the case that the two types of symptoms are expected to exhibit differential relationships with health problems or other outcomes. The researcher is therefore interested in obtaining scores on the two subscales as well as an overall score. In such situations, the researcher would be interested in knowing the degree to which (1) the physical symptom items relate to each other, (2) the cognitive symptom items relate to each other, and (3) the physical symptom items relate to the cognitive symptom items. The relations among physical and among cognitive items should be greater than the relations between physical and cognitive items. If this were not the case, the creation of physical and cognitive scales would not be supported. However, there should be some relation between the items in the physical and cognitive sets. If not, the creation of a total score would not be warranted.

You may be thinking that examination of correlations among all the items would provide this information. This is true, but with even a moderate number of items for each subscale the number of correlations to be compared would overwhelm the cognitive capacity of most researchers. This is where factor analysis is useful. Factor analytic methods provide a way of sorting out the items based on the relative magnitude of their intercorrelations. Items that are highly correlated with each other form *factors*. The factors are based on the shared variance among the items. In other words, the factors represent whatever it is that the items have in common. The degree to which the items share variance with the common factor is measured by their *factor loadings*. These loadings will differ across items because some items are better measures of the factor than others. In our example, the researcher would hypothesize that the physical symptom items would form one factor and the cognitive symptom items another. These two factors would represent the shared variance among the items of the two subscales. And because the two sets of items are hypothesized to be related, the factors should be correlated. To the degree that these relations hold, the researcher's hypotheses are supported. These relations are diagrammed in Figure 6.1. In the figure, the circles represent the two factors, and the squares represent the items. Arrows emanating from the two factors to the items represent the factor loadings, or the relationships between the items and their factors. Finally, the curved arrow between the two factors indicates that they are correlated.[2]

How does all this relate to scale development? Suppose that 10 items were developed for the cognitive subscale but that 3 of these items had very low loadings. Because low loadings indicate that the item is not a good measure of the factor, the researcher may decide to eliminate or rewrite these 3 items. Of course, as with all of the item analy-

---

[2] For those familiar with such diagrams, I have left out the measurement error or uniqueness terms for simplicity. These will be introduced in Chapter 12.

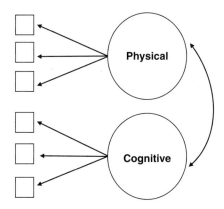

FIGURE 6.1. Two-factor model of anxiety.

sis methods discussed in this chapter, such decisions should not be made lightly. All of the available information should be considered in making decisions about item retention or deletion. However, the magnitude of factor loadings is certainly one piece of information that might be considered. In Chapter 12 I present a more thorough discussion of factor analysis and provide more detail on how to use information from this method in the scale development process.

Summary of Analyses for Noncognitive Items

Perhaps the most basic procedure for evaluating the performance of noncognitive items is the examination of a frequency distribution showing the number of respondents choosing each response option. Examination of such distributions can reveal problems such as the "piling up" of responses onto one or two options, suggesting that the item is not differentiating among respondents. A large number of responses on the neutral or middle response category may be an indication that respondents are confused by the item. Measures of skewness and kurtosis can be used to detect similar problems. Measures of skewness indicate the degree to which responses are concentrated on either the right-hand (negative skew) or left-hand (positive skew) side of the distribution. Such asymmetry indicates that most respondents are choosing the same, or similar, response options. High positive kurtosis values are also signs that responses are concentrated at one point on the response scale, whereas negative kurtosis values indicate a more even spread of responses across the scale.

Examination of item intercorrelation matrices provides basic information on the degree to which items relate to each other. Because scale items have been developed to measure the same construct, they would be expected to intercorrelate, and inspection of these correlations is a straightforward way to evaluate the degree to which items hang together. Low correlations among items may be signs of confusing or poorly written items, or of the existence of subdimensions of the construct being measured. With large numbers of items, examination of all interitem correlations may be overwhelming, however. In such cases, examination of item–total correlations can be useful. These are correlations of each item with the total score and should be high to the extent that items are intercorrelated. An index commonly referred to as alpha-if-item-deleted provides information on the degree to which internal consistency, as measured by coefficient alpha, would change if the item were removed from the total score. If an item is a good one, alpha should decrease upon deletion of the item. Items for which alpha would increase upon deletion are therefore detrimental. Such items may not be measuring the same construct as the other items, may lack variance, or may be confusing to respondents.

For situations in which the scale is to be used to predict an outcome or to differentiate among groups (such as for diagnostic purposes), the degree to which items relate to the outcome of interest or result in different item scores for those in different diagnostic categories is typically of interest. Items can have little diagnostic value if those with very different diagnostic classifications obtain the same scores. Similarly, items on scales to be used for predictive purposes are of little use if they do not relate to the outcome of interest. Items designed to be used for these purposes are therefore often chosen on the basis of their predictive or diagnostic utility. However, two caveats about such approaches should be noted. First, choosing items *solely* on the basis of these criteria can result in nonsensical scales. Second, reliance on such criteria can result in low values of internal consistency reliability indices. As with all aspects of the scale development process, researchers should take a balanced approach, incorporating a variety of procedures in choosing items for the final scale.

USE OF ITEM ANALYSIS INFORMATION

This chapter has presented a great deal of information relevant to determining the quality of cognitive and noncognitive items. In this section, I briefly discuss how to "put it all together"—that is, how to use this information for scale development or revision. As noted in Chapter 3, item analyses should always be conducted as part of the test development process. Information gleaned from these analyses can then be used to select the best items for the final scale. However, those developing scales should be aware that item analysis information can be quite unstable if the sample size used is inadequate. This is because much of the information used in item analysis is based on either item means or interitem correlations. If small samples of respondents are used, data from even one person with an aberrant response pattern can change the results quite dramatically. Correlation coefficients are particularly prone to such instability, such that values of correlations based on small samples can be quite different from sample to sample. Interestingly, however, correlations with large absolute magnitudes (i.e., closer to −1.0 or +1.0) are less variable across samples than are weaker correlations. Thus, somewhat smaller samples can be used if interitem correlations are large. Although Nunnally (1978) and Clark and Watson (1995) have recommended sample sizes of 300 when estimating correlations, Johanson and Brooks (2010) suggest a minimum sample size of 30 for preliminary item analyses based on a pilot sample. Hertzog (2008) recommends somewhat larger sample sizes of 50–80 for pilot studies involving estimation of item–total correlations, coefficient alpha, and/or test–retest reliability coefficients. Of course, these guidelines depend on the interitem correlations, with lower correlations requiring larger sample sizes for precise estimates.

Even if a large sample is used, researchers should exercise caution in deleting items based on item analysis information from a single sample. It is always possible that items exhibiting poor performance in one sample may perform adequately in another. In my view, many of those developing scales are much too cavalier in their willingness to delete items on the basis of information obtained from one, often insufficient, sample of respondents. Unless review of item wording or match to the original test specifications reveals that such items are confusing or irrelevant to the construct being measured, it would be better to flag the offending items but retain them for further study. If, in subsequent studies, the items continue to misbehave, they can then be deleted. However, because items were presumably written to tap into some important aspect of the construct of interest, it is important to consider the implications of such deletions for the overall balance of the scale. For example, if most of the deleted items were written to measure one aspect of the construct, the researcher must think carefully about whether that aspect is really relevant. If so, more (and, one would hope, better) items should be written to maintain the integrity of that subscale.

This example brings up a larger issue in the use of item analysis results: determination of items to be included on the final scale should not be made on the basis of item analysis statistics alone. Although scale developers will have carefully considered issues of content balance as part of their initial planning (see Chapter 3), we have seen how unconsidered reliance on item analysis statistics alone could wreak havoc on one's carefully planned scale. Thus, any decisions to delete items must be balanced with considerations of overall content representativeness. However, as Loevinger (1957) and others have pointed out, scale developers should not focus on content issues alone; both content coverage and item quality must be considered.

As in all aspects of scale development and evaluation, the purpose of the test must be kept in mind when determining which items to keep and which to delete. If the test is to be used for prediction of outcomes or to make diagnoses, preference should be given to items that best differentiate among groups or best predict the desired outcome, even if the intercorrelations of these items are not as strong as those of other, less predictive items. However, this does not mean that information about interitem correlations can be ignored; it is still important that items show some level of correlation. To take a concrete example, suppose that items 1 and 6 from the ADHD items discussed in a previous section were being considered for inclusion in a scale designed to be used for diagnosing ADHD. Item 1 clearly differentiates better between children with and without ADHD. However, item 1 may have an item–total correlation of .3, whereas the item–total correlation of item 6 is .5. In this case, it would still be better to choose item 1 over item 6 because item 1 is best at doing what the scale is supposed to do: differentiate those with and without ADHD. And item 1 still correlates reasonably with the other items.

TABLE 6.4. Example of Matching Items to Obtain Equivalent Test Forms

Item	P	D	Form
1	.30	.41	A
2	.32	.42	B
3	.45	.53	A
4	.43	.52	B
5	.37	.45	A
6	.39	.44	B
7	.80	.29	A
8	.77	.30	B

Another way item analysis information can be used is in the creation of different forms of a scale. Having different forms is particularly useful in educational testing or program evaluation, in which progress might be measured by administering a test before and after instruction or other intervention. In such cases, researchers should use different forms of the test because it is likely respondents will remember at least some of the questions from pre- to posttest. Another example in which multiple test forms are desirable is that of large-scale achievement tests, which often have several different forms to discourage cheating. The need for different test forms is not limited to the educational domain, however. Researchers measuring attitudes or personality variables for studies that involve a pre- and posttest might also want to use different test forms to circumvent memory effects.

If multiple test forms are desired, sufficient items for all forms should be developed, pilot-tested, and subjected to item analyses. Items can then be assigned to forms in such a way that both item content and statistical properties are balanced across forms. As an example, suppose that eight cognitive items are available to measure content domain A. The difficulty (P) and discrimination (D) values of the fictitious items are shown in Table 6.4. Each pair of consecutive items (e.g., 1 and 2, 3 and 4) has been matched on difficulty and discrimination values. If one item from each pair is assigned to a different test form, the two forms should be fairly well matched in terms of difficult and discriminatory power. Although the matching shown in Table 6.4 is not perfect, it should suffice for classroom testing or for scales to be used for research purposes. Tests used in "high-stakes" decisions, such as for college admissions or professional certification decisions, would be subjected to the much more rigorous methods of creating equivalent scales, discussed in Chapter 18. However, the basic concept would be the same.

EXERCISES

1. What are two reasons that difficulty values for standardized achievement tests usually range from about 0.3 to 0.7?

2. What are two assumptions underlying formula scoring (corrections for guessing)?

3. Calculate the difficulty (*P*) and discrimination (*D*) values for the following hypothetical multiple-choice items. An asterisk next to a response option indicates it is the correct answer.

Item 1

	A	B	C*	D	Total
High	1	17	0	0	18
Low	5	9	4	0	18

Item 2

	A	B	C	D*	Total
High	3	5	4	6	18
Low	3	3	7	5	18

Item 3

	A	B	C*	D	Total
High	0	0	18	0	18
Low	2	2	12	2	18

Item 4

	A*	B	C	D	Total
High	8	1	8	1	18
Low	3	4	7	4	18

Item 5

	A	B*	C	D	Total
High	0	2	0	16	18
Low	4	5	4	5	18

4. Comment on the performance of the distractors for Item 5.

5. Comment on the possible problem(s) with each item and support your comments with evidence from the item analysis.

6. Which item do you think is performing worst? Explain.

The 10 items shown here were developed to measure attitudes toward same-sex marriage. The items were answered on a Likert scale ranging from 1 = "strongly disagree" to 5 = "strongly agree." Five items (4, 6, 8, 9, and 10) were re-coded so that a higher total score on the scale would indicate a more positive attitude toward same-sex marriage.

For these items, 1 ("strongly disagree") was re-coded to 5 ("strongly agree"), 2 ("disagree") was re-coded to 4 ("agree"), and so on.

Attitude toward Same-Sex Marriage Items

1. Civil unions between same-sex couples should be legal.

2. Same-sex couples should be able to adopt children together.

3. People in same-sex civil unions should have the same benefits as those in heterosexual marriages.

4. Same-sex marriage is morally wrong. (R)

5. Same-sex marriage should be legal in order to allow homosexual partners to have the same rights as heterosexual partners.

6. The homosexual culture has a negative effect on society. (R)

7. To ensure equal rights and to satisfy the heterosexual population who is against gay marriage, civil unions should be legal in all 50 states.

8. Same-sex marriage should not be legalized, but civil unions that provide tax benefits should be allowed in order to be fair. (R)

9. There is more support for same-sex civil unions in today's society then there was 30 years ago. (R)

10. Many people disapprove of same-sex marriages. (R)

The corrected item–total correlations and values of alpha if item deleted are shown in Figure 6.2. Values of descriptive statistics and each item's frequency distribution are also shown. The value of coefficient alpha for the 10-item scale is .858. Use this information to answer Questions 7–11.

7. Which three items are performing worst in terms of their contribution to the total scale score? Explain why you chose these items.

8. Examine the wording for the three items you chose in Question 7. Do these provide any clues about why these items have performed so poorly? Explain.

9. Examine the frequency distributions for the three items you chose in Question 7. Do these provide any additional clues about why these items have performed so poorly? Explain.

10. Based on the information provided, are there any items that may have been confusing or difficult to answer? Explain.

11. Most of the items have negative kurtosis values.

   a. What type of distribution is indicated by a negative kurtosis value?

   b. Is negative kurtosis problematic for attitude items? Why or why not?

Item	Corrected item–total correlation	Value of coefficient alpha if item deleted
Item 1	.849	.817
Item 2	.785	.823
Item 3	.737	.829
Item 4	.844	.817
Item 5	.736	.829
Item 6	.818	.823
Item 7	.460	.854
Item 8	−.011	.889
Item 9	.086	.873
Item 10	.208	.866

Statistic	Item 1	Item 2	Item 3	Item 4	Item 5	Item 6	Item 7	Item 8	Item 9	Item 10
Mean	3.52	3.25	3.59	3.24	3.08	3.61	3.17	3.33	1.96	1.74
SD	1.44	1.48	1.35	1.49	1.49	1.27	1.27	1.25	0.78	0.70
Skewness	−0.64	−0.27	−0.64	−0.27	−0.03	−0.52	−0.22	−0.18	0.62	0.78
Kurtosis	−0.99	−1.32	−0.84	−1.38	−1.48	−0.81	−0.81	−0.92	0.20	0.81

Item 1*

Response option	Frequency	Percentage	Cumulative percentage
1. Strongly disagree	15	15.8	15.8
2. Disagree	11	11.6	27.4
3. Neutral	9	9.5	36.8
4. Agree	30	31.6	68.4
5. Strongly agree	30	31.6	100.0
Total	95	100.0	

Item 2

Response option	Frequency	Percentage	Cumulative percentage
1. Strongly disagree	18	18.9	18.9
2. Disagree	13	13.7	32.6
3. Neutral	18	18.9	51.6
4. Agree	19	20.0	71.6
5. Strongly agree	27	28.4	100.0
Total	95	100.0	

FIGURE 6.2. Item statistics for Questions 7–11. (Continued)

Item 3

Response option	Frequency	Percentage	Cumulative percentage
1. Strongly disagree	10	10.8	10.8
2. Disagree	13	14.0	24.7
3. Neutral	12	12.9	37.6
4. Agree	28	30.1	67.7
5. Strongly agree	30	32.3	100.0
Missing	2	2.1	
Total	93	100.0	

Item 4**

Response option	Frequency	Percentage	Cumulative percentage
1. Strongly disagree	18	19.1	19.1
2. Disagree	15	16.0	35.1
3. Neutral	13	13.8	48.9
4. Agree	22	23.4	72.3
5. Strongly agree	26	27.7	100.0
Missing	1	1.1	
Total	94	100.0	

Item 5

Response option	Frequency	Percentage	Cumulative percentage
1. Strongly disagree	18	18.9	18.9
2. Disagree	23	24.2	43.2
3. Neutral	11	11.6	54.7
4. Agree	19	20.0	74.7
5. Strongly agree	24	25.3	100.0
Total	94	100.0	

Item 6**

Response option	Frequency	Percentage	Cumulative percentage
1. Strongly disagree	7	7.4	7.4
2. Disagree	13	13.7	21.1
3. Neutral	21	22.1	43.2
4. Agree	23	24.2	67.4
5. Strongly agree	31	32.6	100.0
Total	95	100.0	

FIGURE 6.2. Continued.

Item 7

Response option	Frequency	Percentage	Cumulative percentage
1. Strongly disagree	13	14.6	14.6
2. Disagree	10	11.2	25.8
3. Neutral	31	34.8	60.7
4. Agree	19	21.3	82.0
5. Strongly agree	16	18.0	100.0
Missing	6	6.3	
Total	89	100.0	

Item 8**

Response option	Frequency	Percentage	Cumulative percentage
1. Strongly disagree	8	8.5	8.5
2. Disagree	16	17.0	25.5
3. Neutral	29	30.9	56.4
4. Agree	19	20.2	76.6
5. Strongly agree	22	23.4	100.0
Missing	1	1.1	
Total	94	100.0	

Item 9**

Response option	Frequency	Percentage	Cumulative percentage
1. Strongly disagree	27	28.4	28.4
2. Disagree	49	51.6	80.0
3. Neutral	15	15.8	95.8
4. Agree	4	4.2	100.0
5. Strongly agree	0	0.0	100.0
Total	95	100.0	

Item 10**

Response option	Frequency	Percentage	Cumulative percentage
1. Strongly disagree	36	38.3	38.3
2. Disagree	48	51.1	88.4
3. Neutral	8	8.5	97.9
4. Agree	2	2.1	100.0
5. Strongly agree	0	0.0	100.0
Missing	1		
Total	94	100.0	

* Total, percentage, and cumulative percentages are based on the number of nonmissing responses; ** item was reverse-coded.

Part II
Reliability and Validity

Introduction to Reliability and the Classical Test Theory Model

This is the first of four chapters on the important psychometric property of reliability. In this chapter, I define reliability and explain why it is important in measurement. I then introduce the *classical test theory* (CTT) model, on which the original definitions of reliability were based. In the context of this model, I discuss the concepts of measurement error and true and observed scores. I also define *parallel*, *tau-equivalent*, and *congeneric* tests, and use CTT concepts to derive the classical definition of reliability as the correlation between two parallel tests.

WHAT IS RELIABILITY?

When we say a person is reliable, we usually mean that he or she is dependable or trustworthy. A similar interpretation applies in measurement theory. Test scores that are *reliable* are dependable, or trustworthy, in the sense that we would obtain very similar scores if we were to repeat the test. For example, it is well known that measures of blood pressure can fluctuate across readings, even if these are taken at about the same time and location. Does this mean that one of the blood pressure readings is right and the others are wrong? No; the fluctuations are thought to be random in the sense that they would not occur again in the same way, even if the conditions were the same. So, we do not necessarily expect that the readings will be exactly the same each time. However, because readings do fluctuate, several blood pressure readings are sometimes taken to obtain a more accurate overall measure. Similarly, tests are not usually based on just one item. Instead, scores on multiple items are averaged together to obtain a total score. This is because respondents may respond in an idiosyncratic fashion to any one item. For example, an item may be misread, or a respondent may react to a particular wording used in the item. So, as with blood pressure readings, multiple items are typically used in order to obtain multiple "trials" or measurements. In both of these situations, however, we would probably be concerned if the blood pressure readings or test item scores were very different from each other. If this were the case, we would likely have less faith in the results obtained, as we would not know which of the disparate results to trust. In testing, such inconsistent measures are said to be *unreliable*. *Reliability* is a crucial property of test scores because it provides some assurance that we would obtain similar scores if we were to measure again in the same way.

Implicit in the previous blood pressure and testing examples is the idea of dependability or consistency across some condition. In the blood pressure example, the condition over which scores might vary is time. With tests, the condition of interest is often the test items themselves. Responses to some test items may be inconsistent with the others due to confusing or idiosyncratic wording, and inclusion of such items on a test could "throw off" the overall score. Another situation in which consistency across items is an issue is that in which different forms of a test are available. The availability of different forms of a test is useful for situations in which researchers want to administer a pre- and posttest, but do not want to use the same test version because respondents may remember their answers to the first test and simply answer in the same way. In achievement testing, different forms are often used in an effort to thwart cheating. When different forms of a test are used, it is important that the forms are equivalent in terms of difficulty as well as content coverage. Inconsistencies across test forms in these aspects are likely to result in a lack of equivalence among forms. Items must therefore be chosen carefully such that respondents would obtain very similar scores regardless of the form used. However, even scores from carefully developed test forms will still differ somewhat, owing to individualistic reactions to particular items.

Time is another condition over which test scores might vary. In many situations, tests are used to select people for employment, awards, advanced training, or admission to college or other educational programs, or to predict future performance in a job, training program, or academic program. In all of these situations, the focus of the prediction or selection is on something that will happen in the future. However, suppose that, owing to a flaw in our measurement procedures, people's scores changed radically between the time they took the test and the time they were selected, or the predicted event occurred. In this case, the selection/prediction decisions would be wrong because we would be using scores that were no longer accurate measures of the construct of interest. When making selection/prediction decisions, therefore, we must use measures that are known to be stable across time. Reliability coefficients that measure consistency across test items, test forms, and testing occasions are discussed in more detail in the next chapter.

A final condition over which scores may vary is that of raters. In some cases, scores are obtained through the use of observations of behavior in either a naturalistic situation, such as observing student nurses give an injection, or in a more contrived situation, such as requiring students to make a speech. Raters code these behaviors using some type of rubric to obtain numerical scores. In other cases, students provide products such as artwork or essays, which are then rated. In all of these cases, consistency of scoring across raters is usually of interest. Even when raters are trained to score in exactly the same way, a momentary lapse of attention or slight differences in raters' interpretations of the rating rubric will result in unwanted score fluctuations. Coefficients designed to assess consistency of scores across different raters are discussed in Chapters 9 and 10.

I note at the outset that reliability is not defined for a single person's score. Rather, reliability coefficients assess the average consistency of scores for an entire group of interest. Values of reliability coefficients will be high when people respond consistently across different conditions, such as on different items or test forms, or different testing occasions. Note, however, that this does not imply that people must all obtain the same scores for reliability to be high. Instead, a high reliability coefficient indicates that respondents have obtained similar *patterns of scores* across different conditions. Some people may obtain low scores and some may obtain high scores, but as long those with low scores obtain similarly low scores across items, test forms, occasions, or raters, and those with high scores obtain similar scores across conditions, reliability should be high. If the pattern described here seems very similar to the underlying mechanism for a high correlation, that's because it is. In fact, many reliability coefficients are nothing more than correlation coefficients, and others are functions of correlations. You may recall that calculation of correlation coefficients requires some degree of variability in the variables being correlated. The same is true for reliability coefficients. If everyone obtained the same score, we would not be able to tell if the pattern of scores was consistent across conditions because there would be only one pattern. Thus, there must be some variability in scores to calculate reliability coefficients.

To summarize, the term *reliability* in the context of measurement theory refers to the dependability or consistency of measurements across conditions. As the previous examples indicate, however, the conditions across which consistency is measured vary. In some situations, such as with blood pressure, consistency across items is irrelevant, but consistency across occasions may be important. With paper-and-pencil tests, consistency across items is often of greatest concern.

Because the conditions across which scores may fluctuate depend on the type of measurement being taken, different ways of assessing reliability have been proposed. *Test–retest reliability* measures, sometimes called *coefficients of stability*, are obtained when the researcher is concerned with consistency of scores over time. *Alternate forms reliability* measures, or *coefficients of equivalence*, are of interest for situations in which there are multiple test forms designed to provide equivalent scores. *Internal consistency* measures of reliability reflect the degree to which the items on a test are interrelated. Internal consistency is important for any test that contains multiple items that will be summed or averaged to obtain a total score. These coefficients are discussed in Chapter 8. Finally, measures of *interrater agreement*, discussed in Chapter 9, assess the degree to which scores are consistent across raters.

The type of reliability evidence that is important for a given situation depends on the sources of inconsistency that are of interest. In measurement theory, inconsistencies across test items, occasions, and raters are known as *measurement errors*, and a theory known as *classical test theory* is used to describe the effects of measurement error on test scores. Here, the term *error* does not refer to a mistake or incorrect answer, but to the types of inconsistencies described in the previous paragraphs. Because the concept of measurement error and the tenets of classical test theory are fundamental to reliability theory, I discuss these in some detail in the following section. In Chapter 8, I discuss each of the types of reliability evidence in turn.

MEASUREMENT ERROR AND CTT

CTT is based on Equation 7.1 which, though simple, has had a far-reaching impact on current concepts of reliability. According to CTT, any respondent's observed score, X, can be formulated as follows:

$$X = T + E \tag{7.1}$$

where X represents the observed score. The term *observed* does not mean that we can literally observe the value of, for example, a person's level of depression by looking at them. Instead it refers to the values that have been assigned on the basis of the measurement instrument being used. For example, assigning scores to each item on a Likert-type attitude scale and summing or averaging these scores would provide the observed attitude score. So, the observed scores are simply the values, or scores, we have obtained with our measurement instrument. The term E represents the part of the score that is due to error or to inconsistencies in measurement, as discussed in the previous section. Essentially, errors are random influences on test scores. For example, a respondent may have a momentary lapse of attention and misread a question, or not feel well on the day of the test, or be distracted by noises outside the testing room. All of these occurrences will likely affect the test scores, but they are random in the sense that, if the respondent were to be tested again, they would not reoccur. Finally, the term T refers to a respondent's *true score*. The true score is an important, though hypothetical, entity in classical test theory. It represents the score a respondent would obtain if our measurements were free of all error. The fact that measurements are never completely free of error is what makes the true score hypothetical rather than observed.

Equation 7.1 represents the conceptualization that, in CTT, a respondent's observed score is made up of two parts: the true score and the error score. The true score can be conceptualized as the average score that would be obtained if we were able to give a test to a respondent hundreds of times, wiping out her or his memory after each testing. Because the error scores are assumed to be random, some errors would cause the observed score to be higher than the true score, but some would cause it to be lower. Thus, the errors should cancel each other out across the hundreds of tests, and the average across all the tests should be the true score. Figure 7.1 provides a representation of this concept. As can be seen from the figure, observed scores vary around the true score. The amount by which observed scores differ from the true score is the error score. The dashed lines labeled X1 and X2 represent two possible observed scores. X1 is closer to the true score, and therefore has less error than does X2.

The description of the true score as the average score over repeated testings, though not literally possible, is useful because it introduces some additional CTT concepts. One of these is that the true score remains constant across different conditions. This means that the only reason observed scores vary across conditions is that different amounts of error are present on different occasions, test forms or items, or for different raters. So, differences in a person's observed scores, assuming the person's true score has not

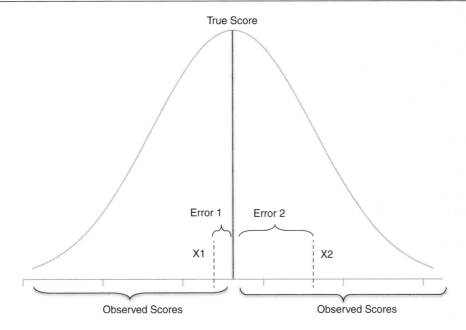

FIGURE 7.1. The distribution of observed scores around the true score.

changed, are due only to differences in their error scores, not to differences in their true score. Another implication of this scenario is that error scores are conceptualized as being random; if this were not the case, they would not cancel each other out over repeated testing, and the average of the repeated scores would not be equal to the true score. As noted previously, it is indeed the case that in CTT error scores are assumed to be random, resulting in an approximately normal distribution of observed scores around the true score as pictured in Figure 7.1. Although I have referred in this paragraph to multiple scores obtained from a single person, CTT also posits that error scores are random *across* people. For example, just because one person might be particularly tired when taking a test, resulting in a large error score, there is no reason to think that others would be as well. Thus, error scores are considered to be random (and normally distributed) across people.

Having said this, systematic errors are also possible. For example, some raters might be too lenient, some persons' blood pressure might always be higher in the afternoon than in the morning, and some students might be much better at guessing on multiple-choice items than others. Fluctuations due to these sources would be considered error because they are not due to the construct being measured. But they are not random in the sense that, if the testing were repeated, they would not happen again in the same way. On the contrary, lenient raters tend to be lenient in most situations, and students who are good at guessing do not confine this behavior to randomly chosen tests. Hence, systematic errors do not contribute to inconsistencies in observed scores. However, they do result in observed scores that are inaccurate because such scores reflect the influence of both the systematic error and true levels of the construct. But, because systematic error does not result in inconsistencies in scores, it has more to do with the *validity* than the reliability of scores.

MORE ON CTT

In mathematical parlance, the *expectation* or *expected value* of a variable describes the mean of that variable. In CTT it is useful to think of the mean as an expectation because of the way in which the true score is often defined. Recall from the previous section that the true score is defined as the mean of a distribution of observed scores based on multiple testings. Thus, the true score represents our expectation of what the observed score would be if we could obtain such a distribution. In a very real sense, the observed score differs from the true score because the observed score is based on limited information. For example, if we were able to administer all possible test items under every possible set of conditions, the amount of error in our test scores or observational ratings would decrease to zero. The true score therefore represents our expectation of what the score value would be if we had unlimited information. In mathematical terms, we state that the true score is the expected value of the observed score, or

$$T_j = \varepsilon X_j \qquad (7.2)$$

where T_j represents the true score of respondent j, ε stands for expectation, and X_j represents the observed score of respondent j.

From Equation 7.1, we can define respondent j's error score, E_j, as

$$E_j = X_j - T_j \qquad (7.3)$$

Thus, error is defined as simply the difference between a person's observed and true scores, as depicted in Figure 7.1. The expected value of the errors is

$$\varepsilon E_j = \varepsilon(X_j - T_j) \qquad (7.4)$$

which can be written as

$$\varepsilon E_j = \varepsilon X_j - \varepsilon T_j \qquad (7.5)$$

Recall that individuals' true scores do not fluctuate across conditions[1]; according to CTT, fluctuations in observed scores are due only to error. Thus, the true score is a constant. The expectation of a constant is simply that constant (it would not make sense to say,

---

[1]This assumes, of course, that no intervention or other occurrence has changed respondents' true scores.

for example, that the expected value of 12 is anything other than 12). So, Equation 7.5 becomes

$$\varepsilon E_j = \varepsilon X_j - T_j \tag{7.6}$$

And because the expectation of the observed scores is the true score, we find that

$$\varepsilon E_j = T_j - T_j = 0 \tag{7.7}$$

This is an important result because it means that, over repeated testing, the average of the errors for any respondent will be zero. Of course, on any *single* testing the error will not be zero. One purpose of a reliability coefficient is to estimate how much error there is likely to be in a given situation.

Properties of True and Error Scores in CTT

There are three commonly cited properties of true and error scores in CTT:

1. The mean of the errors for a population of respondents is equal to zero.
2. The correlation between true and error scores for a population of respondents is zero.
3. The correlation between the error scores obtained from two separate tests, or on two separate occasions using the same test, is zero.

The first of these properties was demonstrated through Equations 7.2–7.7 for an individual and holds in the same way across people, as noted previously. Points 2 and 3 follow from the assumption that error scores are random. Random quantities cannot correlate with anything for the simple reason that they are random. A high value on one random variable may be associated with a high value on another variable but is just as likely to be associated with a low, medium, or any other value of the other variable. In short, there is no pattern to the relations of random variables, which follows from the definition of randomness. As an example, I generated a scatterplot of hypothetical true scores and random error scores, shown in Figure 7.2. As can be seen from the figure, the correlation between the true scores and random error scores appears to be (and, in fact, is) zero. This illustrates the fact that error scores will not be correlated with true scores because they are random variables and therefore do not correlate with anything.

As noted in the previous section, systematic errors are also possible. However, systematic errors do not result in inconsistent scores and so do not generally result in lower reliability.[2] In CTT, therefore, the focus is on random rather than systematic errors.

---

[2] Although systematic errors will not generally result in lower reliability, such errors can be correlated across items. If this is the case, reliability values will be inflated. This point is discussed in a later chapter.

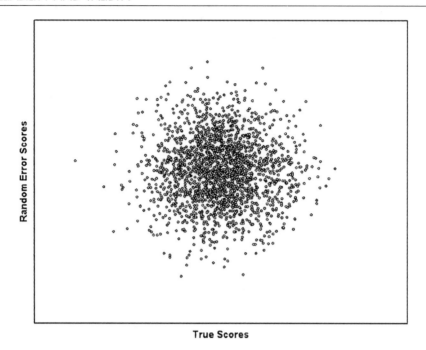

FIGURE 7.2. Scatterplot of hypothetical true scores and random error scores.

THE CTT DEFINITION OF RELIABILITY

These three properties of true and error scores allow for the derivation of a reliability coefficient based on CTT. The concept of reliability has previously been described as the consistency or dependability of test scores. Within the context of CTT, reliability can also be thought of as the extent to which observed scores reflect true rather than error scores. This conceptualization is congruent with the conceptualization of reliability as a measure of consistency because it is only error that makes observed scores inconsistent with each other. Thus, the more the observed scores reflect true scores and not error, the more consistent they will be. In addition, the extent to which observed scores reflect true, rather than error, scores is often what those using the scores want to know. For example, a researcher may wonder whether an observed difference in scores between two respondents is due to error or whether it reflects a difference in the respondents' true scores. Or a teacher may want to know whether students' observed scores are close to their true scores or are largely reflections of random error.

In other words, both the researcher and the teacher are interested in the correlation between true and observed scores. Of course, it is not really possible to compute this correlation because we only have the observed scores; the true scores are hypothetical. However, such a correlation represents yet another way of thinking about reliability. And as will be shown in a later section, psychometricians have developed ways to estimate this correlation using only observed scores. First, however, I begin with a brief derivation of the theoretical correlation between true and observed scores, known in

CTT as the *reliability index*. I note at the outset that the equations involved in these derivations are not intended to be used for actual computations. One reason for this is that these equations are based on the true score, which is not available. Instead, the equations that follow are the beginning steps in a process that translates the conceptual definition of reliability as the correlation between true and observed scores to a more practical quantity that can be computed from two observed scores.

CORRELATION BETWEEN TRUE AND OBSERVED SCORES: THE RELIABILITY INDEX

Recall from your introductory statistics class that the correlation between two variables is equal to

$$\rho_{xy} = \frac{\sum xy}{N\sigma_X\sigma_Y} \tag{7.8}$$

Here, x and y are in deviation score form; that is, they are expressed as deviations from their means (e.g., as $X = \overline{X}$ and $Y = \overline{Y}$). This is done simply to make the derivations easier. Substituting t for y, the correlation between true and observed scores would be

$$\rho_{xt} = \frac{\sum xt}{N\sigma_X\sigma_T} \tag{7.9}$$

Because $x = t + e$, Equation 7.9 can be written as

$$\rho_{xt} = \frac{\sum (t+e)t}{N\sigma_X\sigma_T} \tag{7.10}$$

Expanding the expression in Equation 7.10 results in

$$\rho_{xt} = \frac{\sum t^2}{N\sigma_X\sigma_T} + \frac{\sum te}{N\sigma_X\sigma_T} \tag{7.11}$$

The second term in Equation 7.11 can be shown to equal zero (see Crocker & Algina, 1986, p. 114), so the equation simplifies to

$$\rho_{xt} = \frac{\sum t^2}{N\sigma_X\sigma_T} \tag{7.12}$$

Note that the term $(\Sigma t^2)/N$ in Equation 7.12 is simply the variance of T (remember that t represents the deviation of T from its mean). Replacing those terms with the variance of T results in

$$\rho_{xt} = \frac{\sigma_T^2}{\sigma_X\sigma_T} \tag{7.13}$$

By dividing the numerator and denominator by σ_T, this simplifies to

$$\rho_{xt} = \frac{\sigma_T}{\sigma_X} \qquad (7.14)$$

Thus, the correlation between true and observed scores, ρ_{xt}, which I defined as reliability, is equivalent to the ratio of the standard deviations of true to observed scores.

Although this formulation is of interest theoretically as a definition of reliability, it is of little use to researchers who are interested in actually calculating a reliability coefficient. This is, of course, because we do not know the true score. However, suppose we had two scores for each respondent, obtained from two different forms of a test or from the same test administered at two different time points. The two observed scores would then be estimates of the same true score, and their correlation could be used to estimate reliability. The logic behind this is as follows. Each observed score is composed of a true score and an error component. However, because the errors are random, they cannot correlate with each other. Therefore, if the two observed scores correlate, it must be because the true scores are correlated, as the errors cannot be correlated. So, the correlation between two observed scores that are measuring the same thing can be taken as an estimate of ρ_{xt}. This idea is developed more formally in a later section. However, before doing so it is necessary to define *parallel*, *tau-equivalent*, and *congeneric measures*.

PARALLEL, TAU-EQUIVALENT, AND CONGENERIC MEASURES

In CTT, measures of the same thing (note that these measures can be items, subtests, or tests) can be classified by their levels of similarity. In this section, I define four levels of similarity: parallel, tau-equivalent, essentially tau-equivalent, and congeneric. Their properties are summarized in Box 7.1. Note that these levels are hierarchical in the sense that the highest level (parallel) requires the most similarity, whereas levels lower in the hierarchy allow for less similarity in test properties. For example, parallel measures must have equal true score variances, whereas congeneric measures do not require this.

One useful way of thinking about these levels is in terms of the relationships between the true scores of pairs of measures (Komaroff, 1997). In CTT, the basic relationship between the true scores on two measures (t_i and t_j) is

$$t_i = a_{ij} + b_{ij}t_j \qquad (7.15)$$

If the term b_{ij} is not zero, the two measures have different "amounts" of true score. If the term a_{ij} is not zero, the true score means of the measures differ. The terms a_{ij} and b_{ij} are subscripted for both measures (i and j), indicating that these constants can differ across pairs of measures (although they may also be the same across all pairs of measures).

BOX 7.1

Properties of Parallel, Tau-Equivalent, Essentially Tau-Equivalent, and Congeneric Measures

Type of measure	μ_X	σ_X^2	σ_T^2	σ_E^2	σ_{X_1,X_2}	ρ_{X_1,X_2}	Relationship between true scores
Parallel	Must be equal	Must be equal	Must be equal	Must be equal	Must be equal	Must be equal	$t_i = 0 + 1*t_i$
Tau-equivalent	Must be equal	May be equal or unequal	Must be equal	May be equal or unequal	Must be equal	May be equal or unequal	$t_i = 0 + 1*t_i$
Essentially tau-equivalent	May be equal or unequal	May be equal or unequal	Must be equal	May be equal or unequal	Must be equal	May be equal or unequal	$t_i = a_{ij} + 1*t_i$
Congeneric	May be equal or unequal	May be equal or unequal	May be equal or unequal	May be equal or unequal	May be equal or unequal	May be equal or unequal	$t_i = a_{ij} + b_{ij}*t_i$

Parallel[3] *measures* have the strongest type of similarity. For parallel measures, $a_{ij} = 0$ and $b_{ij} = 1$ for all pairs of measures. This means that the true scores of all measures are exactly equal. Because of this, the true score variances of the measures will also be equal. Parallel measures also have equal error variances. These properties (equal true score means, equal true score variances, and equal error variances) imply that parallel measures will also have equal observed score means and equal observed score variances, and that their observed scores will have equal correlations with each other. The last-named property follows from the fact that observed scores on parallel measures are perfectly linearly related. Parallel measures therefore tap into a common construct and measure that construct with the same sensitivity and precision.

Tau-equivalent measures (sometimes referred to as *true-score equivalent measures*) have a slightly weaker form of similarity than parallel measures. Like parallel measures, tau-equivalent measures have $a_{ij} = 0$ and $b_{ij} = 1$ for all pairs of measures, meaning that they have equal true score variances. However, tau-equivalent measures need not have equal error variances. Note that tau-equivalence does not *require* unequal error variances; it simply *allows for* unequal error variances. Tau-equivalence therefore relaxes the constraint that error variances must be equal. Therefore, although tau-equivalent measures must have equal true score variances, they may or may not all have equal observed score variances. Tau-equivalent measures also have equal true score (and observed score) covariances with each other. For those unfamiliar with covariances, a covariance is simply an unstandardized correlation. Recall that correlations are standardized in the sense that they must have values between −1.0 and +1.0. However, covariances are not standardized in this way and can take on any value. But covariances are measures of the relations between two variables, just as correlations are. The only difference is in their metric, or scale. Box 7.2 illustrates the covariance and how it is different from the correlation. The columns in the box show values for two variables, X and Y, followed by the quantities needed to calculate the covariance and correlation: the sum of squared deviations from the mean for X and Y (the *sum of squares*, or *SS*) and the product of the deviations of X and Y from their means (the *sum of products*, or *SP*).

Essentially tau-equivalent measures represent a slightly weaker form of tau-equivalence in which $a_{ij} \neq 0$ but $b_{ij} = 1$. This means that the true scores of essentially tau-equivalent measures may differ by an additive constant. For example, in a pair of essentially tau-equivalent measures, one true score might equal 2 plus the other. Although essential tau-equivalence *allows for* constant differences across true scores, it does not *require* this. Some items in a tau-equivalent set may have true score means that differ by a constant and some may not. Note that if two true scores differ by a constant, they would still be perfectly linearly related. And although such true scores could have different means, they would not have different variances. Thus, their true score variances would be the same, although observed score variances could be different because essentially

---

[3] The definition of parallelism presented here is sometimes referred to as *strict parallelism*. This is in contrast to *parallelism*, in which the item means need not be equal.

BOX 7.2

Computations for Covariance and Correlation

X	Y	$(X-\bar{X})^2$	$(Y-\bar{Y})^2$	$(X-\bar{X})(Y-\bar{Y})$
50	40	196	4	−28
20	50	256	64	−128
40	30	16	144	−48
30	40	36	4	12
40	50	16	64	32

$\bar{X}=36$ $\bar{Y}=42$ $\sum(X-\bar{X})^2=520$ $\sum(Y-\bar{Y})^2=280$ $\sum(X-\bar{X})(Y-\bar{Y})=-160$

$$\sigma_X=\sqrt{\frac{520}{5}}=10.20 \qquad \sigma_Y=\sqrt{\frac{280}{5}}=7.48$$

$$\text{cov}_{xy}=\frac{\sum(X-\bar{X})(Y-\bar{Y})}{n}=\frac{-160}{5}=-32$$

$$\rho_{xy}=\frac{\sum(X-\bar{X})(Y-\bar{Y})}{N\sigma_X\sigma_Y}=\frac{-160}{5(10.2)(7.48)}=-.42$$

---

tau-equivalent measures can have different error variances. True scores of essentially tau-equivalent measures are perfectly linearly related, so essentially tau-equivalent measures would have equal true score covariances with each other. However, neither tau-equivalent nor essentially tau-equivalent scores will have equal correlations. This is because they can have different observed score variances and standard deviations, so the denominator of the formula shown in Box 7.2 could differ across measures.

Finally, for *congeneric* measures, $a_{ij} \neq 0$ and $b_{ij} \neq 1$. For congeneric measures, all restrictions are relaxed. Congeneric measures are not assumed to have equal error variances, equal true score variances, equal observed score variances, equal observed score covariances, equal observed score correlations, or equal means. Congeneric measures thus have the least restrictive assumptions and as a result, such measures can differ more than those in any other classification.

RELIABILITY AS THE CORRELATION BETWEEN SCORES ON PARALLEL TESTS

As noted in the previous sections, the quantity ρ_{xt} is only of theoretical interest because true scores can never be obtained in practice. However, the correlation between two parallel tests can be shown to be equivalent to the correlation between true and observed scores. In this section, this equivalence is shown mathematically. I begin by expressing the observed scores for two parallel tests as

$$x_1 = t_1 + e_1$$
$$x_2 = t_2 + e_2$$

The correlation between these two scores (assuming, as before, that the X values are expressed as deviations from their means) is

$$\rho_{X_1 X_2} = \frac{\sum x_1 x_2}{N \sigma_{X_1} \sigma_{X_2}} \tag{7.16}$$

As before, I replace the x values with their equivalent forms $t + e$ to obtain

$$\rho_{X_1 X_2} = \frac{\sum (t_1 + e_1)(t_2 + e_2)}{N \sigma_{X_1} \sigma_{X_2}} \tag{7.17}$$

Expanding this expression yields

$$\rho_{X_1 X_2} = \frac{\sum t_1 t_2}{N \sigma_{X_1} \sigma_{X_2}} + \frac{\sum t_1 e_2}{N \sigma_{X_1} \sigma_{X_2}} \frac{\sum t_2 e_1}{N \sigma_{X_1} \sigma_{X_2}} + \frac{\sum e_1 e_2}{N \sigma_{X_1} \sigma_{X_2}} \tag{7.18}$$

The last three terms can be shown to equal zero, because they involve relations of error scores with either true scores or with other error scores (see Crocker & Algina, 1986, p. 116 for a more detailed explanation). Recall from a previous section that error scores cannot be correlated with anything because they are assumed to be random. Also, remember that parallel tests have equal true scores and equal observed score variances and standard deviations (i.e., $t_1 = t_2$ and $\sigma_{X_1} = \sigma_{X_2}$. Given these facts, the expression in Equation 7.18 simplifies to

$$\rho_{X_1 X_2} = \frac{\sum t^2}{N \sigma_X^2} \tag{7.19}$$

Finally, because $(\sum t^2)/N = \sigma_T^2$, the expression becomes

$$\rho_{X_1 X_2} = \frac{\sigma_T^2}{\sigma_X^2} \tag{7.20}$$

The expression in Equation 7.20 is known as the reliability coefficient, a measure of the proportion of variance in the observed scores (X) that is due to differences in the true scores (T). If a test is reported to have a reliability coefficient of .90, this can be interpreted to mean that .90, or 90% of the variance in observed scores is due to true score variation (and, conversely, that only 10% is due to error).

The reliability coefficient expressed in Equation 7.20 is more useful than the purely theoretical expression in Equation 7.14 because it can be obtained from observed scores on two parallel tests. However, the reliability coefficient of Equation 7.20 is still somewhat theoretical because it is based on the very strong assumptions of parallel tests. In applied testing situations, it is unlikely that two tests will be strictly parallel, and to the extent that they are not, the reliability coefficient from Equation 7.20 will underestimate the true reliability. Thus, although the reliability coefficient just derived provides a useful starting point, it is not commonly used in practice. The chapters that follow discuss several methods of obtaining reliability coefficients that are based on less restrictive assumptions.

SUMMARY

The concept of reliability is central to measurement theory because it has to do with the degree to which scores are consistent across conditions such as different sets of items, test forms, or testing occasions. Any test score represents a snapshot of behavior obtained from a limited set of the conditions of interest. For example, when interpreting a score based on 20 addition items, a teacher is not typically interested in students' ability to answer only these 20 items. Instead, the teacher is usually interested in students' scores because they are an indication of students' likely performance on other, similar items. If such generalizations cannot be made, scores are of limited use.

In this chapter, I discussed the theoretical underpinnings of reliability, which are rooted in CTT. The CTT model is a simple, yet powerful, one in which observed scores are posited to be the sum of a true score and an error score. The error part of a person's score is the part attributable to any random process, such as fatigue, inattention, mismarking the answer sheet, or confusion in interpreting an item. Although such processes will affect a person's responses on a particular testing, these effects are random in the sense that they would not occur in the same way upon retesting. The true score is, hypothetically, the average score persons would obtain if they were to take a test over and over again, with their memory reset after each testing. The true score is hypothesized to remain constant across repeated testings. Because the observed score is the sum of the true and error scores, it follows that fluctuations in observed scores are the result of fluctuations in error scores.

Theoretically, reliability is defined as the correlation between true and observed scores, or, equivalently, as one minus the correlation between error and observed scores. A practical problem with such a definition is that true scores are not available, as they exist only in theory. To obtain a real-life reliability coefficient, we must resort to other methods of obtaining measures of reliability. In this chapter I have described how this can be done by correlating the scores on two parallel tests. Parallel tests are those with equal true score means and equal true, error, and observed score variances. Because the assumptions of parallel tests are quite stringent, other methods of assessing reliability have been developed in which these assumptions are relaxed somewhat. Other methods of assessing reliability are discussed in the next chapter.

EXERCISES

1. Define the quantities X, T, and E from CTT. How are these related?

2. According to CTT, if a test is perfectly reliable:

    a. What should the correlation between T and X equal? Why?

    b. Which should be larger: the variance of X or the variance of T? Why?

3. The reliability index ρ_{xt} is the correlation between observed (X) and true (T) scores.

    a. Why is this index only of theoretical interest?

    b. In what sense is the correlation between X and T a measure of reliability?

4. Instead of correlating observed and true scores, reliability can be assessed by correlating two observed scores. What is the logic behind this?

5. Which of the following is a correct interpretation of a reliability coefficient (as defined in Equation 7.20) of .80? (Choose all that are true.)

    a. 80% of the variance in the observed scores is due to true score differences.

    b. A person's true score is equal to his or her observed score 80% of the time.

    c. 20% of the differences in observed scores is due to error.

6. The data in Table 7.1 are observed score means and variances for 5 test items. Are these items likely parallel, tau-equivalent, or congeneric? Explain.

TABLE 7.1. Observed Score Means and Variances for Question 6

Item	1	2	3	4	5
Mean	1.2	2.7	5.0	4.9	4.1
Variance	1.5	1.0	0.5	1.2	1.4

7. What is the difference between tau-equivalence and essential tau-equivalence?

8. The reliability coefficient from Equation 7.20 is based on the assumption that items are (choose one):

    a. congeneric

    b. essentially tau-equivalent

c. parallel

d. tau-equivalent

9. If the assumption from Question 8 is violated, the reliability coefficient from Equation 7.20 will be:

a. overestimated.

b. neither over- nor underestimated.

c. underestimated.

8

Methods of Assessing Reliability

As pointed out in Chapter 7, there are many conditions over which test scores can vary. In some situations, researchers might be interested in determining how much scores would vary across different sets of items, while in other situations interest might center on inconsistencies across different time points or raters. Because of this, different methods of assessing reliability have been developed that take into account different types of random error. As noted in Chapter 7, some of these methods are based on assumptions that are not as strict as those of parallel measures.

In this chapter, I discuss reliability coefficients that are appropriate for assessing inconsistencies or random errors due to differences in items, in time points, and in test forms. In the previous chapter, I introduced these as, respectively, *coefficients of internal consistency*, *coefficients of stability*, and *coefficients of equivalence*. Following the discussion of these coefficients, I introduce and discuss the *standard error of measurement*, which can be used to determine the approximate amount of error in an individual score. Finally, I discuss the issues inherent in assessing the *reliability of difference scores*. Difference scores, as the name implies, are the difference between two scores obtained at different time points and are of interest when measuring growth or change across time.

INTERNAL CONSISTENCY

One source of error in test scores is the items themselves. Violation of the item-writing conventions discussed in Chapters 4 and 5 can result in problems such as confusing wording, items that are irrelevant to the construct, vocabulary that is unfamiliar to respondents, or cognitive items that have more than one answer. Problems such as these will result in inconsistent responses for two reasons. First, not all respondents will be affected in the same manner by such wording. Second, such wording interferes with respondents' ability to express their true level of the construct. Internal consistency coefficients assess the degree to which responses are consistent across items within a scale. Such coefficients are based on the idea, discussed in Chapter 7, that a correlation between two observed scores that measure the same construct will reflect their shared true score variance, and not shared error variance. This is because errors are assumed to be random and therefore should not have any shared variance. Even when there is only one form of a test, there will still be error due to inconsistencies across item responses. For such situations, reliability coefficients have been developed that are based on the idea that any test with multiple items can be considered as a composite of the scores on all the individual items. In this sense, the items are treated as multiple "mini-forms" of the test. Reliability coefficients are then developed as the reliability of a composite composed of all the items. Because such widely used reliability coefficients as coefficient alpha are based on the framework of the reliability of a composite, this framework is covered in detail in the following sections.

Reliability of a Composite

An early approach to estimating the reliability of a test was to split the test into two halves and correlate the resulting two scores. This approach mimics that of correlating scores on two parallel forms of a test, or on two scores from the same test obtained at different times, but it can be used in situations where neither scores from two test forms nor scores from two test administrations are available. In theory, the test could be split into thirds, fourths, or any fraction, with the ultimate split being one in which each item is treated as a sort of "mini-test." The latter is the approach taken in developing coefficient alpha. I begin here with a general development of the reliability of a composite of parallel parts, which could consist of any fraction of the test. First, here are some rules governing composite scores:

1. The reliability of a composite consisting of component parts $(A + B + C + \cdots + K)$, where A–K are the components, is equal to the variance of the true scores divided by the variance of the observed scores. This follows from our earlier definition of reliability as the ratio of true to observed score variance.

2. The variance of a composite is equal to the sum of the k variances (one for each component) plus the sum of the $k(k-1)$ covariances of the components $(A, B, C, \text{etc.})$ with each other. There are only $k(k-1)$ covariances because the diagonal of a covariance matrix contains the covariances of each variable with itself; these are the variances of the variables. There are k variances, which have already been accounted for as the sum of the k variances. Therefore, they are not included in the sum of the covariances, leaving $k(k-1)$ covariance elements in the matrix.

As an example, a composite of $(A + B + C)$ would have a variance equal to the expectation (remember that word?):

$$E(A+B+C)(A+B+C) = E(A^2 + AB + AC + B^2 + BA + BC + C^2 + CA + CB) \quad (8.1)$$

The expectations of A^2, B^2, and C^2 are their variances, and the expectations of terms such as AB and BC are the covariances. So, you can verify that there are k (in this case, three) variance terms and $k(k-1)$, or six covariance terms (two each of AB, AC, and BC). Recall that in a correlation or covariance matrix, the values below the diagonal will also appear above the diagonal, yielding two of each correlation or covariance element (i.e., AB and BA).

The numerator and denominator of the reliability coefficient described in point 1 above are σ^2_{TC} and σ^2_{XC} where the subscripts TC and XC refer to the true and observed scores of the composite. As stated in point 2, the observed score variance of a composite is equal to the sum of the k variances plus the sum of the $k(k-1)$ covariances, or

$$\sigma^2_{XC} = \sigma^2_A + \sigma^2_B + \cdots + \sigma^2_k + \sum_{i \neq j} \rho_{ij} \sigma_i \sigma_j \quad (8.2)$$

The term $\rho_{ij}\sigma_i\sigma_j$ is one way of expressing the covariance between components i and j (recall that a covariance is a correlation, ρ_{ij}, that is "unstandardized" by multiplying it by the standard deviations of components i and j). Because all of the components are parallel, all of their correlations ρ_{ij} are equal. In addition, all of their variances are equal. This results in

$$\sigma^2_{XC} = k\sigma^2_i + k(k-1)\rho_{ij}\sigma^2_i \quad (8.3)$$

Factoring out the term $k\sigma^2_i$ yields

$$\sigma^2_{XC} = k\sigma^2_i\left[1 + (k-1)\rho_{ij}\right] \quad (8.4)$$

Recall from a previous section that, for parallel measures, ρ_{ij} is the reliability coefficient (the correlation between scores on two parallel measures). So, Equation 8.4 can be rewritten as

$$\sigma^2_{XC} = k\sigma^2_i\left[1 + (k-1)\rho_{ii'}\right] \quad (8.5)$$

Here, and in the remainder of the book, I use the term $\rho_{ii'}$ for reliability. The expression in Equation 8.5 represents the observed score variance of a composite made up of parallel measures. Next, I obtain the true score variance of a composite in a similar fashion as

$$\sigma^2_{TC} = \sigma^2_{T_A} + \sigma^2_{T_B} + \cdots + \sigma^2_{T_k} + \sum_{i \neq j} \rho_{T_iT_j}\sigma_{T_i}\sigma_{T_j} \quad (8.6)$$

Because the components are parallel and because true scores on parallel tests correlate perfectly, the terms $\rho_{T_iT_j}$ are all equal to 1, the $\sigma^2_{T_k}$ are all equal, and the σ_{T_i} terms are all equal. This allows simplification of Equation 8.6 to

$$\sigma_{TC}^2 = k\sigma_{T_i}^2 + k(k-1)\sigma_{T_i}^2 \tag{8.7}$$

The expression in Equation 8.7 simplifies to

$$\sigma_{TC}^2 = k\sigma_{T_i}^2 + k^2\sigma_{T_i}^2 - k\sigma_{T_i}^2 = k^2\sigma_{T_i}^2 \tag{8.8}$$

This is the true score variance of a composite of k parallel measures and the numerator of the formula for the reliability of such a composite. Putting together the numerator in Equation 8.8 with the denominator from Equation 8.5 gives the reliability of a composite as

$$\rho_{CC'} = \frac{k^2\sigma_{T_i}^2}{k\sigma_i^2\left[1+(k-1)\rho_{ii'}\right]} \tag{8.9}$$

Note that the expression in Equation 8.9 contains the ratio $\sigma_{T_i}^2/\sigma_i^2$, or the ratio of true to observed score variance, which is the reliability $\rho_{ii'}$. Equation 8.9 therefore simplifies to

$$\rho_{CC'} = \frac{k^2\rho_{ii'}}{k\left[1+(k-1)\rho_{ii'}\right]} = \frac{k\rho_{ii'}}{1+(k-1)\rho_{ii'}} \tag{8.10}$$

The Spearman–Brown Prophecy Formula and Split-Half Reliability

The final expression in Equation 8.10 is the reliability of a composite made up of parallel components. This formula shows that the reliability of a composite is a function of the reliability of a single component and the number of components.

If the test is split into two equal halves, the value of k from that formula will be equal to two, and the formula becomes

$$\rho_{CC'} = \frac{2\rho_{ii'}}{1+\rho_{ii'}} \tag{8.11}$$

The formula in Equation 8.11 is known as the *corrected* or *adjusted split-half reliability*. One way to obtain an internal consistency reliability coefficient is to split a test in half and correlate the two halves. The correlation between the two halves is the quantity ρ_{ii} in Equation 8.11. However, note that this quantity is the reliability of only half a test; to estimate what the reliability of the full test would be, this value must be adjusted by applying Equation 8.11. This is sometimes referred to as "stepping up" the reliability coefficient obtained from correlating the two half tests. Although such coefficients are often reported in the literature, I agree with McDonald (1999), who states that there is "no good reason" (p. 95) to use Equation 8.11 to estimate reliability. This is because (1) this formulation does not use all of the available information in the test, being based on only half the test, and (2) it does not yield a unique estimate because there are many ways in which a test could be split in half. Coefficient alpha, discussed in the next section, was developed, in part, as an effort to overcome these problems.

The formula in Equation 8.10 is also known as the *Spearman–Brown prophecy formula* because it can be used to estimate, or "prophesy" how the value of a reliability coefficient will change as the number of components changes. For example, suppose that the reliability of one component, or item, is .5 and there are three components, or items ($k = 3$). Then,

$$\rho_{CC} = \frac{3(.5)}{1+(3-1).5} = \frac{1.5}{2} = .75$$

By including three components rather than just one, reliability increases from .5 to .75. More generally, k is often taken to be the factor by which the number of components or items on a test changes. If a 10-item test with a reliability of .8 were reduced to 5 items, k would be .5, and the reliability of the new 5-item composite would be

$$\rho_{CC} = \frac{.5(.8)}{1+(1-.5).8} = \frac{.4}{1-.4} = \frac{.4}{.6} \cong .67$$

Here, k is .5 because the number of items changes from 10 to 5, so the factor by which the number of components changes is .5.

Coefficient Alpha

I have noted two problems with estimating reliability through the split-half method; it is not based on all the available information, and it does not yield a unique value. In addition, recall that the formulation of composite reliability in the previous section was premised on the assumption that all components were parallel. In real life, however, this assumption is not likely to hold, as components may very well have different observed score, true score, and error variances. This is particularly true if the components are individual items on a test rather than randomly created half-tests. If the assumptions of parallelism do not hold, the quantity obtained from Equation 8.10 will be an underestimate of the true reliability of the test. In practice, a researcher would not know the exact amount by which reliability was underestimated, but the greater the departure from parallelism, the greater the underestimation.

Cronbach (1951) developed a formula that is now generally referred to as *coefficient alpha* (α) or *Cronbach's alpha* (although Cronbach himself did not use the latter term). The formula for coefficient alpha is based on all of the items in a test; no splitting of the test is required. In his 1951 paper, Cronbach showed that coefficient alpha was equivalent to the average of all possible split halves of a test. Thus, alpha overcomes the first two problems noted in the previous section (failure to use all of the information and to yield a unique value) and is therefore preferable to split-half reliability coefficients in nearly all situations (one exception is noted later in this chapter). Cronbach did not specifically address the issue of parallelism. Instead, Cronbach (1951; Cronbach & Shavelson, 2004) noted that he developed alpha on the basis of a *domain sampling model* in which items are randomly sampled from a domain of items that all measure the same construct. If such random sampling truly holds, items should be randomly equivalent and will therefore meet the assumptions of parallelism.

Lord and Novick (1968), however, showed that coefficient alpha provides an accurate estimate of reliability under weaker assumptions than those of parallelism. Specifically, Lord and Novick showed, based on a proof from Guttman (1945), that coefficient alpha will be equal to the true reliability of a test if items are (at least) essentially tau-equivalent. As noted previously, the assumptions of essential tau-equivalence are weaker than those of parallelism; essentially, tau-equivalent measures have true score means that differ by (at most) an additive constant and can have different error variances. If essential tau-equivalence does not hold, coefficient alpha is said to be a *lower bound* of reliability; that is, the true reliability may be higher than alpha. Because of this, the formula for alpha is typically presented as an inequality, and its derivation is based on the following statements about inequalities.

If items or components of a test are not strictly parallel, the following inequalities hold:

1. The true score variance of at least one component will be greater than or equal to the covariance of that component with any other component. In symbols, $\sigma^2_{T_j} \geq \text{cov}_{ij}$.

2. The sum of the true score variances will be greater than or equal to twice their covariances: $\sigma^2_{T_i} + \sigma^2_{T_j} \geq 2\text{cov}_{T_iT_j}$. (For the mathematically minded, this is based on the Cauchy–Schwartz inequality.) This and the previous point follow from the fact that the covariance of two true scores can be expressed as $\rho_{T_iT_j}\sigma_{T_i}\sigma_{T_j}$, and if tests are parallel $\rho_{T_iT_j}$ is equal to one and the variances (and standard deviations) of the two true scores will be equal. The quantity $2\text{cov}_{T_iT_j}$ would therefore be equal to $2(1)\sigma_{T_i}\sigma_{T_j}$, and because σ_{T_i} and σ_{T_j} are equal for parallel measures, $\sigma_{T_i}\sigma_{T_j}$ is equivalent to σ^2_T. The expression on the right-hand side of the inequality can therefore be written as $2\sigma^2_T$. On the left-hand side of the inequality, $\sigma^2_{T_i}$ and $\sigma^2_{T_j}$ are equal, so the expression $\sigma^2_{T_i} + \sigma^2_{T_j}$ can be written as $2\sigma^2_T$. These reexpressions show that, if the components are parallel, the inequality becomes an equality. However, if the two tests are not parallel, $\rho_{T_iT_j}$ will be less than one, and the right-hand side of the inequality must be less than the left-hand side.

3. The sum of the k true score variances will be greater than or equal to the sum of the $k(k-1)$ covariances divided by $k-1$:

$$\sum \sigma^2_{T_i} \geq \frac{\sum_{i \neq j} \text{cov}_{T_iT_j}}{k-1}$$

Though perhaps not obvious, this is simply an extension of point 2 to situations with more than two components.

A final fact I will use in obtaining coefficient alpha is that the covariances among observed scores are equal to the covariances among true scores: $\text{cov}_{ij} = \text{cov}_{T_iT_j}$. I can therefore substitute cov_{ij} for $\text{cov}_{T_iT_j}$ in points 1–3 as well as in the derivations that follow. Armed with these facts, I can now proceed to the derivation of coefficient alpha (Based on that presented in Crocker & Algina, 1986, p. 121) as a lower bound to reliability.

In these derivations, I make use of population values of parameters (σ), resulting in a population value of coefficient alpha. In practice, population values of parameters are replaced by their sample estimates to obtain sample values of alpha.

To begin, then, the sum of the true score covariances among the k components is added to each side of the inequality in point 3 to yield

$$\sum \sigma_{T_i}^2 + \sum_{i \neq j} \text{cov}_{ij} \geq \frac{\sum_{i \neq j} \text{cov}_{ij}}{k-1} + \sum_{i \neq j} \text{cov}_{ij} \tag{8.12}$$

On the right-hand side of Equation 8.12, a common denominator can be obtained as

$$\frac{\sum_{i \neq j} \text{cov}_{ij}}{k-1} + \frac{(k-1)\sum_{i \neq j} \text{cov}_{ij}}{k-1} = \frac{\sum_{i \neq j} \text{cov}_{ij}}{k-1} + \frac{k\sum_{i \neq j} \text{cov}_{ij}}{k-1} - \frac{\sum_{i \neq j} \text{cov}_{ij}}{k-1} = \frac{k}{k-1}\sum_{i \neq j} \text{cov}_{ij}$$
$$\tag{8.13}$$

(Note that the first and last terms after the first equals sign cancel out.)

The left-hand side of Equation 8.12 is equal to our earlier definition of the variance of a composite (the sum of the variances plus the sum of the covariances), although in this case these are the variances and covariances of the true scores (remember that the covariances of the true scores are equal to the covariances of the observed scores). I therefore express the term to the left of the inequality as $\sigma_{T_c}^2$ and, substituting this expression into Equation 8.12, rewrite the original equation as

$$\sigma_{T_c}^2 \geq \frac{k}{k-1}\sum_{i \neq j} \text{cov}_{ij} \tag{8.14}$$

Dividing both sides of the equation by the observed variance of the composite, σ_C^2, yields the definition for the reliability of a composite.

$$\frac{\sigma_{T_c}^2}{\sigma_C^2} \geq \frac{k}{k-1}\left(\frac{\sum_{i \neq j} \text{cov}_{ij}}{\sigma_C^2}\right) \tag{8.15}$$

Because $\sigma_C^2 = \sum \sigma_i^2 + \sum_{i \neq j} \text{cov}_{ij}$ and therefore $\sum_{i \neq j} \text{cov}_{ij} = \sigma_C^2 - \sum \sigma_i^2$, I can substitute the latter term for the numerator in the right-hand side of Equation 8.15, yielding

$$\frac{\sigma_{T_c}^2}{\sigma_C^2} \geq \frac{k}{k-1}\left(\frac{\sigma_C^2 - \sum \sigma_i^2}{\sigma_C^2}\right) \tag{8.16}$$

Because the same term appears in both the numerator and denominator of the expression within parentheses, Equation 8.16 can be simplified to

$$\rho_{CC} \geq \frac{k}{k-1}\left(1 - \frac{\sum \sigma_i^2}{\sigma_C^2}\right) \tag{8.17}$$

This is the formula for coefficient alpha, which can be seen as a general expression for the reliability of a composite consisting of k components, or, more commonly, of tests consisting of k items.

Like all reliability coefficients, alpha ranges from zero to one, with higher values indicating greater reliability. The term $\Sigma \sigma_i^2$ is the sum of the k item variances, and the term σ_C^2 is the variance of the total test score. (In general, this is written as σ_X^2, but I have used σ_C^2 to emphasize that coefficient alpha is based on the rules for the reliability of a composite.) You may wonder why the total test variance would not be simply the sum of the item variances. The answer stems from the earlier definition of the variance of a composite as the sum of the component variances *plus* the sum of the component covariances. The term σ_C^2 contains both the variances *and* *covariances* of the items, whereas the term $\Sigma \sigma_i^2$ contains only the item variances. We can therefore formulate alpha as

$$\rho_{CC} \geq \frac{k}{k-1}\left(1 - \frac{\sum \sigma_i^2}{\sum_{i \neq j} \mathrm{cov}_{ij} + \sum \sigma_i^2}\right) \tag{8.18}$$

Though not as straightforward computationally, this expression is useful because it shows how alpha is influenced by the item covariances. If the item covariances were all 0, the last fraction in Equation 8.18 would equal 1, and reliability would be 0. The denominator of the last term is greater than the numerator to the extent that item covariances are greater than 0; the larger they are, the greater the reliability. This makes sense when we consider that alpha is a measure of internal consistency, or interrelatedness, of the items. Answers to items that are highly related to each other will be more consistent and should therefore yield more reliable test scores. This is, in part, what coefficient alpha reflects. Thus, alpha and other internal consistency coefficients are largely a function of the correlations, or covariances, among items.

Although not as obvious, alpha is also affected by the number of items on the test. This is because, as the number of items increases, the number of elements in $\Sigma \sigma_i^2$ (the sum of item variances) increases at a much slower rate than the number of elements comprising σ_C^2 (the sum of item variances plus the sum of item covariances). For example, with five items, there are five item variances in $\Sigma \sigma_i^2$, but there are five variances plus $5(5-1)$, or 20, covariances in σ_C^2. With 10 items, there are 10 variances plus $10(10-1)$, or 90, item covariances in σ_C^2. Thus, the sheer number of item covariances can contribute substantially to the magnitude of σ_C^2 relative to $\Sigma \sigma_i^2$. Although it may seem as though the effect of the number of items would be conveyed through the term $k/(k-1)$ in the formula for coefficient alpha, DeVellis (2003, p. 35) explains that this ratio is simply a correction for the fact that the numerator and denominator are based on different numbers of elements.

Given the discussion above, you can see that high values of coefficient alpha will be obtained when (1) items are highly intercorrelated, (2) there are many items, or (3) both. Thus, one way in which researchers can increase the alpha value for scores from a particular test is by increasing the number of items on the test. However, this does not mean that items can be added willy-nilly in the expectation that alpha values will increase; the items added must be at least equal in quality to those already on the scale for this to happen. Another way to increase the value of alpha is to use items that are highly correlated. That is, the items added must have correlations with the original items that are at least as high as those among the original items.

However, Green and Yang (2009) make the valid point that choosing only the most highly correlated items can lead to extremely narrow scales. Consider, for example, the following five-item scale:

1. I enjoy measurement theory.
2. Measurement theory is the best thing since sliced bread.
3. Measurement theory really makes my day.
4. If it weren't for measurement theory, I don't know what I'd do.
5. I can't get enough of measurement theory.[1]

Although I am sure you will agree that such a scale would have many intriguing applications, it would not yield a particularly broad perspective on feelings toward measurement theory. However, responses to these items would likely be quite consistent, resulting in a high alpha value even though there are only five items.

Alpha and Unidimensionality

A related issue has to do with the relation, if any, between alpha and *unidimensionality*. As its name implies, unidimensionality is the extent to which a scale measures only one dimension. This may seem like a simple notion. Unfortunately, in the context of internal consistency, it is not. This is because, like many aspects of measurement theory, it depends on one's interpretation. For example, scales measuring overall cognitive ability often have many subscales, representing different cognitive dimensions such as verbal ability, fluid reasoning, and visual-spatial ability. These subscales are considered to be separable dimensions of cognitive ability, although many are highly intercorrelated. But respondents often receive both an overall general cognitive ability score and scores on each subscale. So, is cognitive ability unidimensional, or is it multidimensional? In one sense, this is a theoretical question. However, the answer to this question is of concern for users of reliability coefficients such as alpha because values of such coefficients will be lower to the extent that scales are not unidimensional. This follows from the fact that coefficient alpha is a function of the correlations among items, and these correlations are likely to be lower for items measuring different dimensions.

Yet, multidimensional tests are not doomed to have low values of alpha. On the contrary, Green, Lissitz, and Mulaik (1977) showed that coefficient alpha can be as high

---

[1] You may recall from Chapter 5 that it is generally not a good idea to include extreme items such as items 2–5 on a scale (see Chapter 5 for an explanation). I use the items here simply to illustrate a point (and to amuse myself).

as .81 for a 10-item test with two completely uncorrelated dimensions. Thus, although alpha values will generally be higher for unidimensional tests, unidimensionality is *not* necessary for obtaining high values of alpha. Thus, it is *not correct* to interpret a high alpha value as an indication that a test is unidimensional. In fact, the study by Green and colleagues shows that high values of alpha can be obtained from either unidimensional or multidimensional tests. Alpha measures the interrelatedness of the items on a test; not of unidimensionality. It is also not the case that high values of alpha indicate that items are measuring the same thing. Items can have high intercorrelations for many reasons, only one of which is that they measure the same thing. However, the converse of the previous statement is true; if items are *not* related, it is difficult to argue that they are measuring a common construct.

Measurement experts disagree on whether the use of coefficient alpha requires the items to be unidimensional. In addition to the argument that values of alpha tend to be lower for multidimensional scales, some experts contend that total scores obtained from multidimensional items are inherently uninterpretable because such scores combine different dimensions, or aspects, of the construct being measured. However, Cronbach himself (1951) stated that it is not necessary for all items to be "factorially similar" for scores to be interpretable; it is just necessary that a large proportion of the covariation among the items is due to a *general* or overall factor. Such general factors are measures of the shared variance among all the subscales or dimensions of the scale. Perhaps the most well-known such factor is the so-called g, or general cognitive ability, factor. g is a measure of the general factor that is common to all dimensions of cognitive ability, whereas the individual subscales such as verbal ability, fluid reasoning, and visual-spatial ability measure more narrowly defined dimensions. Although overall alpha values will be underestimated to some extent for such multidimensional scales, Cronbach states that unless subdimensions of items are relatively uncorrelated, underestimation will not be "serious" (p. 320). Revelle and Zinbarg (2009) also seem relatively comfortable with the use of alpha for tests consisting of a general dimension and several subdimensions. Raykov and Shrout (2002) are less positive about this practice, however, arguing that alpha should not be used with tests that are not strictly unidimensional because such scales are more complex and difficult to interpret.

My own view is that coefficient alpha should be calculated at the level at which test scores are to be interpreted. If subscale scores are to be interpreted, it is important to know the value of coefficient alpha for these. By the same token, if an overall or general factor score is to be interpreted, alpha values for that score should be obtained. If both types of score will be reported, reliability values should be obtained for each.

Criticisms of Coefficient Alpha

Recall that, if items are at least essentially tau-equivalent, coefficient alpha is equal to reliability. However, if items do not meet the assumptions of tau-equivalence, alpha is a lower bound to the true reliability value. This means that alpha will underestimate the true reliability value in such cases. Because alpha is not equal to reliability when essential tau-equivalence is violated, researchers such as Sijtsma (2009) have criticized the use of alpha, stating that other coefficients provide a better estimate of the true reliability value. The alternative index recommended by Sijtsma is known as the *greatest lower bound* (glb). Unfortunately, this index may not be useful in many applied situations because of its large sample size requirements: a sample of 1,000 is needed to obtain unbiased estimates, and this if for a test of only 10 items. An even larger N is needed with more items.

Other researchers (Green & Yang, 2009; McDonald, 1999; Raykov & Marcoulides, 2011; Revelle & Zinbarg, 2009) recommend the use of *coefficient omega*, which can be obtained using confirmatory factor analysis (CFA) methods. However, the sample size needed to use these methods is somewhat larger than that needed to compute coefficient alpha. (I discuss coefficient omega and show how to use structural equation modeling software to estimate it in Chapter 13.)

Although both coefficient omega and the glb will provide more accurate estimates of reliability than alpha for measures that violate essential tau-equivalence, researchers have shown that such violations often have minimal impact. For example, Raykov (1997) has shown that if a scale is composed of at least eight items with intercorrelations of at least .60 and factor loading values differing by no more than .20, coefficient alpha will underestimate the true reliability by, at most, .02. Of course, as the differences among loading values increase and/or the correlations among items decrease, the discrepancy between alpha and true reliability will increase. However, as Raykov's work shows, in many applications, the differences between alpha and true reliability will be minimal.

Effects of Correlated Measurement Errors

Another situation in which coefficient alpha results in a biased estimate of the true reliability is that in which the measurement errors of items are correlated. Although in CTT errors are assumed to be uncorrelated with each other, many researchers have pointed out situations in which it is reasonable to assume that errors might be correlated (Cole, Ciesla, & Steiger, 2007; Fleishman & Benson, 1987; Rozeboom, 1966). For example, in cognitive tests, several items are sometimes based on the same stimulus materials, such as a graph, figure, or reading passage. Respondents who interpret this material incorrectly will likely make similar errors on all of the items. On noncognitive tests, similarities in the wording of items can result in correlated errors because the wording similarity can induce similarities in response patterns. Correlations among errors will increase the observed interitem correlations, which will in turn increase coefficient alpha. As Komaroff (1997) puts it, covariation among errors will "masquerade" as covariance among true scores.

In the formulation of coefficient alpha, it is not possible to separate true score covariance from error covariance, as both serve to increase the overall item covariance. Several studies (e.g., Green & Hershberger, 2000; Gu, Little, & Kingston, 2013; Komaroff, 1997;

Zimmerman, Zumbo, & Lalonde, 1993) have shown that violations of the assumption that errors are uncorrelated result in overestimation of coefficient alpha. As might be expected, this overestimation increases as the (positive) correlations among error scores and the number of such correlations increase. You may wonder whether the inflation of coefficient alpha resulting from correlated errors could cancel out the underestimation caused by violations of essential tau-equivalence. This can indeed happen, as shown in the studies conducted by Gu and colleagues (2013) and by Komaroff (1997). However, given that in practice researchers are not likely to be able to accurately predict the extent of such violations, it is probably not wise to rely on this cancellation effect in the hope of obtaining an unbiased value of alpha. Having said this, I do recommend that researchers consider possible violations of both assumptions when interpreting reported values of alpha. For those who wish to evaluate such assumptions for their own data, the procedures outlined in Chapter 13 can be used to test for violations of both essential tau-equivalence and measurement error independence.

Other Internal Consistency Coefficients

In this section, I discuss two earlier formulations of alpha-like coefficients that are sometimes seen in the literature. Both were developed by Küder and Richardson (1937) in an article in which they produced a series of coefficients. Those discussed here were the 20th and 21st in the series, aptly referred to as KR-20 and KR-21.

KR-20

KR-20 is appropriate for situations in which items are *dichotomously scored*, that is, scored as simply right/wrong or agree/disagree. The formula for KR-20 is

$$\text{KR-20} = \frac{k}{k-1}\left(1 - \frac{\sum p_i q_i}{\sigma_C^2}\right) \tag{8.19}$$

A comparison of this formula with that in Equation 8.17 reveals that the only difference is the replacement of the term $\sum \sigma_i^2$ in Equation 8.17 with the term $\sum p_i q_i$ in the formula for KR-20. The term p_i is the proportion of respondents with correct (or agree) answers, and the term q_i is simply $1 - p_i$. The product $p_i q_i$ is the variance of a dichotomously scored item. Thus, KR-20 is really the same quantity as coefficient alpha, but it applies to the special situation in which items are dichotomously scored with variances equal to $p_i q_i$. If a researcher were washed up on a desert island and had to calculate an internal consistency coefficient by hand, KR-20 would be much easier to compute than alpha because the former coefficient requires only a simple multiplication to obtain the item variance. At the time Küder and Richardson derived KR-20, computers were not in existence, so ease of calculation was a great advantage. Nowadays, however, statistics packages such as SPSS and SAS can easily calculate such coefficients from one's raw data. When using these packages, the distinction between alpha and KR-20 is somewhat blurred, as the programs will simply default to KR-20 if the data are dichotomously scored. Although the coefficient will still be labeled as alpha in the computer output, it is, strictly speaking, actually KR-20. This is really of no consequence; I point it out only to avoid confusion for those using such packages.

KR-21

KR-21 is also a modification of coefficient alpha, based on the assumption that all items have the same mean, or difficulty level. This assumption is clearly untenable for most, if not all, tests, and I present KR-21 here only for historical reasons. In the dark ages before computers, or even calculators, KR-21 was sometimes calculated instead of coefficient alpha because it was much easier to compute by hand. The formula for KR-21 is

$$\text{KR-}21 = \frac{k}{k-1}\left(1 - \frac{\mu(k-\mu)}{k\sigma_C^2}\right)$$ (8.20)

where μ is the mean of the total test scores and k is the number of items on the test (as before). Clearly, it is easier to calculate KR-21 than to compute coefficient alpha, as KR-21 only requires one to know the mean and variance of the total test scores and the number of items; item–level variances are not needed. However, such ease of computation is now a nonissue, given the widespread availability of statistical packages for computers.

Recommended Values for Internal Consistency Indices

How high should values of alpha (or related indices such as KR-20) be? I hesitate to give an answer to this question because estimates of alpha can be affected by many things, such as the purpose of the test, the heterogeneity of the sample from which it was obtained, the conditions of testing, and the number of items. These factors are discussed in a subsequent section of this chapter. Because the determination of an appropriate level of reliability is reliant on so many factors, the guidelines given in this chapter should be taken as only rough approximations. There is no substitute for thoroughly thinking through the context of testing and purposes to which the test will be put and for using these to guide decisions about values of reliability coefficients.

Guidelines for alpha values vary, but Raykov and Marcoulides (2011) recommend values of at least .80. Nunnally's (1978) recommendations are somewhat more nuanced. He provides the following guidelines: .70 for scales in the initial stages of development; .80 for "basic research scales," and .90 as minimum for use in clinical settings. Kaplan and Sarcuzzo (2001) suggest values of up to .95 for clinical settings. The higher values for clinical decisions reflect the serious consequences of such decisions and the need for correspondingly higher standards. The same argument for higher reliabilities could be

made in the context of educational tests that are used for student placement, graduation, or remediation decisions or for licensure or certification tests. Indeed, any test that
will be used to make consequential decisions about students, clients, patients, or others
should contain as little error as possible.

Factors Affecting Internal Consistency Coefficient Values

Item Correlation Levels

Several factors affecting estimates of internal consistency coefficients such as alpha
have already been noted. Such coefficients are based on the intercorrelations of the
items and as such will obviously be affected by them, with higher interitem correlations yielding higher values for internal consistency coefficients. In addition, as
explained previously, values will increase with the number of items. The effects of
adding items to an existing test can be estimated by the Spearman–Brown prophecy
formula from Equation 8.10. However, two caveats apply. First, the items added must
correlate at least as well with the existing items as the existing items correlate with
each other. Second, there is a point of diminishing returns; Kormorita and Graham
(1965) showed that increases in the value of coefficient alpha as a function of the number of items begin to level off at about 19 items. After this point, adding more items
to a test does not provide much of an increase in alpha values. Estimates of internal
consistency coefficients are also affected by the dimensionality of the test, with unidimensional tests generally yielding higher values. However, this is because, overall,
items on multidimensional tests tend to have lower correlations with each other than
do items on unidimensional tests. By definition, items on multidimensional tests are
more correlated with the other items on their dimension than with items on a different dimension.

Level of Sample Heterogeneity

In addition to these factors, estimates of internal consistency coefficients can be affected
by how heterogeneous the sample is with regard to the construct being measured. A
common misconception is that, because reliability has to do with consistency, reliability
estimates will be higher when obtained from a sample in which respondents have very
similar scores. However, nothing could be further from the truth. As Traub and Rowley
(1991, p. 178) point out, reliability can be thought of as the ability of a test to make reliable distinctions among respondents with regard to the construct being measured. Such
distinctions are only possible if respondents have different scores. In fact, the greater
the differences among scores, the easier it is to differentiate respondents based on these
scores. Another way of thinking about this is that, because reliability is the ratio of
true to observed score variance, a low reliability coefficient means that either the error
variance is large or the true score variance is small (or both). Because the error variance
is considered to be random, it should not differ very much sample to sample. However,

samples could differ in true score variance, and the sample with less variance in true scores will yield a lower reliability estimate than the sample with more true score variance, given comparable amounts of error variance.

This is similar to the phenomenon of *restriction of range* of the correlation coefficient, which occurs when a sample lacks variability on one or both of the variables being correlated, resulting in a lower estimate of the correlation coefficient than would have been obtained if the range were not restricted. In the context of reliability coefficients, a similar phenomenon can occur if respondents' scores are restricted in some way. For example, if only students in accelerated or advanced placement classes are selected, scores on cognitive tests are likely to be uniformly high. This will restrict the range of the scores and result in a lower estimate of the reliability coefficient than would have been obtained from a sample with more variation. Similar examples include selecting respondents based on high levels of job performance, blood pressure, or other variables. It should be noted, however, that a sample that is restricted in some way will not *necessarily* yield less variable scores. Variation in scores will be affected only if the variable on which the sample is restricted is related to the scores of interest. As an example, a sample consisting only of weight lifters may well yield restricted scores on measures of strength, but not necessarily on scores of cognitive ability (despite stereotypical notions to the contrary).

The moral of the story is that those reporting reliability estimates should always accompany these estimates with a full description of the sample from which these were obtained. This approach will allow those reading the report to better understand why values may be unusually high or low. It also provides a basis for researchers using the scale to evaluate whether the reliability estimate might be higher or lower for the sample with which they plan to use the scale.

Reliability as a Property of Test Scores from a Particular Sample

In a very real sense, sample estimates of reliability coefficients are just that—estimates. Sample reliability coefficients are estimates of the population reliability value for a particular type of score in a particular population, and these sample estimates vary in the same manner as sample estimates of other population values. This is why contemporary discussions of reliability emphasize that reliability is not a property of the test itself, but of the scores from the test that are obtained from a particular sample. In writing about reliability coefficients, therefore, readers are advised to use language such as "The reliability coefficient estimated from the scores on Test X for our sample was XX" rather than "The reliability of Text X is. . . ." Researchers should always include a description of the sample from which scores were obtained because this will help to put the obtained reliability coefficient value into the proper context.

Effects of Item Type on Internal Consistency

Another factor affecting estimates of internal consistency for cognitive tests is the type of item. Specifically, so-called *objective* item formats such as multiple choice or true–false tend to result in more reliable tests (Traub & Rowley, 1991) than do essay or short-answer items. This is the case for two reasons. First, objective items can be answered more quickly, and so tests based on such items tend to contain more items. As noted earlier, adding items generally results in higher reliability. Second, objective item types are, as the name implies, scored in a more objective manner than essay or other performance items, and this also results in higher reliability coefficients because inconsistencies in scoring, a form of error, are reduced.

Effects of Speededness on Internal Consistency

Another aspect of cognitive tests noted in Chapter 3 is the level of test speededness. Until fairly recently, conventional wisdom held that coefficients of internal consistency such as alpha should *not* be used with highly speeded tests. To understand the reasoning on which this recommendation was based, recall that on pure speed tests, the items are fairly easy. Thus, respondents will answer correctly on those items they are able to reach, but not-reached items will be scored as incorrect. For this reason, respondents' scores on the answered items will be very consistent (all correct) and scores on the not-reached items will also be very consistent (all incorrect), and this pattern will be consistent across respondents. Such response patterns will result in spuriously high estimates of alpha and other internal consistency coefficients. That is, high values of coefficient alpha will be obtained not because of similarities in item content but because of the speeded nature of the test.

However, Attali (2005) has pointed out that this reasoning assumes respondents will not guess on the not-reached items but will instead simply skip them. If respondents were to randomly guess at the answers to not-reached items, responses would not be consistent, as some guesses would be successful and some would not. Under such a scenario, values of coefficient alpha would be *lower* for speeded tests. Attali noted that the overall effect of speededness on coefficient alpha would depend on the number of item pairs on which respondents (1) answered both items (AA pattern), (2) guessed on both items (GG pattern), or (3) guessed on one item but not on another (AG pattern). Item pairs on which the majority of respondents exhibited AA and GG patterns would have inflated correlations, whereas those on which respondents exhibited AG patterns would have deflated correlations. So, if the number of AA and GG patterns was greater than the number of AG patterns, coefficient alpha would be inflated. If the number of AG patterns was greater, coefficient alpha would be deflated. Attali argued that, for speeded tests, the number of AG patterns would be greater than the number of AA or GG patterns.

In response to Attali (2005), Wise and DeMars (2009) brought up the interesting point that guessing does not occur only on speeded tests. These researchers noted that guessing is also common in low-stakes tests on which the results have little consequence for respondents. And unlike on speeded tests for which guessing is seen only for not-reached items at the end of the test, guessing on low-stakes tests occurs throughout the test. The significance of this finding is that it provides for the possibility of more AA and GG patterns, thus inflating values of coefficient alpha. Wise and

DeMars provide data from low-stakes tests showing that coefficient alpha is indeed higher for low-stakes tests on which rapid guessing occurs. The effects of test speededness are therefore not as straightforward as previously believed, and researchers should think carefully about the possible ramifications of speededness and of rapid guessing on testing outcomes.

Effects of Level of Standardization on Internal Consistency

Finally, the level of standardization of the testing procedures will affect internal consistency coefficients. Thorndike (2005) points out that when testing companies obtain the reliability coefficients reported in test manuals, aspects of test standardization such as the test setting, the instructions given, and the test proctoring are typically much stricter than those that are used in practice. As a result, estimates of reliability coefficients reported in test manuals are often somewhat higher than those obtained in more typical settings. One specific aspect of the testing procedure that can have a substantial effect on reliability estimates from cognitive tests is the instructions about guessing. Because respondents differ in their propensity to guess, all respondents should be provided with specific instructions about whether or not they should guess. Such instructions may even include information about situations in which guessing is more likely to result in a correct answer (e.g., if the respondent can eliminate one or more of the distractors in a multiple-choice test). A related issue in the context of noncognitive tests is the degree to which respondents interpret the response options in the same way. As noted in Chapter 5, labeling each response option can help to ensure similar interpretations across respondents, as can ensuring questions are clear and unambiguous.

The next section presents examples of the computations for coefficient alpha using two different sets of data designed to illustrate the effects of several of the factors just discussed.

Computational Examples for Coefficient Alpha

Table 8.1 shows fictitious answers of 20 respondents to six items. Note that, although respondents differ in their item responses and total scores, the *pattern* of responses is quite similar across respondents. Responses are consistently higher for items 4, 5, and 6 than for items 1, 2, and 3. It is this type of consistency that is measured by coefficient alpha. Given this consistency, the estimate of coefficient alpha can be expected to be quite high, even though the number of items is fairly small. For the data in Table 8.1, alpha would be calculated as

$$\alpha = \left(\frac{6}{5}\right)\left(1 - \frac{1.25 + 1.54 + 1.61 + 1.79 + 1.25 + 1.35}{49.05}\right) = \frac{6}{5}\left(1 - \frac{8.79}{49.05}\right) = 0.985$$

TABLE 8.1. Data Showing Consistency across Item Responses

Respondent	Item 1	Item 2	Item 3	Item 4	Item 5	Item 6	Total score (X)
1	1	1	1	2	2	2	9
2	1	1	1	2	2	2	9
3	1	1	2	2	2	2	10
4	1	1	1	1	2	2	8
5	2	2	2	3	3	3	15
6	2	2	2	3	3	3	15
7	2	2	3	3	3	3	16
8	2	2	2	2	3	3	14
9	3	3	3	4	4	4	21
10	3	3	3	4	4	4	21
11	3	3	4	4	4	4	22
12	3	3	3	3	4	4	20
13	4	4	4	5	5	5	27
14	4	4	4	5	5	5	27
15	4	4	5	5	5	5	28
16	4	4	4	4	5	5	26
17	4	5	5	5	5	5	29
18	2	4	2	5	4	5	22
19	1	1	1	1	2	2	8
20	2	2	2	2	3	3	14
	σ_i^2 (item variances)						σ_C^2 (total test variance)
	1.25	1.54	1.61	1.79	1.25	1.35	49.05

As expected, the estimate of coefficient alpha is very high; in fact, it is close to perfect! This is because of the response consistency noted previously.

In contrast to the data in Table 8.1, the data in Table 8.2 show little consistency in the response patterns of the 20 respondents. Some have high scores for items 4, 5, and 6, others' highest scores are for items 1, 2, and 3, and still others have scores of about equal magnitude on all of the items. Note also that the total scores across respondents are quite similar, resulting in a total score variance that is quite a bit lower than that for the data in Table 8.1. All of these things should contribute to a lower estimated value of alpha.

Sure enough, you can see from the following calculations that the estimate of alpha is quite low for these data:

$$\alpha = \left(\frac{6}{5}\right)\left(1 - \frac{1.03 + 0.39 + 0.39 + 0.53 + 1.45 + 1.04}{7.25}\right) = \frac{6}{5}\left(1 - \frac{4.83}{7.25}\right) = 0.401$$

TABLE 8.2. Data Showing a Lack of Consistency across Item Responses

Respondent	Item 1	Item 2	Item 3	Item 4	Item 5	Item 6	Total score (X)
1	1	2	3	4	5	4	19
2	1	3	2	4	2	5	17
3	1	2	3	5	4	4	19
4	2	2	2	4	4	4	18
5	2	3	3	4	4	5	21
6	1	2	3	4	5	5	20
7	1	3	3	5	5	4	21
8	2	2	3	4	5	4	20
9	3	3	3	3	2	3	17
10	2	2	3	3	5	4	19
11	2	3	3	4	3	3	18
12	4	2	3	2	3	3	17
13	3	3	4	3	1	3	17
14	1	2	3	3	5	4	18
15	1	2	2	4	5	4	18
16	4	3	3	4	5	5	24
17	1	1	1	3	4	2	12
18	1	1	2	3	3	2	12
19	3	2	3	4	4	2	18
20	1	2	3	3	5	2	16

	σ_i^2 (item variances)						σ_C^2 (total test variance)
	1.03	0.39	0.39	0.53	1.45	1.04	7.25

TEST–RETEST RELIABILITY

Test–retest reliability is concerned with the consistency, or stability, of test scores across different time points. This type of reliability is important for situations in which scores will be obtained at different times and compared, such as in a pre–posttest situation. Test–retest reliability information is also important for situations in which test scores will be used for diagnosis, selection, or placement decisions. When test scores are used in making such decisions, the outcome, in the form of a treatment or placement, does not typically occur immediately but is delayed to some extent. For example, tests used to determine placement of college students into an appropriate math class are typically given the summer prior to their matriculation, but the students do not take the math class until the following fall or spring semester. A lack of stability in the test scores could mean that students would have achieved very different scores if they had been tested earlier or later in the summer. If this were the case, the placements made on the basis of those scores would be incorrect and students would spend a semester in a course that was too easy or too difficult for them. The same logic applies to tests used for diagnosis and selection decisions.

For such situations, it is very important that information regarding the stability of test scores is obtained *before* using the test. Unless the test is known to yield stable scores ahead of time, it is not possible to discern whether poor placements or diagnoses are the result of instability in test scores, changes in levels of the construct (e.g., students learning more math content after being tested), or both. Test scores can change across time because of (1) lack of reliability of the measure being used, (2) changes in respondents' true levels of the construct being measured, or (3) a combination of these. Test–retest reliability is concerned with the first of these, but in a typical test–retest reliability study it is not possible to determine whether differences in scores are due to 1, 2, or 3.

To take another example, suppose researchers are conducting a study in which respondents take part in an intervention designed to improve their ability to monitor their own health. A measure of this ability is developed and administered before and after the intervention. However, respondents' scores are no different after the intervention than before. Is this because ability levels have not changed, or because the measure was unstable and therefore unable to detect changes, or both? Again, without knowing a priori that the scale yields scores that are stable across time, there is no way to answer this question.

For situations involving pre–post comparisons of scores or use of scores to make decisions about placement, diagnosis, or selection, researchers must therefore either choose measures that are known to yield consistent scores across time or be prepared to obtain such evidence themselves. In the latter case, the researcher should first administer the scale of interest to the same respondents at two (or more) time points with no intervention or treatment in between. Ideally, the length of time between the two administrations should be the same as that which will elapse between the pre- and post-test or between the scale administration and the eventual placement or selection. The reliability coefficient, known in this case as a *coefficient of stability,* is simply the correlation between the two scores. If this coefficient is sufficiently high, the researcher is justified in basing decisions regarding pre–post changes, diagnosis, or placement on the test scores. If, however, the coefficient is low, it will not be possible for the researcher to unambiguously interpret pre–post differences or to make defensible decisions regarding future placement or treatment.

Because assessment of the stability of a test can be confounded with actual changes in respondents' true levels of the construct, test–retest reliability is *not* appropriate for measurement of constructs that are not known to be stable. Measures of mood, or of constructs that are known to be context dependent, are not appropriate candidates for test–retest studies. Recall that the purpose of this type of reliability is *not* to determine whether the construct being measured is stable; rather, it is to determine whether the measurements of the construct are stable. However, stability coefficients are not capable of differentiating between these two sources of instability, so researchers must know a priori that the construct is a stable one. Having said this, many constructs of interest in the social sciences are considered to be relatively stable across fairly long time periods, such as creativity, cognitive ability, and some personality characteristics.

Factors Affecting Coefficients of Stability

Because estimates of stability coefficients are simply correlations between scores obtained at two different time points, anything that affects correlation coefficients can affect these estimates. This includes factors such as restriction of range, which was discussed in a previous section. Readers may also recall that if the relationship between two variables is not linear, the commonly used Pearson correlation will typically underestimate the strength of the relationship.

Floor and Ceiling Effects

Both restriction of range and nonlinearity could occur in the context of stability or other reliability coefficients if the test had an insufficient *floor* or *ceiling*. A test with an insufficiently low floor is one on which there is not a sufficient number of items at the low end of the scale. For example, cognitive tests that are too difficult for low-ability respondents may yield very restricted (and low) scores because respondents are unable to answer the majority of the items. A test with an insufficiently high ceiling is one on which there are not enough items at the high end, such as a cognitive test that is too easy or an attitude scale on which respondents agree with most items. Such tests are problematic from a test construction point of view because they do not allow for differentiation among respondents at the low end (floor effect) or high end (ceiling effect) of the scale. In addition, scores from such tests taken at two different time points will be nonlinearly related due to their skewed distributions.

Length of Time between Test Administrations

Because estimates of stability coefficients are based on scores obtained at different times, the length of time between the two test administrations can have a large effect on their values. Recall that values of stability coefficients are affected by (1) changes in true scores, (2) instability due to unreliability of measures, or (3) both of these factors. Changes in true scores can occur because respondents have learned more or changed their attitudes or behaviors in ways that result in actual changes in the construct being measured. For example, if attitudes toward vegetarianism are being measured, some respondents may have viewed a video or television program on animal welfare, or spoken to friends with strong attitudes about the topic and changed their attitudes based on these experiences. If health-related behaviors are being measured, respondents may have become more health conscious because of a friend or family member's illness. These are changes in true scores, as they represent changes in actual attitudes or behaviors.

At the same time, scores could change between time points because some of the items on the measurement instrument are confusing or ambiguous, so that respondents interpret them differently on the two occasions. Or items may require respondents to provide information about the number of times they engaged in a particular behavior. In such cases, respondents may not remember accurately and may err on the side of caution on one occasion while overestimating on another. This will result in different scores on the two occasions, but these differences are due to the unreliability of the measurement instrument. In practice, it is often difficult to know whether changes from one time point to the next represent changes in true scores or are due to unreliability. It may be possible to determine whether respondents' true scores have changed by obtaining information on activities that may have resulted in such changes. Interviews or questionnaires could be used for this purpose. However, the researcher would have to anticipate the collection of such information. For studies in which the time interval is long, allowing ample time for changes in true scores, or the construct under study is thought to be particularly amenable to change, incorporating the collection of such additional information into the research plan may be useful.

Note that, over time, changes in true scores become more likely. This is because opportunities for exposure to media, learning resources, and the opinions of others increase with time. Measurement of attitudes on two consecutive days does not leave much room for attitude change, but over the course of a year change would be more likely. Thus, when planning test–retest reliability studies, researchers must pay careful attention to choosing a reasonable length of time. Researchers studying young children will likely choose shorter time periods than researchers studying adults because young children develop at a much faster rate. As noted previously, researchers planning to use tests for purposes of selection, diagnosis, or prediction should choose time intervals that are consistent with those over which the decision will elapse. For example, researchers developing a math placement test that will be taken by entering college students in June for placement into math courses in September would want to know that scores will be stable over the June to September interval. If not, scores obtained in June may not be predictive of students' needs in September. Thus, it would be important to show that scores are stable over a four-month period. (Of course, some students may learn more math content over the summer, but such vagaries are unavoidable in testing.)

Memory and Practice Effects

Another factor that must be kept in mind in determining an appropriate time interval is the possibility of memory or practice effects. This consideration is particularly salient for situations involving a pre- and posttest. If the test is such that practice involved in taking the test at time one is enough to increase the score at time two, a longer time interval may be desired. One example is a speeded test in which respondents have to hit a certain key on a keyboard as fast as possible. If the test is repeated later in the day or on the next day, the practice effect from the pretest might increase scores for some respondents, making it appear as though scores are inconsistent. Similarly, if respondents can remember answers from the pretest and therefore obtain higher scores on the posttest, scores would appear to be unreliable. Therefore, in planning studies for tests on which practice or memory may affect scores, researchers should conduct some pilot studies to determine an appropriate length of time.

Sensitization Effects

Finally, responding to a test on the first administration may sensitize or otherwise affect respondents in such a way that they answer differently on the next administration. This is most likely to happen with attitude or opinion measures. For example, respondents may be administered a scale measuring an attitude about which they have not thought very much. In the process of answering the questions on the scale, respondents may begin to think more about the issues and perhaps even to research these issues afterward. Because such sensitization will not occur for all respondents in the same way, however, this would result in inconsistent changes in scores.

Because the time period can have a substantial influence on estimates of stability coefficients, those reporting such estimates should always report the time interval over which the estimate was obtained. In addition, as noted previously, relevant characteristics of the sample should be reported. Those choosing tests should pay careful attention to both the value of the coefficient and the time period reported. As users of tests should recognize, high values can often be obtained by choosing an unreasonably short time interval. The interval used should also be congruent with that over which the test will be used to make predictions or placement decisions. If it is not, the test user should take this into account in interpreting the reported estimate of the coefficient. In general, the longer the time interval between tests, the lower the coefficient will be. Therefore, if the use for which the test is planned will require a longer interval, test users should recognize that the reported coefficient may be an overestimate.

Recommended Values for Coefficients of Stability

How high should stability coefficients be? The higher the better, but Crocker and Algina (1986, p. 133) state that "well-constructed" noncognitive scales can yield scores with coefficients in the .80s, and scores from aptitude tests can have values into the .90s. Of course, the length of the time interval over which the values were obtained will have a significant bearing on this magnitude. Researchers should take this into account when interpreting stability coefficients, realizing that values would likely be higher if the time interval had been shorter, and lower if the time interval had been longer. The important point here is that the time interval used for computation of the coefficient should be congruent with the time period of interest to the researcher.

ALTERNATE FORMS RELIABILITY

In many situations, more than one version of a test is available. These versions are designed to be interchangeable, such that the particular version taken does not influence respondents' scores. Such *alternate forms* of tests are perhaps most common in educational testing, in which multiple forms of tests are often prepared in an effort to prevent cheating. Researchers may also use alternate forms in studies involving pre- and posttests. In particular, if researchers are concerned that respondents may benefit from practice or memory effects, as discussed in the previous section, they may develop two or more versions of the test to circumvent such effects. Whenever two or more test forms are designed to be used interchangeably, a crucial question is whether scores are consistent across the different forms. If they are not, respondents may be unfairly advantaged or disadvantaged by having a form that is easier or more difficult. In pre–post situations, a lack of equivalence among forms may result in incorrect conclusions about the extent to which scores have changed. It is therefore critical to determine the degree to which alternate forms are equivalent.

The most important sources of measurement error for alternate forms of cognitive tests are differences in the content, difficulty, and cognitive complexity of items. For noncognitive tests, differences in content and intensity of the items are of concern. Those developing alternate forms of a test typically use several procedures designed to ensure equivalence of forms. First, the forms should be based on the same table of specifications (see Chapter 3). This can help to ensure that the forms contain the same proportions of items across both the content domains and the cognitive or noncognitive levels of the items. As a simple example, if a math test is designed to have 40% of the questions on addition and 60% on subtraction, these proportions should be reflected on all forms. Similarly, the proportions of items at the various levels of cognitive complexity or affective intensity should be equivalent across forms. In addition to matching items on these characteristics, test developers also match items on difficulty and discrimination levels. For noncognitive items, recall that difficulty is analogous to the item mean, so noncognitive items could be matched on this index. To continue our simple example, if two forms of the math test are to be developed, test developers should first choose several items from each cell of the table of specifications. These items would then be matched on difficulty and discrimination values, and the two items with the most similar values would be assigned to form 1 and form 2. This process would be continued until the two forms were complete. More sophisticated strategies, typically used in high-stakes and/or large-scale testing, are discussed in Chapter 18.

Coefficients that assess the similarity of two or more test forms are called *coefficients of equivalence*, and this type of reliability is sometimes referred to as *alternate forms* or *equivalent forms reliability*. Estimates of equivalence coefficients are obtained by administering the two forms of interest to the same respondents and then correlating the two sets of scores. Although the coefficient itself is straightforward, there are some issues to be considered in obtaining the two scores. First, as readers can imagine, having to respond to two cognitive tests may be something of a burden on respondents. This is particularly true if the tests are long, as is often the case in the cognitive arena. Second, the tests should ideally be administered back to back, or at least with only a short time interval in between, to prevent the possible infiltration of the types of time-related inconsistencies discussed in the previous section. This poses an additional burden on respondents and introduces the possibility of fatigue. If respondents are more fatigued when responding to form A than to form B, this can introduce artifactual inconsistencies in scores. One way to circumvent this problem is to allow a short time period between administrations of the two forms. Another possible remedy is to divide the respondents into two groups and counterbalance the order of administration of the two forms, with one group taking form A first and the other taking form B first. Although this approach will not eliminate fatigue effects, it should ensure that the fatigue effects on each form are equivalent. Another issue is that respondents may obtain higher scores on the second form they are administered because they had a chance to practice answering similar items on the first form. Also, items on the first form may have suggested answers to items on the second form. Counterbalancing would help to even out such practice or memory effects across the two forms.

Factors Affecting Coefficients of Equivalence

The main concern in alternate forms reliability is differences in content, difficulty (or intensity, for noncognitive items), and cognitive complexity (for cognitive items) across test forms. Such differences can clearly result in a lack of equivalence across forms. In addition, estimates of equivalence coefficients are correlations and are subject to all the factors affecting correlations discussed previously. Specifically, a lack of heterogeneity of the sample from which these coefficients are estimated will result in lower values than would be obtained from a more heterogeneous sample. If the two scores being correlated have a nonlinear relationship, as can be the case when scores display floor or ceiling effects, this will also result in underestimation. Because coefficients of equivalence are often computed for cognitive tests, some of the factors discussed in the context of internal consistency become relevant. For example, tests consisting of multiple-choice items will typically result in higher reliability estimates than more subjectively scored tests, such as those based on essay or short-answer items, or on performances. Higher levels of standardization of the testing procedures will also result in higher estimates of these coefficients. Finally, values for coefficients of equivalence will typically be higher for tests with more, rather than fewer, items. This is because any inconsistencies due to idiosyncrasies of the items will be more likely to cancel out across a larger set of items.

Recommended Values for Coefficients of Equivalence

Coefficients of equivalence are generally quite high. Raykov and Marcoulides (2011) state that values should be at least .80 and preferably in the .90s. Crocker and Algina (1986) found that manuals for most standardized achievement tests report values ranging from the .80s to the .90s. Given the high-stakes nature of most achievement tests, values should be as high as possible, and in my view it is not unreasonable to expect values in the .90s for such tests. For noncognitive tests, or tests with few items, values may be in the .80s. However, with careful construction of alternate forms, values should not be much lower than .80.

COMBINING ALTERNATE FORMS AND TEST-RETEST RELIABILITY

In some situations, researchers may be interested in using different forms of an instrument at different time points. For example, the research may involve a pre- and post-test, but the researcher is unwilling to use the same form for each because of concerns over practice or memory effects, or cheating. The researcher's interest is therefore in the extent to which scores are consistent over *both* time and forms. To obtain information on the extent of these combined sources of measurement error, the two forms should be administered to the same sample of respondents at two occasions that are separated by the time interval of interest. Test forms should be counterbalanced, with one group of respondents receiving form A first and the other form B. The correlation between scores from the two administrations is the coefficient of interest, sometimes referred to as a *coefficient of stability and equivalence.*

Factors Affecting Coefficients of Equivalence and Stability

Because the coefficient of equivalence and stability is essentially a combination of the two coefficients from which it takes its name, all of the factors affecting these two coefficients will affect it. However, because only one coefficient is obtained, it is not possible to determine the relative contributions of inconsistencies across time and inconsistencies across forms. For this reason, researchers may want to consider the use of generalizability theory, discussed in Chapter 10, for situations involving more than one source of measurement error. The use of generalizability theory and its associated indices allow researchers to ascertain the relative degree to which test scores are affected by each source of error.

Recommended Values for Coefficients of Equivalence and Stability

Estimated values for coefficients of equivalence and stability are typically lower than those for either stability or equivalence alone because they combine the two sources of score inconsistencies. However, this should not be taken as a reason to avoid obtaining such coefficients. If the research or testing situation of interest is one in which scores will be obtained both from different forms and at different time points, it is important to know the likely level of reliability that can be expected. If this level is low, the researcher could take steps to increase the reliability level by improving the equivalence of the two forms and/or eliminating other sources of error. If this is not possible, test users should adjust their levels of confidence in the scores accordingly. Values for coefficients of equivalence and stability should be at least .70, and values of .80 are not unreasonable.

THE STANDARD ERROR OF MEASUREMENT

The reliability coefficients discussed thus far are useful for summarizing the reliability of a set of test scores for a group of people. But they do not provide direct information about how accurate an individual's observed score might be as an indicator of their true score. Because under CTT, errors are considered to be random both across and within individuals, it is never possible to know the exact amount of error in a given person's score. However, we can use the reliability coefficient to estimate the amount of error in a score. This information is provided by the *standard error of measurement* (*SEM*), defined as the standard deviation of an individual's observed scores around their true score. Recall from the beginning sections of this chapter that, according to classical test theory, each person's hypothetical distribution of observed scores is posited to vary randomly around their true score, as depicted in Figure 7.1 in Chapter 7. The *SEM* can be thought of as the average of the deviations of a person's observed scores from their true score, or as the average standard deviation of the observed/true score differences. And because the differences between observed and true scores are defined as measurement errors under CTT, the *SEM* is the average of these distributions of measurement errors. In other words, the *SEM* represents the average amount of error in scores, across people. Given this fact, the *SEM* must be related to the error scores defined in CTT, or, more specifically, to their variance. In fact, the *SEM* can be shown to be the standard deviation of the error scores. Recall that in CTT the relation between observed, true, and error scores is defined as

$$X = T + E \tag{8.21}$$

Because the true and error scores are assumed to be uncorrelated, the variances of observed, true, and error scores are also uncorrelated and have a simple additive relationships, as shown here:

$$\sigma_X^2 = \sigma_T^2 + \sigma_E^2 \tag{8.22}$$

To obtain the *SEM*, first divide both sides of the equation by σ_X^2, which yields

$$\frac{\sigma_T^2}{\sigma_X^2} + \frac{\sigma_E^2}{\sigma_X^2} = \frac{\sigma_X^2}{\sigma_X^2} \tag{8.23}$$

Note that the last term is equal to 1 and the first term is our earlier definition of reliability. The expression therefore simplifies to

$$\rho_{XX'} + \frac{\sigma_E^2}{\sigma_X^2} = 1 \tag{8.24}$$

By subtracting $\rho_{xx'}$, I obtain

$$\frac{\sigma_E^2}{\sigma_X^2} = 1 - \rho_{xx'} \tag{8.25}$$

Multiplying each side by σ_X^2 and taking the square root of each side, I obtain the *SEM* as

$$SEM = \sigma_E = \sigma_X \sqrt{1 - \rho_{xx'}} \tag{8.26}$$

The quantity in Equation 8.26 is based on population parameters and therefore yields the population value of the *SEM*. In practice, sample estimates of the total score standard deviation (S_X) and of the reliability are substituted for the population values to obtain sample estimates of the *SEM*. The *SEM* can be interpreted as the average amount of error in a given test score or as the average deviation of any observed score from its corresponding true score.

Factors Affecting the *SEM*

Estimates of the *SEM* are influenced by two things: the estimated reliability of the test scores and the sample standard deviation or level of variability of the observed test scores. The latter influence reflects the fact that the *SEM* must be interpreted relative to the amount of total variability in the test scores of the sample. For example, a *SEM* of 6 might be considered small if the sample's total score $SD(S_X)$ were 100, but if S_X were 10, the same estimated *SEM* would indicate a large amount of error. This is because the range of the *SEM* is *not* from 0 to 1, as many incorrectly suppose, but from 0 to S_X, which can be seen by using Equation 8.26 to determine the value of the *SEM* for situations in which reliability is perfect (i.e., 1.0) and in which reliability is 0. These situations should correspond to the lowest and highest possible values of the *SEM* because measurement error and reliability are inversely related. Inserting 1 as the reliability value in Equation 8.26 yields a value of 0 for the *SEM*. This indicates that there is no error in test scores or that observed scores are exactly the same as their corresponding true scores. This statement makes sense because this is what a reliability estimate of 1.0 means. Inserting a value of 0 for reliability yields a value of σ_X for the *SEM*. This value indicates that the standard deviation of the error scores is equal to the *SD* of the observed scores—that is, that *all* of the variation in observed scores is due to error. The *SEM* thus has a range from 0 to the standard deviation of the test.

Using the *SEM* to Place Confidence Intervals around Scores

If the distribution of errors of measurement is assumed to be normal, the *SEM* can be used to place confidence intervals (CIs) around true score values using the properties of the normal distribution. That is, a 95% CI could be obtained by taking the true score plus and minus 1.96 (or, simply 2.0) times the *SEM*, or a 68% CI could be obtained by taking ±1 *SEM*. The only glitch in this procedure is that we would like to put a confidence interval around the true score, but only the observed score is available. However, McDonald (1999) has argued that X is an unbiased estimate of T, assuming that the error variance is the same across respondents. If errors are random, the assumption of equal error variances is plausible because there may be no particular reason to think that some respondents would have more random error than others. And because X is an unbiased estimator of T, it makes sense to use X in place of T and to place the CI around X. (For a somewhat more formal argument, see Crocker & Algina, 1986, p. 123.) The interpretation of such a CI is that an individual's true score would be expected to lie within ±1 *SEM* of their observed score with 68% probability or that the true score would be within ±2 SEMs with 95% probability.

For example, suppose that in a particular sample the standard deviation of a test was 10 and the reliability of the test was .84. The *SEM* would be $10\sqrt{1-.84} = 10\sqrt{.16} = 10 \times .4 = 4$. If a person's score was 20, we could have 68% confidence that the interval 20 ± 4, or 16–24 would contain their true score, or 95% confidence that their true score would be in the interval 12–28. You may be surprised that this interval is so wide, given the relatively high reliability. However, it illustrates the amount of imprecision associated with many test scores. Had the reliability been .95, the *SEM* would be about 2.2 points, and the CIs much more narrow. Most test scores do not attain this level of reliability, however, and readers should therefore keep in mind that observed scores are often only a rough estimate of a person's true level of the construct being measured.

Such considerations are particularly important for situations in which scores are used for high-stakes decisions. Assume that in our earlier example, test scores were to be used to select job applicants for employment based on a cutoff score of 23. For an applicant with a score of 20, the 95% confidence interval around the applicant's score includes the score of 23. This indicates that such an applicant may well have a true score that falls at (or even above) the cutoff. Figure 8.1 shows the 95% CIs as shaded areas around scores of 20 and 23. The figure shows that the CIs (shown as shaded areas in the figure) for the two scores overlap considerably.

Sample Dependence of Reliability Coefficients and the *SEM*

As noted previously, the *SEM* is useful for estimating the amount of error that is likely to be present in an individual score. It is also useful to take the *SEM* into account when comparing scores across individuals on the same test because doing so helps to guard against overinterpreting small differences in scores. However, it is not appropriate to compare the SEMs from different tests, except in the unlikely case that the test standard deviations are exactly the same. This is because the *SEM* of a test is dependent on both the reliability of the test scores and their standard deviation. If it is of interest to compare two or more tests, reliability coefficients, not SEMs, should form the basis of comparison.

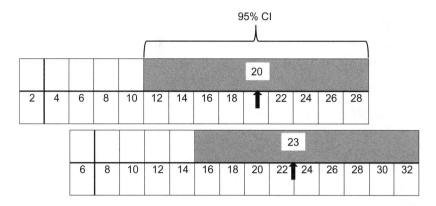

FIGURE 8.1. Overlap in confidence intervals of two scores.

Somewhat paradoxically, however, it should be noted that reliability coefficients are sample dependent, whereas the *SEM* is less so. To understand why, consider the makeup of reliability and *SEM* coefficients. Reliability coefficients are ratios of true score to observed score (or true plus error) variance. The amount of observed score variance can differ across samples because of restriction of range or other factors that operate to increase or decrease the variance in observed scores. However, this decreased (or increased) variance in scores is likely due to decreased (or increased) variance in respondents' true scores. It is difficult to argue that changes in variance are a result of changes in random error that occur in one sample but not in another. Such an explanation seems at odds with the concept of randomness. Thus, changes in observed score variance will generally be the result of changes in true score variance, but the same amount of error variance. Given that reliability coefficients are estimates of the ratio $\sigma_T^2/(\sigma_T^2 + \sigma_E^2)$, situations in which true score variance decreases and error variance stays the same will clearly result in lower values. Turning to the *SEM*, recall that this quantity is simply σ_E, which is, conceptually, the standard deviation of the error scores. As just discussed, the variance (or standard deviation) of errors should not differ across samples. The *SEM* should therefore not be sample dependent.[2]

RELIABILITY OF DIFFERENCE SCORES

In some situations, researchers are interested not in the score on one test, but in the difference between an individual's scores on two different tests. Perhaps the most common of these situations is when growth or change is of interest, as in a pre–post testing

---

[2] Some readers may wonder how this is possible, given that the observed score standard deviation (σ_X) is part of the formula for the *SEM*. However, keep in mind that the reliability estimate σ_T^2/σ_X^2 is also part of the formula, and the presence of the term σ_X^2 in the denominator largely serves to offset the σ_X term. Strictly speaking, this is only true of the squared *SEM* (σ_E^2), but the overall effect is still that the *SEM* is largely sample independent.

situation. The difference between two scores is simply $D_i = X_{i_1} - X_{i_2}$, where D_i represents the difference score and X_{i_1} and X_{i_2} are scores at times 1 and 2 for individual i. If decisions are based on the difference scores, then it is the reliability of these differences, rather than the individual reliabilities of the two X scores, that must be taken into account. However, as has been widely discussed in the measurement literature, the reliability of differences between two scores can be lower than the reliability of the individual scores. This is typically explained by pointing out that a difference score will be affected by measurement error in both X_1 and X_2, and so will have more error than either score individually.

Although this is true to some extent, difference scores will not always be unreliable. The reliability of difference scores is affected by the reliability of the two individual scores and by the correlation between the scores. Specifically, the reliability of difference scores will increase with the reliability of the two scores and will decrease as the correlation between the two scores increases. It is intuitive that differences between two unreliable measures will themselves be unreliable. What is not so intuitive, however, is why a high correlation between the two measures would result in low reliability for difference scores. To help you understand this phenomenon, I present both the formulaic and conceptual definitions of the reliability of difference scores. Note that, although the formulations are based on population parameters, in practice the population parameters would be replaced by their sample estimates to obtain estimates of the reliability of difference scores for a particular sample.

Following the theoretical definition of reliability presented earlier in this chapter, the reliability of a difference score is the ratio of the true variance in difference scores to the observed variance in difference scores, or

$$\rho_{DD'} = \frac{\sigma_{T_2-T_1}^2}{\sigma_{X_2-X_1}^2} = \frac{\sigma_{T_2-T_1}^2}{\sigma_{T_2-T_1}^2 + \sigma_{E_1-E_2}^2} \tag{8.27}$$

The observed difference score is defined above, and its variance is

$$\sigma_{X_2-X_1}^2 = \sigma_{X_1}^2 + \sigma_{X_2}^2 - 2\sigma_{X_1 X_2} \tag{8.28}$$

The variance of the true difference score would be defined similarly as

$$\sigma_{T_2-T_1}^2 = \sigma_{T_1}^2 + \sigma_{T_2}^2 - 2\sigma_{T_1 T_2} \tag{8.29}$$

The ratio of the variance of true score differences to that of observed score differences provides a theoretical expression for the reliability of difference scores, but this expression would not be estimable because it contains expressions for the true scores, which are not, of course, available. However, recall that the true score variance is the reliable part of the observed score variance, so the true score variances can be calculated as $\sigma_T^2 = \rho_{XX'}\sigma_X^2$. Also, the covariance of true scores is the same as the covariance of their corresponding observed scores because the random error part of the score should not covary with anything. Thus, $\sigma_{T_1 T_2}$ equals $\sigma_{X_1 X_2}$. I can therefore express the reliability of difference scores as

$$\rho_{DD'} = \frac{\rho_{X_1 X_1'} \sigma_{X_1}^2 + \rho_{X_2 X_2'} \sigma_{X_2}^2 - 2\rho_{X_1 X_2} \sigma_{X_1} \sigma_{X_2}}{\sigma_{X_1}^2 + \sigma_{X_2}^2 - 2\rho_{X_1 X_2} \sigma_{X_1} \sigma_{X_2}} \tag{8.30}$$

In Equation 8.30, $\rho_{X_1 X_1'}$ and $\rho_{X_2 X_2'}$ are the reliabilities of X_1 and X_2, and $\rho_{X_1 X_2}$ is the correlation between X_1 and X_2. Ignoring for a moment the parts of the numerator and denominator after the minus signs, we can see that the reliability of difference scores functions in the same way as the reliability of single scores: reliability increases as true score variance increases relative to observed score variance, as would be expected.

The term after the minus sign $(2\rho_{X_1 X_2} \sigma_{X_1} \sigma_{X_2})$ is equal to twice the covariance between the two scores. Because this term is subtracted in both the numerator and denominator, you can see that the sums of both true and observed score variances are reduced by an amount proportional to the covariance between X_1 and X_2. The reliability of difference scores is therefore higher when the two X values are less correlated. To demonstrate this effect, I computed the reliability of difference scores for the hypothetical pre- and posttest data in Table 8.3, assuming different values for the correlation between the two X values.

As the table shows, reliability indeed decreases as the strength of the correlation between the two scores increases. Why does this happen? The answer has to do with the concept of variation in difference scores, as explained by Rogosa and Willett (1983; see also Rogosa, Brandt, & Zimowski, 1982; Zimmerman, 2009). Variation in difference scores means that not all respondents change at the same rate. Some respondents may change quite a bit, whereas others may not change at all. Figure 8.2 represents a situation in which there is considerable variance in difference scores. If, however, all respondents change in a similar way, there will be little variation in difference scores, as depicted in Figure 8.3. You can see from the parallel lines in Figure 8.3 that all respondents changed by exactly the same amount. The reliability is low in this case because it is not possible to accurately rank-order respondents in terms of their amount of change.

TABLE 8.3. Reliability of Difference Scores as Correlation between Scores Varies

	X_1		X_2	
Test variance	$\sigma_{X_1}^2 = 3$		$\sigma_{X_2}^2 = 5$	
Test reliability	$\rho_{X_1 X_1'} = .80$		$\rho_{X_2 X_2'} = .90$	
	Reliability of difference score			
Correlation between tests	$\rho_{X_1 X_2} = .2$	$\rho_{X_1 X_2} = .4$	$\rho_{X_1 X_2} = .6$	
Difference score reliability	$\rho_{DD'} = .83$	$\rho_{DD'} = .76$	$\rho_{DD'} = .67$	

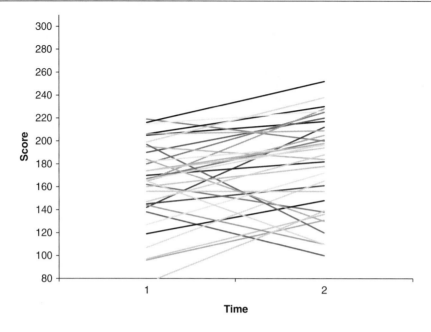

FIGURE 8.2. Scores at two time points with large variance in difference scores.

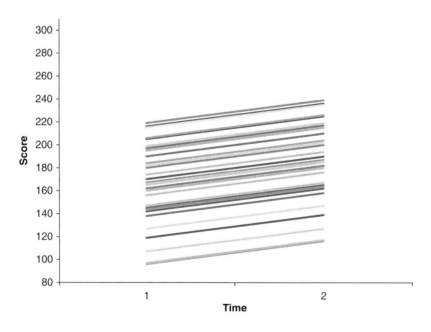

FIGURE 8.3. Scores at two time points with no variance in difference scores.

Note that this represents a restriction of range, which affects the reliability coefficient in the same way as discussed previously for other types of reliability.

But how is this related to the effect of the correlation between the two scores on difference score reliability? Consider the graph in Figure 8.3, in which change is constant across respondents. In this case, X_1 and X_2 are highly correlated because each person's score on X_1 differs from his or her score on X_2 by the same amount. In fact, the two sets of scores are correlated perfectly. Note that this perfect correlation between scores is what results in the lack of variability in difference scores. It must be the case that more highly correlated scores will result in less variability in difference scores, because, by definition, two sets of scores that are highly correlated differ by similar amounts; this is what results in their high correlation. So, as the correlation between the two scores increases, the amount of variability in difference scores decreases. Conversely, two scores that are not as highly correlated will have more variability in differences between the two. This is illustrated in Figure 8.2, in which the two sets of scores have a correlation of .58. This set of scores will have a higher difference score reliability than those in Figure 8.3 because in this case it is possible to accurately rank-order respondents on their amount of change.

It is important to note that low reliability of difference scores does not necessarily imply that the change score for any individual is estimated imprecisely (Rogosa et al., 1982). As Nunnally and Bernstein (1994) point out, the difference between observed scores is an unbiased estimate of the difference in true scores (given the typical assumption that measurement errors average to zero). Low reliability of difference scores implies a lack of precision in rank ordering people on the basis of their difference scores, not necessarily a lack of precision of any individual score. Nevertheless, in making decisions about individuals on the basis of difference scores, it is advisable to consider the *SEMs* of the two scores in determining whether the difference between the two scores is within the range of measurement error.

Finally, it is possible to use the techniques of CFA to estimate the reliability of difference scores. CFA methods provide a way to disattenuate scores from the effects of measurement error, essentially allowing for correlation of the true scores rather than the observed scores. This is accomplished by estimating the amount of measurement error in each variable and isolating it in a residual term that is uncorrelated with other variables in the model. (I discuss CFA procedures in more detail in Chapter 13.)

SUMMARY

Testing situations vary widely in both purpose and testing conditions. Consequently, reliability coefficients that focus on different sources of error, resulting from different testing conditions, have been developed. In some cases, response fluctuations across different items are the main source of measurement error. Coefficients of internal consistency were developed to assess measurement error resulting from this type of inconsistency. Internal consistency is important whenever response consistency across items is of interest, as is the case for most scales. In this chapter, I have discussed several internal consistency coefficients, including coefficient alpha, KR-20, and KR-21. The latter two coefficients can be seen as special cases of coefficient alpha. Coefficients of equivalence assess the consistency of scores across different forms designed to measure the same construct. These coefficients are simply the correlation of scores from the two forms, and will be high to the extent that the two test forms are parallel. Researchers should expect high (and positive) coefficients of equivalence for different forms of a test. Coefficients of stability assess the consistency of scores across different occasions and are obtained by correlating scores from the same scale obtained on two different occasions. This type of coefficient is important for scales that are used for the purposes of prediction or classification, or for any situation in which score interpretation carries with it the assumption that measurement should be stable across time. Coefficients of stability are not appropriate for constructs that are known to be unstable, such as state anxiety, or that are expected to change as a result of some type of intervention.

It is important to note that decisions regarding the type(s) of reliability that are important should not be based on the type of data available. Instead, the type of reliability information should match the purpose of the test and should be capable of measuring the type of measurement error that is most likely to result. For example, if a test is to be used to predict future outcomes, it is imperative for researchers to know a priori that the test measures consistently across the time period of interest. If such evidence is not available, researchers must conduct a test–retest reliability study to obtain it. It is neither appropriate nor ethical to state that such information is not necessary simply because it is not available.

In this chapter, I have also introduced and discussed the standard error of measurement. In contrast to the reliability coefficient, which assesses the average level of score consistency across a group of people, the *SEM* is an estimate of the average amount of error in an individual score.

Finally, I discussed the issues inherent in assessing the reliability of difference scores. These are measures of the difference between two scores obtained at different time points and are of interest when measuring growth or change across time. The difference score reliability coefficient measures the degree to which variation in difference scores is due to variation in true scores rather than to error. The reliability of difference scores is affected by the individual reliabilities of the two scores involved, as well as the correlation between the two scores. Difference score reliability increases as individual score reliabilities increase but decreases as the correlation between the two scores increases.

EXERCISES

Questions 1 and 2 are based on the two datasets in Table 8.4. Each dataset contains the hypothetical scores of 10 people on six items.

TABLE 8.4. Hypothetical Scores for Questions 1 and 2

Dataset 1

Person	Item 1	Item 2	Item 3	Item 4	Item 5	Item 6	Total score
1	5	5	2	5	5	1	23
2	5	2	5	5	2	2	21
3	5	5	3	3	1	1	18
4	5	5	5	5	1	2	23
5	4	4	4	2	3	3	20
6	4	5	5	2	2	2	20
7	3	5	4	2	4	4	22
8	4	4	2	4	3	3	20
9	3	3	3	1	2	2	14
10	3	3	3	1	2	2	14
Variance	0.77	1.21	1.38	2.67	1.61	0.84	10.72

Dataset 2

Person	Item 1	Item 2	Item 3	Item 4	Item 5	Item 6	Total score
1	3	3	4	4	4	4	22
2	3	3	3	3	4	4	20
3	4	4	4	5	5	5	27
4	4	4	4	5	5	5	27
5	4	4	5	5	5	5	28
6	4	4	4	4	5	5	26
7	4	5	5	5	5	5	29
8	2	4	2	5	4	5	22
9	1	1	1	1	2	2	8
10	3	3	3	1	4	4	18
Variance	1.07	1.17	1.61	2.62	0.90	0.93	40.23

1. Without doing any calculations, which dataset should have the highest value of coefficient alpha? Why?

2. Calculate the value of coefficient alpha for each dataset. Do the values support your answers from Question 1?

3. What sources of error, or inconsistency, are measured by each of the following types of reliability?

   a. Internal consistency

   b. Test–retest

   c. Alternate forms

4. What are the differences and similarities between coefficient alpha and adjusted split-half reliability coefficients?

5. Which type of test should yield more reliable scores: a classroom test or a standardized achievement test? Why?

6. Which would yield a higher value for internal consistency reliability: scores from a very easy achievement test or scores from a test of medium difficulty? Why?

7. Would it be appropriate to obtain a test–retest reliability coefficient over a 1-hour period for scores on an achievement test? Why or why not?

8. A testing company has developed two versions of a math placement test. The company wants to investigate the extent to which students' scores are similar across the two tests. What type of reliability coefficient is most appropriate for this situation? Describe a procedure they could use to collect this information.

9. Amanda is interested in whether social workers have higher scores on a scale measuring altruism than the general population. She finds that social workers do indeed have scores on the altruism scale that are, on average, at the 90th percentile and above. However, she also finds that the value of coefficient alpha for her sample of social workers is lower than the value of .85 that has been reported for the scale in the general population. What is the most likely reason for the lower value of coefficient alpha?

10. Officials at a local college administer a study skills scale to students during their summer orientation and use students' test scores to place them into noncredit study skills classes for the fall semester. If students receive a study skills score of 30 or more, they are exempt from the class. If they receive a score of 10 or lower, they must take a year-long class, and if they receive a score between 11 and 29, they must take a semester-long class. What type of reliability coefficient is important to obtain in this situation? Explain.

11. The test–retest reliability coefficient value for a memory test is .60. The test authors explain this low value by indicating that the test has a "low ceiling," meaning that many respondents obtained the highest score possible. How could this have affected the test–retest coefficient?

12. Allison administered a measure of statistics self-efficacy on the first day and the last day of her semester-long introductory statistics course. The statistics self-efficacy scale was designed to measure students' levels of confidence that they could perform various statistics tasks, such as distinguishing between population parameters and sample statistics and identifying factors affecting statistical power. Allison computed a coefficient of stability and obtained a value of .31.

   a. What is the most likely reason for this low value?

   b. Is test–retest reliability appropriate for this situation? Why or why not?

13. Explain why the reliability of difference scores is lower when scores on the two tests are highly correlated than when the scores have a low correlation.

14. The *SEM* of a test is 5 points. A person has an observed score of 55. Create an interval around the observed score such that we could have 95% confidence that the person's true score is contained in the interval.

15. Test A has an *SEM* of 2 points. Test B has an *SEM* of 5 points. Is Test A more reliable than Test B? Why or why not?

16. If the reliability of a 20-item test is .80, what would the reliability be if:

    a. the test length was doubled?

    b. the number of test items was increased to 60?

    c. the number of test items was decreased to 10?

9

Interrater Agreement and Reliability

In many situations, the skills or performances of interest cannot easily be measured by a paper-and-pencil instrument. Instead, a performance or product is rated by trained judges, or raters. You may be familiar with controversies surrounding Olympic judges' ratings of ice-skating or gymnastics performances. These controversies involved suggestions that some judges provided ratings favoring athletes from their home country. This is an example of the main source of measurement error in ratings: that of inconsistencies in scores due to the raters themselves. *Interrater reliability* and *interrater agreement* are concerned with the degree to which ratings obtained from different raters are consistent and these are important for any situation in which scores are provided through a rating method. Ratings can be of performance, such as sports or job-related skills, musical or dramatic performances, or driving ability, of products such as essays, artwork, or business plans, or of behavior, as when behaviors are observed or videotaped and rated. Examples of behaviors include observations of classrooms to rate occurrences of disruptive behavior or caretakers' observations of patients' levels of functioning. In all of these situations, it is important that a person's score not be dependent on a particular rater. Instead, scores provided by different raters should be consistent with one another.

Lack of consistency across raters can occur for many reasons, including poor training of raters, unclear rating rubrics, and rater bias. Ratings are usually based on some type of rubric, and they should be as clear and explicit as possible (see Chapter 4). Even with an excellent rubric, however, rater training will still be necessary. This training should allow raters to practice using the rubric and to ask any questions they may have. Raters may need clarification about the meaning of a specific rating category or about how one rating category differs from another. Ideally, raters should practice on a set of products or performances that have been preselected to represent the full range of scores. This type of practice will allow raters to better understand the differences among the rating levels. Raters should also be warned to guard against rater biases such as harshness or leniency and the halo effect. The halo effect involves the tendency of raters to give higher ratings to those who have done well in the past (see Chapter 4). Rater "drift" is the tendency of raters to stray from the rubric and often increases with the length of time since training. Because of this tendency, it is a good idea to conduct refresher training sessions if ratings take place over an extended length of time.

Even when rubrics are clear and raters are well trained, some inconsistencies in ratings are inevitable. This is because raters, being human, can be expected to be somewhat idiosyncratic in their ratings. This is similar to the case of paper-and-pencil instruments, in which items written to measure the same construct will nevertheless invoke somewhat different responses. Because of these inconsistencies, it is essential to assess the level of interrater agreement and/or reliability whenever raters are used. Although the terms *interrater agreement* and *interrater reliability* are sometimes used synonymously in the literature, they are not the same thing (see Tinsley & Weiss, 1975, for an excellent discussion). As noted by LeBreton and Senter (2008), both of these measure the similarity of ratings, but they differ in how similarity is defined. Indices of interrater agreement measure the extent to which different raters provide the same rating. Interrater reliability measures assess the degree to which ratings provided by different raters result in the same relative rank order of individuals. Table 9.1 shows hypothetical ratings of 10 people provided by three raters on a 5-point rating scale. As can be seen from the table, Raters 1 and 2 are in perfect agreement about the ratings of 7 of the 10 people. Thus, their interrater agreement would be fairly high. In contrast, the ratings of Raters 1 and 3 do not agree for most of the people, so their level of interrater agreement would be low. However, the ratings of the latter pair do result in the same rank ordering of people from low to high, so their level of interrater reliability would be high.

As this example shows, interrater agreement and interrater reliability indices assess different quantities and will not necessarily agree with each other. Because interrater reliability indices are correlational in nature, they are affected by range restriction.

TABLE 9.1. Hypothetical Ratings of 10 People by Three Raters

Person	Rater 1	Rater 2	Rater 3
1	1	1	1
2	2	1	3
3	2	2	3
4	3	3	4
5	3	2	4
6	3	3	4
7	4	4	4
8	4	3	5
9	5	5	5
10	5	5	5

If raters use only a small portion of the rating scale, interrater reliability may be low simply because of the resulting range restriction. However, interrater agreement may be high because it is easier for raters to agree when fewer rating categories are used than when more categories are used.

MEASURES OF INTERRATER AGREEMENT

Nominal Agreement

Interrater agreement measures are based on the proportion of agreements in ratings given by two raters. Because they are based on proportions, agreement measures are appropriate for data at any level of measurement. The simplest of the interrater agreement indices is the proportion of times that raters agree, which Frick and Semmel (1978) refer to as *nominal agreement*. These authors provide the following formula for nominal agreement:

$$P_o = \frac{1}{N} \sum_{i=1}^{c} n_{ii} \tag{9.1}$$

where N is the total number of ratings and n_{ii} is the number on the diagonal of the two-by-two matrix that cross-classifies the ratings provided by the two raters. Summation is across rating categories (c). This formula is probably more easily understood through an example. Table 9.2 shows the two-way table of hypothetical ratings on a 5-point scale obtained from Raters 1 and 2 from Table 9.1. The diagonal entries (n_{ii}) in the table are bolded for ease of reference. Note that these represent agreements between the two raters. The notations n_{i+} and n_{+i} in the table refer to the row and column totals, respectively. Using Equation 9.1, P_o is calculated as

$$P_o = \frac{1}{10}(1+1+2+1+2) = \frac{7}{10} = .7$$

This is simply the proportion of agreements between the two raters. Nominal agreement can range from zero, indicating a complete lack of agreement, to one, indicating perfect agreement between raters.

TABLE 9.2. Hypothetical Ratings by Two Raters

Rater 1	Rater 2					n_{i+}
	1	2	3	4	5	
1	**1**	0	0	0	0	1
2	1	**1**	0	0	0	2
3	0	1	**2**	0	0	3
4	0	0	1	**1**	0	2
5	0	0	0	0	**2**	2
n_{+i}	2	2	3	1	2	10

Three problems have been noted with measures of nominal agreement (Frick & Semmel, 1978; Tinsley & Weiss, 1975). First, nominal agreement is quite stringent in that it requires raters to agree exactly. With a small number of rating categories, this may not be an unreasonable expectation, but as the number of categories increases, exact agreement becomes more difficult. For example, Tinsley and Weiss provide an example of a 9-point rating scale of counselor's empathy levels. With this many rating categories, it can be difficult for raters to agree on the exact meaning of each category, which results in rating inconsistencies. Tinsley and Weiss describe two indices that allow researchers to define adjacent agreements as "in agreement." However, indices based on adjacent agreements are somewhat complicated computationally. Researchers could accomplish the same purpose in a less sophisticated manner by simply combining adjacent categories before calculating P_o. Note, however, that this is only appropriate for ratings at the ordinal level of measurement or above; collapsing nominal ratings such as "pass" and "fail" is nonsensical.

A second problem with P_o is that it does not indicate whether the two raters are rating correctly. For example, raters could agree because both are rating everyone as a "1" or otherwise misusing the rating scale. To some extent, this is a validity issue, because it has to do with the degree to which ratings can be interpreted in the intended manner. If a researcher's interest lies in comparing each rater's score to that of an expert rater, P_o can be calculated with one of the two raters being the expert. Frick and Semmel (1978) refer to this as *criterion-related agreement*.

Cohen's Kappa

The third problem with measures of nominal agreement is that they do not take into account the fact that raters could agree simply by chance. For a two-category rating scale, two raters assigning scores completely at random would be expected to agree about 50% of the time. Because of this, indices that "correct for" or remove the proportion of agreement due to chance have been proposed. The most commonly used of these indices was developed by Cohen (1960) and is known as *Cohen's kappa* or simply *kappa*. Kappa is calculated as

$$\kappa = \frac{P_o - P_c}{1 - P_c} \tag{9.2}$$

where P_o is the nominal agreement from Equation 9.1 and P_c is the expected chance agreement between the two raters, calculated as

$$P_c = \frac{1}{N^2} \sum_{i=1}^{c} \left(n_{i+}\right)\left(n_{+i}\right) \tag{9.3}$$

Recall that n_{i+} and n_{+i} refer to the row and column totals of the two-by-two table of ratings. N is the total number of people being rated. Thus, the notation after the summation sign indicates that, for each rating category, the row total should be multiplied by the column total, and these products should be summed across categories. From Equation 9.2

you can see that kappa will reach its maximum value of 1.0 when P_o is equal to 1. To the degree that nominal agreement (P_o) is not perfect, kappa will be less than 1, with a minimum value of 0. Because of the correction for chance, kappa will always have a lower value than P_o for the same data. For the example data in Table 9.2, P_c is equal to

$$P_c = \frac{1}{N^2}\sum_{i=1}^{c}(n_{i+})(n_{+i}) = \frac{1}{10^2}\left[(2\times 1)+(2\times 2)+(3\times 3)+(1\times 2)+(2\times 2)\right]$$

$$= \frac{1}{100}(2+4+9+2+4) = \frac{21}{100} = .21$$

P_o was previously calculated as .7, so kappa is equal to

$$\kappa = \frac{P_o - P_c}{1 - P_c} = \frac{.7 - .21}{1 - .21} = \frac{.49}{.79} = .62$$

Kappa can be interpreted as the amount of rater agreement that is above what would be expected by chance, expressed as a proportion of the maximum possible agreement beyond chance. As this statement makes obvious, the interpretation of kappa is not as straightforward as that of P_o.

As noted by Sim and Wright (2005), kappa is affected by the prevalence of a positive, or high, rating. Table 9.3, adapted from their article, illustrates this phenomenon. The table shows the cross-classification of ratings from two raters of whether a symptom is present or absent. On the left-hand side, the overall prevalence, or proportion of cases in which the symptom is present, is high (27), whereas on the right-hand side the prevalence is much lower (15). As you can see in the values at the bottom of the table, the high-prevalence situation results in higher values of P_c, and therefore lower values of kappa, than does the low-prevalence situation, even though the nominal agreement value is .83 for both situations. This example shows that kappa will be lower when the prevalence of a positive event (in this case, a rating of "present") is very high. The same phenomenon would occur if the prevalence of a positive event were very low. As Sim and Wright point out, the effect of the prevalence level is greater for large than for small values of kappa. This phenomenon should be kept in mind when interpreting values of kappa in situations for which the data tend to be concentrated in a single rating category.

TABLE 9.3. Hypothetical Data Illustrating the Prevalence Effect on Values of Cohen's Kappa

| | High prevalence | | | Low prevalence | | |
| | Rater 1 | | | Rater 1 | | |
Rater 2	Present	Absent	n_{i+}	Present	Absent	n_{i+}
Present	24	2	26	13	3	16
Absent	3	1	4	2	12	14
n_{+i}	27	3	30	15	15	30
	$P_o = .83$	$P_c = .79$	$\kappa = .19$	$P_o = .83$	$P_c = .50$	$\kappa = .66$

If the marginal values (n_{i+} and n_{+i}) are equal across raters, kappa values have a range from −1.0 to 1.0. If the marginal values are not equal, the range of kappa is more restricted. Negative values of kappa indicate that agreement is worse than would be expected by chance, and values of 1.0 indicate perfect agreement. Kappa values of 0 do not indicate a complete lack of agreement but instead mean that agreement is exactly the same as what would be expected by chance.

Although interrater agreement measures have been discussed in the context of two raters, several versions of kappa that can accommodate more than two raters have been developed. Fleiss (1971) extended kappa to accommodate multiple raters in the specific case in which each person is rated by the same number of raters, but the raters are not necessarily the same for each person. Light (1971) proposes extensions of various agreement measures, including kappa, to situations with more than two raters. Finally, Conger (1980) discusses the indices developed by Fleiss and Light and integrates these into a common framework.

MEASURES OF INTERRATER RELIABILITY

Stemler (2004) discussed several measures of interrater reliability, including coefficient alpha, correlational measures such as the Pearson correlation, and the *intraclass correlation* (ICC). The Pearson and other measures of correlation only allow for calculation of consistency between two raters. In contrast, both alpha and the ICC allow for calculation of consistency across any number of raters. Because software for obtaining both alpha and ICCs are readily available, there seems little point in using correlational measures to assess interrater reliability because these are restricted to use with only two raters.

Coefficient Alpha

Recall from Chapter 8 that coefficient alpha assesses consistency of responses across items. Given that interrater reliability refers to the consistency of ratings across judges, it seems reasonable to use alpha in this situation. In this case, alpha would be computed as usual, except that raters would be treated as "items." For the three raters in Table 9.1, calculating alpha in this way results in a value of .96. This is in clear contrast to the much lower P_o values of .70, .40, and .40 for rater pairs 1 and 2, 1 and 3, and 2 and 3. The difference reflects the fact that measures of interrater agreement, such as P_o, assess the absolute level of agreement whereas measures of interrater reliability assess the degree to which ratings from multiple judges result in the same relative order of scores. In other words, interrater reliability measures consistency, not absolute agreement, of ratings.

Intraclass Correlation

The ICC is based on an analysis of variance (ANOVA) framework in which persons (or ratees) and raters are the independent variables and the set of scores assigned to each person by each rater is the dependent variable. For example, Table 9.1 shows that each person has three scores, one from each rater. Calculation of the ICC requires recasting Table 9.1 into the format of Table 9.4 (commands for accomplishing this in the SPSS and R programs are provided in Shrout & Lane, 2012, but note that the SPSS reliability module will do this automatically). Note that each person is now listed three times, once for each rater. Codes for the raters (1, 2, and 3) are in the second column, and the score assigned to each person by each rater is shown in the last column.

TABLE 9.4. Data from Table 9.1 Reformulated for Calculation of an ICC

Person	Rater	Score
1	1	1
1	2	1
1	3	1
2	1	2
2	2	1
2	3	3
3	1	2
3	2	2
3	3	3
4	1	3
4	2	3
4	3	4
5	1	3
5	2	2
5	3	4
6	1	3
6	2	3
6	3	4
7	1	4
7	2	4
7	3	4
8	1	4
8	2	3
8	3	5
9	1	5
9	2	5
9	3	5
10	1	5
10	2	5
10	3	5

ICCs are based on the ratio of between-subjects variance to total (between-subjects plus error) variance (although in a subsequent section I point out an exception to this definition). Thus, ICCs are based on an ANOVA framework. Unlike in ANOVA, however, when using ICCs to assess interrater reliability, the focus is not on obtaining F-tests or other tests of significance but on the values of the ICC itself. For interrater reliability, the error, or within-subject variance, represents differences in the ratings of the same person by two or more raters. For example, Person 2 received ratings of 2, 1, and 3 from the three raters. In a reliability framework, such inconsistencies across raters are considered to be error variance. As in ANOVA, the between-subjects variance is calculated as the sum of the squared differences between a person's average score across the three raters and the overall, or grand mean, calculated as the average of all 30 (3 raters × 10 people) scores. Because between-subjects variance is based on the average rating for each person, it is considered to be an estimate of the true score a person would have obtained if rated by all possible raters. Recall that a true score was defined conceptually as the expected score a person would obtain across all items, raters, occasions, or other sources of error. It is in this sense that the between-subjects variance represents the true score variance. ICC measures of reliability thus parallel the classical test theory definition of reliability as the ratio of true score to observed score (or total) variance.

Decisions Involved in Choosing an ICC Design

As pointed out in a classic article by Shrout and Fleiss (1979) and elaborated on by McGraw and Wong (1996), there are several versions of the ICC. Researchers must be aware of the differences among these versions to make an informed choice about the most appropriate coefficient for their situation.

Most of the decisions researchers must make in choosing an appropriate ICC have to do with the design of the study. One such consideration is whether there is one set of raters, all of whom rate each person, or whether people are rated by different sets of raters. Under the first scenario (all raters rate all people), raters are said to be *crossed* with persons. If each person is rated by a different set of raters, raters are said to be *nested* within people. For example, one family member and one friend might rate each person, so the raters would be different for each person, resulting in raters nested within persons. Or the same two teachers might rate each student, resulting in raters crossed with persons.

Another consideration is whether raters are considered to be *fixed* or *random*. Raters are fixed if they are the only raters of interest or if they constitute the entire group of possible raters. If raters are fixed, there is no need to generalize to any larger population of raters. For example, if a company has hired three consultants to rate all of its employees and no other raters will ever be used, raters would be fixed. If raters are considered to constitute a random effect, the assumption is that they are a random subset of all possible raters, at least theoretically. In the previous example, if the company randomly selected raters from among the supervisory staff rather than always using the same three raters, raters would be considered random.

A third consideration has to do with the type of reliability in which a researcher is interested. ICCs can measure either *consistency* or *absolute agreement* of ratings. Consistency measures are appropriate when interest is in norm-referenced decisions involving comparisons among peoples' scores. In such situations, what is important is the degree to which scores assigned by different raters result in the same rank ordering of people. For this type of reliability, the fact that one rater's ratings are generally more stringent or lenient than those of another does not matter because the ratings will still result in the same rank ordering, or comparison, of people. For example, suppose three applicants apply for an award for which they are rated by two raters. If Rater A gives the three applicants ratings of 10, 8, and 6 and Rater B gives ratings of 8, 6, and 4, the applicants are ranked in the same order by both raters, so if the highest rated applicant is to receive the award, the differences between the ratings does not matter. For consistency-type reliability, therefore, differences among raters are not considered to be a source of error, as is reflected in the formulas for these ICCs.

Absolute agreement is of interest for any situation in which it is important that raters agree in their numerical ratings. Decisions requiring absolute agreement are analogous to those referred to as criterion-referenced decisions in Chapter 2. One example of such a situation is that in which raters are being trained and it is of interest to determine their level of agreement with an expert rater. The question being addressed under an absolute agreement definition is whether the raters can be considered to be interchangeable. The interchangeability of raters is often of interest for studies in which different raters rate different people because a high level of absolute agreement indicates that ratees would not be advantaged or disadvantaged by being assigned to one rater rather than another. When absolute agreement is of interest, differences among raters are considered to be a source of error, so rater variance is included in the error term for this ICC.

ICC Designs

If raters are nested within people, only a one-way ANOVA of the person effect can be estimated. This design is called a *one-way random* design because persons are always assumed to be random. The nesting of raters within people results in a confounding of raters with people, so a separate rater effect cannot be computed. Estimation of rater effects would require a crossed design in which everyone was rated by the same raters. Nested designs therefore preclude answering questions about how much raters vary in their ratings. Instead of being estimated as a separate effect, the rater effect will be subsumed in the error or residual term, resulting in larger error variance and a smaller ICC than in other designs. Researchers should be aware of these limitations before designing an interrater reliability study.

If raters are crossed with persons, *two-way* designs are possible in which separate person and rater effects can be estimated. In these designs, raters can be either fixed or random; this specification does not affect the calculation of the ICC. However, it does affect its interpretation because with random effects generalization to other raters is possible, whereas with fixed effects such generalizations are not justified. Two-way designs in which raters are random are referred to as *two-way random effects models*; designs with fixed raters are known as *two-way mixed effects models*.

Two-way designs can yield ICCs that measure either the expected reliability of one rater or expected reliability based on the average score across two or more raters. If scores are to be assigned on the basis of only one rating, then averages across multiple raters are not of interest. However, in most situations in which people are rated by more than one rater, the ratings are averaged to obtain a score. For example, if ratings are to be used for high-stakes decisions such as graduation from high school, promotion in a job, or admittance into graduate school, scores should be based on multiple ratings as this will generally result in higher reliability. On the other hand, if ratings are made by teachers for use in their own classrooms, a single rating by that teacher would typically be used.

Table 9.5 is based on Table 5 in the article by McGraw and Wong (1996) and shows the ANOVA-like formulas for calculating various ICCs that differ according to whether the design is one-way or two-way, whether raters are crossed or nested, whether an absolute or consistency definition is desired, and whether the reliability of a single rating or an average rating will be used. These formulas are based on variance components, or, to use ANOVA terminology, mean squares (MS) for the various effects. In Table 9.5, MS_B represents between-subjects variance, MS_W represents within-subjects variance, and MS_R represents rater variance. For two-way designs, MS_W can be broken down into residual error variance (MS_E) and rater variance (MS_R). For the one-way design, no separate rater variance estimate is possible, and the error variance is referred to as within-subjects variance (MS_W). Finally, note in Table 9.5 that although in general ICCs are computed as a ratio of between-subjects variance to total variance, this is not the case for the reliability of an average rating when using the consistency definition. This is because raters are not considered to be a source of error in this design, so the denominator does not include a term for rater variance. For these designs, the denominator of the ICC formula is therefore not a measure of total variance. Because of this inconsistency, McGraw and Wong (1996) define the ICC as the proportion of variance attributable to the "object of measurement," where the object of measurement is simply the person (or other entity) being rated.

Calculations for ICC Designs

To illustrate the calculations, I used the SPSS syntax provided in Shrout and Lane (2012) to obtain estimates of the mean squares for the data in Table 9.4. The results are shown in Table 9.6. Note that because the data are from a two-way design, the within-persons variance can be broken down into variance between raters (MS_R) and residual variance (MS_E). As pointed out previously, if raters had been nested in persons, only an overall error term combining rater and residual variance would be possible (MS_W). The fact that no separate rater variance term is available for the one-way (nested) design is the reason that consistency formulas are not available for that design. Table 9.7 uses the MS estimates from Table 9.6 to illustrate the computations for each of the designs in Table 9.5.

TABLE 9.5. ICC Formulas for One-Way and Two-Way Models

Model	Raters nested or crossed?	Absolute or consistency decision?	Formula for single rating	Formula for average rating
One-way random	Nested	Absolute	$\dfrac{MS_B - MS_W}{MS_B + (k-1)MS_W}$	$\dfrac{MS_B - MS_W}{MS_B}$
		Consistency	N/A	N/A
Two-way random	Crossed	Absolute	$\dfrac{MS_B - MS_E}{MS_B + (k-1)MS_E + \frac{k}{n}\left(MS_R - MS_E\right)}$	$\dfrac{MS_B - MS_E}{MS_B + \left(MS_R - MS_E\right)/n}$
		Consistency	$\dfrac{MS_B - MS_E}{MS_B + (k-1)MS_E}$	$\dfrac{MS_B - MS_E}{MS_B}$
Two-way mixed	Crossed	Absolute	$\dfrac{MS_B - MS_E}{MS_B + (k-1)MS_E + \frac{k}{n}\left(MS_R - MS_E\right)}$	$\dfrac{MS_B - MS_E}{MS_B + \left(MS_R - MS_E\right)/n}$
		Consistency	$\dfrac{MS_B - MS_E}{MS_B + (k-1)MS_E}$	$\dfrac{MS_B - MS_E}{MS_B}$

Note. k, number of raters; *n,* number of people rated.

TABLE 9.6. Mean Squares for Data in Table 9.1

Source of variance	SS	df	MS	
Between persons	44.30	9	4.92	(MS_B)
Within persons	8.00	20	0.40	
Between raters	4.20	2	2.10	(MS_R)
Residual	3.80	18	0.21	(MS_E)

The ICC for the one-way random design for a single rating is .79, indicating that 79% of the variance in ratings is due to true differences in scores rather than to error. This value increases to .92 for average ratings, indicating that when a person's score is based on the average score across raters rather than a single rating, 92% of the variance in scores is due to true score variance. Note that the coefficients for average measures will always be higher than those for single ratings. This is to be expected because an average score based on multiple ratings will always be more reliable than a score based on a single rating. With multiple ratings, rater idiosyncrasies would be expected to average out, whereas with single ratings this is not possible. This is directly analogous to the internal consistency situation in which measures with more items have higher reliability than those with fewer items (assuming the items are of equal quality), as demonstrated by the Spearman–Brown formula introduced in Chapter 8. Also note in Table 9.7 that the ICCs based on a consistency definition are higher than those based on an absolute agreement definition. Again, this is to be expected because, as noted previously, rater variability is not considered measurement error when calculating consistency coefficients, whereas it is considered to be error for absolute agreement coefficients. Thus, the latter coefficients will always be smaller in magnitude than the former (unless rater variability equals 0).

Finally, note that the ICC value for consistency in the two-way random design is the same as that calculated previously for coefficient alpha. This is because the two indices are measures of the same thing. To understand why the two indices are the same, recall that when calculating coefficient alpha, items are always completely crossed with people and are considered to be random rather than fixed. In addition, recall that coefficient alpha is used for norm-referenced (consistency) rather than criterion-referenced (absolute), decision making. In ICC terms, therefore, coefficient alpha is the same as an ICC for a two-way random, consistency design.

SUMMARY

In this chapter, I have discussed reliability for situations involving raters. I distinguished between interrater agreement and interrater reliability. Interrater agreement measures the degree to which the *numerical ratings* provided by different raters are in agreement, whereas interrater reliability measures the degree to which the scores from different raters would result in the same *rank ordering* of those being rated. Whether interrater agreement or interrater reliability is of interest will depend on the research questions to

TABLE 9.7. Computation of ICCs for One-Way and Two-Way Designs

Model	Raters nested or crossed?	Absolute or consistency decision?	Formula for single rating	Formula for average rating
One-way random	Nested	Absolute	$\dfrac{MS_B - MS_w}{MS_B + (k-1)MS_w}$ $=\dfrac{4.92-.40}{4.92+(3-1).40}=.79$	$\dfrac{MS_B - MS_w}{MS_B}$ $=\dfrac{4.92-.40}{4.92}=.92$
		Consistency	N/A	N/A
Two-way random	Crossed	Absolute	$\dfrac{MS_B - MS_E}{MS_B + (k-1)MS_E + \frac{k}{n}(MS_R - MS_E)}$ $=\dfrac{4.92-.21}{4.92+2(21)+\frac{3}{10}(2.10-.21)}$ $=.80$	$\dfrac{MS_B - MS_E}{MS_B + \frac{(MS_R - MS_E)}{n}}$ $=\dfrac{4.92-.21}{4.92+\frac{(2.10-.21)}{10}}$ $=.92$
		Consistency	$\dfrac{MS_B - MS_E}{MS_B + (k-1)MS_E}$ $=\dfrac{4.92-.21}{4.92+(3-1).21}$ $=.88$	$\dfrac{MS_B - MS_E}{MS_B}$ $=\dfrac{4.92-.21}{4.92}$ $=.96$
Two-way mixed	Crossed	Absolute	Same as for two-way random	
		Consistency		

Note. k, number of raters; *n*, number of people rated.

be answered. For example, multiple raters may code videotapes of children's playground behavior to determine the prevalence of aggressive actions. Interest in this study may be focused on determining the overall number of aggressive acts committed. In this scenario, researchers would likely be interested in absolute agreement because if raters did not agree on whether an aggressive act had been committed, the number of aggressive acts could be under- or overestimated. In contrast, if interest centered on rank ordering children in terms of their levels of aggression, absolute agreement would not be critical. In this case, researchers may be more interested in determining the degree to which raters rank-order the children in the same way. Of course, researchers may be interested in both, and there is no reason that both interrater agreement and interrater reliability cannot be calculated. The important point is that the type of interrater consistency obtained should match the research question of interest.

I discussed several coefficients of interrater agreement. Nominal agreement coefficients measure the degree to which two raters provide exactly the same scores. Because two raters may agree simply by chance, some researchers prefer to calculate Cohen's kappa, which adjusts for such chance agreement. Kappa can be affected by prevalence or a preponderance of ratings in one category. Given that all other things are equal, kappa will be lower for high-prevalence than for low-prevalence situations. This should be kept in mind when interpreting the kappa coefficient.

There are several methods of assessing interrater reliability. Stemler (2004) discusses three of these methods: Pearson correlations, coefficient alpha, and the intraclass coefficient (ICC). Although correlating scores from two raters is a simple way of assessing interrater reliability, correlations are limited by the fact that they can accommodate only two raters. Coefficient alpha and the ICC can accommodate multiple raters, and because of their greater flexibility, I focused on these. Using coefficient alpha to assess interrater reliability simply requires raters to be treated as items. Alpha can then be calculated in the usual manner.

Calculation of ICCs is based on an ANOVA framework in which persons and items are treated as independent variables and scores are the dependent variable. Unlike in ANOVA, the focus in calculation of ICCs is on estimating the between- and within-variance components rather than on F-tests and statistical inference. The between-persons variance is analogous to true score variance in classical test theory, whereas the within variance is analogous to error variance. The ICC is the ratio of the between-persons variance to the total (between plus within) variance, and in this sense it is analogous to the CTT definition of reliability as the ratio of true score to total score variance.

Researchers using ICCs to assess interrater reliability must make several choices about the design of their studies. Researchers must determine whether raters should be considered as random or fixed. The random designation applies to raters considered to be representative of other possible raters and in this sense to be a random sample of the raters of interest. Raters are considered to be fixed if they are the only raters that could be used or are of interest. It is important to note that designating raters as fixed does not allow the researcher to generalize results to any other raters. Raters can also be either crossed with persons or nested within persons. If all raters rate all people, raters are crossed with people, whereas if a different set of raters rates each person, raters are nested within persons. In the latter case, it is not possible to estimate a separate variance component for raters because the rater effect is confounded with the rater by person interaction and is subsumed into the error term. Finally, ICCs can be calculated for either consistency or absolute decisions. Consistency decisions are those in which comparisons across people are of interest, and are analogous to the norm-referenced decisions discussed in Chapter 2. Absolute decisions are those in which it is important that the numerical ratings provided by different raters are in strict agreement.

EXERCISES

1. What is the difference between interrater agreement and interrater reliability?

2. For each of the following situations, indicate whether interrater reliability or interrater agreement is most appropriate.

   a. Students' gymnastics skills are rated by three different raters; each rater assigns a score to each student. The gymnastics coach wants to know whether students are rank-ordered differently by the different raters.

   b. Noelle is training raters. At the end of the training she compares the ratings of each trainee to those of an expert rater. She would like to know how closely each trainee's ratings match those of the expert.

   c. Four officials at the Bandalos widget factory are rating employees' widget-making skills. The officials want to choose the employee with the most highly rated widget-making skills for special recognition. Should the officials be more concerned about interrater reliability or interrater agreement?

Table 9.8 shows the cross tabulation of ratings given by two raters. Ratings ranged from 1 to 4.

TABLE 9.8. Rater Data for Questions 3–4

Rater 2	Rater 1				
	1	2	3	4	Row total
1	5	2	1	0	8
2	1	14	3	1	19
3	1	2	8	2	13
4	0	0	3	7	10
Column total	7	18	15	10	40

3. Calculate nominal agreement for these data.

4. Calculate Cohen's kappa for these data.

5. In the calculations from Questions 3 and 4, the value for nominal agreement is higher than that for Cohen's kappa. Will this always be the case? Why or why not?

6. A clinical supervisor gives a counseling student high ratings when observing her clinical skills. However, the supervisor's rating is influenced, in part, by the fact that the student received a high score on her paper-and-pencil test. What is the name of this type of rating error?

7. What is a criterion-related agreement? When would this type of agreement be of interest?

8. Explain how coefficient alpha can be calculated from rating data.

9. For each of the following situations, state whether the raters are fixed or random and whether they are crossed or nested.

   a. Employees' job skills are rated by a team of three supervisors. Each supervisor on the team rates each employee. Ratings are completed every six months, with different teams of randomly selected supervisors used each time.

   b. Parents rate their child's level of cooperativeness.

   c. Teachers' classroom management skills are rated by teams of two raters. A different team of raters is assigned to rate each teacher.

10. Using the data in Table 9.9, calculate ICCs for the following designs. Note that there are 4 raters rating 15 people.

TABLE 9.9. ANOVA Table for Question 10

Source of variance	SS	df	MS
Between persons	84.00	14	6.00
Within persons	45.00	45	1.00
Between raters	24.00	3	8.00
Residual	21.00	42	0.50

   a. Two-way random design for an absolute decision using the formula for a single rating.

   b. Two-way random design for an absolute decision using the formula for an average rating.

11. Would the ICCs for average ratings be lower, higher, or equal to those for single ratings? Why?

12. Would the ICCs for a consistency decision be lower, higher, or equal to those for an absolute decision? Why?

Generalizability Theory

The discussion of ICCs in Chapter 9 provides a good lead-in to the concepts of *generalizability theory* (*G theory*). This is because many of the issues discussed in the context of ICCs, such as determining whether raters are fixed or random, whether the design is crossed or nested, and whether absolute agreement or consistency is needed, are also relevant in G theory. Basically, the G theory framework is the same as that underlying the computation of ICCs used to determine interrater reliability. The difference is that G theory can be used to assess the impact of *multiple* sources of error, whereas the ICCs discussed in Chapter 9 only assess error due to one source (typically raters). Thus, the G theory framework is much more comprehensive than that underlying either ICC computation or reliability coefficients based on classical test theory (CTT). In fact, the ICC framework is a special case of the more general G theory methodology. In the following sections, I first describe the basic tenets and terminology of G theory and then illustrate the computations and interpretations for some common models. I distinguish between generalizability studies (G studies) and decision studies (D studies) and define the two reliability-like coefficients used to assess the reliability, or, in G theory parlance, the dependability of scores: the G and phi (ϕ) coefficients.

BASIC CONCEPTS AND TERMINOLOGY

In G theory, the concept of *generalizability* or *dependability* replaces that of reliability as used in CTT. But the two concepts are analogous in the following way. In CTT, interest is in assessing the degree to which the observed scores obtained from different sets of items, on different occasions, or from different test forms are sufficiently similar that they can be regarded as measures of the same true score. In G theory, interest is in the degree to which the observed scores obtained under one set of conditions can be generalized to the average score that might be obtained across a more broadly defined set of acceptable conditions, known as the *universe of admissible operations* (UAO). In G theory, the degree to which scores can be generalized across different sets of conditions is termed *dependability* or *generalizability*.

G theory differs from CTT in several ways. First, whereas CTT provides reliability coefficients that assess only one source of measurement error, G theory allows for the simultaneous estimation of multiple sources of error. This allows researchers to compare the amounts of error contributed by different sources. Also, because multiple sources of error variance are estimated in G theory, the reliability-like coefficients obtained can incorporate all of these, providing a more realistic picture of the dependability of measures across combinations of error conditions. Second, G theory provides a method for estimating the number of items, raters, occasions, or other sources of measurement error needed to obtain acceptable levels of reliability. Although in CTT the number of items needed to obtain acceptable levels of reliability can be estimated using the Spearman–Brown prophecy formula presented in Chapter 8, that formula can accommodate only a single source of error. Third, G theory includes two types of studies: G studies, in which the magnitude of various sources of error are estimated, and D studies, in which the information obtained from a G study is used to determine the number of raters, items, occasions, or other error conditions needed to optimize dependability for a particular decision. Fourth, G theory provides two types of reliability coefficients: one that is appropriate for use in making norm-referenced decisions and one appropriate for making criterion-referenced decisions. The reliability coefficients discussed in Chapters 7 and 8 are appropriate only for norm-referenced decisions (although reliability coefficients for criterion-referenced testing are available). Differences between the G theory and CTT frameworks are summarized in Table 10.1.

G theory also differs from CTT in terminology. These terminology differences are due to differences in the conceptualization of reliability in the two theories. Whereas in CTT researchers' interest is in the degree to which examinees' observed scores are reflective of their true scores, in G theory interest is in how accurately observed scores obtained under a particular set of conditions (e.g., different items, raters, occasions) will generalize across the defined universe of conditions in the UAO. Instead of providing a list of terminology and definitions, I use the following scenario to introduce G theory terminology.

FACETS, OBJECTS OF MEASUREMENT, AND UNIVERSE SCORES

Consider a situation in which nursing students are assessed on several different tasks by different raters. Students' performances may differ across tasks, with some doing best on one skill and others on another. Students' performance may also be assessed differently by different raters, with one rater providing higher ratings than another. In G theory, sources of error such as differences across raters and tasks are termed *facets*, and their levels are referred to as *conditions*. The entities yielding scores, in this case the students, are known as the *objects of measurement* and are not considered as facets.

TABLE 10.1. Differences between G Theory and CTT

G theory	CTT
Provides estimates of multiple sources of measurement error in one analysis.	Can estimate only one source of measurement error at a time.
Dependability coefficients take into account all measured sources of measurement error.	Reliability coefficients take into account only one source of error at a time.
Provides a method for estimating how many levels of each source of error are needed to obtain acceptable dependability levels.	The Spearman–Brown formula can provide estimates of the number of levels of one source of error (usually items) needed to obtain acceptable reliability levels.
Provides dependability coefficients for both norm-referenced and criterion-referenced decisions from the same data.	Most commonly used reliability coefficients are appropriate for norm-referenced rather than criterion-referenced tests.

All facets of interest and their conditions make up the universe of admissible operations, which is defined by the researcher to include all measurements considered acceptable. For example, the researcher would likely be willing to accept ratings from any qualified rater, but ratings from random people wandering in off the street with no knowledge of nursing would probably not be considered acceptable and would not be within the universe of admissible operations. Similarly, the nursing faculty would likely have identified the types of tasks on which the students would be assessed. Other tasks, such as those involved in woodworking or computer programming, though useful, would not be considered admissible for the purposes of the assessment. However, any rating of an admissible task from an admissible rater would be within the universe.

Although any rating from an admissible rater of any admissible task provides some indication of a student's skill in nursing, typically ratings differ over raters and over tasks. This means that the inclusion of multiple raters, tasks, occasions, or other facets introduce a certain amount of error into students' scores in addition to providing information on their level of skill. If all the raters use their scoring rubric in a similarly conscientious fashion, and if the tasks are all similar in difficulty, the amount of error due to raters and tasks will be small. In such cases, the interpretation of a student's score need not be qualified by stating that it is a score from a specific rater, on specific tasks. Instead, we can assume that the student would obtain similar scores if rated by other raters on other tasks. Stated another way, we have evidence that scores will *generalize* across raters and tasks, and that scores are thus *dependable* or reliable. To use more G theory terminology, a high level of dependability indicates that scores obtained under a particular set of conditions will generalize to a student's *universe score*. The universe score is analogous to the true score in CTT and can be conceptualized as the average score a student would obtain if tested repeatedly under all possible sets of conditions in the UAO. As the name implies, the ability to make such generalizations is the raison d'être for G theory.

Crossed and Nested Facets

I have already introduced several other aspects of G theory terminology in the context of the ICC used in assessing interrater reliability. Facets can be *crossed* or *nested*. Crossed facets are those in which all conditions of one facet are observed with all conditions of another. For example, if all raters rated all tasks, raters and tasks would be crossed. Facets can also be crossed with the objects of measurement. If all students completed all the tasks and all raters rated all tasks, the design would be *fully or completely crossed*. *Nested* conditions are those in which two or more conditions from one facet are associated with each condition of another facet (or of the object of measurement) and different conditions of that facet are associated with each condition of the other. Suppose that the tasks being rated in the nursing example were quite time consuming to rate. The faculty might decide that a different set of raters would rate each task. In this case, two or more raters are associated with each task, and there is a different set of raters for each task. Raters are therefore nested within tasks.

Random and Fixed Facets

Facets can be *random* or *fixed*. Random facets are those in which the conditions used in the study are assumed to be interchangeable with any others within the universe of admissible operations. Note that this does not mean the conditions must literally be randomly sampled from the universe (although this would certainly qualify the facet as random). Instead, it means that the researcher considers the conditions to be exchangeable in the sense that they are all members of the same UAO. In the nursing example, raters would be random if researchers considered ratings provided by one rater to be exchangeable with ratings provided by another. Treating a facet as random allows researchers to generalize to all other conditions of that facet within the UAO. Fixed facets are those that contain either all of the possible conditions in the universe or all of the conditions to which the researcher wants to generalize. For example, if the tasks included in the nursing assessment were the only tasks of interest, task would be a fixed facet. Although a design in which tasks were fixed would not allow for generalization to other tasks, this should not be an issue because there would be no need for such generalizations. In some cases, facets are fixed "naturally" because the conditions included are the only conditions possible. To take a silly example, if students' hair color was considered to be a source of error, it would constitute a fixed facet because there would be no need to generalize beyond the hair colors brown, black, blonde, and red (assuming the UAO were restricted to natural rather than artificially induced hair colors). A less facetious, and common, example is that in which a test consists of several established subtests. Here the facet of subtests would be fixed rather than random because there are no additional subtests to which generalizations might be made.

G STUDIES AND D STUDIES

As noted previously, G theory encompasses two types of studies: G studies and D studies. The purpose of a G study is to obtain as much information as possible on the magnitude of sources of error that are of interest. In the D study, the researcher uses information on the magnitude of various sources of error obtained from the G study to design a measurement scenario in which the desired level of dependability is achieved with the smallest number of conditions. This is done by estimating how much levels of dependability would increase with different combinations of facet conditions, much as the Spearman–Brown prophecy formula introduced in Chapter 8 estimates the increase in reliability achieved by adding more items to a test. In a D study, the researcher can estimate the increase in dependability that would result from adding more conditions of various facets. For example, the researcher could determine whether increasing the number of raters, the number of tasks, or both, would optimize dependability. The G study should define the universe of admissible operations as broadly as possible because a broadly defined UAO allows for a broader range of D study possibilities. I elaborate on this point in a later section. Another reason for adopting a broad definition of the UAO, according to Brennan (1992, p. 32), is that a large sample of G study conditions will yield more stable estimates of the variance accounted for by each facet.

In the D study, researchers must decide what type of decision (relative or absolute) will be made and define the *universe of generalization*. The universe of generalization is, as the name implies, that to which the researcher wants to generalize once the measurement scenario is finalized. This universe may or may not be the same as the universe of admissible operations. Although the universe of generalization cannot go beyond the conditions of the G study, it can restrict those conditions in some way. For example, after obtaining information about the various sources of measurement error from the G study, a researcher may decide to fix a facet in the D study that was considered random in the G study by limiting that facet to only some of the possible conditions. Or the researcher may decide that a nested design would better serve the intended measurement purpose than the crossed design used in the G study.

THE G THEORY MODEL

At this point, you may have perceived certain similarities between the G theory model and the ANOVA model. In fact, G theory is based on the same model as ANOVA and divides the variance in scores into parts due to each source of error and to the object of measurement. The facets in G theory are analogous to factors in ANOVA, and as in ANOVA their effects are sometimes called *main effects*. There can be multiple facets, and the fully crossed design will include the interactions among the facets. For a simple design in which persons are crossed with raters, the variance due to raters, to persons (known as *universe score variance*), and to the person-by-rater interaction can be estimated. However, the person-by-rater variance is confounded with the residual term.

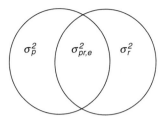

FIGURE 10.1. Venn diagram showing the decomposition of variance for a one-facet, crossed, $p \times r$ design.

This is because in a G theory design, facets are typically crossed with persons, and this results in a design in which each cell contains only one person's score. More generally, for any G theory design, the highest order interaction will be confounded with the residual. The residual also includes any random error and any systematic sources of error that were not included in the design. For example, if the nursing students had been assessed on several occasions, and occasions were not included as a facet in the design, any variance due to occasions would be relegated to the variance component for error.

Let us examine the variance components of the person-by-rater design in more detail. This is a one-facet, crossed design because there is only one facet (raters; remember that persons are the object of measurement and not a facet), and raters are crossed with persons, with every person rated by every rater. There are three sources of variation for this design: variation due to persons, raters, and the person-by-rater interaction. The last-named effect is confounded with the residual or overall error term, as noted previously. Because these sources of variance are independent, they can be decomposed into separate variance components.

Equation 10.1 shows the decomposition of the observed score variance for the person-by-rater design ($\sigma^2(X_{pr})$) into that due to persons (σ_p^2), raters (σ_r^2), and person-by-rater interaction and residual ($\sigma_{pr,e}^2$).

$$\sigma^2\left(X_{pr}\right) = \sigma_p^2 + \sigma_r^2 + \sigma_{pr,e}^2 \tag{10.1}$$

The person variance, known as the *universe score* variance, is the average deviation of peoples' universe scores from the overall, or grand mean, and indicates how much scores vary across people. The rater variance measures the degree to which people's scores differ across raters, on average. The last term is a combination of variance due to the interaction of persons by raters and residual or unmeasured variance. The interaction variance will be large when raters rate different people in different ways. For example, if Casey gives her highest scores to students 1, 2, and 3, and Kat gives students 4, 5, and 6 her highest scores, the result will be some level of person-by-rater interaction. The residual variance assesses the amount of random error and of any unmeasured sources of variance. Venn diagrams such as that in Figure 10.1 are often used to show the variance partitioning in G theory designs. The diagram in Figure 10.1 depicts the person-by-rater design and shows the decomposition of the sources of variation just discussed.

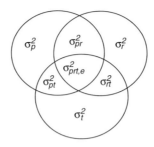

FIGURE 10.2. Venn diagram showing the decomposition of variance for a two-facet, crossed, $p \times r \times t$ design.

The statistical model underlying the one-facet design can be extended to designs with any number of facets. As in ANOVA, additional facets bring with them additional main effects and additional interaction terms. The highest order interaction, whatever it is, will always be confounded with the error term. Recall that in the initial nursing student example, each student completed several tasks, all of which were rated by several raters. The result is a two-facet, fully crossed, $p \times r \times t$ design, in which raters and tasks are the two facets and students (persons) are the object of measurement. The observed score variance can be decomposed into components due to the main effects of person, rater, and task, the person-by-rater interaction, person-by-task interaction, rater-by-task interaction, and the three-way person-by-rater-by-task variance, which would be confounded with the overall error term. This decomposition is shown in Equation 10.2 and Figure 10.2.

$$\sigma^2\left(X_{prt}\right) = \sigma_p^2 + \sigma_r^2 + \sigma_t^2 + \sigma_{pr}^2 + \sigma_{pt}^2 + \sigma_{rt}^2 + \sigma_{prt,e}^2 \qquad (10.2)$$

The person, rater, and person-by-rater variances are defined in the same way as in the one-facet model. The task variance measures the degree to which students' scores vary across tasks, on average. The person-by-task variance indicates the degree to which students find the tasks differentially difficult. For example, Kate may receive her highest score on one task, whereas Thai receives his highest score on another. The rater-by-task variance indicates the degree to which the raters rate different tasks differentially. Sancho may give higher ratings to a particular task, while Kristen gives high ratings to another. Finally, the three-way variance indicates the extent to which students obtain differential scores on different tasks that are rated differentially. This variance component also includes the residual or overall error term.

COMPUTATION OF VARIANCE COMPONENTS

While there are several similarities between G theory and ANOVA, there are also two important differences. First, although in ANOVA the focus is on testing the statistical significance of effects, this is not of interest in G theory. Rather, the focus in G theory is on estimation of the amounts of variance due to different sources of error, on comparison of the relative magnitudes of different sources of error, and on the development of a measurement design to maximize dependability. Those familiar with ANOVA models will recall that the F-tests are based on the mean squares for the factor and for the error, or residual. Because of the different focus in G theory, *variance components* rather than mean squares are computed. These variance components are estimated from *expected mean squares* (EMS). Expected mean squares estimate the value of a mean square that would be obtained by analyzing repeated samples, using the same G theory design and averaging across the resulting mean squares. The EMS is therefore the expected value, or average, of the mean square across all conditions in the universe of generalization, or the "universe" value of the mean square within the UAO. Estimates of the variance components can be obtained by substituting sample estimates of the MS from ANOVA into the equations provided in the next section.

G theory variance components are derived from the expected mean squares algebraically (see Crocker & Algina, 1986, or Shavelson & Webb, 1991, for derivations of some of these) and are different for each design. For the simple one- and two-facet crossed designs in our examples, the derivations are straightforward, but they increase in complexity with more facets and with nested designs or those with fixed facets. Although variance components for simple designs can be calculated by hand or by using a spreadsheet, specialized programs are generally used to obtain those from more complex designs. A variety of programs developed by Robert Brennan and his colleagues are available for free download (www.education.uiowa.edu/centers/casma/computer-programs). These programs compute not only the variance components, but also the two dependability coefficients discussed later in this chapter.

Computation of Variance Components for a One-Facet Design

In this section, I present the formulas for the one- and two-facet designs in the previous examples. For the one-facet person-by-rater design, the estimated variance components are calculated as follows:

$$\hat{\sigma}_p^2 = \left(MS_p - MS_{pr,e}\right) / n_r$$

$$\hat{\sigma}_r^2 = \left(MS_r - MS_{pr,e}\right) / n_p \qquad (10.3)$$

$$\hat{\sigma}_{pr,e}^2 = MS_e$$

The mean squares (MS_p, MS_r, and $MS_{pr,e}$) on which the estimated variance components are based are those from an ANOVA in which persons and raters are included as factors, and scores are the dependent variables. The data must be set up in the same way as for calculation of the ICC for interrater reliability, as shown in Table 10.2. The variance component for the combined two-way interaction/error term ($\sigma_{pr,e}^2$) is the same as the ANOVA interaction term. However, as noted previously, it will be confounded with the residual because there is only one person in each cell (e.g., each person is rated by each rater, so the person-by-rater cells contain only the score of one person rated by one rater, as shown in Table 10.2).

Also note from Equations 10.3 that the error MS is subtracted from the MS for the main effect (person or rater). This is because the expected mean squares from which the variance components are derived, being theoretical averages across repeated random samples, contain sampling error, which must be subtracted to obtain a "pure" measure of the person or rater variance. The resulting difference is then divided by the number of conditions in the other facet. This is because the variance for a facet is calculated by averaging across all other conditions in the other facet. In G theory, the estimated variance components represent the variance attributable to only one condition of the other facet, and this is obtained by dividing by the number of conditions of that facet. The resulting variance components are measures of the degree to which the scores provided by a single, randomly selected level of the facet are expected to differ from the mean rating across all levels. This indicates how much error is inherent in generalizing from a person's score from a single level to that person's universe score (their average across all conditions and levels in the universe).

The calculations and resultant values for the one-facet design are shown in Table 10.3, based on the data in Table 10.2. There are 12 students and three raters, so $n_p = 12$ and $n_r = 3$. The last column of Table 10.3 shows each estimated variance component expressed as a percentage of the total variance. You may recall from introductory statistics that variances depend on the scale of the variables from which they are calculated. This lack of standardization means that they can only be interpreted in a relative manner. In G theory, this is done by expressing the variance components as percentages of the total amount of variation. To obtain these percentages, I simply added the values of all the variance components (including that for error), divided the estimated variance component for each effect by this total, and multiplied by 100.

The variance due to persons is by far the largest, at 63%. The person, or universe score variance is roughly analogous to true score variance in classical test theory. The relatively large amount of universe score variance indicates that nursing students varied systematically in their performance. The percentage of variance due to raters is quite small—only 1%. This indicates that the raters were quite consistent in their average ratings. The remaining variance is due to random measurement error and the interaction of persons by raters (remember that these are confounded). Person–rater interactions indicate that different raters were more or less lenient for different students. However, we do not know from the error–interaction variance term whether random error or person–rater interaction accounts for most of the 36% of the variance in scores.

Another way to interpret variance components is to take the square root of each component. This provides a measure of the deviation of a score from the mean of that facet. For example, the rater variance component is .05, and its square root of .22 means that, on average, ratings vary about .22 of a point across raters. This is quite good given that ratings were made on a 6-point scale.

TABLE 10.2. Data for One-Facet Person × Rater Design

Person	Rater	Score
1	1	3.0
1	2	5.0
1	3	4.0
2	1	3.0
2	2	5.0
2	3	5.0
3	1	1.0
3	2	1.0
3	3	2.0
4	1	3.0
4	2	1.0
4	3	2.0
5	1	6.0
5	2	5.0
5	3	5.0
6	1	1.0
6	2	2.0
6	3	5.0
7	1	3.0
7	2	5.0
7	3	5.0
8	1	5.0
8	2	4.0
8	3	5.0
9	1	3.0
9	2	1.0
9	3	3.0
10	1	4.0
10	2	3.0
10	3	5.0
11	1	3.0
11	2	4.0
11	3	3.0
12	1	2.0
12	2	2.0
12	3	2.0

TABLE 10.3. Estimated Variance Components for the One-Facet, Crossed $p \times r$ Design

Source of variation	Mean square (MS)	Estimated variance component	Percentage of total variance
Persons (p)	10.80	(10.8 − 1.72)/3 = 3.03	63
Raters (r)	2.37	(2.37 − 1.72)/12 = 0.05	1
Persons × raters, error (pr,e)	1.72	1.72	36
Total		4.80	100

Computation of Variance Components for a Two-Facet Design

The computation of variance components for a two-facet design is a fairly straightforward extension of that for the one-facet design. I illustrate the process with an example in which the person-by-rater design is extended to include the task facet, with three conditions representing three different tasks. All students are rated on all tasks by all raters, resulting in a fully crossed two-facet design ($p \times r \times t$). The rules for obtaining the estimated variance components are as follows. For main effects, subtract the MS for any two-way interaction of that facet with any other facet, and add the error MS. Divide this quantity by the product of the number of conditions of the facets with which the main-effect facet interacts (or by the number of people if the interaction is with persons). For example, for the person main effect, subtract the interaction MS for the person-by-rater and person-by-task effects from the person MS and add the error MS. Then divide by the number of raters (3) times the number of tasks (3). For the two-way interactions, subtract the error MS from the interaction MS and divide this difference by the number of conditions of the facet(s) that is(are) *not* involved in the interaction. For example, for the person-by-rater effect, subtract the error MS from the person-by-rater mean square, and divide by the number of tasks (3). The formulas and calculations for this design are shown in Table 10.4.

Note that the estimated variance component for raters is negative. There are two possible reasons that negative estimates of variance components might be obtained. One of these reasons is that the G theory model is misspecified, which would happen if an important facet had been left out of the design. In this example, students were actually rated on two occasions, but for simplicity I averaged the two occasions in analyzing the data. It may be that omitting the occasion facet resulted in misspecification and in the negative variance estimate. If so, this is an indication that I should reanalyze the data using a three-facet (rater, task, and occasion) design. The second reason for negative estimates of variance components is sampling error. If the population value of the variance is very small, a negative estimate could be obtained in a sample because of sampling error around the population value. In this example, the number of students is relatively small, which would result in a relatively large amount of sampling variation, so this may account for the negative estimate. The small magnitude of the negative estimate also

TABLE 10.4. Estimated Variance Components for the Two-Facet, Crossed $p \times r \times t$ Design

Source of variation	Mean square (MS)	Variance component equation	Estimated variance component	Percentage of total variance
Persons (p)	11.72	$\hat{\sigma}_p^2 = \dfrac{\left(MS_p - MS_{pr} - MS_{pt} + MS_{prt,e}\right)}{n_r n_t}$	$\dfrac{\left(11.72 - 2.06 - 1.00 + .64\right)}{3(3)} = 1.03$	44.3
Raters (r)	2.07	$\hat{\sigma}_r^2 = \dfrac{\left(MS_r - MS_{pr} - MS_{rt} + MS_{prt,e}\right)}{n_p n_t}$	$\dfrac{\left(2.07 - 2.06 - .79 + .64\right)}{12(3)} = -0.004$	0
Tasks (t)	3.34	$\hat{\sigma}_t^2 = \dfrac{\left(MS_t - MS_{pt} - MS_{rt} + MS_{prt,e}\right)}{n_p n_r}$	$\dfrac{\left(3.34 - 1.00 - .79 + .64\right)}{12(3)} = 0.06$	2.6
pr	2.06	$\hat{\sigma}_{pr}^2 = \dfrac{\left(MS_{pr} - MS_{prt,e}\right)}{n_t}$	$\dfrac{\left(2.06 - .64\right)}{3} = 0.47$	20.2
pt	1.00	$\hat{\sigma}_{pt}^2 = \dfrac{\left(MS_{pt} - MS_{prt,e}\right)}{n_r}$	$\dfrac{\left(1.00 - .64\right)}{3} = 0.12$	5.2
rt	0.79	$\hat{\sigma}_{rt}^2 = \dfrac{\left(MS_{rt} - MS_{prt,e}\right)}{n_p}$	$\dfrac{\left(.79 - .64\right)}{12} = 0.01$	0.4
(prt,e)	0.64	$\hat{\sigma}_{prt,e}^2 = MS_{prt,e}$	0.64	27.5
Total			2.85	100

suggests that sampling error may be the culprit. When negative estimates are obtained and are presumed to be due to sampling error, they can be set to zero (Cronbach, Gleser, Nanda, & Rajaratnam, 1972). As long as the negative variance estimate is close to zero, as it is in this case and is due to sampling error, this should not result in any bias in the other estimates, so I have taken that approach here.

Although the variance component for persons is the largest at about 44%, the person-by-rater interaction accounts for about 20% of the variance. This indicates that different raters rated students differentially. Some raters tended to give high ratings to some students, whereas other raters tended to give low ratings to the same students. In the one-facet design, this effect was confounded with the overall error term. One advantage of the two-facet design is that I can now obtain an estimate of this effect. Note that the error term is considerably smaller in the two-facet than in the one-facet design, reflecting the fact that the person-by-rater interaction as well as any variance due to tasks has been removed from the error term in this two-facet design. The percentage of variance accounted for by the main effects of rater and task are very small. Recall that the variance components represent the variance associated with a single condition of each facet.

For these two facets, the relatively small estimated variance components indicate that the tasks are fairly equal in difficulty and the raters gave fairly equal percentages of high and low ratings. However, when interactions are present, as in this example, these must be considered when interpreting the main effects. I have already noted that the person-by-rater interaction variance is relatively large. The person-by-task variance component is much smaller at 5.2%, indicating that students perform differentially across tasks, although not to any great extent. The task-by-rater interaction variance component is near zero, indicating that the raters do not rate tasks differentially.

Variance Components for Nested Designs

Nested facets are those in which multiple conditions of the facet are associated with each condition of another facet *and* the associated conditions of the nested facet are different for each condition of the other facet. An example may help to clarify. In the previous design, each student responded to each task. But suppose that there are many tasks and that these tasks are quite time consuming for students. In this case, the nursing instructors may decide to administer only two tasks to each student, with each student completing different tasks. Because multiple (two) tasks are associated with each student and the tasks are different for each student, tasks are nested in students. As another example, if tasks are time consuming to rate, the nursing instructors may decide to assign a limited number of tasks to each rater, with each rater providing ratings for a different set of tasks. This would result in tasks being nested within raters because multiple tasks are associated with each rater, and each rater rates a different set of tasks. These examples illustrate that facets can be nested either within the object of measurement (students) or within another facet.

Nested designs are indicated by the notation $t{:}p$, or $t(p)$, meaning that tasks (t) are nested within students (p), or $t{:}r$ for a design in which tasks are nested within raters. Note that if, in the $t{:}p$ design, only one task had been assigned to each student, tasks and students would be completely confounded. In that case, there would be no way to obtain an unconfounded variance component for either because we would have no way of knowing whether a particular student received a higher score because she was assigned an easier task or whether the task appeared to be easier because it was assigned to a particularly competent student. This is why *multiple* conditions of the nested facet must be associated with each condition of the other facet.

Nested facets can occur by design, as in the preceding examples. Cost, time, or other considerations may dictate that not all students perform all tasks or are rated by all raters. Nested facets could also occur naturally, as when items are nested within subtests. In this situation, multiple items are associated with each subtest, and each subtest has different items. It would not make sense to cross items with subtests if, for example, the subtests measured different areas of content knowledge. In such a situation, a nested design is the only reasonable choice. Although nested designs may be preferable for practical or logistical reasons or may be unavoidable in the case of

TABLE 10.5. Estimated Variance Components for the One-Facet, Nested *t:p* Design

Source of variation	Mean square (*MS*)	Estimated variance component	Percentage of total variance
Persons (*p*)	12.0	$(12 - 1.5)/2 = 5.3$	78
Tasks, persons × tasks, error (*t,pt,e*)	1.5	1.5	22
Total		6.8	100

naturally nested facets, they have a disadvantage relative to crossed designs. This disadvantage is that the main effects of nested facets are confounded with those of the facet (or object of measurement) in which they are nested. In the *t:p* design, there is no way to determine the main effect of tasks independent of the main effect of students because each task was completed by only one student. Thus, the task effect becomes part of the student-by-task interaction. And because that interaction is confounded with the error term in this one-facet design, the variance due to task, student by task, and error would all be combined.

Table 10.5 shows the estimated variance components for a hypothetical *t:p* design. Note that the only variance components are for persons and error. The variance component for persons is calculated in the usual way, by subtracting the error *MS* from the person *MS*. The only difference is that, instead of dividing by the total number of tasks across persons, the result is divided by the number of tasks each person completed. In our example, this is two. The estimated variance component for persons accounts for the lion's share of the variance (78%), indicating that much of the total variation is due to differences in people's universe scores. The drawback of the nested design is that neither the variance due to tasks nor the variance due to the person by task can be estimated.

Nested designs are often part of more complicated two- (or more) facet designs, opening up a large array of nesting possibilities. For example, tasks could be nested within students as before but both crossed with raters. In this design, students would be assigned different sets of tasks, but all of the tasks from all of the students would be rated by all of the raters, resulting in an $r \times (t:p)$ design, or tasks nested within students, all crossed with raters, design. Or a different set of raters might rate each task, with all students performing all tasks, yielding a design in which raters are nested within tasks and tasks are crossed with students ($p \times (r:t)$). As in the one-facet nested design, the main effect for the nested effect cannot be estimated independently of the effect in which it is nested. In addition, for two-facet designs, the interaction of the crossed and nested facets is confounded with the three-way interaction/error term. Thus, nested two-facet designs result in some loss of information because all sources of variation in scores cannot be estimated. The formulas to calculate variance components for nested designs can become quite complicated. Shavelson and Webb (1991) provide the expected *MS* for

TABLE 10.6. Nested Two-Facet Designs and Estimable Variance Components

Source of variance	Design			
	$r \times (t{:}p)$	$p \times (r{:}t)$	$t{:}(p \times r)$	$t{:}r{:}p$
P	σ_p^2	σ_p^2	σ_p^2	σ_p^2
R	σ_r^2	$\sigma_{r,rt}^2$	σ_r^2	$\sigma_{r,pr}^2$
T	$\sigma_{t,pt}^2$	σ_t^2	X	X
pr	σ_{pr}^2	X	σ_{pr}^2	$\sigma_{r,pr}^2$
pt	$\sigma_{t,pt}^2$	σ_{pt}^2	X	X
rt	X	$\sigma_{r,rt}^2$	X	X
prt,e	$\sigma_{rt,prt,e}^2$	$\sigma_{pr,prt,e}^2$	$\sigma_{t,pt,rt,prt,e}^2$	$\sigma_{t,pt,rt,prt,e}^2$

Note. X indicates that the variance component is not estimable in the designated design.

some of these designs, but in general, complicated algorithms are needed that are probably best left to computer programs designed for this purpose.

Table 10.6 shows some nested two-facet design possibilities for the nursing example, along with the variance components that can (and cannot) be estimated. Variance components that are confounded are indicated by subscripts on the variances. For example, in the $r \times (t{:}p)$ design, task and person-by-task variance are confounded, as indicated by the variance component subscripts of t,pt ($\sigma_{t,pt}^2$). Variance components that cannot be estimated in a particular design are indicated with an X. The $r \times (t{:}p)$ and $p \times (r{:}t)$ designs have been discussed previously. In these two designs, variance components for the two facets within parentheses are confounded. In addition, the interactions of the facet appearing before the "X" (the crossed facet) and the nested facet (the facet appearing before the ":" cannot be estimated. The $t{:}(p \times r)$ design is one in which all students are rated by all raters, but each student completes only a subset of the tasks. In this design, the nested task effect cannot be estimated, nor can its interactions with persons or raters. All of these effects are relegated to the overall error term. The last design is one that is fully nested, $t{:}r{:}p$. In this design, each rater rates only a subset of the tasks ($t{:}r$) and each person is rated by only a subset of the raters ($r{:}p$) on a subset of tasks. In this design, variance components for several facets and interactions are inestimable. The rater and person-by-rater effects are confounded. Only the person effect can be independently estimated.

Variance Components for Designs with Fixed Facets

The designs discussed thus far have been for *random* effects. In some cases, however, it is more appropriate to consider facets as *fixed*. The conditions of random facets are considered to be exchangeable with any other condition from the universe of admissible operations. This implies that we should be able to generalize from a particular set of conditions to any other set of conditions from the same universe. For example, we should be able to generalize from students' performances on one set of test items or tasks to their performances on another set. Fixed effects are different in that their conditions constitute the entirety of the condition within the universe, or at least the only conditions that are of interest. For example, if a test had four subtests covering specified areas of content, and these four content areas exhausted the content of interest, subtests would constitute a fixed facet. Similarly, if we were only interested in the ratings from particular raters and no others, the rater facet would be considered fixed.

Note that fixing a facet precludes the ability to generalize to other conditions of the facet, so defining raters as a fixed facet would curtail the ability to generalize to other raters. Fixed facets contribute to universe score variance rather than to error variance. Fixing a facet results in a narrower universe of generalization, and generalizing to a narrower universe is less error prone than generalizing to a broad universe. Of course, a broader universe may still be preferred because it allows for generalizability to a wider universe of operations. In any design, some facets can be random and others fixed. Designs with both fixed and random facets are called *mixed* designs. However, all facets cannot be fixed, as this would defeat the purpose of G theory, which is to, well, generalize from the facet conditions in a study to the broader facet universe.

Variance components involving fixed facets are obtained by averaging across conditions of the fixed facet. Suppose in a one-facet student-by-rater design I had determined that raters were fixed. To obtain the variance component for students, I would average across raters. This makes sense if the raters are considered to be interchangeable, as is typical, because the average score across raters should provide a better estimate of a student's score. In some situations, averaging across conditions of the fixed facet may not be defensible. For example, suppose that the nursing students in the earlier example were rated in two different content areas: clinical skills and interaction with patients. Some students may be very good at clinical skills such as administering injections and calculating medication dosages, but perform quite differently in patient interactions. Other students may have the opposite pattern, and some may be good (or bad) at both. If the nursing instructors were interested in the separate effects for clinical skills and patient interactions, it would be entirely reasonable to conduct a separate G study for each content area. In this case, the variance components would be estimated in the same way as illustrated previously for random effects. However, the content area facet would drop out of the design because it would consist of only one condition for each of the two G studies.

If it does make sense to average over conditions, this can be accomplished as follows. First, obtain the MS's by treating all facets as random, and estimate the variance components as shown in the previous examples for fully random designs. Then recalculate each of the variance components for the random effects by adding to each component its interaction with the fixed effect, divided by the number of conditions of the fixed effect. As an example, I modify the earlier nursing student example by introducing a hypothetical content area facet, consisting of the aforementioned areas of clinical skills and patient interactions. This facet is considered to be fixed because clinical skills and patient communication are the only areas in which students receive performance ratings (for other content areas, I will suppose they take written examinations). All students are rated by all raters on both content areas, so the design is fully crossed and mixed, with students and raters random and content area fixed.

Table 10.7 illustrates the variance component calculations for the $p \times r \times c$ design with c fixed. The first step is to calculate the estimated variance components for the random design. The variance components are those for students (p), raters (r), content area (c), student by rater (pr), student by content area (pc), content area by rater (cr), and error (prc,e), and the estimates for the random design are shown on the left-hand side of the table. On the right-hand side of the table, I show the calculations for the mixed-effects design. I recalculated the estimated variance components for persons, raters, and error by adding in a component due to the fixed effect, c. The mixed-effects variance components are designated with an asterisk after the effect (p^*). The formulas for these effects are

$$\hat{\sigma}_{p^*}^2 = \hat{\sigma}_p^2 + \frac{\hat{\sigma}_{pc}^2}{n_c} \tag{10.4}$$

$$\hat{\sigma}_{r^*}^2 = \hat{\sigma}_r^2 + \frac{\hat{\sigma}_{rc}^2}{n_c} \tag{10.5}$$

$$\hat{\sigma}_{pr,e^*}^2 = \hat{\sigma}_{pr}^2 + \frac{\hat{\sigma}_{prc,e}^2}{n_c} \tag{10.6}$$

The percentages of variance due to each effect in the mixed design are then recalculated based on the new variance components. Note that there are no averaged variance components for the person-by-content area or rater-by-content area effects. Also, the error term no longer includes the three-way interaction, but instead contains the two-way interaction between the random effects ($\sigma_{pr,e}^2$). These changes occur because the variation due to pc, rc, and prc has been reallocated to the new averaged variance components. These are important changes because we are no longer able to estimate these three interaction effects. In addition, it is not possible to estimate the variation due to content area.

In the fully random design (left-hand side of the table), the person-by-rater interaction accounts for a relatively large proportion of variance (29%). This indicates that raters provide differential ratings, with students receiving high ratings from one rater and low ratings from another. Thus, if only one rater rated students, students' scores would depend to a considerable extent on the rater to which they were assigned. In the fully random design, over 16% of the variation in scores is due to content area. This indicates that the content areas differ in overall difficulty. The person-by-content area interaction accounts for 8% of the variance, indicating that students find the content areas differentially difficult, to some extent. The rater-by-content variance is slightly negative and is set to zero.

TABLE 10.7. Estimated Variance Components for the $p \times r \times c$ Design with c Fixed

Random design		Mixed design with c fixed		
Source of variation	Estimated variance component	Source of variation	Estimated variance component	Percentage of total variance
Persons (σ_p^2)	0.10	Persons ($\hat{\sigma}_{p\cdot}^2$)	$\hat{\sigma}_{p\cdot}^2 = \hat{\sigma}_p^2 + \dfrac{\hat{\sigma}_{pc}^2}{n_c} = .10 + \dfrac{.16}{2} = .18$	15.3
Raters (σ_r^2)	0.02	Raters ($\hat{\sigma}_{r\cdot}^2$)	$\hat{\sigma}_{r\cdot}^2 = \hat{\sigma}_r^2 + \dfrac{\hat{\sigma}_{rc}^2}{n_c} = .02 + \dfrac{0}{2} = .02$	1.7
Content area (σ_c^2)	0.33			
$p \times r$ (σ_{pr}^2)	0.58	Error ($\hat{\sigma}_{pr,e\cdot}^2$)	$\hat{\sigma}_{pr,e\cdot}^2 = \hat{\sigma}_{pr}^2 + \dfrac{\hat{\sigma}_{prc,e}^2}{n_c} = .58 + \dfrac{.81}{2} = .98$	83.0
$p \times c$ (σ_{pc}^2)	0.16			
$r \times c$ (σ_{rc}^2)	−0.04*			
Error ($\sigma_{prc,e}^2$)	0.81			
Total	2.00		1.18	100

*Negative variance estimate is set to 0.

In the mixed design with content area treated as fixed, the effects for students and raters are averaged across the two content areas. The variation due to interactions with content area is added to the main effects for students and raters. Thus, both the student and rater effects will generally account for larger percentages of variance than in the fully random design. In our example, however, the rater variance does not change because the rater-by-content area variance component has been set to zero. The percentages of variance accounted for by both the person and rater effects are relatively small, and the error component is by far the largest. These results indicate that there may be additional sources of variation that should be incorporated into the design, such as occasion. The fact that content area accounts for a relatively large percentage of the variance in the random design suggests that students' scores differ across the two areas. It may therefore be better to analyze the content areas separately, breaking the design into two person-by-rater crossed designs. This can be accomplished using the procedures for estimating variance components for random effects illustrated previously. The results of these analyses are presented in Table 10.8.

Things look a bit better when we analyze the two content areas separately. For both content areas, the variance due to students' universe scores (σ_p^2) is higher than in the fully random design. The percentage of universe score variance is higher for clinical skills, indicating that students' performance is more variable in this area than in patient communication. Variance due to raters is negligible, indicating that raters are consistent in their scoring, and this holds true for both content areas. However, the

TABLE 10.8. Estimated Variance Components for the *p* × *r* × *c* Design with *c* Fixed, Analyzing Content Areas Separately

Source of variation	Clinical skills		Patient communication	
	Estimated variance component	Percentage of total variance	Estimated variance component	Percentage of total variance
Persons (σ_p^2)	0.70	40.5	0.38	23.2
Raters (σ_r^2)	0.50	0.6	−0.03*	0
Error ($\sigma_{pr,e}^2$)	1.02	58.9	1.26	76.8
Total	1.73	100	1.64	100

*Negative variance estimate is set to 0.

error component still accounts for the largest amount of variance, suggesting that there are some unaccounted-for sources of variation and/or large person-by-rater interactions.

DECISION STUDIES

In G theory a distinction is made between D studies and G studies. The purpose of the G study is to provide estimates of the magnitudes of different sources of error in the form of estimated variance components, as in the previous examples. As should be clear at this point, G studies that incorporate completely crossed designs with random facets yield the most information on the various sources of error. This is because these are the only designs in which all sources of variance and their interactions can be estimated (except, of course, the highest order interaction, which is always confounded with the overall error variance). After the variance components have been estimated, these can be incorporated into a D study to design a measurement situation in which error is minimized as much as possible.

In the D study, various options for the number of raters, tasks, content areas, and so on can be tried out to determine how many of each are needed to achieve the desired level of dependability. Such information is important because, in addition to the effects of different numbers of raters, tasks, and other facets on the error variance and resulting reliability coefficients, practical and logistical considerations will also enter into any decisions about the optimal measurement design. If tasks are difficult to construct and time consuming to administer, this will put constraints on the number that can be used. If it is expensive and time consuming to train raters, it may not be cost effective to increase their numbers. For example, after examining the various possibilities in D studies, the researcher may determine that a measurement scenario in which one or more effects are nested or fixed will yield an adequate level of dependability, and that such a design will save time and money. Thus, devoting extra resources to the G study may pay off in the long run by allowing for exploration of a larger number of D study possibilities, some of which may be more cost effective than others. For instance, the zero variance for raters in the previous G study might seem to suggest that increases in the number of raters would yield negligible increases in dependability. However, if the person-by-rater effect is relatively large, it may be worth increasing the number of raters in an attempt to decrease the magnitude of that component. Increasing the number of raters might therefore prove to be a cost-effective strategy. However, if tasks accounted for a large proportion of variance, and they were inexpensive to develop and not too time consuming to administer and score, increasing the number of tasks might be a better option.

Such options can be explored in the D study in a manner similar to the use of the Spearman–Brown prophecy formula in CTT. Recall that the Spearman–Brown formula "prophesies" the extent to which internal consistency will increase or decrease as the number of items on a test is changed. D study methods work in a similar manner but are more flexible because they can incorporate more than one source of error.

Relative and Absolute Interpretations

Another consideration in the D study is whether the decision to be made is *absolute* or *relative*. As noted in Chapter 9 in discussing the ICC, relative decisions are those in which norm referencing, or comparing students' scores to those of the group, is of interest. More generally, relative interpretations are of interest when individual differences are important. This includes situations in which the scores resulting from the measurement situation will be correlated with other variables, or in which group comparisons will be made. Absolute decisions are those in which comparison to a standard, or criterion referencing, is of interest. Absolute decisions are those in which test takers must meet a certain criterion score to pass a course, move to the next level of instruction, or be licensed or certified. Of course, it is possible that scores could be used to make both absolute and relative decisions.

G theory provides two coefficients that assess the dependability, or reliability, of scores for either relative or absolute decisions. The first of these coefficients, known as the generalizability, or G coefficient, is analogous to the reliability coefficient from CTT. Similar to coefficients from CTT, the G coefficient is appropriate for norm-referenced or relative decisions. For a one-facet person-by-item design in which items are treated as a random facet, the G coefficient is equivalent to coefficient alpha, as well as to the ICC for a two-way design for a consistency decision, averaged across items. The second G theory coefficient for assessing dependability of scores is known as the phi (ϕ) coefficient, or *index of dependability*, and is appropriate for situations in which an absolute decision is to be made.

Calculating the G and Phi Coefficients

Because the two coefficients were designed for use with different types of decisions, error is defined differently for the two. For the G coefficient, only sources of variation that would change people's relative standing within the group are included as error. This means that the main effects of facets, such as error due to raters or tasks, are not included in the error term for the G coefficient. Recall that a rater or task effect indicates that people, on average, receive lower scores from some raters, or on some tasks, than on others. But as long as this is true for all people, on average, the rater effect will not affect people's scores differentially. If, however, there are differential effects of facets on persons, such as when people perform differentially across tasks, the people's rank orders will be affected. Note that the latter scenario is one in which there is a person-by-task interaction. Because only variation that would change people's relative standing is considered as error when calculating the G coefficient, only interactions of persons with another facet (but not interactions among facets that do not include persons) are included in the error component. This includes the overall error term, as it includes the highest order interaction of persons with all of the facets.

Error is defined differently for absolute decisions because absolute decisions are affected by all types of error. For example, if a task is particularly difficult or a rater is particularly stringent, scores will be correspondingly lower for those paired with that task or rater. In addition, the interactions of persons with facets also affect scores, for the same reasons described earlier. For absolute decisions, therefore, all sources of variation (except variation due to persons) and their interactions, both with persons and with each other, are included in the error component. I use the data from the two-facet completely crossed and random design in Table 10.4 to illustrate the components of relative and absolute error variance and their calculations. These components are shown in Table 10.9, in which the variance components contributing to each type of error variance are indicated by an X. In this example, the values of relative and absolute error variance are quite similar (.27 and .29, respectively). This is because the quantities included in the calculations for absolute, but not in relative, error variance ($\hat{\sigma}_r^2$, $\hat{\sigma}_t^2$, and $\hat{\sigma}_{rt}^2$) are all quite small in magnitude. Of course, this will not always be the case, and the two error variances, and their corresponding coefficients, can be quite different.

Once the appropriate error variance (relative or absolute) is calculated, the estimated G coefficient and index of dependability (ϕ) are calculated as

$$G = \frac{\hat{\sigma}_p^2}{\hat{\sigma}_p^2 + \hat{\sigma}_{\text{REL}}^2} \quad (10.7)$$

$$\phi = \frac{\hat{\sigma}_p^2}{\hat{\sigma}_p^2 + \hat{\sigma}_{\text{ABS}}^2} \quad (10.8)$$

Note that both the G and ϕ coefficients are reliability-like in that they are ratios of the universe score variance σ_p^2 (analogous to true score variance) to the expected observed score variance (universe plus error variance). Similar to reliability indices for classical test theory, the G coefficient is an estimate of the squared correlation between observed and universe scores. However, Shavelson and Webb (1991) note that, because the denominator of the ϕ coefficient does not approximate the expected observed score variance, that coefficient is not an estimate of the squared correlation between observed

TABLE 10.9. Computation of Error Variances and Dependability Coefficients for Relative and Absolute Decisions

Source of variation	Estimated variance component	Variance components included in relative error variance	Variance components included in relative absolute error variance
Persons (p)	1.03		
Raters (r)	0		X
Tasks (t)	0.06		X
pr	0.47	X	X
pt	0.12	X	X
rt	0.01		X
(prt,e)	0.64	X	X

$$\hat{\sigma}^2_{REL} = \frac{\hat{\sigma}^2_{pr}}{n_r} + \frac{\hat{\sigma}^2_{pt}}{n_t} + \frac{\hat{\sigma}^2_{prt,e}}{n_r n_t} = \frac{.47}{3} + \frac{.12}{3} + \frac{.64}{3(3)} = .16 + .04 + .07 = .27$$

$$\hat{\sigma}^2_{ABS} = \frac{\hat{\sigma}^2_{r}}{n_r} + \frac{\hat{\sigma}^2_{t}}{n_t} + \frac{\hat{\sigma}^2_{pr}}{n_r} + \frac{\hat{\sigma}^2_{pt}}{n_t} + \frac{\hat{\sigma}^2_{rt}}{n_r n_t} \frac{\hat{\sigma}^2_{prt,e}}{n_r n_t} = \frac{0}{3} + \frac{.06}{3} + \frac{.47}{3} + \frac{.12}{3} + \frac{.01}{9} + \frac{.64}{3(3)}$$

$$= 0 + 0.02 + 0.16 + 0.04 + 0.001 + 0.07 = 0.29$$

Note. X indicates that the variance component is not included in the error variance.

and universe scores, and it is not strictly correct to call it a reliability coefficient. Having said that, it is quite similar to one. As noted earlier, there are many similarities between G theory and the ICCs introduced in Chapter 9. One such similarity is that the G coefficient for a one-way random design is equivalent to the ICC for a two-way consistency design based on average ratings. And both of these are equal to coefficient alpha for an analysis in which raters are treated as items.

Use of the D Study to Determine the Optimal Test Design

An important purpose of the D study is to estimate how much the error would increase or decrease if the number of conditions in each facet were changed. For example, given the relatively large estimated variance component for the person-by-rater interaction, I might consider increasing the number of raters in an attempt to average out the differential ratings across students and obtain greater dependability. This is directly analogous to increasing internal consistency reliability by adding more items to a test, as discussed in Chapter 8. Recall from that chapter that the Spearman–Brown formula can be used to estimate what the increase in reliability would be if items were added to a test. In G theory, a similar process can be used. The procedure is simply to divide each component in the absolute or relative error term by different values of the number of conditions for the facet of interest. For example, if I wanted to determine how much error would decrease, and the G and ϕ coefficients would increase, if five raters were used instead of three, I would simply substitute five into the denominators of calculations for variance components involving raters.

It may seem odd that I can simply act as though there were five raters instead of three, as though wishful thinking would make it so. To understand the reasoning behind this position, it is important to understand that the G study variance component for raters is our best estimate of the *average* amount of variability due to raters, regardless of the number of raters. Although the G study variance is an average across three raters, we should have obtained the same estimate of rater variance if we had averaged across five or any number of raters. This is true because raters are all part of the same UAO, and as such, estimates based on different samples or numbers of raters should be equivalent (within sampling error). Because the G study variance component is averaged across raters, it provides an estimate of the degree to which the score provided by a single, randomly selected rater is expected to differ from the average score across all raters, regardless of the number of raters on which it is based. The same logic holds for the other variance components. Each variance component from the G study is therefore treated as an estimate for a single condition of each facet. In the D study, the G study variance components are divided by different numbers of conditions to estimate the amount of error that might be obtained with more raters, tasks, or numbers of other facets. In D study calculations, it is common to replace the symbol n for sample size with the symbol n' to indicate that the n to be used can be changed to different values, depending on the number of conditions on which scores might be based. Variance components involving persons, however, are not divided by the number of people. This is because interest is in the score for an individual person, and not in the average score across the entire group.

Table 10.10 illustrates the process of trying out different numbers of tasks and raters using the data from Table 10.9. As can be seen from the table, absolute error will always be greater than or equal to relative error because it includes more components. It is also clear from the formulas for relative and absolute error that these will decrease as more conditions are added because the components making up the error variance are divided by the number of conditions. In our example, the additional sources of error included in σ_{ABS}^2 (variance due to raters, tasks, and rater by task interaction) are all quite small (or zero, in the case of rater variance), so the relative and absolute error variances are quite similar in magnitude. Of course, this will not always be the case and will depend on the magnitude of the additional components.

Based on the information in Table 10.10, a design with four raters and three tasks would provide levels of dependability above .80 for both relative and absolute decisions. If greater dependability is needed, more raters and tasks could be used. Of course, the combinations shown in Table 10.10 are not exhaustive of the possible options, and the researcher would likely want to try out others. Readers can confirm that using three raters and three tasks would yield G and ϕ coefficients of .79 and .78, respectively. There is, of course, a point of diminishing returns. Increasing the number of raters and tasks to five of each would yield G and ϕ coefficients of .88 and .87, respectively, but increasing to six conditions for each facet increases the coefficients by only about .02, to .90 and .89.

TABLE 10.10. Decision Studies for the $p \times r \times t$ Design with Random Facets

	G study		D studies		
$n'_r =$	1	1	2	3	4
Source of variation $\quad n'_t =$	1	1	1	2	3
Persons (p)		1.03	1.03	1.03	1.03
Raters (r)		0	0	0	0
Tasks (t)		0.06	0.06	0.03	0.02
Pr		0.47	0.24	0.16	0.12
Pt		0.12	0.12	0.06	0.04
Rt		0.01	0.01	0.00	0.00
(prt,e)		0.64	0.32	0.11	0.05
Relative error variance		1.23	0.68	0.33	0.21
($\hat{\sigma}^2_{ABS}$)					
Absolute error variance		1.30	0.75	0.36	0.23
($\hat{\sigma}^2_{REL}$)					
G		0.46	0.60	0.76	0.83
ϕ		0.44	0.58	0.74	0.82

Decision Studies with Nested or Fixed Facets

The computations illustrated thus far have been based on a design in which the facets of both the G and D studies were crossed and random. If the G study design includes nested and/or fixed facets, the guidelines for calculating relative and absolute error remain the same, but the variances for the facets and their interactions are calculated according to the rules for the nested and/or fixed designs. Each component of the error variance is still divided by n'_i, the number of conditions of interest, which will not necessarily be the same as the number of conditions in the G study. The G and ϕ coefficients are also calculated in the usual way, using the formulas in Equations 10.7 and 10.8. However, because some of the sources of variance in nested G studies are confounded, it would not be possible to estimate the effects of increasing or decreasing the number of conditions for these facets and/or interactions. For example, suppose that tasks were nested in students, as in an earlier example. In this situation, it would be possible to estimate the effects of increasing the number of tasks per student, but the task variance estimate would be confounded with the task-by-student interaction. Thus, it would not be possible to determine whether increasing the number of tasks would affect only the variance due to tasks or the variance due to the student-by-task interaction.

If the G study had a fixed facet, the variance due to the fixed facet would essentially drop out of the design because analyses either would be based on the average across the conditions of the fixed facet or would be conducted separately for each fixed-facet condition. The variance due to any interactions with the fixed facet would therefore not be estimable. In the D study, it would therefore not be possible to estimate the effect of varying the number of conditions of the fixed facet on the relative or absolute error variance. However, the effects of changing the number of conditions of any random facets could still be explored in the usual way.

As you have seen, G studies based on completely crossed designs with random facets provide the greatest number of options for D study explorations. This is why crossed and random effects should be included in the G study whenever possible. G studies based on crossed and random facets can be used to estimate D study variance components for a wide variety of designs. If the G study is based on a completely crossed and random design, D studies with nested or fixed effects could be estimated in addition to those with crossed and random effects. Due to space considerations, I present only a brief summary of the rules for estimating variance components for nested (or partially nested) D studies from crossed G studies:

1. Calculate the D study variance component for each facet that is confounded due to nesting as the sum of the individual variance components from the (crossed) G study. For example, in a one-facet G study design with students crossed with raters, the variance components are σ_p^2, σ_r^2, and $\sigma_{pr,e}^2$. Suppose researchers are considered nesting students within raters, and would like to estimate D study variance components for the nested design. The D study variance components would be σ_p^2 and $\sigma_{r,pr,e}^2$. To obtain the latter variance component from the G study variance components, simply add together $\sigma_r^2 + \sigma_{pr,e}^2$.

2. The variance components for any unconfounded variance components remain the same for the D and G studies.

Shavelson and Webb (1991) and other texts provide more detailed examples for a variety of designs.

SUMMARY

G theory provides a comprehensive framework for estimating the impact of multiple sources of measurement error simultaneously. G theory is based on an ANOVA framework in which ANOVA factors are termed facets and their levels are known as conditions. For example, students might be rated on a set of tasks, by a set of raters, on various occasions. Tasks, raters, and occasions might all contribute to measurement error and would be considered facets in the G theory design. The variance due to these facets and to their interactions could be estimated, and their relative contributions to measurement error variance assessed.

The G theory concept of *generalizability* or *dependability* is analogous to the CTT concept of reliability. In G theory, interest is in the degree to which observed scores obtained under one set of conditions can be generalized to the average score that might be obtained across a more broadly defined set of acceptable conditions, known as the UAO. The UAO is defined by the researcher to include all conditions that would yield acceptable scores. The degree to which scores generalize from the observed conditions to the UAO is termed *dependability*. High levels of dependability indicate that scores obtained under the observed conditions will generalize to people's *universe scores*. The universe score is analogous to the true score in CTT and can be conceptualized as the average score a person would obtain if tested repeatedly under all possible combinations of conditions in the UAO.

Facets are classified in different ways, based on parallel designations in ANOVA designs. One distinction is between facets that are fixed and random. Conditions of random facets are considered to be interchangeable with any others within the UAO. Random facets therefore allow for generalization to other conditions within the UAO. In contrast, conditions of fixed facets are either the only conditions possible or the only conditions of interest. Treating a facet as fixed thus restricts the UAO to only the conditions included and precludes generalization to other conditions. Facets can also be crossed or nested. Two facets are crossed if every condition of one facet is observed with every condition of the other. For example, if every rater rated every task, raters and tasks would be crossed. One facet is nested within another if multiple conditions of the nested facet are associated with each level of the other and different levels of the nested facet are associated with each level of the other. Raters would be nested within tasks if a different set of raters rated each task.

In G theory, a distinction is made between G studies and D studies. The purpose of the G study is to estimate the relative magnitudes of different sources of error. These estimates can then be used in the D study to estimate the number of conditions in each facet that would be needed to obtain desired levels of dependability. This process is similar to use of the Spearman–Brown prophecy formula in CTT. The G theory framework, however, allows for estimation of the effects of more than one source of error. In the G study, the researcher should define the universe of admissible operations as broadly as possible because doing so opens up the largest array of possibilities that can be explored in the D study. The final product of the D study is a measurement design that minimizes error and optimizes dependability with the smallest possible number of conditions for each facet. Of course, practical and logistical considerations must also be taken into account in the measurement design. For example, raters may be expensive to train and to employ. In this situation, minimizing the number of raters needed while still obtaining acceptable levels of dependability would be a likely goal. This goal could be accomplished in the D study by estimating how many raters would be needed to obtain the desired level of dependability.

Finally, G theory yields dependability coefficients for both relative and absolute measurement decisions. Relative decisions are those involving comparisons of peoples' scores to those of others. Relative decisions include norm-referenced decisions, such as selecting those with the highest or lowest scores in the group, as well as situations in which statistical procedures involving comparisons, such as those based on mean differences or correlations, are of interest. Absolute decisions are those in which scores are compared to an external standard, such as a set passing percentage. Absolute decisions are typically associated with decisions involving licensure, certification, and other credentialing because these involve set passing scores. An advantage of G theory is that dependability coefficients for both types of decisions are available. The G coefficient is appropriate for relative decisions, and the ϕ coefficient is appropriate for absolute decisions. Measurement error is defined differently for the two coefficients. For the G coefficient, only interactions of persons with facets are included, whereas for the ϕ coefficient, all facets and interactions are included.

EXERCISES

Questions 1–5 refer to the following scenario: The Center for Entrepreneurship is evaluating candidates for an academic scholarship. Candidates are each rated on the same three elements: a written essay about their entrepreneurial spirit, a 10-minute presentation about their proposed project, and an "elevator pitch" in which the applicants try to sell their idea in one minute. The same four raters provide a score for each element and for each applicant.

1. What is the object of measurement?

2. How many facets are there? What are they?

3. Is the design crossed or nested? Explain.

4. Are the facets random or fixed? Explain.

5. List the sources of variability and provide an interpretation of what each source represents.

6. Explain the difference between relative and absolute decisions. Which variance components are included in the error variance for each type of decision?

7. What is the difference between a G study and a D study?

8. Using the data in Table 10.10, calculate the values of the G and phi coefficients for the following situations:

   a. Three raters and three tasks

   b. Three raters and four tasks

   c. Five raters and five tasks

9. Suppose tasks had been nested within raters for the G study design in Table 10.10. How would this have changed the variance components that could be estimated?

10. Suppose that tasks were a fixed rather than a random facet in the G study design shown in Table 10.10. How would this have changed the variance components that could be estimated?

11

Validity

Suppose you have taken an online test designed to measure where you fall on the introversion/extroversion continuum. You receive the results and are surprised to learn that your score pegs you as an extrovert, as you had always thought of yourself as an introvert. You show the results to your friends and find that they, too, have always seen you as an introvert. This causes you and your friends to question whether the test is really measuring introversion/extroversion and whether the interpretation that you are an introvert is, in fact, justifiable. In psychometric terms, you and your friends question the *validity* of the test. Validity is arguably the most important quality of a test because it has to do with the fundamental measurement issue of what our measurement instruments are really measuring. This may seem a straightforward question, but measurement specialists have long been engaged in discussions about how validity should be defined, how it should be assessed, and what aspects of the testing process should be included under the heading of validity. Although these discussions have resulted in something approaching consensus in some areas, other issues continue to be hotly debated in psychometric circles.

In the following sections, I describe the "traditional" forms of validity evidence: *content*, *criterion-related*, and *construct*, as these are the focus of many of the recent debates. In doing so, I put these into historical context, briefly explaining how the different conceptualizations came about. I then discuss current conceptualizations of validity, with an emphasis on how these differ from the traditional views. In the final section, I turn to the types of validity evidence emphasized in the most recent edition (2014) of the *Standards for Educational and Psychological Measurement* (referred to hereafter as the *Standards*), which is a joint publication of the American Educational Research Association (AERA), the American Psychological Association (APA), and the National Council on Measurement in Education (NCME), and is widely considered to be one of the most authoritative sources on measurement standards in the social sciences.

VALIDITY DEFINED

Currently, no definition of *validity* is accepted by all players in the validity debate. The following definition is taken from the *Standards:* "Validity refers to the degree to which evidence and theory support the interpretations of test scores for proposed uses of tests" (AERA, APA, & NCME, p. 11). Validity thus has to do with the underlying rationale for our interpretations and uses of test scores. In other words, validity has to do with both the *meaning* of test scores and how we use them. As such, validity is justifiably "the most fundamental consideration in developing tests and evaluating tests," as stated in the *Standards* (p. 11). Returning to my earlier example, I might conclude, based on the extroversion test score described previously, that I am much more extroverted than I had ever realized. However, making such an inference from an online test of dubious origin may not be justified. Psychometrically speaking, it may be that the test simply does not yield scores that allow for such an inference. Suppose a company decided to hire salespeople on the basis of high scores on this extroversion test, with the rationale that extroverted people should make the best salespeople. Would doing so achieve the company's goal of obtaining the best salespeople? Probably not, if the scores do not really indicate a person's level of extroversion (and ignoring for now the fact that extroverted people may not actually make the best salespeople). These examples are meant to illustrate the types of "interpretations of test scores for proposed uses of tests" alluded to in the *Standards'* validity definition. But what about commonly used tests, such as those designed to measure one's intelligence, college aptitude, perceived level of pain, or other attributes? Do these have validity for their intended interpretations and uses? And how can we tell? These are the types of questions I address in this chapter.

TRADITIONAL FORMS OF VALIDITY EVIDENCE: A HISTORICAL PERSPECTIVE

Early conceptualizations of test validity focused on the degree to which a test measured "what it is supposed to measure," as stated in an early definition attributed to Garrett (1939, as quoted by Sireci, 2009, p. 22). However, the definition of validity as a determination of whether a test measures what it purports to measure is problematic for at least two reasons. First, a test could "measure what it purports to measure" and still not be good for any useful purpose. To go back to the extroversion example, the developers of the fictitious online test could say that, according to their definition, the term *extroversion* simply means someone who speaks in a loud voice. Items on their instrument could be things like "People say I talk too loudly." Thus, the extroversion test would be measuring what it purports to measure. If that were the end of it, there would be no cause for concern. However, tests are usually developed to be used in some way, such as to predict future behavior or status, or to assess a person's qualifications or suitability for a job or training course. This is what is emphasized by the part of the definition from the *Standards* that says "interpretations of test scores for proposed uses of tests" (2014). If I were to use the "loud voice" extroversion test to, for example, predict who would make a good telemarketer, I would likely meet with little success. This is because the test would be unlikely to result in accurate predictions.

Another reason the definition of test validity as "measuring what it's supposed to measure" was found to be inadequate was that, given the slippery nature of social science constructs, it is often not possible to pin down a particular construct to determine whether a test measures it. As Urbina (2014) points out, although a limited number of constructs, such as narrowly defined content knowledge (e.g., single-digit addition) or skills such as speed or accuracy in typing, are fairly straightforward to define, most social science constructs do not fall into this category. But defining validity as the extent to which tests measure what they are supposed to measure implies that the items included on a test completely define the construct being measured. This can result in definitions that are not particularly useful. Urbina cites as an illustration Boring's (1923) definition of intelligence as "whatever it is that intelligence tests measure." Cliff (1989) called this the *nominalistic fallacy,* or the fallacy of assuming that a test measures something simply because its name implies that it does. The extroversion test alluded to previously is a case in point.

In an attempt to get around the issues inherent in this early definition of validity, a new definition emerged in which validity came to be operationalized as the degree to which scores on the test correlated with scores on another measure of the same attribute. As Guilford (1946), famously stated, "a test is valid for anything with which it correlates" (p. 429). The idea here was that, if there were a "gold standard" of the construct (often, an earlier test), and if scores on the test correlated with that gold standard, the test could be inferred to be a measure of the construct. Note that this is a variety of the "if it walks like a duck and quacks like a duck, it must be a duck" argument. The problem was, of course, that there was no gold standard for most constructs, probably because if there were it may not have been necessary to create the test in the first place. Despite these problems, the correlational view of validity held sway through the 1950s. As noted by many validity researchers (e.g., Angoff, 1988; Borsboom, Cramer, Kievit, Scholten, & Franić, 2009; McDonald, 1999; Newton & Shaw, 2013; Sireci, 2009), this was largely due to the influence of the scientific paradigm of that time. At the time, these early definitions of validity were introduced, the correlation coefficient was a fairly new development (by Karl Pearson in 1896) and was no doubt seen as quite state of the art. At the same time, the prevailing philosophical paradigm was based on logical positivism, which emphasized the use of empiricism, verification, and logical analysis in scientific inquiry, and influenced, among other things, the behaviorist movement of the time. The correlation coefficient provided a means of obtaining empirical and verifiable evidence of validity, so it is not surprising that early validity theorists should have seized upon it as the ideal method for obtaining validity evidence.

Original Validity Types

The first edition of the *Standards* (at that time titled the *Technical Recommendations for Psychological Tests and Diagnostic Techniques* [APA, 1954]) defined four types of validity: *content, predictive, concurrent,* and *construct.* Of these, predictive and concurrent validity reflected the emphasis on correlations, as both types of validity were evidenced by the correlations or regression coefficients of the test of interest with some criterion. These two forms of validity evidence were later subsumed under the heading of *criterion-related* validity. Predictive validity was defined as the correlation between scores on the test of interest (the predictor) with values of a criterion obtained at some point in the future. A widely known example is that of the SAT test, which is purported to predict college grade point average (GPA). In this case, the criterion is students' college GPA, and the predictive validity evidence is the correlation or regression coefficient that measures the relationship between SAT scores and GPA. *Concurrent validity* was defined in a similar fashion, except that, as the name implies, scores on the predictor and on the criterion were obtained at the same time. This type of validity was typically of interest for situations in which one test was proposed as a measure of the same attribute as the other. For example, a newly developed ability test that could be administered in a group format might be proposed as a substitute for a more time-consuming individually administered ability test. For this substitution to be viable, the test developers would have to demonstrate that the group-administered test measured the same attribute(s) as the individually administered test. A high correlation between scores from the two tests would serve as evidence.

Consistent with the empirical orientation of the time, the criteria in predictive validity situations were typically observable or behaviorally defined variables, such as job performance or success in school. Although satisfying the logical positivists, the use of such criteria was problematic on several levels. Job performance measures such as supervisor ratings, for example, often lacked validity evidence themselves. In addition, rating criteria are often inconsistently applied, resulting in a lack of reliability. Other measures of performance, such as the number of widgets produced, were found to measure only a part (and perhaps not the most important part) of job performance. Jenkins, who served during World War II in the Navy Department where he helped to develop tests to select combat pilots, wrote in the aftermath of that war that "there is always the danger that the investigator may accept some convenient measure (especially if it be objective and quantifiable) only to find ultimately that the performance which produces this measure is merely a part, and perhaps an unimportant part, of the total field performance desired" (1946, p. 97). As an example, Jenkins used a situation in which piloting skills might serve as a criterion because they could be objectively scored, but tests of judgment and emotional adjustment, though arguably at least as important, may not be included as criteria because of the greater difficulty in measuring these qualities.

Such observations led researchers such as Jenkins (1946) and Rulon (1946) to suggest that in some situations it is the content of the test and the cognitive processes required to produce a correct answer that is important, not the degree to which the test can predict a criterion. These considerations led to a new type of validity, which came to be called *content validity*. In achievement testing, for example, test scores are taken as indications of the amount of content knowledge examinees have learned, along with the level of cognitive processing skill they have attained. In such situations, interest is naturally focused on the match between the content of the test and the cognitive processes it elicits with the content and processes that have been taught. If the content and processing skills examinees have been taught are not the same as, or at least similar to, those on the test, it is difficult to make inferences about what students have learned. If, however, a content match can be demonstrated, this information would be much more useful than the degree to which the test predicts scores on, say, another test. Thus, content validity emerged in the 1954 *Standards* as a new type of validity, useful for any situation in which the content and/or processes measured by the test were of primary importance. Achievement and aptitude tests were most commonly included in this category.

Finally, as noted by Angoff (1988, p. 25), "it was no coincidence that the 1954 *Standards* listed construct validity . . . as one of the four types." The inclusion of construct validity was more or less assured by the presence on the Joint Committee of Lee Cronbach and Paul Meehl, whose seminal article "Construct Validity in Psychological Tests" (1955) introduced this concept to the world. As the authors stated, "construct validation is involved whenever a test is to be interpreted as a measure of some attribute or quality which is not 'operationally defined'" (p. 282). They go on to state that "when an investigator believes that no criterion available to him is fully valid, he perforce becomes interested in construct validity. . . . Construct validity must be investigated whenever no criterion or universe of content is accepted as entirely adequate to define the construct being measured" (p. 282). These statements suggest that construct validity was seen as the option of last resort, to be used with those troublesome tests that were simply not amenable to content or criterion-related validation. The fact that evidence based on inspection of test content or correlations with criteria was not appropriate for this new type of validity made it clear that new types of evidence were needed.

To meet this need, Cronbach and Meehl (1955) proposed several forms of evidence that might fill the bill. Evidence based on group differences would be appropriate for situations in which two or more groups might be expected to score differently. For example, in measuring attitudes toward gun control, we might expect that those who own guns would have more positive attitudes than those who do not. Correlations of test scores with scores from other tests of the same attribute could also provide evidence of construct validity. In the eyes of Cronbach and Meehl, however, the most sophisticated evidence for construct validity was the elaboration and testing of a *nomological network* in which the construct was embedded. As they stated, "Scientifically speaking, to 'make clear what something *is*' means to set forth the laws in which it occurs. We shall refer to the interlocking system of laws which constitute a theory as a *nomological network*" (p. 290, italics in the original). They go on to specify that such a network must contain at least some observable (i.e., not latent) variables. As Borsboom and colleagues (2009) noted, the idea of the nomological network reflected the logical positivism of the time and mimicked the belief expressed in physics and other physical sciences that the meaning of a theoretical term was provided by the laws that governed its relationship with other things (preferably observable things). It is not surprising that psychologists, who were at that time struggling to gain acceptance for their field as a credible science, would adopt the epistemological stance of the more established physical sciences. Whatever its origins, however, the nomological network remains a valuable heuristic for organizing the theory and empirical findings through which the nature of a construct is understood. Shepard (1997) notes that this type of organizing framework is "quintessentially the model of scientific theory testing" (p. 7), which emphasizes the similarities between validity research and plain old scientific research.

Although Cronbach and Meehl (1955) seem to have felt, based on the statements quoted previously, that construct validity was only applicable when content or criterion-related evidence was inadequate or unattainable, in their very next sentence they state that "determining what psychological constructs account for test performance is desirable for almost any test" (p. 282). Sireci (2009) ascribes this seeming ambivalence about the utility of construct validity to the fact that Cronbach and Meehl, having just introduced the concept, were hesitant about overstating its usefulness. As it turned out, however, they need not have worried, as others were more than willing to so for them. Loevinger (1957), never one to mince words, stated flatly that "since predictive, concurrent, and content validities are all essentially *ad hoc*, construct validity is the whole of validity from a scientific point of view" (p. 636). Loevinger's argument was essentially that none of the other forms of validity required the development of theories that would advance scientific knowledge about the attribute of interest. She likened the difference between criterion-related and construct validities to the difference between learning how to boil an egg through trial and error and learning how to boil an egg by developing an understanding of the chemistry of protein molecules. In this context, she stated:

> The argument against classical criterion-related psychometrics is thus two-fold: it contributes no more to the science of psychology than rules for boiling an egg contribute to the science of chemistry. And the number of genuine egg-boiling decisions which clinicians and psychotechnologists face is small compared with the number of situations where a deeper knowledge of psychological theory would be helpful. (p. 641)

Arguments against the "Tripartite" View of Validity

Several years later, Loevinger's argument was taken even further by Messick (1989), who stated that "construct validity embraces almost all forms of validity evidence" (p. 17). By "almost all" Messick excludes only the appraisal of social consequences, although later in his nearly 90-page chapter, he brings these, too, into the fold of the "unified" view of test validity. I discuss Messick's views in more detail later in this chapter. For now, suffice it to say that in a series of papers (Messick, 1965, 1975, 1980, 1981, 1988), he argued against the traditional "tripartite" view in which content, criterion-related (which subsumed predictive and concurrent), and construct validity were treated as separate but equal frameworks for test validation. Instead, Messick has argued that, because information obtained from both content and criterion-related validity studies contributes to our understanding of the meaning of test scores, and because construct validity is concerned with the meaning of test scores, both content and criterion-related evidence contribute to construct validity and should not be considered as separate "types" of validity.

Instead, all available evidence should be integrated into an overall judgment about the meaning of test scores.

Others have argued against the tripartite view of validity on more pragmatic grounds. For example, Anastasi (1986) argued that the separation of validity into three "types" leads researchers to feel that they must "tick them off in checklist fashion" (p. 2), regardless of the purpose of the test. She goes on to rail against the view that "once this tripartite coverage was accomplished, there was the relaxed feeling that validation requirements had been met." (p. 2). Anastasi's argument reflects a widely held view that the segmentation of validity into different "types" has led some researchers to practice what has been termed a "weak program" of validation (e.g., Benson, 1998). In such a program, validity evidence is accumulated in piecemeal fashion without giving sufficient (if any) thought to the types of validity evidence that would contribute most to our understanding of the attribute being measured and how it could be used. Instead, the researcher's efforts simply focus on obtaining evidence from each of the "three C's," regardless of whether this evidence helps to illuminate the meaning of test scores. In contrast, the "strong program" of validation research bears a striking resemblance to the conduct of research in general. The strong program is focused on developing and testing a theory of the attribute being measured, creating a test that reflects this theory, and accumulating evidence specific to the proposed uses of the test (i.e., can it really indicate who would make a good salesperson?) and the proposed interpretations to be made from scores (i.e., does a high score really indicate higher levels of extroversion?).

CURRENT CONCEPTUALIZATIONS OF VALIDITY

In the previous section, I reviewed the history of the traditional tripartite view of validity, which divided validity evidence into the three C's of content, criterion-related, and construct. However, the concept of validity has evolved considerably over the past few decades, and modern validity theory is no longer congruent with the tripartite view. In this section, I therefore discuss the most important aspects of current validity theory, while at the same time introducing some of the current theorists. Because these views are increasingly represented in the measurement literature and will likely dominate that literature in the near future, it is important for you to have an understanding of their major themes. These include the general (though not universal) preference for a unified view of validity; the focus on test score inferences and uses rather than on the test itself; the focus on explanation and cognitive theory in validity studies; and the inclusion of test consequences and values in the validity framework.

The Unified View of Validity

The unified view of validity is now widely held, and it has become more common to refer simply to "validity" rather than to any "type" of validity, as evidenced by this statement from the most recent version of the *Standards*:

Validity is a unitary concept. It is the degree to which all the accumulated evidence supports the intended interpretation of test scores for the proposed use. Like the 1999 *Standards*, this edition refers to types of validity evidence, rather than distinct types of validity. To emphasize this distinction, the treatment that follows does not follow historical nomenclature (i.e., the use of the terms *content validity* or *predictive validity*). (2014, p. 14)

This quotation from the *Standards* illustrates several features common to current conceptualizations of test validity. First, following the work of Loevinger (1957), Messick (1975, 1980, 1981, 1988), and others, the term *validity* is now used in its broad sense to refer to all forms of evidence that support the intended interpretations and uses of a test. "Types" of validity such as content-related and criterion-related are subsumed under this broad definition because these contribute to validity in the broader sense of the term. As Messick (1989) states, "Validity is an integrated evaluative judgment of the degree to which empirical evidence and theoretical rationales support the *adequacy* and *appropriateness* of *inferences* and *actions* based on test scores or other modes of assessment (p. 13, original emphasis). Thus, most modern conceptualizations of validity emphasize an integration of all forms of evidence that are useful in elucidating the meaning(s) that can be attached to test scores. It is up to the test user to evaluate the available evidence to judge the degree to which his or her intended interpretation or use is appropriate.

Another unifying theme in Messick's work is the argument that all threats to construct validity are subsumed under the headings of *construct-irrelevant variance* and *construct underrepresentation*. Construct-irrelevant variance is irrelevant in the sense that, although it contributes variability to test scores, this added variability is not due to differences in the construct of interest. Instead, the additional variance is due to sources other than the construct being measured. For instance, some examinees might obtain higher scores on essay questions because of a greater ability to bluff their way through an answer, not because they have greater knowledge or skill. Construct underrepresentation refers to situations in which a test does not completely capture all salient aspects of the construct of interest. Underrepresentation can result from a narrowing of the content of a test. For example, a test of managerial skills might include many items measuring knowledge of budgeting processes but only two items on personnel management. Underrepresentation can also result from a mismatch of the skills elicited by the type of item used with the skills that are of real interest. In the previous example, suppose that both personnel management items were multiple choice. It could be argued that skills in this area are best demonstrated by having examinees respond to scenarios describing personnel issues, or by actual performance in handling a sticky personnel problem. In these examples, the construct of managerial skill would be doubly underrepresented owing to underrepresentation of both content and response processes.

Focus on Interpretation and Use of Test Scores

Another important aspect of current validity theory, illustrated by the previous quotation from Messick (1989), is that it is not the test itself that is validated but the inferences made from test scores or the uses for which the test is intended. As Newton and Shaw (2013) point out, every edition of the *Standards* since the first (1954) has specified that statements about validity are made about the interpretations for particular types of decisions. For example, making inferences about the spelling knowledge of third-grade students on the basis of a third-grade spelling test would likely be supported by available validity evidence. In contrast, making inferences about students' intelligence or likelihood of success in later life on the basis of the same test would not be supported. With regard to test usage, validity evidence might support the use of the test in making classroom decisions about spelling instruction, such as whether remediation is required for some students. However, use of the test to determine which students should be required to repeat the third grade would not be supported. The view that the appropriate object of validation is the inferences made from test scores and not the test itself is widely, though not universally, accepted (Moss, 1992; Shepard, 1993; Zumbo, 2009). Some validity theorists, most notably Borsboom and his colleagues (Borsboom, Mellenbergh, & van Heerden, 2004; Borsboom et al., 2009), disagree with the view that it is the interpretation of a test that is validated, preferring the original definition of validity as the extent to which a test measures what it purports to measure. Borsboom and colleagues state that "the notion of a test score interpretation is too general," applying to "every possible inference concerning test scores" (p. 139). That is, a score can be interpreted in an infinite number of ways, only some of which make sense. Borsboom and his colleagues argue that this makes it difficult to pin down exactly what is meant by test validity.

My own view on the issue of whether validity applies to the test itself or to the interpretations of test scores aligns with that of Markus (2014), who refers to this issue as a nonproductive "pseudo-argument." Markus points out that validity does not refer to a test or an interpretation in isolation, but rather to a relationship between the test, the test scores, the test interpretation, and the test use. That is, a test can be considered valid in the context of one scoring/interpretation/use but not another. Going back to the earlier example of a spelling test, the test would likely be considered valid in a scoring/interpretation/use context in which it is scored correctly (scoring), and the scores are interpreted as indications of spelling knowledge (interpretation) and used to determine which students need more practice in spelling (use). In contrast, the same test would likely be considered invalid in a context in which correct answers to easy spelling words received twice as many score points than answers to difficult words (scoring), or test scores were interpreted as indications of intelligence (interpretation), or if scores were used to determine placement in gifted programs (use). Markus's view is in alignment with Gorin's (2007) definition that "validity is the extent to which test scores provide answers to targeted questions" (p. 456), where by "targeted" Gorin means the test/test score/interpretation/use relationship noted by Markus.

Finally, through its reference to "the accumulated evidence," the definition in the *Standards* emphasizes that obtaining validity evidence is a *process* rather than a single study from which a dichotomous "valid/not valid" decision is made. The attributes researchers attempt to measure in the social sciences are typically latent constructs that, by their very nature, are somewhat elusive. There is thus no definitive study that can pin down, once and for all, the meaning of a construct such as "intelligence" or "creativity." As some validity theorists have noted, the process of conducting validity studies is very similar to that of conducting research studies in general. Students are taught in their introductory statistics courses that it is not possible to "prove" the null hypothesis but only to disprove it. However, if enough studies accumulate in which the evidence is supportive of a given research hypothesis, we begin to give some credence to that hypothesis. In the same way, it is not possible to *prove* that a test is valid for some purpose, although it is possible to provide evidence that it is not valid for such a purpose. And, as is the case with research studies, the more evidence that accumulates in support of a proposed use of a test, the more credence we are likely to give that use. This is why test validation is best thought of as a program of research in which one attempts to obtain a body of evidence that, taken as a whole, would support the intended uses of and inferences from the test scores.

Focus on Explanation and Cognitive Models

Early tests of achievement were based on theories of learning in which knowledge was thought to be accumulated incrementally. According to such theories, students must first learn factual and procedural information and, when such knowledge is sufficient, can then progress to higher-level skills such as reasoning with, synthesizing, and expanding upon the knowledge. However, more recent learning theories have moved beyond such so-called behaviorist theories of learning and focus more on aspects of learning such as how learners organize information in long-term memory in structures known as *schemas*. Research into learners' schemas in areas such as physics (Chi, Glaser, & Rees, 1982) and chess (Chase & Simon, 1973) has shown that those who are experts in an area have much more sophisticated schematic structures than novices. In the book *Knowing What Students Know* (National Research Council, 2001), it is argued that more detailed theories that take into account learners' organizational schemas, common misconceptions, and response processes are necessary to make accurate inferences about student learning. Contributors to this book point out that to make valid inferences about learners' knowledge, researchers must have an explicit cognitive model of learning based on what is known about how people learn in the domain of interest. Such a model might be more or less detailed, depending on the state of cognitive research in the particular domain and on the complexity of the knowledge or skills being tested, with more complex tasks requiring more detailed models. A cognitive model should include specification of how learners at different levels organize, apply, and transfer knowledge. Although a full explication of cognitive models is outside the scope of this book, it is important to understand this basic framework because such models are central to the thinking of several current validity theorists (i.e., Embretson, 1998, Embretson & Gorin, 2001; Gorin, 2005, 2006; Mislevy, Steinberg, & Almond, 2003).

Cognitive models have been the focus of so much attention in achievement testing because they provide instructors with specific information on learners' strengths, weaknesses, and misconceptions. A common criticism of many current tests of knowledge is that they do not, in general, provide such information. For example, if a student answers a question incorrectly, it is often difficult to determine the exact source of the problem. It could be that the student did not understand the question, did not possess needed factual information, knew that information but was unable to integrate it to arrive at the correct answer, or any of a host of other possible reasons. Such difficulties occur because many achievement tests have not been based on cognitive models that explicate common misconceptions in the domain, what the knowledge structures of novices and experts look like, and how students progress from basic to more advanced knowledge states. Tests that are based on such cognitive models are much more suited to the job of providing detailed information on learners' levels of knowledge and skill.

Inclusion of Values and Test Consequences in the Validity Framework

One of the more contentious aspects of modern validity theory is the focus on value implications of test scores and consequences of testing. As noted by Kane (2013), among others, the arguments regarding consequences are not about whether the consequences of testing are important to consider when making test-based decisions. Instead, the issues center on whether consequences should be included as part of validity, and if so, whether test developers or test users are responsible for evaluating these. As Kane and other theorists have noted, consequences have always been an important consideration in evaluating tests, for the simple reason that tests are usually given with the expectation that they will yield certain positive consequences (e.g., selecting the most capable employees, preventing unqualified people from entering professions, determining the best type of therapy for a client). Because the main purpose of validation is to determine the likelihood that these benefits will be realized, Kane argues that consequences should be included as part of a validity research program. As Shepard (1997) puts it, once test use is brought into the validity arena, we are "obliged to think about effects or consequences" (p. 6).

Values in Testing

Messick (1995) famously stated, "Validity judgments *are* value judgments" (p. 748). By this he meant that value implications are an inherent part of the meaning of scores, and, because validity has to do with understanding what scores mean, values are inextricably linked to validity judgments. To take a concrete example, we as a society attach certain meanings to construct names such as "assertiveness" and "intelligence; if we did not, we would not be interested in measuring them in the first place. However, the implications of low or high scores often go considerably beyond simple statements such as "Sancho has a high level of assertiveness" or "Jon has lower than average achievement." If Sancho had been female, we might attach a different meaning to his high assertiveness score.

And the fact that Jon received a low score on an achievement test will likely result in his being labeled a low performer or as being in need of remediation—a label that may follow him for the rest of his life. As is well known, such labels can have important implications for one's education. In response to arguments that the inclusion of values under the umbrella of validity would unduly complicate the concept, Messick (1989, 1995) has explained that the inclusion of value implications is not meant to *add anything to* the conceptualization of validity, but rather to make explicit an aspect of validity that is often hidden. The importance of making values explicit is that the implications attached to test scores are then exposed and can be openly debated.

Another aspect of value implications is the broader societal value that was the impetus for obtaining the scores in the first place. The fact that a school, organization, or society at large is interested in a particular type of test score implies that some value, either positive or negative, is associated with the construct being measured. For example, the fact that colleges use aptitude tests as part of their college admissions criteria implies that high aptitude is valued. In fact, this value is so firmly entrenched in our society that you may wonder why I even bother to point it out. But as Shepard (1993) notes, colleges could put more weight on other criteria, such as obtaining a diverse student body. Diversity is also a value espoused by many in American society, but the fact that aptitude is typically weighted more heavily than diversity considerations in college admissions may indicate the value placed on each in educational institutions. As another example, admission to medical school is very competitive, typically requiring high scores on the Medical College Admission Test (MCAT). This reflects the appropriately high value placed on medical knowledge for doctors. However, the emphasis on high levels of medical knowledge may result in less emphasis being placed on attributes such as compassion and communication skills, which many patients feel are also valuable. These examples illustrate Messick's (1995) point that, if such values are not made explicit, those using test scores may not consider whether the values inherent in their testing process are, in fact, the most important ones.

OBTAINING EVIDENCE OF VALIDITY

In this section, I descend from the philosophical heights of validity conceptualizations to the more practical matters of what constitutes validity evidence and what types of evidence are most relevant to different testing situations. I begin by introducing the argument-based approach to validity (Cronbach, 1988; Kane, 1992, 2013). Although this approach was originally suggested by Cronbach (1988), Kane's work has done much to popularize the argument-based approach to validity. Space considerations preclude a full account of the intricacies of this approach, but I hope that the abbreviated version presented here is still useful in demonstrating how to make a basic validity argument. I encourage you to consult the original articles for more details on this useful approach. After introducing the argument-based approach, I discuss the five sources of validity evidence outlined in the *Standards* (2014): evidence based on test content, evidence based on response processes, evidence based on internal structure, evidence based on relations to other variables, and evidence for consequences of testing. Each of these is illustrated with a fictitious example.

Introduction to the Argument-Based Approach to Validity

Recall that validity is defined as "the degree to which evidence and theory support the interpretations of test scores for proposed uses of tests" (AERA, APA, & NCME, 2014). This definition implies that it is not possible to obtain evidence to support all possible interpretations or uses of a test. Tests are interpreted and used in many ways, some of which are justifiable and some of which are not. The first step in test validation, therefore, is to specify the intended interpretation(s) and use(s) of the test scores. This should be accompanied by an explanation of how the proposed interpretation is relevant to the proposed use of the test. Suppose that I wanted to develop a test of the ability to generate sound research hypotheses, which I will call the GOSH (Generation of Sound Hypotheses) test. I propose to use this test in selecting students for graduate school. My proposed interpretation of the test scores is that those with higher scores on the test have a greater ability to generate sound research hypotheses. The rationale behind the use of these test scores is that students in graduate school will be engaged in research of some kind, and the ability to generate research hypotheses is crucial to conducting research. Thus, students who do well on the GOSH test should be more successful in graduate school than students who do not.

You may already have identified several problems with my description of the GOSH and its proposed interpretation and usage. For one thing, what do I mean by "*sound research hypotheses*"? Before proceeding with my development of the test, I would have to fully define what is meant by "sound" research hypotheses and identify the skills and knowledge that make up the ability to generate these. Another issue is that not all graduate students are engaged in research that requires the generation of research hypotheses, sound or otherwise. Students in the performing arts, for example, may more likely be engaged in practicing for performances than in hypothesis generation. Thus, my test may not be useful in selecting students for such programs.

This example, and my accompanying critique, represent a streamlined version of Kane's (1992, 2013) argument-based approach to test validation. According to Kane (2013), "The core idea [of the argument-based approach] is to state the proposed interpretation and use explicitly and in some detail, and then to evaluate the plausibility of these proposals" (p. 1). The statements about proposed interpretations and use constitute the validity argument. Claims about validity then depend on the degree to which the accumulated validity evidence supports the claims made in this argument. As I pointed out in the context of the GOSH test, arguments about test interpretations and use are based on a series of assumptions and inferences. For example, I may have initially assumed that the GOSH could be used for selecting students for any type of graduate program. A related underlying assumption of the GOSH is that students in all graduate programs use the same skills and knowledge to generate research hypotheses. This may not be the case, however. Although knowledge of the research process is likely necessary in hypothesis generation, content knowledge is also clearly important. Content knowledge will, by definition, vary across content areas. Thus, some of the assumptions underlying my argument are likely to be violated. If so, my claims that GOSH scores can be interpreted as measures of general hypothesis-generating ability and used to select students for graduate school will not be supported.

Types of Validity Evidence

In the following sections, I describe the five types of validity evidence outlined in the *Standards* (2014): (1) *evidence based on test content*, (2) *evidence based on response processes*, (3) *evidence based on internal structure*, (4) *evidence based on relations to other variables*, and (5) *evidence for consequences of testing*, and I illustrate them using the fictitious GOSH test. Table 11.1 shows the five types of evidence, the general type of validity argument addressed by each, and illustrative methods for obtaining each type of evidence. In the last column I indicate how these relate to the traditional "three C's" (content, criterion-related, and construct validity). Although the tabular format necessitates presenting them separately, the five types of validity evidence are relevant to different aspects of the validity argument and are not intended to be viewed as different "types of validity." Instead, all five types contribute in some way to our understanding of the meaning of test scores, and this meaning is at the heart of validity. However, different types of evidence are needed because test scores may be interpreted and used in different ways, necessitating different validity arguments with different underlying assumptions. The type of evidence that best supports an argument for one use or interpretation may not support others, as is illustrated in the following section. Similarly, support for a particular interpretive/use argument may not require all types of evidence. As Kane (2013) points out, simpler claims regarding interpretation and use of scores require less support than more ambitious claims. Thus, although some types of evidence are often associated with certain types of tests, no type of evidence is exclusive to a particular test type. Researchers should determine the types of evidence that are appropriate based on the type of interpretation and use to be made.

Evidence Based on Test Content

Evidence based on content has to do with the degree to which the content included on a test provides an adequate representation of the domain to be measured. In most, if not all, testing situations, it is not possible to include every item that is part of a construct's domain. For example, the inclusion of every possible two-digit addition item on a test of addition knowledge would clearly result in a prohibitively lengthy test. As noted in Chapter 3, researchers are interested in the responses to specific test items because these responses are thought to be representative of the broader domain. That is,

TABLE 11.1. Types of Validity Evidence with Associated Validity Arguments and Methods

Evidence based on:	Validity argument	Examples of methods for obtaining evidence	Mapping to traditional forms of validity
Test content	Test contains a set of items that are appropriate for measuring the construct	• Table of specifications • Expert review of content/cognitive processes • Identification of possible construct-irrelevant variance • Identification of possible construct underrepresentation	Content
Response processes	Test items tap into the intended cognitive processes	• Specification of chain of reasoning from item responses to desired inferences • Think-aloud protocols • Eye tracking • Response time • Expert–novice studies • Concept maps • Manipulation of item features and other experimental studies	Construct
Internal structure	Relations among test items mirror those expected from theory	• Item and subscale intercorrelations • Internal consistency • Exploratory and confirmatory factor analysis • Item response theory • Generalizability theory • Studies of differential item functioning	Construct

Relations to other variables	Relations of test scores to other variables mirror those expected from theory	• Test–criterion relations
		  ○ Correlations with other scales or variables
		  ○ Predictive
		  ○ Concurrent
		  ○ Sensitivity and specificity
		• Group differences
		• Convergent and discriminant relations
		• Identification of method variance
		• Multitrait–multimethod matrices
			Criterion-related

Consequences of testing	Intended consequences are realized; unintended consequences are not due to test invalidity	• Determination of whether intended benefits accrue • Identification of unintended outcomes ○ Determination of whether unintended outcomes are due to test irrelevance or construct underrepresentation	Not included

researchers are not so much interested in a student's specific ability to add 17 + 11, but in the broader ability to add two-digit numbers. Thus, researchers interested in evidence based on test content are interested in the degree to which the test items constitute a representative sample of the domain of interest, from which inferences about that domain can reasonably be drawn. Evidence based on test content is therefore relevant to any validity argument that scores can be interpreted and used as representative measures of the knowledge, skills, abilities, or other attributes that make up an identifiable domain. Achievement and employment tests fall into this category, as do certification and licensure tests.

Anastasi and Urbina (1997) state that evidence of content validity is not appropriate for tests of aptitude or personality because "these tests bear less intrinsic resemblance to the behavior domain they are trying to sample than do achievement tests" (p. 117). Certainly, it is easier to delineate the relevant content for tests of knowledge or skill than for tests of aptitude or personality, because tests of knowledge are typically based on a common curriculum or set of experiences. In contrast, content on personality and aptitude tests is often based on a particular theory. For example, a personality test based on the Big Five theory of personality would be quite different from one written by a theorist who did not subscribe to that theory. Thus, in my view, content evidence is relevant to personality and aptitude tests, but definition of the content domain is likely to be more theory-based than curriculum-based. And there will likely be less agreement among researchers about what constitutes an appropriate content domain for such tests than for achievement tests.

In all cases, however, evidence based on content begins with a detailed definition of the domain of interest. For achievement tests, this often takes the form of a table of specifications. Items are then written to reflect these specifications, as discussed in Chapter 3. Such tables delineate both the content to be covered and the cognitive level at which items should be written. Similar tables could be prepared for personality tests, although this is seldom done in practice. More commonly, content for personality tests is based on the researcher's understanding of the theory underlying the construct or on diagnostic criteria, if relevant. For tests assessing job-related knowledge or skills, a job or task analysis should be conducted. In these analyses, the knowledge and skills underlying commonly performed tasks in a particular job are evaluated with the goal of determining which are most important for proficiency on the job.

Once the content domain has been delineated, through a table of specifications, job analysis, personality theory, or diagnostic criteria, it should be reviewed by a panel of experts. The makeup of such a panel will necessarily depend on the content area, but the level of expertise of panel members should be as high as possible. This is because many of the analyses conducted to obtain content-based evidence depend on this expertise. One common form of content-based evidence is that in which panel members independently match the items to the original table of specifications. Crocker and Algina (1986) suggest that the matching process be structured by supplying panel members with copies of the table of specifications and the test items and asking them to write the number of each item in the cell to which they think it belongs. Experts could also be asked to rate the items' relevance and importance for the domain. For employment tests, experts could be asked to rate how important each of the test's items or tasks is to successful performance in the job. Information from such ratings or matching processes can be summarized by computing the average rating, the percentage of matches overall and in each content area or cognitive level, and/or the percentages of items the experts felt were unimportant to performance or did not match the table of specifications. Agreement among the experts' assignments or ratings of items could also be calculated, using the methods for interrater agreement described in Chapter 9. Additional information can be obtained by asking experts to suggest other content areas or job tasks that should be included. For licensure or certification tests, some knowledge or skill areas may be considered more important than others. In such cases, experts should consider whether the areas considered most important are appropriately represented by more items. Finally, in addition to matching the items to the table of specification, experts are often asked to rate items in terms of their clarity and freedom from bias or stereotyping. Because these require different types of expertise, different panels are often convened for these tasks, as noted in the discussion of these aspects of the item review process in Chapter 3.

Construct Underrepresentation and Construct-Irrelevant Variance

Although Messick (1989) stated that the presence of construct underrepresentation and construct-irrelevant variance threaten all validity claims, these two threats are particularly associated with evidence based on content. As discussed previously, construct underrepresentation refers to a situation in which test content is defined too narrowly, leaving out important aspects of the construct. For example, the GOSH test is a measure of the ability to generate sound hypotheses. Suppose that students were provided with a question, such as "Why do young people join gangs?" and asked to generate as many hypotheses as possible. Their score on the GOSH test could then be calculated as the number of hypotheses generated. However, this approach does not include any measurement of the *soundness* of the research hypotheses and would thus not represent an important aspect of the ability to generate sound research hypotheses. Construct underrepresentation can also occur if a test covers the intended content adequately but does not do so at the intended cognitive level. For example, a licensure test for physicians that requires memorization of facts but has no items requiring application of these facts to diagnose diseases would result in underrepresentation of the appropriate knowledge domain.

Construct-irrelevant variance occurs when test scores are influenced by factors that are not part of the intended construct. This is problematic because when irrelevant features of an item affect people's scores, we cannot be sure of the meaning of these scores. The scores are now influenced by both the construct of interest and the irrelevant source, but we do not know how much influence each has on a given score. In the context of achievement testing, Messick (1989) defines two types of construct-irrelevant variance: construct-irrelevant easiness and construct-irrelevant difficulty. The first occurs when features of the test items that are irrelevant to the construct being measured make them easier for some examinees. For example, the correct answer for a multiple-choice item may contain a grammatical clue or be longer than the other options, as discussed in Chapter 4. Students who are test-wise are then likely to choose the correct answer even if they do not have the requisite content knowledge. Or there may be examples in the test items with which some examinees are very familiar, making these items easier for such examinees. If the GOSH test included the question on gang membership mentioned previously, examinees who were familiar with gangs would likely have an advantage. Construct-irrelevant difficulty, in contrast, occurs when features of the item that are irrelevant to the construct being measured make the item more difficult for some examinees. A classic example is the inclusion of overly complex language in achievement test items. Some students, notably those whose first language is not English, may fail to answer correctly not because they lack the content knowledge but because they do not understand the question. Unless the purpose of the test is to measure language ability, language complexity should be kept to a minimum to avoid contamination by this source of irrelevancy.

For personality or attitude measures, construct-irrelevant variance is introduced if responses are influenced by social desirability, a tendency to respond in an extreme fashion, or other response styles. Some respondents have trouble answering negatively oriented questions, as discussed in Chapter 5. Others may not read the questions carefully or may deliberately misrepresent themselves. All such tendencies will result in scores that are contaminated with some degree of construct-irrelevant variance. Messick (1989; see also Shadish, Cook, & Campbell, 2002, p. 452) points out that construct-irrelevant variance due to social desirability or other response artifacts occurs because of *mono-operation bias*, or using only one method to measure an attribute. These authors suggest that researchers use several methods of measurement, such as self-reports, ratings by others, and behavioral observations. One advantage of using different measurement methods is that each method provides a somewhat different view, thus triangulating on the construct. In addition, when such measures are combined, the construct-irrelevant variance should wash out because only the construct-relevant variance will be correlated across methods.

Evidence Based on Response Processes

Interpretations of item responses typically presuppose that respondents have used certain cognitive processes to produce their answers. For example, cognitive theories of responses to noncognitive items assume that respondents have read and understood the question, searched their memory for relevant information, integrated this information into an answer, and correctly mapped this answer onto the response options provided. However, what if the respondent has simply chosen the middle response option without even reading the item, or otherwise satisficed (Krosnick, 1991; see Chapter 5). Such responses should engender doubt about whether the question has measured the intended construct. In the context of achievement testing in mathematics, it is common to use word problems that require a student to determine which type of solution is required. But what if a student has memorized key features of such problems that allow for determining the appropriate solution strategy without using the intended reasoning processes? Such responses would not allow for inferences about the student's level of the reasoning ability of interest.

These scenarios illustrate the importance of understanding the response processes used to produce answers to test items. In many situations, inferences about the meaning of test scores center on the response processes used. If our proposed score interpretations are based on the assumption that certain cognitive processes have been used, these inferences are on shaky ground if this assumption has not been met. Embretson (1983) refers to this aspect of validity as *construct representation,* which she defines as being concerned with "identifying the theoretical mechanisms that underlie item responses, such as information processes, strategies, and knowledge stores" (1983, p. 179). Although Embretson's work is in the area of ability testing, it is important to point out that the same principles can be applied to personality or other noncognitive testing situations.

As Mislevy and his colleagues (Mislevy, 1994; Mislevy, Steinberg, & Almond, 2003; Mislevy, Steinberg, Breyer, Almond, & Johnson, 2002) note, the relevance of item responses and their value in supporting our inferences depends on the chain of reasoning that leads from item responses to the claims or inferences that we wish to make. In the context of the GOSH test, the chain of reasoning might be something like this: "I observe that a student has produced a number of well-reasoned hypotheses based on the scenario given. Based on past experience, I have confidence that the student would likely be able to do this in future situations. I therefore infer that the student has the ability to generate sound research hypotheses in general." Such inferences from responses to some type of stimulus are made every day by physicians, psychologists, social workers, and employers. The stimuli may take the form of responses to interview questions, results of medical tests, observations of behavior or nonverbal communications, or performance of a task. The inference may be based on scientific theory, empirical data, subject-matter expertise, or personal experience. My example from the GOSH test represents a very basic reasoning chain, whereas the examples described by Mislevy and colleagues (2003) are much more complex. For example, Mislevy and colleagues would likely identify the specific cognitive processes needed to produce reasonable hypotheses, such as the abilities to keep the scenario in memory, search memory stores for relevant information, combine the information into a hypothesis, and judge the reasonableness of the generated hypotheses. Nevertheless, my example illustrates the basic process of reasoning from evidence.

One part of this process is to rule out alternative explanations for the observations. If the student in the GOSH example has not been able to generate a single hypothesis, I might reason that the student lacked the ability to do so. However, another explanation is that the student did have the ability but lacked the motivation to use it, or had hypothesis-generating ability but was completely unfamiliar with the scenario provided. You might recognize that these explanations represent construct-irrelevant variance in that they result in variations in performance that are not due to the attribute of interest. Construct-irrelevant variance is problematic because it does not contribute to measurement of the attribute of interest. Or, in the words of Mislevy and colleagues (2003), construct-irrelevant variance does not accumulate. These authors note that a total test score is more informative than a score from a single item because each item score provides a nugget of information that contributes to the attribute of interest. These nuggets of information are cumulated in the total test score, yielding a total score that is the sum of what the items have in common (which, we hope, is the attribute of interest). Because construct-irrelevant variance is not relevant to this common attribute, it does not cumulate across items and therefore does not contribute to measurement of that attribute. As Mislevy and colleagues point out, "the more examinees differ from one another on the knowledge that does not accumulate, the less accurate are the scores over the same number of items. A cardinal principle of our view of assessment design is that what accumulates over tasks should be intentional rather than accidental" (p. 50). Although this statement was made in the context of achievement testing, the same principle applies to any type of test in which item responses are combined in some way. How does one make sure that what is captured by a total score is "intentional rather than accidental"? One way is to devise test items, tasks, or performances in such a way that the aspect of the attribute intended to be measured is isolated as much as possible. That is, make sure that influences of extraneous features such as reading ability, motivation, and contextual variables such as the physical setting or test instructions are minimized to the extent possible. Such test standardization practices are discussed in Chapter 3, but in the framework described by Mislevy and his colleagues, standardization is taken to new heights.

Another way in which researchers can design assessments that capture intentional rather than accidental variance is to determine the influences on item difficulty and generate items in which these influences are manipulated systematically. This is the approach taken by Embretson (1998), who has pioneered this type of item generation in her work on spatial ability. Embretson's approach is to build validity into the test during the item development process by manipulating item features known or hypothesized to affect response processes. For example, in her work on measurement of abstract reasoning, Embretson developed items consisting of matrices of shapes or symbols, similar to those used on Raven's Advanced Progressive Matrices (APM) test (Raven, Court, & Raven, 1992). She manipulated item features such as the number of characteristics that varied across the sequence of symbols and the manner in which these characteristics changed across rows or columns of the matrix. She then used a mathematical model called a *cognitive item response theory model* to test the degree to which the manipulated item features affected item difficulty.

Although the work of Mislevy (Mislevy, 1994; Mislevy et al., 2002, 2003) and Embretson (1998) has been in the area of achievement and ability testing, there is no reason that similar approaches could not be used in the noncognitive arena. Note that the approaches described by these researchers build validity into the test during the item development phase. That is, items are specifically engineered to test hypotheses about the constructs of interest, such as the nature of the cognitive processes underlying item responses. Items could also be designed to reflect features thought to affect the task's difficulty level or, for noncognitive items, the intensity level. Doing this requires a fairly well-developed theory that would point to the characteristics to be manipulated. As Embretson points out, most currently used tests are not based on such theories. Instead, achievement and aptitude tests have been based on manipulation of relatively simple content and cognitive features (e.g., Bloom's taxonomy; see Chapter 3). And although most tests assume that items measure only a single piece of knowledge or a single skill, it is certainly possible to design items that tap into multiple sources of knowledge, skill, or ability (for more on this subject, see Chapter 15). This allows the items to "multitask," and provides more information than more traditional items that tap into only one skill.

In the view of Borsboom and colleagues (2009), evidence about response processes is crucial for validity. They argue that validity is concerned with whether "a measurement instrument for an attribute has the property that it is *sensitive* to differences in the attribute; that is, when the attribute differs over objects then the measurement procedure gives a different outcome" (p. 148, original emphasis). They go on to point out that this requires the researcher to understand the underlying response processes and how these processes are influenced by variations in the attribute being measured, which they refer to as "how the test works" (p. 149). Borsboom and his colleagues are not alone in their focus on response processes. As Gorin (2006) states, "In comparison to earlier theories of assessment design . . . recent test development frameworks rely more heavily on cognition than ever before" (p. 21). The work of researchers such as Embretson (1983, 1998), Gorin (2005, 2006, 2007), Mislevy (1994, 1996; Mislevy et al., 2003), and Wilson (Wilson & Sloane, 2000) exemplify this trend of focusing on how test items "work."

Of course, in some situations the underlying response processes are not crucial to our inferences. The GOSH test may be a case in point. If my only interest is in *whether* students are able to generate sound hypotheses for a given scenario, *how* they do so may be immaterial. I might argue that for a student to succeed in graduate school, the important thing is that students are able to come up with research hypotheses in some way, but it does not really matter how they do so (assuming, of course, that it is not by plagiarizing the ideas of others). The important question to ask in determining whether cognitive process evidence is relevant to a particular testing situation is, "For the inference I wish to make, does the response process matter?" If the answer is "yes," evidence based on response processes is needed.

The current focus on process models for item responses is an exciting development in the testing world and has already resulted in better understandings of the mechanisms by which respondents arrive at answers to test items. However, understanding this process is, as Borsboom and colleagues (1999) point out, "no small matter," as it requires the researcher to "explicate what the property's structure or underlying process is and how this structure or process influences the measurement instrument to result in variations in the measurement outcomes. This seems to be a very daunting task indeed for many psychological properties that researchers claim to measure" (p. 148). I agree with Borsboom et al. that this is a daunting task because it requires the researcher to have a theory of how variations in the attribute of interest produce variations in responses. As these researchers imply, such theories are rare in the area of psychology and likely in most social science areas. Perhaps the most progress in developing such theories has been made in certain areas of achievement testing. Much of this research has focused on explicating what it is that makes some types of test items more difficult than others. Such models have been developed in such areas as physics (Chi, Feltovich, & Glaser, 1981; Chi & Van Lehn, 1991), reading comprehension (Gorin, 2005; Gorin & Embretson, 2006), children's math learning (Brown & Burton, 1978; Griffin & Case, 2007), and abstract reasoning (Embretson, 1998). But, as noted in the book *Knowing What Students Know* (National Research Council, 2001), much more work is needed in this area (p. 179).

Developing Process Models

How, then, does one go about developing such process models? The best place to start is with the theory underlying the construct and/or empirical studies of the phenomenon of interest. Theory can help in understanding the types of processes respondents might use in answering. For example, the cognitive process model of responding to attitude items described by Sudman and colleagues (1996; see Chapter 5) is a good starting place for developing a model of noncognitive response processes. Much of Embretson's (1998) work on abstract reasoning relied on the theories of Carpenter, Just, and Shell (1990), which suggested that working memory capacity was the primary cognitive resource needed for solving matrix problems. Empirical studies in which respondents are asked to say their thought processes out loud as they solve a problem or respond to a noncognitive item can be rich sources of information (see Ericsson & Simon, 1984). In the context of the GOSH test, for example, such *think-alouds* might provide insight into the ways students judge the "soundness" of a hypothesis.

A related method is the *analysis of reasons* in which respondents are asked to provide rationales for their responses. For achievement items, such rationales would provide insight into the algorithms, reasoning processes, and/or cognitive schema underlying students' responses. For noncognitive items, rationales might refer to the types of considerations respondents deliberated in forming their answers, how these were weighted to yield a single response, and/or how the response was mapped onto the rating scale provided.

An *analysis of errors* could also be used for cognitive items. In this method, students' incorrect responses are examined in an attempt to make inferences about possible misconceptions, improper application of algorithms, or faulty reasoning.

Expert–novice studies are designed to elucidate features of the knowledge structures that differentiate beginners from experts in a particular area. Studies of this type have revealed that experts and novices do not simply differ in their *amounts* of knowledge, but in how this knowledge is organized (e.g., Chi et al., 1981, 1982). This suggests that research might profitably be focused on the *schemas* or knowledge representation systems, through which experts and novices encode and organize their knowledge. One way of doing this is to ask respondents to create a *concept map* of a set of terms, problems, or other information that depicts the respondents' understanding of how these are related.

In the 1982 study by Chi and colleagues, experts and novices were asked to create concept maps showing the organizational structure underlying a series of problems in mechanics.

Experimental studies, such as those used by Embretson (1998), can be used to manipulate characteristics of items to determine whether these characteristics affect items responses in expected ways. For example, items features thought to affect the ability to generate a response to a noncognitive item, such as the complexity or familiarity of the attribute, could be manipulated systematically to determine their effects on responses. In some cases, it is possible to manipulate the attribute itself to determine whether responses show a corresponding change. This has been done in studies of test anxiety, in which the construct has been measured during a regular class session and again after a difficult examination has been given. Experimental studies might also involve tracking eye movements or the time taken to respond to an item. Eye-tracking studies can be used to study such things as reading comprehension, by showing specific parts of the text on which readers focus (or fail to focus) and how long this focus lasts. Longer periods of focus may be indicative of greater complexity of the material or of greater interest in the material. Response time measures can be used in similar ways. Items that are more difficult or complex should engender correspondingly longer response times. If this is not the case, it may be that respondents are responding randomly or otherwise lack engagement in the material. In studies of the GOSH, I might vary the complexity of the scenarios to determine whether response times increase with complexity, as expected. I might also track respondents' eye movements in an effort to determine the specific part of the scenario on which respondents focused, or whether respondents reread parts of the scenario in the process of producing their answer.

Evidence Based on Internal Structure

Some tests are designed to measure a single *dimension*, or narrow aspect of a test, such as the propensity to buy a particular type of product or ability to add two-digit numbers. Other tests are designed to measure broader, multidimensional constructs such as general intelligence. Many personality constructs are thought to be multidimensional, such as Sarason's (1984) conceptualization of test anxiety, which posits four test anxiety dimensions: worry, bodily arousal, tension, and test-irrelevant thinking. Tests are typically based on theory, either implicit or explicit, about the dimensionality of the construct being measured, and our interpretations of test scores are based on this assumed dimensionality. We might, for example, refer to the "worry" component of test anxiety or to specific abilities such as spatial ability, and we might make inferences on the basis of these narrower dimensions. Because these inferences assume a specific dimensional structure for the test, it is important to determine whether the test items actually form the separate, identifiable dimensions that are hypothesized. Determining the degree to which test items live up to our dimensional expectations is therefore an important type of validity evidence. Such evidence is crucial in determining the degree to which we are justified in interpreting test scores as representing the posited dimensions. In the 2014

Standards, this type of evidence is referred to as "evidence based on internal structure" but is closely related to what Messick (1995) and Loevinger (1957) referred to as the "structural aspect of validity."

Types of Internal Structure Evidence

At the most basic level, evidence about a test's internal structure could be obtained by examining the pattern of intercorrelations among the items. At the very least, items developed to measure the same dimension should have some level of positive correlation (after re-coding negatively oriented items, if needed; see Chapter 5). Correlations among items on a test considered to be unidimensional should be fairly uniform in magnitude. This is because items on a unidimensional scale should all tap into the same construct, in more or less the same way. Of course, each item will be somewhat idiosyncratic simply because it is worded differently from the other items. However, this should not result in patterns in which some items are much more highly correlated than others. A heterogeneous pattern of correlations would suggest that the more highly correlated items share a source of variance that is not shared by the less highly correlated items. The presence of this additional variance may be evidence that the construct is not unidimensional after all and that the highly correlated items represent one or more narrower subdimensions. Another possibility is that the additional variance is due to construct-irrelevant sources, such as similarity in wording or some type of method effect.

Items on a multidimensional scale should exhibit fairly uniform patterns of interitem correlations *within a dimension*, and these within-dimension correlations should be higher than the across-dimension correlations of the items. Such a pattern is shown in Table 11.2, which depicts the intercorrelations of nine items. As can be seen from the table, items 1–3 are much more highly correlated with each other than with the other six items. The same is true for items 4–6 and 7–9. This pattern suggests that the items are tapping into three different dimensions.

TABLE 11.2. Hypothetical Intercorrelations of Nine Items Measuring Three Dimensions

	Item 1	Item 2	Item 3	Item 4	Item 5	Item 6	Item 7	Item 8	Item 9
Item 1	1.0								
Item 2	.60	1.0							
Item 3	.50	.70	1.0						
Item 4	.20	.30	.15	1.0					
Item 5	.15	.20	.20	.60	1.0				
Item 6	.10	.20	.25	.65	.70	1.0			
Item 7	.20	.25	.10	.25	.20	.25	1.0		
Item 8	.30	.10	.15	.20	.20	.15	.55	1.0	
Item 9	.20	.15	.20	.15	.10	.20	.60	.65	1.0

Note that I have not said anything about how high the correlations should be. Intuitively, it may seem that correlations among items measuring the same dimension should be as high as possible. However, as Cronbach and Meehl (1955) have pointed out, high interitem correlations support validity inferences only if they are theoretically warranted. In other words, the theory underlying the construct should determine the appropriate level of interitem correlations. It should be kept in mind that scales based on highly correlated items will be quite narrowly focused. In the case of the GOSH test, asking students to generate hypotheses for two very similar scenarios would yield a much more limited measure of hypothesis-generating ability than use of two very different scenarios. But the scores based on the similar scenarios would be more highly correlated than those based on the different scenarios. Of course, narrowly focused tests based on highly correlated items might be appropriate in some situations. For example, items on scales designed to measure respondents' attitudes about a specific topic, or items developed to measure employees' ability to perform a specific skill within a limited context would be expected to correlate very highly. Messick (1989) suggests that indices of internal consistency, such as coefficient alpha, can be used to provide evidence about internal structure. As he states, "This is relevant validity information because the degree of homogeneity in the test . . . should be commensurate with the degree of homogeneity theoretically expected for the construct in question" (p. 51). Thus, the main point with regard to internal structure analysis is that the structure, whatever it is, should align with theoretical expectations.

Factor Analytic Evidence.   Another common form of evidence based on internal structure is that obtained from *factor analytic* procedures. Because I discuss these procedures in detail in Chapters 12 and 13, I will provide only a brief description here. In essence, factor analytic methods answer the question, "What is causing the item scores to correlate in the particular way we observe?" In factor analysis, the answer to this question is that the scores are correlated due to a common cause: the factor(s) or attributes being measured. In other words, respondents vary in their levels of the factors being measured, and these differences in factor levels cause them to provide different responses. For instance, a respondent with a high level of anxiety will provide different answers to items on an anxiety measure than a respondent with low anxiety. Thus, factors cause respondents to answer in particular ways, and this will result in particular patterns of correlations among the items. As another example, note that the pattern of correlations in Table 11.2 suggests three factors.

The input to most factor analytic methods is the matrix of interitem correlations. Factor analytic methods parse these correlations into blocks that represent highly correlated sets of items. This is done by transforming the interitem correlations into a set of *factor loadings* that measure the relation between the factor and the variable. In *exploratory factor analysis* (EFA), researchers can either allow the number of factors to be determined by the computer software being used or can specify that a specific number of factors be obtained. In either case, the loadings of each variable on each factor are estimated. Researchers examine these loadings to determine whether the items written to measure a specific factor all have high loadings on that factor and lower loadings on other factors. In *confirmatory factor analysis* (CFA) the researcher must prespecify the number of factors and the variables associated with each. Both EFA and CFA can help researchers understand both the number and composition of the latent constructs underlying the variables of interest.

Validity arguments based on factor analytic evidence could take several forms. Scales in the social sciences are often designed to measure multiple dimensions, and if so, evidence of this multidimensionality should be provided. A common validity argument is that the hypothesized number of factors will be found *and* that the hypothesized items will load on each. Support for such an argument provides evidence for the hypothesized dimensionality of the test. For example, evidence that the items on Sarason's (1984) measure of test anxiety, the Reactions to Test (RTT) scale loaded as expected onto the four posited test anxiety factors would support interpretations and use of the scores on these factors as measures of worry, test-irrelevant thinking, and so on.

IRT Evidence.   IRT methods constitute another set of procedures for examining the degree to which test items conform to a hypothesized structure. Because I discuss IRT methods in Chapter 14, I provide only a brief description here. These methods are similar to those of CFA, but whereas the use of CFA methods assumes that items are measured on a continuous scale, IRT methods are generally applied to dichotomously scored items, such as those commonly found on achievement tests (but see Chapter 14 for extensions to items with multiple scoring categories). IRT models can be used to estimate the probability that an examinee with a given level of ability will answer an item correctly. As discussed in Chapter 14, there are different IRT models, distinguished by the inclusion of different item parameters. The most basic IRT model includes one parameter, known as the difficulty parameter, which is analogous to the difficulty index in classical test theory (see Chapter 6). Thus, IRT models can be used to provide evidence for validity arguments about the relative difficulty of items on a test. For example, I might hypothesize that it will be much more difficult to generate hypotheses for one GOSH scenario than for another scenario. I may therefore make a validity argument that examinees who obtain a high score on the difficult scenario have more ability than those with low scores. This argument would be supported if the IRT difficulty parameters for the two scenarios conformed to my hypotheses.

IRT methods are also commonly used to determine whether items are biased, or, in IRT parlance, whether items exhibit *differential item functioning* (DIF). Although readers may think of item bias as occurring when examinees from different ethnic- or gender-based groups obtain different scores, this is not how bias is defined in the measurement literature. Instead, as discussed in Chapter 16, DIF is described as a situation in which examinees from different groups *who have the same level of ability or achievement* obtain different scores. The distinction in italics is necessary because groups may have valid differences in construct levels. For example, students in the fifth grade would likely do better on a general math test than students in the second grade because fifth graders have more math knowledge. However, this would not be considered bias because we would expect fifth graders to know more. In the same way, groups may differ in knowledge because of such things as differential curricula or opportunities to learn the material. Such differences would not be considered as reflective of test bias because they stem from construct-relevant differences in the construct of interest. In contrast, bias or DIF reflects the influence of construct-irrelevant variation on item responses. A common example is the presence of unnecessarily complex language in a mathematics item. Some test takers may miss the item not because they do not understand the mathematics, but because they do not understand the language. Thus, the presence of DIF suggests that some irrelevant construct (such as language ability) is being measured along with the intended construct.

DIF studies are relevant to validity because they can be used to ferret out sources of construct-irrelevant variance that may otherwise remain hidden. In addition, validity arguments typically make the assumption that the items on a test measure the same construct for all groups of interest—an assumption that is called into question if DIF is present.

Generalizability Theory Evidence. Finally, *generalizability theory* was discussed in Chapter 10 as a method for assessing the extent to which scores are affected by different sources of measurement error. For example, students' writing skills might be assessed by requiring them to write essays in different genres, and these essays might be rated by different raters. The extent to which students' scores are similar across the different genres provides evidence about the breadth of their skills within the writing domain. It may be that some students perform well in narrative writing but not in persuasive writing. It may also be the case that scores obtained from different raters are dissimilar, suggesting that we cannot legitimately generalize scores from one rater to those of other raters. Thus, generalizability theory analyses provide information on the limits that should be placed on our interpretations of scores. Because this information informs the meaning we can make from test scores, it is relevant to test validity.

Evidence Based on Relations to Other Variables

In many cases, interpretations and uses of test scores rely on their relation with other variables. For example, a test may be used to predict which job applicants will make the best employees. Or the theory underlying a test might suggest that those with a specific psychological diagnosis, such as depression, should obtain higher scores than those without such a diagnosis. Such relations are measured by correlation coefficients or regression coefficients from either linear or logistic regression, or by tests of mean differences in test scores across groups, with the choice among the methods depending on the types of variables involved. Categories of evidence discussed in the *Standards* include *test–criterion relationships*, *group differences*, and *convergent and discriminant evidence*. Test–criterion relationships refer to situations in which test scores are used to predict future performance or current status on some criterion. For example, recall that I proposed using the fictitious GOSH test as a means of selecting students for graduate school, arguing that students with high scores on the GOSH test should be more successful than those with low scores. My validity argument is therefore that GOSH scores are predictive of graduate school success. To back up this claim, I would have to demonstrate empirically that GOSH scores are predictive of the criterion of graduate school success—an example of the prediction of future performance.

As an example of the prediction of current status, suppose that a researcher develops a multiple-choice test designed to assess the same skills as the GOSH test. If the GOSH test were an established instrument, the researcher's validity argument might be that scores on her test are highly correlated with, or predictive of, scores on the GOSH, and are therefore measuring the same construct. Of course, to back up her argument, the researcher would have to show that scores on her test are, in fact, highly correlated with scores on the GOSH test. Another type of test–criterion relationship involves the use of test scores for assigning individuals to different treatments, jobs, or educational programs. Within the educational system, for example, tests are sometimes used to determine whether students should take an advanced placement or remedial class. The logic behind such placements is that students with higher scores are more likely to benefit from an advanced placement course, whereas students with lower scores will benefit from remediation before moving on in the curriculum. The validity of this type of test use depends on the degree to which the hypothesized benefits actually accrue. If students assigned to the remedial class would actually have done well in the advanced placement class and/or if students assigned to the advanced placement class are unable to keep up in that class, doubt would be cast on these uses and interpretations of the test scores.

Some validity arguments are predicated on hypotheses that respondents in different groups should score differently. This is common for tests designed to identify those with a particular mental disorder. For such tests, the validity argument is that the scores of those diagnosed with the disorder should differ from the scores of those without such a diagnosis. For example, an appropriate form of validity evidence for a test designed to measure social anxiety would involve comparing the scores of those who had been independently diagnosed with social anxiety and those who had not been. Such studies are commonly referred to as *known groups* studies. Clearly, if scores of the two groups do not differ, the test is of little use in diagnosis, so evidence of group differences is essential for such tests.

Finally, validity arguments involving *convergent and discriminant evidence* state that test scores should be related to scores from other tests of the same or similar constructs (convergent evidence) and should be less strongly related to scores from tests measuring dissimilar constructs (discriminant evidence). For instance, if a researcher wanted to show that scores on an attitude measure were not influenced by social desirability, attitude scores could be correlated with scores on a measure of social desirability. A correlation close to zero would provide the desired discriminant evidence. In the context of the GOSH test, it might be argued that GOSH scores should be related to scores on a test of inductive reasoning (convergent) but should not be related to writing ability (discriminant).

In the following sections, I briefly discuss the types of evidence relevant to arguments based on test–criterion relationships, group differences, and convergent and discriminant relationships. I also highlight practical considerations in designing studies to obtain such evidence.

Test–Criterion Relationships

Recall my earlier proposal to use the fictitious GOSH test as a means of selecting students for graduate school, on the basis that students with high scores on the GOSH test should be more successful than those with low scores. However, it would be foolish to accept this claim without any evidence to back it up. To obtain such evidence, I would have to show empirically that those with high GOSH scores are more successful in graduate school than those with low scores. Arguments that test scores can be used to predict such things as success in education or training programs or performance in employment settings are common in the testing arena. Such claims underlie the use of test scores to select those who will be admitted to college or given a job. In these situations, evidence of the test's predictive ability is crucial to the validity argument. If the test does not predict success, using it as a selection tool is questionable, at best. Another form of test–criterion relationship is that in which scores on two tests or on a test and a criterion are obtained concurrently. Evidence of concurrent test relationships is necessary whenever it is argued that one test can be used as an alternative to another, as in my example of the multiple-choice GOSH test. Other examples are the development of a shorter form of a longer test or a less expensive measure designed as an alternative to an existing, more expensive test. An example from the latter category might involve a paper-and-pencil test of anxiety proposed as an alternative to an existing physiological test. If the shorter or less expensive test is intended to replace the longer or more expensive test, there must be empirical evidence showing that scores from the two tests are highly correlated. Another situation in which concurrent evidence is relevant is that of psychodiagnostic tests. Such tests are often validated against the clinician's diagnosis. If the test yields the same diagnosis as the clinician, use of the test for diagnostic decisions is supported.

Issues with Test–Criterion Relationships

Selection of an Appropriate Criterion.   A common issue with evidence based on test–criterion relationships is the selection of an appropriate criterion. When a new test is suggested as a substitute for an existing test, as in concurrent validity situations, selection of the criterion is straightforward as the criterion is simply the existing test. For tests purported to predict a particular outcome, such as success in school or on the job, however, obtaining scores on an appropriate criterion can be problematic. In my previous example of the GOSH test, I stated that GOSH scores should be related to success in graduate school. In presenting that example, I skirted the issue of what I meant by "success in graduate school," but if I were to actually conduct such a study success would have to be defined. Does success in graduate school mean a high GPA, the number of conference presentations or research publications produced, the number of citations of a student's research, all of these, or something else? GPA and number of citations have the advantages of being easily obtained and quantifiable but may not correspond to what many people think of as "success." Number of presentations or publications is arguably more closely related to the ability to generate sound hypotheses because such products presumably are based on such hypotheses. But should all presentations be weighted the same, or should international presentations count more than local presentations?

Similar questions arise in other areas in which tests are hypothesized to predict performance, such as employment testing. What should the criterion be for a test designed to identify the best employees? Actual performance on the job is probably the most relevant criterion, but how should it be measured? In most cases, this is not as straightforward as counting the number of widgets produced. One possible criterion is supervisor ratings, but as readers who have held jobs can imagine, such ratings may not always be accurate reflections of performance. One commonly discussed influence on supervisor ratings is *criterion contamination*, which occurs when supervisors know employees' scores on the employment test and allow this knowledge to affect the ratings they give. This is similar to the halo effect discussed in Chapter 4.

Restriction of Range.   As noted previously, evidence for test-criterion relations typically takes the form of a correlation or regression coefficient and is therefore subject to the factors influencing these coefficients. Restriction of range, as discussed in Chapter 8, occurs whenever the full range of scores on either the predictor or criterion variable (or both) is not obtained. Because the whole point of using tests for selection purposes is to choose the highest (or in some cases, the lowest) scorers, restriction of range is almost always an issue. Recall that restriction of range in either the predictor test or the criterion can result in lower values of the correlation coefficient than would be obtained if the full range of scores was available. Thus, the true correlation of the test with a criterion may be higher than that obtained from a restricted sample.

Other Factors Attenuating Predictor–Criterion Relations.   Another potential issue is that commonly used correlation coefficients such as Pearson's correlation are based on the assumption that the relation between the predictor and criterion is linear. This may not be the case in many situations. For example, suppose that a performance requires a certain level of ability but after that point, having more ability does not increase performance. In this case, performance will increase with ability up to the requisite level, but the relationship will then remain constant, resulting in a nonlinear pattern. Another attenuating factor in predictor–criterion relations is a lack of reliability in either. In general, the relation between a predictor test and a criterion will be attenuated to the extent that either the predictor or criterion is not measured reliably. This effect is ubiquitous in measurement theory, as evidenced by Equation 11.1, which provides the relation between the predictor–criterion correlation and the reliabilities of the two.

$$\rho_{XY} \leq \sqrt{\rho_{XX'}\rho_{YY'}} \tag{11.1}$$

ρ_{XY} is the correlation between predictor and criterion, and $\rho_{XX'}$ and $\rho_{YY'}$ are the reliabilities of the two. Equation 11.1 shows that the correlation between two scores is restricted by their reliabilities. When measuring such relationships, what we would really like to know is the correlation between the two true scores, or the correlation between the error-free measures of X and Y ($\rho_{t_X t_Y}$) The so-called correction for attenuation formula in Equation 11.2 provides an estimate of the correlation between the true scores of X and Y; that is, it is the correlation we would have obtained if the measures were perfectly reliable. Note that the observed score correlation (ρ_{XY}) is adjusted upward by dividing it by a function of the reliabilities of the two scores. This makes sense conceptually because the correlation between the true scores should be higher than that between the observed scores to the extent that the observed scores are unreliable.

$$\rho_{t_X t_Y} = \frac{\rho_{XY}}{\sqrt{\rho_{XX'} \rho_{YY'}}} \tag{11.2}$$

However, as noted by Crocker and Algina (1986), researchers rarely, if ever, have perfectly reliable measures in practice, so Equation 11.2 yields an overestimate of the correlation that would be obtained from actual tests. McDonald (1999), however, points out that "in many applications, we wish to know how well the given test predicts, in spite of its measurement properties" (p. 227), and Equation 11.2 answers this question.

Logistic Regression

The discussion to this point has been based on the assumption that both the test score and the criterion can be treated as continuous. However, in some situations, the outcome to be predicted takes the form of categories, such as whether a person passes or fails, responds to treatment or not, or drops out or does not drop out of school. With categorical outcomes, the overarching validity argument is that the test can accurately classify respondents into the correct category. To obtain evidence supportive of this argument, researchers would administer the test to respondents and obtain information on their subsequent status on the categorical variable. A regression method such as logistic regression, which is suitable for categorical outcomes, would then be used to determine the degree to which the test accurately predicts the outcome. Although space concerns preclude a full treatment of logistic regression here, readers unfamiliar with logistic and other regression techniques suitable for categorical data are referred to Cohen, Cohen, West, and Aiken (2003) or other regression texts. However, because the topic of classification accuracy, which is relevant to measurement validity, is not covered in depth in most regression texts, I include a brief discussion of this topic in the following paragraphs.

Classification Accuracy. One outcome of logistic regression models is the predicted probability, given a particular score on the test, that a respondent is either "positive" (passes, drops out, responds to treatment) or "negative" (fails, does not drop out, does not respond to treatment). Note that for dichotomous outcomes, only one probability is obtained because the probability of a negative classification is simply one minus the probability of a positive classification (because the probabilities must sum to one). Cut scores are chosen by first determining a probability above which a person would be classified as a "positive" and below which the person would be classified as a "negative." For example, probabilities of 0.6 or above might be considered as a positive, and probabilities less than 0.6 as negatives. After deciding on this probability, the logistic regression equation can be used to determine the test score that corresponds to that probability. This score is then set as the cut score for classifying people as positives or negatives. Classification accuracy can then be determined by comparing the results of these classifications to the actual status of the person.

With a dichotomous (two-category) outcome, there are four possible outcomes: classification of a person as being in the positive category either correctly (*true positive*) or incorrectly (*false positive*), and classification of a person as being in the negative category either correctly (*true negative*) or incorrectly (*false negative*). These four terms give rise to two further specifications: *sensitivity*, or *true positive rate*, and *specificity*, or *true negative rate*. Sensitivity is calculated as the number of true positive classifications divided by the total number of actual positive outcomes (i.e., number of true positive + false negative classifications). Sensitivity measures answer the question, "Of those with observed positive outcomes, what proportion were correctly classified as positive on the basis of the test?" Specificity is calculated as the number of true negatives divided by the total number of actual negative outcomes (i.e., true negatives + false positives) and addresses the question, "Of those with observed negative outcomes, what proportion was correctly classified as negative on the basis of the test?" The calculations for sensitivity and specificity are illustrated in Table 11.3.

In this illustration, the sensitivity of the test, or the proportion correctly classified as having a positive outcome, is .7, or 70%. The specificity, or proportion correctly classified as having a negative outcome, is .9, or 90%. Is this good? The answer to this question depends on the relative consequences of false positives and false negatives in any given situation. The terms *sensitivity* and *specificity* were originally developed in the context of medical studies. In those studies, a "positive" outcome is usually the presence of a disease (although this does not seem particularly positive), so a false positive would

TABLE 11.3. Numbers of Respondents Correctly and Incorrectly Classified by a Test

Predicted outcome (based on test)	Actual outcome		Total predicted positive and negative
	Positive	Negative	
Positive	True positives (TP) = 35	False positives (FP) = 5	40
Negative	False negatives (FN) = 15	True negatives (TN) = 45	60
Total actual positive or negative	50	50	Total N = 100

$$\text{Sensitivity} = \frac{TP}{TP+FN} = \frac{35}{50} = .7 \qquad \text{Specificity} = \frac{TN}{TN+FP} = \frac{45}{50} = .9$$

mean a patient is classified as having a disease when it is not really present, and a false negative would mean that the patient is not classified as having the disease when it really is present. In this case, a false negative is probably more consequential than a false positive because a person classified as a false negative would not receive needed treatment, whereas a false positive would likely be identified as such upon further testing. In educational settings, sensitivity and specificity are often calculated for the purpose of diagnosing learning disabilities. Because students diagnosed with such disabilities usually receive additional resources, it could be argued that a false negative classification is more serious than a false positive. Whereas a false positive diagnosis would result in a student receiving unneeded services, a false negative diagnosis would result in needed services being withheld.

Although ideally we would prefer to minimize both false positives and false negatives, this is possible only if the test is 100% accurate, which is an unlikely scenario. The interplay between false positives and false negatives can be seen from Figure 11.1, which shows the proportions of true and false positives and negatives for three different test cut points. Recall that decisions regarding classification of a respondent as positive or negative are made on the basis of a particular cut score on the predictor test. These cut scores can be chosen by the test user to minimize false positives or false negatives. In Figure 11.1, three cut scores are shown as vertical lines in the center of the figure. The shaded ellipse represents the obtained test scores and outcomes. The cut score represented by the heavy black line in the center of the figure would balance false positives and negatives fairly evenly. Choice of the lower cut point to the left would minimize false negatives but increase false positives, whereas the higher cut point to the right would minimize false positives at the expense of false negatives. This is somewhat similar to the situation in statistical hypothesis testing, in which minimization of Type I errors comes at the expense of Type II errors. To determine the "optimal" cut score, therefore, researchers must first decide whether it is more important to minimize false positives or false negatives. Researchers can then try out different cut scores, using them to make positive and negative classification decisions, and calculating the sensitivity and specificity values for each. To illustrate, I constructed the hypothetical data in Table 11.4 in which dropout status is predicted by a test score. Three different cut scores on the test are used to determine dropout status: low, medium, and high. Numbers in the body of the table represent the number of people with each dropout status.

As can be seen in Table 11.4, use of the low cut score maximizes sensitivity (.98), or the proportion of true positives, and minimizes the proportion of false negatives (.02). In this scenario, a true positive is a student who is predicted to drop out and does drop out, whereas a false negative is a student who is not predicted to drop out but actually does. Use of the high cut score results in the greatest specificity (.97), or the largest proportion of students correctly predicted not to drop out. The proportion of false positives, or students who are predicted to drop out but do not, is lowest using the high cut score at 0.03. Use of the medium cut score results in the largest combined total for sensitivity and specificity. This cut score would therefore result in the greatest number of students being correctly classified overall. If test users were most concerned with minimizing false positives, the

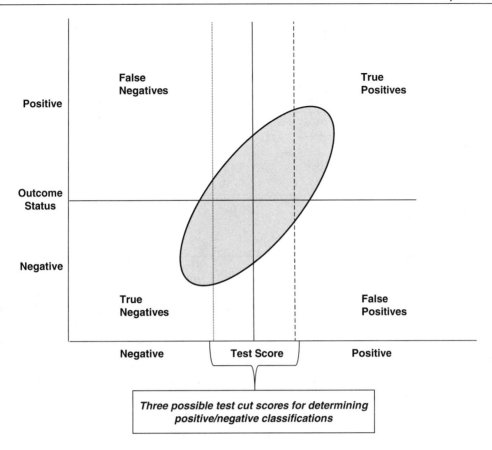

FIGURE 11.1. False positives and false negatives for three different cut scores.

high cut score should be used, whereas if false negatives were of most concern, the low cut score should be used. If test users want to obtain the largest number of correct decisions overall, the medium cut score should be used. Note that these results are consistent with Figure 11.1, which shows that the number of false positives decreases as the cut score increases, and the number of false negatives decreases as the cut score decreases.

As is evident from the previous discussion, selection of a cut point involves a trade-off between sensitivity and specificity. Table 11.4 shows these values for three possible cut points, but a more fine-grained examination of the relationship between the two can be obtained from a *receiver operator characteristic* (ROC) *curve*, which plots the percentage of true positives (sensitivity) against the percentages of false positives (1 – specificity) for each possible cut score. The ROC curve thus provides a graphical way of showing the percentages of true positives and false positives for each possible cut score.

Group Differences

Evidence about group differences is relevant in any situation for which logic or theory (or, one hopes, both) dictates that one group should obtain higher scores than

TABLE 11.4. Determination of Dropout Status Using Three Cut Points

Predicted outcome	Low cut score		Medium cut score		High cut score	
	Actual outcome					
	Dropout	No dropout	Dropout	No dropout	Dropout	No dropout
Dropout	98	78	82	28	37	6
No dropout	2	122	18	172	63	194
Total	100	200	100	200	100	200
Sensitivity	98/100 = .98		82/100 = .82		37/100 = .37	
Specificity	122/200 = .61		172/200 = .86		194/200 = .97	
Sensitivity + specificity	1.59		1.68		1.34	

another on the test of interest. For example, those clinically diagnosed with depression would be expected to obtain higher (more depressed) scores on a depression scale than those who were not so diagnosed. Or, I might expect that scientists would obtain higher scores on the GOSH test than would professional wrestlers because scientists have presumably had more practice than wrestlers in hypothesis generation. Studies of group differences, typically referred to as *known groups* studies, can shed light on score interpretation and use. If diagnosed and nondiagnosed groups were found to have equivalent mean scores on a depression instrument, this would call into question the meaning of scores as measures of depression. If on one hand, students who had taken a measurement theory course and those who had not taken such a course obtained the same scores on a test of that content, I would be hesitant to use that test to assign grades in my measurement theory course. On the other hand, if the expected group differences were found, the meaning of the scores as measures of the intended construct would be enhanced.

Another type of differences are *within-person differences*, or differences in scores obtained from people at two or more different times. Many skills and abilities, such as motor coordination and reading ability, increase steadily throughout childhood. Other abilities increase up to a certain point and then decrease. For instance, vocabulary generally increases throughout early adulthood, reaches its peak in middle age, and declines slowly after that point. Reasoning ability shows a similar pattern but declines more quickly after its peak in late adolescence. In the case of the GOSH test, I would expect students' hypotheses to become increasingly sophisticated throughout their school careers, possibly reaching a peak in adulthood and then leveling off. For constructs such as these that are expected to change in a particular way across time, longitudinal studies can provide evidence for the validity of scores. A finding that scores change over time as expected would support interpretations of the scores as measures of the intended construct.

Convergent and Discriminant Evidence

An important aspect of the theory surrounding a construct is an explication of its expected relations with other constructs as well as with observed variables. These relations are important to understanding a construct because they help to situate the construct within existing theory. In addition, explication of a construct's network of relations provides a basis for distinguishing it from similar constructs. Finally, knowledge of such networks helps in understanding a construct's possible utility for practical purposes such as prediction, and for theoretical purposes such as elaboration of related theories. Explication of this network of relations is sometimes referred to as embedding the construct in a *nomological network*. As discussed earlier in this chapter, the concept of a nomological network was introduced in the classic article by Cronbach and Meehl (1955), who defined it as "the interlocking system of laws which constitute a theory" (p. 290). In this section, I focus on two important features of a construct's relations: its *convergence* with other constructs and its *discriminability* from other constructs.

Constructs are often hypothesized to share certain characteristics with other constructs. If such similarities make up part of the theory underlying a construct, evidence of such convergence is relevant. For example, depression and anxiety are both considered to be aspects of negative affect, and they often covary. An empirical finding of independence between scores from scales purported to measure depression and anxiety would likely cause researchers to question whether the scales used to measure one or both of these were valid. *Discriminant evidence* refers to the fact that constructs should not be redundant; that is, a construct should not be a reformulation of another construct. Thus, researchers proposing a construct such as test anxiety must be prepared to differentiate it from an existing construct such as performance anxiety. In the case of the GOSH test, I would have to explain how generating sound hypotheses differs from the broader construct of inductive reasoning or from creativity.

Messick (1989) defines *trait validity* as the notion that "constructs should not be uniquely tied to any particular method of measurement nor should they be unduly redundant with other constructs" (p. 46). The second part of this definition refers to discriminant evidence. In the first part of the definition, Messick refers to the fact that different methods of measurement can yield scores that are quite dissimilar. For example, it is well known in educational measurement that students can score quite differently on essay and multiple-choice tests of the same content because these testing formats require different types of knowledge and response processes. Similarly, measures of personality based on self-reports and on reports by others may show little convergence. The extent to which scores diverge across different methods of measurement is referred to as *method variance*. In general, the presence of method variance is undesirable because it suggests that scores are tied to a specific type of measurement, and this narrows the interpretation of the construct. Ideally, we would like to see scores converge across different methods of measurement.

In a classic article, Campbell and Fiske (1959) introduced the *multitrait–multimethod* (MTMM) *matrix* as a way of simultaneously assessing the degree to which measures of the same construct using different methods converge (lack of method variance) and the degree to which measures of different, but related, constructs converge (convergent evidence). To construct an MTMM matrix, a researcher obtains scores on traits, or constructs, that are similar but differentiable. All of the traits are measured by at least two methods, such as self and peer ratings, paper-and-pencil measures and observations, or whatever methods are appropriate. Correlations among all the traits measured by all methods are then entered into a matrix. A hypothetical MTMM matrix for the GOSH is shown in Table 11.5. In the matrix, there are three traits or constructs: ability to generate sound hypotheses (GOSH), ability to reason inductively (ARI), and creativity (CRE). Although the three constructs are likely related, my hypothesis is that they are differentiable. Thus, although I expect that they will be positively correlated, their correlations should not be so high as to suggest that they are measuring the same construct. Each of the three traits is measured by two methods: a written, open-ended test and a multiple-choice test. Ideally, three or more methods would be used. I illustrate the concept with only two methods here simply for ease in presentation.

The entries in the table are as follows: The diagonal entries in parentheses are the reliability values for each trait/method combination (i.e., the value of .79 is the reliability coefficient for the GOSH measured by an open-ended test). The bolded values on the bottom left-hand side (.60, etc.) are the so-called *validity coefficients*, or the *monotrait–heteromethod coefficients*. These are correlations of the same trait measured by different methods and should be high if method variance is not excessive. Low values indicate that scores lack generalizability across methods. That is, an examinee could obtain very different scores from the open-ended and multiple-choice tests. The coefficients in Table 11.5 are reasonably high, given that open-ended tests likely measure a different aspect of the three traits than can be measured using a multiple-choice test. These validity coefficients should be larger than the *heterotrait–monomethod coefficients* shown in the triangles enclosed in solid lines. The heterotrait–monomethod coefficients are correlations of different traits measured by the same method and should be lower than correlations of the same trait measured by different methods (e.g., the validity coefficients). If this is not the case, it would indicate that substantial method variance exists,

TABLE 11.5. Hypothetical MTMM Matrix

	Traits	Method 1: Open-ended			Method 2: Multiple-choice		
		A1	B1	C1	A2	B2	C2
Method 1: Open-ended	A1: GOSH	(.79)					
	B1: ARI	.40	(.75)				
	C1: CRE	.30	.20	(.70)			
Method 2: Multiple-choice	A2: GOSH	.60	.35	.25	(.85)		
	B2: ARI	.25	.65	.20	.45	(.83)	
	C2: CRE	.20	.20	.50	.35	.25	(.80)

resulting in high correlations among same-method measures, even though these are not measuring the same thing. In Table 11.5, the heterotrait–monomethod coefficients are lower than the validity coefficients, indicating that method variance is not a substantial problem. Finally, the *heterotrait–heteromethod coefficients* shown in triangles enclosed in dashed lines should be the lowest in the table, because these are correlations among measures that share neither trait nor method. This is the case in Table 11.5, as the heterotrait–heteromethod coefficients are lower than either their heterotrait–monomethod or monotrait–heteromethod (validity) counterparts.

At this point, you may be wondering how to determine whether a given correlation should be considered "high" or "low." The answer is that these are relative terms and depend on the particular application. One advantage of the MMTM is that it provides some context for determining what is high or low. With a matrix, the monotrait–heteromethod (validity) correlations should be highest, heterotrait–heteromethod correlations should be lowest, and heterotrait–monomethod correlations should be somewhere in between. It is this pattern of correlations, rather than their absolute sizes that is important. In the current example, I relied on the interocular method, more commonly known as eyeballing, to discern this pattern. However, methods of CFA described in Chapter 13 can provide more rigorous tests of MTMM structures.

Evidence Based on Consequences of Testing

Although not all theorists agree that test consequences fall under the purview of validity, evidence for consequences of testing has been included in the latest version of the *Standards*, so here I include examples of the possible forms such evidence might take. Before doing so, however, I provide a brief overview of recent discussions of consequences in testing. In a previous section I alluded to the fact that tests are typically given with the expectation that they will yield certain positive consequences (e.g., selecting the most capable employees, preventing unqualified people from entering professions, determining the best type of therapy for a client). In these examples, the consequences share two important features. First, they are *intended* consequences; that is, the purpose of testing, at least in part, is to accrue these benefits. Second, they are *positive* consequences, in the sense that the benefits of testing (obtaining qualified employees) outweigh the negative consequences (e.g., potential employees who did not do well on the test but have important job skills not measured by the test may not be hired).

In contrast, much of the recent theorizing in the area of test consequences has focused on those consequences that are unintended and negative. For example, if medical school admissions decisions were based solely on high scores on the MCAT, this may have the unintended consequence of yielding doctors who lack communication skills (although I am not, of course, suggesting this is the case). A commonly cited unintended consequence of state-level achievement testing is that such testing programs result in a narrowing of the curriculum to focus only on the material included on the test. Turning to negative testing consequences, situations in which the test scores of certain gender- or ethnic-based groups result in their being selected at lower rates for jobs or scholarships, or at higher rates for remedial classes (known as *adverse impact*), are common examples.

Although consequences originally entered into the validity framework in their positive form, more recently the focus has shifted to studies designed to detect negative consequences of testing. In addition, the topics of whether such studies should be included in the validity framework and of whether a finding of negative consequences invalidates a test are the subjects of much discussion. There is no consensus on these issues, but most theorists feel that a validity study should, at the very least, include information on whether negative consequences are outweighed by positive consequences. If there are negative consequences, the test and testing procedures should be investigated to determine whether these consequences are due to a source of invalidity in the test. For example, if students whose first language is not English obtain low scores on a math test because the test contains many word problems, the test probably will not yield valid inferences about such students' math achievement. Thus, the negative consequence of these students' obtaining low scores would be due to a source of invalidity in the test. Note, however, that this would not necessarily affect the inferences that could be made about the math achievement of students who are native English speakers; valid inferences may still be made on the basis of these students' scores.

As noted in an earlier section, many theorists have argued for the consideration of test consequences as part of test validity. Others, however, argue that the concept of validity is already sufficiently complex and that the inclusion of yet another aspect of validity overburdens the concept. For example, Mehrens (1997) stated that proponents of the inclusion of consequences under the validity heading apparently feel that "one should confound the results of using data in a decision-making process (which is what I think is what such individuals mean by consequential validity) with the accuracy of the inference about the amount of the characteristic an individual has" (p. 17). Mehrens notes that such a confounding of concepts may not be a good idea. He goes on to point out that consequences are, by definition, tied to a specific use of a test but that valid inferences can be made whether or not the test is used for some purpose. Thus, he argues that (some) test inferences may be valid even if negative consequences accrue from (some) test uses.

Others have argued that consequences are important but should not be included under the validity heading. These researchers have argued instead that terms such as *utility* (Lissitz & Samuelsen, 2007), *evaluation* (Shadish et al., 2002), *overall quality* (Borsboom et al., 2004), or *justification* (Cizek, 2012a) be used instead. Theorists such as Markus (2014) state that consequences have a bearing on test use whether or not they are included in one's definition of validity. If they are not included in one's definition of validity, consequences are simply discussed separately. Markus points out that inclusion of consequences in the validity definition helps to ensure that consequences are not overlooked or marginalized and makes it easier to link consequences to sources of test invalidity. Markus feels that exclusion of consequences from the validity definition would remove the investigation of consequences from the purview of those gathering validity evidence and make these the responsibility of others (such as schools or other organizations), which may or may not be a good thing.

This leads us to the final point of contention in the consequences-as-part-of-validity debate: if consequences are to be included as part of validity, who should be responsible for investigating these? Clearly, unintended consequences are more difficult to investigate than intended consequences for the simple reason that we do not necessarily know what the unintended consequences are. Kane (2013) argues that, because consequences are tied to test use, test users are in the best position to evaluate them. Test developers, however, often have greater technical expertise and more experience in testing issues, and so may be better at spotting potential consequences. Haertel (2013) suggests that those in academic disciplines such as sociology, anthropology, economics, and law, may, depending on the nature of the test, be able to help identify likely consequences. He suggests that testing experts work together with colleagues in these areas, as well as with interested stakeholders, to carry out studies of test consequences. The inclusion of stakeholders in the process is important because arguments about consequences depend on values, and for the argument to persuade stakeholders (e.g., parents, employers, health care professionals, members of the general public), the stakeholders must share the values of the test developers.

Intended Testing Consequences

Suppose I argue that using the GOSH test in graduate school admissions decisions will result in a greater likelihood of selecting students who will graduate within a specified time-frame. Such claims are common in testing because tests are typically used in the expectation that they will yield some type of benefit. These claims may be either explicit, as in my GOSH test claim, or implicit. Explicit claims can and should be evaluated to determine whether the anticipated benefits actually accrue, and if so, whether these can reasonably be attributed to use of the test. Simply showing that students with high GOSH scores graduate within a certain amount of time does not completely verify my claim because students with low GOSH scores might graduate in the same amount of time. To rule out this possibility, I would have to show empirically that students with low GOSH scores take longer to graduate. If high GOSH scores are required for admission to an institution, I may not be able to obtain graduation information from low GOSH scorers. However, I may be able to find a school in which the GOSH test is not used for admission, give the test to all the students, keep track of their times to graduation, and determine whether the expected pattern occurs. Or I could make a strong logical argument in which I show that the skills measured by the GOSH are the same as those used by successful graduate students.

In some cases, so-called *extra-test* claims are made. These are claims that go beyond the interpretations and uses of test scores specified by the test developers. For example, one argument for the use of performance assessments in lieu of paper-and-pencil tests was that performance assessments would be fairer tests of the knowledge of minority students. Unfortunately, there appears to be no evidence that this is the case (Linn, Baker, & Dunbar, 1991). As noted in the *Standards*, those making such claims are responsible for providing evidence that they actually accrue. Because such claims are outside the specified interpretations and uses of test scores, additional studies would likely be required to obtain evidence to support them. For example, if I were to claim that use of the GOSH test in graduate school admissions would enhance the reputation of graduate programs, I would need some data to back up this claim. Because data on people's perceptions of academic programs are not commonly collected, I would have to conduct research studies to gather this evidence.

Unintended Testing Consequences

As discussed earlier in some detail, the use of tests can have both intended and unintended consequences. For example, given the extended-answer format of the hypothetical GOSH test, it would likely be expensive and time consuming to score. If so, this may add to the cost of an admissions application for programs using the test. Admissions decisions might also be delayed because of the time needed to score the test. As in any use of testing, these negative consequences would have to be weighed against the anticipated positive consequences in making a decision about whether to use the test. A commonly discussed unintended consequence in educational and employment testing is the presence of score differences for groups defined by gender, race, ethnicity, age, or disability status. As noted in the *Standards*, "In such cases . . . it is important to distinguish between evidence that is directly relevant to validity and evidence that may inform decisions about social policy but falls outside the realm of validity." For example, selection tests for positions as firefighters require applicants to carry heavy weights, and there may be members of some groups, such as women and older adults, who are not able to do so. However, the ability to carry heavy weights is clearly necessary for carrying out the job of a firefighter, so the fact that members of some groups are disproportionately represented does not imply any lack of validity of the test. But, in addition to physically fighting fires, firefighters are required to interact with the public. Suppose that women were found to be better at these interactions than men (not that I am suggesting this is the case). If a measure of public-interaction ability were not included in the test battery, fewer women might be hired as firefighters. This unintended consequence can be traced to construct underrepresentation—a source of invalidity—and is thus relevant to validity concerns.

Of course, unintended consequences are not always negative. For example, in many states, teachers are hired to score assessments given as part of the state's testing program. In this way, teachers meet other teachers from around the state and gain knowledge of their teaching practices. In addition, teachers obtain a better understanding of the state's testing program. Such consequences of the test, though not necessarily intended, are clearly positive. Therefore, in evaluating evidence based on consequences, all of the consequences, both positive and negative, must be weighed to make an overall judgment. One piece of evidence that should be included in such a calculation is the consequence of *not testing*. In the firefighter example, officials may decide that the consequences of testing are sufficiently onerous that the test should not be used. In that case, however, how would firefighters be selected? Should all applicants be hired on a trial basis, and those who are successful given permanent jobs? This option has a certain appeal but would not be cost effective because many more applicants than needed would be trained, at considerable expense. Another test battery could be developed, but this would also be expensive. Thus, as in any judgment, decisions regarding the use of tests must involve careful weighing of the pros and cons.

SUMMARY

The *Standards* (2014) suggest five types of validity evidence: evidence based on test content; evidence based on response processes; evidence based on internal structure; evidence based on relations to other variables; and evidence for consequences of testing. The basic validity argument underlying evidence based on test content is that the items on the test are appropriate for measuring the construct in terms of both content and cognitive level. Evidence for this can take the form of the match of items to the test blueprint, or table of specifications; expert reviews of the test content and of the cognitive processes required; and identification of any sources of construct irrelevance or construct underrepresentation. Evidence based on response processes should address the degree to which test items require respondents to use the cognitive processes that were intended. For example, if a respondent is able to adequately answer a critical thinking item by simply reciting factual information from memory, the intended cognitive process has not been evoked. Evidence based on response processes can be obtained from think-aloud protocols in which respondents are asked to verbalize their thoughts as they respond to items; tracking respondents' eye movements and/or response times as they answer questions; studies comparing the performance and response strategies of experts and novices; respondents' concept maps; and experimental studies in which item features thought to affect responding are systematically manipulated. Researchers should also specify the logic model that underlies the processes through which item responses are thought to lead to the desired inferences.

The validity argument underlying evidence based on internal structure is, broadly speaking, that the relations among items, and among items and subtests, mirror those expected from theory. Such evidence may take the form of item and/or subscale intercorrelations, internal consistency coefficients for items thought to form an identifiable scale, results from exploratory and confirmatory factor analyses, item response theory and/or generalizability theory, and DIF studies. Establishing evidence based on relations of test scores to other variables should be based on a theory explicating how and why test scores should relate to other variables. This theory should include information about the expected direction and strength of the hypothesized relations. The evidence can take many forms, such as correlations of test scores with the hypothesized variables, prediction of outcomes, differences among groups thought to differ on the construct being measured, or studies designed to reveal the extent, if any, of contamination resulting from method effects.

Finally, evidence of the consequences of testing should be reported whenever possible. Both positive and negative consequences of testing should be discussed, so that potential test users can make an informed decision about whether the positive are likely to outweigh the negative in a particular testing situation. Although researchers cannot be expected to anticipate every possible consequence, careful consideration of likely positive or negative consequences may bring to light possibilities that had not previously been thought of. Such an exercise might therefore be a valuable addition to the validation process. Evidence based on consequences can also be focused on the degree to which intended benefits of testing actually accrue. If unintended consequences are found, researchers should determine, to the degree possible, whether these are due to sources of test invalidity such as test irrelevance or construct underrepresentation. Negative consequences that are due to such sources undermine the validity of the test and suggest that the test should be modified to avoid these consequences. Alternatively, such negative consequences might alter the interpretations that can be made or the ways in which the test can be used.

EXERCISES

1. What, if anything, is problematic with the definition of validity as the degree to which a test "measures what it's supposed to measure"?

2. What is the "tripartite" view of measurement validity? What is one objection that has been raised against this view?

Questions 3–10 refer to the following hypothetical situation: A researcher has developed a test to measure problem-solving imagination (PSI), defined as "the ability to imagine new solutions to existing problems." The PSI consists of short descriptions of existing problems to which test takers respond by writing as many possible solutions as possible within a given time limit. These responses are scored by trained raters in three areas: (a) number of ideas, (b) creativity of ideas, and (c) likelihood of success of the ideas. PSI subscale scores are provided in each of the three areas, and an overall score, which is an equally weighted average of subscale scores, is also provided. The proposed interpretation of PSI total score is that higher scores indicate greater levels of problem-solving imagination. The PSI has been designed for use in research on imagination and problem solving. The test developer does not recommend use of the PSI for selection or classification decisions.

3. Could construct-irrelevant variance could be a threat to the validity of this test? Why or why not?

4. Could construct underrepresentation be a threat to the validity of this test? Why or why not?

5. As one form of validity evidence, the test developer showed that scores on the PSI were related to tests of creativity, problem solving, and imagination, as shown in Table 11.6. Is this evidence persuasive? Why or why not? What other information would be useful in evaluating this evidence?

TABLE 11.6. Correlation Values for Question 5

	Creativity	Problem solving	Imagination
Correlation of PSI with:	.60	.33	.65

6. The developer of the PSI would like to design a study to obtain validity evidence based on response processes. Give an example of this type of evidence that would be relevant to the PSI.

7. The developer of the PSI obtained correlations among the three subscale scores as evidence of validity based on internal structure. The correlations are shown in Table 11.7, with values of interrater agreement (nominal agreement) shown in parentheses on the diagonal.

TABLE 11.7. Correlations among PSI Subscores

	Number of ideas (Number)	Creativity of ideas (Creativity)	Likelihood of success of ideas (Success)
Number	(.95)		
Creativity	.68	(.60)	
Success	.25	.34	(.53)

a. Do these correlations support the validity of PSI scores as measures of problem solving imagination? Why or why not?

b. The correlations between Number and Success and between Creativity and Success are quite low. Why might this be?

8. The test developer did not provide any evidence showing that PSI scores were predictive of a particular outcome, such as success in gifted education programs. Is this problematic? Why or why not?

9. What are some possible consequences (either positive or negative) of using the PSI?

10. Suppose that the test developer decided that the PSI could be used to select students for special educational programs for gifted children. How, if at all, would this change your answer to Question 9?

Part III

Advanced Topics in Measurement Theory

12

Exploratory Factor Analysis

You may be familiar with theories of intelligence that suggest there are anywhere between two (Horn & Cattell, 1967) and eight (Gardner, 1983) different types of intellectual ability. For example, the *Woodcock–Johnson III Tests of Cognitive Abilities* standard battery (McGrew & Woodcock, 2001) yields scores on various abilities such as verbal comprehension, spatial relations, and auditory working memory, each of which is measured by a different set of items. But how do we know that these items are really tapping into these different abilities instead of one single ability? Does the "verbal comprehension" scale really measure only verbal comprehension? Clearly, answers to such questions will influence how we interpret scores from these scales. For example, if the verbal comprehension scale also included some items that measured spatial relations, this would complicate our interpretation of the scale and might make it less useful for our intended purpose. You may recognize from your reading of Chapter 11 that this is a validity issue. If scale dimensionality is not "as advertised," our interpretations and use of the scales are compromised. To take another situation, suppose that a researcher has created a scale to measure empathy. She is interested in determining whether the scale items break down into smaller subsets representing differentiable aspects of empathy. The researcher hopes that this will help her to understand the underlying nature of the empathy construct. As a final example, a researcher is interested in the Big Five personality traits: openness, conscientiousness, extraversion, agreeableness, and neuroticism. He has collected data on aspects of these traits from many different personality inventories and wants to see whether the interrelations among them are consistent with the Big Five dimensions.

Each of these situations—obtaining evidence for the hypothesized structure of a scale, generating theory about a construct, and verifying theories about dimensionality—can be addressed by *factor analysis*. Broadly speaking, the purpose of factor analytic techniques is to help us to understand the number and nature of the dimensions, or *factors*, underlying a set of variables. These factors are *latent* or unobserved, in the sense that we cannot obtain values for them directly but instead must infer their values indirectly from responses to items or other behaviors thought to tap into them. Factor analytic studies address questions such as "How many factors are there?", "What do these factors represent?", and "Are these factors consistent with my theory?"

Note that these questions range from being quite exploratory ("How many factors?") to confirmatory (consistency with theory). An analysis in which the researcher attempts to answer such basic questions as how many factors are represented by a set of variables would likely use *exploratory factor analysis* (EFA). In contrast, a researcher may hypothesize a particular number of factors that represent distinct aspects of a construct, based on theory or prior research, and write items to measure each factor. In this type of situation, the researcher already has a hypothesis about the number of factors underlying the items and about which items measure each factor. This researcher may therefore ask questions such as "Am I right about the number of factors?" and "Do the items I wrote to measure Factor A really do so?" Because researchers asking such questions can specify the number of factors and the variables that measure each of these ahead of time, they may take advantage of the model-testing capabilities of *confirmatory factor analysis* (CFA).

THE EFA–CFA DISTINCTION

As the previous examples illustrate, factor analysis can be conducted in an exploratory or a confirmatory fashion. The CFA model is much more restrictive than that of EFA, so most experts recommend that EFA be used for situations in which minimal research has been conducted regarding the structure of the construct or scale of interest and that CFA be used for situations in which there is strong theory and/or prior research to guide specification of the factor model. Researchers using EFA are typically in the beginning stages of scale development and may not have firm hypotheses about the number or nature of the factors underlying responses to their items. Researchers using CFA must be able to specify both the number of factors that are expected and the variables that measure them. There is also a practical distinction between EFA and CFA in terms of the software that can be used. EFA can be conducted using any standard statistical software package, such as SPSS or SAS. CFA is a *structural equation modeling* (SEM) method, and requires specialized SEM software. Aside from the software requirements, however, the EFA–CFA dichotomy is not always clear-cut. Instead, most research falls on a continuum between exploratory and confirmatory. A researcher may have created a scale based on strong theory and/or previous research and may therefore have good reason to hypothesize that there will be a certain number of factors and what these factors will be. Such a researcher could choose either EFA or CFA to evaluate the factor structure (number and nature of the factors) underlying the items.

Speaking more broadly, it is possible to use EFA in a confirmatory manner or to use CFA in an exploratory manner. For example, researchers employing EFA often have strong theory to support a particular factor model, with hypotheses about the number of factors, the variables that should load on these, and even the level of correlation among the factors. Such researchers may opt to use EFA rather than CFA, but this would represent a more confirmatory use of the method. Another researcher may decide to use CFA to analyze data on a newly developed scale. Although the researcher has strong hypotheses about the number and nature of the factors that he wished to test using CFA, he is open to other possibilities because his hypotheses have not yet been empirically supported. Thus, his analysis is somewhat exploratory, even though it is based on CFA methods. In this chapter, I focus on EFA; CFA is discussed in Chapter 13. Although the two methods share many features, they are sufficiently different as to warrant separate treatment.

THE EFA MODEL

The use of factor analysis (either exploratory or confirmatory) implies the existence of a model that underlies the observed correlations or covariances among scores on a set of variables. Such models represent a researcher's hypotheses about the structure that resulted in the observed covariation among the variables. In factor analysis, the word *structure* refers to the features of the factor model, including how many factors there are, which variables load on each, and whether the factors are intercorrelated. To illustrate, consider the correlations among six variables in Table 12.1. As can be seen from the table, there are two distinct groups of variables. X_1–X_3 have fairly high correlations with each other, as do X_4–X_6. Note, however, that the two groups of variables do not correlate with each other; that is, the correlations of X_1–X_3 with X_4–X_6 are zero. If these data were submitted to a factor analysis, it would yield two factors: those corresponding to the X_1–X_3 and X_4–X_6 groups of variables. Thus, factors are subgroupings of variables that are differentiable on the basis of their intercorrelations. Variables forming a factor will show stronger correlations with each other than with variables forming another factor. The variables in Table 12.1 represent an extreme case in which the variables for the different factors have no cross correlation.

TABLE 12.1. Hypothetical Correlations of Six Variables Representing Two Uncorrelated Factors

	X_1	X_2	X_3	X_4	X_5	X_6
X_1	1.00					
X_2	0.70	1.00				
X_3	0.65	0.75	1.00			
X_4	0.00	0.00	0.00	1.00		
X_5	0.00	0.00	0.00	0.65	1.00	
X_6	0.00	0.00	0.00	0.75	0.60	1.00

The EFA Model: Diagrammatic Form

In essence, then, factor analysis is about patterns of correlations. However, factor analysis goes beyond simple *observations* of correlational patterns and attempts to provide an explanation for these patterns. Factor analytic methods answer the question, "Why are these variables correlated in the way we observe?" In factor analysis, the answer to this question is that the variables are correlated through a common cause: the factor(s). This is illustrated by the *path diagram* in Figure 12.1, which represents a factor model for the data in Table 12.1. I use diagrammatic conventions that are common in CFA, but that are also useful for EFA. The six variable scores (X_1–X_6) are represented by boxes, and the two factors are represented by circles. There are also six error terms designated (for reasons I explain later) by the letter "u."

Note that there are single-headed arrows, labeled with lower-case letters, which run *from* the factors *to* the variable scores. These arrows indicate that, according to the factor analytic model, changes in the factors drive changes in the variable scores. For example, suppose the variables are measures of respondents' underlying levels of depression and the factors represent two aspects of depression, such as somatic and physical complaints. According to the factor model, increases or decreases in one's level of depression are the direct cause of corresponding increases or decreases in responses to the variables. Someone with a high level of depression would answer items on a depression scale differently than someone with a low level of depression. In addition, the fact that the same aspect, or factor, of depression is driving the responses to X_1, X_2, and X_3 is what causes them to be correlated. Responses to variables X_4–X_6 are correlated for a similar reason. You may recall from your regression class that one reason variables can be correlated is that they have a common cause. This is the case in factor analysis, in which the factor serves as the common cause. It is in this sense that the factors provide an explanation for the item intercorrelations.

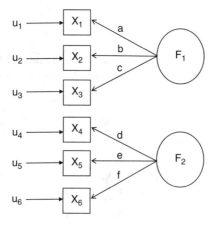

FIGURE 12.1. Factor model for six variables with two uncorrelated factors.

The part of the variance in X_1–X_6 that is accounted for by the two factors is known as the *common variance*. However, note that there are also single-headed arrows from the "u" terms to the X's. These represent an additional influence on each of the X's: a residual or error component. These are residuals in the sense that they represent the part of the variable score that is *not* explained by the variable's relationship with the factor. In EFA, the residual components are typically called *uniquenesses* because they represent the unique, or idiosyncratic, variance in the variable scores. Recall from Table 12.1 that, although the variables X_1–X_3 and X_4–X_6 have high intercorrelations, they are not perfectly correlated. This means that some of the variability in each variable score is *not* due to the factor. As an example, responses to scale items will always have some unique variation because items are typically written to tap into slightly different aspects of a construct. Items may also have idiosyncratic wording or phraseology that makes them different from other items. These differences result in some lack of correlation among the items, which is reflected in the residual or uniqueness component. In addition to capturing the unique or idiosyncratic part of the item score, the unique variance also captures random error, or lack of reliability, in the items. The uniqueness component is therefore a combination of specific, or unique, variability across individuals and variability due to random error.

In Figure 12.1, there is no arrow connecting the two factors. In path analytic diagrams, the lack of such an arrow indicates that the two factors are hypothesized to be uncorrelated. In most social science applications, however, factors are correlated with each other. This is likely true for the depression example because somatic and physical symptoms often co-occur. Correlations among the factors imply some level of correlation across the two sets of variables.

To see why this is so, I briefly introduce one of the three *path-tracing rules* developed by Sewall Wright (1921, 1934). The tracing rules are the rules for valid ways of moving between two variables in a path diagram. One of these rules is that it is permissible to move backward (i.e., opposite to the direction in which the arrow points) and then forward (in the direction of the arrow), but not forward and then backward. Referring to Figure 12.1, this means that we can move from X_1 to X_2 by going backward along path "a" and then forward along path "b." Note that this allows X_1 and X_2 to be correlated by their common cause, F_1. In fact, the reason for the "backward, then forward" rule is just that: to allow variables to be connected, or correlated, through common causes. Using this rule, you can see that X_2 and X_3 can be connected by going through paths b and c, X_5 and X_6 can be connected by going through paths e and f, and so on. However, note that no path allows a connection between X_1 and X_4, or between any of the variables related to F_1 and any of those related to F_2. The implication is that the two sets of variables are assumed to be uncorrelated. This is an appropriate model for the data in Table 12.1 because the two sets of variables are not correlated. However, suppose that the correlations were instead those shown in Table 12.2.

The data in Table 12.2 show some correlation between X_1–X_3 and X_4–X_6, although the correlations *within* the two sets are still much larger in magnitude than the correlations *across* the two sets. Even so, the model of Figure 12.1 is no longer a good

TABLE 12.2. Hypothetical Correlations of Six Variables Representing Two Correlated Factors

	X_1	X_2	X_3	X_4	X_5	X_6
X_1	1.00					
X_2	0.70	1.00				
X_3	0.65	0.75	1.00			
X_4	0.20	0.05	0.25	1.00		
X_5	0.15	0.10	0.15	0.65	1.00	
X_6	0.10	0.20	0.20	0.75	0.60	1.00

representation of the relations among the variables because it does not allow for any correlations at all across the two sets. For the data in Table 12.2, the model in Figure 12.1 can be modified by adding a curved double-headed arrow between F_1 and F_2, as shown in Figure 12.2. Curved, double-headed arrows indicate correlations rather than the causal or directional relationships that are indicated by straight, single-headed arrows. The curved arrow between F_1 and F_2 therefore represents a correlation between the two factors. With regard to the tracing rules, double-headed arrows are not subject to the "backwards and forwards" rules for single-headed arrows; movement can be in either direction. This means that we can navigate between X_1 and X_4 by going backward along path a, through path g, and moseying forward along path d, thus allowing X_1 and X_4 to be related. Of course, the same logic applies to any correlations of variables in the set X_1–X_3 with those in set X_4–X_6. The model depicted in Figure 12.2 is therefore more appropriate for the data in Table 12.2 because it allows for these "cross-factor" variable correlations.

As one last alternative, the data in Table 12.2 could be represented by allowing paths from each of the factors to each of the X's, as in Figure 12.3. Because in EFA it is

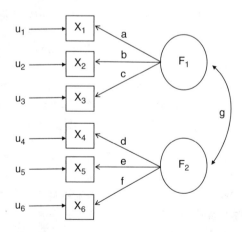

FIGURE 12.2. Factor model for six variables with two correlated factors.

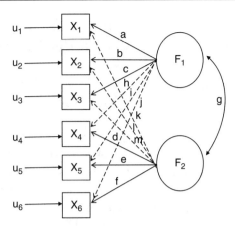

FIGURE 12.3. Factor model for six cross-loading variables with two correlated factors.

not possible to prespecify which variables measure which factors, models in EFA typically take the form of that in Figure 12.3. This is because, even though the researcher may hypothesize that variables will relate to only one of the factors, in reality variables have an annoying tendency to relate to completely unanticipated factors, for reasons elaborated in a later section.

Factor Loadings

The relations between variables and factors are called *loadings* or *coefficients*. When squared, loadings represent the amount of variance in the variable that is due to, or explained by, the factor. Loadings thus quantify the extent to which the variable and factor are related. Variables that have loadings on more than one factor are referred to as *cross-loading* variables. When variables cross-load, the largest loading for a variable is referred to as its *primary loading* and the smaller loadings are referred to as its *secondary loadings*. For the data in Table 12.2, the loadings of X_1–X_3 on F_1 and those of X_4–X_6 on F_2 would be larger than the loadings of these variables on the other factor. The loadings shown as solid lines in Figure 12.3 are therefore the primary loadings, and those shown as dashed lines are the secondary loadings. In Figure 12.3, I have included a curved arrow between the two factors. However, as can be seen by applying the "backward, then forward" tracing rule to Figure 12.3, variables in the two sets can cross-correlate even if there is not a curved arrow between F_1 and F_2. For example, X_1 and X_4 can be related by moving up path a to F_1 and then down path h from F_1 to X_4.

The EFA Model: Equation Form

Note that each of the variables in Figures 12.1–12.3 has two types of influences on it: those from the factors, represented by the loadings, and those from the uniquenesses.

This implies that each variable score consists of shared or common variance that is due to the factors and unshared variance that is due to the uniquenesses. This can be expressed in equation form as

$$X_{iv} = w_{v1}F_{1i} + w_{v2}F_{2i} + \ldots + w_{vf}F_{fi} + U_{iv} \qquad (12.1)$$

Ignoring the subscripts for the moment, we see that X represents the value of an observed variable, such as an item or subscale on a test, F represents the factor, or latent variable measured by the X's, w measures the relationship of variable X to factor F, and U is the uniqueness, or measurement error. Equation 12.1 is similar to the regression equation $Y = a + bX + e$, in which Y is replaced by X, b is replaced by w, X is replaced by F, and e is replaced by U. However, one big difference between the two is that, whereas X in the regression equation is an observed variable, the F in Equation 12.1 is an unobserved, or latent variable. The factor scores F represent hypothetical scores that people are thought to have and that drive the values of the X_{iv}, as discussed in the previous section. Similar to a regression equation, Equation 12.1 shows how values of the X variables can be broken down into weighted scores on the factors ($w * F$) plus an error term (U).

In Equation 12.1, the X variables are assumed to be expressed as z-scores. Although this is typical, it is not required. (It is also not necessary for researchers to convert their variables into z-score form before analyzing their data. This is taken care of by the data analysis program.) Variables are expressed as z-scores here only to simplify the equations somewhat. Given this z-score form, X_{iv} represents the score of a person i on variable v, expressed as a z-score. The influence of the factors on each variable score is represented by terms of the form $w_{vf}F_{fi}$. The term w_{vf} is the weight, or loading. It is subscripted with v for variable and f for factor, so that w_{vf} stands for the loading of variable v on factor f. Note that these subscripts imply that each variable (subscript v) can have a different loading on each factor (subscript f), as is usually the case. In Figures 12.2 and 12.3, the loading terms w_{vf} are represented by the arrows labeled with lowercase letters. These loadings represent the degree to which the variable is related to, or taps into, the factor. The term F_{fi} is the score on factor f of person i. Note from the subscripting of the F_{fi} scores that people (i) can have scores that are different from other people's and that an individual person can have different scores on different factors. Finally, the term U_{iv} is the score of person i on the unique factor for variable v. These terms are represented in Figures 12.2 and 12.3 as u_1–u_6. Note that the uniquenesses can vary across both people and variables.

Equation 12.1 represents the variable score (X) of one person. However, the purpose of factor analysis is to represent the relationships among variable scores across all respondents. Thus, scores on all of the X's are collected for all respondents, and the relations among variables are summarized for the set of respondents in the form of a correlation matrix, as shown in Tables 12.1 and 12.2. In factor analysis, it is this correlation matrix of the variable scores that is usually analyzed, rather than the raw data.

The correlation matrix of the X's can be obtained by multiplying the right-hand side of Equation 12.1 by itself. This yields the following matrix equation[1]:

$$\Sigma_X = \Lambda\Phi\Lambda' + \Theta_\delta \qquad (12.2)$$

Here, Σ_X is the matrix of correlations among the variable values, as in Table 12.1 or 12.2. The Λ matrix contains the loadings of each variable on each factor. This matrix therefore consists of a row for each variable (v) and a column for each factor (f). The matrix Φ contains the factor correlations. It therefore has f rows and f columns. For the models in Figures 12.2 and 12.3, Φ would have two rows and two columns, and the value of the path g would be shown below the diagonal. Typically, only the lower part (*below the diagonal*) of the matrix Φ is shown because the values in the upper part (*above the diagonal*) would be the same. This is because correlation matrices are *symmetric*; that is, the parts of the matrix below and above the diagonal are the same (i.e., the correlation of X_1 and X_2 is the same as the correlation of X_2 and X_1). And because it is a correlation matrix, the values on the diagonal of the Φ matrix are 1.0. Finally, θ_δ is a matrix of the uniquenesses, or measurement error variances. As can be seen from the absence of any curved arrows connecting the uniquenesses in Figures 12.1–12.3, these components are assumed to be uncorrelated, making θ_δ a diagonal matrix. In other words, only the variances of the uniquenesses (the values on the diagonal) are estimated in EFA models; no covariation among uniquenesses is allowed in the EFA model. From Equation 12.2 it can be seen that the correlations among variable scores can be broken down into components due to the factors, represented by Λ, to the correlations or covariances among the factors, or Φ, and to the uniqueness (θ_δ). The parts represented by Λ and Φ make up the shared, or common, variance among the variables, whereas the uniquenesses represent the variance that is not shared.

Factor analysis can thus be seen as a method of modeling the covariation among a set of observed variable scores as a function of one or more factors, the correlations (if any) among these factors, and variance unique to each variable. This means that each correlation between the variables in Tables 12.1 and 12.2 can be obtained from combinations of these parameters. For example, based on the model shown in Figure 12.1, the only allowable way to navigate between X_1 and X_2 is to "travel" up path a to X_1 and down path b to X_2. The correlation between X_1 and X_2 should therefore be equal to $a * b$, according to this model. Correlations between other pairs of variables in Figure 12.1 can be obtained in analogous ways. Note that the model in Figure 12.1 implies that the correlations between variables loading on F_1 and those loading on F_2 are equal to zero. This is because there are no possible paths between these pairs of variables. The model in Figure 12.2, however, allows for correlations between the F_1 and F_2 variables. The correlation between X_1 and X_4 should be equal to $a * g * d$. Correlations among other

---

[1] I do not assume knowledge of matrix algebra in this chapter. However, those who would like a basic introduction to the topic in the context of factor analysis can refer to Gorsuch (1983, ch. 3) or Mulaik (2010, ch. 2).

pairs of variables loading on F_1 and F_2 can be obtained in a similar fashion. The model in Figure 12.3 is somewhat more complicated, as it allows for each variable to load on each factor. This, in turn, allows for more than one way to travel from one variable to another. For example, I can get from X_1 to X_2 through paths a and b. I can also go through paths a, g, and l. The correlation of X_1 and X_2 would therefore be equal to $a * b$ plus $a * g * l$. This illustrates the path-tracing rule that, when there are multiple pathways between a pair of variables, their correlation should be equal to the sum of the products of all the paths involved. As another illustration, the pathways between X_3 and X_5 are $c * i$ and $c * g * e$, and their correlation should be equal to $c * i + c * g * e$. As a final example, to get from X_1 to X_4, I can go through a, then g, and then d, and I can also go through a and then h. The correlation between X_1 and X_4 should therefore be equal to $a * h + a * g * d$.

A Note on Model Fit

Note that in these examples I say the correlations "should" be equal to the sum of the products of the coefficients involved. This is because an incorrect factor model will not accurately reproduce the variable correlations. For example, if the true factor model contained correlated factors, as shown in Figure 12.2 and Table 12.2, but the uncorrelated factor model in Figure 12.1 was specified in error, the specified model would not be able to account for the correlations among the X_1–X_3 and X_4–X_6 sets of variables. Although I could still take the products of the existing loadings, they would not be equal to the correlations in Table 12.2. The difference between the actual variable correlations, such as those in Table 12.2, and those we calculate based on the pathways in our model (referred to as the *reproduced* or *fitted correlations*) forms the basis of *model fit*. A factor model that reproduces the observed correlations well is said to have good fit, whereas a model yielding reproduced correlations that are discrepant from the observed correlations is said to fit poorly. I elaborate on model fit in Chapter 13 in the context of CFA. In most EFA applications, model fit has not been an issue. This is because most software programs that estimate EFA models have not provided model fit information. However, programs such as M*plus* have begun to provide this information, so I expect interest in EFA model fit to increase in the future.

STEPS IN CONDUCTING EFA

Conducting an EFA involves several steps. Although I present the following steps in a particular order, you should keep in mind that EFA is an exploratory method, and it may be the case that some of the steps may be repeated or their order varied to fit the researcher's needs. In this and subsequent sections, I discuss the steps in conducting a factor analysis:

1. Preparing the data
2. Extracting the factors

3. Determining the number of factors to retain

4. Rotating the factors

5. Interpreting the factors (here researchers may repeat steps 2–4 if they are not satisfied with the solution)

6. Replicating or confirming of the results

I motivate my discussion of these steps through an example factor analysis based on data from the 2012 General Social Survey. These data come from responses to the following statements about the work of scientists:

1. A scientist usually works alone. (ALONE)

2. Scientific researchers are dedicated people who work for the good of humanity. (GOOD)

3. Scientists don't get as much fun out of life as other people do. (NOFUN)

4. Scientists are helping to solve challenging problems. (HELP)

5. Scientists are apt to be odd and peculiar people. (ODD)

6. Most scientists want to work on things that will make life better for the average person. (BETTER)

7. Scientists are not likely to be very religious people. (NORELIGN)

8. Scientists have few interests other than their work. (NOINTRST)

9. A job as a scientist would be boring. (BORING)

All statements were answered on a Likert scale on which 1 = "strongly agree," 2 = "agree," 3 = "disagree," and 4 = "strongly disagree." Strictly speaking, these data are not ideal for a factor analysis because of the 1–4 Likert scaling. As discussed in a later section, most commonly used estimation methods for EFA are based on the assumption that data are continuous, and scales with only four categories do not really meet this assumption. The data serve pedagogical purposes well in other ways, however, so I use them for this example with the caveat that factor loadings and correlations will likely be somewhat underestimated, due to the restricted scale of the data. Correlations among the nine "Attitudes about Scientists" variables are shown in Table 12.3.

Extracting the Factors

You may have noticed that I skipped the first step: data preparation. I have done so because, even though it would be the first step in the analysis, the data preparation step raises issues that are better discussed after I have introduced some additional concepts and terminology. I therefore return to discussion of data requirements later in the chapter and begin with the second step: *factor extraction*. Factor extraction is the process of obtaining values for the factor model parameters in Equation 12.2.

TABLE 12.3. Intercorrelations of Attitudes about Scientists Variables

	NOINTRST	ODD	NOFUN	BORING	ALONE	NORELIGN	BETTER	GOOD	HELP
NOINTRST	1.00								
ODD	.504	1.00							
NOFUN	.454	.388	1.00						
BORING	.286	.303	.261	1.00					
ALONE	.351	.216	.260	.252	1.00				
NORELIGN	.292	.311	.264	.090	.096	1.00			
BETTER	.123	.138	.113	−.136	.076	.067	1.00		
GOOD	.049	.029	.046	−.131	.031	.051	.470	1.00	
HELP	.006	.027	.007	−.231	−.010	.046	.425	.402	1.00

Recall that Equation 12.2 shows how the variable correlations can be broken down into parts due to the factors and their intercorrelations (the common variance) and to unique variance. The factor extraction process therefore seeks to parse the variable correlations into these common and unique parts. It is important to note that it is the variable *correlations* and not the individual scores that are analyzed in a factor analysis. Factor analytic procedures therefore begin by creating a correlation matrix from the raw scores. Another goal of factor analysis is to obtain factors that account for as much of the covariation among the variables as possible. Most extraction methods therefore proceed by first extracting the factor that explains the most covariation. The next factor to be extracted is that which accounts for the largest amount of the remaining covariation. Successive factors are extracted in a similar manner.

Using the data in Table 12.3 as an example, we see two sets of variables with relatively high intercorrelations. I indicate the two sets of variables by shading the relevant cells in Table 12.3. The first set contains the variables NOINTRST, ODD, NOFUN, BORING, ALONE, and, to some extent, NORELIGN, and the other is composed of BETTER, GOOD, and HELP. The latter set of variables appears to tap into feelings about the degree to which scientists help society in a broad sense. The first set is composed of items about the nature of scientists and their work. Parenthetically, I found it interesting that all these characteristics are at least somewhat negative, but I will refrain from any additional social commentary. The pattern of correlations in Table 12.3 suggests that two factors might be extracted: one that accounts for the covariation among NOINTRST, ODD, NOFUN, BORING, ALONE, and NORELIGN and one that accounts for the covariation among BETTER, GOOD, and HELP. The first factor would likely be that based on the first set of variables because these variables account for more covariation than the second set. There are many methods of factor extraction, and in the following sections I briefly describe some of the most popular. First, however, I discuss the issue of estimating the variable *communalities*.

Communalities

Variable *communalities* are measures of the common or shared variance among the variables. Because the object of factor analysis is to explain, or account for, the correlations or covariation among the variables, it is only the common variance that is of interest. The unique variances can be thought of as a sort of by-product of the analysis and are not the focus of the analysis. An important part of most extraction methods is therefore to obtain estimates of the variables' communalities. The correlation matrix being analyzed is then *reduced* by replacing the ones on the diagonal with estimates of the communalities. The effect of this replacement is to restrict the analysis to the common variance, so that the obtained factors will be based only on that part of the variance. In factor analysis, it is the reduced correlation matrix rather than the original correlation matrix that is analyzed.

Obtaining the communalities is slightly problematic in that they cannot be directly calculated. Instead, *iterative* methods are used that begin with some reasonable estimate of the communalities and then proceed to a series of steps, or *iterations*, in which the communalities are updated until the best estimates are obtained. Iterative methods are therefore a way of zeroing in on the best estimates of the communalities. A common beginning value in the iteration process is the squared multiple correlation of each variable with all of the other variables. A given number of factors is extracted based on these initial communalities, and new communalities are computed by taking advantage of an important mathematical relationship between the communalities and the factor loadings. Recall that the squared factor loadings are measures of the amount of variance in a variable that is shared with the factors, or of the variable's common variance. Thus, each loading represents the variance shared between a variable and a single factor, while each communality represents the variance that the variable shares with all of the factors. The communality for each variable is therefore the sum of the variable's squared loadings across all the factors[2] (assuming that the factors are uncorrelated, as they are in the initial extraction of factors).

Getting back to the iteration process, at each iteration the communalities are recomputed as the sum of each variable's squared loadings. These communalities are compared to those from the previous iteration. If there are differences between the two sets of communalities, another iteration is conducted. Iterations continue until little or no change in communality estimates occurs, at which point the iterations are said to have *converged* and the communalities at this final iteration are taken as the best estimates. Communalities for the nine Attitudes about Scientists variables are shown in Table 12.4. On the whole, these values are fairly low. For example, the communality for the variable "alone" is only .16, indicating that it shares only 16% of its variance with the factors. The low communalities suggest that any factor solution obtained from these variables is likely to be somewhat weak.

---

[2] This assumes that the factors are uncorrelated, as they are when they are initially extracted. In a later section, I discuss how factors can rotate to relax this orthogonality constraint.

TABLE 12.4. Communalities for Attitudes about Scientists Variables

ALONE	.160
BETTER	.314
BORING	.217
NOFUN	.272
GOOD	.273
HELP	.259
ODD	.337
NORELIGN	.138
NOINTRST	.387

Principal Axis Factor Extraction

Principal axis factor (PAF) extraction is based on an *eigenanalysis* of the reduced correlation matrix. Basically, an eigenanalysis breaks down the reduced correlation matrix into sets of *eigenvalues* (S) and *eigenvectors* (A). This is sometimes referred to as an *eigen-decomposition* because it decomposes the matrix into S and A. Although matrices can be decomposed in many ways, the eigen-decomposition, or PAF solution, has some special properties that make it very useful for factor analysis. First, each eigenvalue corresponds to a set of variables that have high intercorrelations with each other. To put it another way, each eigenvalue is a measure of the variance that is common to a particular set of variables. Eigenvalues therefore correspond to factors, making eigen-decomposition perfectly suited to factor analysis. Second, the factors yielded by PAF solutions will extract the maximum amount of covariation possible from the reduced correlation matrix. No other method of factor extraction will result in more explained covariance. PAF solutions are therefore very similar to *least squares* solutions in the sense that they will reproduce the original correlations among the variables as closely as possible. A third property of an eigen-decomposition is that it yields uncorrelated, or *orthogonal* factors. This is because the common variance accounted for by each factor is subtracted out of the correlation matrix before the next factor is extracted. That is, each factor after the first is extracted from the *residual* correlation matrix obtained by removing the common variance accounted for by previous factors. And, as in regression, this residual variance is uncorrelated with the explained or common variance accounted for by the factors. Thus, each successive factor extracts the common variance that has not been accounted for by previous factors and is uncorrelated with them.

Principal Component Analysis

Principal component analysis (PCA) is similar to PAF in that both are *principal solutions*. Principal solutions are those that extract the maximum common variance possible from a correlation matrix. So, principal solutions are least squares solutions that will reproduce the original correlations better than any other solution. PCA has these properties, as does PAF. However, there is an important difference between PCA and PAF. PCA is a *component* solution rather than a factor solution. In component solutions, the diagonal of the correlation matrix is not replaced with communalities as in factor solutions. Instead, the correlation matrix is analyzed "as is" with 1's on the diagonal. This means that, in component analysis, *all* of the variance in the variables, rather than just the common variance, is analyzed. There is therefore no uniqueness term in the equation for component analysis. This equation is otherwise identical to that for factor analysis, as can be seen by comparing Equation 12.1 with the analogous equation for component analysis shown in Equation 12.3.

$$X_{iv} = w_{v1}C_{1i} + w_{v2}C_{2i} + \cdots + w_{vf}C_{fi} \qquad (12.3)$$

In Equation 12.3, I have replaced the F for *factor* with a C for *component* to emphasize that, although factors and components are similar entities, they have important differences. Components are not just composed of shared variance, but also contain the unique and random error variance that is relegated to the uniqueness term in factor analysis. As noted by MacCallum (2009), the implication of this is that factor analysis will account for the variable correlations better than component analysis, whereas component analysis will account for more variance. The reason for the latter point is that PCA analyzes the full (unreduced) correlation matrix that contains both common and unique variance. It is therefore based on more variance than is PAF.

Another difference between component and factor analysis is more philosophical. Factors are thought to represent latent entities that transcend the variables being analyzed. That is, the latent variables represented by factors are thought to exist independently of the variables that measure them. For example, intelligence would not cease to exist if we did not have scales to measure it. In this sense, then, factors are, at least theoretically, more than the sum of their parts. The same is not true of components, however. Components are optimally weighted composites of the variables being analyzed. By "optimally weighted" I mean that each variable is weighted according to its correlations with the other variables. Variables with high correlations receive higher weights than those with lower correlations. In component analysis, we could say that "what you see is what you get."

The Factor versus Component Debate

Methodologists do not agree about whether factor or component analysis should be used (e.g., Velicer & Jackson, 1990; Widaman, 1993). In fact, an entire special issue of the journal *Multivariate Behavioral Research* (1990; Vol. 25, No. 1) was devoted to this subject, and many other articles have been devoted to this topic. Velicer and Jackson (1990) argue that factor and component analyses typically yield the same results and that it does not much matter which is used. If we put aside the philosophical differences between the two analyses, there is some truth to this statement. Recall that the difference between the two analyses is that in component analysis a correlation matrix with values of 1.0 on the diagonal is analyzed, whereas in factor analysis a reduced correlation matrix with communalities on the diagonal is analyzed. Therefore, the closer the communalities are to 1.0, the more similar results of the two analyses will be. Communalities reflect the variable intercorrelations, and as these correlations increase, communalities will become closer to 1.0. Thus, the two analyses will yield similar results when variables are highly correlated.

Another influence on the similarity of factor and component analysis results is the number of variables. This similarity has to do with the number of the diagonal elements in the correlation matrix relative to the number of off-diagonal elements. The number of diagonal elements in a correlation matrix is equal to the number of variables, k. However, the number of nonredundant off-diagonal elements (correlations) is equal to $k(k-1)/2$ (remember that correlation matrices are symmetric, so we do not count both the above- and below-diagonal elements as separate pieces of information). If there are 5 variables, there will be 5 diagonal and $5(5-1)/2$ or 10 nonredundant off-diagonal elements. But if there are 20 variables, there will be 20 diagonal and $20(20-1)/2$ or 190 off-diagonal elements. This illustrates that the ratio of diagonal to off-diagonal elements becomes much smaller as the number of variables increases. Consequently, the contribution of the off-diagonal elements to the solution begins to overwhelm that of the diagonal elements as k increases. Because it is only the diagonal elements that cause the two to differ, factor and component solutions tend to produce more similar results when there are more variables in the analysis.

In my view, the choice between factor and component analyses should be based on one's research purpose. Factor analysis is appropriate for situations in which the researcher's aim is to explain and model the correlations among a set of variables. These aims are congruent with the goals of theory generation and/or testing. Component analysis is appropriate for situations in which a researcher wants to boil down the variables into a smaller set of components that contain as much of the variables' variance as possible. As one example, a researcher may have data on many variables related to "neighborhood quality," such as the median home price, the number of parks, libraries, and other recreational outlets, information about the local schools, and so on. The researcher is conducting a regression analysis and wants to use this neighborhood quality information to predict some outcome but is not interested in the effects of each individual variable. Instead, the researcher would like to have a composite of the neighborhood quality variables to use in the analysis. A component analysis would produce such a composite. Another situation in which a component analysis would be useful is that in which a researcher has multiple measures of the same thing. Because these measures are likely to be highly collinear, she does not want to use the individual variables as predictors. Using a component analysis, however, she could combine the multiple measures into an optimally weighted component and use the component as a predictor in lieu of the individual variables.

Maximum Likelihood and Unweighted Least Squares Factor Extraction

Whereas PAF and PCA extraction methods are based on an eigen-decomposition of the correlation matrix, maximum likelihood (ML) and unweighted least squares (ULS) extraction methods take a different approach. In both ML and ULS, the factors are extracted in such a way that the resulting parameter estimates (loadings and factor correlations) can reproduce the original correlations[3] as closely as possible. This is done in an iterative fashion by "trying out" different sets of estimates and using them to reproduce the original correlations, in the manner illustrated previously with path diagrams. The reproduced correlations are compared to the original correlations, and if they are not sufficiently close, a new set of estimates is obtained and tried out. This iterative process continues until *convergence* is reached—that is, until the estimates from adjacent iterations do not differ by more than a small amount (e.g., .000001). Note that this is similar to the iteration process for communalities described previously.

Although ML and ULS extraction methods are similar conceptually, they differ in the way they define the "closeness" of the reproduced and original correlation matrices. In ULS, the *discrepancy function,* or quantity that measures the difference between the two matrices, is simply the sum of the squared differences between the two. ULS extraction will always result in factors that account for the original correlations as well as possible. And even though PAF and ULS operate somewhat differently, the goal of both methods is to extract the maximum variance from the data. If the PAF solution is based on iterated communalities, as described previously, the ULS and PAF solutions will become more and more similar as sample size increases (MacCallum, 2009). Thus, for a sufficiently large sample size, ULS and PAF extraction will yield the same results.

In contrast to ULS, ML methods seek estimates of the population parameters that *maximize* the *likelihood* of obtaining the observed correlations (hence the name). In other words, in ML estimation, the idea is to find estimates that are most likely to have produced the observed correlations. Thus, unlike other methods of extraction, ML estimation methods explicitly take into account the fact that a sample and not a population correlation matrix is being analyzed. This means that ML methods take sampling error into account in the estimation process. In order to do so, ML methods also assume a particular distribution for the data: the multivariate normal distribution. Although the need to assume multivariate normality may seem to be a disadvantage, it has certain benefits. Most importantly, it allows standard errors of the parameter estimates to be obtained, which in turn allows for tests of statistical significance. Such tests are not generally available for other methods of extraction.[4]

Although in some situations ML and ULS will yield very similar solutions, Briggs and MacCallum (2003) have shown that loading estimates from the two can be quite different. This is because, as alluded to earlier, ML estimation is based on the assumptions that the factor model holds exactly in the population and that any error is the result of

---

[3]Although many applications of ML estimation methods require use of a covariance, rather than a correlation matrix, EFA applications are *scale invariant*. This means that either a covariance or correlation matrix can be analyzed.

[4]Although standard errors for factor analytic methods other than maximum likelihood have been derived, the computations are intensive and have not been programmed into most general-use statistical packages. However, the program CEFA (Browne, Cudeck, Tateneni, & Mels, 2008) does provide standard errors for coefficients. It can be downloaded from Browne's website at *http://faculty.psy.ohio-state.edu/browne/ programs.htm*. M*plus* and other programs also provide coefficient standard errors.

sampling error. The implication of the latter assumption is that ML estimation will allow more discrepancy in the fit of small than of large correlations, resulting in better estimation of the large correlations. This is because small correlations have more sampling error than large correlations and are therefore expected to fluctuate more around their population values. When calculating the differences between the original and reproduced correlations, ML will therefore weight discrepancies involving large correlations more heavily than those involving small correlations because small correlation are assumed to be less reliable (e.g., have more sampling error). The upshot is that factors with low loadings may not be estimated well in ML because they are based on relatively smaller correlations. ULS, on the other hand, weights all the differences equally and should therefore result in better recovery of factors with low loadings. Briggs and MacCallum have shown empirically that ULS does result in better recovery of known factor loadings than ML when the sample size was small (100) and when the factor model was incorrect (i.e., when the wrong number of factors was extracted).

Determining the Number of Factors to Retain

Recall that the purpose of EFA is to explain the covariation among the variables with a set of factors, under the assumption that the number of factors will be smaller than the number of variables. Accordingly, researchers must come to some decision about how many factors to retain. Numerous methods are available to aid in this decision. Note that I say "aid in this decision" rather than "make this decision" because methods of determining the number of factors are, in the end, only heuristic devices. This is because there is no "true" number of factors. In part, this is because researchers typically work with sample data, which may not reflect the number of factors in the population. However, even if population data were available, it is unlikely that a model with a particular number of factors would completely account for all of the covariation among a set of variables. Even in the population, so-called *nuisance factors* based on wording similarities or other irrelevant variable characteristics might be present, and unless these nuisance factors are all retained, the original variable correlations will not be perfectly reproduced.

In the sections that follow, I briefly describe several methods for determining the number of factors to retain that are commonly used and/or have been found to perform well in simulation studies (note that these two criteria are not necessarily the same). These are the eigenvalue greater than 1 (K1) rule, the scree plot, parallel analysis (PA; Horn, 1965), and one newer method known as the Hull method (Lorenzo-Seva, Timmerman, & Kiers, 2011).

The K1 Criterion

The eigenvalue greater than one rule is often referred to as the "K1" criterion, after its originator Henry Kaiser (1960). Based on earlier work by Guttman (1954), Kaiser was able to show mathematically that "for a principal component to have positive . . . reliability, it is necessary and sufficient that the associated eigenvalue be greater than one" (1960, p. 145). Kaiser therefore argued that a component should at least have an eigenvalue greater than one or it would be unreliable. However, note that Kaiser's argument is about components, not factors. When used in factor analysis, use of the K1 criterion will typically result in overestimation of the number of factors. However, the K1 criterion is the default method for determining the number of factors in both the SAS and SPSS computer packages and, as such, is still commonly used. For the scientist data, the eigenvalues for the first four factors are 2.53, 1.95, 0.95, and 0.73. Based on the K1 criterion, two factors would be extracted.

The Scree Plot

The scree plot (Cattell, 1966) is a graph in which the eigenvalues are plotted on the Y axis and the number of factors are plotted on the X axis. The first factor extracted will always have the largest eigenvalue as it accounts for the most common variance. Eigenvalues for subsequent factors will decrease with each factor extracted. The eigenvalues for the first few factors will therefore be large, suggesting strong factors, and the latter eigenvalues will be progressively smaller. In a typical plot, there will be a bend, or "elbow" after which the eigenvalues begin to level out. This bend represents a point at which a line drawn through the eigenvalues would change in slope. Cattell (1966) likened the eigenvalues after the bend to the rubble, or scree, at the bottom of a cliff, thus giving the test its name. To use the scree plot, examine the plot to determine the number of factors before the elbow. This is taken as the suggested number of factors. Figure 12.4 shows the scree plot for the Attitudes about Scientists scale. The elbow, or change in slope, comes at factor 3, suggesting that the appropriate number of factors is two, the number before the elbow. I find it useful to put a piece of paper or other straight-edge along the points beginning at the elbow, as illustrated by the dashed line drawn from the third to the last point in Figure 12.4. If the points after the elbow tend to fall on this line, the number of factors before the elbow is probably appropriate. If not, more factors may be needed. For the line drawn in Figure 12.4, the first point after the elbow is somewhat distant from the line, suggesting that another factor may be needed. However, the scree plot does not dip much between the third and fourth points, suggesting that the third factor would be relatively weak. I extracted three factors to see if this would be the case and did find that the third factor had only two loadings of moderate size, indicating a weak factor.

Parallel Analysis

Like the K1 criterion and the scree plot, PA is based on the eigenvalues of a correlation (or reduced correlation) matrix. However, instead of comparing eigenvalues to one, as with the K1 criterion, in the PA procedure eigenvalues are compared to the average eigenvalue obtained from sets of randomly generated data. Specifically, random datasets of the same size (i.e., same number of people and variables) as the dataset being

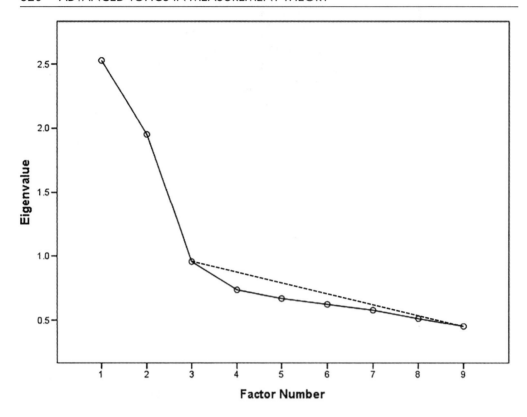

FIGURE 12.4. Scree plot for Attitudes about Scientists scale.

analyzed are generated, and correlation matrices are created from each of these random datasets. Eigenvalues are obtained from each correlation matrix, creating a distribution of eigenvalues. This distribution of random eigenvalues forms an empirical sampling distribution to which the real data eigenvalues can be compared. If the eigenvalues from the real data are greater than those from the random data, this suggests that the real data eigenvalue is greater than would be expected by chance. As discussed in a subsequent section, PA has been found to perform well in selecting the true number of factors. Although PA is not provided by widely used statistical packages such as SAS and SPSS, Kevin O'Connor has provided macros that can be used with both packages to obtain PA results (available at *https://people.ok.ubc.ca/brioconn/nfactors/nfactors.html*). In addition, the free Factor program by Lorenzo-Seva and Ferrando (available at *http://psico.fcep.urv.es/utilitats/factor/index.html*) implements PA as well as other recently developed methods for determining the number of factors. I used one of O'Connor's macros to obtain the PA results for the scientist data in Table 12.3. The PA results are shown in Table 12.5. These macros allow the researcher to specify whether factor or component analysis will be used. For factor analysis, the reduced correlation matrix is used to obtain the eigenvalues; for component analysis the full correlation matrix is used. I specified factor analysis in obtaining the results shown in Table 12.5.

TABLE 12.5. Parallel Analysis Results for Attitudes about Scientists Scale

Number of factors	Real data eigenvalue	Mean of random eigenvalues	95th percentile of random eigenvalues
1	1.816	.267	.356
2	1.227	.185	.244
3	.127	.124	.171
4	−.047	.068	.108
5	−.090	.012	.046
6	−.114	−.041	−.013
7	−.148	−.083	−.052
8	−.179	−.138	−.094
9	−.237	−.195	−.151

Table 12.5 depicts the real data eigenvalues and both the mean and the 95th percentile of the random eigenvalues for each factor. Although Horn (1965), the originator of the procedure, originally suggested using the mean value of the random eigenvalues for each factor as the value to which the real data eigenvalues should be compared, Glorfeld (1995) suggested that the 95th percentile may be a better cutoff value. This is because, although the PA procedure is generally considered to be quite accurate, some researchers have found that it tends to suggest too many factors (Cho, Li, & Bandalos, 2009; Glorfeld, 1995; Humphreys & Montanelli, 1975; Timmerman & Lorenzo-Seva, 2011; Zwick & Velicer, 1986). Use of a higher cutoff such as the 95th percentile should diminish this tendency. In addition, as Glorfeld (1995) explains, his suggestion is based on the logic that using the average eigenvalue as a cutoff is analogous to setting α to .50 in hypothesis-testing situations, whereas using the 95th percentile is analogous to setting α equal to .05, as is more common. As can be seen from the table, PA suggests two factors based on the 95th percentile. Using the mean of the random eigenvalues as a cutoff, PA suggests three factors but only marginally. Note that the real data eigenvalues differ from those obtained earlier for the K1 criterion and scree plot. This is because in both SPSS and SAS, eigenvalues for the K1 and scree plot are based on the full (unreduced) correlation matrix. These values will be underestimates of the values that would be obtained based on the reduced correlation matrix. In fact, the last eigenvalues from a reduced correlation matrix will typically be negative, as are the last six eigenvalues in Table 12.5.

The Hull Method

The Hull method (Lorenzo-Seva et al., 2011) is a relatively new technique that attempts to balance goodness-of-fit with parsimony. Parsimony is operationalized as degrees of freedom which, for statistical tests of EFA models, increase with the number of factors.

At a basic level, goodness-of-fit refers to the degree to which the reproduced correlations match the original correlations. Goodness-of-fit is a hot topic in structural equation modeling (SEM), a family of model-testing procedures that includes CFA, and a plethora of goodness-of-fit indices have been developed in that context. I discuss some of these indices in Chapter 13. The Factor program is currently the only program that provides the Hull method, and this program offers several choices of goodness-of-fit measures (see Lorenzo-Seva et al., 2011, for details). Based on studies conducted by the program's developers, the *comparative fit index* (CFI; see Chapter 13) appears to be the best overall choice.

In the Hull method, goodness-of-fit values are plotted on the Y axis and a measure of parsimony on the X axis in a two-dimensional graph. Because degrees of freedom increase with the number of factors in EFA, these can be used as the parsimony measures on the X axis. This plot yields a curve that tends to increase sharply up to a certain number of degrees of freedom and then increase more slowly or even level off. This pattern reflects the fact that goodness-of-fit increases with the number of factors up to a point, but after this point adding more factors is not justified because of the smaller improvements in fit. The idea is to locate the point at which goodness-of-fit and the number of factors are optimally balanced, indicated by the sharpest elbow (i.e., a big increase followed by a small increase, or elbow).

The calculations for the Hull method are rather involved but are taken care of by the Factor program. This program allows researchers to specify either component analysis or one of several methods for factor analysis. In addition to results for the Hull method, the program can also provide results from PA. I used the Factor program to obtain Hull method results for the scientist data, specifying ULS factor extraction with the CFI as the goodness-of-fit measure. The results are shown in Table 12.6, which shows the goodness-of-fit values, degrees of freedom, and Hull test value (denoted the "Scree test value" on the output from the Factor program). The Hull test value is computed from the goodness-of-fit value and degrees of freedom for each number of factors (see Lorenzo-Seva et al., 2011, for details). The number of factors associated with the highest test value is considered optimal. Results of the Hull method correspond

TABLE 12.6. Hull Method Results for Attitudes about Scientists Scale Based on the CFI and ULS Extraction

Number of factors	Goodness-of-fit value	Degrees of freedom	Hull test value
0	0.000	9	0.000
1	0.621	18	1.483
2	0.993	26	28.282[a]
3	1.004	33	0.000

[a]Advised number of common factors: 2.

to those from the scree test and PA in suggesting that a two-factor solution is optimal for the scientist data.

Comparison of Methods for Determining the Number of Factors

The performance of K1, the scree plot, PA, and the Hull method in determining the number of factors has been investigated in several studies (Horn, 1965; Humphreys & Montanelli, 1975; Lorenzo-Seva et al., 2011; Velicer, Eaton, Fava, 2000; Zwick & Velicer, 1986). In these studies, the PA procedure has been found to perform best in terms of accurately identifying the true number of factors, whereas K1 consistently performs worst, with the scree plot falling somewhere in between. However, these studies have been based on generated data in which the factors are known to be uncorrelated. With correlated factors, methods of determining the number of factors will likely be less accurate. This possibility was investigated in a recent study by Lorenzo-Seva and colleagues (2011) that included the Hull method, PA, and several other methods, and manipulated, among other things, the numbers of factors and of variables and the level of correlation among the factors. The Hull method accurately identified the correct number of factors 97% of the time across all data conditions (using the CFI as the goodness-of-fit index). PA had an overall accuracy rate of 81% across all conditions. As expected, the performance of both the Hull and PA methods was adversely affected by the presence of high correlations among the factors; however, overall accuracy decreased to only 79% for PA and to 93% for the Hull method when factor correlations were .40. Accuracy was also affected by the number of factors, and it decreased as the number of factors increased for both methods. However, increases in the number of factors could be offset by increases in the sample size. For example, with five factors, accuracy rates for PA were 78% with a sample size of 100 but increased to 95% for a sample size of 200. For the Hull method, the corresponding percentages were 76% and 87%.

Use of Multiple Criteria for Determining the Number of Factors

Because the accuracy of methods for determining the number of factors differs across data conditions, decisions regarding the number of factors to retain should never be based on one criterion alone. Instead, researchers should routinely examine the scree plot as well as results from PA and the Hull method. Ideally, these methods will converge on a particular number of factors, as was the case with the scientist data. However, this is often not the case. For the common situation in which the number of factors is ambiguous, researchers should explore various numbers of factors. Keep in mind that EFA is an exploratory technique, which implies that researchers are permitted, and even encouraged, to explore solutions with different numbers of factors. For example, suppose that implementation of different methods suggested three, four, and five factors. All of these solutions should be obtained, as well as solutions with two and six factors and any number of factors suggested by theory and/or prior research. Interpretability and consistency with theory should then be assessed for all the solutions. In the end, the overriding criteria for choosing a particular number of factors are interpretability and theoretical relevance because a factor solution is useful only if it can be interpreted in a meaningful way. This is why it is important to relate factor analytic results to existing theory as much as possible.

Under- and Overfactoring

Although both underfactoring (extracting fewer factors than are needed) and overfactoring (extracting more factors than are needed) can be problematic, underfactoring is generally thought to be the worse of the two options. This is mainly because overfactored solutions are typically quite easy to identify. In overfactored solutions, the last factor(s) is (are) characterized by only one or two strong loadings. These weak factors can occur for several reasons. Items that share certain words or phrases may tend to factor together, a phenomenon known as a *bloated specific* (Cattell & Tsujioka, 1964). Variables obtained using the same method can also form separate factors. For example, in cognitive testing it is sometimes found that multiple-choice and essay items tend to factor together, regardless of content. Or noncognitive items that are negatively worded may tend to cluster together. All of these causes of bloated specifics will result in overfactoring, and most are easily detected from an inspection of either the content or wording of the variables or of the variable distributions. If overfactoring is suspected, researchers should obtain a solution with one (or more) fewer factor(s). Ideally, the variables that loaded on the additional factors will then be "forced" onto other factors in an interpretable manner. If this does not occur, the variables making up the last factor may be pointing to a "real" factor, but there are insufficient variables to capture it. In this case, researchers will need to conduct additional studies in which they obtain additional variables to measure the factor. A final possible reason for overfactoring is that factors can sometimes form because of similarities in item distributions rather than similarities in item content. That is, variables that are positively skewed and those that are negatively skewed may form separate factors, regardless of their content. If distribution-based factors are suspected, this possibility can easily be investigated by examining descriptive statistics for the variables.

When too few factors are extracted, it may be difficult to interpret the factors. This is because underfactoring usually results in two or more factors being combined into one. Such factors can sometimes be identified by examining the content of the variables loading on them. However, to form a factor in the first place, these variables must have some level of correlation, and it may therefore be difficult to determine those that may form a separate factor. This is one reason solutions with more factors than anticipated should always be examined, as such solutions may "peel off" variables from one factor to form another. Of course, a finding of fewer factors than anticipated may also indicate that aspects of the construct that were thought to be distinguishable are not. If this is the case, the researcher may have to rethink the theory on which the original hypothesis about the number of factors was based. Alternatively, the expected separate factors may exist, but the variables used to measure these factors may not be pure measures of them. If so, the variables will likely cross–load onto a related factor or factors. A final possibility is that there are not sufficient variables to "bring out" the particular aspect of the factor. In this case, more variables would have to obtained.

Example with Attitudes about Scientists Data

Results from the scree plot, PA (based on the 95th percentile), and the Hull method suggest two factors for the Attitudes about Scientists data. In addition, the two-factor solution makes sense. Recall that in an earlier section it was noted that the variables appeared to be tapping into two different aspects of people's feelings about scientists: purported characteristics of scientists (NOINTRST, ODD, NOFUN, BORING, ALONE, and NORELIGN) and people's feelings about the degree to which scientists help society (BETTER, GOOD, and HELP). These two aspects were supported by the two-factor solution, in which the variables loaded on two factors defined by these two sets of variables. Because PA based on the mean of the random eigenvalues supported a three-factor solution, I also looked into this. In the three-factor solution, the variables ALONE ("A scientist usually works alone") and BORING ("A job as a scientist would be boring.") split off from the "characteristics of scientists" factor to form their own factor. It is possible that working alone would result in a boring job or that boring people tend to work alone, so these results make some sense. However, the three-factor solution shows signs of overfactoring because it is loaded by only two variables. If I were developing this scale and felt that this aspect of attitudes about scientists merited further study, I might write more items having to do with the perceived loneliness and boredom aspect of scientists' jobs. Given the available items, however, I decided that two items were not sufficient to measure this aspect and that it also made sense for these two items to belong to the "characteristics" factor. I therefore decided on the two-factor solution.

Percentage of Variance Accounted For

Table 12.7 shows the percentages of variance accounted for by the two factors, based on PAF extraction. This table is adapted from the SPSS output. Values in the three columns under "initial eigenvalues" provide, respectively, the eigenvalue for each possible factor, the percentage of variance in the variables that is accounted for by each factor, and the cumulative percentage of variance accounted for by sets of factors. I briefly discussed eigenvalues in a previous section. If variables were completely uncorrelated, each variable would have an eigenvalue of 1.0, and a separate factor would be needed for every variable. When variables are correlated, however, some of their variance is shared, and this is reflected in their eigenvalues. The more shared variance there is, the larger the eigenvalue will be. But because the eigenvalues must sum to the number of variables, if some eigenvalues are larger, some must be correspondingly smaller. This reflects the fact that eigenvalues partition the variables' variance to correspond to their levels of correlation.

TABLE 12.7. Percentages of Variance Accounted for by Two-Factor Solution for the Attitudes about Scientists Scale

	Total variance explained					
	Initial eigenvalues			Extraction sums of squared loadings		
Factor	Eigenvalue	% of variance	Cumulative % of variance	Sum of squared loadings	% of variance	Cumulative % of variance
1	2.528	28.089	28.089	1.924	21.374	21.374
2	1.952	21.689	49.778	1.376	15.285	36.658
3	0.954	10.604	60.382			
4	0.735	8.168	68.550			
5	0.668	7.420	75.969			
6	0.622	6.915	82.885			
7	0.577	6.416	89.301			
8	0.512	5.685	94.985			
9	0.451	5.015	100.000			

The percentage of variance accounted for is calculated as the eigenvalue divided by the number of variables (nine, in this case), multiplied by 100. The logic behind dividing by the number of variables is that, before any factor extraction is done, each variable in a correlation matrix accounts for one unit of variance. Summing the 1's across all variables therefore gives us the total amount of variance possible. So, dividing by the number of variables is the same as dividing by the total amount of variance. For our example, the first percentage is equal to 2.528/9 ∗ 100, or 28.089%. The remaining values in this column can be obtained in the same way. Values in the third column represent the *cumulative percentage* of variance accounted for by a particular factor plus all the previous factors. These are obtained by simply summing the values in the percentage of variance column. Cumulative percentage values can be useful for determining the practical utility of including a factor. For example, the first two factors account for nearly 50% of the variance in the nine Attitudes about Scientists variables. If the third factor were to be retained, about 10% more of the total variance would be explained. Although the percentage of variance explained is an important piece of information, decisions about the number of factors to extract should take into account multiple criteria, including the interpretability of the factors, as noted earlier.

A Note on Eigenvalues from the Reduced Correlation Matrix

Note that even though these values are based on PAF extraction, the eigenvalues sum to nine (the number of variables) because the full, rather than the reduced, correlation matrix was analyzed. As you now know, in PAF and other factor analysis methods the reduced correlation matrix is analyzed, so it makes intuitive sense that the eigenvalues from that matrix should be used to calculate the percentages of explained variance. However, even in factor analysis, percentages of variance are based on the eigenvalues from the unreduced correlation matrix. The reasons for this are somewhat technical but have to do with the fact that in factor analysis some eigenvalues can be negative. This is because the reduced correlation matrix analyzed in factor analysis is not a "real" correlation matrix, and therefore does not have to obey the usual rules about eigenvalues, one of which is that they must be positive. Negative eigenvalues are problematic for variance partitioning, however. Using the calculations illustrated previously, a factor with a negative eigenvalue would have a negative percentage of variance, and a negative percentage is not possible. As a result, eigenvalues are obtained from the unreduced correlation matrix for both factor and component analysis.

You may be wondering about the values in the table under "extraction sums of squared loadings." Unlike the values under "initial eigenvalues," these values are obtained from the reduced correlation matrix for factor analysis solutions. (For component analysis solutions, the values under this heading are still calculated from the full correlation matrix, as would be expected, and because of this will match the values in the first three columns.) The values for factor analyses are obtained from the reduced correlation matrix, so the eigenvalues are not "true" eigenvalues, for the reasons discussed previously. Because of this, the values under the "extraction sums of squared loadings" values are not obtained from the eigenvalues, but are instead calculated from the loadings on the designated number of factors (two, in our example). For example, the eigenvalue-like values in the first column of this section (1.924 and 1.376) were obtained by squaring the factor loadings for each factor and summing these to obtain a total value for each factor (hence the heading "extraction sums of squared loadings"). The values are treated as "pseudo-eigenvalues," and the percentages of variance and cumulative percentages of variance are obtained from these in the usual way (dividing by the total number of variables, multiplying by 100, etc.). However, because they are based on loadings obtained from a factor analysis, these "pseudo-eigenvalues" will be smaller than the "real" eigenvalues in the first section of the table. Recall that the reduced correlation matrix used in factor analysis contains only the shared variance among the variables, omitting the unique variance. Thus, loadings in factor analysis are based on only the shared variance and so cannot account for all of the variance contained in the "real" eigenvalue. Note that this is only the case for factor analysis. If I had obtained a solution based on component analysis, the values in the two sections of Table 12.7 would have been the same.

Rotating the Factors

Recall that the purpose of factor (and component) analysis is to extract as much of the (co)variance among the items as possible and to reconfigure this covariation into factors. Note, however, that this purpose says nothing about producing factors that are interpretable. As an example, consider the correlation matrix in Table 12.8. Without actually carrying out the analysis, we might think that there would be two factors: one based on the

TABLE 12.8. Hypothetical Data for Four Variables

	X_1	X_2	X_3	X_4
X_1	1.0			
X_2	.70	1.0		
X_3	.30	.30	1.0	
X_4	.30	.30	.60	1.0

high correlation between X_1 and X_2 and one based on the correlation between X_3 and X_4. We might, for example, expect loadings such as:

	Factor 1	Factor 2
X_1	.80	.20
X_2	.80	.20
X_3	.20	.75
X_4	.20	.75

But because the goal of factor analysis is to reproduce *all of* the (co)variance and not just the largest covariances, this is not the solution we would get. This is because X_1 and X_2 do have some covariance with X_3 and X_4, and this must be considered in producing a solution that accounts for the maximum amount of variance. The actual solution obtained from PAF extraction would be:

	Factor 1	Factor 2
X_1	.75	−.38
X_2	.75	−.38
X_3	.63	.45
X_4	.63	.45

All of the variables contribute to the first factor, although X_1 and X_2 contribute slightly more. This is because all four variables are correlated, to some extent, but X_1 and X_2 are slightly more intercorrelated than X_3 and X_4. Then, because the first factor does not really differentiate X_1 and X_2 from X_3 and X_4, the second factor separates these by giving the first two negative loadings. Factors with both positive and negative loadings are sometimes called *bipolar factors*. Note that in our example the negative loadings of X_1 and X_2 are artifactual because all of the variables are positively correlated. That is, X_1 and X_2 have received negative loadings only in order to differentiate them from X_3 and X_4. The fact that variables can obtain negative loadings even though all correlations are positive can be quite confusing, but it is due only to the mathematics behind the initial solution. This can be seen from the plot in Figure 12.5, in which the two

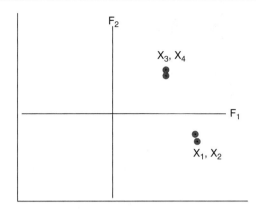

FIGURE 12.5. Plot of four variables in two-factor space.

variable pairs X_1, X_2 and X_3, X_4 are plotted against the two factors. As can be seen in the figure, all four variables fall toward the positive end of Factor 1, represented as a horizontal line. In contrast, the X_1, X_2 cluster falls on the negative side of F_2, represented as a vertical line.

Although the solution shown above reproduces the variance quite well, it is difficult to interpret. This is where rotation comes in. The purpose of rotation is to orient the two factor axes in such a way that the variables are more clearly aligned with a particular factor. In Figure 12.5, neither of the factor axes goes through the clusters of points. However, the two factor axes could be reoriented, or *rotated*, so that they do, as in Figure 12.6. As can be seen from the figure, the rotated factor axes, represented by dashed lines, now pass right through the two clusters of variables. This is what is meant by *rotation* of factors. The factor axes are literally rotated in multidimensional space so that they come as close as possible to the clusters of variables. The loadings for this solution are:

	Factor 1	Factor 2
X_1	.84	.00
X_2	.84	.00
X_3	.00	.77
X_4	.00	.77

This solution is much easier to interpret: Factor 1 is composed of X_1 and X_2, and Factor 2 is composed of X_3 and X_4. Of course, rotated solutions will not always be this clear. The results here are due to the fact that there are only four variables and these have a very clear pattern of correlations. Having said that, solutions for most data can be made more interpretable by rotating the factors, and for this reason solutions are almost always rotated in practice. It is therefore important to know something about how rotation works and about the different kinds of rotations available.

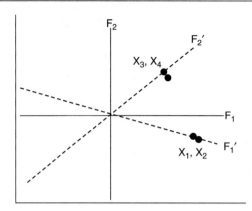

FIGURE 12.6. Plot of two rotated factors.

How Does Rotation Work?

As noted previously, the purpose of rotation is to make the factor solution more interpretable. One way of doing so is to minimize the number of factors on which a variable loads. This is known as minimizing *variable complexity*. Another way is to minimize the number of variables loading on each factor, known as minimizing *factor complexity*. Both of these criteria are illustrated in the previous example. In the unrotated loading matrix, all four variables loaded on both factors. However, in the rotated solution, X_1 and X_2 loaded only on Factor 1, thus minimizing their variable complexity. And only two variables loaded on each factor, minimizing factor complexity. As can be seen in this example, it is possible to minimize both variable and factor complexity; however, as the factor structure becomes more complex, this becomes more difficult.

Many popular *orthogonal* rotations, or rotations that yield uncorrelated factors, can be seen as part of the *Crawford–Ferguson family*, which is based on minimization of the criterion in Equation 12.4.

$$(1-\kappa)\sum_{i=1}^{v}\sum_{j=1}^{f}\sum_{l\neq j}^{f}\lambda_{ij}^2\lambda_{il}^2 + \kappa\sum_{j=1}^{f}\sum_{i=l}^{v}\sum_{k\neq i}^{v}\lambda_{ij}^2\lambda_{kj}^2 \qquad (12.4)$$

Although the equation may look quite menacing, it is really just a function of the loadings (λ) summed across variables (v) and factors (f). The part of the equation before the "+" sign minimizes variable complexity by summing the product of each variable's squared loadings across factors. Here, variables are subscripted with i and k, and factors are subscripted with j and l. Note that summing the products of (squared) loadings across factors does measure variable complexity because this quantity increases with the number of factors on which a variable loads. For example, if a variable loads on four factors, four squared loadings will be summed, whereas if a variable only loads on one factor, only one squared loading enters the sum. The part of the equation after the "+" sign minimizes factor complexity by taking the sum of each factor's squared loadings across the variables. Again, this is a good measure of factor complexity because it will be higher for factors on which more variables load.

The balance between variable and factor complexity is controlled by the κ term in Equation 12.4. Setting κ to 1 focuses the solution completely on factor complexity, whereas setting it to 0 results in minimization of only variable complexity. Setting κ somewhere between 0 and 1 results in more of a balance of variable and factor complexity. In the following sections I briefly review some of the more commonly used rotations. As part of this review, I also discuss the criteria for *simple structure* proposed by Thurstone (1947).

Types of Rotation

Orthogonal and Oblique Rotations

Rotations come in two basic varieties: *orthogonal* and *oblique*. The difference between the two is that orthogonal rotations result in factors that are uncorrelated, whereas oblique rotations allow factors to be correlated. Note that oblique rotations do not *force* factors to be correlated; they simply allow for correlations if these result in lower variable and/ or factor complexity. When oblique rotations are chosen, a matrix of correlations among the factors is obtained along with the factor loadings. If the factors turn out not to be correlated, the factor correlations will be zero and the results obtained will be the same as those from an orthogonal rotation.

In choosing between the two types of rotation, researchers should consider whether theory suggests that factors should be correlated or uncorrelated; this consideration should drive their choice. Many researchers have argued for the use of oblique rather than orthogonal rotations on the basis of the fact that, in the social sciences, factors are very likely to be correlated (Bandalos & Finney, 2010; Floyd & Widaman, 1995; Preacher & MacCallum, 2003). Also, if no theory is available to guide this choice, an oblique rotation is a safe choice because if the factors are not correlated, an oblique rotation "defaults" to an orthogonal one, as noted in the previous paragraph. For this reason, many experts have little use for orthogonal rotations. For example, Comrey and Lee (1992) stated that "given the advantages of oblique rotation over orthogonal rotation, we see little justification for using orthogonal rotation as a general approach to achieving solutions with simple structure" (p. 283).

Researchers sometimes operate under the mistaken belief that orthogonal rotations result in solutions with fewer cross-loadings than do oblique rotations, thus rendering the factor solution easier to interpret. As it turns out, nothing could be further from the truth. As Comrey and Lee (1992, p. 287) state, "It is sometimes thought that this retention of statistically independent factors 'cleans up' and clarifies solutions, making them easier to interpret. Unfortunately, this intuition is exactly the opposite of what the methodological literature suggests." That is, orthogonal solutions actually result in *more* rather than fewer cross-loadings. To see why this is true, we need go no farther than Figure 12.2, which, using our newly learned terminology, we can now say represents an oblique solution because of the correlational arrow between the two factors. Now suppose that the correlational arrow (g) were removed, but that variables X_1 and X_6 were actually correlated. In this situation, the only way for the X_1–X_6 correlation to manifest itself would be through a cross-loading of X_6 on F_1, or of X_1 on F_2 (or both). This is because the only other possible avenue, that of going through paths a, g, and f, would no longer be an option. Thus, when variables are correlated across factors but the factors are forced to be orthogonal, cross-loadings will be the inevitable result.

Simple Structure

Factor rotations are *indeterminate* by nature. This means that there is no one rotation that can be considered to yield the "correct" or "true" solution. To see why this is so, refer back to Figure 12.2. As I noted in that section, the correlation between variables X_1 and X_4 could be reproduced by going up path a, through the double-headed arrow g, and through path d. The values of paths a and d might be estimated as .6 each, and the value of path g as .55. This would yield a correlation of .6 * .55 * .6, or .198, which comes fairly close to the actual value of the X_1, X_2 correlation of .20. However, values of .5 for a and d and .8 for g would yield about the same value. In fact, there is an infinite number of sets of values that would yield the same result. This is what is meant by an *unidentified* or *indeterminate solution*. In some cases, lack of identification can be resolved by putting restrictions, or conditions, on the solution. Thurstone (1947) proposed five such restrictions to help in the identification of factor rotations. These are known as rules for *simple structure* because they result in a matrix of loadings with lower variable or factor complexity (or both). The five restrictions are as follows:

1. Each variable should have at least one loading of zero.
2. Each factor should have at least *f* zero loadings, where *f* is the number of variables.
3. For every pair of factors there should be several variables that load on one but not the other.
4. If there are more than four factors, every pair of factors should have several variables with zero loadings on both factors.
5. For every pair of factors there should be only a few variables that load on both.

Although Browne (2001) cites Yates (1987) as pointing out that Thurstone originally intended the first criterion to be the most important in determining simple structure, the majority of published factor analytic studies focus on the fifth, that is, on minimizing the number of cross-loadings. However, as Sass and Schmidt (2010) observed, this focus on minimizing cross-loadings may not be appropriate. This is because when variables are correlated across factors, as they usually are, minimizing cross-loadings will have the effect of increasing correlations among factors. (Those who are interested can work out the reason for this using the logic presented previously in the context of cross-loadings and orthogonal factors.) Also, choosing a solution with the fewest cross-loadings will prevent the researcher from identifying variables that really do relate to more than one factor. Such so-called *complex* variables may yield insight about the nature of the factors that would not be possible if solutions with cross-loading variables were ignored. Finally, it is often useful during scale development to identify variables that cross-load. In some cases, such variables are removed from the scale in order to obtain "pure" measures with unambiguous interpretations. However, such clarity may be obtained at the cost of creating overly narrow measures. If the construct is itself narrowly defined, this is appropriate, but if the construct is complex the removal of cross-loading variables may result in an oversimplified representation.

Orthogonal Rotations.   *Varimax* is the most commonly used orthogonal rotation,[5] perhaps because it is the default option in popular statistical packages such as SAS and SPSS. Varimax can be seen as a member of the Crawford–Ferguson family of rotations with a kappa value of $1/v$, where v is the number of variables. Analytically, varimax attempts to maximize the variance of the squared loadings across factors (hence the name). Maximization of the variance across loadings is a common rotation criterion because in order to maximize variance across loadings, small loadings must be made smaller and/or high loadings higher, thus maximizing simple structure. In varimax rotation, this results in the variance among variables being spread more evenly across factors, such that no one factor has a preponderance of high loadings. Another result of the varimax criterion is that it tends to minimize the tendency to obtain a *general factor*. A general factor is one on which the majority of the variables load, and because of this it will account for the most variance. In some cases, general factors are supported by theory, as with the construct of intelligence. In most intelligence theories, a general intelligence, sometimes referred to as *g*, is posited. This factor is hypothesized to be superordinate to various so-called *group factors* that are based on more specific abilities such as those involving spatial or language skills. Varimax rotations tend to build up the group factors at the expense of the general factor. As a result, researchers hypothesizing a general factor may want to steer clear of varimax rotations.

   Quartimax minimizes the number of factors on which a variable loads, thus reducing the number of cross-loadings and minimizing variable complexity. Quartimax can be viewed as a member of the Crawford–Ferguson family, with kappa = 0. In contrast to varimax rotations, quartimax rotations tend to produce a large general factor, as this is one way of minimizing variable complexity (if there is only one factor, variables cannot load on multiple factors). Thus, quartimax avoids cross-loadings by merging variables that tap into separate factors into a general factor. Therefore, if theory supports the existence of a general factor, quartimax may be just what the doctor ordered.

Oblique Rotations.   As explained in Mulaik (2010, pp. 326–327), the *oblimin* rotation was proposed by Kaiser (1958) as an oblique version of the varimax rotation. As an oblique rotation, oblimin allows for factors to be correlated, with the degree of correlation

---

[5] Although the original varimax rotation was orthogonal and orthogonal versions are still widely used, modern EFA software also includes oblique versions of varimax.

controlled by a parameter known as delta. Gorsuch (1983) recommends varying delta systematically between values of 1 and −4 and selecting the solution that yields the best simple structure. (However, delta is implemented somewhat differently across statistical packages. In SPSS, for example, the highest allowable value is .8.) If researchers have hypotheses about the expected level of factor correlation, they can use this information to choose a value for delta. Higher (positive) values of delta will produce more highly correlated factors, and lower (negative) values will produce lower correlations. A delta value of zero yields a moderate level of factor correlation.

Promax rotations are obtained by allowing an existing orthogonal rotation (usually varimax or quartimax) to be oblique. This may result in a better simple structure because relaxing the orthogonality constraint allows for moderate and low loadings to be forced even lower, while maintaining high loadings at relatively high levels. Note that this will tend to reduce both variable and factor complexity. Mathematically, this is done by raising the loadings to powers greater than two (recall that in the Crawford–Ferguson criterion, loadings are squared). This has the desired effect of increasing the discrepancy between the low and high loadings. For example, if loadings on a particular factor were 0.2, 0.4, and 0.8, raising these to a power of four would result in 0.0016, 0.0256, and 0.4096. Whereas the original loading of 0.8 is four times the size of the lowest loading of 0.8, when the loadings are raised to the fourth power, 0.4096 is 256 times the size of 0.0016! Gorsuch (1983) notes that the higher the power to which loadings are raised, the more highly correlated the resulting factors will be. So, as with oblimin rotations, researchers can control the level of correlation to some extent.

Choosing a Rotation

As noted previously, the main distinction for rotations is that between orthogonal and oblique solutions. The choice between the two should be guided by theoretical considerations about the extent, if any, to which the factors should be correlated. If there is no theory to guide this choice, researchers should feel free to try both and choose a solution on the basis of interpretability. Interpretability is, after all, the reason that rotation is done in the first place. This logic can be extended to the choices among the various orthogonal or oblique rotations. Although these often yield very similar results, I recommend that researchers explore different options and choose the most interpretable and theoretically defensible result. As pointed out in a previous section, EFA is an exploratory procedure, so it is permissible, and even recommended, that researchers explore different solutions before coming to a final decision.

Pattern and Structure Coefficients

Up to this point, I have referred to factor "loadings" without providing any indication that there may be more than one type. I have been somewhat remiss in this regard, however, because when an oblique rotation is used, two types of loadings, or coefficients, are obtained. These are known as *pattern loadings* or *coefficients* and *structure loadings* or *coefficients*. *Pattern coefficients* are essentially regression weights for predicting the variables from the factors. In other words, they are the weights, or w values, in Equation 12.1. The pattern coefficients are calculated by holding constant all of the other factors, as in the calculation of regression coefficients for multiple predictors. Pattern coefficients therefore represent the *unique* relationship of a factor to a variable, with all the other factors partialed out or held constant. More specifically, the squared pattern coefficients represent the amount of variance in each variable that is explained by a particular factor. *Structure coefficients* are measures of the correlation of a variable with a factor. These coefficients are the product of the pattern coefficients and factor correlations. If the factors are uncorrelated, the pattern and structure coefficients are the same. However, if the factors are correlated (i.e., if an oblique rotation is obtained), the structure coefficients assess both the unique relationships of the factors with the variables *and* the additional amount of relationship introduced by the overlap among the factors.

Methodologists disagree about which coefficients should be used for interpretation of the factors. Some (Gorsuch, 1983; Graham, Guthrie, & Thompson, 2003; Nunnally & Bernstein, 1994; Thompson, 1997) adamantly state that both structure and pattern coefficients should be reported and used in interpreting the factors. Graham and colleagues (2003) present hypothetical situations in which a researcher, upon seeing that a variable has a small pattern coefficient for a particular factor, might incorrectly assume it is not related to that factor. If the factors are correlated, however, the variable with a low pattern coefficient might be related to the factor through the factor correlations and would therefore have a much higher structure coefficient. Interpretation of pattern and structure coefficients could therefore result in different conclusions about the relationship of a variable to a factor. Arguing against the use of structure coefficients, Mulaik (2010) points out that if researchers incorporate information from both the pattern coefficients and factor correlations into their interpretations, adding information about structure coefficients is redundant as these are simply the product of the former two sources of information. He therefore states that "for this reason, some factor analysts only rely upon the factor-pattern coefficients and the correlations among the factor for interpretation of the factors" (p. 138). This is a valid argument, as can be seen clearly from Figure 12.2: even though X_1 is not directly related to F_2 by its pattern loading, it would still have some relationship to F_2 because of the correlation between F_1 and F_2. Nevertheless, this is easy to forget when one is looking at a pattern matrix, so when factors are rotated obliquely, researchers should present both the pattern and structure matrices, or alternatively, the pattern matrix and the factor correlations. Table 12.9 shows the pattern and structure coefficients from an oblimin rotation (with delta set to 0) of the Attitudes about Scientists data. As can be seen from the table, the pattern and structure coefficient values are very similar for these data. This is due to the extremely low correlation (.023) between the two factors.

A Second Example

As another example, I analyzed data from a version of the Achievement Goal Questionnaire (AGQ; Elliot & McGregor, 2001) as revised in a study by Finney, Pieper, and

TABLE 12.9. Pattern and Structure Coefficients for the Attitude toward Scientists Scale

| | Pattern coefficients | | Structure coefficients | |
| | Factor | | Factor | |
Item	1	2	1	2
ALONE	.418	−.002	.418	.007
BETTER	.125	.696	.141	.699
BORING	.448	−.291	.442	−.281
NOFUN	.608	.037	.609	.051
GOOD	.026	.637	.040	.638
HELP	−.041	.636	−.026	.635
ODD	.662	.044	.663	.059
NORELIGN	.379	.068	.381	.077
NOINTRST	.750	.039	.751	.056

Barron (2004). There are 12 items designed to measure four aspects of achievement goal orientation: mastery–approach (MAP), mastery–avoidance (MAV), performance–approach (PAP), and performance–avoidance (PAV). Briefly, mastery achievement goals are those in which students are motivated by a desire to learn the material, whereas performance goals are those in which students are motivated by a desire to perform better than others. The items are as follows.

1. My goal this semester is to get better grades than most of the other students. (PAP)

2. It is important for me to do well compared to other students this semester. (PAP)

3. I want to do better than other students this semester. (PAP)

4. I just want to avoid doing poorly compared to other students this semester. (PAV)

5. The fear of performing poorly is what motivates me. (PAV)

6. My goal this semester is to avoid performing poorly compared to other students. (PAV)

7. I'm afraid that I may not understand the content of my courses as thoroughly as I'd like. (MAV)

8. I worry that I may not learn all that I possibly could this semester. (MAV)

9. I am definitely concerned that I may not learn all that I can this semester. (MAV)

10. Completely mastering the material in my courses is important to me this semester. (MAP)

11. I want to learn as much as possible this semester. (MAP)

12. The most important thing for me this semester is to understand the content in my courses as thoroughly as possible. (MAP)

I analyzed data from these 12 items using PAF extraction and an oblimin rotation with delta set to zero, as in the previous example of the Attitudes about Scientists data. The pattern and structure matrices are shown in Table 12.10, and the correlations among the factors are shown in Table 12.11.

The pattern and structure coefficients of the three highest loadings for each factor are fairly similar. For example, for item 1, the pattern and structure coefficients for PAP are .813 and .817. However, some of the items have low pattern coefficients but much higher structure coefficients for a factor. Looking at item 3, the pattern and structure coefficients for PAV are .009 and .321, respectively. The structure coefficient is higher than the pattern coefficient because of the relatively high correlation between the PAP and PAV factors, seen in Table 12.11. The correlation drives up the structure coefficient

TABLE 12.10. Pattern and Structure Coefficients for the AGQ Scale

Item	Pattern coefficients				Structure coefficients			
	PAP	MAV	MAP	PAV	PAP	MAV	MAP	PAV
1	.813	−.032	.039	−.011	.817	.024	.239	.251
2	.784	.007	.022	.124	.832	.113	.236	.391
3	.858	.064	−.012	.009	.862	.120	.225	.321
4	.000	−.115	.029	.745	.249	.195	.065	.701
5	.035	.162	−.012	.460	.196	.349	.074	.537
6	.200	.063	−.023	.604	.400	.316	.094	.695
7	−.130	.420	.018	.276	−.006	.528	.106	.405
8	.065	.817	.050	−.027	.121	.822	.255	.332
9	.035	.808	.002	−.062	.066	.785	.194	.278
10	.120	−.042	.657	.006	.288	.121	.678	.084
11	.018	.017	.781	−.080	.193	.168	.782	−.001
12	−.102	.043	.720	.065	.108	.230	.710	.109

TABLE 12.11. Correlations among the AGQ Factors

Factor	PAP	MAV	MAP	PAV
PAP	1.000			
MAV	.064	1.000		
MAP	.257	.233	1.000	
PAV	.334	.407	.084	1.000

for the loading of item 3 on PAV (and for the other two PAP items on PAV). Similar effects can be seen for other coefficients in Table 12.10.

Interpreting the Factors

After the number of factors has been chosen and the factors have been extracted and rotated, the work of interpretation begins. Interpretation involves examining the pattern and/or structure coefficients for each factor in an attempt to determine what the factor represents. Specifically, researchers examine the variables that have high coefficients for a factor to determine what these variables have in common. Variables with higher coefficients are given more weight in determining what the factor represents. If structure coefficients are used, researchers should keep in mind that a high value can be obtained due to a strong relationship of the variable to the factor, a strong correlation between factors, or both.

To determine which variables can be considered to load on each factor, the researcher must choose a threshold at which coefficients will be considered as salient. It is common to use pattern coefficient values such as .3 or .4 for this purpose. The reasoning behind this (such as it is) is that the squared coefficient represents the proportion of the variance in a variable that is accounted for by a factor. Coefficients of .3 indicate that a proportion of .09, or nearly 10%, of the variance in the variable is explained by the factor. Parenthetically, some researchers suggest a cutoff of .32, so that the explained variance is at least 10%. Ten percent may not seem a particularly high amount of explained variance, but keep in mind that variables can have substantial amounts of unreliable variance and of unique or idiosyncratic variance. Also, if variables cross-load, their variance must be spread around to more factors. Even so, an explained variance of 10% certainly represents a lower bound for indicating that a variable should be considered as part of a factor. Of course, such thresholds are, to some degree, arbitrary, and it is reasonable to choose a higher threshold for situations in which variables are known or expected to be more highly correlated. For example, items on scales measuring narrowly defined constructs will typically have high coefficients because such items will tend to be highly correlated. Whatever value is chosen, it is important for researchers to establish thresholds for salient coefficients a priori. Failure to do so may lead to self-serving choices, such as setting a threshold of .35 after observing that a number of variables that do not conform to one's theory have loadings of .34.

As an example, I refer to the coefficients from the Attitudes about Scientists data in Table 12.9. As noted previously, the factors are nearly orthogonal with a correlation of only .023, so the factor and structure coefficients are very similar. Because the variables are not strongly correlated, I adopted a cutoff value of .3. For the first factor, the variables not interesting, odd, not much fun, boring, tending to work alone, and not being religious have pattern coefficients higher than the cutoff. The similarity among these variables is that they represent putative characteristics of scientists. For the second factor, the variables making the world a better place, working for the good of humanity, and helping to solve problems load higher than the cutoff. These variables represent scientists' contributions to society. I might therefore call the two factors something like "Personal Characteristics" and "Contributions." This solution largely meets the requirements for simple structure. The variable "boring" comes close to cross-loading on the second factor, but other variables have very low cross-loadings. With regard to the other simple structure criteria, each row and column has several values that are close to zero, and criterion 3 is met because each variable has a small loading on one factor but not on the other. Criterion 4 is not relevant because there are only two factors.

Although the practice of interpreting factors on the basis of high pattern (or structure) coefficients is quite common, it should be pointed out that most experts in factor analysis would argue that the observed variables cannot uniquely characterize the nature of a factor (e.g., Mulaik, 2010, p. 384). This may seem confusing, as characterizing the nature of factors using observed variables is exactly what most people think is the purpose of factor analysis. To understand why experts would disagree, a brief diversion into the topic of *factor score indeterminacy* is needed.

Factor Score Indeterminacy

To explain the concept of indeterminacy in factor scores, I go back to Equation 12.1. That equation shows that the variable scores (X) are additive functions of the factor scores (F), which are weighted by the loadings (w), plus the uniquenesses (U). Taking a simplified version of Equation 12.1 with just one factor as an illustration, we have

$$X_{iv} = w_v F_i + U_{iv} \tag{12.5}$$

The values of X_{iv} are a person's scores on the variables, so for a given set of data these are fixed values (e.g., they cannot be changed). The values of w_v, F_i, and U_{iv}, however, can conceivably take on any value, as long as the equation adds up to the value of X_{iv}. Even if we knew the population values of the weights, or loadings (w_v), the values of F_i and U_{iv} would still be *indeterminate* in the sense that they could take on any values that added up to the value of X_{iv} and the equation would still be satisfied. A simple example of such an indeterminacy is the equality 2X + Y = 10. An infinite number of values will work in this equation (X = 4, Y = 2; X = 3, Y = 4; X = −1, Y = 12, etc.). The solution is indeterminate because we have only one equation, but two unknowns (X and Y). If we had another equation that must also be satisfied, we could obtain a solution. For example, if we knew that X must equal 2Y, the first solution (X = 4; Y = 2) is the only one that would work.

In factor analysis there is a version of Equation 12.5 for each variable, and there is a uniqueness for each. For each of these equations, there are thus two unknowns: F_i and U_{iv}. Even though the same F_i appears in all the equations, estimates of that factor score in each equation are still subject to the vagaries of the uniquenesses. If there were an infinite number of variables, and thus of equations, it might be possible to pin down the value of F_i, but as there are not, the factor scores remain indeterminate.

Grice (2001) provides an introduction to the factor score indeterminacy issue and gives formulas for the computation of various indices to measure this indeterminacy. The good news is that factor score indeterminacy diminishes with high variable communalities and with more variables per factor. Therefore, to some extent, researchers have a degree of control over the determinacy of their factors through their choice of variables used in their analyses. Researchers should keep in mind that theoretical arguments can also be brought to bear on one's interpretation of factors. Those who are able to provide a theory-based explanation for what is common to a set of variables with high loadings on a factor are clearly in a stronger position to defend their interpretation of that factor than those who can show only the high loadings with no theory to back them up. Mulaik (2010) gives as an example Spearman's (1904, 1927) "discovery" of g, or general intelligence, stating that

> Spearman (1904, 1927) did not discover g using factor analysis. He did not . . . know about eigenvectors and eigenvalues. He presumed from a conceptual analysis of the mental operations he believed were involved in performing on certain tasks that they would have a mental factor in common. (p. 395)

Let us get back to the original issue, that the observed variables cannot uniquely characterize the nature of a factor. Although a researcher cannot hope to do this with one EFA study, evidence of the nature of the factor accumulates as more studies are done, as Mulaik (2010) explains in some detail. According to Mulaik, this is the nature of science, which advances as information about a phenomenon is obtained. Such information may either support or disconfirm earlier ideas about the phenomenon but in either case will cause scientific concepts to "become increasingly better anchored in experience" (2010, p. 395).

EFA Results as Evidence of Measurement Validity

I used the data for the Attitudes about Scientists example simply for illustrative purposes, with no particular hypotheses about the factor structure. Typically, however, EFA is used to aid the scale development process and/or to obtain validity evidence based on internal structure. Use of EFA during scale development involves examining the pattern and/or structure coefficients to determine whether items load on the expected factors, whether there are undesirable cross-loadings, or whether any of the obtained coefficients fail to meet the cutoff criterion for saliency. Although it is common practice to eliminate cross-loading items or items with low coefficients from the scale, I do not recommend dropping items until such results are replicated on an independent sample. This is because the results of correlational procedures such as factor analysis can be quite unstable, particularly with small samples and/or with poorly correlated items. Thus, items can fail to load simply because of idiosyncrasies in the data. It is therefore prudent to defer such decisions until results can be verified on another sample.

It is also common for researchers to use EFA to obtain evidence about the hypothesized structure of a particular construct, such as intelligence or self-concept. This type of research may not involve scale development. Instead, researchers may collect data using existing measures and factor analyze the data to see whether theoretically supported structures are supported. Results of such studies can both advance theory and provide support (or lack of support) for validity arguments underlying interpretations and use of the measures used. Claims of measurement validity could be supported by obtaining the expected number of factors and the expected pattern of loadings. If the anticipated number of factors is obtained, and the hypothesized variables are found to load on each, this does support validity arguments regarding both the dimensionality of the construct and the nature of its components. However, as Benson (1998) points out, the results of a factor analytic study do not necessarily provide plausible information about what a factor is measuring. This is because, although the nature of factors can be tentatively inferred from the content of the items loading on them (given the caveats regarding indeterminacy discussed previously), correlations among the items are also driven by the processes involved in responding to them. For example, loadings can reflect shared variance due to similarities in wording, or shared susceptibility to response styles. Items that are negatively worded often share more variance with each other than with items that are positively worded, and many studies have found that such items tend to form artifactual factors (e.g., Barnette, 2000; Marsh, 1986; Motl et al., 2000; Pilotte & Gable, 1990). The possibility for such artifactual factors, sometimes referred to as *nuisance factors*, should be kept in mind when interpreting the results of an EFA.

As noted by Mulaik (2010), factor analytic studies should be part of an ongoing program of research in which each study builds on the next. Subsequent studies might test the factor interpretations formed in previous studies by incorporating new variables that should load on the factors if the interpretations are accurate. As a simple example, I could conduct a follow-up to the Attitudes about Scientists EFA, adding in variables that I think should measure either the "Personal Characteristics" or the "Contributions" factor. A finding that these variables loaded as expected would support my interpretation of the factors. If the initial study suggested the possibility of an additional factor, variables chosen to flesh out this factor could be added. Another common extension of an initial EFA is that of determining whether a factor solution that was supported with a sample from one population will be replicated in a sample from a population that differs in terms of age, sex, ethnicity, cultural background, or other characteristics. Factor solutions from different samples can be compared statistically in the CFA framework. In EFA, differences in factor solutions are typically compared in a more descriptive manner, by noting differences in the pattern or magnitudes of factor coefficients and correlations.

Data Requirements for EFA

I end this chapter with a discussion of some practical matters in EFA analysis: methods for determining whether a correlation matrix is appropriate for factoring, how variable distributions can affect EFA results, and how large a sample size is needed.

Suitability of a Correlation Matrix for Factoring

Recall that factor analysis is based on the premise that the variables share variance and that this shared variance can be translated into factors. Given this premise, it is important to determine up front whether the shared variance in a matrix is sufficient for factor analysis to proceed. Two procedures that are often used to determine the amenability of a correlation matrix to factoring are the Kaiser–Meyer–Olkin (KMO) measure of sample adequacy and Bartlett's test of sphericity. The KMO is a ratio of the sum of the squared correlations of all possible pairs of variables to the sum of these squared correlations, plus the sum of the squared correlations with the effects of all other variables partialed out. The logic behind this is that if the variables are highly correlated, the partial correlations should be very small, resulting in a KMO ratio close to 1.0. The less correlation among the variables, the higher the partial correlations and the lower the KMO ratio. Kaiser (1974), who was something of a wit, provided the following guidelines to indicate a matrix's amenability to factoring:

.90s—marvelous

.80s—meritorious

.70s—middling

.60s—mediocre

.50s—miserable

<.50—unacceptable

Bartlett's test of sphericity is a test of whether the correlation matrix is an identity matrix. An identity matrix has ones on its diagonal and zeros on its off-diagonal, so if a correlation matrix were an identity matrix, the variables would be completely uncorrelated with each other; clearly an undesirable state of affairs for factoring. The null and alternative hypotheses for Bartlett's test are

$$H_0: R = I$$

$$H_1: R \neq I$$

where R is the correlation matrix. Because an identity matrix would be useless for factoring, the researcher would like to reject H_0 in favor of H_1 and conclude that the matrix is not an identity matrix. Bartlett's test is distributed as chi-square with degrees of freedom equal to $v(v - 1)/2$, where v is the number of variables. This is a very powerful test, and with a large enough sample size (which we usually have in factor analysis), even very small differences from an identity matrix will result in rejection of the null hypothesis.

Distributional Assumptions for EFA

As noted in a previous section, most EFA estimation methods are not based on strict assumptions about the distributions of the variables to be analyzed. This means that the variable distributions are not required to be normal for most EFA methods. The reason is that EFA does not typically involve statistical testing of model parameters or of the model as a whole (although such tests are possible; see McDonald, 1999, pp. 169–170). However, this lack of distributional assumptions is somewhat misleading because it does not necessarily mean that variable distributions have no effect on the results obtained from EFA. On the contrary, it has been known for some time that variables with similar levels of skew and/or kurtosis can form artifactual factors, sometimes known as *difficulty factors* (e.g., McDonald & Ahlawat, 1974). This occurs because variables with similar distributions tend to be more highly correlated with each other than with differently distributed variables, even though the variables may have no similarity in content. The severity of this problem increases with the level of nonnormality. Artifactual factors are unlikely to occur if variable distributions are not severely nonnormal (i.e., values of skewness and kurtosis are less than |2.0|, although some authors suggest kurtosis can be as high as 7.0). If they do occur, however, non-normally distributed variables can result in the retention of difficulty factors, which can be confusing unless researchers can correctly identify these as being due to distributional artifacts. This is one reason that authors such as Nunnally and Bernstein (1994; see also Bernstein & Teng, 1989) argue against the use of individual items in EFA, preferring the analysis of scales or subscales. These authors point out that items are less continuous and more subject to non-normality than scales or subscales.

To illustrate this type of effect, I created data on which items 1–6 measure one factor and items 7–12 measure a second factor. The items' distributions differ; all of the odd-numbered items have uniform, or rectangular distributions (skewness of 0 and kurtosis of approximately –2.0), and all of the even-numbered items have positively skewed distributions (skewness ranging from 3–4 and kurtosis ranging from 5–14). I analyzed these data using a principal components extraction with a varimax rotation (the factors were created to be uncorrelated) and obtained the solution shown in Table 12.12.

Component 1 is based on variables 1–6 and corresponds to the first component I generated. Component 2 should be based on variables 7–12, but instead variables 7, 9, and 11 have high coefficients and variables 1, 3, and 5 have loadings that are lower in magnitude but that would still be considered salient. Thus, component 2 is based on the similarity in these items' distributions. And where did the third component come from, given that I only generated a two-component solution? Looking at the variables with high coefficients, you can see these are variables 8, 10, and 12. Putting all of this information together, it appears that the generated component 2 has been split into two parts, represented by the obtained components 2 and 3. The obtained component 2 is loaded by the odd-numbered, or uniformly distributed variables, and the obtained

TABLE 12.12. Factor Coefficients from Variables with Different Distributions

	Component 1	Component 2	Component 3
V1	.691	.348	−.080
V2	.625	−.047	.309
V3	.676	.353	−.014
V4	.644	−.118	.377
V5	.677	.347	−.056
V6	.598	−.085	.407
V7	.131	.722	.248
V8	.062	.253	.697
V9	.120	.709	.259
V10	.103	.280	.668
V11	.094	.743	.206
V12	.143	.224	.711

component 3 is loaded by the even-numbered, or positively skewed variables. These two components are therefore driven by the artifact of the variables' distributions.

These effects are exacerbated because I generated these data to have only two categories. Because EFA estimation is typically based on analysis of Pearson product–moment (PPM) correlation matrices, violations of the assumptions underlying PPM correlations can result in bias in EFA parameter estimates. More specifically, use of PPM correlations is based on the assumptions that the variables are continuous and have a linear relationship with the factors. Both of these assumptions are violated if data have only a small number of response categories, such as those resulting from dichotomously ("yes/no") or ordinally scored (Likert-type) questions. These violations result in underestimation of the relationships among variables and, consequently, of the pattern and/or structure coefficients. The reason for this underestimation is that PPM correlations cannot completely capture the nonlinear relationships among the dichotomous or ordinal variables or their regression on a continuous factor. Thus, values of pattern and structure coefficients, factor correlations, and the amount of variance explained by the factor solution will all be underestimated when data are not continuous. This bias increases as the number of response categories decreases, but with five or more ordered categories it should be minimal. Thus, researchers working with data based on fewer than five response categories should consider using item response theory (IRT; see Chapter 14) in lieu of EFA because IRT methods were specifically designed for modeling relationships among such variables. Alternatively, so-called categorical least squares (cat-LS) estimation methods available in structural equation modeling programs have been found to perform well with noncontinuous data (see Finney & DiStefano, 2013).

Sample-Size Requirements

Recent studies (Hogarty, Hines, Kromrey, Ferron, & Mumford, 2005; MacCallum, Widaman, Preacher, & Hong, 2001; MacCallum et al., 1999; Velicer & Fava, 1998) have shown that the sample size needed to obtain accurate estimates of factor coefficients depends on the level of communality of the variables, the number of variables per factor, and the interaction of these two characteristics. If communalities are high, researchers can obtain accurate estimates of factor loadings with sample sizes as small as 100, whereas with lower communalities samples sizes of 500 would be needed. Previous rules of thumb indicated that the sample size needed was an increasing function of the number of variables in the analysis, resulting in sample size recommendations of 5, 10, or even 20 times the number of variables. In contrast, the studies by Hogarty and colleagues (2005) and MacCallum and colleagues (1999, 2001) have shown that more accurate estimates of loadings are obtained when the number of variables per factor is increased, even if the sample size stays the same. These researchers thus found that it was better to have more than fewer variables per factor. Of course, results are never simple, and the results from these studies were no exception. More specifically, the level of communality and the number of variables per factor interacted such that, if communalities were high (averaging .7), the number of variables per factor had little effect on the accuracy of estimation. Thus, variables with high communalities could compensate, to some extent, for having fewer variables per factor.

In terms of specific recommendations, these studies suggest that samples of 100 may be sufficient to obtain accurate estimates for solutions with three factors, *if* the factors are measured by at least three to four variables each *and* variable communalities are between .6 and .8. However, these communality values are quite high. For example, loadings of approximately .71 and .3 on two uncorrelated factors would be needed to yield a communality of .6 (recall that the communality of a variable is equal to the sum of its squared loadings). In most social science applications, loadings are often well below this level. If communalities are lower than .5, sample sizes of at least 300 would be needed. Larger sample sizes are also needed if there are more factors. If there were seven factors, a sample size of 500 would be needed to obtain accurate parameter estimates in a situation with communalities less than .5 and at least three to four variables per factor.

SUMMARY

EFA is used in many measurement pursuits, including scale development and revision and the generation and testing of theories based on variable interrelations. At its core, factor analysis is a method for parsing out clusters of variables that share a common source of variance. The underlying philosophy of factor analysis is based on the idea that the shared variance among such clusters of variables is due to the fact that they are all caused by the same factor. Such factors are often thought to represent latent constructs, and factor analysis is seen as a way to shed light on the nature of such constructs.

Factor analysis can therefore be an important tool for generating and/or testing theories involving latent constructs. Because of its exploratory nature, however, factor analysis does not provide strict tests of such theories. In fact, in many cases the results of a factor analytic study raise more questions than they answer. This is why some researchers see EFA as well suited to the generation of theory (e.g., Haig, 2005). Strict tests of factor structures and the theories they represent are better accommodated by CFA.

EXERCISES

1. What are some research situations in which exploratory factor analysis is useful?

2. What is represented by the u term in Equation 12.1?

Questions 3–6 refer to the correlation matrix in Table 12.13.

TABLE 12.13. Correlation Matrix for Questions 3–6

	X_1	X_2	X_3	X_4	X_5	X_6	X_7	X_8	X_9
X_1	1.0								
X_2	.70	1.0							
X_3	.75	.80	1.0						
X_4	.20	.15	.18	1.0					
X_5	.22	.21	.20	.76	1.0				
X_6	.17	.20	.23	.78	.80	1.0			
X_7	.20	.19	.22	.23	.15	.76	1.0		
X_8	.22	.18	.16	.15	.21	.20	.65	1.0	
X_9	.18	.24	.13	.16	.16	.15	.66	.71	1.0

3. If these data were factor analyzed, how many factors would there be? Why?

4. Would correlated or uncorrelated factors provide the best model for these data? Why?

5. Draw the path diagram for the model you indicated in Questions 3 and 4. Include only primary loadings for each variable (e.g., show only one loading for each factor, even if you think there may be some secondary loadings). In your model, indicate what each element (circles, arrows, etc.) represents.

6. Using your path diagram from Question 5, explain how you can use Wright's tracing rules to trace from:

   a. X_1 to X_3

   b. X_3 to X_6

   c. X_5 to X_8

7. What is the main difference between PAF analysis and PCA analysis?

Questions 8–16 refer to the following results, which are based on the responses of approximately 1,000 students to the 10 items on the Rosenberg Self-Esteem Scale (RSE;

Rosenberg, 1989). The wording of the 10 items is shown here. Each item is followed by either a P or an N, indicating that it is either positively or negatively oriented. A positively oriented item is one for which agreement indicates positive self-esteem, whereas a negative item is one for which agreement indicates negative self-esteem. Although the negatively oriented items are often recoded prior to analysis, I did not recode them for these analyses.

The RSE was developed to measure a single self-esteem factor. However, I obtained results from the Hull method for determining the number of factors as well as the scree plot to see if these might suggest a different number of factors.

1. I feel that I'm a person of worth, at least on an equal plane with others. (P)

2. I feel that I have a number of good qualities. (P)

3. All in all, I am inclined to feel that I am a failure. (N)

4. I am able to do things as well as most other people. (P)

5. I feel I do not have much to be proud of. (N)

6. I take a positive attitude toward myself. (P)

7. On the whole, I am satisfied with myself. (P)

8. I wish I could have more respect for myself. (N)

9. I certainly feel useless at times. (N)

10. At times I think I am no good at all. (N)

I obtained a PAF solution with an oblimin rotation. Selected results are shown in Table 12.14.

TABLE 12.14. Selected Results from PAF Analysis for Questions 8–10

	Total variance explained					
	Initial eigenvalues			Extraction sums of squared loadings		
Factor	Eigenvalue	% of variance	Cumulative % of variance	Sum of squared loadings	% of variance	Cumulative %
1	5.399	53.990	53.990	4.973	49.729	49.729
2	1.051	10.508	64.498	.644	6.441	56.170
3	.689	6.886	71.383			
4	.582	5.819	77.202			
5	.543	5.434	82.636			
6	.433	4.326	86.962			
7	.406	4.060	91.022			
8	.351	3.508	94.530			
9	.283	2.833	97.363			
10	.264	2.637	100.000			

8. Explain how the initial percentage of variance for Factor 1 (53.99%) is calculated. What does this value represent?

9. Why is the percentage of variance for Factor 1 under "extraction sums of squared loadings" different from the value under "initial eigenvalues"?

10. If extraction were based on the K1 criterion, how many factors would be extracted? Why?

11. Results obtained from the Hull method of determining the number of factors are shown here. How many factors does this method suggest?

Number of factors	Goodness-of-fit values	Degrees of freedom	Scree test values
0	0.000	10	0.000
1	0.873	20	9.500
2	0.956	29	0.000

12. The scree plot is shown in Figure 12.7. How many factors does it suggest?

13. Based on the results from the K1 criterion, the Hull procedure, and the scree plot, how many factors would you recommend? Why?

14. What is the difference between an orthogonal and an oblique rotation?

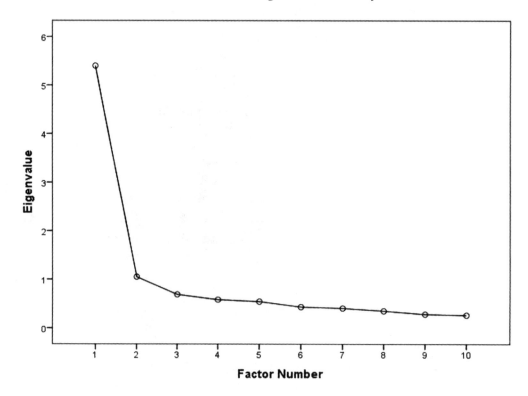

FIGURE 12.7. Scree plot for Question 12.

15. The oblimin-rotated factor pattern matrix for a two-factor solution is shown in Table 12.15. What do you think is driving the separation of the items onto the two factors?

TABLE 12.15. Factor Pattern Matrix for Question 15

Item	Factor 1	Factor 2
2	−.908	.121
1	−.697	−.003
4	−.583	−.027
6	−.561	−.322
7	−.509	−.310
9	−.079	.873
10	−.038	.830
8	.142	.612
3	.294	.452
5	.402	.408

16. What is the difference between a pattern matrix and a structure matrix? For this example, the two factors are correlated at .67. How would this affect the differences between the pattern and structure matrices?

Confirmatory Factor Analysis

DIFFERENCES BETWEEN EXPLORATORY AND CONFIRMATORY FACTOR ANALYSES

In Chapter 12, I discussed EFA, and noted that EFA has many similarities to *confirmatory factor analysis* (CFA). Both are methods for transforming the observed relations among a set of variables into a broader set of underlying factors. Both methods therefore provide an answer to the question, "Why are these variables related to each other in the particular way we observe?" In CFA, as in EFA, the answer to this question is that the variables are related to a set of factors, and it is these factors that are driving the variables' intercorrelations. One difference between the two is that in CFA the factor solution can be tested statistically, whereas EFA is, as the name suggests, a more exploratory procedure. Because of this it is sometimes said that EFA is more appropriate for theory generation and CFA is more appropriate for theory testing. Although this is true to some extent, the exploratory/confirmatory distinction is not a strict dichotomy. Instead, it is probably more correct to think of purely exploratory and purely confirmatory analyses as forming two ends of a continuum. Along this continuum lie analyses that combine features of both. Thus, EFA is sometimes used in a confirmatory manner, and CFA is sometimes used in an exploratory manner. Having said this, many experts recommend that EFA be used for situations in which minimal research on the construct or scale of interest has been conducted and that CFA be used for situations in which strong theory and/or prior research are available to guide specification of the factor model.

There are two basic reasons for this recommendation. First, in CFA the researcher *must* specify the entire factor structure. This means that the researcher must specify which variables load (and do not load) on which factor(s), which factors are correlated (if any), and whether any of the *measurement error variances* (called uniquenesses in EFA) should be correlated. If there is no theory or prior research to guide decisions about the CFA structure, researchers could easily become overwhelmed by these choices. In EFA, however, the researcher does not have to make such choices for the simple reason that these choices are not allowed. For example, in EFA all variables are free to load on all of the factors. Thus, researchers cannot specify the exact pattern of loadings a priori even if they want to do so. Although in EFA factors can be correlated or not correlated, all factors must either be correlated or all must be uncorrelated; there is no "mixing and matching" allowed. Finally, uniquenesses (or measurement error variances, as they are called in CFA) are not allowed to be correlated in EFA. In CFA, however, measurement error covariances are allowed.

The second reason that CFA is recommended only when theory/prior research is available is that if the model is specified incorrectly, the researcher may be able to tell from the CFA output that *something* is wrong but may not be able to identify what. The worse the initial model specification, the more difficult it can be to determine the source of the problem. This problem is exacerbated by the fact that, unlike EFA, CFA is *not* an exploratory method. Instead, CFA allows for statistical tests of a hypothesized model structure that indicate whether that structure is consistent with the variables' observed interrelations.[1] Because CFA involves statistical significance testing, it is not appropriate to test multiple factor structures, unless these are hypothesized a priori. This, then, is another difference between EFA and CFA. In EFA, researchers are encouraged to try out different numbers of factors and rotations that might be suggested by the results of previous analyses. In CFA, however, this would be tantamount to obtaining the results of a statistical test and then changing one's hypothesis on the basis of that information. This, you should remember from Statistics 101, is a statistical testing no-no.

ADVANTAGES OF CFA

For situations in which researchers have sufficient knowledge to feel confident in proposing a factor model, CFA has definite advantages over EFA. As noted previously, CFA allows for the researcher to completely specify which variables should load on which factor. It also allows researchers to specify which factors should be correlated. Thus, a researcher could specify that some factors are correlated and others are not, if this is suggested by theory or previous research. It is also possible to specify that measurement errors between pairs of variables covary. Although measurement errors are usually hypothesized to be random, the uniquenesses, or measurement error variances, actually contain both random and systematic variance (see Chapter 12). Random values should not correlate with anything, but systematic values may. As an example, suppose that a scale is administered at different time points, as in a longitudinal study. It may be reasonable to think that the measurement errors for the same variable measured at different times will be correlated. This could happen because respondents made the same type of mistake or because their answers were influenced by the same response set at both times.

[1] Some EFA programs, such as CEFA (Browne, Cudeck, Tateneni, & Mels, 2008), do allow for statistical testing.

Because CFA allows for detailed specification of a factor model, it can be very valuable in psychometric studies. In particular, CFA is often used to provide evidence of measurement validity. For example, if a researcher obtained the expected pattern of loadings, this would be evidence in support of the internal structure of a scale. If the scale contained more than one factor, researchers could also examine the correlations among factors to determine the degree to which these correlations are consistent with theoretical expectations. As noted in Chapter 12, however, researchers should be mindful of Benson's (1998) point that the results of a factor analytic study do not provide definitive information about the meaning of factors. This is due in part to the fact that interpretations of factor meaning are somewhat subjective. Two researchers interpreting the same results may not agree on the meaning of all the factors. Another reason that factor meaning cannot be definitively identified from factor analytic results is that covariation among the items can be influenced by noncontent forces, such as wording similarities or shared susceptibility to response styles. Finally, CFA results are influenced by the particular population from which they are derived. There is no guarantee that the results obtained from one population will be found again in another. This is especially true if the populations differ on characteristics that are relevant to the construct being measured. To take an obvious example, CFA results from a measure of racial identity are very likely to vary across respondents of different races.

CFA methods can also be used to obtain reliability estimates. In particular, CFA methods can be used to compute estimates of *coefficient omega* (McDonald, 1999), an estimate of reliability that does not require the assumption of tau-equivalence. You may remember from Chapter 8 that if variable scores are not tau-equivalent, use of coefficient alpha will underestimate the true reliability of the scale. Coefficient omega does not have this limitation and requires only that variable scores are congeneric. CFA methods can also be used to obtain statistical tests of the assumptions of tau-equivalence and parallelism of items.

As described in the previous paragraphs, EFA and CFA differ in terms of their position on the exploratory/confirmatory continuum and in terms of the degree to which aspects of the factor model can be specified a priori. Because of these differences, EFA and CFA are typically used for somewhat different purposes. However, the basic purpose of providing an explanation for the observed covariation among a set of variables, as operationalized by the factors and their intercorrelations, is the same in both approaches. Both approaches are also based on the same equation, and in both approaches the factor model is assessed by the degree to which it accounts for the variable intercorrelations or covariances.

CFA MODEL AND EQUATIONS

To illustrate these similarities, I use the model shown in Figure 13.1, which is identical to that in Figure 12.2. You may notice, however, that I have changed the names of the parameters to correspond to the Greek letters commonly used in CFA. The loading

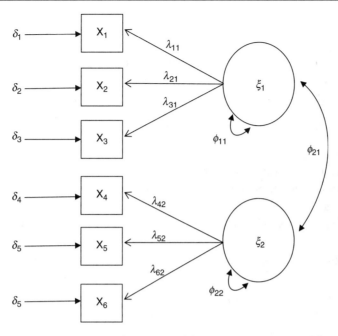

FIGURE 13.1. CFA model for six variables with two correlated factors.

coefficients are represented by λ, factors are represented by ξ (or sometimes η), and factor correlations by ϕ. The small double-headed arrows next to each factor symbolize the factor variances. Measurement errors have two representations: the measurement errors themselves are represented by ε (or sometimes δ), but the *variances* of the measurement errors are represented by θ_ε or θ_δ. For easy reference, these symbols, along with their spelling and definitions, are shown in Box 13.1. Note also that the symbols in Figure 13.1 are subscripted. For measurement errors and measurement error variances, the subscript simply refers to the number of the variable. For loadings, the subscripts are for the

BOX 13.1

Greek Letters Used in CFA

CFA symbol	Spelling	What it represents
λ	Lambda	Factor (pattern) loading
ε or δ	Epsilon or delta	Measurement error
θ_ε or θ_δ	Theta epsilon or theta delta	Measurement error variance
ξ or η	Ksi or eta	Factor scores
ϕ	Phi	Factor correlation

variable and the factor (in that order). For example, λ_{21} refers to the loading of variable 2 on factor 1 (ξ_1). The factor correlations are subscripted by the numbers of the factors involved. For example, Φ_{21} is the correlation between factors 1 and 2 (this subscripting follows the convention of putting the largest number—2—first).

As in EFA, the relations shown in Figure 13.1 can be expressed in equation form as

$$X_{iv} = \lambda_{v1}\xi_{1i} + \lambda_{v2}\xi_{2i} + \cdots + \lambda_{vf}\xi_{fi} + \delta_{iv} \qquad (13.1)$$

In Equation 13.1, X_{iv} is subscripted with i for person and v for variable. You may recall that in the similar equation for EFA, the X variables were assumed to be in z-score form. In CFA, as in most structural equation modeling, this is not the case, and variables are typically analyzed in their original metrics. Because variable means are often not of interest in CFA,[2] variables are often expressed as deviations from their means (i.e., $x = X - \overline{X}$), but not as z-scores, in equations such as Equation 13.1. Perhaps more importantly, a covariance rather than a correlation matrix is analyzed in CFA (although raw data can also be used and are required for some of the more complex structural equation modeling analyses). Recall from Chapter 7 that a covariance matrix is an unstandardized correlation matrix. The diagonal of a covariance matrix contains the variables' variances, and the off-diagonal elements (the covariances) are measures of the variables' relations, as are correlations, but covariances are not constrained to fall between −1.0 and +1.0. Because a covariance rather than a correlation matrix is analyzed, estimates of loadings and other parameters are typically reported in an *unstandardized* form in the output from most CFA software packages. However, standardized coefficients can also be obtained. The difference is that for standardized estimates a pattern or loading coefficient can be interpreted as the number of standard deviation units the variable would change if the value of the factor changed by one standard deviation, holding all other factors constant. For unstandardized pattern loadings, the interpretation is in terms of "raw" variable units. That is, the pattern coefficient is the number of its units the variable would change if the factor changed by one of its units. Here, the units of the variable are simply its raw score units. If the variable were, for example, age, the units would be years.

Getting back to Equation 13.1, the interpretation is the same as that in EFA: the term λ_{vf} is the pattern loading coefficient of variable v on factor f, ξ_{fi} is the score of person i on factor (ξ) f, and δ_{iv} is person i's error or uniqueness score on variable v. As in EFA, Equation 13.1 represents the variable score (X) of only one person, but in CFA/EFA our interest is in explaining the relations among all the variables across all respondents. Consequently, the covariance matrix of the scores is obtained and analyzed in CFA. A covariance matrix can be obtained as the expectation of Equation 13.1 multiplied by itself (see Hayduk, 1987, pp. 109–110 for a step-by-step account), but because the error

---

[2] There are, however, situations where means are of interest (e.g., with categorical data or in multiple-group comparisons).

scores (δs) are assumed to be independent of each other and of the factor scores (ξs), the covariance matrix obtained from Equation 13.1 simplifies to

$$\Sigma_X = \Lambda\Phi\Lambda' + \Theta_\delta \qquad (13.2)$$

Note that this expression is identical to the equation for EFA, except that here Σ_X is the covariance matrix of the X's, rather than their correlation matrix. The interpretation of Equation 13.2 is very similar to that in EFA. The Λ matrix contains the pattern or loading coefficients relating the variables to the factors and has a row for each variable and a column for each factor. Because CFA results in a default solution that is unstandardized, the matrix Φ contains the factor covariances, rather than their correlations (as in EFA). Thus, the Φ matrix contains the factor variances on the diagonal and their covariances on the off-diagonal. However, factor correlations can be obtained if a standardized solution is requested. Finally, Θ_δ is a matrix of the measurement error variances (and covariances, if specified). The Θ_δ matrix has v rows and v columns, with the variances of the error or uniqueness scores on the diagonal. Although in EFA correlations among these errors are not permitted, in CFA it is possible to estimate covariances between pairs of error scores. If estimated, these would be shown below the diagonal.

The model in Figure 13.1 indicates that correlations among variables X_1–X_6 are posited to be caused by two factors and that these factors are correlated. As in EFA, respondents' scores on the variables are thought to be caused by the factors. That is, those with high levels of a factor will have a higher score on the related variables than those with low levels of the factor. In CFA, as in EFA, the covariation among a set of observed variable scores is modeled as a function of one or more factors, the covariances (if any) among these factors, and the measurement error variances (and possibly measurement error covariances). This means that each covariance between a pair of variables can be obtained from combinations of these parameters, using the backward, then forwards path-tracing rule illustrated in Chapter 12.

Recall that this rule states that it is permissible to move backward (i.e., in a direction opposite to the way the arrow is pointing) and then forward. For example, for the model in Figure 13.1, it is possible to navigate from X_1 to X_3 by going backward along the path labeled λ_{11}, through ξ_1, and forward along path λ_{31}. This backward, then forward rule allows X_1 and X_3 to be related through their common cause, ξ_1. If the model is a good one, the covariance between X_1 and X_3 should be equal to $\lambda_{11} * \phi_{11} * \lambda_{31}$. Note that this differs from the EFA equation by including the term ϕ_{11}, the variance of factor 1. This is because CFA is based on covariances, whereas EFA is typically based on correlations. In the correlation metric, ϕ_{11} is equal to 1.0, but in the covariance metric it is the variance of factor 1. Because we must pass through ξ_1 to get from X_1 to X_3, its variance must be included in the equation. Similarly, the covariance between X_1 and X_4 would be obtained by the sequence of paths λ_{11}, ϕ_{21}, λ_{42}, and their covariance should equal the product of those three values. As in Chapter 12, I say the covariances *should* equal the products of the associated coefficients because this will not always be the case. For example, if ξ_1 and ξ_2 were not modeled as correlated, the path ϕ_{21} would be omitted from

TABLE 13.1. Pattern Coefficients for the Model in Figure 13.1

Variable	Factor ξ_1	ξ_2
X_1	λ_{11}	0
X_2	λ_{21}	0
X_3	λ_{31}	0
X_4	0	λ_{42}
X_5	0	λ_{52}
X_6	0	λ_{62}

the model, and there would be no way to get from X_1 to X_4. Their *reproduced* or *model implied* covariance would therefore be zero. If some covariation actually existed between the two variables, it would not be reproduced by a model with uncorrelated factors.

Although the backward then forward rule for CFA is essentially the same as in EFA, there are two important modifications. I have already mentioned the first of these. Although in EFA it is assumed that the factors have variances of 1.0, this need not be the case in CFA. This affects our path tracing because if a path goes into a factor and then back out, the factor's variance must be included in the calculations. Technically, this was the case for EFA as well, but because those variances were equal to 1.0, it had no effect on the calculations. Second, in CFA the matrix of pattern coefficients is typically restricted such that each variable only loads on its posited factor, with coefficients for all other factors set equal to zero. This is the pattern modeled in Figure 13.1. The matrix of pattern coefficients for the CFA model in Figure 13.1 is shown in Table 13.1. Note that only three pattern coefficients for each factor will be estimated, and the other three will be *fixed*, or set to zero.

The restricted pattern of loadings, in which potential cross-loadings are set to zero, is a major difference between the EFA and CFA models. In EFA, it is not possible to make such restrictions, and each variable can potentially load on each factor. Note that this has implications for path tracing, as in CFA there are typically no cross-loadings that make it possible to navigate among variables loading on different factors. This means that the only way to account for covariation among such variables is through the factor covariances (and variance). As discussed in the previous paragraph, for example, the covariance between X_1 and X_4 would be obtained by multiplying together the paths λ_{11}, ϕ_{21}, and λ_{42}. If, however, X_1 cross-loaded onto ξ_2 (λ_{12}), this would allow for an additional tracing between X_1 and X_4. Because this tracing goes through ξ_2, the variance of that factor must be taken into account, yielding $\lambda_{12} * \phi_{22} * \lambda_{42}$. Thus, because it includes more cross-loadings, the EFA model allows more possibilities for reproducing the observed variable covariances than does the CFA model. The upshot of this difference is quite important: it means that CFA has fewer "chances" to reproduce the covariances accurately. And as we shall see later in this chapter, this has implications for the fit of the model.

TABLE 13.2. Model Implied Covariances and Variances for the Model in Figure 13.1

Variable pair	Model-implied covariance	Variable pair	Model-implied covariance
X_1X_2	$Cov_{x1x2} = \lambda_{11}\phi_{11}\lambda_{21}$	X_3X_6	$Cov_{x3x6} = \lambda_{31}\phi_{21}\lambda_{62}$
X_1X_3	$Cov_{x1x3} = \lambda_{11}\phi_{11}\lambda_{31}$	X_4X_5	$Cov_{x4x5} = \lambda_{42}\phi_{22}\lambda_{52}$
X_1X_4	$Cov_{x1x4} = \lambda_{11}\phi_{21}\lambda_{42}$	X_4X_6	$Cov_{x4x6} = \lambda_{42}\phi_{22}\lambda_{62}$
X_1X_5	$Cov_{x1x5} = \lambda_{11}\phi_{21}\lambda_{52}$	X_5X_6	$Cov_{x5x6} = \lambda_{52}\phi_{22}\lambda_{62}$
X_1X_6	$Cov_{x1x6} = \lambda_{11}\phi_{21}\lambda_{62}$	Variable	Model-implied variance
X_2X_3	$Cov_{x2x3} = \lambda_{21}\phi_{11}\lambda_{31}$	X_1	$VAR_{X1} = \lambda^2_{11}\phi_{11} + \theta_{\delta1}$
X_2X_4	$Cov_{x2x4} = \lambda_{21}\phi_{21}\lambda_{42}$	X_2	$VAR_{X2} = \lambda^2_{21}\phi_{11} + \theta_{\delta2}$
X_2X_5	$Cov_{x2x5} = \lambda_{21}\phi_{21}\lambda_{52}$	X_3	$VAR_{X3} = \lambda^2_{31}\phi_{11} + \theta_{\delta3}$
X_2X_6	$Cov_{x2x6} = \lambda_{21}\phi_{21}\lambda_{62}$	X_4	$VAR_{X4} = \lambda^2_{42}\phi_{22} + \theta_{\delta4}$
X_3X_4	$Cov_{x3x4} = \lambda_{31}\phi_{21}\lambda_{42}$	X_5	$VAR_{X5} = \lambda^2_{52}\phi_{22} + \theta_{\delta5}$
X_3X_5	$Cov_{x3x5} = \lambda_{31}\phi_{21}\lambda_{52}$	X_6	$VAR_{X6} = \lambda^2_{62}\phi_{22} + \theta_{\delta6}$

In Table 13.2, I show each pair of variables and its model-implied covariance, which I have obtained by using path tracing based on the model in Figure 13.1. I also show the model-implied variance of each variable. Recall that the model-implied or reproduced variances and covariances are those that would be obtained on the basis of a particular model, using path tracing. You may want to review path tracing from Chapter 12 if you encounter problems in reproducing these calculations. To refresh your memory, I provide two examples here from the model shown in Figure 13.1. To obtain the model-implied covariance between X_1 and X_2, I can trace along path λ_{11}, through ξ_1 (remember that in CFA this means we must include the variance of ξ_1, ϕ_{11}), and then back down to X_2 along path λ_{21}. The model-implied covariance would therefore equal $\lambda_{11} * \phi_{11} * \lambda_{21}$. To obtain the model-implied covariance between X_1 and X_4, I would trace along path λ_{11}, through ϕ_{21}, and down λ_{42}. This path would therefore equal $\lambda_{11} * \phi_{21} * \lambda_{42}$.

STEPS IN CONDUCTING A CFA

As with EFA, conducting a CFA study involves several steps:

1. Data preparation
2. Model specification
3. Model identification
4. Estimation of model parameters
5. Model testing
6. Respecification of the model

In the next sections, I illustrate these steps using the Achievement Goal Questionnaire (Elliot & McGregor, 2001) data from Chapter 12. The response scale ranged from 1 = "not at all true of me" to 7 = "very true of me". The data were collected as part of a study by Finney and colleagues (2004) who were interested in determining whether the factor structure reported by Elliot and McGregor (2001) could be replicated in a general, rather than a specific, academic context. To test this notion, Finney and colleagues asked respondents to answer in terms of their performance "in your college classes this semester" rather than in a specific class. The items are:

1. My goal this semester is to get better grades than most of the other students.

2. It is important for me to do well compared to other students this semester.

3. I want to do better than other students this semester.

4. I just want to avoid doing poorly compared to other students this semester.

5. The fear of performing poorly is what motivates me.

6. My goal this semester is to avoid performing poorly compared to other students.

7. I'm afraid that I may not understand the content of my courses as thoroughly as I'd like.

8. I worry that I may not learn all that I possibly could this semester.

9. I am definitely concerned that I may not learn all that I can this semester.

10. Completely mastering the material in my courses is important to me this semester.

11. I want to learn as much as possible this semester.

12. The most important thing for me this semester is to understand the content in my courses as thoroughly as possible.

Finney and colleagues (2004) hypothesized that there would be four factors, based on the work on Elliot and McGregor (2001): performance approach, measured by variables 1–3; performance avoidance, measured by variables 4–6; mastery avoidance, measured by variables 7–9; and mastery approach, measured by variables 10–12. "Performance" goals are those in which students are motivated by a desire to do well in comparison to others. In contrast, "Mastery" goals are those in which students are motivated by a desire to understand the course content. "Approach" goals are concerned with reaching a goal, such as getting good grades, or learning material, whereas "avoidance" goals are concerned with escaping negative outcomes, such as performing poorly or failing to learn course material. Correlations among these variables are shown Table 13.3, in which I have highlighted the blocks of correlations among the variables hypothesized to measure the same factor. I have included the variables' standard deviations at the bottom of Table 13.3 for those interested in reproducing the analyses in this chapter. CFA software programs can create a covariance matrix from a matrix of correlations and a vector of standard deviations, thus allowing you to reproduce my covariance-based analyses.

TABLE 13.3. Intercorrelations among Goal Orientation Variables

	I1	I2	I3	I4	I5	I6	I7	I8	I9	I10	I11	I12
I1	1.00											
I2	.690	1.00										
I3	.702	.712	1.00									
I4	.166	.245	.188	1.00								
I5	.163	.248	.179	.380	1.00							
I6	.293	.421	.416	.482	.377	1.00						
I7	−.040	.068	.021	.227	.328	.238	1.00					
I8	.143	.212	.217	.218	.280	.325	.386	1.00				
I9	.078	.145	.163	.119	.254	.301	.335	.651	1.00			
I10	.280	.254	.223	.039	.066	.059	.018	.152	.129	1.00		
I11	.182	.202	.186	.012	−.008	.051	.052	.202	.177	.558	1.00	
I12	.112	.154	.128	.029	.021	.084	.160	.221	.205	.483	.580	1.00
Standard deviations	1.55	1.53	1.56	1.94	1.68	.172	1.42	1.50	1.61	1.18	0.98	1.20

Before beginning the example, it is necessary to comment on the use of the same dataset for both the EFA and CFA. It is not good research practice to conduct both EFA and CFA on the same dataset. In fact, methodologists (myself included) are quite vocal in their opposition to this practice. The reason is that using CFA to "confirm" a factor solution obtained through an EFA of the same data capitalizes on chance because the initial EFA will be fit to the idiosyncrasies of the sample data. If those same data are used for the CFA, the same idiosyncrasies that influenced the EFA structure will of course be present. This means that the EFA-derived CFA model will fit the data better than it would have fit data from another sample. Essentially, conducting an EFA and then "confirming" the solution with a CFA on the same set of data is the same thing as obtaining a t-test of two means, finding that mean one is higher than mean two, and then rerunning the t-test to test whether mean one is higher than mean two. There is no point to such a test: we already know the answer, so it is not really a test. The only "test" that is occurring here is, possibly, a test that our computer program is working properly.

Fortunately, the goal orientation dataset is quite large, with over 2,000 cases, so I was able to split the file in half. The analyses presented in Chapter 12 were based on one-half of the cases, and in this chapter I use the other half to conduct the CFA. Although such split half sampling does not provide information about how well the results might replicate in other samples, it does avoid the capitalization on chance described in the previous paragraph.

Model Specification

As in Chapter 12, I will skip the data preparation step for now because some of the issues involved in data preparation will be clearer after you are familiar with the

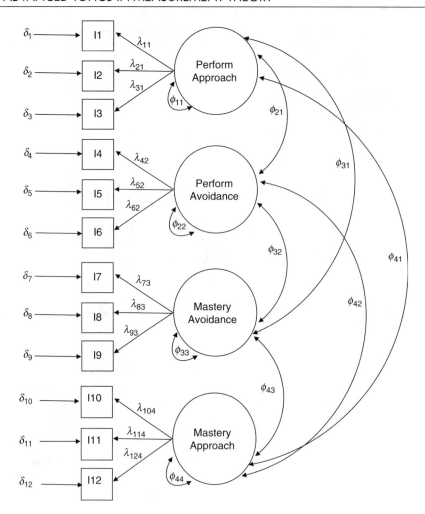

FIGURE 13.2. CFA model for the Achievement Goal items.

overall CFA process. I therefore begin with the *model specification* step. By model specification, I simply mean enumerating the various paths to be included (and not included)
in the CFA model. This is typically done by drawing a path diagram that shows all the
paths to be included in the model. Alternatively, the matrices corresponding to each
type of model parameter (loading coefficients, factor covariances, measurement error
variances and covariances) can be constructed. I illustrate both approaches. The CFA
path diagram for the Goal Orientation variables is shown in Figure 13.2. The model
specifies that variables I1 through I3 should load on the "Performance Approach" factor,
variables I4–I6 on "Performance Avoidance," I7–I9 on "Mastery Avoidance," and I10–I12
on "Mastery Approach," as specified by the theory put forth by Elliot and McGregor
(2001). Note that there are no cross-loadings specified; that is, all cross-loadings are
fixed to zero. In the form of a matrix, this loading pattern would be specified as

Variable	Papp	Pavoid	Mavoid	Mapp
I1	λ_{11}	0	0	0
I2	λ_{21}	0	0	0
I3	λ_{31}	0	0	0
I4	0	λ_{42}	0	0
I5	0	λ_{52}	0	0
I6	0	λ_{62}	0	0
I7	0	0	λ_{73}	0
I8	0	0	λ_{83}	0
I9	0	0	λ_{93}	0
I10	0	0	0	λ_{104}
I11	0	0	0	λ_{114}
I12	0	0	0	λ_{124}

The phi, or factor covariance matrix, is specified as

	Papp	Pavoid	Mavoid	Mapp
Papp	ϕ_{11}			
Pavoid	ϕ_{21}	ϕ_{22}		
Mavoid	ϕ_{31}	ϕ_{32}	ϕ_{33}	
Mapp	ϕ_{41}	ϕ_{42}	ϕ_{43}	ϕ_{44}

The symbols on the diagonal of the matrix (ϕ_{11}, ϕ_{22}, ϕ_{33}, and ϕ_{44}) represent the variances of the four factors. The symbols below the diagonal (ϕ_{21}, etc.) represent the covariances of the four factors. Because covariance matrices are symmetric, the values above the diagonal would be the same as those below and are therefore not typically shown. Finally, the covariance matrix of measurement errors, or θ_δ (theta-delta) matrix, is specified as

	δ_1	δ_2	δ_3	δ_4	δ_5	δ_6	δ_7	δ_8	δ_9	δ_{10}	δ_{11}	δ_{12}
δ_1	$\theta_{\delta 11}$											
δ_2	0	$\theta_{\delta 22}$										
δ_3	0	0	$\theta_{\delta 33}$									
δ_4	0	0	0	$\theta_{\delta 44}$								
δ_5	0	0	0	0	$\theta_{\delta 55}$							
δ_6	0	0	0	0	0	$\theta_{\delta 66}$						
δ_7	0	0	0	0	0	0	$\theta_{\delta 77}$					

Continued

	δ_1	δ_2	δ_3	δ_4	δ_5	δ_6	δ_7	δ_8	δ_9	δ_{10}	δ_{11}	δ_{12}
δ_8	0	0	0	0	0	0	0	$\theta_{\delta 88}$				
δ_9	0	0	0	0	0	0	0	0	$\theta_{\delta 99}$			
δ_{10}	0	0	0	0	0	0	0	0	0	$\theta_{\delta 1010}$		
δ_{11}	0	0	0	0	0	0	0	0	0	0	$\theta_{\delta 1111}$	
δ_{12}	0	0	0	0	0	0	0	0	0	0	0	$\theta_{\delta 1212}$

The variances of the measurement errors are shown on the diagonal of the matrix. In a typical CFA specification, these are the only parameters estimated in the θ_δ matrix; measurement error covariances are not usually included. This is indicated here by the presence of zeros on the off-diagonal. However, in CFA it is possible to specify that measurement errors covary. For example, if the measurement errors for items 1 and 2 were allowed to covary, this would be indicated symbolically as $\theta_{\delta_{21}}$ and diagrammatically by including a curved arrow between δ_1 and δ_2 in Figure 13.2.

Model Identification

I briefly discussed the issue of *model identification* in Chapter 12, in the context of factor rotations. In a nutshell, identification has to do with whether unique values for the parameters in Λ, Φ, and θ_δ can be obtained. In algebra, for example, it is not possible to solve the equation $2x + y = 10$ uniquely. There are many possible solutions, such as $x = 1$; $y = 8$ or $x = 5$; $y = 0$. However, none of these solutions is *unique* in the sense that it is better in some way than any other solution. In order to make the solution unique, we need more information, in the form of more equations. For example, if we also knew that $x = 2y$, then x must be 4 and y must be 2 because this is the only solution that will satisfy both equations. The solution $x = 4$ and $y = 2$ is therefore unique. Note that with two unknowns (x and y) and one piece of information ($2x + y = 10$) we were unable to solve uniquely for values of x and y, but with two unknowns and two pieces of information, we were able to do so. The former situation (more unknowns than information) is referred to as an *unidentified* or *underidentified solution*, whereas the latter situation (the same number of unknowns as pieces of information) is referred to as a *just-identified solution*. An *overidentified solution* is one for which there is more information than unknowns. With overidentified solutions, more than one solution is possible. This may seem problematic because in algebra we are used to having one and only one solution to a problem. However, consider the case of regression, in which there are typically many more pieces of information (in the form of data points or observations) than there are parameters to estimate (in the form of the intercept and the slopes, or *b*-values, for each X variable). Although it is possible to conduct a regression with two variables and two observations, you may recall that this would result in a perfectly fitting line, as in the following diagram.

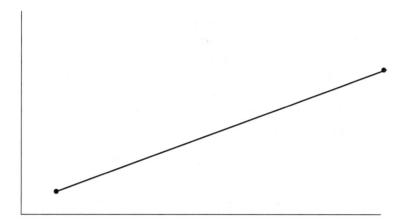

Regardless of where the two points fall, a straight line will always connect them perfectly. However, you may also recall that it is considered poor research practice to conduct a regression on two variables with only two observations because a straight line *has* to fit. This is not because the two variables are perfectly correlated in reality, but because the solution is just-identified. In a just-identified solution, not only is there only one solution, but that solution has to be exact (recall that this was the case with two unknowns and two equations as well). This means that just-identified models will always fit the data perfectly. What would an overidentified solution look like in regression? It would be the typical regression with many more observations than unknowns, as illustrated in the following diagram.

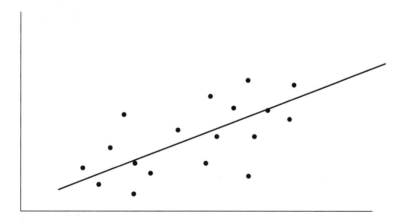

In this situation, a regression line can still be fit. However, the fact that all data points do not necessarily fall directly on the line allows us to *test* the line to determine how well it fits all the data points. Note that such a test was not possible when there were only two data points. Thus, instead of being problematic, overidentified solutions are desirable because they allow for tests of the parameter estimates that are obtained. In fact, these extra data points are what provide us with *degrees of freedom*, with which you are likely familiar.

Getting back to CFA, in that analysis and in path modeling in general, the model of interest must be either just-identified or overidentified. Solutions cannot be obtained for underidentified models. In CFA, our information is the number of variances and covariances in the variable covariance matrix, rather than the number of equations. Our unknowns are the parameter values in Λ, Φ, and θ_δ that we want to estimate. There must therefore be at least as many variance/covariance elements as there are parameter values to be estimated. Recall that a covariance matrix consists of the variances of the variables (on the diagonal) and the covariances of the variables on the off-diagonal. Because the elements below and above the diagonal are mirror images, only one set (below or above the diagonal) is counted. In any covariance matrix with v variables, there are $v(v + 1)/2$ variance and covariance elements. For the 12 Goal Orientation items, this is equal to $12(12 + 1)/2$, or 78 variance/covariance elements. This is the number of pieces of information available for a CFA of the Goal Orientation data. Turning to the number of unknowns, we can count up the parameter values to be estimated from the parameter matrices for Λ, Φ, and θ_δ. These are 12 loadings, 4 factor variances, 6 factor covariances, and 12 measurement error variances, for a grand total of 34 parameters to be estimated. The CFA model therefore *may be* overidentified. I say it "may be" because there are additional considerations in identifying a CFA model, which I discuss in the subsequent sections. Also, as I discuss later in this chapter, degrees of freedom for CFA models are tied to the identification process in that the degrees of freedom are calculated as the number of variance/covariance elements minus the number of parameters to be estimated. Thus, overidentified models will always have positive degrees of freedom, whereas just-identified models have zero degrees of freedom. As you may suspect, underidentified models have negative degrees of freedom.

Setting the Factor Metric

An additional identification issue that must be resolved for CFA models has to do with the factor variances. Recall that the factors are latent, which means that they are not directly measured and must be inferred from information on the observed variables. Unlike observed variables, latent variables have no real scale of measurement. For example, what is the "true" scale of a latent variable such as "propensity to purchase product X" or "leadership ability"? With well-known latent variables, such as intelligence, we often think of the latent variable as having the scale of measurement assigned to it. In the case of intelligence, that scale has a mean of 100 and an SD of 15 or 16. However, this is not its "real" metric, or scale of measurement, because latent variables, being latent, have no "real" metric. It is simply the metric that was assigned to a particular intelligence scale by its developer. Because latent variables have no inherent metrics, the researcher must assign metrics to them. Choosing such metrics is not as momentous a decision as it may sound, however, because such metrics are arbitrary and are typically chosen on the basis of convenience. The z-score metric with a mean of zero and standard deviation (and variance) of one is the standard choice for latent variables. Under this metric, the (unstandardized) loading coefficients would be interpreted as the number of units the variable score would change for a change of one *SD* in the factor. Also, the factor covariance matrix Φ would become a correlation matrix.

Another commonly used method of setting the factor metric is to "give" the factor the metric of one of the variables. This is accomplished by setting the loading of that variable to one. Typically, the variable chosen as the metric-giver (sometimes known as the *reference* variable) is the first variable loading on each factor. In Figure 13.2, this would be I1 for the first factor, I4 for the second, and so on. If factor metrics are set in this way, unstandardized loading coefficients would be interpreted as the number of units the variable score would change for a one-unit change in the factor, where the unit of the factor is the same as that of the metric-giving variable. If that variable were measured in pounds, or inches, or on a 1–5 Likert-type scale, the factor would have the same scale. Note that once the metric of the factors is set by either fixing their variances to one or by fixing one of their loadings to one, the parameters being set are no longer estimated. Thus, instead of having 34 parameters to estimate in our example model (12 loadings, 12 measurement error variances, 4 factor variances, and 6 factor covariances), there are now only 30. Setting the factor variances to one, there would be 12 loadings, 12 measurement error variances, *zero* factor variances, and 6 factor covariances (now factor correlations) to estimate, for a total of 30 parameters. Setting a factor loading to one for each factor, there would be 8 loadings, 12 measurement error variances, 4 factor variances, and 6 factor covariances to estimate, for the same total of 30. Note that either method of setting the factor metric will result in the same number of parameters to be estimated. The degrees of freedom for our model would be 78 (variance and covariance elements) minus 30 (parameters to estimate), or 48.

For the most part, the two methods of setting the factor metric will yield the same results. Models based on the two metrics will provide the same reproduced covariances, and therefore the same fit to the data (I discuss model fit in a later section). Although the two methods will yield different *unstandardized* parameter values, CFA programs also provide *completely standardized* parameter values, and these will be equivalent across the two methods. Completely standardized values are those in which both the observed variables and the factors are scaled as *z*-scores. In a completely standardized solution, loading coefficients represent the number of *SD* units the variable score would change for a change of 1 *SD* in the factor. Finally, the two methods of setting the factor metric will result in different standard errors for the parameter estimates. The reasons for this are somewhat technical, but interested readers are encouraged to consult Gonzalez and Griffin (2001) for an excellent explanation.

Back to Identification of a CFA Model

Although identification of CFA models does require that there are more pieces of information (variances and covariances of the observed variables) than unknowns (parameters to be estimated), this is a *necessary* but not *sufficient* condition, meaning that this condition must hold to have any chance of model identification, but that it does not

guarantee identification. Bollen (1989), in his classic text on structural equation modeling, provides the following three rules for the identification of CFA models:

1. Three or more variables load on each factor.
2. Each variable loads on only one factor.
3. Measurement error variances are not correlated.

These rules are sufficient, meaning that if they are met, identification is guaranteed. But
they are not necessary; a model might be identified if some of the conditions are not met.
For models that do not meet these three conditions, you should consult Bollen.

Taking the model in Figure 13.2 as an example, we see that each of the four factors
has three variables loading on it, each of the 12 variables loads on only one of the factors,
and the measurement errors are not correlated. Thus, our model will be identified, and
we can continue with estimation of the model parameters. However, note that these
rules are sufficient but not necessary, meaning that a model can still be identified if the
rules are not entirely met.

Estimation of Model Parameters

Table 13.2 shows the equations that would be obtained by using the tracing rules to
obtain the variances and covariances of the six variables from the model in Figure 13.1.
To solve for the parameter estimates, the quantities on the right-hand side of the equals
sign in each equation (involving the elements of Λ, Φ, and θ_δ) would be set equal to
the value of the observed covariance or variance on the left-hand side of the equals
sign. These equations would then be solved simultaneously to obtain the parameter estimates. Those who are familiar with matrix algebra may recognize this as the problem
of solving a system of equations. However, in most cases the system is too complex to
obtain a solution computationally. Instead, iterative methods are used. These methods
proceed as follows:

1. Iterations begin by inserting some reasonable "starting values" for the elements
   of Λ, Φ, and θ_δ.
2. The reproduced covariance matrix is then calculated using Equation 13.2.
3. The reproduced covariance matrix is compared to the observed covariance
   matrix of the variables.
4. If the two matrices are not sufficiently close, the estimates are adjusted, and
   steps 2–4 are repeated.
5. When the reproduced and observed covariance matrices are sufficiently close,
   the iterations are said to have "converged" and the process ends. The estimates
   from that step are taken as the final parameter estimates.

The difference between S, the observed sample covariance matrix, and $\Sigma(\hat{\theta})$, the model-implied covariance matrix (sometimes called the "reproduced" or "fitted" covariance matrix) forms the basis of a *discrepancy*, or *fit function*. In least squares regression, the sum of the squared distances from the observed data points to the regression line, known as the least squares criterion, is minimized during estimation. Analogously, in estimating CFA parameters, the discrepancy $\left(S - \Sigma(\hat{\theta})\right)$ is minimized. The symbol $\Sigma(\hat{\theta})$ is a common way of denoting the model-implied covariance matrix. The parameter estimates are sometimes collectively referred to as θ, so the notation $\Sigma(\hat{\theta})$ denotes the covariance matrix that is reproduced from the parameter estimates in θ. The notation $\left(S - \Sigma(\hat{\theta})\right)$ therefore represents the differences between the elements of the sample covariance and the reproduced covariance matrix.

Discrepancy Functions, Weight Matrices, and Estimation Methods

Several different discrepancy functions are used in CFA, and they lead to different forms of estimation. However, the basis for all of these functions is the discrepancy, or residual $\left(S - \Sigma(\hat{\theta})\right)$. The differences among the various discrepancy functions are due to differences in their *weight matrices*. The purpose of a weight matrix is, as its name implies, to weight the elements of the discrepancy function $\left(S - \Sigma(\hat{\theta})\right)$. Specifically, the squared discrepancies are weighted by the inverse of a weight matrix in such a way that their sum is minimized. A chi-square statistic can then be obtained as $(n - 1)F$, where n is the sample size and F is the minimum value of the (weighted) discrepancy function.

Why Weight?

You may wonder why weighting is needed. In general, weighting is done to compensate for some adverse characteristic of the observed data. For example, you may recall that in ordinary least squares (OLS) regression, the variability of a variable (Y) is assumed to be the same at all values of another variable (X). In other words, Y values are not more spread out at some values of X than at others. This is the assumption of homoscedasticity. However, what if this assumption does not hold? In this case, prediction will be less accurate for some X values than others. *Weighted least squares* (WLS) estimation gets around this problem by weighting each residual, or discrepancy between Y and $\hat{Y}$, by the inverse of its variance. Residuals with large variances are given small weights, and residuals with small variances are given larger weights. This results in regression coefficients that will yield the smallest sum of the (weighted) squared residuals and the smallest standard errors of estimate (see Cohen, Cohen, West, & Aiken, 2003, pp. 146–147).

CFA estimation methods use analogous types of weighting, and differences in weight matrices result in different types of estimation. Although a full discussion of estimation methods is beyond the scope of this chapter, I briefly discuss some commonly used forms of estimation. Table 13.4 provides information on the weight matrices for each of the four estimation methods discussed, along with brief comments on their use. Interested readers should consult sources such as Finney and DiStefano (2013) and

TABLE 13.4. Summary of CFA Estimation Methods

Estimation method	Weight matrix	Comments
Unweighted least squares (ULS)	$W = I$; the weight matrix is the identity matrix	Because the weight matrix is an identity matrix, all residuals are weighted equally. This can cause problems if variables are on very different scales.
Generalized least squares (GLS)	$W = S$; the weight matrix is the sample covariance matrix	Research has shown that GLS can result in biased parameter estimates and inaccurate assessment of model fit if the model is misspecified.
Maximum likelihood (ML)	$W = \Sigma(\hat{\theta})$; the weight matrix is the reproduced covariance matrix	Research has shown that ML estimates and model fit indices will be more accurate than those from GLS estimates if the model is misspecified.
Weighted least squares (WLS), also referred to as asymptotically distribution-free (ADF)	$W =$ asymptotic covariance matrix of the observed sample covariances. This matrix takes non-normality of the variables (specifically, nonzero kurtosis) into account.	This method was developed to yield unbiased estimates, standard errors, and fit index values for data that are non-normally distributed. However, research has shown that, unless the sample size is very large (at least 2000), WLS will yield biased parameter estimates, standard errors, and fit index values.

Finney, DiStefano, and Kopp (2016) for more information on estimation methods in CFA and SEM.

Estimation Methods

Unweighted Least Squares Estimation

Unweighted least squares (ULS) estimate is analogous to OLS estimation in regression. In ULS, the simple sum of the squared discrepancies between S and $\Sigma(\hat{\theta})$ is minimized. The weight matrix is the *identity matrix*, which serves as a number "1" in matrix algebra. This means that each of the squared discrepancies is weighted equally, as in OLS. The main problem with this approach is that, if some variables have much larger metrics than others, they will also tend to have larger residuals. These larger residuals will receive more weight in the solution due to their larger magnitude, so that the final parameter values may be driven more by the variables with larger metrics. As an example, if systolic and diastolic blood pressure, waist circumference, and a measure on a 1–5 Likert-type scale were used as indicators of the latent variable "metabolic syndrome," residuals involving the Likert-scaled variable would have less weight simply because that variable is on a smaller metric.

Another disadvantage of ULS is that it is not as *efficient* as the other estimation methods to be described. In statistics, *efficiency* refers to the amount of sampling variability associated with an estimator. Estimators that are more efficient will have smaller standard errors, indicating that the parameter estimates will be more tightly clustered around their population values. Efficiency is therefore a good property for an estimator to possess because greater efficiency translates into smaller standard errors and more precise estimates. And because standard errors are typically the denominators of test statistics, greater efficiency means larger values of test statistics. Finally, greater efficiency means that the confidence intervals around parameter estimates will be smaller, indicating that we have zeroed in more closely on the parameter value.

Although not as efficient as other estimation methods, ULS parameter estimates are *consistent*, which means that as sample size increases the values of the sample statistics get closer and closer to the value of the population parameter. Thus, for example, as sample size increases, values of the estimated loadings will become closer and closer to values of the population loadings. Finally, one advantage of ULS over other methods of estimation is that it will often converge to yield parameter estimates when other methods will not. Recall from the earlier discussion that CFA estimation methods typically work in an iterative fashion, systematically improving the parameter estimates until no further improvements can be made. At this point, the estimation is said to have converged. In some cases, however, estimation does not converge, and a final set of estimates cannot be obtained. Such *nonconvergence* problems can be due to a model that is simply not right for the data, or there can be problems with the data, such as influences of outliers or a sample size that is too small. ULS estimation is less prone to such nonconvergence problems and can therefore be used for situations in which other estimation methods fail to converge. Researchers can then use the ULS estimates in a diagnostic manner in trying to identify the source of the convergence problem (see Wöthke, 1993, for more detail).

Generalized Least Squares Estimation

Generalized least squares (GLS) estimation is similar to ULS, except that the squared discrepancies between the observed and reproduced covariances are weighted by the observed variances and covariances. That is, the observed covariance matrix S is used as the weight matrix. The advantage of this type of weighting is that it adjusts for differences in metrics among the variables. Like ULS, GLS is a consistent estimator, but GLS has the advantage of being more efficient (e.g., having smaller standard errors) than ULS. However, recent studies have found that when the CFA model is misspecified, GLS can produce biased parameter estimates and inaccurate measures of the goodness-of-fit of the overall model. A *misspecified* model is one in which the model is incorrect in some way. For example, the model may specify the wrong number of factors, or it may specify a pattern of loadings that is not correct. For more information on the performance of GLS with misspecified models, you can consult the studies by Olsson, Troye, and Howell (1999) and Olsson, Foss, Troye, and Howell (2000).

Maximum Likelihood Estimation

Maximum likelihood (ML) estimation is by far the most widely used method of estimation for CFA. ML estimators are unbiased (e.g., they yield estimates that are, on average, neither too high nor too low), consistent, and efficient. The weight matrix for ML estimation is $\Sigma(\hat{\theta})$, the reproduced covariance matrix. Recall that during the iterative estimation process for CFA, new parameter estimates are produced at each iteration. It follows that a new reproduced covariance matrix ($\Sigma(\hat{\theta})$) is also produced at each iteration because the reproduced matrix is created from the parameter estimates. The upshot of using the reproduced matrix as a weight matrix is that, unlike GLS estimates, ML estimates are generally unbiased even if the CFA model is misspecified. This is because the weight matrix for ML is updated at each iteration and is therefore tailored to weight the residuals optimally.

As explained by Enders (2005), ML estimation does not work by minimizing the sum of the squared residuals as do ULS and GLS. Instead, ML attempts to find parameter estimates that are most likely to have produced the observed covariance matrix. Both ML and GLS estimation are based on the assumption that the observed variables are normally distributed.[3] The two methods described next were developed for situations in which this assumption does not hold.

Weighted Least Squares Estimation

Weighted least squares (WLS), sometimes called *asymptotically distribution-free* (ADF), estimation (Browne, 1984), was developed for situations in which the observed variables are not normally distributed. Theoretically, therefore, if the observed variables' distributions deviate from normality, this should not affect the parameter estimates or fit of the model when WLS estimation is used. The fit function for WLS estimation is similar to that of GLS in that it minimizes the sum of the (weighted) squared residuals. However, the weight matrix used in WLS estimation is more complicated than those for GLS or ML because it is designed to adjust for the effects of non-normality. It does this by including information about the level of kurtosis in the observed variables. If variables are normally distributed, all of the information necessary for estimation is contained in their variances and covariances. However, if variables are not normally distributed, the variances and covariances do not contain all the necessary information, and information about the variables' kurtosis must be added. This additional information is contained in the weight matrix for WLS, which is called the *asymptotic covariance matrix* (ACM). The ACM is much larger than the weight matrices used in GLS or ML estimation. In the latter forms of estimation, the weight matrices have v rows and v columns, where v is the number of variables. The ACM, however, has $v(v + 1)/2$ rows and columns. For a CFA with 20 variables, the ACM would be a 210×210 matrix, much larger than the

---

[3]Specifically, the *endogenous* or dependent observed variables are assumed to have a multivariate normal distribution. GLS estimation is actually based on the slightly weaker assumption that variables have no excess kurtosis (see Bollen, 1989, p. 114).

20 × 20 weight matrices for ML or GLS. The size of the weight matrix leads to some issues with WLS estimation. Because the weight matrix is so large, *very* large sample sizes are needed (at least 2,000 for even a small number of variables and 5,000 for more reasonably sized CFAs). If the sample size is too small, WLS will result in biased parameter estimates, poor fit to the data, and inaccurate standard errors (Bandalos, 2014; Chou & Bentler, 1995; Curran, West, & Finch, 1996). As if this were not bad enough, model fit indices from WLS, like those from GLS, may indicate that a model fits well when it is actually misspecified (Curran et al., 1996; Foss, Jöreskog, & Olsson, 2011; Olsson, Foss, & Troye, 2003; Olsson et al., 2000). So what is a poor researcher afflicted with non-normally distributed data and a small sample size to do?

Satorra–Bentler Adjustments

Fortunately, an ad-hoc method developed by Satorra and Bentler (1988) appears to work quite well with non-normally distributed data. This is not an estimation method per se but rather an adjustment that can be applied to existing estimators such as ML, GLS, and WLS to correct the chi-square goodness-of-fit statistic and the standard errors of model parameter estimates for the detrimental effects of non-normality. The adjustments to the chi-square test statistics and standard errors are known collectively as the Satorra–Bentler (S–B) scaled chi-square and robust standard errors. Studies have shown that, with non-normally distributed data, the S–B scaled chi-square appears to be a more accurate measure of how well the model fits than the (unadjusted) chi-square value obtained from ML estimation (Chou, Bentler, & Satorra, 1991; Curran, West, & Finch, 1996; Hu, Bentler, & Kano, 1992; Yu & Muthén, 2002). Similarly, the S–B robust standard errors have exhibited greater accuracy than ML standard errors when the variables have non-normal distributions (Chou & Bentler, 1995; Chou et al., 1991). Based on this research, the S–B adjusted chi-square and standard errors are typically recommended for situations in which data are not normally distributed and a large sample size is not available.

A Note on Estimation with Noncontinuous Data

All of the estimation methods just described were designed for use with continuous variables. If variables are measured dichotomously (e.g., yes/no; agree/disagree; right/wrong) or are measured on a response scale with only a few categories (sometimes referred to as a *coarsely categorized* scale), these estimation methods will yield biased parameter estimates and standard errors and incorrect measures of model fit. How many categories are too few? In general, research in this area suggests that if there are five or more ordered categories on the response scale, there will be little bias in the measures of model fit and parameter estimates (Bandalos, 2014; Dolan, 1994; Flora & Curran, 2004; Muthén & Kaplan, 1985; Rhemtulla, Brosseau-Liard, & Savalei, 2012). Thus, many methodologists argue that data based on five or more categories can be treated as continuous, with little loss of information. With four or

TITLE:	CFA of goal orientation data;
DATA:	file is goal2.dat;
	format is free;
VARIABLE:	names are i1 i2 i3 i4 i5 i6 i7 i8 i9 i10 i11 i12;
MODEL:	perfapp by i1 i2 i3;
	peravoid by i4 i5 i6;
	masavoid by i7 i8 i9;
	masapp by i10 i11 i12;
OUTPUT:	sampstat stand residual;

FIGURE 13.3. M*plus* syntax for CFA of the Goal Orientation data.

fewer categories, however, specialized measurement models should be used. One of these is the *item response theory* (IRT) model, discussed in Chapter 14. Estimation methods for noncontinuous data exist for CFA but are beyond the scope of this chapter. I refer you to the chapters by Finney and DiStefano (2013) for more information on CFA estimation methods for noncontinuous data.

Example of Model Estimation

I illustrate the process of estimation using the Goal Orientation data. The model, shown previously in Figure 13.2, consists of four factors: Performance Approach, Performance Avoidance, Mastery Avoidance, and Mastery Approach, each measured by three variables. The four factors are hypothesized to intercorrelate, and there are no covariances among errors posited. Armed with this information, I used the M*plus* program (Muthén & Muthén, 1998–2010) to estimate the model. M*plus* is a popular program for SEM analyses, but many other programs are available, including LISREL (Jöreskog & Sorböm, 2006), EQS (Bentler, 2004), and freeware programs available through the R statistical package such as *lavaan* and OpenMx. My purpose in this chapter is not to introduce you to statistical software, but rather to explicate the concepts underlying CFA. I include the M*plus* code in Figure 13.3 to give you a sense of how such analyses are specified. Those interested in an introduction to the M*plus* program should consult the book by Byrne (2011).

I first note some general characteristics of M*plus* syntax. Note that each command must end in a semicolon. The words at the beginning of each line (TITLE, etc.) are commands and must be spelled exactly as indicated and followed with colons (:). Commands need not be written in capital letters; I do so here only to set them off. The TITLE line is optional, and simply causes the title following the command to be printed at the top of the output. Data must be read from a separate (external) file (my data are in a file called "goal2.dat"). I find it easiest to write data out as tab-delimited. In this format, values for each variable are separated by spaces (indicated by the statement "format is free"). This is the easiest format to read into M*plus*. If data are not delimited by spaces, the user must provide a Fortran format statement.

	Estimate	S.E.	Est./S.E.	Two-tailed P-value
PERFAPP BY				
I1	0.812	0.014	58.457	0.000
I2	0.850	0.013	65.661	0.000
I3	0.850	0.013	66.189	0.000
PERAVOID BY				
I4	0.591	0.027	22.029	0.000
I5	0.526	0.030	17.572	0.000
I6	0.797	0.024	32.857	0.000
MASAVOID BY				
I7	0.462	0.029	16.163	0.000
I8	0.855	0.021	41.273	0.000
I9	0.756	0.021	35.574	0.000
MASAPP BY				
I10	0.691	0.022	30.834	0.000
I11	0.811	0.020	40.333	0.000
I12	0.708	0.022	32.591	0.000
PERAVOID WITH				
PERFAPP	0.523	0.031	16.685	0.000
MASAVOID WITH				
PERFAPP	0.238	0.035	6.722	0.000
PERAVOID	0.502	0.034	14.563	0.000
MASAPP WITH				
PERFAPP	0.301	0.035	8.610	0.000
PERAVOID	0.086	0.041	2.094	0.036
MASAVOID	0.297	0.036	8.139	0.000

FIGURE 13.4. Completely standardized parameter estimates from Goal Orientation data.

VARIANCES

PERFAPP	1.000	0.000	999.000	999.000
PERAVOID	1.000	0.000	999.000	999.000
MASAVOID	1.000	0.000	999.000	999.000
MASAPP	1.000	0.000	999.000	999.000

RESIDUAL VARIANCES

I1	0.341	0.023	15.148	0.000
I2	0.278	0.022	12.629	0.000
I3	0.278	0.022	12.734	0.000
I4	0.651	0.032	20.560	0.000
I5	0.723	0.032	22.930	0.000
I6	0.364	0.039	9.409	0.000
I7	0.787	0.026	29.850	0.000
I8	0.269	0.035	7.608	0.000
I9	0.429	0.032	13.357	0.000
I10	0.522	0.031	16.864	0.000
I11	0.342	0.033	10.491	0.000
I12	0.498	0.031	16.191	0.000

FIGURE 13.4. Continued

In the VARIABLE command, I provide the names of the 12 variables. Names must be eight characters or fewer. It is crucial that the variable names are in the same order as the variables in the external data file because the program will assume that this is the case. If they are not, any subsequent references to the variable names will result in the wrong variable being used. The MODEL command specifies the CFA model. Here, the "BY" keyword indicates "measured by." The statement "perfapp by i1 i2 i3;" indicates that the variables i1, i2, and i3 should load on the factor perfapp. Note that another function of this set of statements is to provide names for the factors.

Finally, the OUTPUT command specifies that the sample statistics (sampstat), the standardized solution (stand) and the model residuals (residual) should be printed in the output. The sample statistics consist of the variable means and their covariance and correlation matrices. The model residuals are the differences between each observed covariance and its corresponding reproduced covariance. By default, M*plus* prints the unstandardized parameter estimates rather than the standardized estimates. Unstandardized estimates are analogous to *b*-values in regression, whereas standardized estimates are analogous to beta-values. Because standardized values are typically obtained from EFA solutions, researchers typically report CFA parameter estimates in standardized format as well. The completely standardized parameter estimates (referred to as STDYX Standardization in M*plus*) for the Goal Orientation data are shown in Figure 13.4.

R-SQUARE

Observed variable	Estimate	S.E.	Est./S.E.	Two-tailed P-value
I1	0.659	0.023	29.228	0.000
I2	0.722	0.022	32.830	0.000
I3	0.722	0.022	33.094	0.000
I4	0.349	0.032	11.015	0.000
I5	0.277	0.032	8.786	0.000
I6	0.636	0.039	16.429	0.000
I7	0.213	0.026	8.082	0.000
I8	0.731	0.035	20.637	0.000
I9	0.571	0.032	17.787	0.000
I10	0.478	0.031	15.417	0.000
I11	0.658	0.033	20.167	0.000
I12	0.502	0.031	16.295	0.000

FIGURE 13.5. R^2 values for the Goal Orientation data.

The values in the columns are, in order from left to right, the (completely standardized) parameter estimate ("estimate"), the standard error of the parameter estimate (S.E.), the value of the z-test that the parameter value is equal to zero (the parameter estimate divided by its standard error, Est/S.E.), and the two-tailed p-value associated with the z-test.

The first four sets of values are the factor loadings, indicated by the keyword BY. These values are all reasonably high, indicating that the variables relate fairly strongly to the factors. The relations among the factors are shown next. In Mplus, the keyword "with" indicates a correlation or covariance. Because this is a standardized solution, these values are correlations. As might be expected from theory, the two Performance factors (performance approach and performance avoidance) are correlated most highly, followed by the two Avoidance factors (mastery avoidance and performance avoidance). The mastery approach and performance avoidance factors are least correlated. The four factor variances are shown next. These are all equal to 1.0 because of the standardization. Finally, the measurement error variances (termed *residual variances* in Mplus) are shown. In a completely standardized solution, these are equal to $1 - \lambda^2$ (one minus the squared loading) for each variable. Taking I2 as an example, 1.0 minus its squared loading ($.85^2 = .7225$) equals its measurement error variance (.278), within rounding error. This must be the case because the squared loading and the measurement error variance account for all of the variance in a variable and so must sum to the variance of that variable. In a completely standardized solution, the variance of each variable is set to 1.0, so the sum of the squared loading and the measurement error variance must be equal to 1.0. It follows that the measurement error variance must be equal to $1 - \lambda^2$.

The z-tests of the factor loadings are not particularly strong indications of the variable's strength as a measure of the factor. This is because they simply test whether the loading is equal to zero, which is quite a low standard. More useful in this regard are the R^2 values. These are measures of the proportion of variance in a variable that is accounted for by the factor. In the completely standardized solution, these are simply the squared loadings of each variable. Figure 13.5 shows the R^2 values for the 12 Goal Orientation variables.

Model Testing

Model testing in CFA is the process of determining whether the model as a whole "fits the data." In CFA and structural equation modeling more generally, a model that fits the data is one in which the model-implied, or reproduced, covariances match the actual sample covariances. Table 13.2 showed the model-implied covariances for each variable pair from Figure 13.1. Calculation of the various measures of model fit in CFA is based on the discrepancies between the model-implied and sample covariances. As explained in the context of parameter estimation, these discrepancies form the basis of a *fit* or *discrepancy function*, which is simply the average of the squared differences between the actual and model-implied covariances. If the model fits the data perfectly, these discrepancies will be zero. In most applications, however, there will be small discrepancies due to sampling error, so that even if the model is correct in the population, it will not fit perfectly in the sample.

Of course, in most CFA applications, the model is not completely correct, even in the population. As noted previously, this is because the typical CFA model, in which each variable loads on only one factor, is very restrictive. If you have conducted EFAs or have read Chapter 12, you are aware that variables rarely have the decency to load on only one factor but instead often spread themselves willy-nilly across multiple factors. In CFA, however, all of these cross-loadings are forced to be exactly zero. Although this is the primary cause of lack of fit, or misspecification, in most CFA models, many other misspecifications are common as well. These include specifying an incorrect number of factors and specifying that measurement error covariances are zero when they are not. However, the fact that it is difficult to obtain good fit for CFA models does not mean that researchers can simply ignore the poor fit of a model. On the contrary, poor model fit means that the model as specified is not able to fully explain the covariation among the variables. Researchers should therefore make every effort to determine why the model failed to fit. Such investigations will lead to a better understanding of how the variables are related, which is, after all, the purpose of conducting factor analytic research in the first place. The fit indices discussed in this section are known as *global fit indices* because they assess the fit of the model as a whole. If the model fails to fit, researchers must use information on *local fit* to determine the source(s) of this lack of fit.

The last, but certainly not least, reason to assess fit is that an ill-fitting model is misspecified, and misspecified models result in biased parameter estimates. This is somewhat similar to a multiple regression analysis in which some important predictors have been omitted. If these predictors were added into the model, parameter (b or *beta*) values for the variables in the initial analysis would likely change. The initial set of parameter values would thus be biased. The same thing is true in CFA modeling. If the model is misspecified, parameter estimate bias is likely.

Assessment of Fit in CFA

The original fit statistic is the chi-square test. As noted in the previous section on estimation, this test is computed in CFA as

$$\chi^2 = (n-1) \times F \qquad (13.3)$$

where n is the sample size[4] and F is the minimum value of the discrepancy function. If the model fits perfectly, F, and therefore the chi-square value, will be zero. The chi-square test is one of the only measures of fit that has an inferential test associated with it. That is, the chi-square test can be used to test the null hypothesis $H_0 : \Sigma = \Sigma(\hat{\theta})$, or that, in the population, the observed covariance matrix Σ is equal to the model-implied matrix $\Sigma(\hat{\theta})$. Thus, the null hypothesis states that the model fits. If the value of the chi-square statistic is greater than the chi-square critical value, based on the degrees of freedom for the model (the calculation of which was discussed previously), the null hypothesis that the model fits the data is rejected. Note that, unlike the case with other statistical tests, in CFA model testing the hoped-for decision is a failure to reject, as this would mean that the model fits the data. Rejection of the null hypothesis indicates that the model does not fit.

The utility of the chi-square test of fit has been, and continues to be, hotly debated in the SEM literature (for a widely cited installment of this debate, see the entire issue of *Personality and Individual Differences*, 2007, 42(5)). Briefly, the debate has to do with the extent to which the chi-square statistic should be relied upon for assessment of model fit. Researchers at one end of the debate spectrum argue that the chi-square statistic is the only fit index that rigorously tests the fit of the model, and therefore it is the only fit index that should be considered. Researchers at the other end of the spectrum feel that the chi-square test is overly rigorous and that other indices, described here, are more useful in assessing model fit. The truth, as in most debates, is probably somewhere in between. I agree with Kline (2011) who urges researchers to be their "model's toughest critic" (p. 191) by holding to high standards of model fit. At the same time, Kline notes that researchers should use their judgment and knowledge of the theory underlying their models to make sense of the variety of information on model fit provided by most computer programs.

---

[4] Although $(n-1)$ is used in most SEM programs, the M*plus* program calculates the chi-square index using n.

Criticisms of the Chi-Square Statistic

One of the main criticisms of the chi-square statistic is that it tests the hypothesis that the model fits perfectly in the population ($H_0 : \Sigma = \Sigma(\hat{\theta})$). However, MacCallum (1990), among others, has noted that it is unlikely that models will fit perfectly. You need only think about weather or economic forecasting models to realize that human knowledge has not yet reached the point at which specification of a perfect model is possible. In the social sciences, it is difficult to think of any area in which researchers would claim to completely understand the vagaries of human behavior. Thus, a more reasonable claim is that models fit only approximately.

Another issue with the chi-square test statistic is that, because it is computed as $n-1$ (or n) times F, it is highly dependent on sample size. With samples of the size needed to estimate CFA models, even small discrepancies between S and $\Sigma(\hat{\theta})$ could be statistically significant. Of course, this is true of all statistical tests and is one reason that effect sizes should be reported. In the case of CFA model testing, however, the dependence of the chi-square statistic on sample size results in a great deal of power to reject the null hypothesis. But recall that this is a hypothesis that the researcher does not want to reject. This so-called reversal of the null and alternative hypotheses, coupled with the influence of sample size, typically results in a very high level of power. This can result in rejection of models due to levels of misspecification that are so small researchers may consider them negligible. A final issue with the chi-square statistic is that it is based on the assumption that the variables are normally distributed (or, more correctly, that they follow a multivariate normal distribution; more on this in a later section). If this assumption does not hold, the chi-square value will be too high, and the researcher will be more likely to conclude that the model does not fit.

Fit Indices

These issues do not exempt researchers from paying attention to the chi-square statistic. However, such issues have resulted in what sometimes seems to be an entire cottage industry for the production of other *fit indices*. Of these, I discuss the *standardized root mean square residual* (SRMSR), the *root mean square error of approximation* (RMSEA; Steiger, 1990), and the *comparative fit index* (CFI; Bentler, 1990). I have chosen these indices from among the many possible ones because they have performed well in widely cited simulation studies (Hu & Bentler, 1998, 1999; but see critiques of these studies by Fan & Sivo, 2005, 2007; Sivo, Fan, Witta, & Willse, 2006).

The SRMSR is an intuitively appealing measure of fit, as it is calculated directly from the discrepancies between S and $\Sigma(\hat{\theta})$. Specifically, the root mean square residual (RMSR) is the square root of the average of the squared discrepancies. Because S and $\Sigma(\hat{\theta})$ are covariance matrices, however, the discrepancies are in a covariance metric, making the RMSR difficult to interpret. To solve this problem, a standardized version, (the SRMSR) is computed by transforming both S and $\Sigma(\hat{\theta})$ into correlation matrices, thus putting the SRMSR into a correlation metric. SRMSR values of 0 indicate no discrepancy, and increasingly higher values indicate increasingly greater levels of average discrepancy between the two matrices. Hu and Bentler (1999) stated that SRMSR values ≤ .08 generally indicate acceptable fit of a model, and values ≤ .05 are sometimes taken to indicate "good" model fit. However, as Kline (2011) states, researchers must keep in mind that the SRMSR is the *average* residual, so some residuals might be much larger. Programs that estimate CFA models will print out the full matrix of $S - \Sigma(\hat{\theta})$ discrepancies. Researchers should examine these discrepancies to determine which of the variable covariances result in the greatest values. Doing so can help researchers to determine the source of model misfit.

The RMSEA (Steiger, 1990) is based on the *noncentrality parameter* $\chi^2 - df$. If a model fits well, its chi-square value should be equal to its degrees of freedom (*df*). As model fit worsens, the model's chi-square value increases relative to its degrees of freedom, and the noncentrality parameter increases. The RMSEA attempts to balance model fit as measured by the noncentrality parameter, with *parsimony*, operationalized as the model degrees of freedom. The reason for incorporating parsimony is that a model can be made to fit better by arbitrarily adding in more parameters (recall that a just-identified model will always fit perfectly). Thus, any model can be made to fit well by simply adding more parameters. As more parameters are added to a model, the model's degrees of freedom decrease, so the RMSEA "penalizes" models by dividing the noncentrality parameter (representing model fit) by its degrees of freedom (representing parsimony). The full formula is

$$\text{RMSEA} = \sqrt{\frac{\chi^2 - df}{df(n-1)}} \qquad (13.4)$$

The formula in Equation 13.4 shows that the RMSEA will equal zero if a model's chi-square value equals its degrees of freedom (e.g., if a model fits well). As a side note, it is possible for a model's chi-square value to be less than its degrees of freedom. If this happens, the quantity in the numerator is set to zero. The denominator of the formula shows that the RMSEA will decrease as model degrees of freedom, sample size, or both increase. Remember that more model degrees of freedom mean fewer model parameters, so this part of the formula penalizes models with more parameters. Small values of the RMSEA indicate good fit, and larger values indicate poor fit. Browne and Cudeck (1993) have suggested that values of ≤ .05 indicate good model fit. Hu and Bentler (1999) have suggested values of ≤ .06. You should keep in mind, however, that these suggestions are based on either the writers' experience or on computer simulation studies and cannot be expected to apply to every possible situation. Although they can used as guides, researchers should use all of the information available (such as model residuals) to detect possible sources of lack of fit.

The CFI (Bentler, 1990) is one of a class of indices that assess the relative improvement in the fit of one's model over that of a *baseline* model. The baseline model is one in which all of the parameters are set to zero, implying that the variables are all uncorrelated with each other. Thus, the baseline model is really more of a nonmodel, or the lack of a model. You may wonder why such a silly model would be chosen for comparison because at the very least we would hope our model would fit better than no model at all. As far as I can tell, there are two reasons. One is tradition; this is the model that has always been used. The second reason is that the null model must be one that can be calculated for a broad range of models, including every model in the structural equation modeling family, and not many baseline models would fill this bill. The silliness of the baseline model aside, the CFI is calculated as

$$\text{CFI} = 1 - \frac{\chi_M^2 - df_M}{\chi_B^2 - df_B} \tag{13.5}$$

Here, the subscripts M and B refer to the model of interest and the baseline model, respectively. You should recognize the quantity $\chi^2 - df$ as the noncentrality parameter, a measure of model (lack of) fit. Recall that a well-fitting model should have a chi-square value equal to its degrees of freedom. If the model of interest fits well, the quantity in the numerator of the right-hand side should equal 0, and the CFI will equal 1.0, its optimal value. To the extent that the model of interest does not fit, chi-square will be greater than degrees of freedom (although it is possible for it to be less; in this case, the noncentrality parameter is set to zero). Of course, the baseline model will likely not fit either, and it should fit much worse than the model of interest. The ratio after the minus sign should therefore be less than 1.0. CFI values range from 0 to 1.0 and can be interpreted as the relative improvement in fit of the model of interest over that of the baseline model. Hu and Bentler (1999) suggest that values of .95 indicate good fit. As before, however, this value is not set in stone and should be taken as a guideline rather than a firm rule.

Because these fit indices measure model fit in different ways, no one index should be used in isolation to assess model fit. Instead, information from all of the fit indices, including the chi-square, should be integrated in assessing model fit. If any one of the indices indicates a lack of fit, this possibility should be investigated. To illustrate the use of fit indices, I show the values obtained from the Goal Orientation data in Figure 13.6.

The chi-square value is significant, indicating the model does not fit the data. The RMSEA value is a bit over the .06 guideline suggested by Hu and Bentler (1999), and the CFI value is slightly below their suggested value of .95 for that index. Only the SRMSR suggests a good fit at .046. Taken as a whole, these values indicate that there is some misspecification in the model, though it may be minimal.

Chi-Square Difference Tests

A common test in CFA is one in which the fit of a model with more factors, such as a two-factor model, is compared to the fit of a model with fewer factors, such as a one-factor model. Although a model with more parameters will always fit better, it may not fit *significantly* better in a statistical sense. In practical terms, the inclusion of additional factors may not be justified if these do not result in significantly better fit, as this would not provide enough model-fit bang for the degrees-of-freedom buck. A chi-square

Chi-square test of model fit

Value	283.977
Degrees of freedom	48
P-value	0.0000

RMSEA (root mean square error of approximation)

Estimate	0.069

CFI/TLI

CFI	0.946
TLI	0.926

SRMR (standardized root mean square residual)

Value	0.046

FIGURE 13.6. Selected fit index values for Goal Orientation factor model.

difference ($\Delta\chi^2$) test can be used to compare the fit of two models, as long as the two models are *nested*. Models are nested if one model can be derived from another by setting one or more parameters to some fixed value (usually either 1.0 or 0). Taking the model in Figure 13.1 as an example, if I set the factor correlation to 1.0, the model becomes, for all intents and purposes, a one-factor model. Although researchers sometimes mistakenly treat models with different variables or different numbers of variables as nested models, this is incorrect. Nested models must be based on exactly the same variables (as well as the parameter restrictions just explained).

Although chi-square difference tests are widely used to determine if a model with more factors fits significantly better than a model with fewer factors, such tests are not quite as straightforward as is often assumed. As explained by Stoel, Garre, Dolan, and van den Wittenboer (2006), this is because such tests are based on setting a parameter at its *boundary*. Parameter boundaries are essentially limits on the value the parameter can have. For example, the boundaries for correlations are −1.0 and +1.0, because their values are limited to this range. When parameters are constrained at their boundary, the usual critical values for the chi-square test do not hold. Chi-square difference tests comparing models with different numbers of factors fall into this category because they involve setting one or more factor correlations to 1.0. Therefore, critical values for these comparisons must be obtained from a distribution called the chi-bar distribution. The usual chi-square critical values will be too high, resulting in a greater chance of Type II errors. These critical values can be quite complicated to work out, but Stoel and colleagues provide values for some common cases and give instructions on how to obtain the correct critical values for other situations.

TABLE 13.5. Hypothetical Chi-Square Difference Test Results for One- versus Two-Factor Models

Model	χ^2	df	$\Delta\chi2$
One factor	12	9	
Two factor	10	8	2 (1)

To obtain the difference chi-square values, first obtain the chi-square values and degrees of freedom for the two models to be compared. The chi-square difference value is then calculated as the difference between the two chi-square values with degrees of freedom equal to their difference in degrees of freedom.[5] The resulting chi-square difference value should then be compared to the appropriate critical value from the chi-bar distribution (Stoel et al., 2006). To make things more concrete, suppose that I estimated the two-factor model in Figure 13.1 and obtained a chi-square value of 10. This six-variable model has 8 degrees of freedom (you are encouraged to do the calculations as an exercise). Suppose that I then estimated a one-factor model, which resulted in a chi-square value of 12. The one-factor model would have one more degree of freedom than the two-factor model (obtained from setting the factor correlation equal to 1.0). Its degrees of freedom would therefore be 9. Armed with this information, I could perform a chi-square difference test of the hypothesis that the two models fit the data equally well. The alternative hypothesis is that the two-factor model fits significantly better than the one-factor model. Values for chi-square difference tests are often shown in tables, as illustrated in Table 13.5.

The chi-square difference between the one- and two-factor models is 2, with 1 degree of freedom. The correct critical value for this test, presented in Stoel and colleagues (2006), is 2.71. Note that this is quite a bit lower than the usual $\chi^2(1)$ critical value of 3.84. In this example, the obtained chi-square difference value of 2 is not greater than the 2.71 critical value, so I would not reject the hypothesis that the two models fit equally well. Put another way, the two-factor model does not fit significantly better than the one-factor model, so the one-factor model would be preferred on the basis of parsimony.

Respecification of the Model

As noted previously, CFA models often do not fit the data well. When this happens, researchers understandably seek to determine the reason. Developing an understanding of the reasons for lack of fit is good practice for at least two reasons. First, better understanding the relations among variables thought to represent a particular construct

---

[5]For some estimation methods, calculation of chi-square difference tests is not quite this simple. You should refer to references for the particular software being used, such as this note from the M*plus* website: http://www.statmodel.com/chidiff.shtml.

should lead to a better understanding of that construct. Such work can advance theory in the substantive area of interest. Second, study of lack of fit at the item level may reveal flaws in the items themselves. Such flaws can result in item-level responses that do not fully reflect the construct of interest, thus impinging on the measurement validity of the scales. A better understanding of how item selection and wording affect validity can, one hopes, lead to improvements in scale development practices.

Given such heady prospects for changing the world through a better understanding of CFA lack of fit, you may be surprised that methods used in this enterprise have been widely criticized. This is not as great a paradox as it seems, however, because criticisms of these methods are not leveled at their use in *understanding* sources of misfit. Rather, criticism is aimed at their use in *model modification* (Hutchinson, 1998; MacCallum, Roznowski, & Necowitz, 1992). Model modification is the practice of using the information obtained from investigations of the sources of lack of fit to add parameters to the model with the goal of obtaining a better fit. One problem with this practice is that it changes the original model tested by the researcher. And because in CFA the model represents one's research hypothesis, this amounts to changing one's hypothesis after having looked at the data. You may recall that this is frowned upon in statistics. In the following sections, I briefly discuss two sources of information that can help researchers understand the reasons for model lack of fit: *residuals* and *model modification indices*.

Model Residuals

One intuitive source of information on model lack of fit is the matrix of model residuals. These residuals are simply the discrepancies between S and $\Sigma(\hat{\theta})$. Because S and $\Sigma(\hat{\theta})$ are covariance matrices, the "raw" residuals are in a covariance metric, making them difficult to interpret. Therefore, researchers often look at the standardized residuals, in which the discrepancies are transformed into z-scores. Typically, standardized values > |2.0| are taken to be "large" and indicative of possible misfit. However, note that transformation of the residuals into z-scores involves dividing them by functions of their standard deviations. I point this out because with a large sample size, these standard deviations can be quite small, resulting in larger residuals. This fact should be kept in mind when examining the standardized residuals. I reproduce some of the largest standardized residuals from the Goal Orientation CFA in Table 13.6.

I have also included the wording of the items and the factor on which they were expected to measure so that I can demonstrate the process of thinking through the possible reasons that covariances between these items might be misspecified. In interpreting these residuals, keep in mind that a positive residual indicates that the covariance between the two items was *underpredicted* (the actual covariance was larger than the reproduced covariance), and a negative residual indicates that the covariance was *overpredicted* (the actual covariance was smaller than the reproduced covariance). Taking the covariance between I2 and I6 as an example of a positive residual (underpredicted covariance), note that the two items refer to "doing well compared to other students" and "not doing poorly compared to other students," respectively. Although the two items

TABLE 13.6. Selected Standardized Residuals from Goal Orientation CFA

Variable pair	Standardized residual	Item wording
I2, I3	−22.299	I2: It is important for me to do well compared to other students this semester. PAP I3: I want to do better than other students this semester. PAP
I5, I7	7.180	I5: The fear of performing poorly is what motivates me. PAV I7: I'm afraid that I may not understand the content of my courses as thoroughly as I'd like. MAV
I2, I6	5.594	I2: It is important for me to do well compared to other students this semester. PAP I6: My goal this semester is to avoid performing poorly compared to other students. PAV
I5, I6	−5.125	I5: The fear of performing poorly is what motivates me. PAV I6: My goal this semester is to avoid performing poorly compared to other students. PAV
I3, I6	5.079	I3: I want to do better than other students this semester. PAP I6: My goal this semester is to avoid performing poorly compared to other students. PAV
I4, I9	−5.034	I4: I just want to avoid doing poorly compared to other students this semester. PAV I9: I am definitely concerned that I may not learn all that I can this semester. MAV
I1, I10	4.900	I1: My goal this semester is to get better grades than most of the other students. PAP I10: Completely mastering the material in my courses is important to me this semester. MAP
I1, I7	−4.722	I1: My goal this semester is to get better grades than most of the other students. PAP I7: I'm afraid that I may not understand the content of my courses as thoroughly as I'd like. MAV
I11, I12	4.700	I11: I want to learn as much as possible this semester. MAP I12: The most important thing for me this semester is to understand the content in my courses as thoroughly as possible. MAP
I4, I5	4.495	I4: I just want to avoid doing poorly compared to other students this semester. PAV I5: The fear of performing poorly is what motivates me. PAV
I1, I3	4.252	I1: My goal this semester is to get better grades than most of the other students. PAP I3: I want to do better than other students this semester. PAP

are measures of different factors, they clearly have something in common: one's performance in comparison to that of other students. This, and the fact that both items contain the wording "compared to other students," have likely resulted in a higher correlation between the two than would be expected by the fact that they are loaded on different factors. Although some of the covariance between I2 and I6 can be accounted for by the correlation between their respective factors, this is apparently not sufficient to account for all of it.

The I4 and I9 covariance is one that was overpredicted, having a large negative residual. These items load on different factors; I4 loads on Performance Avoidance and I9 on Mastery Avoidance. From the correlation matrix in Table 13.3, I can see that the correlation between these two items is quite small—only .119. This is the lowest correlation among the three Performance Avoidance and the three Mastery Avoidance variables. Because the correlations among the other variables measuring the two factors are higher, the correlation between the two factors is relatively high (.502). However, because this correlation does not reflect the lower correlation between I4 and I9, it results in an overprediction of the relationship between these two variables. This can be seen by multiplying the values implied by the tracing rules: the two loadings are .571 (I4) and .756 (I9), so the reproduced correlation is .571 * .502 * .756. If the factor correlation of .502 had been lower, reflecting the low correlation between the two items, the reproduced correlation would have been closer to the two variables' actual correlation.

Although these reasons may explain the large residuals for these two pairs of items, there is really no way to know for sure. Understanding the reasons for large residuals involves some detective work in which the researcher must piece together knowledge about the theory on which the model is based, the way respondents might be expected to answer, information about the specific sample used, and knowledge of item writing principles, and put these all together to paint as complete a picture as possible. This may seem a lot of work, but the reward is a better understanding of the relations among the variables of interest, as well as possibly better item writing in the future.

Model Modification Indices

Model modification indices, often referred to as MIs, are measures of the amount by which the chi-square value would decrease if a particular parameter were added to the model. Thus, rather than being associated with a specific covariance between two variables, as are residuals, MIs suggest specific model parameters that are not in the model (such as cross-loadings or measurement error covariances) that could be added to improve model fit. One criticism of MIs is that they are based only on statistical considerations about what would result in decreases in the chi-square value. The parameters being suggested may not make any sense from a theoretical point of view. The fact that MIs suggest a parameter should be added to the model does not mean that researchers *must*, or even should, add that parameter. That is, researchers should simply treat MIs as another resource that can be used to understand the reasons for lack of fit. To motivate the discussion, I include some of the highest MIs from the Goal Orientation CFA in Table 13.7. Also included in this table are the *expected parameter change* (EPC) values. These are the *estimated* values of the suggested parameter, if it were to be added to the model. Note that I highlight the word "estimated" because the actual values obtained if the parameter is included in the model can be somewhat different. Kaplan (1990; Kaplan & Wenger, 1993) recommends reporting the EPC values along with the MIs.

TABLE 13.7. Selected Modification Indices from Goal Orientation CFA

Suggested parameter	Value of MI	Completely standardized EPC	Item wording
Measurement error covariance I5,I7	40.37	.214	I5: The fear of performing poorly is what motivates me. (PAV) I7: I'm afraid that I may not understand the content of my courses as thoroughly as I'd like. (MAV)
Measurement error covariance I5,I6	33.83	−.591	I5: The fear of performing poorly is what motivates me. (PAV) I6: My goal this semester is to avoid performing poorly compared to other students. (PAV)
Cross-loading of I1 on PAV	30.61	−.174	I1: My goal this semester is to get better grades than most of the other students. (PAP)
Measurement error covariance I4,I9	23.21	−.189	I4: I just want to avoid doing poorly compared to other students this semester. (PAV) I9: I am definitely concerned that I may not learn all that I can this semester. (MAV)
Cross-loading of I6 on PAP	22.76	.239	I6: My goal this semester is to avoid performing poorly compared to other students. (PAV)
Cross-loading of I10 on PAP	20.22	.135	I10: Completely mastering the material in my courses is important to me this semester. (MAP)

His rationale is that MIs can have different levels of power for different parameters in the model. Because of this, an MI can be high, even though the value of the parameter it suggests may be negligible. Thus, researchers should consider values of the MIs and the EPCs when trying to understand model lack of fit. Table 13.7 presents the completely standardized EPCs, which are analogous to the completely standardized parameter estimates discussed in a previous section.

When interpreting MI values, researchers should keep in mind the value of the model chi-square. For the Goal Orientation CFA, this value is nearly 284, which is highly significant. None of the MI-suggested parameters would, if added, decrease the overall chi-square enough to yield a nonsignificant value. Thus, none of the individual parameters, if added, would result in good model fit, as assessed by the chi-square test. You may notice that the MI results are fairly consistent with the information obtained from the residuals. For example, the largest MI is for a measurement error covariance between I5 and I7, which, if added, would result in a decrease in chi-square of over 40 and a completely standardized value of .214 for the suggested covariance. This parallels the residual results, in which the standardized residual for these items' covariance was quite large at 7.18. Although this residual was not the largest one found, keep in mind that the size of model residuals is influenced by the standard deviations of the two items as well as the $S - \Sigma(\hat{\theta})$ discrepancy between them. Hence, residuals and MIs will not typically result in the same rank ordering, although they will often relate to the same items.

The positive value of the I5, I7 standardized residual indicates that the covariance was underpredicted. The addition of a measurement error covariance with a positive value would add to the reproduced covariance of the two items, which is the reason for the MI-suggested parameter. That is, the MI is suggesting a way in which the covariance of the two items might be bumped up and better reproduced. Of course, that is not the only way this improvement could be accomplished. I5 could be allowed to cross-load onto I7's factor (MAV) or I7 onto I5's (PAV). Such cross-loadings would allow for an addition to the reproduced covariance between the two items. I point this out to illustrate one criticism of MIs, which is that they do not suggest the *only* parameter that might improve model fit or the most theoretically appropriate. Returning to the suggested measurement error covariance, it is instructive to examine the wording of the two items. At first blush, the reason these two items covary more than would be expected from the model may not be obvious. However, in inspecting the wording of all 12 Goal Orientation items, I noticed that I5 and I7 are the only ones that refer to fear or to being afraid. It may be that this reference to fear caused respondents to answer these items more similarly than had this reference not been used in both.

In contrast to the positive expected value of the measurement error covariance suggested by the MI for I5 and I7, the expected value for the MI-suggested measurement error covariance of I4 and I9 is negative in value. This is consistent with the negative standardized residual for these two items, which indicates that their covariance has been overpredicted. Thus, the MI is suggesting a way in which the covariance for these two items could be deflated by adding a negative value (the negative measurement error covariance) to the equation for reproducing their covariance.

As one final example, a large MI (30.61) was obtained for the cross-loading of the Performance Approach item I1 onto the Performance Avoidance factor. If allowed, the completely standardized expected value of the cross-loading would be –.174. This value is fairly negligible for a factor loading. If it resulted from an EFA, it would be dismissed as being below the .3 or .4 cutoff criteria that are commonly used. However, note from Table 13.6 that the standardized residual of I1 with I7 (which is an indicator of Performance Avoidance) is –4.722, indicating that the I1, I7 covariance is overestimated. The addition of a negative loading for I1 onto I7's factor would be a way to deflate this covariance and obtain a closer match between the actual and reproduced covariances. Again, this is not the only way to accomplish this goal and does not necessarily make sense theoretically. Statistically, however, it would "work" in the sense of reducing the model chi-square value, which is the objective of MIs.

Caveats in Using Residuals and MIs

A fair amount of research has been done on the use of MIs (Hutchinson, 1998; Kaplan, 1990; Kaplan & Wenger, 1993; MacCallum, 1986; MacCallum et al., 1992; Silvia & MacCallum, 1988). In general, researchers have found that adding parameters on the basis of MIs does not lead researchers to the true model in many cases. This was especially true if the initial model was badly misspecified and/or if the sample size was low (this varied across studies, but most researchers found that a sample size of at least 300–400 was necessary to obtain accurate results). In part, the poor performance of MIs is due to the fact that there is usually more than one parameter that could be added to "correct" the reproduced covariance between a pair of variables. For example, adding a cross-loading and adding a measurement error covariance may accomplish the same purpose. To complicate matters even further, the misspecification may be due to a combination of two or more parameters, necessitating the addition of multiple parameters. This can be quite difficult to detect. A related issue is that, if a parameter is added on the basis of a high MI and/or residual value, the other MIs/residuals are no longer accurate. If parameters are added to the model, the analysis must be rerun and new MIs/residuals obtained. These MIs/residuals will not be the same as those originally obtained because the addition of a parameter to the model will change things in the same way that the addition of a predictor to a regression model will change the original b- or beta-values.

Another problem with MIs is that adding parameters on the basis of either MIs or residuals capitalizes on chance. This is because, by looking at MIs and/or residuals and then adding in the suggested parameter(s), the researcher is changing her hypothesis on the basis of "data peeking." This is similar to a situation in which a researcher hypothesizes a mean difference on test scores between men and women, runs a t-test to determine which group has a higher mean score, and then states her research hypothesis. In such "research" no real hypothesis is being tested, and the usual p-values are not valid.

Having pointed out these issues, I return to my initial points about the use of MIs and residuals. If used cautiously, these statistics can provide information that can help researchers to better understand the relations among the variables being modeled and the reasons for lack of fit in the model. This information can result in a better understanding of both the theory underlying the construct being measured and the response patterns invoked by the items. Ultimately, such information can lead to enhancements of both theory and measurement practice. I therefore see no need to shun MIs/residuals. Instead, I encourage their use to these ends. I do, however, caution you to use such information carefully. I do not, in general, recommend that parameters be added on the basis of information obtained from residuals or MIs. On the rare occasions in which this might be justified, the respecified model must be treated tentatively until the utility of the respecification is confirmed using a separate dataset. Although the cavalier addition of parameters on the basis of MIs/residuals should be avoided, a suggested addition may sometimes make good theoretical sense. The researcher making such a modification would bear the responsibility for explaining how information from MIs/residuals was used to inform the addition and why the addition is theoretically justified.

DATA PREPARATION AND CFA ASSUMPTIONS

In this section, I get down to the nitty-gritty issues of data screening, sample size, and choice of variables to use in a CFA.

Normality of Variable Distributions

Unlike EFA, CFA is an inferential method, meaning that statistical tests of both parameters and the model as a whole can be obtained. Because of this, most estimation methods in CFA are based on the assumption that variables have a multivariate normal distribution. This assumption is stronger than the assumption that each variable's univariate distribution is normal. Although univariate normality is necessary for multivariate normality to hold, multivariate normality also requires that all linear combinations of the variables have normal distributions. As noted previously in the sections on estimation and model testing, violations of this assumption can result in underestimation of standard errors, inflation of chi-square values, and bias in other model fit indices. Researchers should therefore screen their data for both univariate and multivariate normality. Methodologists have suggested that values of univariate skewness and kurtosis values should be less than |2.0| (some researchers suggest a more liberal standard of less than |7.0| for kurtosis) and values of multivariate kurtosis such as Mardia's normalized coefficient should be less than 3.0. If levels of non-normality are outside these guidelines, the ADF estimation method or Satorra–Bentler adjustments should be used. For the goal orientation data, univariate skewness and kurtosis values were less than |2.0| for all variables, and the value of Mardia's normalized coefficient was 1.17, well below the upper guideline of 3.0. I therefore felt that the assumption of multivariate normality had not been (seriously) violated.

Variable Scales

As with EFA, the scales of the observed variables can also affect results. In particular, estimation methods such as ML and GLS are based on the assumption that variables are continuous as well as multivariately normally distributed. So-called coarsely categorized variables with few scale points can result in biased parameter estimates in CFA. Most important for CFA, factor loadings based on such variables are likely to be underestimated. However, the term *continuous* can be taken with a small grain of salt. Variables with five or more scale points will generally result in minimal bias. Researchers working with variables that have fewer than 5 scale points should consider the use of estimation methods specifically designed for such data. These include item response theory (IRT) methods (see Chapter 14) and specialized estimation methods within structural equation modeling (see Finney & DiStefano, 2013). The goal orientation items have 7 scale points, so I felt fairly comfortable in treating these as continuous data.

Outliers

Data should also be screened for outliers. This is because the presence of outliers can distort the factor structure of the data. A univariate outlier is a case with a variable score that is much higher or lower than the scores of other cases. These can be detected by examining the z-scores for each case. Multivariate outliers are cases with a *pattern* of variable scores that is different from that of the other cases. For example, an individual might respond positively to one item and negatively to another, whereas other respondents answer positively to both items. If the variables being analyzed are scale scores, the same type of pattern can occur. That is, if the prevailing pattern of responses on two scales represents a positive relationship (e.g., people tend to score high on both scales or low on both scales), a person who has a low score on one scale and a high score on the other would be an outlier. Of course, in CFA there are typically many variables, resulting in much more complicated patterns. Regardless of the number of variables, however, Mahalanobis D or D^2 can be used to identify multivariate outliers.

Once outliers have been identified, the difficult question is what to do about them. The answer depends on the nature of the outliers. If outliers are determined to be due to a data entry mistake or to random or other erroneous responding, cases with outlying responses can be deleted from the dataset. It is often difficult to make such determinations, however. In such situations, it is common for researchers to obtain results from data both with and without the outlying cases. If the results are similar, there is little reason to delete the outliers. If the outlying cases alter the results, however, it may be worth the researcher's time to consider why these cases do not follow the typical pattern. Assuming the outlying responses were made in good faith (e.g., no random responding or malingering), they represent interesting variations on the theoretically expected pattern of responses. As such, they may help researchers to extend or amend their theories.

In screening the goal orientation data, I found seven outlying cases. Given that the overall sample size was 1,022, I did not think it likely that these seven cases would have much of an effect on the results of my CFA. Just to be sure, however, I estimated the CFA model using a dataset in which the seven outlying cases were removed. As I expected, differences in the results were negligible. Parameter estimates differed only in the second decimal place (if at all), and the fit index values were virtually unchanged.

Missing Data

Missing data is another problem that is likely to come up in CFA analyses. Although listwise deletion (omitting a case with a missing value on any variable in the analysis) and pairwise deletion (omitting a case only from those statistics on which they have missing data) are commonly used approaches, most CFA software packages allow for more sophisticated approaches. A full description of these methods is beyond the scope of this chapter, but interested readers are encouraged to consult the book by Enders (2010) and the references therein. Briefly, however, the two "modern" approaches that are most widely used are so-called "full information" maximum likelihood (FIML) and methods based on *multiple imputation* (MI). In the FIML method, missing values are not *imputed* or estimated. Instead, parameter estimates are obtained from the information available from each case for the variables involved in the parameter being estimated. That is, each case provides information based on its nonmissing values. If a case has data on X1 and X2 but not on X3, it would contribute to estimation of the X1, X2 covariance, but not the

X1, X3, or X2, X3 covariances. In MI, regression-based methods are used to impute, or fill in, the missing values. Both methods assume that data are missing at random (MAR), meaning that the missing values for a variable do not depend on values of that variable. For example, if a respondent refuses to answer a question about alcohol consumption because he drinks so much he is embarrassed to respond, his response is *not* missing at random, because it depends on the value of the very thing being measured. However, if the person fails to answer because he is too young to drink and is afraid he will get into trouble for reporting that he does, his missing value is due to age, and not to the amount of alcohol he consumes. The missingness in that case would be considered MAR. I was fortunate in that the goal orientation data contained no missing cases, and thus no missing data treatment was necessary.

Sampling Method

Researchers should specify the sampling method that was used to obtain the data. Most commonly used computer packages for structural equation modeling analyses allow the researcher to specify sampling weights for data obtained via stratified sampling methods and allow for nested or hierarchical models that accommodate data obtained from clustered samples. Researchers using such sampling techniques should therefore employ the proper methodology.

Sample Size

With regard to sample size, the guidelines presented in Chapter 12 for EFA also apply to CFA. To refresh your memory, I summarize these guidelines here. These sample-size guidelines are based on computer simulation studies (Hogarty et al., 2005; MacCallum et al., 1999, 2001; Velicer & Fava, 1998), the major finding of which was that the sample size needed to obtain accurate parameter estimates depends on the level of communality of the variables, the number of variables per factor, and the interaction of these two characteristics. In the context of a typical CFA, in which variables are specified to load on only one factor, a variable's communality is simply its squared loading. With strong loadings (extrapolating from the studies cited, this works out to be at least .8) and three to four variables per factor, researchers can obtain accurate estimates of factor loadings with sample sizes as small as 100. Of course, loadings are typically lower than .8, so larger sample sizes are typically necessary. According to the studies by Hogarty and colleagues (2005) and MacCallum and colleagues (1999, 2001) a sample size of at least 300 would be needed if loadings were .7, and sample sizes of at least 500 would be necessary for lower loadings. However, these studies have also shown that more accurate estimates of loadings were obtained when the number of variables per factor was increased, even if the sample and loading size stayed the same. But the level of communality and the number of variables per factor interacted in such a way that, if communalities were high (averaging .6, or CFA loadings of at least .77), the number of variables per factor had little effect on accuracy of estimation. The rough guidelines just presented were obtained from three-factor solutions. With more factors, larger sample sizes are needed.

Researchers can obtain more precise estimates of the sample size needed for a CFA model of interest by using simple Monte Carlo, or simulation studies. Although they may sound daunting, such studies are fairly easy to do. Interested readers can consult Brown (2006, ch. 10), who devotes an entire chapter to this topic, and includes example syntax for popular structural equation modeling programs. As noted previously, the goal orientation dataset is quite large, and even after splitting it in half for the purpose of estimating both EFA and CFA, there were still over 1,000 cases in each half—a sample size that should be more than adequate based on any guidelines.

CFA-BASED RELIABILITY ESTIMATION[6]

As noted previously, CFA methods can be used to estimate a coefficient of internal consistency known as *coefficient omega* (McDonald, 1999). Most psychometricians consider omega to be more accurate than coefficient alpha as an index of internal consistency because it does not require the assumption of tau-equivalence. Box 13.2 shows the specifications for parallel, tau-equivalent, and congeneric measures in factor analytic terms. Recall that these levels are hierarchical in the sense that the highest level (parallel) requires the most similarity, whereas levels lower in the hierarchy require fewer things to be equal. In the CFA context, I specify whether loadings, error variances, or variables means are required to be equal for each model. (Although the variable means are often not of interest in CFA models, I include them for comparison to Box 7.1). In the last column of Box 13.2, I indicate the implication of these specifications for the model-implied covariance matrix. For example, because parallel measures have equal (unstandardized) loadings and error variances, they should result in equal reproduced variances ($\sigma_{ii}^2 = \sigma_{jj}^2$) and covariances ($\sigma_{ij} = \sigma_{i'j'}$) for all items. Both tau-equivalent and essentially tau-equivalent measures should have equal model-implied covariances, but because their error variances are not required to be equal, they may have different observed score variances. For congeneric measures, neither the observed score variances nor the covariances need be equal. Note that item means do not come into play in the equivalencies for variances and covariances, because they do not affect estimates of the variances and covariances. However, parallel and tau-equivalent measures must have equal item means, so I include tests of these in the section below.

Tests of Parameter Estimate Equivalence

As noted in the previous section, structural equation modeling software can be used to test assumptions such as tau-equivalence and parallelism. Running the M*plus* commands

---

[6] This section may be omitted without loss of continuity.

BOX 13.2

Properties of Parallel, Tau-Equivalent, and Congeneric Measures in Factor Analytic Terms

Type of measure	Loadings (λ)	Means (μ)	Measurement error variances (θ^2_δ)	Model-implied variances and covariances
Parallel	Must be equal	Must be equal	Must be equal	Variances must be equal; covariances must be equal
Tau-equivalent	Must be equal	Must be equal	May be equal or unequal	Variances may be equal or unequal; covariances must be equal
Essentially tau-equivalent	Must be equal	May be equal or unequal	May be equal or unequal	Variances may be equal or unequal; covariances must be equal
Congeneric	May be equal or unequal	May be equal or unequal	May be equal or unequal	Variances may be equal or unequal; covariances may be equal or unequal

in Figure 13.3 provides the results for a congeneric model. This is the "default" model in M*plus* and other programs and does not impose any equality constraints on the model parameters. Tests for tau-equivalence and parallelism can be obtained by making a few modifications to the M*plus* program. Note that the tau-equivalent and parallel models are nested within the congeneric model because they can be obtained from that model by constraining the loadings and/or measurement error variances to be equal. I illustrate the commands to impose such constraints in Figure 13.7. Strictly speaking, tests for tau-equivalence and parallelism should be based on a unidimensional model. Although the goal orientation model, having four factors, does not meet this requirement, the model is used here for the purpose of illustration. However, instead of testing for tau-equivalent and parallelism *across* factors, these properties are tested *within* each of the four factors, as illustrated in Figure 13.7.

The numbers within parentheses in the MODEL command indicate that the preceding parameters should all have the same value. For example, the syntax "perfapp by i1 * i2 i3; (1);" means that the loading estimates for i1, i2, and i3 on the Performance Approach factor should all be equal. Similar specifications for the other three factors

TITLE: test for parallelism/tau-equivalent of goal orientation data;

DATA: file is goal2.dat;
            format is free;

VARIABLE: names are i1 i2 i3 i4 i5 i6 i7 i8 i9 i10 i11 i12;
            missing all (8,9,10);

MODEL:
! The commands below set the loadings for each item equal to each other.
            perfapp by i1* i2 i3 (1);
            peravoid by i4* i5 i6 (2);
            masavoid by i7* i8 i9 (3);
            masapp by i10* i11 i12 (4);

! The next set of commands sets the means for each item equal to each other.
            [i1 i2 i3] (5);
            [i4 i5 i6] (6);
            [i7 i8 i9] (7);
            [i10 i11 i12] (8);

! The two sets of commands above (for loadings and item means) will provide a test of tau-equivalence;
! The next set of commands set the measurement error variances for items equal to each other.
Adding these commands to the two previous sets of commands will provide a test of parallelism;
            !i1 i2 i3 (9);
            !i4 i5 i6 (10);
            !i7 i8 i9 (11);
            !i10 i11 i12 (12);

! Because all of the loadings are estimated, the factor variances must be set to 1.0
            perfapp@1; peravoid@1; masavoid@1; masapp@1;
OUTPUT: sampstat residual stand modindices;

FIGURE 13.7. M*plus* syntax for tau-equivalent and parallel models.

follow. For tau-equivalent models, item means must also be equal. This equality is specified by adding the next set of commands, beginning with the line "[i1 i2 i3] (5);." In Mplus, placing variable names within square brackets indicates that means should be estimated. The asterisk after variable names i1, i4, i7, and i10 are included to override the Mplus default specification for setting the factor metric. Recall that there are two ways to do this: (1) set the factor variances(s) to 1.0 or (2) set the loading of one variable per factor to 1.0. Mplus uses the latter method by setting the loading of the first variable loading on each factor to 1.0. However, to test equivalence of the factor loadings I want to estimate all of these. Placing an asterisk after the name of the first variable for each factor overrides the default Mplus specification and allows all loadings to be estimated. Note that I now must specify that the factor variances should be set to 1.0, which I have done in the line beginning "perfapp@1." Inclusion of only these sets of MODEL commands will result in a test of tau-equivalence because the measurement error variances are allowed to differ across items by default. Adding the next four lines provides a test of parallelism. Similar to the loading commands, the syntax

TABLE 13.8. Chi-Square Differences Test Results for Congeneric, Tau-Equivalent, and Parallel Models

Model	χ^2	df	$\Delta \chi^2$ (df)
Congeneric	283.98	48	
Tau-equivalent	1371.05	64	1087.07* (16)
Parallel	1582.01	72	210.96* (8)

*$p < .0001$.

"i1 i2 i3 (5);" indicates that estimates of the measurement error variances for i1, i2, and i3 should all be equal.

Table 13.8 shows the chi-square difference tests for the congeneric, tau-equivalent, and parallel models. The chi-square value for the tau-equivalent model is significantly higher than that of the congeneric model, indicating that it fits significantly worse. This means that the loadings are not equal within factors and that tau-equivalence within factors is not supported. It is therefore not possible for the items to be parallel. However, the chi-square value for the parallel model, which adds equal measurement error variances, is significantly higher than that of the tau-equivalent model, so the measurement error variances within each factor are not equal in any case. These findings are not surprising because a quick look back at the parameter estimates in Figure 13.4 illustrates that loadings and measurement error variances within the four factors are quite different.

Calculation of Coefficient Omega

Given that the goal orientation items cannot be considered tau-equivalent even within a given factor, coefficient alpha will result in an underestimate of the reliability for these items. As noted previously, coefficient omega is a less restrictive index of internal consistency. However, use of coefficient omega does require that the items are unidimensional. This assumption also underlies coefficient alpha, although definitions of unidimensionality can be somewhat loose, as discussed in Chapter 8. For the purposes of illustration, I demonstrate the M*plus* syntax for coefficient omega using only one of the four goal orientation factors, thus satisfying the assumption of unidimensionality. Coefficient omega is based on the factor analysis model and uses estimates of the loadings and measurement error variances to calculate reliability. Specifically, the formula for omega is

$$\omega = \frac{\left(\Sigma \lambda_i\right)^2}{\left(\Sigma \lambda_i\right)^2 + \left(\Sigma \theta_{\delta_i}^2\right)} \tag{13.6}$$

The quantity in the numerator is the sum (across all items) of the loadings, squared (note that this is not the same thing as the sum of the squared loadings). This represents the

TITLE: coefficient omega for goal orientation data;

DATA: file is goal2.dat;
                format is free;

VARIABLE: names are i1 i2 i3 i4 i5 i6 i7 i8 i9 i10 i11 i12;

! The command below selects out the three Performance Approach items;
                usevariables = i7 i8 i9;

! The names in parentheses (P1, etc.) are used to provide names for the parameters;

MODEL: masavoid by i7*(P1);
                masavoid by i8-i9 (P2-P3);
                i7 – i9 (P4-P6);
                masavoid@1;

! The model constraint commands compute omega according to equation 3;

! The NEW command indicates that a new parameter is being computed;

MODEL CONSTRAINT:
                new (omega);
                omega = (P1 + P2 + P3)**2/((P1 + P2 + P3)**2 + P4 + P5 + P6);

! The specification "cinterval" on the OUTPUT line indicates that confidence intervals should be computed.

OUTPUT: cinterval;

FIGURE 13.8. M*plus* syntax to obtain coefficient omega.

part of the variance in each variable that is due to the factor, or the true score variance. The quantity in the denominator is the true score variance plus the sum of the measurement error variances ($\Sigma\delta_i^2$). The denominator therefore represents the total score variance. The formula for omega is thus consistent with the definitional formula of reliability as true score variance divided by total variance.

Figure 13.8 shows the M*plus* syntax used to obtain coefficient omega for the items on the Mastery Avoidance factor. As noted in the syntax in Figure 13.8, labels in parentheses are used to assign names to the various parameter estimates. The three loadings are labeled P1–P3, and the three measurement error variances are labeled P4–P6. These labels allow the parameter estimates to be used in the MODEL CONSTRAINT command to compute coefficient omega. Finally, the specification "cinterval" in the OUTPUT command indicates that confidence intervals for the parameter estimates, including coefficient omega, should be computed. This is useful because confidence intervals for reliability coefficients are not symmetric and are therefore difficult to compute by hand.

For these three Mastery Avoidance items, the omega value estimated by M*plus* was .749, with a 95% confidence interval of .723–.775. In contrast, the value of coefficient alpha was .719, illustrating that if measures are not (at least) tau-equivalent, alpha will underestimate the true level of internal consistency.

SUMMARY

Whereas in exploratory analyses researchers can specify, at most, only the number of factors, in confirmatory analyses researchers *must* specify all model parameters. This means that researchers conducting CFAs must have a good grasp of the theory underlying the measures to be analyzed. In addition, most methodologists recommend that confirmatory analyses be conducted only after preliminary exploratory work has been done on the measures of interest, such that researchers feel comfortable in their understanding of the factor structure. Of course, these are not strict rules. In some cases, theory may be sufficiently strong that researchers decide to proceed directly to CFA. In other cases, although many previous analyses of the measures may have been done, these analyses may have been inconclusive. In such situations, researchers may well decide to conduct more exploratory analyses.

In addition to specifying the model, researchers conducting CFAs must pay attention to the identification, estimation, and testing of the model. Identification of a model is the process of determining whether unique values of model parameters can be found. CFA models will be identified if (1) there are at least three variables measuring each factor, (2) each variable loads on only one factor, and (3) none of the measurement errors covary. Although these conditions are sufficient for identification, models can be identified if one or more of the conditions is not met. This should be determined on a case-by-case basis. Estimation is the process of solving for the model parameters. The most commonly used estimation method for CFA is maximum likelihood analysis, but I have also discussed unweighted and generalized least squares estimation, as well as asymptotically distribution free methods of estimation. Although maximum likelihood is the best choice in many situations, data characteristics such as non-normally distributed or noncontinuous variable distributions may dictate other choices.

Assessment of model fit is an important aspect of CFA for two reasons. First, lack of fit is a sign of model misspecification, and model misspecification can result in biased parameter estimates. Second, the model represents the researcher's theory about how the variables of interest are related, so a test of the model is tantamount to a test of this theory. Finding a lack of fit may indicate that the theory is in need of revision. Researchers faced with poorly fitting models may opt to use devices such as residuals or modification indices to help in understanding the reasons for misfit. I encourage researchers to use these devices to better understand the variable interrelations and the reasons for lack of fit. However, respecifying the model on the basis of these values using the same sample data is poor research practice. Researchers who want to respecify their models on the basis of residuals or MIs should conduct the respecified analyses on a separate sample and should only make those modifications that are theoretically defensible. Keep in mind that changing one's model represents a change in one's theory and should not be done lightly (if at all). Along these lines, guidelines for reporting the results of a CFA can be found in Bandalos and Finney's (2010) chapter. This chapter is also useful for those reviewing CFA manuscripts.

Finally, I discussed the use of CFA methodology for assessing the psychometric properties of measures. CFA methods are widely used to obtain support for measurement validity. Obtaining parameter estimates that are congruent with one's theory (assuming the model fits the data) provides evidence in support of the internal structure of the test. Validity evidence based on relations with other variables can also be obtained by embedding such variables in the model to determine whether they have the anticipated convergent or discriminant relations with the measures of interest. Less widely known are procedures for testing measurement properties such as the parallelism or tau-equivalence of measures. Such tests are quite easy to conduct using most CFA software, and I have illustrated these using the M*plus* software package. I also illustrated the calculation of omega, a coefficient of internal consistency that is based on the factor analysis model. Omega is recommended over coefficient alpha for most situations because it is not based on the somewhat strict assumption that measures are at least essentially tau-equivalent. To calculate coefficient omega, measures need only be congeneric; that is, they need only measure the same unidimensional factor. However, because calculation of omega is based on CFA model parameters, the CFA model should have a good fit to the data. If not, the parameter estimates used to calculate omega may be biased, resulting in biased values of omega. Also, estimation of CFA models requires a larger sample size than does calculation of coefficient alpha. Thus, researchers should consider sample-size requirements in deciding which of the two coefficients would result in the most accurate values for their situation.

EXERCISES

1. What do the following Greek symbols used in CFA represent?

   a. δ

   b. ξ

   c. λ

Questions 2–7 refer to the model in Figure 13.9.

2. Write out the equations for the model-implied covariances and variances for the following:

   a. X_2X_3 covariance

   b. X_4X_9 covariance

   c. X_5 variance

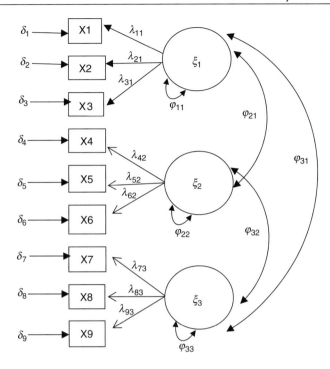

FIGURE 13.9. CFA model for Questions 2–7.

3. Write out the matrix of model-implied loadings (i.e., a matrix indicating which loadings will be estimated and which loadings will not be estimated) for this model.

4. Is the matrix of measurement error covariances diagonal or nondiagonal? Why?

5. Is the model identified? Explain why or why not.

6. Assume that the factor variances have been set to 1.0 to identify the model. How many degrees of freedom does the model have?

7. Now assume that, instead of setting the factor variances to 1.0, the first loading for each of the three factors has been set to 1.0 for identification of the model. How does this change the model degrees of freedom?

8. What are the weight matrices for the following methods of estimation?

   a. Maximum likelihood (ML)

   b. Unweighted least squares (ULS)

   c. Generalized least squares (GLS)

   d. Weighted least squares (WLS)

	Estimate	S.E.	Est./S.E.	Two-tailed P-value
RSE BY				
R1	0.490	0.023	20.960	0.000
R2	0.501	0.021	23.940	0.000
R3	-0.683	0.029	-23.559	0.000
R4	0.479	0.027	17.927	0.000
R5	-0.722	0.028	-25.644	0.000
R6	0.779	0.027	29.252	0.000
R7	0.746	0.028	26.534	0.000
R8	-1.038	0.045	-23.319	0.000
R9	-1.014	0.042	-23.893	0.000
R10	-0.970	0.041	-23.931	0.000
		Variances		
RSE	1.000	0.000	999.000	999.000
		Residual Variances		
R1	0.367	0.018	20.514	0.000
R2	0.266	0.014	19.711	0.000
R3	0.524	0.026	19.990	0.000
R4	0.518	0.025	21.056	0.000
R5	0.457	0.024	19.413	0.000
R6	0.338	0.019	17.785	0.000
R7	0.435	0.023	19.058	0.000
R8	1.242	0.062	20.078	0.000
R9	1.091	0.056	19.585	0.000
R10	0.981	0.050	19.476	0.000

FIGURE 13.10. Parameter estimates for Questions 10 and 11.

9. What is the purpose of a Satorra–Bentler type adjustment?

Questions 10 and 11 refer to the completely standardized parameter estimates shown in Figure 13.10. These estimates were obtained from a CFA of data from the 10 Rosenberg Self-Esteem items in which I specified that all items load on a single factor. The data are the same as those used in the exercises for Chapter 12. Please refer to those exercises for the wording of the 10 items.

10. Are the loading values (shown first in the output) statistically significant? Indicate how you knew.

11. The R^2 values for each item are not shown but can be obtained by a simple calculation.

    a. What is the R^2 value for R3?

    b. What does the R^2 value represent? (i.e., interpret this value)

12. The fit index values for this model are shown in Figure 13.11. Do these values indicate that the model fits the data well? Why or why not?

Chi-square test of model fit

Value	656.203
Degrees of freedom	35
P-value	0.0000

RMSEA (root mean square error of approximation)

Estimate	0.134

CFI/TLI

CFI	0.872
TLI	0.835

SRMR (standardized root mean square residual)

Value	0.057

FIGURE 13.11. Selected fit index values for Question 12.

Some of the largest values of the standardized residuals for this model are shown in Table 13.9. Use this information to answer Questions 13 and 14.

TABLE 13.9. Selected Standardized Residuals for Questions 13 and 14

Variable pair	Standardized residual	Item wording
R9, R10	11.210	R9: I certainly feel useless at times. R10: At times I think I am no good at all.
R1, R2	7.965	R1: I feel that I'm a person of worth, at least on an equal plane with others. R2: I feel that I have a number of good qualities.
R2, R4	7.289	R2: I feel that I have a number of good qualities. R4: I am able to do things as well as most people.

13. Values of the standardized residuals are all positive. What does this indicate?

14. What do you think is causing the large residuals for these items?

Some of the larger modification index values are shown in Table 13.10. Use this information to answer Questions 15 and 16.

TABLE 13.10. Selected Modification Index Values for Questions 15 and 16

Suggested parameter	Value of MI	Completely standardized EPC	Item wording
Measurement error covariance R9, R10	256.73	.584	R9: I certainly feel useless at times. R10: At times I think I am no good at all.
Measurement error covariance R1, R2	96.17	.346	R1: I feel that I'm a person of worth, at least on an equal plane with others. R2: I feel that I have a number of good qualities.
Measurement error covariance R2, R4	74.09	.299	R2: I feel that I have a number of good qualities. R4: I am able to do things as well as most people.
Measurement error covariance R6, R7	59.35	.309	R6: I take a positive attitude toward myself. R7: On the whole, I am satisfied with myself.

15. What is an EPC? What is the difference between an EPC value and a completely standardized EPC value?

16. The item pairs resulting in the largest MIs also resulted in large standardized residuals. Will this always be the case? Why or why not?

17. What arguments have been advanced against changing a model on the basis of information from residuals and modification indices?

Item Response Theory

with Christine E. DeMars

Many of you learned to know and love the CTT model in reading Chapter 7. I can understand why, as the CTT model has much to recommend it. It is a relatively simple model: it is easy to understand, and it does not make too many unreasonable assumptions. However, the CTT model also has some disadvantages, as summarized by Hambleton, Swaminathan, and Rogers (1991, ch. 1). One disadvantage is that in CTT estimates of item difficulty and discrimination are group dependent. As discussed in Chapter 6, the difficulty of a test item under the CTT model is equal to the proportion of examinees in a particular group (representing a particular population) who get the item right. However, if the difficulty had been obtained from a group of examinees with higher ability, the item would appear easier and the item difficulty would be higher (remember that in CTT easier items have higher difficulty values). The same idea holds for discrimination values because these, too, are calculated from data on a particular group of examinees. This makes it quite tricky to compare the difficulty and discrimination values of items that have been administered to different groups, unless we know the groups have the same average ability (and therefore represent the same population).

A related problem is that examinees' scores are dependent on the particular test they are administered. This may seem obvious, as a test score in CTT is, of course, a function of examinees' scores on the individual test items. But if easier or harder test items had been used, examinees' scores would change accordingly. And if some examinees took an easier test and some took a harder test, we could not compare their scores, even if the two tests were based on the same material and table of specifications. So, in CTT, estimates of examinee ability are dependent on the item parameters, and estimates of item parameters are dependent on the ability of the group to which the items are administered. The test-dependence of examinees' ability estimates and the ability-dependence of item parameter estimates imply that examinee ability and item parameter values are

Christine E. DeMars, PhD, is Professor in the Department of Graduate Psychology and a senior assessment specialist in the Center for Assessment and Research Studies at James Madison University.

confounded. Ideally, item parameter estimates would be independent of the group to which they were administered, and examinee ability would be independent of the items. Unfortunately, such independence is very difficult to achieve under the CTT framework.

Estimates of reliability coefficients and of the standard error of estimate in CTT are also group-dependent. Estimates of coefficient alpha, for example, are based on the item and test-score variances of the group to whom the test was administered. The standard error of measurement for a test is calculated from the estimated reliability value, and the test-score variance of the group. Thus, estimates of both the reliability and standard error of measurement would change if they were calculated from different items from the same domain and/or a different group of examinees. Again, this may seem obvious, but the fact that tests administered to different groups can have different amounts of error makes it difficult to compare scores across groups. Similarly, the fact that tests based on different sets of items can have different amounts of error makes it difficult to compare scores across different versions of a test. Of course, the problem is compounded if different versions of a test are administered to different groups. A final issue is that in CTT only one standard error of measurement is typically obtained for a test. This is problematic because in reality the amount of measurement error is greater at some score levels than at others. Although it is possible to estimate the amount of error at each score level using CTT (see Feldt & Brennan, 1989), the procedures for doing so are not widely known.

Finally, although CTT models make fairly minimal assumptions, recall that estimates of reliability for these models are based on the assumption that item scores are parallel (for split-half or alternate form reliability estimates) or tau-equivalent (for coefficient alpha estimates). As noted in Chapter 7, these assumptions, though necessary, are not likely to hold in practice.

The methods of *item response theory* (IRT) described in this chapter can alleviate some of these problems. Under the IRT model, item parameter estimates can be linearly transformed in such a way that scores obtained from different groups or from different sets of items are on the same scale. Thus, if the IRT model fits, item parameter estimates are not dependent on the group from which they were obtained, and examinee ability estimates are not dependent on the particular items chosen to be on the test. IRT methods also allow for items to be targeted to specific score levels. For example, in creating a test with a specific passing point such as a licensure or certification test, items that discriminate best at the cut point can be chosen, thus minimizing measurement error at that crucial point. The fact that item difficulty levels are invariant across groups is also invaluable in creating parallel test forms. Finally, measurement error in IRT models can differ across score levels.

The advantages of IRT models make them particularly useful for some measurement applications, including computerized adaptive testing, equating test forms, and detecting differential item functioning (DIF). These applications are discussed at the end of this chapter. In the next section, we describe the IRT function that relates items to the construct being measured. We then describe the most commonly used unidimensional models known as the one-parameter or Rasch model, the two-parameter model, and the three-parameter model. We then briefly discuss extensions of these models to items with more than two response categories, known as polytomous items, as well as extensions to data with more than one dimension.

ITEM RESPONSE FUNCTIONS FOR IRT

Item response theory is used to model the probability of a correct response to an item (or agreement with an item, for attitude or personality scales), conditional on the level of the construct measured. This chapter refers to the level of the construct being measured as *ability* or *proficiency*, but it could be any psychological construct. Sometimes the term *latent trait* is used for generality; in this context, *latent* means that the ability is estimated as a function of the person's pattern of responses and the item parameters, and it is not simply the observed or number correct score. In IRT, each item is characterized by an item response function (IRF; also known as the item characteristic curve, or ICC). These IRFs model the relation between ability and the probability of a correct answer to the item. This is similar to the function that relates scores on the factor to item responses in factor analysis. However, in factor analysis the item responses are assumed to be continuous, so the function relating these responses to factor levels is linear. Because item responses in IRT are typically dichotomously (0/1) scored, the IRT function is nonlinear. And instead of modeling the item response, the IRF models the *probability* of a correct response. However, the general idea of the factor analysis and IRT functions is the same.

An example IRF is shown in Figure 14.1. Ability, symbolized by θ, is on the horizontal axis, and the probability of a correct response is on the vertical axis. In IRT, it is common to scale ability using a metric similar to that of z-scores, with a mean of 0 and an *SD* of 1 (although note that the θ scale is not the same thing as the z-score scale based on the observed scores). In Figure 14.1, the probability of answering correctly is 25% for examinees with θ values of –1, or those scoring one *SD* below the mean, compared with a probability of 90% for those with θ values of 1 (scoring 1 *SD* above the mean). This illustrates the usual pattern of IRFs: a person with high ability should have a high probability of obtaining a correct answer, whereas a person with low ability should have a low probability. Of course, this relationship also depends on the characteristics of the item. If an item is easy, even those with low ability may have a high probability of obtaining a correct answer.

Note that the IRF is S-shaped. This is because the probability of a correct answer does not increase linearly with ability. Instead, examinees will have a very low probability of answering an item correctly unless they have the requisite amount of ability. After that point, the probability of answering correctly will increase with ability. However, the probability will not increase indefinitely. For example, if an item is at a medium level of difficulty, as illustrated by the item in Figure 14.1, most examinees above the average range of ability should be able to answer it. After this point, examinees have enough ability to answer the item, so having more ability does not necessarily increase the probability of a correct answer. In Figure 14.1, for example, you can see that having

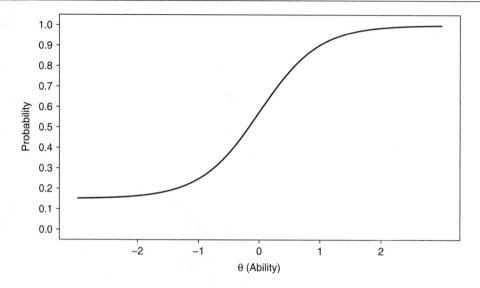

FIGURE 14.1. An IRF for a middle difficulty item.

an ability level greater than 1.0 does not result in much of an increase in the probability of obtaining a correct answer.

IRT MODELS

IRT is most often used for tests that provide one total score, and thus unidimensional IRT models are most common. However, multidimensional IRT models for tests that measure more than one ability are also possible. The most frequently used models for dichotomously scored items are the one-parameter logistic (1PL) or Rasch model, the two-parameter logistic (2PL) model, and the three-parameter logistic (3PL). These models are distinguished by the number of parameters used to model the item response function. Three parameters can be used: the difficulty, or *b*-parameter; the discrimination, or *a*-parameter; and the so-called guessing, or *c*-parameter. The discrimination (*a*) parameter is analogous to the CTT discrimination parameters discussed in Chapter 6. That is, the *a*-parameter indicates how well the item can differentiate among those with different levels of ability. This can be assessed by the steepness of the IRF slope; the steeper the slope, the greater the item's ability to discriminate and the higher the value of the *a*-parameter. However, the discrimination parameter in IRT differs from that in CTT because the item response function in IRT is nonlinear. One consequence of this nonlinearity is that discrimination is not the same at all levels of θ. For example, the item shown in Figure 14.1 discriminates well around a θ value of 0, as indicated by the steepness of the curve in that area. However, the item does not discriminate so well if θ is less than −1 or greater than +1. Because discrimination is not constant across levels of θ, it is defined as the steepness of the curve at its steepest point. In other words, the *a*-parameter indicates how rapidly the IRF curve changes at its steepest point.

The *b*-parameter is labeled the item difficulty and is the point at which the IRF increases most rapidly, or the point of inflection of the IRF curve. Because the *b*-parameter and θ are on the same scale (more about this later), another way of defining the *b*-parameter is as the point at which just over 50% of examinees with $\theta = b$ answer the item correctly. In other words, if $b = 0$, just over 50% of examinees with θ values of 0 should answer the item correctly. The *c*-parameter is the lower asymptote of the function, or the point on the Y axis at which the IRF "bottoms out" on the left-hand side of the graph. If no *c*-parameter is included, the lower asymptote would be zero, indicating that low-ability examinees have no chance of obtaining a correct answer. However, this may not be realistic for items on which examinees could obtain a correct answer by guessing. Because guessing is thought to be a common reason for a nonzero lower asymptote, *c* is often referred to as the guessing, or pseudo-guessing parameter. The *c*-parameter thus allows for the possibility that even examinees with very low ability levels may have some chance of obtaining the correct answer. More generally, the *c*-parameter allows for the lower asymptote of the IRF to be greater than zero, thus accommodating responses from low-ability examinees who may obtain a correct response by guessing or other means not related to the construct being measured (e.g., test-wiseness, luck, cheating).

IRT models can also be used for items with more than two score categories, such as Likert items or short-answer questions that are worth more than one point. Such items are referred to as *polytomous* items. The most frequently used models for polytomous items are the graded response (GR), partial credit (PC), and generalized partial credit (GPC) models.

The One-Parameter Logistic Model

The one-parameter logistic (1PL) model is the simplest IRT model. This model is characterized by the difficulty or *b*-parameter. The *c*-parameter is not included, and all item discrimination (*a*) parameters are assumed to be equal. Thus, only one *a*-parameter is estimated instead of a separate *a*-parameter for each item. This means that all the IRFs for 1PL items would have equal slopes or discrimination and would have lower asymptotes of zero. The 1PL is symbolized as

$$P\left(X_{ij} = 1 \mid \theta, a, b_i\right) = \frac{e^{Da\left(\theta_j - b_i\right)}}{1 + e^{Da\left(\theta_j - b_i\right)}} \tag{14.1}$$

where *P* means probability, $X = 1$ means that the item is correct (or the response is 1), and the symbol | means "conditional on." So we read $P(X_{ij} = 1 \mid \theta_j, a, b_i)$ as: The probability of a correct response to item *i* by examinee *j* conditional on examinee *j*'s ability and the difficulty (b_i) of the item. The wording "conditional on" simply means that the probability of a correct response can (and usually does) depend on the examinee's ability level and the item difficulty. The expression $P(X_{ij} = 1 \mid \theta_j, a, b_i)$ is often shortened to $P(\theta)$, which will be used in the remainder of the model description.

Note that the item discrimination parameter, *a*, is not subscripted in Equation 14.1. This is because in the 1PL all items are assumed to have the same discrimination value. The difficulty or *b*-parameters are subscripted because these parameter values can vary across items. The parameter D is simply a scaling constant, set equal to either 1.0 or 1.7. Setting $D = 1$ puts the a-parameter on the logistic metric; setting it to 1.7 puts the a-parameter on the normal metric.[1] D does not change the value of the b-parameter.

Turning to the other terms in Equation 14.1, the base e is a mathematical constant, approximately 2.72, and the natural log of $e = 1$. These particular values are adopted because they are helpful in describing some natural phenomena, such as the rate of growth of bacteria. Equation 14.1 can be effective in describing the relationship between ability and correct response, but of course the accuracy of the model for any particular item and group of examinees is an empirical question that can be assessed by methods described in a later section.

The Rasch Model

The *Rasch model* is mathematically equivalent to the 1PL model, except that in the Rasch model the a-parameter is fixed to 1 and is completely dropped from the model. Another difference between the Rasch and 1PL models is that whereas the 1PL model may be on either the normal or logistic metric, the Rasch model is always on the logistic metric. As a result, the D term is equal to 1.0 and can be dropped from the equation for the Rasch model. Thus, the Rasch model may be formulated as

$$P\left(X_{ij} = 1 \mid \theta_j, b_i\right) = \frac{e^{\theta_j - b_i}}{1 + e^{\theta_j - b_i}} \tag{14.2}$$

where θ and b are as defined in Equation 14.1. It is also relatively common to use the symbol δ instead of b for the item difficulty and β instead of θ. Rasch (1980) developed the model in terms of log-odds (logits), not probabilities, so the original form was

$$\ln\left(\frac{P(\beta_j)}{1 - P(\beta_j)}\right) = \beta_j - \delta_i$$

which is equivalent to the right-hand side of Equation 14.2. The top panel of Figure 14.2 shows three 1PL or Rasch items. Notice how the response functions have the same shape. If the graph were continued far enough on the left, the probability would approach a lower asymptote of zero for all items. If we change the Y axis to logits, as shown in the bottom panel, the response functions are parallel. Thus, the item response functions are often described as parallel; even though probability functions can never be parallel; only log-odds functions can be.

The Rasch model (and equivalently the 1PL model) has some special properties not obtained in data that follow the 2PL or 3PL models. In the Rasch model, the

---

[1] $D = 1.7$ is sometimes preferred for historical reasons because normal models were developed before logistic models, and changing D to 1.7 for the logistic model leads to an a-parameter that is nearly identical to the a-parameter estimated using the normal model. Use of the normal model requires integration, so when the normal metric is desired, it is easier to *use* the logistic model but include the 1.7 to put the logistic model on the same metric as the normal model.

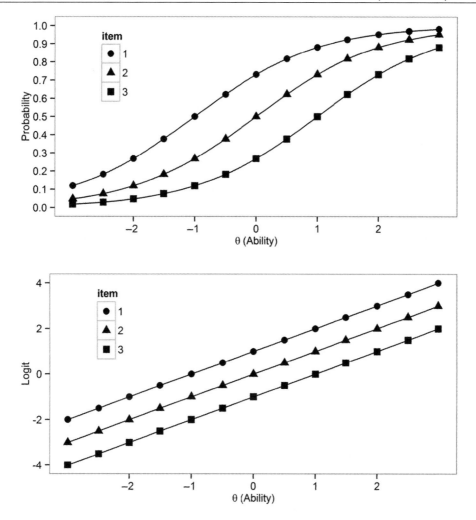

FIGURE 14.2. Example Rasch (1PL) items. The upper panel shows the probability of correct response, and the lower panel shows the logit of the probability (the log-odds of correct response).

observed (number-correct) score is a sufficient statistic for the estimate of θ, and the proportion of correct responses is a sufficient statistic for the estimate of the item difficulty. This means that all examinees with the same observed score on the same test form will have the same estimated θ, regardless of which items were correct. For the 2PL and 3PL models, the estimate of θ depends on which items an examinee answered correctly. The rank order of the θ estimates in the Rasch model is the same as the rank order of observed scores; only the intervals between adjacent values on the two scales differ. Another special property of the Rasch model is known as *specific objectivity*, which means that differences between any two examinees in the log-odds of answering an item correctly is the same for all items. This means that if the θ values of two examinees differ by one unit, their logit values for any item will also differ by 1.

Because of this property, the θs are sometimes referred to as logit scores. Although each examinee's log-odds value will differ from item to item depending on item difficulty, the difference in logits between any two examinees *relative to one another* is constant across items. But note that this property only holds if the data adhere to a Rasch model. Improperly applying the Rasch model to data where the items differ in discrimination or where there is a non-negligible degree of correct guessing will not yield these properties of the Rasch model.

The Two-Parameter Logistic Model

For the two-parameter logistic (2PL) model, the lower asymptote (c) is fixed to zero and thus can be removed from Equation 14.1. This is appropriate when very low ability examinees are unlikely to respond correctly, perhaps because the items are constructed-response or multiple choice, with distractors that are very effective with low-ability examinees. In such situations, examinees may still guess, but they are unlikely to guess correctly. And because the lower asymptote is only affected by correct guessing, the c-parameter would not be needed. The 2PL model is expressed as

$$P\left(x_{ij}=1\mid\theta_j,a_i,b_i\right)=\frac{e^{Da_i\left(\theta_j-b_i\right)}}{1+e^{Da_i\left(\theta_j-b_i\right)}} \tag{14.3}$$

where all terms are as defined for Equation 14.1. However, note that the a-parameter now has an "i" subscript because it can vary across items in the 2PL model. Like the 1PL, the 2PL includes no guessing or c-parameter. In the 2PL model, 50% of examinees at $\theta=b$ are predicted to answer the item correctly. Figure 14.3 shows the item response functions for two pairs of items. The two items in the top panel have equal a-parameters but different b-parameters. (Note that, although the two items in the top panel do not appear to have equal slopes, this is because of their differences in difficulty. If the more difficult item 2 were shifted to the left, the two curves would coincide.) However, $b=-1$ for item 1 and $b=1$ for item 2. Thus, item 2 is more difficult than item 1 because an examinee would need a higher ability ($\theta=1$) to have a 50/50 chance of getting item 2 correct. In the bottom panel, the b-parameters for the two items are equal, but $a=0.8$ for item 1 and $a=1.2$ for item 2. Item 2 is therefore more discriminating, as indicated by the fact that its response function is steeper, at its steepest point.

The Three-Parameter Logistic Model

As its name implies, the three-parameter logistic (3PL) model includes three item parameters, as well as the parameter of ability (θ), which is included in all the IRT models. The 3PL model is symbolized as

$$P\left(x_{ij}=1\mid\theta_j,a_i,b_i,c_i\right)=c_i+\left(1-c_i\right)\frac{e^{Da_i\left(\theta_j-b_i\right)}}{1+e^{Da_i\left(\theta_j-b_i\right)}} \tag{14.4}$$

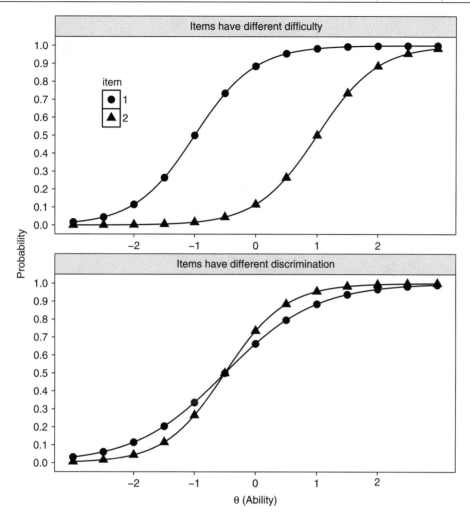

FIGURE 14.3. Example 2PL items.

In Equation 14.4, all terms are as defined previously, but there is one additional item parameter. This is the c-parameter, or lower asymptote of the function. The lower asymptote is the point on the Y axis at which the IRF "bottoms out" on the left-hand side of the graph. As θ becomes very low, $P(\theta)$ approaches c. In other words, the c-parameter allows for the possibility that even examinees with very low ability levels may have some chance of obtaining the correct answer. Sometimes c is called the guessing parameter because one reason that low-ability examinees might respond correctly is by guessing correctly.

Figure 14.4 shows the IRFs for three pairs of items. The first two item pairs, shown in the top and middle panels of Figure 14.4, have the same a- and b-parameters as the items in Figure 14.3. However, a c-parameter has been incorporated for the items in Figure 14.4. The two items shown in the top panel have equal a- and c-parameters. However, as in Figure 14.3, $b = -1$ for item 1 and $b = 1$ for item 2. Notice how $P(\theta)$ is just over

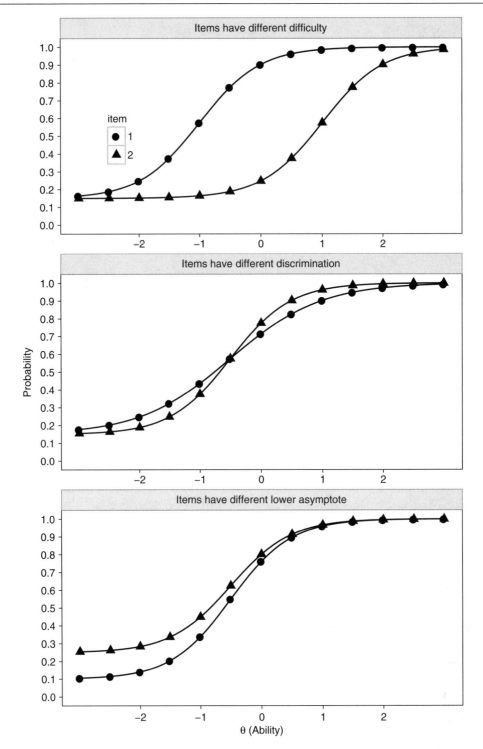

FIGURE 14.4. Example 3PL items.

50% at a θ value of -1 for item 1 and at a θ value of 1 for item 2. This follows from the previous statement that b is the point at which just over 50% of examinees with $\theta = b$ answer the item correctly. The answer hinges on use of the term *just over 50%*, indicating that the percentage will not be exactly 50% for all items. How much greater it is than 50% depends on c. If one conceptualizes the c-parameter as correct guessing, at $\theta = b$, 50% of the examinees guess because they do not know the correct answer, so the proportion of correct answers increases to .5 (the proportion who know the correct answer) plus $.5c$ (the proportion who do not know the correct answer times the probability of guessing the correct answer).

In the middle panel, the two items have equal b- and c-parameters but $a = 0.8$ for item 1 and $a = 1.2$ for item 2. In the bottom panel, the two items have equal a- and b-parameters, but $c = 0.10$ for item 1 and $c = 0.25$ for item 2. Notice how about 10% or 25%, respectively, of very-low-ability examinees (at the far left of graph) are expected to answer the items correctly. This is because examinees have a greater chance of guessing the correct answer on these items. The c-parameter alters the function throughout the range of ability, but this change is most apparent at the low end. Although $b = -0.5$ for both these items, at $\theta = -0.5$, 55% of examinees are predicted to answer item 1 correctly compared to 62.5% for item 2.

IRT Models for Polytomous Items

The 1PL/Rasch/2PL/3PL models apply to dichotomous items, but the 2PL and Rasch models have been extended to scales containing polytomous items (items with more than two response categories, such as short-essay questions or Likert-type items) as well. Some commonly used models for polytomous items are the *graded response* (GR), *partial credit* (PC), and *generalized partial credit* (GPC) models. One important feature of models for polytomous models is that there is no longer only one correct answer. Instead, examinees can obtain 0, 1, 2, 3, or more points for each item. To accommodate this, models for polytomous data have multiple b-parameters. Each of the b-parameters indicates the difficulty associated with a different number of points. In some models, these parameters are known as *thresholds* because they indicate the point at which the probability of scoring in that category *or higher* equals 50%. In other words, the b- or threshold parameters represent the "threshold" of ability over which an examinee must cross to obtain the next higher score. In other models, the multiple b's are known as *step difficulties*. In these models, the b's represent the point at which the probabilities of choosing two adjacent categories are equal.

The Graded Response (GR) Model

Samejima (1969) proposed several models under the general description of graded response, but one of them has been widely adopted and is commonly referred to as the GR model. The function estimated using the GR model is

$$P^*\left(x_{ij} \geq k \mid \theta_j, a_i, b_{ik}\right) = \frac{e^{Da_i\left(\theta_j - b_{ik}\right)}}{1 + e^{Da_i\left(\theta_j - b_{ik}\right)}} \tag{14.5}$$

where θ is again the ability, a_i is the item discrimination for item i, and b_{ik} is the threshold for response category k of item i. As explained in the previous paragraph, the threshold indicates the point at which the probability of scoring in category k or higher is equal to 50%. For example, the top panel of Figure 14.5 shows an item with possible scores of 0 to 3. For this item the threshold for a score of 1 is –1, the threshold for a score of 2 is 0, and the threshold for a score of 3 is 1.5. Notice that a score of 0 is not graphed because the probability of scoring 0 or higher is 100%. So, the number of thresholds for an item with k response categories is $k - 1$ (e.g., there are three thresholds for a four-category item, four thresholds for a five-category item).

Although there are multiple thresholds for polytomous items, in the GR model there is only one a-parameter for each item, so the response functions for each score category within an item have the same shape. Different items, however, may have different

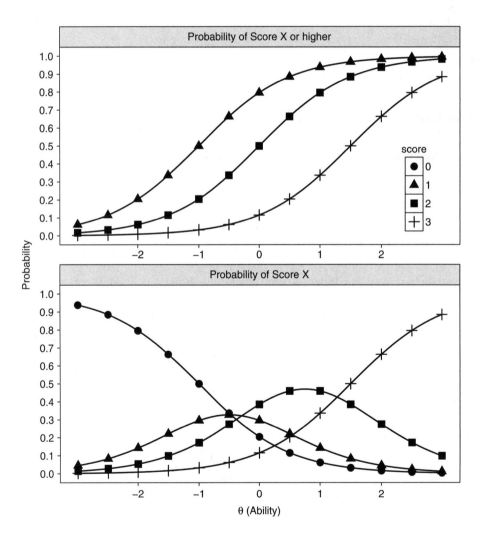

FIGURE 14.5. A graded response model item.

discrimination values. Sometimes the GR model is modified to fix the a-parameters to equality across items (yielding the 1PL version of the GR), but this modified model does not have all the properties of the Rasch model.

After estimating the probability of obtaining each score or higher, $P^*(\theta)$, using Equation 14.5, the probability of scoring in a particular score category X can be obtained as follows. Subtract the probability of scoring in the next-highest-score category from the probability of scoring in that category. The lower panel of Figure 14.5 shows this for the item graphed in the top panel. For example, at $\theta = 0$, the probability of scoring 1 or higher = 0.80 and the probability of scoring 2 or higher = 0.50 (top panel). Therefore, the probability of scoring 1 at theta 0 = 0.80 – 0.50 = 0.30 (lower panel). These calculations can be performed at various values of θ, and the differences can be displayed as a function. Notice that there is now a function for a score of 0 because the probability of scoring a 1 or higher was subtracted from 100% (the probability of 0 or higher).

The Partial Credit (PC) Model

The PC model was developed as an extension of the Rasch model (Masters, 1982). The PC directly models the probability of scoring in category k, not the probability of scoring in category k or higher. Instead of the threshold parameters estimated in the GR model, parameters known as *step difficulties* are estimated in the PC model. The step difficulty indicates the point on the ability scale at which responses in adjacent categories are equally likely. In other words, the step difficulty for a score point is the point at which the line representing its response function crosses the line representing the response function of an adjacent score point. For example, the step difficulties in Figure 14.6 are –1.5, –.5, and 0. Notice how, although four score categories are depicted in the graph, there

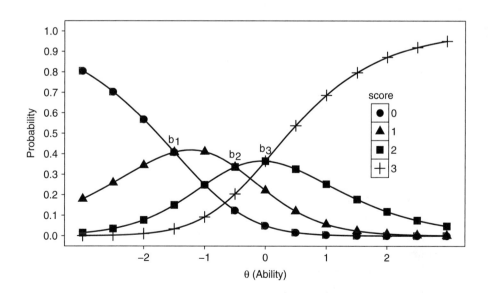

FIGURE 14.6. A partial credit model item.

can only be three step difficulties: the transition between categories 0 and 1, 1 and 2, and 2 and 3. It is important to note that the step difficulties do not have the same meaning as the category thresholds in the GR model and that the two sets of parameters are not equivalent in value.

The PC model is formulated as

$$P\left(x_{ij} = k \mid \theta_j, b_{ik}\right) = \frac{e^{\sum_{x=0}^{k}\left(\theta_j - b_{ix}\right)}}{\sum_{j=0}^{m_i} e^{\sum_{x=0}^{j}\left(\theta_j - b_{ix}\right)}} \tag{14.6}$$

Equation 14.6 models the probability of person j obtaining a score of k on item i, given particular values of θ and b. In this equation, b_{ik} is the step difficulty for score k and m_i is the maximum score for item i. There is no step difficulty for the 0th category. Instead, the term inside the parentheses is defined to be 0 for that category, yielding a numerator of 1.

The Generalized Partial Credit (GPC) Model

The GPC model (Muraki, 1992) extends the PC model by adding an a-parameter that can vary across items. Adding this parameter causes the GPC to lose the special properties of the Rasch model discussed previously. However, if the items really do have different a-values, the PC model would not provide a good match to the data, and the Rasch properties would be lost in any case. Either the logistic or normal scaling ($D = 1$ or 1.7) may be used with the GPC.

Multidimensional IRT Models

Although outside the scope of this chapter, all of the models covered here could be extended to include scales measuring multiple abilities. Such scales are referred to as multidimensional scales and require IRT models that take into account their multidimensionality. Not surprisingly, these models are called multidimensional IRT (MIRT) models and are often referred to as the 3PL-MIRT, 2PL-MIRT, and so on. The 3PL in the label means it is the extension of the 3PL unidimensional IRT model (similarly for the label 2PL). For extensive coverage of MIRT, see Reckase (2009).

INDETERMINACY AND SCALING

As discussed in Chapter 13 in the context of CFA models, the metric of θ and that of the item parameters are arbitrary. This stems from the fact that factors in CFA and θ values in IRT do not have any inherent scale, a property referred to in IRT literature as indeterminancy. Therefore, the researcher must fix the center point (mean) and the unit width of the θ scale. In the 3PL and 2PL models, it is typical to set the mean θ value to 0 and the *SD* to 1 in the sample used to estimate the item parameters. You may recall that this is also one of the ways in which the scale is set for CFA models, and it puts the θ or factor into a *z*-score-like metric. In IRT, the process of estimating the item parameters is called *calibration*, and the sample from which the parameters are estimated is called the *calibration sample*. The θ values may be re-scaled for reporting purposes. For example, on a state's math test covering grades 3–8, the scaling may be chosen such that the mean and *SD* of sixth graders in the norming year are 600 and 50, respectively. The scores for all other grades and future test administrations are calculated relative to the sixth-grade metric. For example, the mean for seventh graders would be higher than 600, and the mean for fifth graders would be lower than 600.

Scaling for the Rasch Model

For the Rasch model, the mean difficulty across all items is typically set to 0, and all *a*-parameters are set to 1. Both the mean and *SD* of θ are then estimated relative to this scale. This is in contrast to the 1PL model, in which the mean of θ is typically fixed to 0 and the *SD* of θ to 1. Suppose a set of items was calibrated with the 1PL model and that the shared *a*-parameter for all items was estimated to be 1.2 and the mean of the *b*-estimates was 0.3. If the items were instead calibrated with the Rasch model, the mean *b* would be fixed at 0, and the *SD* of the θ estimates would be 1.2 (the *a*-parameter from the 1PL scaling). Under this scaling, the mean θ estimate for the Rasch model would be $-0.3(1.2) = -0.36$ to reflect the fact that the average θ was 0.3 *SD* units lower than the average item difficulty. Thus, the scaling of both *b* and θ change, so that whenever $\theta = b$ the probability of correct response is still $= 0.5$. Note that one implication of the Rasch scaling is that the mean and *SD* of ability cannot be fixed, as in the 1PL, 2PL, and 3PL models. Instead, the scale is set by fixing the mean *b*-value to 0 and the common *a*-value to 1. The ideal range of θ can therefore be specified only in relative terms. Graphics are often used in Rasch modeling to illustrate the location of the items relative to the distribution of ability.

Scaling for the 2PL and 3PL Models

For the 2PL and 3PL models, θ is scaled so that a value of 0 indicates a score at the mean of the ability distribution, and a θ value of 1 indicates a score that is one *SD* above the mean. Although θ values are not necessarily normally distributed, many abilities do tend to be approximately normally distributed. For normally distributed abilities, we can invoke the well-known properties of that distribution that approximately 95% of examinees will score between two *SD*s below the mean and two *SD*s above the mean, or between -2 and 2 on a *z*-score metric. And because the item difficulties are on the same scale as the θ values, they should be in this range as well. An item with $b < -2$ would be so easy that even examinees two *SD*s below the mean would have at least a 50% probability of correct response.

The value of the *a*-parameter is harder to interpret than the values of *b* or θ and depends on whether the normal or logistic metric is chosen. In general, however, higher values of the *a*-parameter indicate better discrimination among examinees with different θ values, or, equivalently, a steeper IRF. On the normal metric, *a*-parameters lower than approximately 0.6 or 0.8 might be screened out during pilot-testing because such values would indicate an item that does not differentiate well between examinees with different levels of ability. As a result, it is likely that *a*-parameters on most published tests will be in the range of approximately 0.8 to 2.0 in the normal metric. This is equivalent to approximately 1.3 to 3.4 in the logistic metric.

The *c*-parameter indicates the lower asymptote, or the point at which the probability of obtaining a correct response bottoms out. Although, theoretically, values of *c* could range from 0 to 1.0, typical values are in the range of about 0 to .3. Lord (1980) suggested that on standardized tests the *c*-parameter should be somewhat lower than chance level because the distractors should be functioning effectively.

As noted previously, in IRT the abilities are on the same scale as the item difficulties. One result is that when $\theta = b$, the quantity $(\theta_j - b_i)$ in Equations 14.1–14.3 is 0, and the quantity $e^{Da_i(\theta_j - b_i)}/1 + e^{Da_i(\theta_j - b_i)}$ becomes $e^0/(1 + e^0)$. Because any number raised to the 0th power equals 1, this quantity becomes $1/(1 + 1)$, or 0.5. This yields the result, discussed previously, that 50% of examinees at $\theta = b$ are predicted to respond correctly (plus, for the 3PL model, a small additional percentage due to the *c*-parameter). In terms of the Rasch model, analysts would say that the logits are 0 when $\theta = b$. This is because the logits are the log-odds, and the odds in this case are the probability of a correct answer divided by the probability of an incorrect answer. So, if an examinee has a 50/50 chance of obtaining a correct answer, the odds would be 1, and the log-odds (log of 1.0) would be 0.

INVARIANCE OF PARAMETER ESTIMATES

The introduction to this chapter mentioned that one advantage of IRT models is that the item parameter estimates are invariant across samples—a property known as sample independence. After reading the section on scaling, you may be thinking, "But if you scale the parameters such that θ has a mean of 0 and *SD* of 1 in the calibration sample, and the *b*-parameter is scaled to θ, don't the item parameter estimates have to depend on the sample"? The answer is yes: the *b*-parameters would be lower in a more able sample than in a less able sample, just as in CTT the proportion correct difficulty index *P* would be higher in a more able sample. Similarly, in a more heterogeneous sample, the *a*-parameters will be higher than in a less able sample, just as in CTT the item–total correlations will be higher in a more heterogeneous sample. The difference is that in IRT the parameter estimates should differ only by a linear transformation, and that transformation is the same for all items (aside from calibration or estimation error). So, a more correct way of stating the sample–independence property is that item parameter estimates can be linearly transformed so that they are the same across samples.

For example, we may need to add 0.2 to each of the *b*-parameters from a more able sample to make them approximately equal to the *b*-parameters from the less able sample. Or we may need to multiply each of the *a*-parameters from the less heterogeneous sample by 1.3 to make them approximately equal to the *a*-parameters from the more heterogeneous sample.

Of course, sometimes groups do not just differ in their ability distribution. They may actually differ in their item response functions. Item 1 may be easier than item 2 for men but harder than item 2 for women. This is an illustration of differential item functioning (DIF; discussed in Chapter 16). If the items exhibit DIF, the invariance of item parameter values across samples will not hold.

ESTIMATION

Although it is tempting to think of θ as the z-score corresponding to a person's observed score due to its scaling of a mean of 0 and *SD* of 1, θ does not have such a simple interpretation. Instead, θ values are estimated from an examinee's pattern of responses and the corresponding item parameters. The most common estimation methods currently are maximum likelihood (ML) and Bayesian *expected-a-posteriori* (EAP) scores. Both methods are based on the examinee's *likelihood function*.

A likelihood function expresses the probability, or likelihood, of obtaining a particular pattern of responses, given a particular level of ability. In other words, the likelihood function indicates what the probability of an examinee's response pattern would be if the θ value were –1.0, –1.5, 0, 1.0, or any other value. For IRT models, the likelihood function of a particular response pattern is the product of the probabilities for each item and is symbolized as $L(x_j|\theta)$, where x_j is the vector of responses, or response pattern, for examinee *j*. Table 14.1 shows the item parameters for a 10-item test. The items are arranged in order from the easiest (item 1) to the most difficult (item 10). Figure 14.7 shows the likelihood function for an examinee with the response pattern 1111101100, where 1 and 0 indicate the examinee's correct (1) and incorrect (0) answers to the 10 items. The figure also shows the overall or *joint likelihood* of the entire response pattern. The likelihood functions show the probability of each item response for different values of θ.

For dichotomous items, the likelihood of a correct response is $P(\theta)$, which increases with θ. Because the examinee answered items 1–5, 7, and 8 correctly, the likelihood of a correct response to these items increases with θ, as shown in Figure 14.7. In contrast, the likelihood of an incorrect response is $1 - P(\theta)$, which decreases as θ increases. Because the examinee answered items 6, 9, and 10 incorrectly, the likelihood functions for these items model the likelihood of an incorrect response. This makes the likelihood functions for these items *decrease* as θ increases. If the response pattern includes at least one incorrect response and one correct response, the likelihood of the overall response pattern will usually have a unimodal shape as in this example (shown in the last panel of Figure 14.7). However, with the 3PL model, it is possible to have multiple peaks or a very small peak because of the effects of correct guessing.

TABLE 14.1. Item Parameters for a 10-Item Test

Item	a	b	c
1	2.0	−1.8	0.1
2	1.0	−1.4	0.2
3	0.8	−1.0	0.1
4	1.5	−0.6	0.2
5	2.1	−0.2	0.1
6	1.2	0.2	0.2
7	0.8	0.6	0.1
8	2.3	1.0	0.2
9	1.0	1.4	0.1
10	1.4	1.8	0.2

Note. a's are on the logistic metric. Divide each *a* by 1.7 to obtain the normal metric.

Maximum Likelihood Estimation

The goal of maximum likelihood estimation is to find the θ value at which the likelihood of a particular response pattern is greatest. This is the point at which the likelihood is said to reach its maximum, thus giving the estimation procedure its name. The actual value of this maximum is not of importance; we only need to know it will become increasingly small as the number of items increases. This is because as the number of items increases, so does the number of possible response patterns: thus, the likelihood of any single response pattern becomes very low. The focus in maximum likelihood estimation is on *where* that maximum is located and on how peaked or flat the likelihood surface is. A peaked distribution indicates greater certitude about the examinee's ability level, whereas a flat likelihood distribution indicates that it is difficult to "zero in" on the examinee's ability. This is illustrated in the upper panel of Figure 14.8. This panel shows the likelihood from Figure 14.7 again, along with the likelihoods for two additional examinees with response patterns of 1110000000 (Examinee 2) and 1101000100 (Examinee 3). Notice that Examinee 2's likelihood is the most peaked because this examinee has a clear response pattern, with correct responses on the easiest items and incorrect responses on the hardest items. The fact that the examinee was able to answer all of the easiest items but unable to answer any of the more difficult items is a strong indication that the examinee probably has a fairly low level of ability. In contrast, Examinee 3 was unable to answer most of the more difficult items but unexpectedly got item 8 right. This resulted in a flatter likelihood surface because it is not clear whether the response to item 8 was due to lucky guessing or ability, especially given the examinee's poor performance overall. The θ value at which each pattern's maximum likelihood occurs is indicated by the label "max" in the top panel of Figure 14.8. This θ value is taken as the maximum likelihood score estimate

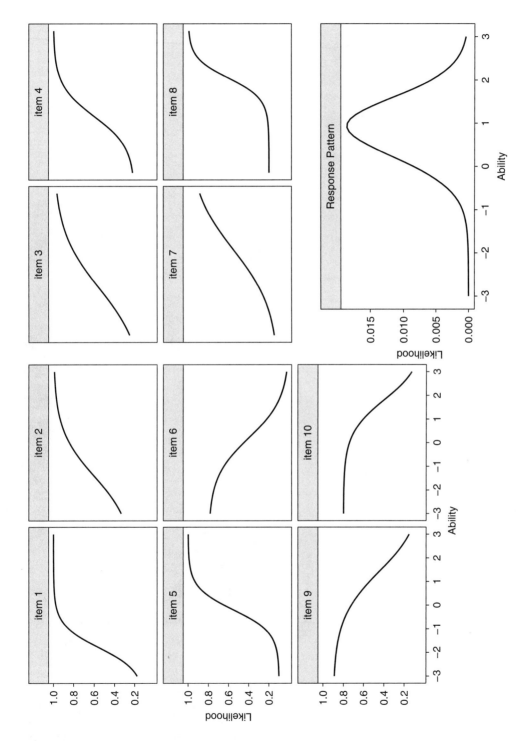

FIGURE 14.7. Likelihood of each item response, along with the likelihood of the response pattern (1111101100).

421

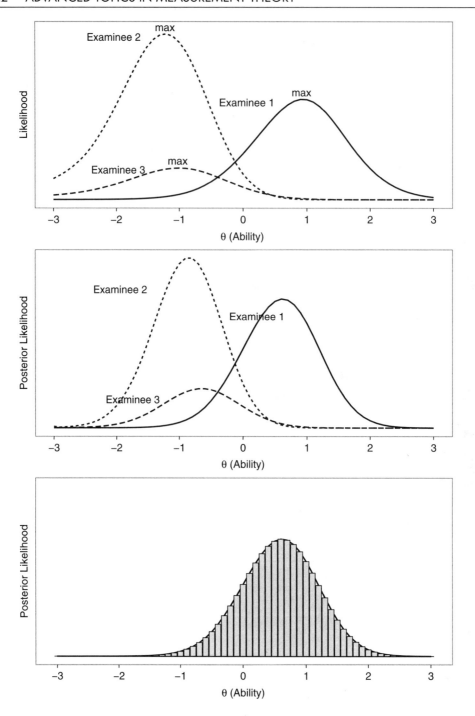

FIGURE 14.8. Likelihood functions for three examinees' response patterns. The top panel shows the likelihood functions—the maximum of the function (labeled max) is the ML estimate of θ. The middle panel shows the posterior likelihood function for the same three response patterns—the maximum of the function is the MAP estimate of θ. The lower panel illustrates the calculation of the EAP estimate of θ for examinee 1, using the posterior likelihood function from the middle panel.

(although it may be transformed to another scale before reporting). Although we do not go into the details here, you may recall that calculus can be used to find the maxima of functions, and this is how the maximum likelihood values are obtained in IRT.

Bayesian Estimation Methods

The Modal-A-Posteriori Estimation

Sometimes maximum likelihood estimation incorporates a *Bayesian prior*. Although full explanation of Bayesian statistics is beyond the scope of this chapter, a very brief synopsis is presented here. In maximum likelihood estimation, the likelihood that is estimated is the likelihood of obtaining a particular response pattern, given a value of θ. However, it could be argued that what we really want to know is the likelihood of a particular θ value, given the response pattern. The latter likelihood is known in Bayesian estimation as the *posterior distribution* and is the quantity estimated in the Bayesian paradigm. In symbols, in Bayesian estimation we estimate $L(\theta|X_j)$ (the likelihood of θ given the response pattern) instead of $L(X_j|\theta)$ (the likelihood of the response pattern given θ).

Bayesian estimation is so-called because it is based on Bayes's theorem: $P(B|A) = P(A|B)P(B)/P(A)$. In words, the probability of B given A is equal to the probability of A given B times the probability of B, divided by the probability of A. In the IRT context, A is the response pattern and B is θ, so $P(A|B)$ is the probability of the response pattern, given a particular θ value; $P(B)$ is the probability distribution of θ; and $P(A)$ is the probability of the response pattern. So, the probability of θ given the response pattern ($P(B|A)$) is equal to the probability of the response pattern, given θ ($P(A|B)$) times the probability of θ ($P(\theta)$), all divided by the probability of the response pattern ($P(A)$). The probability of θ is its distribution or *density function*. Expressed in the form of likelihoods, as is usual, the function is symbolized as $L(\theta|X_j) = L(X_j|\theta)g(\theta)^2$, where $g(\theta)$ is the distribution of θ. The symbol g is often used in statistics for the density function. The distribution $g(\theta)$ is known as the *prior distribution*, or prior, in Bayesian statistics, and as the name implies, its form must be specified a priori. Because in IRT the distribution of θ is usually assumed to be normal with a mean of 0 and *SD* of 1, this is taken as the prior distribution, or density, of θ ($g(\theta)$). The normal density is symbolized as N(0,1).

The posterior distribution $L(\theta|X_j)$ is the likelihood of θ given the response pattern. The middle panel of Figure 14.8 shows each examinee's posterior distribution, obtained by multiplying the examinee's likelihood ($L(X_j|\theta)$) by the N(0,1) density function. The maximum of this posterior distribution is called the *modal-a-posteriori* (MAP) estimate and is estimated using calculus. Notice how the posterior distributions in the middle panel of Figure 14.8 are more tightly concentrated around their means in comparison to the ML distributions in the upper panel. This is the result of multiplying the likelihood times the N(0,1) density, which draws the Bayesian function closer to the mean of the prior distribution (0 in this case). Multiplication of the likelihood by the density is what

---

[2] The full equation includes a scaling factor that makes the area under the likelihood equal 1. This was omitted for simplicity and can be omitted in the estimation as well.

makes the Bayesian function different from the ML function. This difference between the two distributions decreases with the number of items, however. If a test is longer, the likelihood function is more peaked, so multiplying it by the prior has a smaller effect. Because most tests are longer than the 10-item test depicted here, posterior distributions will generally be less impacted by the prior than in the example.

The Expected-A-Posteriori Estimation

An alternative to finding the maximum (mode) of the posterior distribution (MAP) is to find the mean (expected value). This is known as the expected-a-posteriori (EAP) estimate. Because the posterior distribution is a continuous function, the mean is approximated using the *method of quadratures*. This is a general method of approximation used in calculus and is not unique to IRT. The method of quadratures is a way of estimating the area under a curve, and it works by dividing the area under the curve into a series of rectangular areas. Because the area of a rectangle is easier to compute than the area under a curve, this method is useful for situations in which the latter computation is intractable.

Specifically, the method of quadratures involves spacing a number of points throughout the range in which most of the scores are likely to be located. A reasonable range to capture most examinee scores, if the population is centered at 0, is −4 to 4. Within that range, a series of vertical rectangles is drawn, as illustrated in the lower panel of Figure 14.8 for Examinee 1. The θ value at the center of each of the k rectangles is termed the quadrature point or node, and the area of the rectangle is termed the quadrature weight, symbolized as $A(\theta_k)$. If the points are evenly spaced, all of the rectangle widths are equal, so the relative weight depends only on the height of each rectangle, which is the posterior likelihood at that point ($L(\theta_k|X_j)$. The mean (expected value) of the posterior is then obtained by multiplying the θ value at each quadrature point by the posterior likelihood at that same quadrature point and by summing the resulting values across all of the points. The resulting sum is divided by the sum of the weights (if the weights have not already been scaled to sum to one, as is sometimes done).

Because the method of quadrature simply involves dividing the area under a curve into a series of discrete rectangular areas, it is straightforward to apply the method to any shape of prior distribution. Thus, it is not necessary for the prior distribution used in EAP estimation to be normal. For example, the distribution of ability can be estimated from the subgroup to which an examinee belongs, and that distribution can be used as the examinee's prior, even if that distribution is skewed or otherwise non-normal.

Table 14.2 shows the calculations for obtaining the mean and variance of the posterior distribution for Examinee 1. This distribution is shown in the middle and bottom panels of Figure 14.8. The calculations are essentially the same as would be used to find the mean of a grouped frequency table in introductory statistics. However, in a grouped frequency distribution, score values are multiplied by their frequency of occurrence rather than by the posterior likelihood. For example, imagine that out of three basketball free-throws, 10% of your sample made zero baskets, 40% made one, 45% made two, and 5% made three baskets. To compute the mean, you would calculate $.10(0) + .40(1) + .45(2) +.05(3) = 1.45$. As you can see in Table 14.2, the posterior likelihood value (second column) is shown for values of θ between -4.0 and 4.0, at intervals of $.5$. A θ value of 0.5 has the highest likelihood for this response pattern. This makes sense because it is at this value that the graphs for examinee 1 reach their peak. To obtain the mean posterior likelihood for examinee 1, each θ value is multiplied by its posterior likelihood (analogous to the sample proportion), yielding the quantities in the third column of Table 14.2. The average of these values, shown at the bottom of the column, is the mean likelihood or EAP estimate of θ, 0.5758.

The variance of θ can also be calculated from the data in Table 14.2. The necessary quantities are shown in the last column of Table 14.2, and the calculations are described when the standard error of θ is discussed.

TABLE 14.2 Calculation of Mean and *SD* of Examinee 1's Posterior Likelihood

θ_k	Posterior likelihood ($L(\theta_k|x_j)$)	$L(\theta_k|X_j)\theta_k$	$L(\theta_k|X_j) \times (\theta_k - \overline{\theta})^2$
−4.0	0.000000015	−0.0000001	0.0000003
−3.5	0.000000143	−0.0000005	0.0000024
−3.0	0.000001578	−0.0000047	0.0000202
−2.5	0.000018235	−0.0000456	0.0001725
−2.0	0.000202046	−0.0004041	0.0013405
−1.5	0.001893690	−0.0028405	0.0081600
−1.0	0.013803139	−0.0138031	0.0342761
−0.5	0.068901999	−0.0344510	0.0797465
0.0	0.200852835	0.0000000	0.0665966
0.5	0.322129307	0.1610647	0.0018518
1.0	0.267485317	0.2674853	0.0481282
1.5	0.103418164	0.1551272	0.0883303
2.0	0.019211051	0.0384221	0.0389655
2.5	0.001953675	0.0048842	0.0072334
3.0	0.000122578	0.0003677	0.0007203
3.5	0.000005175	0.0000181	0.0000443
4.0	0.000000177	0.0000007	0.0000021
	Sum of weights	Mean	Variance
	0.999999124	0.5758204	0.3755910
			SD (SE of $\hat{\theta}$)
			0.6128548

Maximum Likelihood Estimation for the Rasch, 2PL, and 3PL Models

For the Rasch model, the maximum likelihood will occur at the same θ value for all examinees with the same observed score (this is due to the property of sufficiency discussed previously). However, some ways of earning a given score are more likely than others, so the likelihood values for different response patterns that yield the same ability estimate will be different. As an illustration, the data from Table 14.1 are transformed into data appropriate for a Rasch model. That is, the same b-values are kept for all items but all items' a-values are set to 1 and c-values to 0. The top panel of Figure 14.9 shows the resulting

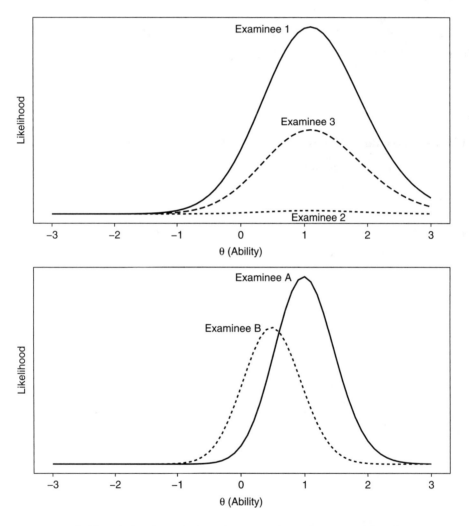

FIGURE 14.9. Likelihood distributions based on Rasch and 2PL models. The upper panel shows the likelihood functions, based on the Rasch model, for three different patterns of seven items correct. All functions reach a maximum at the same θ. The lower panel shows the likelihood functions, based on a 2PL model, for response patterns that varied in the a-parameters of the correct items. Examinee A answered more discriminating items.

Rasch-based likelihoods for three different response patterns, each with seven items correct: 1111111000 (examinee 1), 1101011101 (examinee 2), and 1111110010 (examinee 3). All three functions reach a maximum at $\theta = 1.1$, but the maximum value attained is much lower for examinee 2 because this pattern is very unusual and thus unlikely.

In the 2PL and 3PL models, the shape of the likelihood depends on which items the examinee answered correctly. For the 2PL model, the likelihood will reach a maximum at different theta values for examinees who have the same observed score but different response patterns. This is because in the 2PL model items are differentially weighed by their a-parameters. We created data representing responses to a 20-item test by copying two sets of the b-values from the 10-item test in Table 14.1 and assigning one item in each matched pair of b-values to have an a-value of 0.8 and the other to have an a-value of 1.6 (with $D = 1$). The lower panel of Figure 14.9 shows the likelihood functions obtained from estimating a 2PL model from these data based on the response patterns of two hypothetical examinees. Both examinees answered the first five pairs of items correctly, but Examinee A answered the more discriminating items ($a = 1.6$) in the sixth, seventh, and eighth pairs correctly but the less discriminating items ($a = .8$) in the ninth and tenth pairs incorrectly. Examinee B answered all of the more discriminating items incorrectly. Because of the differences in their responses to the highly discriminating items, Examinee A's maximum occurred at $\theta = 1.0$, whereas Examinee B's maximum was at 0.5.

For the 3PL model, the a-parameter values also vary across examinees. In addition, in this model a correct response to a difficult item has less weight in the likelihood for a low-ability examinee than for a high-ability examinee. This is because the low-ability examinee may have guessed the correct answer. For a given examinee, if two items have equal a's and b's, a correct response to the item with the lower c-value will have a higher weight, especially if the item is difficult relative to the examinee's ability.

This discussion illustrates that the likelihood function of θ depends on the item parameters. Of course, the item parameter values must also be estimated in IRT. However, estimation of the item parameters is quite complicated, and so only a short synopsis is presented here. Interested readers can refer to de Ayala (2009, ch. 4) or Baker and Kim (2004, ch. 6) for more information. In brief, the most common method of item parameter estimation in current use is known as *maximum marginal likelihood* (MML). Just as each response pattern has a likelihood that is a function of θ conditional on the item parameters, each item has a multidimensional likelihood that is a function of θ and the three (or fewer, depending on the model) item parameters. The likelihood is *marginalized*, or averaged, over the values in the θ distribution, and the item parameter values at which the marginal distribution reaches a maximum are estimated using calculus. Figure 14.10 shows the marginal likelihood for a 2PL item (a 3PL item would require four dimensions). The maximum occurs at $a = 1.3$ and $b = 0.5$. The marginalization of the likelihood is approximated by the method of quadratures discussed in the previous section. As discussed in that section, the distribution of θ is also estimated from these quadrature points as part of the process. One advantage of using quadratures for estimation is that it is not necessary to assume that the ability distribution is normal.

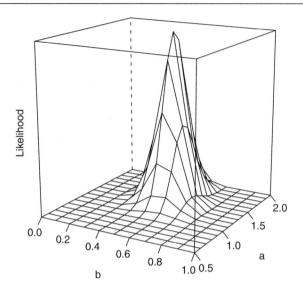

FIGURE 14.10. The marginal likelihood function for a 2PL item.

The distribution of θ estimated from the quadrature points can be used as the prior ability distribution in the EAP estimation of ability for individual examinees. Alternatively, the θs could be estimated using maximum likelihood after the item parameters are estimated.

SAMPLE SIZE REQUIREMENTS

The number of examinees needed to estimate the item parameter values depends on the complexity of the model. Typically, information on how well the parameters are estimated is based on simulation studies of the standard errors of the parameter estimates. The standard errors will decrease as the sample size increases, but at some point the decrease in standard error becomes negligible and the sample size is then considered adequate. The Rasch and 1PL models are often applied with sample sizes as small as 100 or 200 because item difficulties are the easiest parameters to estimate. For the 2PL model, samples of around 250–500 are often recommended (Drasgow, 1989; Harwell & Janosky, 1991; Stone, 1992). Sample sizes of 1,000 or more may be needed for the 3PL model, but smaller samples may give acceptable standard errors, depending on item and sample characteristics and choices made during the item calibration. For example, the c-parameters are easier to estimate for difficult, well-discriminating items than for easy items. Test length also contributes to the accuracy of item parameter estimation. Adding items leads to better estimation of item parameters, but after reaching a test length of 20 to 30 items, further additions will not make much difference to item parameter estimation.

INFORMATION, STANDARD ERROR OF MEASUREMENT, AND RELIABILITY

Maximum Likelihood Estimation

When abilities are estimated using ML, the *test information function*, $I(\theta)$, can be used to indicate the precision, or reliability, of the estimates. The test information is used in IRT estimation to measure the precision or reliability of the test scores. However, instead of having only a single value, as in classical test theory, the test information is a function that varies across ability levels. The test information function is the sum of the information functions from the individual items. It is therefore easy to determine the impact of adding or deleting items to the test form by comparing test information functions with and without particular items. This is analogous to examining values of alpha-if-item-deleted in classical test theory. Calculation of the item information function is complicated. It is the negative of the expected value of the second derivative of the natural log of the item response function $P(\theta)$, which is the probability of correct response as a function of θ. This function is obtained as part of the calculus used in finding the ML estimate of θ, so it is a by-product of the estimation process.

Figure 14.11 shows the item information functions (dashed lines), along with the item response functions (solid lines) for three 2PL items and three 3PL items. Notice the relationship between the two functions: the item information function peaks at the location of the item difficulty for 2PL items (and just above the item difficulty for 3PL items). This makes sense because an item that is matched to an examinee's ability will provide the most information. Items that are too easy will not provide information about how much ability an examinee has. Such items can only indicate that the examinee has at least a minimum level of ability. Similarly, items that are too difficult for an examinee indicate that the examinee does not have sufficient ability to answer the item but do not provide any information about how much ability the examinee does have. The discrimination parameter values also affect the amount of information provided by an item, with larger *a*-values yielding higher levels of information. This is evidenced by the fact that the peak value of the information function is higher for items with higher *a*-parameters and flatter for items with lower *a*-parameters. The same is true in CTT, in which reliability is highest when items are most highly correlated with the total score (e.g., are most discriminating). Finally, adding a nonzero lower asymptote (*c*-parameter) decreases the information for difficult items, particularly for examinees for whom the item is quite difficult. This is because a nonzero lower asymptote indicates that examinees may obtain a correct answer by guessing, and this does not provide any information about their levels of ability. Examinees who find the item more difficult are more likely to guess, so less information is obtained about their ability levels than would be obtained for higher-ability examinees.

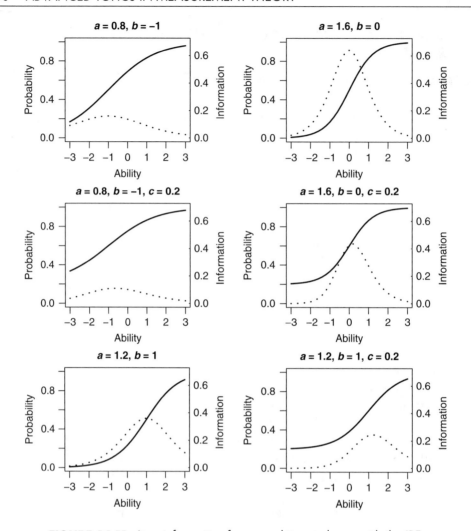

FIGURE 14.11. Item information for several items, shown with the IRF.

Test Information Function

The item information functions are summed to form the test information function. The test information function for the items in Table 14.1 is shown as a solid line in Figure 14.12. Because the b-values for these items were spread evenly around zero, the information is highest for abilities near zero or a little above. Because of the c-parameter, which results in a decrease in information for lower-ability examinees, there is somewhat less information for these examinees than for examinees at the highest ability levels.

The test information function shown in Figure 14.12 is the information function for ML scores. Test information functions can also be obtained for MAP score estimates, except that the second derivative of the prior is added to the information function. If a normal prior was chosen, the second derivative is simply the inverse of the SD of the

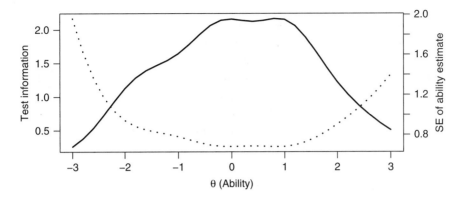

FIGURE 14.12. Test information and standard error of ML estimate of θ.

prior, usually 1. In regions of θ where there is already a large amount of information, adding 1 to the information function will not make much difference. But where there is little information, this information from the prior will make more of a difference. Test length also affects test information. Short tests have less information than long tests, so adding a constant of 1 from the prior will make a larger difference on shorter tests. Earlier, when discussing Figure 14.8 in the Estimation section, an example was shown where the prior distribution made a large contribution to the posterior likelihood for a 10-item test. This occurred because there is not much information in the responses to a 10-item test, so the prior contributed relatively more information.

Standard Error of θ

The standard error of the ML or MAP estimate of θ is the inverse of the square root of the test information function, or $1/\sqrt{I(\theta)}$. This is quite a mouthful but is similar to CTT, in which the standard error of measurement is an inverse function of reliability. This inverse relationship makes sense because the standard error is a measure of lack of information, or error, whereas the test information, or reliability, is a measure of the precision with which θ, or true scores, can be estimated. The standard error function is shown as a dashed line in Figure 14.12. To illustrate the relationship between the standard error and the test information function, note from the figure that as test information increases, the standard error decreases. However, the relationship between the two functions is not linear. This is important because it is the basis for the fact that as the test length increases, each additional item contributes less and less to decreasing the standard error of measurement. That is, for shorter tests adding items results in a greater payoff in terms of decreases in the standard error of θ, but for longer tests adding items results in smaller standard error decreases. You may recall that the same is true in CTT, as can be illustrated by applying the Spearman–Brown prophecy formula with increasing numbers of items.

An important feature of IRT standard errors is that they vary across examinees. This allows for estimation of different standard errors at different levels of θ. Such estimates are more accurate than the "one-size-fits-all" reliability estimates of CTT. For the example test, information is highest and standard errors are lowest for examinees in the middle of the distribution, as you can see from Figure 14.12. As noted previously, this is because the difficulty values for this test ranged from –1.8 to 1.8. Because the item difficulties are targeted to the middle range of ability, the test provides the most information and the lowest standard errors for examinees in that ability range. For example, an examinee with the response pattern 1111101100 (Examinee 1 in Figure 14.8) had an ability estimate of 0.94, which has a standard error of 0.68, as shown in Figure 14.12. In contrast, an examinee with an ability estimate of 3 would have a standard error of 1.40.

EAP Estimation

For EAP estimation, the standard error is calculated somewhat differently than for ML estimation. The posterior distribution used in EAP estimation is the hypothetical distribution of θ values that would be obtained if the examinee were tested over and over again using items with identical parameters. It is no coincidence that this sounds similar to the definition of a true score as the mean of repeated observed scores. The two concepts are equivalent. The posterior distribution is therefore a sort of sampling distribution, and as is true for other parameter estimates, such as the mean or regression coefficient, the SD of the sampling distribution is the standard error of the EAP θ estimate. This standard error was calculated in Table 14.2 for one response pattern, 1111101100, using the same method one would use to calculate the SD from a table of grouped frequencies. Returning to the free-throw example, imagine that out of three basketball free-throws, 10% of your sample made zero baskets, 40% made one, 45% made two, and 5% made three baskets. Recall that the mean of this distribution is 1.45. To compute the variance, you would calculate $0.10(0–1.45)^2 + 0.40(1–1.45)^2 + 0.45(2–1.45)^2 + 0.05(3–1.45)^2 = 0.5475$. Taking the square root yields 0.74 for the SD.

In Table 14.2, θ_k is analogous to the number of baskets scored, and the posterior likelihood ($L(\theta_k|X_j)$) takes the place of the sample proportion. Recall that the mean likelihood, or EAP estimate of θ, was previously calculated to be 0.5758. So, for a θ value of 1.0 the calculation is $0.2674853(1–0.5758204)^2 = 0.2674853(0.1799283) = 0.0481282$. The same calculation is applied to each θ value, and the results are summed to obtain the variance of θ. The square root of this quantity, or the standard error of the θ estimates, is 0.61 as shown at the bottom of Table 14.2. This is somewhat smaller than the standard error for the ML estimate of the same response pattern. The reason for this is that EAP estimates are somewhat more precise than ML estimates because of the inclusion of the prior. In a sense, the prior can be thought of as an additional source of information that helps to obtain more precise estimates.

Item parameter estimates also have their own standard errors, which indicate the precision of the estimate. Thus, when communicating IRT results, it is important to say, "the standard error of the θ estimate" (or $\hat{\theta}$), or "the standard error of the a-parameter," not just "standard error." The standard error of $\hat{\theta}$ may also be called the standard error of measurement (*SEM*) but some researchers prefer to reserve that term only for observed scores, or CTT standard errors.

Sometimes it is desirable to have a single index of the reliability for a sample of examinees. In CTT, the relations between the score reliability and the *SEM* is: reliability $= (\sigma_X^2 - \sigma_e^2)/\sigma_X^2$, where σ_X^2 is the variance of the observed scores and σ_e^2 is the variance of the errors (the squared *SEM*). With real data, sample estimates s_X^2 and s_e^2 are substituted for σ_X^2 and σ_e^2. In IRT, this relationship also applies to ML scores (Green, Bock, Humphreys, Linn, & Reckase, 1984), using s_θ^2 in place of s_X^2.

IRT ASSUMPTIONS

Three broad assumptions underlie IRT models: correct dimensionality, local independence, and functional form.

Correct Dimensionality

As noted previously, IRT models that can accommodate both unidimensional and multidimensional data are available. Here, dimensionality refers to the number of attributes or abilities measured by the test. It will perhaps not surprise you that an assumption underlying the use of unidimensional IRT models is that the data are, in fact, unidimensional. If data violate the unidimensionality assumption, item parameter estimates are likely to be biased. Unidimensionality may be assessed in a number of different ways. Some methods of assessing dimensionality that were discussed in Chapter 12 in the context of EFA are also used in IRT. These include scree plots, parallel analysis, and examination of the relative magnitude of eigenvalues.

One popular method of dimensionality assessment specific to IRT is called DIMTEST, named for the software in which it is implemented (Stout, 2005). This procedure is often run as a check for unidimensionality before implementing IRT. In DIMTEST, examinees are divided into groups with the same observed score, and the covariances among items are calculated for each group. If the observed score is unidimensional, calculating covariances within score-based groups should remove any interitem covariance that is due to differences in levels of that dimension. In essence, calculating covariances within such groups is the same as covarying, or conditioning out any variance due to examinee differences on the dimension being measured (θ). And because under the unidimensional IRT model the covariances among items are posited to be due to differences in levels of θ, item covariances should be zero after these differences are controlled. If the score is not unidimensional, however, conditioning on the ability score will not remove all of the dimensions that might cause items to covary, and the resulting item covariances will not be zero. DIMTEST provides an index known as Stout's T that provides a statistical

ADVANCED TOPICS IN MEASUREMENT THEORY

significance test of the average interitem covariance that remains after controlling for the ability scores. The statistical significance of this test implies that the test is not unidimensional, whereas statistical nonsignificance implies unidimensionality.

Like most statistical assumptions, the assumption of unidimensionality is an ideal rather than an absolute standard. Item responses will always exhibit some degree of multidimensionality, even if all items measure a single construct. This is because dimensionality can be affected by similarities in item wording or difficulty or by response artifacts such as test-wiseness or socially desirable responding. There may also be an overarching *general factor* that subsumes several more specific factors. This is the case, for example, with many intelligence scales, which measure one general or g factor, along with several more specific factors such as spatial ability or vocabulary comprehension. Essentially, the general dimension measured will be a composite of the general factor and the specific or more minor factors. In such situations, there should be little distortion in item parameter estimates as long as one factor is much stronger than any other, more minor factors.

A related issue is that most testing programs change the test form every year or keep multiple test forms for security, and different test forms might produce slightly different composite scores. For example, perhaps on a math test there is a general math ability factor as well as minor factors for geometry, algebra, arithmetic, and statistics. If the mix of these minor factors changed slightly between test forms, the composite score might change, thus impacting the estimated parameters.

Local Independence

The local independence assumption is essentially the same as the assumption, discussed in Chapters 12 and 13 in the context of factor analysis, that the factor is the reason for the correlations among the items. The implication here is that, if the factor were removed or controlled for, the items would no longer be correlated. In IRT, this assumption is known as local independence. In this context, local is used to mean conditional, so local independence means that the items are independent after controlling for, or conditioning on ability. The assumption of local independence is tied to the unidimensionality assumption because if the test is unidimensional, item responses should be locally independent. If shared variance among the items remains after controlling for the ability being measured, there must be some additional dimension (or dimensions) that is causing the shared variance. These additional dimensions may represent either more specific substantive factors or unintended dimensionality due to such factors as wording similarities or, for noncongnitive items, the influences of socially desirable or other response styles.

Yen's (1984) Q_3 is commonly used to detect item pairs that violate local independence. The first step in calculating Yen's Q_3 is to estimate an IRT model. Then for each examinee and each item, the residual between the observed item response (0 or 1 if the item is dichotomous) and the item response predicted by the model, given the examinee's θ estimate, is calculated. The predicted item response is simply the probability of a correct response discussed previously. For example, if $P(\theta_i) = 0.4$ for examinee j, then examinee j's predicted response is 0.4. Thus examinee j's residual for item i would be -0.4 $(0 - 0.4)$ if the item were wrong (0) or 0.6 $(1 - 0.4)$ if the item were right (1). Yen's Q_3 is the correlation, across examinees, of the residuals for each pair of items. The idea is that if an additional dimension is measured by a pair of items, examinees who were higher on that dimension would be more likely to get both items right than predicted based on θ. Examinees who were lower on that dimension would be more likely to get both items wrong than predicted based on θ. Either situation would produce a positive correlation between the residuals. Although Yen's Q_3 is based on Pearson's correlation, it does not follow the same distribution and should therefore not be used as a statistical significance test (Chen & Thissen, 1997). Instead, it should be used as an effect size. Yen (1993) suggested that values of 0.2 or higher might be considered large enough to indicate a violation that could affect the IRT results. For alternative indices for testing statistical significance of pairwise local independence, see Chen and Thissen (1997).

The importance of the local independence assumption can be seen when considering how the likelihood is calculated. Recall that the likelihood of the overall response pattern is the product of the likelihood of the individual item responses. However, this relationship is true only if the responses are conditionally independent. Violating local independence inflates the estimate of the information function (Wainer & Wang, 2000). This means that the scores will appear to be more reliable than they really are. In CTT, coefficient alpha is also inflated by violations of local independence (Sireci, Thissen, & Wainer, 1991). Violation of local independence does not generally bias the θ or b-parameter estimates, but it can lead to overestimates of the c-parameter and either over- or underestimates of the a-parameter, depending on the mix of items (Wainer, Bradlow, & Du, 2000; Wainer & Wang, 2000).

Functional Form

De Ayala (2009) used the term *functional form* to encompass what some authors have separated into multiple assumptions. Simply put, functional form means that the model used (i.e., 1PL, 2PL, 3PL) is the correct model for the data. One implication of this for all IRT models is that the probability of a correct response (or a higher score, for polytomous IRT models) should increase as θ increases. For the 2PL and 1PL/Rasch models, specification of the correct functional form also means that there is no correct guessing or other reason for a lower asymptote. For the 1PL/Rasch model, an additional assumption is that items have equal slopes. The most direct way to test the functional form is to test the *item fit*.

Item Fit

Item fit is a measure of how well the observed item responses match the responses predicted by the model. A similar concept in regression is that respondents' *y*-values will match their predicted *y*-values. One way to assess item fit is to look at plots of the observed and predicted responses. Recall that the predicted response is $P(\theta)$, the probability of a correct response given θ. When creating plots, the observed responses are generally pooled over examinees with similar estimated θs. The plots therefore indicate the proportion of examinees near each θ value who answered correctly. Figure 14.13 shows a plot of the model-predicted proportions for each θ value, represented by a solid line, and the observed proportions of examinees who answered correctly, represented by circles. In this figure you can see that the line deviates most from the circles for the lowest ability and highest ability examinees. The observed proportions (circles) are below the line for these examinees. Thus, these examinees were less likely to respond correctly than the model predicted, whereas the middle-ability examinees were more likely to respond correctly than predicted. Perhaps there is a distractor that is particularly appealing to a few high-ability examinees, leading this group of examinees to obtain a smaller percentage of correct responses than would be expected, given their θ values.

Many indices have been developed to test the statistical significance of the item misfit. One index that seems to have relatively accurate Type I error rates is the Orlando–Thissen (2000) index. To calculate this index, examinees with the same observed score are grouped together. Within each score group, the number of examinees who obtained a correct answer is compared to the number expected to obtain a correct answer, given the IRT model used. The differences between the two quantities are squared, divided by their variance, and summed across score groups. The resulting

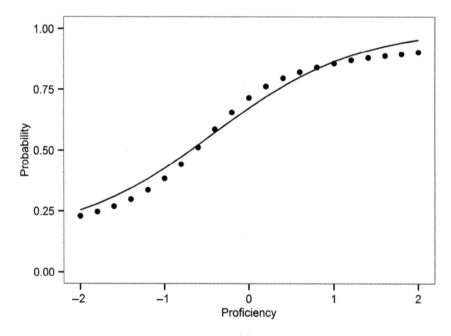

FIGURE 14.13. Graph showing item fit. Model-predicted proportions for each θ value are represented by a solid line; observed proportions of examinees who answered correctly are represented by circles.

index is distributed as χ^2 and thus can be tested for statistical significance. As with any statistical significance test, even if the Type I error rate is accurate, small, inconsequential misfit can be statistically significant in large samples. The Orlando–Thissen index (and other similar item fit indices) has no accompanying effect sizes, but predicted and observed responses for items rejected as misfitting can be plotted to interpret whether the difference is large or small. Unfortunately, there are no guidelines regarding how large a gap between predicted and observed responses should be tolerated. Generally, test developers would be most concerned about differences in regions of θ where there are many examinees.

IRT APPLICATIONS

As discussed at various points throughout this chapter, IRT methods have advantages over CTT methods in the estimation of examinee ability and item parameter values, and the assessment of measurement error. IRT yields estimates of item parameters that are group-invariant, such that item parameter estimates are not specific to the group of examinees from which they were obtained. Neither are estimates of examinee ability dependent on the specific items administered. Moreover, the item information functions obtained through IRT allow test developers to minimize measurement error at specific ability levels. These properties facilitate applications such as test form assembly and computer adaptive testing.

Test Form Assembly

A common application of IRT methods is the assembly of items into test forms that meet desired criteria. One function that may be useful in test assembly is the test characteristic function (TCF; also called the test characteristic curve, TCC). The TCF characterizes the relationship between θ and the predicted observed score. In other words, the TCF shows how the θ values from IRT relate to the predicted scores that are in the original test metric. The TCF is the sum of the item response functions (IRFs): $\Sigma_i P_i(\theta)$, where $P_i(\theta)$ is the probability of correct response on item i, for a given value of θ. The TCF for the item parameters in Table 14.1 is shown in Figure 14.14. The value of the TCF for a given θ is called the *true score* because if the data perfectly fit the model, the predicted score will equal the average observed score (conditional on θ), which corresponds to the concept of true score in CTT. For example, in Figure 14.14, the TCF = 5.81 at $\theta = 0$, so if an examinee with $\theta = 0$ were tested repeatedly, the average of the observed scores would be 5.81. Although a score of 5.81 might seem quite different from a score of 0, recall that the observed scores are on a number-correct metric, whereas the θ values are on a z-score-like metric.

Turning back to test assembly, test developers may want a specific θ to correspond to a particular observed score. For example, in an achievement testing program in which students are classified into categories such as Developing, Proficient, or Advanced, test

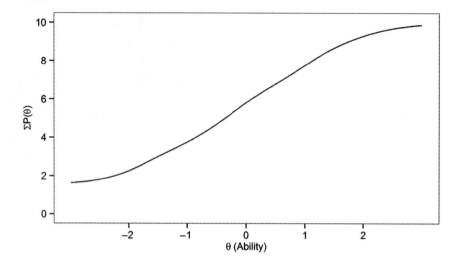

FIGURE 14.14. TCF for item parameters in Table 14.1.

specifications may call for the TCF to reach specific observed score values at the θ values corresponding to the classification cut points. Making such a specification each year the test was given would ensure the same cut-point score values across years.

Additionally, those developing the test would likely want the measurement error to be smallest at the cut points, so the scores that determine an examinee's achievement level classification are as precise as possible. Because of the inverse relationship between the squared standard error and the test information function, the test could be developed to achieve this goal. Recall that the test information function is the sum of the item information functions, so items that yield the highest amount of information at the cut points could be selected to make up the test. Of course, the test developers would also have to make sure the chosen items covered the content specified in the test's table of specifications. Van der Linden and Adema (1998) have developed algorithms that take content considerations into account while maximizing test precision at the desired cut points. Alternatively, psychometricians may adopt a more empirical approach, shifting items in and out of the test until the desired content and accuracy levels are obtained.

Equating

Another application facilitated by the use of IRT is test form equating (see Chapter 18). Equating is used to ensure that different test forms have equal overall difficulty levels. The advantage of using IRT for equating stems from the fact that item difficulty values and θ estimates are on the same scale. This means that, as long as items from different forms have been calibrated to the same metric (for example, with a mean θ value of 0 and

SD of 1), any combination of items from the forms can be combined to make a new form, and the resulting θ estimates will have the same scale. Thus, no additional equating to achieve equal metrics is needed.

Basic details of IRT equating are covered in Chapter 18 and will not be repeated here. In brief, IRT equating is quite similar to linear equating using CTT. The key difference is that in CTT a linear transformation is applied at the test form level, and in IRT the transformation is applied at the item level. Once a large group of items, sometimes called an *item bank*, is on the same metric, any combination of items can be pulled out to make a test form, and multiple test forms will be on the same metric even if there are no common items. The test developers do not have to wait until the test form has been administered and scored to scale it to the same metric as another test form; this will occur automatically because the items are already on the same metric.

In some cases, test developers or users may want to use IRT to equate the forms but then use summed scoring to score the test. The summed score can then be transformed to the test's reporting scale (such as a T-score scale or IQ-type scale) directly. Although this could be done using CTT equating, some test developers prefer the simplicity of scaling all items to a common metric so that they can work out the equating for future test forms before they are administered. The easiest method is labeled *true score equating*, which derives its name from the tradition of calling $\Sigma_i P_i(\theta)$ the true score. In this method, the item parameters for Group 1 are first transformed to the desired metric of Group 2 by finding the appropriate additive and multiplicative constants, and the test characteristic functions are computed for the two test forms to be equated. (For simplicity, assume that these test forms were those administered to Groups 1 and 2, although once the items are calibrated, they could be any combination of items.) The θ that best corresponds to a summed score of X on the TCF for test form 1 is found using calculus. This θ is then plugged into the TCF for test form 2 to estimate the summed score that would theoretically be achieved on test form 2. For example, imagine that a score of 22 on the Y axis of the TCF for test form 1 corresponds to $\theta = -0.58$. And $\theta = -0.58$ corresponds to a score of 22.6 on the TCF for test form 2. The 22.6 would likely be rounded to 23, and a score of 22 on form 1 would be considered equivalent to a score of 23 on form 2.

Computer Adaptive Testing Applications

Computer adaptive testing (CAT) is another common application of IRT. In such tests, examinees are administered different test items depending on their ability level. These ability levels are adjusted throughout the test, based on each examinee's performance. Specifically, in CAT each item is selected based on the examinee's current estimate of θ. Most frequently, the item that would yield the maximum amount of information at an examinee's estimated ability value ($\hat{\theta}$) is selected, subject to content constraints and restrictions in the proportion of examinees that may see the item (known as *item exposure limits*). Note that CATs are not possible without IRT. IRT procedures allow for items to be precalibrated, so that their difficulty and discrimination values are known in advance. This allows for examinees' ability levels to be updated as each item is answered, and the updated ability level for each examinee determines the next item to be administered. Such testing would not be possible under CTT, although approximations have been developed.

CATs are advantageous because they allow examinees to take fewer items while keeping the standard error of measurement at or below the level of a fixed-length test. CAT is particularly useful for measuring the ability of those at the lowest and highest ability levels. Scores at these levels typically have larger standard errors on fixed-length tests because such tests are often designed for examinees at middle-ability levels. This means that most items are in the middle-difficulty range, with fewer items, and therefore less precision, outside this range. With CATs, items can be targeted to the specific ability level of each examinee, resulting in lower standard errors.

Differential Item Functioning Applications

The detection of items that exhibit DIF is another useful application of IRT. Most often, observed score methods such as the Mantel–Haenszel method are used to conduct DIF analyses (see Chapter 16), but IRT is particularly useful for conceptualizing DIF. An item is said to exhibit DIF if examinees who are from different groups, but who are matched on levels of ability, have different probabilities of a correct response. In IRT, these differences in response probabilities manifest themselves as different item response functions. Thus, DIF can be detected by comparing IRFs for different groups. Such comparisons can be done visually, but most DIF detection methods based on IRF comparison use mathematical procedures to determine the magnitude and significance of these differences. However, plotting the IRFs provides a visual display of how large the DIF effect is.

SUMMARY

Item response theory is a complex topic, and one on which many books have been written. This chapter has provided an overview of some basic IRT concepts and models; we refer those of you who would like more in-depth treatments to consult the resources cited in the chapter. One feature of IRT models that gives them an advantage over the CTT model is that IRT models allow for item parameter estimates from different groups to be transformed so that they are on the same scale. In contrast, item parameters from CTT are sample dependent and will not, in general, be comparable across different samples of examinees. A second useful feature of IRT models is that estimates of ability are not dependent on the particular items administered, but they can be compared across examinees who have taken different sets of items. Also, measurement error in IRT is a function of the test information function. This function varies across ability levels and can be used to obtain values of the standard error of ability (θ) for each ability level.

Three IRT models are commonly used to model data from unidimensional tests: the one-parameter, or Rasch model, the two-parameter model, and the three-parameter model. As their names imply, the three models differ in the item parameters included in each. The simplest model is the 1PL/Rasch model, which includes only one item parameter: the difficulty (b) parameter. In the 2PL model, another parameter is added; this is the discrimination (a) parameter. The a-parameter allows for items to differ in the degree to which they can discriminate among examinees with different levels of ability. In the 1PL/Rasch model, all items are assumed to have equal discriminating power, so the a-parameter is not included (or is set to 1 for all items). Finally, the 3PL includes a pseudo-guessing (c) parameter. This parameter allows for the possibility that even examinees with low levels of ability may obtain a correct answer to an item through guessing or other behavior that is not related to their ability. For items on which guessing is likely to occur, such as true–false or multiple-choice items, the 3PL may provide a better model of examinees' response probabilities than the 1PL or 2PL models.

The properties of IRT estimation allow for several useful applications. The fact that IRT item parameter estimates are not sample dependent is very useful for the development of parallel test forms. Items that have equal item parameter values and that measure the same content area can be matched and assigned to different test forms. This is usually accomplished through computer applications that are programmed to select such items from an item bank. It is also possible to select test items in such a way that the standard error of ability is lowest at a particular ability level. This is very useful for licensure, certification, and achievement tests in which examinees must score above a particular cut point to pass the test. In these testing situations, it is crucial for scores at the cut point to be estimated as precisely as possible. Because items are precalibrated in IRT (i.e., item parameters are known), it is possible to select items that discriminate best at the cut point, which results in the smallest amount of error at that point. Another advantage of precalibrated items is the ability to develop CATs, in which examinees are administered items that best match their ability. Ability levels are adjusted up or down as examinees proceed through the test, depending on whether test items are answered correctly or incorrectly. Because of this, examinee ability can be accurately measured with fewer items than would be needed when using a paper-and-pencil test. Other applications in which IRT methods are useful include equating test forms and detecting DIF.

EXERCISES

1. Define the a-, b-, and c-parameters in IRT.

2. Why is the IRF usually S-shaped rather than linear?

Questions 3–5 refer to the item response functions in Figure 14.15.

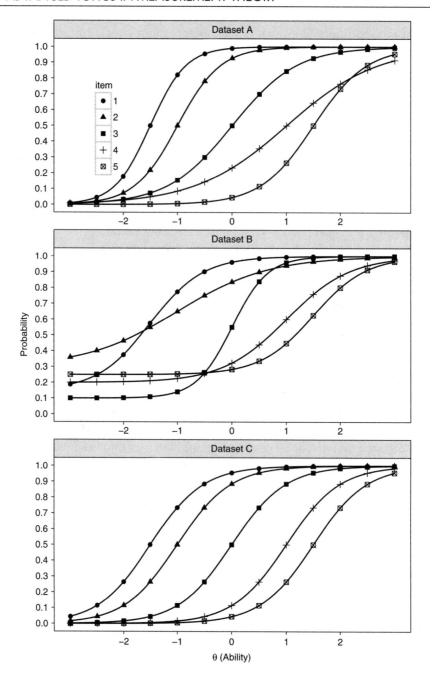

FIGURE 14.15. IRFs for Questions 3–5.

3. Which dataset most likely follows each of these IRT models:

   a. 1PL/Rasch

   b. 2PL

   c. 3PL

4. In Dataset C, which of the five items is most difficult?

5. In Dataset B, which item is most discriminating?

6. In the IRF in Figure 14.16, what is the approximate probability of correct response for an examinee with $\theta = 1$?

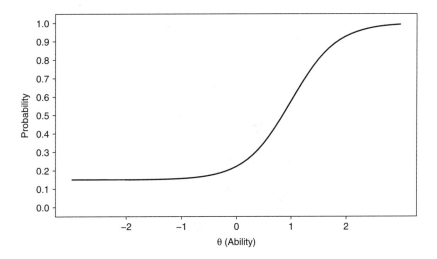

FIGURE 14.16. IRF for Question 6.

7. In Figure 14.17, what is the most likely score for an examinee with $\theta = -0.5$?

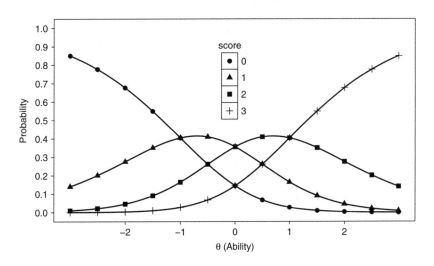

FIGURE 14.17. Graph for Question 7.

8. What is the difference between the partial credit and generalized partial credit models for polytomous data?

Questions 9 and 10 refer to the graph of the log-likelihood for one examinee (Figure 14.18).

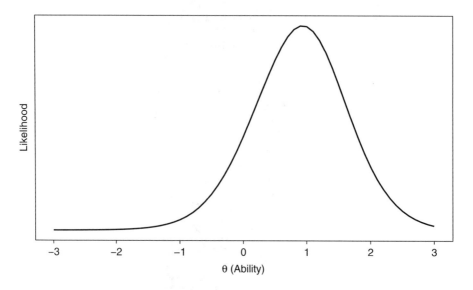

FIGURE 14.18. Log-likelihood graph for Questions 9 and 10.

9. What is the examinee's approximate ML estimate of θ in this graph?

10. If the prior θ distribution were N(0,1) would the MAP estimate of θ be higher or lower than the ML estimate for this examinee?

11. Figure 14.19 shows a test information function. Which θ would correspond to the smallest standard error of measurement?

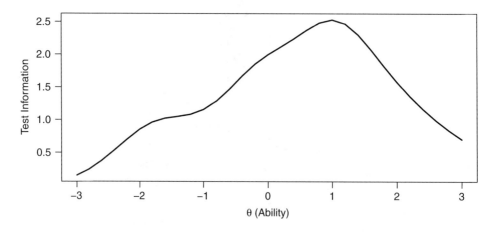

FIGURE 14.19. Graph of test information function for Question 11.

12. Would the test in Question 11 be best suited for classifying students as passing or failing based on a cut score of 1 on the θ scale or for obtaining accurate scores across a broad range of abilities?

13. For the test shown in Question 11, how could the test developers increase the information for low-ability examinees?

14. What is the relationship between test information and reliability?

15. Explain the meaning of the following primary assumptions of IRT.

    a. Correct dimensionality

    b. Local independence

    c. Functional form

16. Which of the assumptions from Question 15 would be violated in each of the following situations?

    a. A test is thought to measure only math ability and is modeled as unidimensional. In reality, however, the test contains several word problems that measure reading ability as well as math ability.

    b. The 2PL model is used for a test on which there is a considerable amount of guessing.

    c. A test measures a broad general factor as well as several minor factors. However, the general factor is much stronger than the minor factors.

Diagnostic Classification Models

with Laine P. Bradshaw

In Chapters 13 and 14, I discussed models in which the latent variable being measured was considered to be continuous. In CFA this latent variable is referred to as a factor, whereas in IRT it is commonly referred to by its Greek name of theta. Examples of such latent variables are depression, management style, and ability to calculate prescription dosages. But what if the latent variable is considered to be categorical rather than continuous? For example, suppose we wanted to know whether a person had a disease or did not have it? In this case, there is no underlying continuum to be measured as with factor or theta values. Models in which the latent variables are considered to be categorical rather than continuous can be estimated using diagnostic classification models (DCMs). Whereas methods based on continuous latent variables, such as EFA/CFA and IRT, allow for locating examinees along a latent continuum, categorical latent variables classify examinees into a latent group (also known as a latent class).

You may wonder how a group can be latent, as most groups with which you are likely familiar, such as those based on sex, race, ethnicity, or assignment to an experimental or control condition, are fairly easy to observe. However, consider the situation in which a teacher must determine whether students have sufficient mastery of a content area to go on to the next level. In this case, the decision is binary—either a student has achieved the mastery level or has not—but this is not evident through observation or other overt means. Instead, the teacher would likely administer some sort of test to students to determine whether they were in the mastery or nonmastery latent class. The class is therefore latent in the sense that it is not directly observable but must be ascertained through responses to test items or other observable behaviors. DCMs aid in such determinations by providing a mathematical model of the probability that a person is in a particular latent classification category, based on their responses to the test items.

Laine P. Bradshaw, PhD, is Associate Professor of Quantitative Methodology in the Department of Educational Psychology at the University of Georgia.

In this chapter, we provide an introduction to the DCM framework. We first describe the theoretical underpinnings of DCMs as a tool to support assessments that seek to provide multiple classifications of examinees according to a specific set of hypothesized latent characteristics. Then we introduce the fundamental form of the item response models and illustrate different types of items that may be specified under the general formulation. The chapter concludes with an explanation of how examinee classifications are estimated and a discussion of how classifications can be interpreted for use in practice.

CATEGORICAL LATENT VARIABLES FOR DCMs

Categorical latent variables are referred to as *attributes* in the DCM literature. Attributes are similar to the latent factors introduced in Chapters 12 and 13, but they differ in two ways. First, attributes are typically considered to be binary. In other words, we assume that there are only two possible states, or categories, of the attribute. Second, attributes are often more narrowly defined than factors. This is because the purpose of determining mastery or nonmastery of attributes is to help in making decisions about whether examinees have mastered specific content areas or exhibit symptoms indicative of a particular psychological disorder. Such decisions require detailed knowledge of a relatively narrow attribute. Attributes may represent, for example, components of a student's mathematics ability, symptoms of depression, or types of purchasing behavior. These attributes are binary in the sense that a student has either mastered a particular math skill or has not mastered it; a person either has a certain symptom of depression or does not have it; and a consumer either has a certain type of purchasing behavior or does not have it.

Test developers often label and interpret these attribute categories in a manner appropriate for the context and use of the test. In educational settings, where attributes are often skills or conceptual understandings, the two categories may be interpreted as mastery and nonmastery. For example, if the attribute is defined as the skill of determining the median of a dataset, students are classified as either masters of finding the median or nonmasters. In psychology, people can be classified as either exhibiting a particular symptom or not exhibiting it. Students taking tests designed to measure state educational standards are often classified into categories such as "emerging" or "proficient." Regardless of the labeling, the two groups differ in terms of their performance on a test, such that one group consistently exhibits the attribute being measured and the other group does not. As discussed in a later section, these determinations are based on examinees' patterns of responses to the test items.

Although classification into two categories is most consistent with the original meaning of the term *diagnosis*—("two" [*dia-*] and "to know" [*-gnosis*]; Rupp, Templin, & Henson, 2010), DCMs can be used to classify examinees into more than two ordered categories. For example, students may be nonmasters, partial masters, or complete masters of finding the median. In this case, the attribute would have three categories, or levels, instead of two. In this chapter, the focus is on DCMs with binary attributes. For readers who wish to understand how to make finer distinctions among the attribute levels, see Templin and Bradshaw (2013) for an example of multicategory attribute DCMs.

WHEN TO USE DCMs

DCMs are appropriate measurement models to use when the test purpose is to *classify* examinees according to one or more attributes, rather than to locate examinees on a continuum, as in IRT or CFA models. Typically, DCMs are used to measure more than one attribute. Often a single, broad trait is dissected into multiple fine-grained traits that constitute the attributes of interest. For example, multiple attributes of the broad traits of ability to subtract with fractions and to carry out multiplicative reasoning, and psychological attributes such as pathological gambling have been estimated in DCM analyses (Bradshaw, Izsák, Templin, & Jacobson, 2014; Tatsuoka, 1990; Templin & Henson, 2006). Tatsuoka (1990) broke the ability to subtract with fractions down into seven attributes, such as the ability to convert a mixed number to a fraction, the ability to borrow one from a whole number, and the ability to simplify a fraction to its lowest terms for a final answer. For this reason, it seems fitting that latent traits for DCMs are referred to as attributes because the term *attribute* connotes a part or characteristic of the whole rather than the whole itself.

In the previous paragraphs, we have stressed that attributes in DCMs are considered to be categorical. Having said that, a researcher may hypothesize that in truth the attributes of interest are continuous but may still use a DCM in which traits are treated as categorical. This might be done for one of two reasons. First, the researcher may want to classify examinees instead of scaling them along a continuum. For example, a teacher may administer a pretest so that she can roughly group students according to ability levels. The teacher may not need to make fine-grained distinctions among ability levels. Instead, she may simply want to know whether students are ready to move on to the next lesson (one level) or not (a second level). Second, a researcher might prefer to treat attributes as categorical because he or she wants to measure multiple dimensions with a single test, but the testing context does not support the measurement of multiple continuous traits. For example, estimation of multidimensional IRT (MIRT) models can be quite complex, requiring a very large sample size and many items for each dimension. In contrast, estimation of multiple DCM attributes is more practicable. For example, if a classroom pretest is administered for a mathematics unit, the purpose of the test may be to measure three distinct skills in the unit, but the teacher cannot devote more than 45 minutes to pretesting, meaning the test length cannot be more than about 20 items. DCMs are more feasible to use in this scenario than are MIRT models.

ATTRIBUTE PROFILES

When a test measures multiple attributes, a DCM classifies examinees according to the pattern of attributes they have mastered. If a test measures A binary attributes (represented by α), there are 2^A possible attribute patterns of mastery and nonmastery into which examinees can be classified. For example, with four attributes, there are 2^4 or 16 possible attribute patterns. The attribute patterns are denoted by $\alpha_e = \left[\alpha_{e1} \alpha_{e2} \ldots \alpha_{eA} \right]$ where $\alpha_{ea} = 1$ if examinee e is a master of Attribute a and is equal to zero otherwise. Thus, attributes are subscripted 1 through A, and examinees are subscripted with the letter e. To illustrate how to decipher such attribute patterns, consider the profile [0101]. This pattern indicates that the examinee is a master of Attributes 2 and 4 but not Attributes 1 and 3. As a succinct summary of the multidimensional test results, the attribute pattern provides a multivariate profile of an examinee's traits and, as such, is commonly referred to as an *attribute profile*.

DIAGNOSTIC CLASSIFICATION MODEL: A CONFIRMATORY LATENT CLASS MODEL

The attribute patterns define a set of mutually exclusive and exhaustive latent groups. Mutually exclusive means that when using DCMs, we assume all examinees are a member of one, and only one, of the latent groups. One purpose of DCM estimation is to optimize the classification of examinees into these groups or latent classes. One feature of an optimal classification scheme is that examinees within a latent group or class are as homogeneous as possible with respect to the construct being measured. Latent class modeling is a statistical technique for accomplishing such classifications, and DCMs are a member of the family of latent class models. Latent class models assume that item responses are independent, conditional on the set of latent classes. This is analogous to the local independence assumption in IRT, which holds that item responses to test items are independent, conditional on latent ability. That is, all of the covariation among item responses is accounted for by the ability (θ) being measured. For DCMs, this assumption means that an examinee's attribute pattern explains all of the covariance in the item responses and there are no other latent traits influencing responses. This implies that the set of attribute patterns is exhaustive; no other latent groups are hypothesized to exist outside of the attribute patterns that are modeled.

The latent groups in DCMs are predetermined according to the attribute patterns. That is, there are hypothesized to be as many latent groups as there are possible attribute patterns. Latent class analyses such as DCMs, in which the number and characteristics of the latent classes are known and defined before the analysis is conducted, are called *restricted* or *confirmatory* analyses. The alternative is an unrestricted or exploratory latent class model in which researchers seek to find the number of latent classes that exist empirically and may hypothesize theoretical justifications for their existence post hoc. Note that this confirmatory/exploratory distinction is directly analogous to that made in factor analysis. In CFA, the researcher specifies the number and nature of the factors a priori, whereas in EFA the researcher allows these determinations to be suggested by the data and attempts to explain the latent factors uncovered in a post-hoc fashion (see Chapters 12 and 13).

THE LATENT CLASS MODEL

Recall that responses to items are assumed to be conditionally independent given an examinee's class membership. Given this assumption, the latent class model for DCMs defines the probability of observing examinee e's response pattern across all items (denoted x_e) as a function of the attribute pattern p of examinee e (α_e) as

$$P\left(X_e = x_e\right) = \sum_{p=1}^{2^A} \upsilon_p \prod_{i=1}^{I} \pi_{i|\alpha_e}^{x_{ei}} \left(1 - \pi_{i|\alpha_e}\right)^{1-x_{ei}} \tag{15.1}$$

This equation has *structural* and *measurement* components. The structural component includes parameters that describe the attributes and how they are related to each other, analogous to the factor correlation matrix in factor analysis. The measurement component includes parameters that describe how attributes are related to items, analogous to the loading parameters in factor analysis. The parameter υ_p is a structural parameter that represents the proportion of examinees who have attribute pattern p, where

$p = 1, \ldots, 2^A$. These proportions sum to 1 $\left(\sum_{p=1}^{2^A} \upsilon_p = 1\right)$ because the attribute patterns

are mutually exclusive and exhaustive (e.g., each examinee has one and only one pattern). The parameter $\pi_{i|\alpha_e}$ is the measurement component of the model that denotes the probability that examinee e provides the correct response for item i ($x_{ei} = 1$), given his or her attribute pattern (α_e). The phrase "given his or her attribute pattern" is important here as it makes clear the fact that the probability of obtaining a correct response depends on whether one has mastered the particular attributes required by the item. The notation $(1 - \pi_{i|\alpha_e})$ is the probability of obtaining an incorrect response. So, the product $\pi_{i|\alpha_e}^{x_{ei}} \left(1 - \pi_{i|\alpha_e}\right)^{1-x_{ei}}$ is the probability of either a correct or an incorrect response, depending on the examinee's item response:

If $x_{ei} = 1$ (correct answer), then $\quad \pi_{i|\alpha_e}^{x_{ei}} \left(1 - \pi_{i|\alpha_e}\right)^{1-x_{ei}} = \pi_{i|\alpha_e}^{1} \left(1 - \pi_{i|\alpha_e}\right)^{0} = \pi_{i|\alpha_e}$

If $x_{ei} = 0$ (incorrect answer), then $\quad \pi_{i|\alpha_e}^{x_{ei}} \left(1 - \pi_{i|\alpha_e}\right)^{1-x_{ei}} = \pi_{i|\alpha_e}^{0} \left(1 - \pi_{i|\alpha_e}\right)^{1} = 1 - \pi_{i|\alpha_e}$

Because the item probabilities are conditionally independent, they can be multiplied together to obtain the probability of the entire response pattern. This is indicated by the notation $\prod_{i=1}^{I}$, which means that the products of $\pi_{i|\alpha_e}^{x_{ei}} \left(1 - \pi_{i|\alpha_e}\right)^{1-x_{ei}}$ are multiplied across all items. Taken as a whole, Equation 15.1 indicates that the probability of observing examinee e's response pattern is the sum, weighted by the p attribute patterns, of the products of the conditional probabilities of each item response.

The vector of attribute pattern proportions, υ_p, can have its own model that specifies how the latent attributes are related (e.g., de la Torre & Douglas, 2004; Hartz, 2002;

Henson & Templin, 2005; Templin & Henson, 2006; Templin, Henson, Templin, & Roussos, 2008; Xu & von Davier, 2008). As indicated previously, this model is known as the *structural model*. For example, one attribute may be a prerequisite for another attribute, which could be modeled by a regression-type relationship between the two attributes when specifying the possible attribute profiles (Templin & Bradshaw, 2014). You do not need a thorough understanding of structural models for DCMs to understand the basics of DCMs presented in this chapter. Similarly, a full understanding of the estimation process for DCMs is beyond the scope of this chapter. Chapters 8, 10, and 11 of the book by Rupp and colleagues (2010) are recommended for those who would like more detailed explanation of these topics.

To form a basis for understanding DCMs, the remainder of this chapter will focus on understanding the item response functions (IRFs) for DCMs. The IRFs comprise the *measurement* component of the model. As noted previously, the measurement components are the parameters that explain how observed item responses are related to latent traits. In Equation 15.1, the item parameter is $\pi_{i|\alpha_e}$ and denotes the probability that examinee e provides the correct response for item i ($X_{ei} = 1$), conditional on his or her attribute pattern (α_e). In this chapter, we will assume the item response is dichotomous ($X_{ei} = 0$ or $X_{ei} = 1$), as would be the case in a true–false or multiple-choice test scored as correct or incorrect. In DCMs, the item response also may be nominal (e.g., unordered categories; Templin, Rupp, Henson, Jang, & Ahmed, 2008), ordinal (Nixon, Ferster, Alagoz, & Templin, 2012), or continuous (Bozard, 2010). In this chapter, we focus on the simplest case, DCMs for dichotomous response data.

IRFs FOR DCMs

You may recall that in IRT the probability of a correct response can be modeled in different ways. The different IRT models (i.e., 1PL, 2PL, 3PL) are characterized by the presence or absence of different item parameters. These differences in parameterization (i.e., the number and type of parameters that are specified as predictors of the item response in the model) result in different IRFs. In the same way, the probability of a correct response for DCMs, $\pi_{i|\alpha_e}$, can be parameterized in various ways. As noted in the previous section, the structural parameters can also have different parameterizations. Because both the measurement (item) and structural models can take different forms, or parameterizations, a wide variety of DCMs are available. As an aside, one difference between the IRT and DCM models is that the IRT model does not include structural parameters, such as the parameter υ_p in DCMs. The structural model in an IRT model is simply the distribution of the latent traits (i.e., normally distributed latent traits). In the following sections, we detail the DCM item response function for a general DCM, known as the *log-linear cognitive diagnosis model* (Henson, Templin, & Willse, 2009).

THE LOG-LINEAR COGNITIVE DIAGNOSIS MODEL: A GENERAL DCM

The measurement part of the DCM models the relations between the expected outcome of the item response (the probability of a correct response) and the presence or absence of the attributes (predictor variables) thought to influence the item response. Before we explain the specifics of the measurement part of the DCM, we first provide a little background on one feature of the model known as the link function.

Link Functions for DCMs

Using DCMs, we want to know the probabilities of correctly answering an item for students with different attribute patterns. Although probabilities range from 0 to 1, a typical linear regression model would yield some predictions that are outside of this range and would not make sense (e.g., a probability of −.75 or 1.25). In statistics, when we want to predict the expected outcome of a binary variable and run into this problem, we predict the *natural log of the odds* of a correct response (known as the *log-odds*) instead of the probability of a correct response. This is because the log odds do not have a restricted range that would cause unrealistic predictions. This technique is called *logistic regression* and is discussed in Chapters 14 and 16 as well as in texts on categorical data analysis (e.g., Agresti, 2002). Understanding logistic regression is helpful for understanding DCMs and IRT models because both DCMs and IRT models are analogous to logistic regression models in which the predictor variables are latent instead of observed.

The odds of a correct response is the ratio of the probability of a correct response to the probability of an incorrect response:

$$\text{Odds} = \frac{P(X_{ei}=1)}{P(X_{ei}=0)}$$

where $P()$ stands for the probability of the quantity in parentheses. To form the log-odds, we take the natural log of the odds:

$$\ln\left(\frac{P(X_{ei}=1)}{P(X_{ei}=0)}\right)$$

Similar to a normally distributed outcome, log-odds are centered at 0 and range from negative infinity to positive infinity. In other words, unlike probabilities, which range from 0 to 1, log-odds have an unrestricted range. Figure 15.1 shows the relationship between the log-odds and probabilities of a correct response. Notice that a log-odds of 0 corresponds to a probability of .50 and that as probabilities increase, the log-odds also increase. You can also see that the log-odds are symmetric around 0: the probabilities of .1 and .9 are both .4 probability units from the probability scale center of .5 and 2.2 log-odds units from the log-odds scale center of 0. While the log-odds technically range from negative infinity to infinity, notice that for the near-zero probability of .01, the log-odds is equal to only −4.6; similarly, for the near-unit probability of .99, the log-odds is

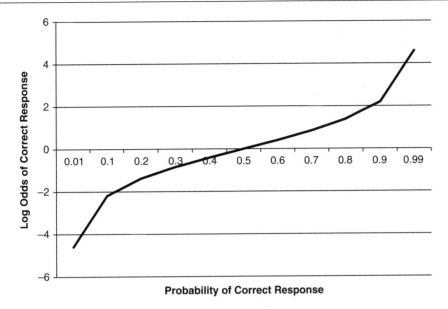

FIGURE 15.1. Relationship of log-odds and probabilities.

equal to 4.6. So, although larger values are possible as probabilities get more extreme, it is more usual for log-odds to range from −5 to 5.

Although log-odds help in modeling binary outcomes, interpreting results in terms of log-odds is not intuitive, so they are typically transformed back into the probability scale as it is easier to interpret. Suppose the log-odds for an item equals k:

$$\ln\left(\frac{P\left(X_{ei}=1\right)}{1-P\left(X_{ei}=1\right)}\right)=k \tag{15.2}$$

With a few algebra steps omitted here, we can solve for $P\left(X_{ei}=1\right)$:

$$\frac{P\left(X_{ei}=1\right)}{1-P\left(X_{ei}=1\right)}=e^{k};\ P\left(X_{ei}=1\right)=\frac{e^{k}}{1+e^{k}} \tag{15.3}$$

where e is a constant equaling approximately 2.718. This equation form probably looks familiar if you have read Chapter 14 on IRT because it is the exact form of an IRT model. For example, you can specify the 1PL IRT model by letting k equal $\theta-b$. For a DCM model, as you will see in the following, k is a function of attributes instead of a continuous ability θ.

A regression model that models an outcome without making a transformation on it (e.g., without transforming probabilities to log-odds) is known as a *general linear model*. Regression models that do transform the outcome using some function like the log-odds are known as *generalized* linear models. There are many generalized linear models, and these differ by the type of function they use to transform the outcome. This transformation function is called the *link function*. The log-odds link function used by the DCM (and by logistic regression models) is called the *logit link function*.

Log-Linear Cognitive Diagnosis Model

The log-linear cognitive diagnosis model (LCDM) is a flexible DCM used to model the conditional item response probabilities $\pi_{i|\alpha_e}$ in Equation 15.1 as a function of a set of attributes. The LCDM is like an IRT model, with the difference that in the IRT model the latent predictor of the item response is a continuous variable, whereas in the LCDM discussed here the latent predictors are binary variables. With continuous predictors, the IRT model is closely related to a linear regression model. With binary predictors, the LCDM is closely related to ANOVA models where group membership predicts an outcome. Binary indicators designate the presence ($\alpha_{ea} = 1$) or absence ($\alpha_{ea} = 0$) of the latent predictors, or the attributes. As in ANOVA, both the effects of individual attributes (simple main effects) and the effects of combinations of attributes (interaction effects) on the item response can be modeled.

The LCDM is a general DCM; that is, it allows for a great deal of flexibility in how the attributes are specified to influence (or predict) the item response. The LCDM shares one common assumption with other DCMs: mastery of additional required attributes cannot lead to a decrease in the probability of a correct response. In other words, examinees who have mastered *more* attributes can never have a *lower* probability of responding correctly than examinees who have mastered *fewer* attributes. This makes sense because it is mastery of the attributes that is hypothesized to drive the item response probabilities: The more attributes one has mastered, the greater the probability of a correct response. This assumption is known as *monotonicity* because the item response probability increases (or stays the same) as the number of required attributes increases, making the IRF a monotonically increasing function. Beyond this assumption, the LCDM does not require any assumptions about how attributes interact with each other on items that measure more than one attribute. Although such assumptions could be made, doing so would require specific constraints to be placed on the LCDM, resulting in a less general model.

Specifications for Attributes and Item–Attribute Relationships

You may have noted that in the previous paragraph we referred to "required attributes." Required attributes are attributes test developers or researchers hypothesize are required to answer an item correctly. This implies that, to correctly specify the DCM, test developers or researchers must have considerable knowledge of the attributes being measured and which of these are required to answer an item. The fact that such a priori specifications must be made is what makes DCMs confirmatory rather than exploratory models. Two types of knowledge about the attributes are required. The researcher must (1) define and delineate the attribute or set of attributes that are measured by the assessment, and (2) specify the attribute or set of attributes that are measured by each item. Both must be done prior to any statistical analysis using the LCDM. Where does such knowledge come from? Ideally, the attributes are defined or operationalized on the basis of expert knowledge and/or empirical theories in domain-specific content areas. For example, teachers familiar with the content area of the assessments and/or researchers in the domain measured by the test items are often consulted. The same sources can be used to specify the attribute(s) measured by each item. These specifications are recorded in an item-by-attribute *Q-matrix* (e.g., Tatsuoka, 1990).

The Q-Matrix

The Q-matrix is the DCM equivalent of the factor loading matrix in factor analysis in that it specifies how latent traits are related to observed responses. The entries in the Q-matrix are denoted by q_{ia}, where $q_{ia} = 1$ if item i measures attribute a and $q_{ia} = 0$ otherwise. A sample Q-matrix for a test with 14 items and three attributes is provided in Table 15.1. The rows represent items, and the columns represent attributes. Items can measure one attribute (known as *simple structure items*) or multiple attributes (known as *complex structure items*). In Table 15.1, each of the first six items measure only one attribute. For example, item 4 measures Attribute 2 ($q_{42} = 1$) and does not measure Attribute 1 ($q_{41} = 0$) or Attribute 3 ($q_{43} = 0$). Items 7 through 12 are complex structure items that

TABLE 15.1. Q-Matrix for Sample Diagnostic Assessment

Item(i)	$q_{i,1}$	$q_{i,2}$	$q_{i,3}$
1	0	0	1
2	0	0	1
3	0	1	0
4	0	1	0
5	1	0	0
6	1	0	0
7	0	1	1
8	0	1	1
9	1	0	1
10	1	0	1
11	1	1	0
12	1	1	0
13	1	1	1
14	1	1	1

measure two attributes. For example, item 7 measures Attribute 2 ($q_{72} = 1$) and Attribute 3 ($q_{73} = 1$). The last two items measure all three attributes.

Figure 15.2 provides a path diagram for the DCM model corresponding to the Q-matrix in Table 15.1. This diagram is similar to those used in CFA and shows that there are three latent attributes, indicated by circles, and 14 observed item responses, indicated by rectangles. The diagram differs from those used in CFA by using bisected circles and rectangles to indicate that the attributes and item responses are binary. The unidirectional arrow from an attribute to an item indicates that the attribute is expected to influence the item response; these arrows correspond to the "1" entries in the Q-matrix. The bidirectional arrows among the attributes indicate that they are correlated. These correlations are discussed in a later section.

Identification of the Q-Matrix

Chapter 13 discussed model identification in the context of CFA models. Q-matrices for the LCDM also have conditions that must be met for model identification. The Q-matrix in Table 15.1 illustrates these conditions. First, note that each attribute is measured by at least one item, as is required for the identification of a diagnostic assessment (as well as by common sense, because it is not clear how attributes could be measured without items). As discussed in the context of CTT, increasing the number of items that measure an attribute will increase the accuracy with which the attribute is measured (assuming the items are good ones). For the Q-matrix in Table 15.1, each attribute is measured by eight items. Simulation studies have shown that the number of items needed to accurately measure each attribute depends on many things, but eight items per attribute is a reasonable minimum in many cases. A second requirement for identification is that

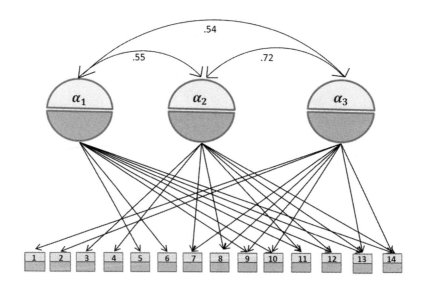

FIGURE 15.2. Path diagram for sample diagnostic assessment.

no attribute is conjoined with another attribute in the Q-matrix. This means that no two attributes are measured by exactly the same items. The problem here is that, if two attributes are conjoined, the model does not have information to distinguish between a latent class of people that has only one of these attributes versus a latent class that has both. Put differently, conjoined attributes violate the identification requirement that the expected response pattern for each posited attribute pattern is unique (Chiu, Douglas, & Li, 2009). The most straightforward way to meet this requirement is to have at least one item for each attribute that measures only that attribute (e.g., one simple structure item for each attribute); however, many Q-matrix structures meet the identification requirement without having a simple structure item for each attribute.

The Q-matrix in Table 15.1 also has some features that are not necessary for identification of a diagnostic assessment. The Q-matrix is *balanced*, meaning the same number of items measure each attribute. The complexity of the items measuring an attribute is also the same for each attribute: Each attribute is measured uniquely by a particular item twice (e.g., by a simple structure item; items 1–6); each attribute is measured twice by an item that also measures one other attribute (items 7–12); and each attribute is measured twice by an item that measures all three attributes (items 13 and 14). These features are not required for DCMS; they were selected for this chapter primarily as a convenience for explaining how to parameterize and interpret results from different types of diagnostic items with a single Q-matrix. In practice, the design of the Q-matrix is important. Balancing the Q-matrix and avoiding overly complex Q-matrices can have positive impacts on the diagnostic assessment results (see Madison & Bradshaw, 2015).

Correct specification of the Q-matrix ensures that the measurement component of the DCM is correct and is imperative to obtain valid interpretations of the estimated model parameters (Rupp & Templin, 2008a). How can correct specification be ensured? One way to provide evidence that an item elicits the attributes specified by the Q-matrix is to use think-aloud protocols in which students think out loud as they solve diagnostic items or verbally explain their thought process after they have completed solving diagnostic items (e.g., Bradshaw et al., 2014; Jang, 2005; Leighton, 2004). Then, prior to conducting DCM analyses, researchers can analyze the qualitative data to provide evidence that either supports the entries in the Q-matrix or suggests changes. There has also been some recent work on statistical methods for evaluating Q-matrices (e.g., de la Torre & Chiu, 2016). The more accurate the Q-matrix is, the more accurate inferences about student mastery will be. Conversely, inaccurate Q-matrices can lead to very inaccurate diagnoses of student mastery.

Back to the IRF

The LCDM IRF defines the probability of answering an item correctly as a function of the examinee's attribute profile. We begin by explaining the IRF for the simplest case: simple structure items that measure only one attribute. Conditional on examinee e's attribute profile (α_e), the LCDM defines the probability that examinee e correctly answers Item i ($X_{ei} = 1$) as

$$P(X_{ei} = 1 \mid \alpha_e) = \frac{\exp\left(\lambda_{i,0} + \lambda_{i,1,(a)}\alpha_{ea}\right)}{1 + \exp\left(\lambda_{i,0} + \lambda_{i,1,(a)}\alpha_{ea}\right)} \tag{15.4}$$

The lamba (λ) parameters are the item parameters, which include the intercept for Item i $(\lambda_{i,0})$ and the main effect for Attribute a on item i $(\lambda_{i,1,(a)})$. In subscripting item parameters, the first number indicates the item i; the second number indicates the parameter type (i.e., 0 for intercept, 1 for main effect); and the parenthetical subscripts indicate the specific attribute to which the main effect refers. We can equivalently write this equation in a way that looks more like a regression equation by solving for the log-odds of a correct response rather than the probability:

$$\log\left(\frac{P(x_{ei} = 1 \mid \alpha_e)}{P(x_{ei} = 0 \mid \alpha_e)}\right) = \lambda_{i,0} + \lambda_{i,1,(a)}\alpha_{ea} \tag{15.5}$$

Writing the IRF this way allows us to interpret the item parameters in an ANOVA-like way. The categorical variables (presence/absence of the attributes) are the (dummy coded) predictors in the model, and the reference group is the class of examinees who have not mastered the attribute measured by the item. As such, the intercept for the item $(\lambda_{i,0})$ represents the log-odds of a correct response for an examinee who is not a master of Attribute a. We can see this result if we substitute the attribute value for an examinee who is not a master of Attribute a (i.e., $\alpha_{ea} = 0$) into Equation 15.5:

$$\log\left(\frac{P(x_{ei} = 1 \mid \alpha_e)}{P(x_{ei} = 0 \mid \alpha_e)}\right) = \lambda_{i,0} + \lambda_{i,1,(a)}(0) = \lambda_{i,0} \tag{15.6}$$

The main effect for the item $(\lambda_{i,1,(a)})$ represents the increase in log-odds of a correct response for an examinee who is a master of Attribute a, which can be shown by substituting $\alpha_{ea} = 1$ into Equation 15.5:

$$\log\left(\frac{P(x_{ei} = 1 \mid \alpha_e)}{P(x_{ei} = 0 \mid \alpha_e)}\right) = \lambda_{i,0} + \lambda_{i,1,(a)}(1) = \lambda_{i,0} + \lambda_{i,1,(a)} \tag{15.7}$$

Comparing Equations 15.6 and 15.7, you can see the difference is that the log-odds for masters of Attribute a is greater than the log-odds for nonmasters by $\lambda_{i,1,(a)}$.

Let's look at an example item to further illustrate the IRF for simple structure items. The Q-matrix in Table 15.1 shows item 4, which measures only Attribute 2. The IRF for item 4 can be expressed as

$$P(X_{e4} = 1 \mid \alpha_e) = \frac{\exp\left(\lambda_{4,0} + \lambda_{4,1,(2)}\alpha_{e2}\right)}{1 + \exp\left(\lambda_{4,0} + \lambda_{4,1,(2)}\alpha_{e2}\right)} \tag{15.8}$$

Table 15.2 provides hypothetical values of the item parameters for all the items shown in Table 15.1 and indicates that the intercept for item 4 equals −1.25. Thus, the log-odds

TABLE 15.2. Item Parameters for Sample Diagnostic Assessment

Item	$\lambda_{i,0}$	$\lambda_{i,1,(1)}$	$\lambda_{i,1,(2)}$	$\lambda_{i,1,(3)}$	$\lambda_{i,2,(1*2)}$	$\lambda_{i,2,(1*3)}$	$\lambda_{i,2,(2*3)}$	$\lambda_{i,3,(1*2*3)}$
1	−1.5	-	-	1.75	-	-	-	-
2	−0.75	-	-	2.75	-	-	-	-
3	−0.25	-	1.5	-	-	-	-	-
4	−1.25	-	4	-	-	-	-	-
5	−2	3.5	-	-	-	-	-	-
6	−2	2.5	-	-	-	-	-	-
7	−1	-	1	2	-	-	1	-
8	−1.25	-	0.75	0.75	-	-	0.75	-
9	−1.5	0	-	0	-	3	-	-
10	−2	1.75	-	1	-	0	-	-
11	−0.75	1	2	-	−1	-	-	-
12	−1.25	3	3	-	−3	-	-	-
13	−1.25	0.50	0.50	0.50	0.25	0.25	0.25	2
14	−2	1.75	1.5	2	0.25	0.25	0.75	0.25

that an examinee who has not mastered Attribute 2 will answer item 4 correctly is equal to −1.25, which corresponds to a probability of 0.22 $\left(\exp(-1.25)/1 + \exp(-1.25) = 0.22 \right)$. For examinees who have mastered Attribute 2, the log-odds increases by 4 (because the main effect of Attribute 2 $\lambda_{i,1,(2)}$ on item 4 equals 4), yielding a log-odds of 2.75 (i.e., −1.25 + 4 = 2.75). This log-odds corresponds to a probability of 0.94.

The item parameter values in Table 15.2 are used to calculate the log-odds of a correct response and the probability of a correct response for each latent class for each of the items on the sample assessment. These are shown in Tables 15.3 and 15.4. In these tables, you can see the values discussed earlier for item 4. For example, Table 15.3 shows that for item 4, the log-odds is equal to 1.25 for attribute patterns with nonmastery of Attribute 2 (Patterns [000], [001], [100], and [101]) and is equal to 2.75 for attribute patterns that do have mastery of Attribute 2 (Patterns [010], [011], [110], and [111]).

The Item Characteristic Bar Chart

Analogous to an item characteristic curve in IRT, an item characteristic bar chart (ICBC) displays the probability of a correct response to an item (shown on the vertical axis) as a function of the latent classifications (as represented by the different bars). The charts for the six simple structure items on the sample diagnostic assessment (items 1–6) are displayed in Figure 15.3. Comparing the charts across this set of items, we see, for example, that item 1 was the most difficult for masters, whereas item 4 was the easiest item for masters. For nonmasters, item 3 was the easiest and items 5 and 6 were the hardest.

TABLE 15.3. Log-Odds of Correct Response for Sample Diagnostic Assessment

Item	Log-odds of a correct response							
	[000]	[001]	[010]	[011]	[100]	[101]	[110]	[111]
1	−1.50	0.25	−1.50	0.25	−1.50	0.25	−1.50	0.25
2	−0.75	2.00	−0.75	2.00	−0.75	2.00	−0.75	2.00
3	−0.25	−0.25	1.25	1.25	−0.25	−0.25	1.25	1.25
4	−1.25	−1.25	2.75	2.75	−1.25	−1.25	2.75	2.75
5	−2.00	−2.00	−2.00	−2.00	1.50	1.50	1.50	1.50
6	−2.00	−2.00	−2.00	−2.00	0.50	0.50	0.50	0.50
7	−1.00	1.00	0.00	3.00	−1.00	1.00	0.00	3.00
8	−1.25	−0.50	−0.50	1.00	−1.25	−0.50	−0.50	1.00
9	−1.50	−1.50	−1.50	−1.50	−1.50	1.50	−1.50	1.50
10	−2.00	−1.00	−2.00	−1.00	−0.25	1.75	−0.25	1.75
11	−0.75	−0.75	1.25	1.25	0.25	0.25	1.25	1.25
12	−1.25	−1.25	1.75	1.75	1.75	1.75	1.75	1.75
13	−1.25	−0.75	−0.75	0.00	−0.75	0.00	0.00	3.00
14	−2.00	0.00	−0.50	2.25	−0.25	2.00	1.50	4.75

TABLE 15.4. Probability of Correct Response for Sample Diagnostic Assessment

Item	Probability of correct response							
	[000]	[001]	[010]	[011]	[100]	[101]	[110]	[111]
1	0.18	0.56	0.18	0.56	0.18	0.56	0.18	0.56
2	0.32	0.88	0.32	0.88	0.32	0.88	0.32	0.88
3	0.44	0.44	0.78	0.78	0.44	0.44	0.78	0.78
4	0.22	0.22	0.94	0.94	0.22	0.22	0.94	0.94
5	0.12	0.12	0.12	0.12	0.82	0.82	0.82	0.82
6	0.12	0.12	0.12	0.12	0.62	0.62	0.62	0.62
7	0.22	0.73	0.50	0.95	0.22	0.73	0.50	0.95
8	0.22	0.38	0.38	0.73	0.22	0.38	0.38	0.73
9	0.18	0.18	0.18	0.18	0.18	0.82	0.18	0.82
10	0.12	0.27	0.12	0.27	0.44	0.85	0.44	0.85
11	0.32	0.32	0.78	0.78	0.56	0.56	0.78	0.78
12	0.22	0.22	0.85	0.85	0.85	0.85	0.85	0.85
13	0.22	0.32	0.32	0.50	0.32	0.50	0.50	0.95
14	0.12	0.50	0.38	0.90	0.44	0.88	0.82	0.99

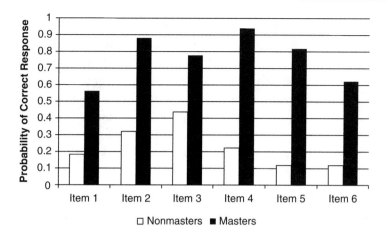

FIGURE 15.3. ICBCs for simple structure items on sample diagnostic assessment.

Notice that Figure 15.3 only displays two item response probabilities, even though there are eight (2^3) latent classes. This is because some of the latent classes have the same item response probabilities. Table 15.4 shows that across the eight latent classes for each of the simple structure items, there are only two (i.e., 2^1) unique item response probabilities. Using item 4 as an example, we see that the probabilities are 0.22 and 0.94. The same result will be obtained for any simple structure item; no matter how many attributes are measured by an assessment, a simple structure item will have only two possible item response probabilities, and each latent class will have one of those probabilities.

IRF for Complex Structure Items

For an item i measuring two attributes (a) and (b), the LCDM expresses the IRF for examinee e as

$$P\left(X_{ei} = 1 \mid \alpha_e\right) = \frac{\exp\left(\lambda_{i,0} + \lambda_{i,1,(a)}\alpha_{ea} + \lambda_{i,1,(b)}\alpha_{eb} + \lambda_{i,2,(a,b)}\alpha_{ea}\alpha_{eb}\right)}{1 + \exp\left(\lambda_{i,0} + \lambda_{i,1,(a)}\alpha_{ea} + \lambda_{i,1,(b)}\alpha_{eb} + \lambda_{i,2,(a,b)}\alpha_{ea}\alpha_{eb}\right)} \quad (15.9)$$

To further explain the LCDM, consider again the Q-matrix provided in Table 15.1. Let's consider an item that measures two attributes. Item 7 measures Attributes 2 and 3, as shown by the Q-matrix entries of $q_{7,2} = 1$ and $q_{7,3} = 1$. Conditional on examinee e's attribute profile (α_e), the LCDM defines the probability that examinee e correctly answers item 7 $(x_{e7} = 1)$ as

$$P\left(X_{e7} = 1 \mid \alpha_e\right) = \frac{\exp\left(\lambda_{7,0} + \lambda_{7,1,(2)}\alpha_{e2} + \lambda_{7,1,(3)}\alpha_{e3} + \lambda_{7,2,(2,3)}\alpha_{e2}\alpha_{e3}\right)}{1 + \exp\left(\lambda_{7,0} + \lambda_{7,1,(2)}\alpha_{e2} + \lambda_{7,1,(3)}\alpha_{e3} + \lambda_{7,2,(2,3)}\alpha_{e2}\alpha_{e3}\right)} \quad (15.10)$$

The lambda (λ) parameters are the item parameters, which include the intercept for item 7 $(\lambda_{7,0})$, the main effect for Attribute 2 on item 7 $(\lambda_{7,1,(2)})$, the main effect for Attribute 3 on item 7 $(\lambda_{7,1,(3)})$, and the interaction effect of Attribute 2 and Attribute 3 on item 7 $(\lambda_{7,2,(2,3)})$. In subscripting item parameters, the first number indicates item i; the second number indicates the parameter type (i.e., 0 for intercept, 1 for main effect, 2 for two-way interaction); and the parenthetical subscripts indicate the specific attribute(s) to which the main effect or interaction refers. As before, we can equivalently write this equation in a way that looks more like a linear model by using the log of the odds of a correct response rather than the probability:

$$\log\left(\frac{P\left(X_{e7}=1\,|\,\alpha_e\right)}{P\left(X_{e7}=0\,|\,\alpha_e\right)}\right)=\lambda_{7,0}+\lambda_{7,1,(2)}\alpha_{e2}+\lambda_{7,1,(3)}\alpha_{e3}+\lambda_{7,2,(2,3)}\alpha_{e2}\alpha_{e3} \quad (15.11)$$

Before explaining how to interpret the item parameters for item 7, suppose the values of the item parameters for the sample diagnostic assessment are those given in Table 15.2. Note that these values are hypothetical and were selected for illustration purposes. Substituting the item parameter values for item 7 into Equation 15.2 yields the function

$$P\left(X_{e7}=1\,|\,\alpha_e\right)=\frac{\exp\left(-1+1\left(\alpha_{e2}\right)+2\left(\alpha_{e3}\right)+1\left(\alpha_{e2}\alpha_{e3}\right)\right)}{1+\exp\left(-1+1\left(\alpha_{e2}\right)+2\left(\alpha_{e3}\right)+1\left(\alpha_{e2}\alpha_{e3}\right)\right)} \quad (15.12)$$

The item parameters in the LCDM are again interpreted analogously to ANOVA parameters, and now the reference group is the class of examinees who have mastered none of the attributes measured by the item. For item 7, the reference group is the group of examinees who have not mastered Attributes 2 or 3 (regardless of their mastery classification for Attribute 1). We can denote this reference group by $[\alpha_1\alpha_2\alpha_3]=[.00]$, where (.) serves as a placeholder for Attribute 1 and indicates that examinees in the reference group can have either a 0 or 1 (nonmastery or mastery) state on Attribute 1 (i.e., an examinee's status on Attribute 1 does not affect her or his probability of correctly answering item 7).

The intercept for the item $(\lambda_{7,0})$ represents the log-odds of a correct response for an examinee who is not a master of either Attribute 2 or 3 (i.e., examinees in class [000] and [100]):

$$\log\left(\frac{P\left(X_{e7}=1\,|\,[.00]\right)}{P\left(X_{e7}=0\,|\,[.00]\right)}\right)=-1 \quad (15.13)$$

On the probability scale used in Equation 15.10, this log-odds can be expressed as

$$P\left(X_{e7}=1\,|\,[.00]\right)=\frac{\exp\left(-1+1(0)+2(0)+1(0*0)\right)}{1+\exp\left(-1+1(0)+2(0)+1(0*0)\right)}=\frac{\exp(-1)}{1+\exp(-1)}=0.27 \quad (15.14)$$

In Equation 15.14, the notation $P\left(X_{e7}=1\,|\,[.00]\right)$ indicates that this is the probability that an examinee in the reference group with attribute profile [.00] (either mastery or nonmastery of Attribute 1 and nonmastery of Attributes 2 and 3) would answer item 7 correctly. The calculation in Equation 15.14 shows that the probability of correct response for these examinees is equal to approximately .27. Thus, not surprisingly, an examinee who has not mastered the requisite attributes has a fairly low chance of answering item 7 correctly. Recall that the intercept parameter for IRT models is known as a difficulty parameter. The intercept for DCMs is akin to a difficulty parameter but is more specific in that it describes the difficulty of the item for nonmasters of the attributes measured by that item. As such, this parameter is more similar to the pseudo-guessing parameter in IRT, describing the probability that an examinee will answer the item correctly without the required attributes that are presumed to produce a correct response.

Turning to the interpretation of the main effects ($\lambda_{7,1,(2)} = 1$ and $\lambda_{7,1,(3)} = 2$), note that these indicate the increase in log-odds of a correct response given mastery of the individual attribute. From Table 15.2 you can see that Attribute 3 has a higher main effect (2.0) than Attribute 2 (1.0). Therefore, the probability of a correct response for examinees with mastery of Attribute 3 and not Attribute 2 (i.e., examinees in class [.01]) will be greater than the probability for examinees with mastery of Attribute 2 and not Attribute 3 (i.e., examinees in class [.10]):

$$P\left(X_{e7} = 1 \mid [.01]\right) = \frac{\exp\left(-1 + 1(0) + 2(1) + 1(0 * 1)\right)}{1 + \exp\left(-1 + 1(0) + 2(1) + 1(0 * 1)\right)} = \frac{\exp(1)}{1 + \exp(1)} = 0.73 \quad (15.15)$$

$$P\left(X_{e7} = 1 \mid [.10]\right) = \frac{\exp\left(-1 + 1(1) + 2(0) + 1(1 * 0)\right)}{1 + \exp\left(-1 + 1(1) + 2(0) + 1(1 * 0)\right)} = \frac{\exp(0)}{1 + \exp(0)} = 0.50 \quad (15.16)$$

The log-odds of a correct response for examinees who have mastered Attribute 3 and not Attribute 2 equals 1 (i.e., the intercept plus the main effect for Attribute 3, or −1 + 2), which corresponds to a probability of 0.73, whereas the log-odds for examinees who have mastered Attribute 2 and not 3 equals 0 (i.e., −1 + 1) and corresponds to a probability of 0.50.

Main effects, as well as the interaction terms to be discussed subsequently, are akin to IRT discrimination parameters or CFA factor loadings, and measure the strength of the relationship between the item and the latent trait of attribute mastery. Because the main effect for Attribute 3 is greater than the main effect for Attribute 2, item 7 can more clearly distinguish between the reference group and profile [.01] than between the reference group and profile [.10]. In comparison to the reference group, those who have mastered only Attribute 3 have a 0.46 (i.e., 0.73 − 0.27) higher probability of answering the item correctly, while those who have mastered only Attribute 2 have a 0.23 (i.e., 0.50 − 0.27) higher probability. Notice that both main effects are positive. This is because the main effects of the LCDM are constrained to be positive to ensure that the monotonicity assumption discussed earlier in this chapter has been met. That is, it ensures that the response probability never decreases as more attributes are mastered. This constraint also follows from the assumption that the item measures the attribute, as is specified by the Q-matrix.

Unlike IRT models, the LCDM also contains parameters that capture any interactions between attributes when more than one attribute is measured by an item.

These interaction terms function similarly to discrimination parameters in the sense that they allow for an additional way in which attribute patterns with only one attribute can be discriminated from attribute patterns with both attributes. To take an example, item 7 measures two attributes, so it could support a two-way interaction term. A positive interaction coefficient indicates that the ability to discriminate between examinees who have mastered only one attribute and examinees who have mastered both attributes is amplified by inclusion of the interaction. That is, differences in the item response probabilities for the two types of examinees increase with the magnitude of the interaction between the two attributes. Conversely, a negative interaction coefficient indicates that the ability to discriminate between examinees who have mastered only one attribute and examinees who have mastered both attributes is decreased by inclusion of the interaction. In this case, differences in the item response probabilities for the two types of examinees decrease with the magnitude of the interaction. The more negative the interaction coefficient, the more similar item response probabilities would be for examinees with one versus both attributes.

For Item 7, the two-way interaction between the two attributes $(\lambda_{7,2,(2,3)})$ is positive (1.0), allowing the log-odds of a correct response to change given mastery of both attributes by the examinee. For examinees who have mastered Attribute 2 and 3, the log-odds of a correct response is equal to 3.0 (i.e., $-1 +1 +2 + 1$), and the probability of a correct response is equal to

$$P\left(X_{e7} = 1 \mid [.11]\right) = \frac{\exp\left(-1+1(1)+2(1)+1(1*1)\right)}{1+\exp\left(-1+1(1)+2(1)+1(1*1)\right)} = \frac{\exp(3.0)}{1+\exp(3.0)} = 0.95 \quad (15.17)$$

For this item, mastering both Attributes 2 and 3 provided an increase of .45 over masters of Attribute 2 only (i.e., subtracting the result in Equation 15.16 from the result in Equation 15.17 yields $0.95 - 0.50 = 0.45$) and of .22 over masters of Attribute 3 only (i.e., subtracting the result in Equation 15.15 from the result in Equation 15.17 yields $0.95 - 0.73 = 0.22$).

As noted previously, the interaction term may be positive, zero, or negative in the LCDM. However, the interaction term cannot be so negative that it would violate the monotonicity assumption. In other words, the absolute values of a negative interaction term cannot be so large that mastering additional attributes measured by an item would lead to a lower response probability for the item. The value of the interaction coefficient is therefore constrained, so that monotonicity is not violated. To illustrate these constraints, consider item 7 again. To satisfy the monotonicity assumption, an examinee who has mastered Attributes 2 and 3 should have a greater (or equal) probability of a correct response on item 7 than an examinee who has mastered only one of the two attributes. For example, we expect $\left(X_{ei} = 1 \mid [.11]\right) \geq P\left(X_{ei} = 1 \mid [.01]\right)$. We therefore constrain the two probabilities such that

$$\frac{\exp\left(\lambda_{7,0}+\lambda_{7,1,(2)}\alpha_{e2}+\lambda_{7,1,(3)}\alpha_{e3}+\lambda_{7,2,(2,3)}\alpha_{e2}\alpha_{e3}\right)}{1+\exp\left(\lambda_{7,0}+\lambda_{7,1,(2)}\alpha_{e2}+\lambda_{7,1,(3)}\alpha_{e3}+\lambda_{7,2,(2,3)}\alpha_{e2}\alpha_{e3}\right)} \geq \frac{\exp\left(\lambda_{7,0}+\lambda_{7,1,(3)}\alpha_{e3}\right)}{1+\exp\left(\lambda_{7,0}+\lambda_{7,1,(3)}\alpha_{e3}\right)} \quad (15.18)$$

or, equivalently,

$$\lambda_{7,0} + \lambda_{7,1,(2)}\alpha_{e2} + \lambda_{7,1,(3)}\alpha_{e3} + \lambda_{7,2,(2,3)}\alpha_{e2}\alpha_{e3} \geq \lambda_{7,0} + \lambda_{7,1,(3)}\alpha_{e3} \qquad (15.19)$$

This simplifies to $\lambda_{7,1,(2)}\alpha_{e2} + \lambda_{7,2,(2,3)}\alpha_{e2}\alpha_{e3} \geq 0$ and finally to $\lambda_{7,1,(2)}\alpha_{e2} \geq -\lambda_{7,2,(2,3)}\alpha_{e2}\alpha_{e3}$. An analogous result could be demonstrated for $P\left(X_{ei} = 1 \,|\, [.11]\right) > P\left(X_{ei} = 1 \,|\, [.10]\right)$ to yield the constraint: $\lambda_{7,1,(3)}\alpha_{e3} \geq -\lambda_{7,2,(2,3)}\alpha_{e2}\alpha_{e3}$. These results demonstrate a constraint for two-way interactions that can be stated more generally as follows: The absolute value of a negative two-way interaction coefficient cannot be greater than the magnitude of either of the two main effects for individual attributes.

For the remaining two-attribute items, the log-odds of a correct response and the probability of a correct response for each latent class for each of the items on the sample assessment are shown in Tables 15.3 and 15.4, respectively. Notice that for item 7, there are four unique log-odds (and probabilities) across the eight latent classes. This is because, for the LCDM, items that measure two attributes will have 2^2 unique response values, no matter how many attributes are measured on the assessment. More generally, items that measure a attributes will have 2^a unique response values. Figure 15.4 provides ICBCs for the items that measure two attributes (items 7–12). Each chart shows the four unique item response probabilities corresponding to the possible patterns of mastery of the two attributes measured by the item.

Fully Extending the IRF for the LCDM

For items measuring three attributes, the IRF is more complex and contains an interaction term, a main effect for each attribute, all possible two-way interactions, and a three-way interaction. For example, the IRF for item 14 is

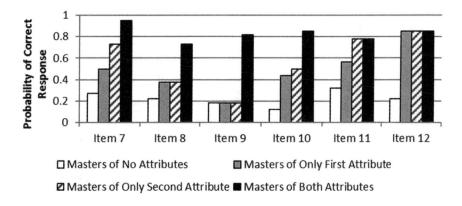

FIGURE 15.4. ICBCs for two-attribute items on sample diagnostic assessment.

$$P\left(X_{e14}=1\,|\,\alpha_e\right)=\frac{\exp(k)}{1+\exp(k)}\qquad(15.20)$$

where

$$k = \lambda_{14,0} + \lambda_{14,1,(1)}\alpha_{e1} + \lambda_{14,1,(2)}\alpha_{e2} + \lambda_{14,1,(3)}\alpha_{e3} + \lambda_{14,2,(1,3)}\alpha_{e1}\alpha_{e3} + \lambda_{14,2,(1,2)}\alpha_{e1}\alpha_{e2}$$
$$+ \lambda_{14,2,(2,3)}\alpha_{e2}\alpha_{e3} + \lambda_{14,3,(1,2,3)}\alpha_{e1}\alpha_{e2}\alpha_{e3}\qquad(15.21)$$

Figure 15.5 provides the ICBCs for the two items that measure three attributes (items 13 and 14). Analogous to Figure 15.4, Figure 15.5 displays the item response probabilities (also shown in Table 15.4) that correspond to the possible patterns of mastery of the three attributes measured by each item, assuming these items have the item parameters values provided in Table 15.2. Notice that for item 14, each of the eight latent classes has a unique item response probability. This result can occur when an item measures all of the attributes measured by the assessment. For item 13, some of the attribute patterns have equal item response probabilities—despite the fact that the item measures the maximum number of attributes—because it is a special case where the main effects are exactly equal for each attribute and the two-way interactions are exactly equal for each attribute pair (see Table 15.2).

The pattern from Equations 15.4, 15.9, and 15.21 can be extrapolated from items measuring one, two, and three attributes to—though it would be tedious—items measuring any number of attributes by adding main effects and interaction terms that correspond to the attributes measured. Henson and colleagues (2009) provided a condensed notation to express the general parameterization for the LCDM that specifies the IRF for an item that measures up to A attributes:

$$P\left(X_{ei}=1\,|\,\alpha_e\right)=\frac{\exp\left(\lambda_{i,0}+\lambda_i^T h(\alpha_e,q_i)\right)}{1+\exp\left(\lambda_{i,0}+\lambda_i^T h(\alpha_e,q_i)\right)}\qquad(15.22)$$

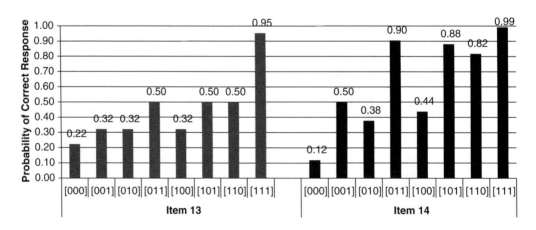

FIGURE 15.5. ICBCs for three-attribute items on sample diagnostic assessment.

The term $\lambda_{i,0}$ is the intercept that quantifies the log-odds of a correct response if examinee e has not mastered any of the attributes measured by Item i. The term $\lambda_i^T h(\alpha_e, q_i)$ is a linear combination of ANOVA-like main and interaction effects of the model. The main effects and interactions are given in the row vector λ_i^T, where T represents the transpose. The term $h(\alpha_e, q_i)$ is a column vector of 0, 1 indicators used to specify whether the main effects and interactions are present for the examinee and item. The term $q_i = [q_{i1}, q_{i2}, \ldots, q_{iA}]^T$ denotes the Q-matrix entries for item i, and $\alpha_e = [\alpha_{e1}, \alpha_{e2}, \ldots, \alpha_{eA}]$, the attribute pattern for examinee e. Thus, an element of $h(\alpha_e, q_i)$ equals 1 if and only if (1) the item measures the attribute(s) corresponding to the effect $(q_{ia}\text{'s} = 1)$, and (2) the examinee has mastered the attribute(s) corresponding to the effect $(\alpha_{ea}\text{'s} = 1)$. Otherwise the element equals zero, which discounts any main effect or interaction effect parameter associated with unmeasured attributes for this item or unmastered attributes in an examinee's attribute pattern. Specifically,

$$\lambda_i^T h(\alpha_e, q_i) = \sum_{a=1}^{A} \lambda_{i,1(a)}(\alpha_{ea} q_{ia}) + \sum_{a=1}^{A-1} \sum_{b=a+1}^{A} \lambda_{i,2(ab)}(\alpha_{ea} \alpha_{eb} q_{ia} q_{ib}) + \cdots \quad (15.23)$$

where $\lambda_{i,1(a)}$ is the main effect for Attribute a for item i, $\lambda_{i,2(ab)}$ is the two-way interaction effect between Attributes a and b for item i, and the ellipses denotes the third through Ath higher-order interactions.

Other General DCMs

The LCDM is built upon the notation used for the general diagnostic model (GDM; von Davier, 2005), a general psychometric model that encompasses, as well as combines, models from different psychometric families, including some familiar IRT models. The LCDM expanded the DCM portion of the GDM specification by including interaction terms in the predictor of the item response. More recently, de la Torre (2009) expanded the LCDM, noting that—analogous to the practice of using linear regression when the outcome is binary—the LCDM could be estimated with the identity link function as well as the logit link function. He referred to the LCDM when any link function is used as the "generalized DINA model" or gDINA model. The gDINA has the same linear predictor form as the LCDM, as represented in Equation 15.23. Its name is counterintuitive, however: while the gDINA model has "DINA" in its name, it does not impose DINA-like restrictions (explained in a subsequent section) on the items by default, though it does allow some items to be DINA-like items in identical fashion to the LCDM as discussed earlier.

We explain the relationships of these general models to the LCDM to help readers make connections within DCM research where the LCDM, GDM, and gDINA frameworks are all used. However, we focus this chapter on the LCDM using the logit link function to keep predictions within probability bounds of 0 to 1, as well as to highlight similarities between DCMs and IRT models that also use the logit link.

SUBMODELS OF THE LCDM

The general expression of the LCDM shown in Equation 15.22 provides a consolidated expression for the family of DCMs. The parameters in the LCDM can be constrained in a number of different ways to yield other DCMs that have different attribute behavior on an item, as demonstrated by Henson and colleagues (2009). Attribute behavior can range from completely noncompensatory to partially compensatory to completely compensatory. Compensatory models are those in which mastery of an additional attribute can compensate, to some extent, for non-mastery of another attribute. Noncompensatory models are those in which mastery of other attributes cannot make up for nonmastery of a necessary attribute.

The Deterministic Inputs Noisy And Gate Model

The deterministic inputs noisy and gate (DINA) model (Haertel, 1989; Junker & Sijtsma, 2001) is a completely noncompensatory model: the mastery of an attribute or subset of attributes does not compensate for the lack of mastery of other attributes. In the DINA model, there are two unique item response probabilities: one for examinees who have mastered all attributes and one for all other examinees. To specify the DINA model using LCDM parameterization, only two item parameters are estimated for each item, an intercept and the highest-order interaction term. All lower-order main effects and interaction terms are constrained to equal zero. Item 9 in our example assessment is a DINA-like item, as can be seen from Table 15.2 and Figure 15.4. Note from Table 15.2 that for this item, both of the main effect parameters have been set to zero, and only the intercept and interaction are estimated. As can be seen from Figure 15.4, this results in only two response probabilities: masters of both Attributes 1 and 3 have a .82 probability of answering the item correctly, and all other examinees have a .18 probability of answering correctly.

In the DINA model, all items on an assessment are constrained to behave like item 9. It is important to note that this type of constraint reflects a strong assumption that all attributes behave in a completely noncompensatory way on every item. Like all statistical model assumptions, this assumption should be verified before interpreting model results. This can be done by comparing the fit of the DINA model and the more general LCDM using nested model comparisons similar to those described in Chapter 13 for CFA models. For more details in the context of model comparisons for DCMs, see Bradshaw (2017).

The Compensatory Reparameterized Unified Model

For compensatory models, mastering additional attributes increases the probability of a correct response. One such compensatory model is the *compensatory reparameterized unified model*, (C-RUM; Hartz, 2002). In the log-linear framework, the C-RUM is expressed as

$$\pi_{i|\alpha_e} = P\left(X_{ie} = 1|\alpha_e\right) = \frac{\exp\left(\lambda_{i,0} + \sum_{a=1}^{A} \lambda_{i,1(a)}(\alpha_{ea}q_{ia})\right)}{1 + \exp\left(\lambda_{i,0} + \sum_{a=1}^{A} \lambda_{i,1(a)}(\alpha_{ea}q_{ia})\right)} \qquad (15.24)$$

There are extensive similarities between the two-parameter MIRT models (Chapter 14) and the C-RUM. For both models, there are no interactions between the latent traits; the model is simply a linear function of an intercept and all relevant traits that are weighted with a discrimination parameter. However, for the C-RUM the latent variable is categorical, whereas in the MIRT model it is continuous. Item 10 is an example of a C-RUM-like item; it has a zero value for the interaction term. Like the DINA model assumptions of zero-valued main effects, the C-RUM assumption of zero-valued interaction terms can be assessed with a comparison of the C-RUM, which is a nested model within the LCDM, with the full LCDM where the interaction terms are estimated.

The Deterministic Inputs Noisy Or Gate Model

The deterministic inputs noisy or gate (DINO) model (Templin & Henson, 2006) is a completely compensatory DCM. The mastery of a single attribute can compensate for the lack of mastery of all other measured attributes. To specify the DINO model in the LCDM framework, the interaction terms are constrained to "cancel out" the added effects of mastering additional attributes in order to keep the log-odds of a correct response the same for any combination of one or more mastered attributes. For example, consider item 12, which measures Attributes 1 and 2 and whose item response function given by the parameters in Table 15.2 equals

$$P\left(X_{ei} = 1 | \alpha_e\right) = \frac{\exp\left(-1.25 + 3\alpha_{e1} + 3\alpha_{e2} - 3\alpha_{e1}\alpha_{e2}\right)}{1 + \exp\left(-1.25 + 3\alpha_{e1} + 3\alpha_{e2} - 3\alpha_{e1}\alpha_{e2}\right)}. \qquad (15.25)$$

In the DINO model, as reflected in Equation 15.25, the main effects and interaction terms are constrained to have the same absolute value, and the interaction term is constrained to be negative. For item 12, this guarantees that the log-odds for profiles [10.], [01.], and [11.] all have the same value of 1.75, as shown in Table 15.3. As illustrated in Figure 15.4, a log-odds of 1.75 corresponds to a 0.85 probability of correct response, which is 0.63 higher than the probability of correct response for examinees who have mastered neither attribute (i.e., profiles [00.]).

Other Models

In addition to the three submodels already described, there are others, including the noisy inputs deterministic and gate (NIDA) model (Maris, 1999), the non-compensatory reparameterized unified model (NC-RUM; e.g., Hartz, 2002), and the noisy inputs deterministic or gate (NIDO) model (Templin, 2006). Other resources provide in-depth reviews of submodels and DCM taxonomies (e.g., DiBello, Roussos, & Stout, 2007; Fu & Li, 2007; Rupp & Templin, 2008b; Rupp et al., 2010).

Which Model Should I Use?

We have introduced the full version of the LCDM, which does not make any assumptions about attribute behavior at the item level, as well as some submodels of the LCDM, which make the same assumption about attribute behavior on every item. The LCDM framework can more generally model different types of attribute behavior on different items, so one item may be a DINO item, another a C-RUM item, and so on (as illustrated by the example parameters in Table 15.2). With so many options, users may want to use a data-based approach to finding a parsimonious version of the LCDM that represents the data well.

One approach that is common in ANOVA-type models is the top-down approach, where the full LCDM (also known as the *saturated* version of the LCDM) is estimated first and parameters that are not statistically significant are then removed. The top-down approach is used because, analogous to ANOVA, the interaction terms in the LCDM should be included in the model unless they are near zero. If not, the main effect parameters will be biased. In this approach, the researcher would begin by estimating the saturated LCDM that includes the interaction terms; this may or may not be the most parsimonious model for representing the data. After the saturated LCDM is estimated, some terms in the model may be statistically nonsignificant. For example, suppose the saturated LCDM was estimated, and the resulting interaction term for item 10 was not statistically significantly different from zero. Analogous to ANOVA techniques where unnecessary interaction terms are removed from the model, the interaction term may be removed from the model if it is found to be nonsignificant. Using this type of top-down approach, we can determine the parameterization for *each* item empirically; there is no reason to constrain attributes to have the same behavior on items across the same test. However, empirically driven specification requires large enough sample sizes to yield adequate power to detect significant effects and minimize the possibility that the findings are idiosyncratic to the sample. Even if the sample is large and representative of the target population for which the test was designed, results should be replicated to provide evidence that the results were not due to chance.

With regard to this issue, the minimum sample size needed to produce accurate and stable estimates of the item parameters, as well as the examinee classifications discussed in the next section, depends on a number of factors. One of the strongest factors influencing sample size is the number of attributes being estimated. As the number of attributes increases, the number of different groups into which examinees are classified grows quickly, necessitating larger sample sizes. Applications of DCMs typically involve a small number of attributes, with a range from three to seven being common. Other factors that influence the necessary sample size include the correlations among the attributes, the complexity of the Q-matrix (how many attributes are being measured by individual items), the test length, and the quality of the items. Specifically, larger sample sizes per attribute are needed for attributes that are less correlated, for more complex Q-matrices, and for items of poorer quality. Test length requirements are discussed in more detail in the following paragraph. At this point, few studies have been completed to inform sample size requirements under the general LCDM. Studies have suggested that with three to five attributes and well-designed assessments, 1,000 examinees can produce reasonably accurate examinee classifications. But, even samples of this size may yield sizable bias in item parameter estimates, particularly in the interaction terms (Bradshaw & Cohen, 2010; Kunina-Habenicht, Rupp, & Wilhelm, 2009, 2012). However, the testing conditions that have been investigated empirically at the time of this writing are but a small fraction of the possible diagnostic test designs that may be realized. Different combinations of the factors influencing sample size listed earlier can interact to produce different sample size needs, so it is particularly difficult to generalize beyond the specific conditions studied in the aforementioned work. Because of these complexities, an empirical analysis akin to an a priori power analysis to determine needed sample size for a given test design has been recommended as part of the diagnostic test design process. Such studies are based on simulated data; for freely available software to conduct such simulations, see Madison, Bradshaw, and Hollingsworth (2014).

In addition to sample size, test length is a critical diagnostic assessment design feature. Studies have shown that DCMs can reliably classify examinees (meeting a reliability threshold of 0.80) into mastery and nonmastery classes, with as few as eight items per attribute in a one-attribute scenario and as few as six items per attribute in a three-attribute scenario (Templin & Bradshaw, 2013). Conceptually, this metric of reliability captures the theoretical consistency of classification (i.e., whether a student receives the same classification of mastery or nonmastery) in a test–retest scenario. Templin and Bradshaw (2013) provide the steps for calculating this reliability measure as the correlation of expected classifications for two independent testing occasions. Similar to the sample-size recommendations already described, the specific assessment design features and the nature of the attributes being assessed can influence minimum test length requirements. Shorter test lengths, however, may push the lower boundary of items required for another critical aspect of a validity argument: construct representation. Developers of diagnostic assessments should keep in mind that the sample of items used to make a diagnosis should adequately represent the target attributes; in some cases, six to eight items may not be sufficient from a content representation perspective, even if this number is enough from a statistical perspective.

EXAMINEE CLASSIFICATIONS

DCMs allow for examinees to be classified into each of the 2^A attribute patterns for an assessment of A attributes. Results provide each examinee with the probability that he or she is in each latent class. The probability that examinee e has profile c is a function of his or her item responses (x_{ei}), the conditional item response probabilities (π_{ic}), and the base rates of latent class membership (v_c), given by (Rupp et al., 2010):

$$P(\alpha_e = \alpha_c \mid x_e) = \frac{v_c \prod_{i=1}^{I} \pi_{ic}^{x_{ie}} (1 - \pi_{ic})^{1-x_{ie}}}{\sum_{k=1}^{C} v_k \prod_{i=1}^{I} \pi_{ik}^{x_{ie}} (1 - \pi_{ik})^{1-x_{ie}}} \qquad (15.26)$$

Examinee classifications can be assigned using a *maximum-a-posteriori* (MAP) estimate or an *expected-a-posteriori* (EAP) estimate (see Chapter 14 for previous discussion of these estimation methods).

The MAP estimates the most likely class for each examinee, $\hat{\alpha}_e = \alpha_m$, such that m is the class for which the probability of being in that class, given the examinee's response pattern $(P(\alpha_e = \alpha_m \mid x_e))$, is highest. Table 15.5 provides hypothetical classifications for 10 examinees on the example diagnostic assessment. The first eight columns represent the attribute pattern probabilities $(P(\alpha_e = \alpha_c \mid x_e))$ for each examinee and class, and the shaded cell for each examinee corresponds to the examinee's most likely class (MAP estimate). For example, Examinee 9 most likely has attribute pattern [000], with probability of 0.64, and there is a 0.22 probability the examinee has pattern [001].

EAP estimates are marginal attribute probabilities, formed by summing the relevant class probabilities for each attribute. For example, in Table 15.6, the marginal probability of mastery of Attribute 1 for an examinee (i.e., the EAP estimate) is equal to the sum of the probabilities the examinee has the attribute patterns that include Attribute 1: [100], [101], [110], and [111]. For Examinee 9, the probability that he or she

TABLE 15.5. Latent Class Membership Estimates for 10 Example Examinees

	$P(\alpha_e = \alpha_c \mid x_e)$								MAP estimate		
e	[000]	[001]	[010]	[011]	[100]	[101]	[110]	[111]	$\hat{\alpha}_{e1}$	$\hat{\alpha}_{e2}$	$\hat{\alpha}_{e3}$
1	0.640	0.120	0.000	0.070	0.100	0.005	0.050	0.015	0	0	0
2	0.015	0.003	0.000	0.480	0.000	0.050	0.005	0.447	0	1	1
3	0.020	0.030	0.000	0.050	0.014	0.006	0.030	0.850	1	1	1
4	0.900	0.000	0.000	0.002	0.010	0.000	0.075	0.013	0	0	0
5	0.052	0.550	0.080	0.170	0.000	0.007	0.087	0.054	0	0	1
6	0.002	0.083	0.000	0.000	0.220	0.675	0.006	0.013	1	0	1
7	0.055	0.002	0.880	0.000	0.005	0.007	0.050	0.000	0	1	0
8	0.004	0.050	0.001	0.106	0.000	0.000	0.020	0.820	1	1	1
9	0.640	0.220	0.060	0.050	0.001	0.005	0.015	0.009	0	0	0
10	0.005	0.001	0.050	0.200	0.030	0.004	0.000	0.710	1	1	1

TABLE 15.6. Marginal Attribute Estimates for Example Examinees

Examinee e	EAP probabilities of mastery			EAP classifications of mastery		
	$P(\hat{\alpha}_{e1})=1$	$P(\hat{\alpha}_{e2})=1$	$P(\hat{\alpha}_{e3})=1$	$\hat{\alpha}_{e1}$	$\hat{\alpha}_{e2}$	$\hat{\alpha}_{e3}$
1	0.170	0.135	0.210	0	0	0
2	0.502	0.933	0.980	1	1	1
3	0.900	0.930	0.936	1	1	1
4	0.098	0.090	0.015	0	0	0
5	0.148	0.391	0.781	0	0	1
6	0.915	0.020	0.772	1	0	1
7	0.063	0.931	0.010	0	1	0
8	0.840	0.946	0.976	1	1	1
9	0.030	0.134	0.284	0	0	0
10	0.744	0.960	0.915	1	1	1

has mastered Attribute 1 is equal to .03, calculated by summing $P(\hat{\alpha}_e \mid x_e) = [100]$, $P(\hat{\alpha}_e \mid x_e) = [101]$, $P(\hat{\alpha}_e \mid x_e) = [110]$, and $P(\hat{\alpha}_e \mid x_e) = [111]$, where $P(\hat{\alpha}_e \mid x_e)$ represents the posterior probability that examinee e is in class c, given examinee e's item responses. The values of these posterior probabilities, given in Table 15.5, sum to 0.03: $0.001 + 0.005 + 0.015 + 0.009 = 0.03$. Thus, the probability that Examinee 9 has mastered Attribute 1 is equal to 0.03, meaning also that the probability that Examinee 9 has not mastered Attribute 1 is equal to 0.97. Because Examinee 9 most likely has not mastered Attribute 1 (i.e., because $0.97 > 0.03$), the EAP estimate classifies Examinee 9 as a nonmaster of Attribute 1.

Looking at all attribute classifications (for either MAP or EAP estimates), we can see that Examinee 9 has not mastered any of the measured attributes. Other examinees, for example, Examinees 3 and 8 have mastered all three attributes. In an educational context, Examinee 9 may need additional instruction on all three attributes, while Examinee 3 may be ready to move on to new material or enrichment activities. For other examinees, the attribute patterns show that examinees have mastered either one or two attributes. For example, Examinee 6 has mastered Attribute 1 and 3 but not Attribute 2. In an educational context, a teacher may use this information to focus time and effort on learning Attribute 2 for Examinee 6.

Individual classification results can be summed across a sample of examinees to estimate the distribution of examinees among the possible latent classes. Figure 15.6 displays hypothetical estimates of the probabilities that a randomly chosen examinee belongs to each class. According to the figure, an examinee would have the greatest probability (0.28) of having profile [111] and the least probability (0.02) of having profile [010]. This distribution can be reexpressed as the tetrachoric correlation between each pair of attributes as shown in Figure 15.2, where correlations of the attribute pairs range from 0.54 to 0.72. The class-specific estimates in Figure 15.6 can also be aggregated to provide the probability of mastery for each attribute as shown in Figure 15.7. These proportions of mastery for individual attributes are the *base rates* of mastery. For example, to determine the base rate for Attribute 1, take the sum of the probability distributions for the classes that include mastery of Attribute 1, the last four classes in Figure 15.6 (i.e., [100], [101], [110], and [111]). This sum (i.e., $0.17 + 0.14 + 0.04 + 0.28$) would yield a base rate of 0.63, as shown in Figure 15.7. This figure shows that the base rates range from 38% mastery for Attribute 2 to 63% mastery for Attribute 1. Again, in an educational context, a teacher may look across at base rates for her classroom of students (or a principal for a particular school) to understand which attributes are less frequently mastered than others. This information may indicate areas where the school curriculum is not as effective or where concepts are more difficult to master.

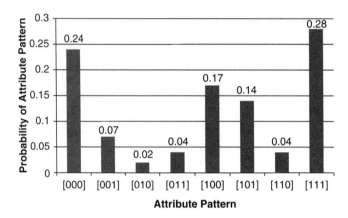

FIGURE 15.6. Latent class membership distribution. Each latent class is defined by a unique attribute pattern indicated by $[\alpha_1\alpha_2\alpha_3]$.

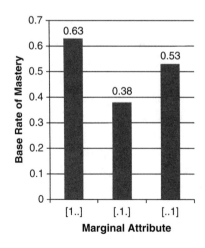

FIGURE 15.7. Marginal attribute mastery.

SUMMARY

This chapter has presented a discussion of the basic tenets of diagnostic classification models (DCMs). DCMs are similar to the factor analysis and item response theory models discussed in Chapters 12–14 in that, broadly speaking, they model the effects of latent variables on responses to items. However, DCMs differ from factor analysis and IRT models in that the latent variables affecting item responses are categorical rather than continuous. Thus, DCMs are used to classify examinees into latent groups known as latent classes, rather than to locate examinees on a continuum as in factor analysis and IRT. As in IRT models, the items used in DCMs are typically dichotomously scored, and because of this the log-odds of the item response rather than the item response itself is modeled. This is in contrast to factor analysis models, in which the variables being modeled are typically considered to be continuous. Another difference of DCMs from both factor analysis and IRT models is that the latent variables thought to affect items responses are often more narrowly defined in DCMs than in factor analysis or IRT models. These latent variables are known as attributes in the DCM nomenclature. Finally, DCMs have both structural and measurement parameters. The structural parameters model the relations among attributes, whereas the measurement parameters describe how the attributes are related to the items.

One of the basic building blocks of DCMs is the attribute profile, which represents an examinee's pattern of attribute mastery. For A binary attributes, there are 2^A attribute profiles, and these define the latent DCM classes. That is, there is one DCM class for each possible attribute pattern. Because these profiles are posited a priori, DCMs are confirmatory rather than explanatory models. Another building block of DCMs is the Q-matrix. This matrix is similar to a factor loading matrix in that it is a representation of how each attribute relates to responses on each item. Unlike factor loading matrices, however, entries in the Q-matrix consist of only 0's and 1's, with a 1 indicating that the attribute is measured by the item and a 0 indicating it is not. Because the Q-matrix forms the basis for the DCM specification, it is crucial that it is based on the best possible information about which attributes are measured by which items. This information can be provided by content experts, and can be verified through think-aloud procedures in which examinees are asked to verbalize their thought processes and problem-solving strategies as they answer the items.

The basic DCM defines the probability of obtaining an observed response pattern across items as a function of the examinee's attribute pattern. The latter is the pattern of an examinee's mastery or nonmastery of the attributes being measured. Because the item responses are dichotomous, estimation of DCMs is based on statistical models that can accommodate such responses, such as the logistic regression model. The log-linear cognitive diagnosis model (LCDM) is a flexible model which, as the name implies, is based on a log-linear, or logistic, function. This model is ANOVA-like in that the predictors are attribute mastery/nonmastery, and are therefore categorical. As in ANOVA models, the LCDM models the (log-odds of) item responses as functions of the main effects and interactions of the attributes. These effects can be interpreted in a manner analogous to those in ANOVA.

The results of DCMs are often displayed in graphs known as item characteristic bar charts which depict the probability of a correct item response as a function of latent class membership. Finally, examinee classification is an important part of DCMs. Examinees can be classified into each of the 2^A attribute patterns for an assessment measuring A attributes. DCM results provide the probabilities that each examinee is a member of each latent class, as a function of the examinee's item response pattern, the conditional item response probabilities, and the base rates of membership in each latent class. These classifications provide teachers, therapists, or others involved in instruction or treatment with a summary of the status of each examinee on each attribute, which can then be used to plan their next steps accordingly.

EXERCISES

1. Fill in each cell of Table 15.7 with either "categorical" or "continuous" to describe how latent variable models differ in terms of the type of observed data they *typically* model.

TABLE 15.7. Table for Question 1

Model	Observed response variable type	Latent predictor variable type
Factor analysis		
IRT		
DCM		

2. What makes a DCM a confirmatory model?

3. Suppose item 1 and item 2 on a test measure the same two attributes. Using the LCDM, the intercept of item 1 on a test is greater than the intercept of item 2. What does this mean?

4. Using the LCDM parameterization, can the intercept for an item be "too big"? Why or why not?

5. Using the LCDM parameterization, can a main effect for a simple structure item be "too small"? Why or why not?

Use Table 15.8 showing LCDM item parameter values to answer Questions 6–16. Zeros indicate that the parameter value was estimated as 0, and "-" indicates that the parameter does not exist because the item does not measure the corresponding attribute. Let $\lambda_{i2(a,a')}$ denote the two-way interaction between Attribute a and Attribute a', the two attributes measured by the item as indicated by the corresponding main effects.

TABLE 15.8. LCDM Item Parameter Values for Questions 6–17

Item	λ_{i0}	$\lambda_{i1(1)}$	$\lambda_{i1(2)}$	$\lambda_{i1(3)}$	$\lambda_{i2(a,a')}$
1	−2.0	1.0	3.0	-	2.0
2	−0.5	0.0	-	0.0	2.0
3	−1.0	-	0.5	2.0	0.5
4	0.5	1.0	-	1.0	−1.0

6. For item 1, are you more likely to answer the item correctly if you're only a master of Attribute 1 or if you're only a master of Attribute 2?

7. Using item parameter symbols (not values from the table), write the LCDM equation for the conditional probability of a correct response (not the log-odds of a correct response) to item 1. Include α's in your equation, to make it general for any attribute pattern.

8. For examinees who have only mastered Attributes 1 and 3, what is the log-odds of a correct response for item 3? For the same examinees, what is the probability of a correct response for item 3?

9. For examinees who have only mastered Attributes 1 and 3, what is the log-odds of an *incorrect* response for item 3? *Hint*: Use Figure 15.1 to think through this question.

10. Examinees with no mastered attributes are most likely to answer which item correctly?

11. This test measures three attributes. How many possible attribute patterns are there?

12. If a test measures *A* attributes, how many possible attribute patterns are there?

13. How many unique item response probabilities will item 1 have across all classes?

14. How many unique item response probabilities would there be for an item that measures three attributes and models all possible attribute interactions?

15. Which item behaves like a DINO model? How do you know?

16. Which attribute patterns have the same item response probability for item 2? What model does this item behave as?

16

Bias, Fairness, and Legal Issues in Testing

Suppose you learn that men obtained higher scores than women on a math placement test used in a local community college. Does this mean the test is biased against women? Possibly, but you would need much more information to determine the test was biased. Psychometrically speaking, a finding that two (or more) groups obtain different average scores on a test is not, in and of itself, proof that the test is biased. For example, suppose that further research revealed that men had, on average, taken more math courses in high school than women had taken. If this was the case, we would expect men to obtain higher scores because, having taken more math courses, they should have more math knowledge and should therefore perform better on the math placement test. This illustrates the importance of considering alternative explanations of differences in test performance before concluding that a test is biased. By identifying the real reason for differential performance, we can have a better idea of how to ameliorate this difference, if desired. Suppose we wanted to increase women's scores so that they were equal to those of men. If we concluded that women's scores were low because the test was biased, the remedy would be to alter the test. However, if the real reason for score differences was the different number of math courses taken by women and men, altering the test would not improve the situation. In that case, what really needs to be altered is course-taking behavior and/or interest in math.

This is not to say that test bias is not a serious issue. On the contrary, the possibility of test bias is of the utmost concern to those who develop, use, or take tests. As explained later in this chapter, the presence of test bias represents a very real threat to test validity. This is because the presence of test bias is an indication that test scores do not have the same meaning for those from different groups. Also, the possibility of test bias can cause the public to question the fairness of testing procedures. This is a legitimate concern, as tests can serve as barriers to admission to higher education programs, selection for jobs, licensure or certification, and other important opportunities. In fact, currently existing definitions of test bias and methods for detecting bias were developed in response to claims of testing practices that were unfair to members of certain racial and ethnic groups.

In this chapter, I discuss test and item bias, methods for detecting bias, and legal issues that arise from claims of bias. I begin by defining the terms *impact*, *test bias*, *item bias*, and *differential item functioning* (DIF). I also briefly allude to the principles of *universal design*, which were developed in an effort to yield tests that are accessible to as many test takers as possible. I then discuss methods for detecting bias at both the test and item level. At the item level, I offer brief explanations of bias detection methods based on contingency tables, such as the Mantel–Haenszel index, and on logistic regression, and provide examples. I also briefly discuss methods based on IRT and CFA. Because IRT and CFA methods are quite similar, I discuss them together, pointing out their differences and similarities. I then discuss reasons that items might exhibit bias, and I provide an overview of judgmental item reviews, sometimes known as *sensitivity reviews*, in which panels of experts examine item wording and content in an attempt to identify items that may result in bias. Finally, I review laws under which tests can be challenged in the United States and describe well-known court cases in which claims of test bias have been made.

IMPACT, ITEM AND TEST BIAS, DIFFERENTIAL ITEM FUNCTIONING, AND FAIRNESS DEFINED

Impact is a term used in the measurement literature for any finding of differences in the average scores of two groups on a test or test item. Impact may be due to (1) true ability differences between the groups, (2) the inclusion of items that are inappropriate or unfair for one of the groups, or (3) other construct-irrelevant aspects of testing such as test instructions or test delivery modes that affect groups differentially. Impact due to true group differences does not imply bias, but impact due to inappropriate items or other testing features does. After finding impact, therefore, the next task is to determine whether the impact was due to actual group differences or to inappropriate items or test features. One way to do this at the item level is to match the two groups on their levels of the construct being measured. If examinees who are from different groups but have the same level of the construct obtain different scores on an item, then reason (1) can be ruled out. For example, if groups of men and women with the same level of math ability had different probabilities of answering a math item correctly, that item would be considered biased. This type of item-level bias is known in the psychometric literature as *differential item functioning* (DIF). Although the terms *item bias* and *DIF* are often used interchangeably, the term *DIF* is preferred in psychometrics because of the negative baggage associated with the term *bias*. Also, bias is usually taken to mean that one group has a lower performance level, on average, than another, whereas DIF can indicate either a lower or higher average performance level.

In measurement contexts, bias is thus defined in terms of its statistical meaning as "a systematic difference between two quantities that should be equal" (Camilli, 2006, p. 225).

Item or test score means from two groups should be equal if the groups have equal levels of the construct being measured. If, after matching the groups on the construct level, the test or item means still differ systematically, test or item bias is implied. So, an item, or a whole test, could be considered biased if two groups that should obtain equal scores do not. Note that I use the term *systematically different* to indicate that such a difference must be found for the entire group, on average; not just for a few people within a group. If one or two people in a given group were to obtain lower scores than expected, we might put this down to measurement error. But if the difference were found across an entire group, on average, measurement error would be an unlikely explanation.

DETECTING TEST AND ITEM BIAS

I base the following discussion of test bias on the *predictive bias* model proposed by Cleary (1968). I focus on this model because it is widely used and relatively easy to understand, but many other models have been proposed (see Cole & Zieky, 2001).

Test Bias

When tests are used to predict future outcomes, such as success in educational or training programs or in a job, it is important that the prediction be as accurate as possible. Implicit in this statement is that the tests predict equally well for all individuals. A test is considered biased if it does not result in the same predictive accuracy (on average) for members of all groups with whom it is used. This type of test bias is sometimes called *differential prediction* because it is assessed by determining whether the predictive relation between test scores and criterion differs across groups. The presence of differential prediction can be assessed from the results of a multiple regression model in which test scores, group membership, and the group by test score interaction are used to predict a criterion of interest. Group membership and the group by test score interaction are entered into the regression equation to allow for differences in group regression lines. The purpose of this analysis is to determine whether the same regression line can be used to predict the criterion for all groups of interest. If not, different regression lines are needed for different groups, and differential prediction is present. To use a common example, SAT scores might be used to predict first-year college GPA, with gender or racial group entered as a grouping variable. To allow for differences in regression lines, a regression would be performed in which SAT scores were entered first into the equation, followed by group membership (dummy or effect coded), with the group membership by SAT scores (group times SAT score) interaction entered last. Here I discuss the simplest situation in which there are only two groups, but the extension to three or more groups is straightforward (for more details, see Cohen, Cohen, West, & Aiken, 2003, pp. 375–383; Pedhazur, 1997, ch. 15).

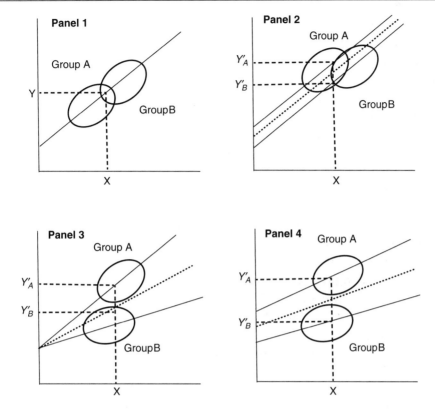

FIGURE 16.1. Scenarios for tests of differential prediction.

When testing for differential prediction, one of four things can happen, as illustrated by the four panels in Figure 16.1. In the figure, Y represents the criterion being predicted, such as GPA, and X represents the test score used as a predictor. Ellipses are used to show the distribution of X and Y scores for each group. From a test bias perspective, the ideal situation is that shown in panel 1, where the same outcome is predicted for a given test score regardless of group membership. Although the two groups shown in panel 1 have different average scores on X and Y, the higher or lower X scores in one group are associated with correspondingly higher or lower values on Y. In other words, the relationship between X and Y is the same for both groups, and the same regression line can be used with both groups. Thus, someone with a given test score would obtain the same predicted criterion value whether he or she was in group A or group B. This is shown by the dashed line that links a given score on X to a predicted score on Y. As can be seen in panel 1, the predicted score is the same regardless of group membership. The situation depicted in this panel therefore indicates a lack of test bias.

Panels 2–4 depict three types of differential prediction: differences in intercept only (panel 2), differences in slope only (panel 3), and differences in both intercept and slope (panel 4). Relating these differences to test bias, a difference in intercepts, as shown in panel 2, indicates that the test systematically over- or underpredicts criterion values for a particular group. Unlike the case in panel 1, where groups differ in average scores but have correspondingly different criterion values, panel 2 shows that, although Group B has higher average test scores, the two groups have equally high average scores on Y. However, the X/Y relation is the same for both groups, as indicated by the parallel regression lines. This situation is the one most often associated with a lack of fairness in testing. Suppose that Group A is a traditionally underrepresented group and Group B is a majority group. In panel 2 you can see that, although the majority group has higher test scores, members of the two groups with the same test score do equally well on the criterion. The dotted regression line in the figure represents the common regression line that would be obtained if the same regression equation were used for both groups. If this common regression line were used, you can see that predictions for Group A would be consistently too low and predictions for Group B would be consistently too high. Members of the underrepresented group would therefore obtain predicted criterion values that underestimate their actual performance. This is sometimes referred to as *intercept bias*.

Panels 3 and 4 show situations in which the slope of the line that relates test scores to the criterion differs across groups. In panel 3, the groups have the same intercept but different slopes, whereas in panel 4 the groups differ in both slope and intercept. Both panels represent *slope bias*, which indicates that the test does not bear the same relation to the criterion in the two groups. In the context of the SAT/GPA example, SAT scores do not predict grades equally well for the two groups. This is problematic because, if a single regression line (shown as a dotted line) were used, the performance of both groups would be predicted incorrectly.

Is there evidence in the literature that intercept and slope bias exist? In one study including nearly 100,000 students who entered college in 1994 or 1995 (Bridgeman, McCamley-Jenkins, & Ervin, 2000), the researchers found that SAT scores underpredicted the grades of women and overpredicted the grades of black and Hispanic students. In another investigation, Young (2001) reviewed over 49 studies of differential prediction involving the SAT and found similar results. Mattern, Patterson, Shaw, Kobrin, and Barbuti (2008) studied over 150,000 students who entered college in 2006. Their findings were quite similar to those of the previous studies. GPA was overpredicted for black, Hispanic, and Native American students and was underpredicted for women. GPAs for white students were also overpredicted, though only slightly. Thus, the SAT does appear to overpredict GPA for black, Hispanic, and Native American students. Also, the SAT has been found to underpredict GPA for women, although the amount of this underprediction is relatively small.

With regard to employment testing, Hunter, Schmidt, and Hunter (1979), in an often-cited study, examined differences in test–criterion relationships for black and white employees taken from 39 published studies.[1] Hunter et al. found that differences in test–criterion relationships occurred at no more than chance level. They concluded that

---

[1] The researchers did not use meta-analysis, as that type of analysis had only recently been developed and was not yet widespread. Instead, they averaged results across studies using a type of chi-square statistic.

"true differential validity is quite uncommon. But it may nevertheless be that specific instances of statistically significant validity differences observed in samples may reflect true differential validity in particular applicant populations" (p. 733). Thus, although differences did not occur any more than might be expected by chance, they did occur in some samples. It should also be noted that Hunter et al. did not study intercept bias, so we do not know whether this type of bias was present in any of the studies they investigated.

Item Bias

As stated in an earlier section, methods for detecting item bias, or DIF, require matching members of the groups of interest on levels of the construct to rule out true differences in construct level as a reason for the DIF. DIF is therefore an *unexpected* difference in item difficulty between groups that is due to something other than the construct of interest. This suggests that DIF is related to test validity because if an item exhibits DIF, it is not measuring the same thing in both groups. The reason may be that the test taps into different dimensions in the two groups, as in the commonly used example in which a math test measures knowledge of English as well as math knowledge for non-native English speakers, but only measures math knowledge for native English speakers. Such unanticipated multidimensionality can result in DIF. In this section, I review several methods of detecting DIF, including methods based on contingency tables, such as the Mantel–Haenszel method, methods based on logistic regression, and IRT- and CFA-based methods. Because the Mantel–Haenszel method is widely used and is relatively easy to compute by hand, I provide a detailed example of its calculation. For the logistic regression and IRT/CFA-based methods, my discussions are more conceptual.

Contingency Table Methods

One way of matching respondents from two groups on the construct of interest is to divide them into categories based on their total test scores. For example, if a test were worth 10 points, respondents could be divided into categories of those scoring 1, 2, 3, and so on, up to a score of 9. Note that there is no need to create categories for scores of 0 or 10 because respondents with these scores will have either missed every item or gotten every item correct. Given this, there can be no DIF for these respondents because their answers would be the same on every item in each group. If the sample size is small, adjacent score categories can be collapsed so that groups are matched by score ranges such as 1–3 and 4–6. This is known as *thick matching*. However, it is best to use *thin matching* (matching at each score point) if possible, because this results in the closest matches. Note that it is not necessary to have equal numbers of people in each score category.

The next step is to construct a table for each score category, with item response (correct or incorrect) represented in the columns and the groups being compared composing the rows, as illustrated in Table 16.1. For each item there will be s such tables, one for each score category. It is common practice to refer to the group for which lower scores are anticipated (e.g., women, members of a minority group) as the *focal group* and the

TABLE 16.1. Item Contingency Table for One Score Category

Group	Item response		Total
	Correct	Incorrect	
Reference (R)	a	b	$N_R = a + b$
Focal (F)	c	d	$N_F = c + d$
Total	$N_C = a + c$	$N_I = b + d$	$N_T = a + b + c + d$

group for which higher scores are anticipated (typically, members of the majority group) as the *reference group* (I use this terminology for the remainder of this chapter). Entries in the table represent the number of test takers falling into each cell. For example, a is the number of people in the reference group who answered the item correctly, whereas c is the number of people in the focal group who answered correctly. N_C is the total number of people who answered correctly. Similarly, N_I, N_R, and N_F are the total numbers who answered incorrectly, the total number in the reference group, and the total number in the focal group. N_T is the overall total.

Mantel–Haenszel Statistic

The Mantel–Haenszel (MH) statistic (Mantel & Haenszel, 1959) is a widely used contingency table method for DIF detection. The MH is based on *odds ratios*. In the context of DIF, the *odds* of a correct answer on an item is the proportion of correct responses divided by the proportion of incorrect responses, or $p(\text{correct})/p(\text{incorrect})$, where p represents proportion. For example, suppose that in the reference group, 100 people got the item correct and 50 people got the item incorrect. $p(\text{correct})$ equals 100/150, or 0.67, and $p(\text{incorrect})$ equals 50/150, or 0.33. The odds would then be 0.67/0.33, or 2, meaning that examinees are twice as likely to get the item correct as to get it incorrect.

An odds ratio is the ratio of the odds for one group to the odds for another group, or $\text{odds}_1/\text{odds}_2$. By convention, the odds for the reference group is put in the numerator and the odds for the focal group in the denominator. In terms of the entries in Table 16.1, the odds for the reference group could be written as $(a/b)/N_T$. For the focal group, the odds would be $(c/d)/N_T$. The odds ratio for item i is the ratio of the odds for the reference group divided by the odds for the focal group, or

$$\alpha_i = \frac{(a/b)/N_T}{(c/d)/N_T} = \frac{ad/N_T}{bc/N_T} \tag{16.1}$$

An odds ratio of 1 indicates that there is no difference in the proportions of examinees in the reference and focal groups who get the item right for that particular score category. An odds ratio greater than 1 indicates that the reference group performed better than the focal group (had higher odds of getting the item right), whereas an odds ratio below 1 indicates that the focal group performed better.

Note that the odds ratio in Equation 16.1 is for only one score category. However, the MH statistic is based on the odds ratio across all categories, known as the *common odds ratio*. To obtain the common odds ratio, the values are summed across all score categories. The formula for the common odds ratio is shown in Equation 16.2. In Equation 16.2, summation is over the score categories (s), and N_s is the number of people in a particular score category.

$$\hat{\alpha}_{MH} = \frac{\sum_s a_s d_s / N_s}{\sum_s b_s c_s / N_s} \tag{16.2}$$

I use the data in Table 16.2 to demonstrate calculation of the MH common odds ratio. For simplicity, I have included only four score categories in the example, but typically tables would be constructed across all score points.

As can be seen from the table, the value of $\hat{\alpha}_{MH}$ is 1.46, which indicates that the odds of getting the item right for those in the reference group is 1.46 times the odds in the focal group. One problem with the common odds ratio, $\hat{\alpha}_{MH}$, is that it is not bounded. Its upper range is, at least theoretically, infinity because one group could have infinitely greater odds than another of getting an item right. Also, because $\hat{\alpha}_{MH}$ is a ratio, it cannot be zero, and therefore its range is bounded at zero at the lower end. To get around these obstacles, $\hat{\alpha}_{MH}$ is often transformed by taking its natural logarithm and multiplying by -2.35. This transformation may seem a bit odd, but it puts $\hat{\alpha}_{MH}$ onto the widely used delta (Δ) scale developed by the Educational Testing Service. Applying this transformation to the $\hat{\alpha}_{MH}$ value of 1.46 yields $-2.35 * ln(1.46) = -.89$. Angoff (1993) notes that this transformation reverses the direction of the MH index so that it is equal to zero if there is no DIF, has positive values if the item favors the focal group and negative values if it favors the reference group. This is somewhat confusing, as in the original metric, higher values of $\hat{\alpha}_{MH}$ indicate that the item favors the reference group. Nevertheless, the delta metric is commonly used, mainly because ETS has developed cutoff values for determining what constitutes low, medium, and high DIF. These cutoff values involve the use of both $\hat{\alpha}_{MH}$ and the Mantel–Haenszel chi-square statistic, to which I turn next.

Values of $\hat{\alpha}_{MH}$ and Δ can be thought of as effect sizes that measure the relative magnitude of DIF values from different items. Although there is a statistical test of $\hat{\alpha}_{MH}$ (see Dorans & Holland, 1993), the Mantel–Haenszel chi-square statistic ($\chi^2 MH$) is typically used to test the hypothesis that the common odds ratio $\hat{\alpha}_{MH}$ is equal to one. Note that this is the value we would expect to obtain if the odds ratios were equal in the two groups, indicating no difference across groups in the odds of answering correctly, or more succinctly, no DIF. The Mantel–Haenszel chi-square is calculated as

$$\chi^2_{MH} = \frac{\left[\left| \sum_s a_s - \sum_s E(a_s) \right| - .5 \right]^2}{\sum_s Var(a_s)} \tag{16.3}$$

TABLE 16.2. Hypothetical Data for Four Score Categories Illustrating Calculation of the Mantel–Haenszel Common Odds Ratio

Frequency of item response

Group	Total score = 1			Total score = 2			Total score = 3			Total score = 4		
	Correct	Incorrect	Total	Correct	Incorrect	Total	Correct	Incorrect	Total	Correct	Incorrect	Total
Reference	20	50	70	30	40	70	50	20	70	60	10	70
Focal	5	25	30	10	20	30	20	10	30	25	5	30
Total	25	75	100	40	60	100	70	30	100	85	15	100
$\dfrac{a_s d_s}{N_s}$		$\dfrac{20(25)}{100}=5$			$\dfrac{30(20)}{100}=6$			$\dfrac{50(10)}{100}=5$			$\dfrac{60(5)}{100}=3$	
$\dfrac{b_s c_s}{N_s}$		$\dfrac{50(5)}{100}=2.5$			$\dfrac{40(10)}{100}=4$			$\dfrac{20(20)}{100}=4$			$\dfrac{10(25)}{100}=2.5$	

$$\sum_s \frac{a_s d_s}{N_s} \qquad 5+6+5+3=19$$

$$\sum_s \frac{b_s c_s}{N_s} \qquad 2.5+4+4+2.5=13$$

$$\alpha_{MH} \qquad \frac{19}{13}=1.46$$

As in the formula for $\hat{\alpha}_{MH}$, summation is taken over all the score categories (s), and a_s is the number of people in score category s who are in cell a (those answering correctly in the reference group). $E(a_s)$ and $Var(a_s)$ are the expected value (mean) and variance of a under the null hypothesis that there is no relation between the item score and group membership, conditional on total score.[2] The formulas for the mean and SD are shown in Equations 16.4 and 16.5. In these equations, N_{R_s}, N_{F_s}, N_{C_s}, and N_{I_s} are the total numbers of people in the reference group and the focal group, and the total numbers of people getting the item correct and incorrect, respectively, in score category s, and N_{T_s} is the overall total for category s (in our example, the overall total is 100 for each score category, but the total N could differ across categories).[3]

$$E(a_s) = \frac{N_{R_s} N_{C_s}}{N_{T_s}} \tag{16.4}$$

$$Var(a_s) = \frac{N_{R_s} N_{C_s} N_{F_s} N_{I_s}}{N_{T_s}^2 (N_{T_s} - 1)} \tag{16.5}$$

I show the calculations for χ^2_{MH} in Table 16.3. The first step is to calculate the expected values and variances for each score category. These values are then summed across categories and entered into Equation 16.3. The value of χ^2_{MH} is 1.86. The Mantel–Haenszel chi-square has one degree of freedom and can therefore be compared to a chi-square critical value with one degree of freedom to determine statistical significance. At the 0.05 level of significance, the critical value is 3.84. I would therefore fail to reject the hypothesis that the two groups have equal odds ratios, which suggests an absence of DIF for this item. This is not surprising, as you can see from Table 16.3 that the proportions of correct answers are quite similar for the reference and focal group members across all categories.

ETS uses the following classification system, which has now been adopted by many research organizations, for categorizing DIF into low (level A), medium (level B), and high (level C) levels.

---

[2] You may wonder why the MH chi-square calculations are based on only cell a of Table 16.1. The reason is that, as with any two-by-two chi-square table, the count in one cell determines the counts in all the others, assuming the marginal values are fixed. For example, for a total $N = 100$ in Table 16.2, given that the column and row totals are 25, 75, 70, and 30, if the count in cell a is 20, the count in cell b must be 50 (to add to the row total of 70), the count in cell c must be 5 (to add to the column total of 25), and the count in cell d must be 25.

[3] The -0.5 in Equation 16.3 is called a continuity correction and may or may not be included in a particular statistical program. For example, both SAS and SPSS calculate the MH index and chi-square, but SPSS incorporates the correction for continuity in the chi-square and SAS does not. Paek (2010) shows empirically that omitting the correction alleviates the overconservativeness typically found for shorter tests.

TABLE 16.3. Calculation of Mantel–Haenszel Chi-Square Statistic

	Stratum 1			Stratum 2			Stratum 3			Stratum 4		
					Frequency of item response							
Group	Correct	Incorrect	Total	Correct	Incorrect	Total	Correct	Incorrect	Total	Correct	Incorrect	Total
Reference	20	50	70	30	40	70	50	20	70	60	10	70
Focal	5	25	30	10	20	30	20	10	30	25	5	30
Total	25	75	100	40	60	100	70	30	100	85	15	100

$E(a)$

Stratum 1: $E(a_s) = \dfrac{N_{R_s} N_{C_s}}{N_{T_s}} = \dfrac{70(25)}{100} = 17.5$

Stratum 2: $E(a_s) = \dfrac{N_{R_s} N_{C_s}}{N_{T_s}} = \dfrac{70(40)}{100} = 28.0$

Stratum 3: $E(a_s) = \dfrac{N_{R_s} N_{C_s}}{N_{T_s}} = \dfrac{70(70)}{100} = 49.0$

Stratum 4: $E(a_s) = \dfrac{N_{R_s} N_{C_s}}{N_{T_s}} = \dfrac{70(85)}{100} = 59.5$

$Var(a)$

Stratum 1: $Var(a_s) = \dfrac{70(25)(30)(75)}{100^2(100-1)} = \dfrac{3,937,500}{990,000} = 3.98$

Stratum 2: $Var(a_s) = \dfrac{70(40)(30)(60)}{100^2(100-1)} = \dfrac{5,040,000}{990,000} = 5.09$

Stratum 3: $Var(a_s) = \dfrac{70(70)(30)(30)}{100^2(100-1)} = \dfrac{4,410,000}{990,000} = 4.45$

Stratum 4: $Var(a_s) = \dfrac{70(85)(30)(15)}{100^2(100-1)} = \dfrac{2,677,500}{990,000} = 2.70$

$\sum_s a$ $20 + 30 + 50 + 60 = 160$

$\sum_s (E)a$ $17.5 + 28 + 49 + 59.5 = 154$

$\sum_s Var(a)$ $3.98 + 5.09 + 4.45 + 2.70 = 16.22$

$$\chi^2_{MH} = \frac{\left[|160-154| - 0.5\right]^2}{16.22} = \frac{30.25}{16.22} = 1.86$$

488

- Level A: $|\Delta_{MH}| < 1$ and/or χ^2_{MH} not significantly significant
- Level B: $|1 < \Delta_{MH} < 1.5|$ and χ^2_{MH} is statistically significant
- Level C: $|\Delta_{MH}| > 1.5$ and χ^2_{MH} is statistically significant[4]

Based on the ETS system, the example item would be classified as level A because $|\Delta_{MH}|$ is $|-0.89|$, or 0.89, which is less than one, and the χ^2_{MH} value is not statistically significant at the 0.05 level. Items classified as Level A are considered to have little or no DIF. If a large item bank were available, Level A items would be chosen first to create a test. Items with Level B DIF would be used only if there were no Level A items that had the same levels of difficulty and discrimination and measured the same content. Level C items would only be used if the content of the items was essential to the test and there were no Level A or B items that measured the same content (Clauser & Mazor, 1998).

One problem with the MH procedure is that the odds ratios may differ considerably across score categories. This could result in items for which the odds ratios differ for some score categories but not for others, yielding inconsistent evidence of DIF for the item. If the odds ratio for one group is consistently higher than that of the other group, DIF is considered to be *uniform*, and summing across score categories should provide a reasonably accurate picture of the overall amount of DIF. Uniform DIF refers to group differences in the overall difficulty of an item. However, suppose that at some score categories the odds for the reference group are higher but at others the odds for the focal group are higher. In such situations, it is possible that the differences in odds ratios will cancel out across score categories, and the MH may indicate that there is no DIF when there actually is. Situations in which one group is not consistently more likely to answer correctly than the other result in what is known as *nonuniform* DIF. Nonuniform DIF refers to differences in an item's discrimination value across groups. A particularly problematic situation for the MH is that just described: when an item is more difficult for the focal group at some ability levels, but more difficult for the reference group at other ability levels. The MH statistic is not able to detect such nonuniform DIF. It is therefore recommended only for use with uniform DIF. Procedures based on logistic regression and on IRT and CFA methods can handle both uniform and nonuniform DIF. I turn now to these procedures.

Logistic Regression Methods

Logistic regression is a form of regression that is used when the dependent variable is categorical rather than continuous. In this form of regression, the probability of an outcome, rather than the outcome itself, is predicted. In the context of DIF detection, logistic regression is used to test whether the relationship between the test score and the probability of a correct answer to an item is the same for the reference and focal groups. This is very similar to the tests for intercept and slope bias discussed in the section on

---

[4] For Level C items, $|\Delta_{MH}|$ must also be significantly > 1.0, but I do not discuss statistical testing of Δ_{MH} here. See Camilli (2006, p. 238) for the standard error of Δ_{MH}.

test bias, in the sense that differences in the test score/item probability relationship is investigated using regression methods. Specifically, in logistic regression methods, the item probabilities are predicted from the test score, the grouping variable representing focal/reference group membership, and the group by score interaction. However, there are some differences between the logistic regression and test bias procedures. One difference is that, because the analysis is conducted at the item level, the Y variable is the probability of a correct answer on the item, and the variable on the X axis is the test score. That is, in logistic regression analyses to detect DIF, the item probabilities, or more specifically, the *log-odds* or *logits* of these probabilities, are predicted from the test scores. The logit is the natural logarithm of the odds defined earlier in the context of the Mantel–Haenszel statistic, $\ln(p(\text{correct})/p(\text{incorrect}))$. Because the relationship between the item probabilities and the test score is nonlinear, the model parameters cannot be estimated using ordinary least squares. Instead, maximum likelihood estimation is used. I discussed maximum likelihood estimation in Chapter 13. Briefly, this type of estimation uses iterative methods to estimate the parameter values that are most likely to have produced the observed response probabilities.

Note that when using logistic regression methods, it is not necessary to divide respondents into response categories based on their total test scores as in the Mantel–Haenszel procedure. Instead, a series of three sequential logistic regression models is estimated. In the first model, only total scores on X are entered into the equation. In the second model, both X and the grouping variable G are entered, with G typically coded as 0/1 for two groups. Including X in the equation controls for X scores and essentially matches respondents at each score point. In the third model, X, G, and the $X * G$ interaction are included. This process yields the following three logistic regression equations:

$$y' = a + b_1 X$$
$$y' = a + b_1 X + b_2 G \qquad (16.6)$$
$$y' = a + b_1 X + b_2 G + b_3 XG$$

In these equations, the intercept (a) is a measure of the item's difficulty and the slope (b_1) is the item's discrimination. Remember that, in the context of logistic regression, y' is equal to the log-odds defined earlier $\ln(p(\text{correct})/p(\text{incorrect}))$. Coding G as either 0 or 1 in the last equation yields the following equations for the two groups:

$$G = 0 : y' = a + b_1 X + b_2 (0) + b_3 (0 * X) = a + b_1 X \qquad (16.7)$$

$$G = 1 : y' = a + b_1 X + b_2 (1) + b_3 (1 * X) = (a + b_2) + (b_1 + b_3) X \qquad (16.8)$$

By comparing Equations 16.7 and 16.8 for the two groups, you can see that the difficulty values (a and $a + b_2$) differ by an amount equal to b_2, and that the discrimination values (b_1 and $b_1 + b_3$) differ by an amount equal to b_3. Thus, if b_2 is equal to zero, the item difficulties are the same, and if b_3 is equal to zero, the item discrimination values are the same. More specifically, if the test that b_3 equals zero is nonsignificant, the discrimination values, for the two groups are assumed to be the same, ruling out the presence of nonuniform DIF. If the test that b_2 equals zero is nonsignificant, the difficulty values for the two groups are assumed to be the same, ruling out uniform DIF. Logistic regression therefore provides a way to test both types of DIF.

Unlike the case in linear regression, where t- or F-tests are used to determine the significance of the variables, *likelihood ratio tests* are used in logistic regression. The *likelihood* obtained from each regression model is a measure of how likely the observed item probabilities are, given the parameter estimates. Tests of b_2 and b_3 are based on these likelihoods or, more specifically, on the natural logs of their likelihoods, known as *log likelihoods*. Tests for b_2 and b_3 are obtained by subtracting the log likelihood of the model with more variables (I refer to this as the larger model) from the log likelihood of the model with fewer variables (which I refer to as the smaller model), and multiplying by −2, as shown in Equation 16.9.

$$LR = -2\left(LL_{smaller} - LL_{larger}\right) \tag{16.9}$$

The quantity in Equation 16.9 is called the *likelihood ratio* (LR) and the notation LL denotes the log likelihood defined previously. The likelihood ratio is distributed as chi-square with degrees of freedom equal to the difference in the number of parameters in the two models. For example, suppose that the larger model includes X, G, and the $X * G$ interaction and the smaller model includes only X and G; the degrees of freedom are equal to 1 because the models differ by one parameter (the interaction coefficient).

I provide a hypothetical example of a likelihood ratio test for DIF in Table 16.4. Suppose that the data represent one item from a science test given to 800 male (coded 0) and 465 female (coded 1) university students. Science instructors at the university were interested in determining whether the test items exhibited DIF against women. Another way of saying this is that instructors were interested in whether any test items were differentially difficult or differentially discriminating (or both) for women and men who were matched on their total test scores. Here I illustrate the procedure for a single item, but in practice all items would be tested for DIF sequentially. Comparison of the log likelihood values from the model with X only to the model with both X and G yields a LR value of 46.6. This value is distributed as chi-square with one degree of freedom, so

TABLE 16.4. Hypothetical Logistic Regression Results for Testing DIF

Model	LL	# of Parameters estimated	Diff = $LL_{smaller} - LL_{larger}$	LR (−2LLdiff)	*p*-value
X only	−669.9	2[a]			
X and G	−646.6	3	−23.3	46.6	<.0001
X, G, and XG	−643.5	4	−3.1	6.2	.013

[a] Recall that the intercept is estimated for each model, which adds one estimated parameter.

the critical value for the 0.05 level of significance is 3.84. The obtained value is clearly greater than this, so I would reject the hypothesis that the item is equally difficult for women and men with the same test scores. The Mantel–Haenszel chi-square value for the same item is 44.1. Although both values are chi-squares and both test whether the difficulty of the item is equal for men and women, they yield somewhat different results. This is because, whereas in logistic regression the test scores are treated as a continuous variable, in the calculation of the MH chi-square each score point is treated as a discrete category, resulting in a slight loss of power. This power loss is greater if several score points are combined into a single category for the MH procedure.

The odds ratio obtained from the logistic regression (not shown in the table) is 0.364, which indicates that the odds for women are about .36 times the odds for men with the same test scores. That is, the odds that women will answer the item correctly are about a third of those for men. The significant result at this step of the analysis suggests that there is uniform DIF (differences in difficulty) in the item. However, the item may also exhibit nonuniform DIF (differences in discrimination). This is tested in the next step, to which I now turn.

Nonuniform DIF would be indicated if there were differences in the slopes of the lines relating item log odds to total test scores. Differences in slope indicate that the item does not discriminate equally well between those with high and low levels of the construct being measured. Recall that in CTT, the discrimination index is calculated as the difference between proportions of students obtaining a correct answer in the high and low groups. Alternatively, discrimination can be calculated as the correlation of the item score with the total test score. In LR, discrimination differences are tested by comparing the log likelihood of the model that includes X and G to the log likelihood of the model with X, G, and the XG interaction. It is the XG interaction that allows for differences in slope, or discrimination. The LR test value for this comparison is 6.2, which is statistically significant at the 0.05 level, indicating the presence of nonuniform DIF for this item. Thus, although the previous test indicated the odds that women obtained the correct answer on this item were 0.36 times, or about one-third those for men, this is not true across the board. The existence of nonuniform DIF, or differences in discrimination, means that male/female differences in the odds of obtaining a correct answer are not the same across all test scores. It may be that men are more likely to answer correctly at all test scores, but their advantage narrows or widens at some score levels. Or there may be test scores at which women are more likely than men to answer correctly.

As an example, suppose that the relationships between test score and probability of a correct answer for men and women were as shown in Figure 16.2. In this figure, the probability of a correct answer (on the Y axis) is plotted as a function of the total test score, expressed as a z-score (X axis). From Figure 16.2 you can see that men have a higher probability than women of answering correctly at lower test scores. However, at about the mean of the scores (a z-score of 0), things change. After this point, women have a higher probability of a correct answer. This type of pattern, in which the difference in group probabilities does not remain constant across the score spectrum, is what characterizes nonuniform DIF. Such differences are manifested as a difference in

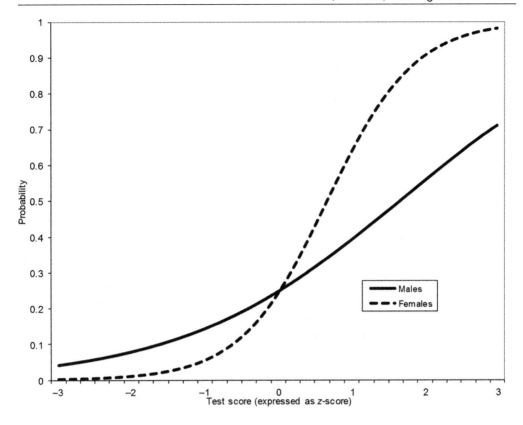

FIGURE 16.2. Plot showing nonuniform DIF for men and women.

slopes, or discrimination values, between the two groups. Contrast this with uniform DIF, as shown in Figure 16.3. In this plot, women have a higher probability of a correct answer across all ability levels, and the difference is fairly constant across levels. One advantage of logistic regression methods is that they offer tests of both uniform and nonuniform DIF.

CFA and IRT Methods

CFA and IRT models were discussed fully in Chapters 13 and 14, respectively, so I provide only a brief introduction in this section. In IRT, a person's response to an item is modeled as a function of the person's level of the construct, referred to as *theta* (θ) in IRT, and of the item's parameter values. The item parameters can include difficulty, discrimination, and what is known as a "pseudo-guessing" parameter. I say "can include" because different IRT models have different parameters. For binary (correct/incorrect) data, there are three such models. The *one-parameter model* includes only a difficulty parameter, usually symbolized as b. The *two-parameter model* adds a discrimination parameter, a. Finally, the *three-parameter model* adds the pseudo-guessing parameter, c. IRT models are based on strict assumptions, such as unidimensionality of the test items, and adequate fit of the IRT model used. The latter assumption requires that the IRT model fit the data in the sense that it is able to account for the observed response probabilities (see Chapter 14 for more detail).

The relationship between theta and the probability of a correct response is represented by the *item characteristic curve* (ICC). This curve is similar to curves from logistic regression in Figures 16.2 and 16.3. One difference is that in IRT the values on the X axis are values of theta rather than of the total test score, as in logistic regression. Also, the mathematical function that relates theta to response probabilities depends on whether a one-, two-, or three-parameter model is used. However, both logistic regression and IRT methods for DIF detection are based on comparing the curves for the focal and reference groups.

In CFA, item responses are modeled as functions of respondents' values on one or more underlying factors, which are characterized by two item parameters, the item loading (λ), which is a measure of discrimination, and the item intercept or threshold (τ), which is a measure of item difficulty. For continuous items, τ is an item intercept, and is interpreted in a manner analogous to the intercept in a regression equation. That is, it is the average score on the item for respondents with factor values of zero. For binary or Likert-type items, τ represents the cut point or threshold between adjacent response categories. This is the point on the underlying response continuum at which a respondent's answer changes from one response category to the next higher response category.

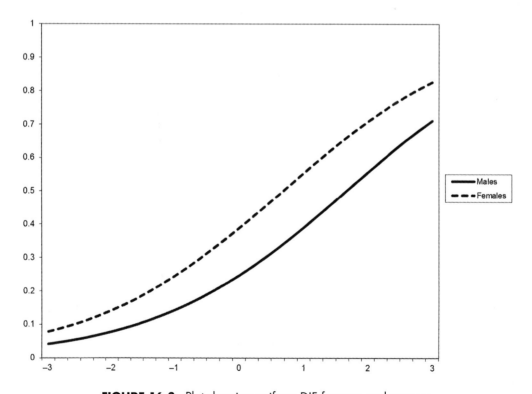

FIGURE 16.3. Plot showing uniform DIF for men and women.

An item with k categories has $k - 1$ thresholds separating the categories. CFA models for continuous items include measurement error variances that represent the variance in item responses that is not accounted for by the factor(s). Although the measurement error variances can be tested for invariance across the reference and focal groups, this is relatively uncommon, so I do not illustrate these tests here.

On one hand, IRT models are typically applied to binary responses, such as those from multiple-choice or true–false items. CFA models, on the other hand, were originally developed for responses considered to be on a continuous scale. However, both IRT and CFA models have been extended to accommodate ordinally scaled items, such as short-answer items with only a few response points or attitude items based on a Likert-type scale. Because of these extensions, IRT and CFA models can, in many cases, be used interchangeably. As discussed by Kamata and Bauer (2008), although the parameter estimates for IRT and CFA models are scaled differently and are obtained from different estimation methods, for many common models parameter values from the two methods can be re-scaled to be equivalent. For example, Kamata and Bauer show how to convert IRT parameter estimates to CFA estimates in the case of the two-parameter IRT model with binary data. Under this model, the threshold and loading parameters in the CFA model can be re-scaled to equal the difficulty and discrimination parameters, respectively, in the IRT model. Thus, in many cases, tests of DIF can be conducted using either the IRT or CFA framework. In the CFA literature, these are known as tests of measurement invariance, whereas in IRT the term *DIF detection* is used. Because the testing procedures are quite similar in the two methods, I discuss DIF testing under both frameworks in this section.

Both IRT and CFA methods assess DIF, or measurement invariance, by constraining item parameter estimates to be equal across groups and then comparing the resulting model fit to that of a model in which the parameter estimates are allowed to differ across groups. These comparisons result in G^2 (in IRT) or chi-square difference (in CFA) tests[5] that are similar to the LR tests for logistic regression discussed in the previous section. Also, both the IRT and CFA frameworks are based on matching those in the reference and focal groups on levels of the construct. This is accomplished by putting the construct, or theta, onto the same scale in both groups. Thus, explicit control by matching groups on total score, as is done in the Mantel–Haenszel method, is not necessary. Although the logic of these tests is the same in IRT and CFA, in IRT each item is typically tested individually, whereas the usual procedure in CFA is to test parameters for all items simultaneously. In both cases, however, tests are conducted by comparing the results from an analysis in which parameters are constrained to be equal across groups to one in which they are not constrained.

In CFA measurement invariance procedures, sets of item parameters are held invariant across groups in a specific order. This results in a series of hierarchical models, each of which adds more invariance constraints to those in the previous model. The first of these models imposes *configural invariance*, which requires that the number of factors

---

[5] See Chapter 13 for an overview of chi-square difference tests in CFA.

TABLE 16.5. Hypothetical Results from CFA Tests of DIF

Model	Chi-square value	Degrees of freedom	Difference in chi-square (df)
Model 1: Configural	65	48	
Model 2: Metric	70	59	5 (11)
Model 3: Scalar	105	71	35 (12)[a]

Note. Differences in the degrees of freedom for the metric and scalar tests are due to setting one loading to 1.0 for identification. Because of this, one degree of freedom is lost for the metric invariance test.
[a] Statistically significant at $p < .001$.

and the pattern of loadings on each factor be the same across groups. Configural invariance does not require that parameter estimates be equal; it requires only that the factor structure be the same across groups. The next model imposes *metric invariance*, in which estimates of all but one of the loading parameters are constrained to be equal across groups. I say "all but one" because the loading for one item must be constrained to 1.0 in both groups to identify the model (see Chapter 13 for more details on identification of CFA models).[6] This constraint is imposed in all models. The fit of the metric invariance model is compared to that of the configural invariance model. If, on one hand, the model imposing metric invariance does not fit significantly worse than the configural invariance model, the conclusion is that the loadings (discrimination values) are equal across groups and there is no nonuniform DIF. If, on the other hand, the metric invariance model fits significantly worse than the configural model, nonuniform DIF exists. The next model to be tested is that imposing *scalar invariance*, in which estimates of both the intercept or threshold parameters and the loading parameters are held invariant across groups. The fit of this model is compared to that of the metric invariance model from the previous step, in which only the loadings were constrained equal. Because the models differ only in whether the threshold/intercept estimates are equal, the difference in fit between the two models provides a test of the equivalence of the thresholds/intercepts, or item difficulty values, across groups. If the scalar invariance model fits significantly worse than the metric invariance model, the conclusion is that the item difficulties differ significantly across groups. If the loading estimates had previously been found to be equivalent across groups, thus ruling out nonuniform DIF, differences in the threshold estimates would indicate the presence of uniform DIF. I provide a hypothetical example of these testing procedures in Table 16.5.

For the hypothetical test in Table 16.5, the results suggest that the items exhibit uniform DIF (scalar noninvariance) but do not exhibit nonuniform DIF (metric invariance). The conclusion regarding a lack of nonuniform DIF (metric invariance) is based on a comparison of the fit of the configural model, in which all parameter estimates are free to vary across groups, to that of the metric invariance model, in which values

---

[6]Alternatively, the factor (theta) variances can be constrained equal across groups and all of the loadings can vary across groups (e.g., see Thompson & Green, 2013).

of the loading or discrimination parameters are constrained to equality across groups. This constraint does not result in a significant decrement in fit, as evidenced by the nonsignificant difference in the two chi-square values. This indicates that estimates of the loadings are not significantly different across groups and rules out the presence of nonuniform DIF. The presence of uniform DIF (scalar noninvariance) is indicated by the statistical significance of the chi-square difference test comparing Models 2 and 3, the metric and scalar invariance models. In Model 2, only the loading estimates are constrained, whereas in Model 3 both the loadings and thresholds/intercepts are constrained. Because the additional constraint involving the thresholds/intercepts results in a significant decrement in fit (χ^2 difference value of 35 with 12 degrees of freedom), I conclude that these estimates differ significantly across groups, indicating the presence of uniform DIF.

The tests illustrated in Table 16.5 are omnibus tests in which loadings (discrimination values) and threshold/intercept (difficulty) estimates for all items are tested for DIF simultaneously. This is the usual procedure in CFA. However, these omnibus tests only indicate whether DIF is present across the entire set of items. In order to determine which items resulted in the overall DIF result, follow-up tests can be conducted in which the parameter estimates for each item are tested individually. Specifically, if the test for the entire set of loadings was statistically significant, a series of models would be estimated in which the loading estimate for one item was allowed to vary across groups. This would be done for each item in turn. The fit of each of these models would be compared to that of a model in which the loadings for all other items were constrained equal across groups. A similar series of tests could be conducted for the threshold/intercept estimates.

In IRT, researchers typically forego the omnibus tests and test each item individually. The IRT-based tests are therefore similar to the follow-up tests for CFA described in the previous paragraph. For each item, a parameter estimate or set of estimates is allowed to vary across groups, and the fit of this model is compared to that of a model in which the estimates are constrained to be equal across groups. Model fit is compared by computing differences in the G^2 goodness-of-fit tests for the two models. The G^2 tests are chi-square tests that are analogous to the chi-square tests used in CFA. Thissen, Steinberg, and Wainer (1993) recommend that tests of IRT parameter estimates be implemented in the following sequence: c (if a three-parameter model is used), a, b. In the first step, the researcher would estimate a model in which estimates of the c-parameters for the two groups were allowed to vary, and would compare the G^2 value of this model to that of a model in which the c-parameters were constrained to be equal. If the unconstrained model fits significantly better than the constrained model, the implication is that the c-parameter estimates differ significantly across groups. The second step is to estimate a model in which both the c- and a-parameter estimates for the two groups are constrained equal. The G^2 value of this model would be compared to that of the previous model constraining the c-parameter values. If the difference in G^2 values is significant, this means that the a-values for the two groups are significantly different and nonuniform DIF is present for the item. In the last step, all three parameter estimates (c, a, and b) are constrained across groups for the item. The fit of this model is compared to that of the model from the second step. If the difference in G^2 is significant, estimates of b differ significantly across groups for that item.

Although this procedure is commonly used, other procedures have been suggested as well. Thissen (2001) recommended first testing all three parameters for each item simultaneously and conducting the series of tests for the invariance of individual parameter estimates as follow-ups. More recently, Woods, Cai, and Wang (2013) suggested another IRT method for comparing item parameter estimates. The sequence of steps for this procedure is as follows. In the first step, the parameters for an item (a, b, and c) are constrained to be equal across groups. As part of this step, the mean and variance of ability (θ) are estimated in the focal group but are fixed at 0 and 1, respectively, in the reference group. In the second step, the mean and variance of theta in each group are fixed to the estimates from the first step and the item parameters are estimated separately for each group. Fixing the theta means and variances to the values from the first step is done so that the item parameters will be on the same scale, and thus will be comparable across groups. Estimation of item parameters across groups results in two sets of item parameters. These differences can be arranged into a column, or vector, that can be tested by essentially dividing[7] it by the matrix of standard errors of the item parameters. Such a test is known as a multivariate Wald test and results in an omnibus test of the equivalence of all three item parameter estimates that can be followed up by tests of individual parameter estimates, as described previously.

CHOOSING A DIF DETECTION METHOD

Several considerations are relevant to the choice of a DIF detection method, notably: (1) sensitivity to DIF, (2) sample-size requirements, and (3) assumptions of the method. As noted previously, contingency table methods such as Mantel–Haenszel are sensitive only to uniform DIF, whereas logistic regression and IRT/CFA methods can detect both uniform and nonuniform DIF. Both the Mantel–Haenszel and logistic regression procedures can be used with sample sizes as low as 200 per group (Camilli & Shepard, 1994). Larger sample sizes may be needed for IRT and CFA methods, but these will depend on both the number of items and the specific model used. For these methods, sample sizes in each group must be sufficient to accurately estimate all parameters. With regard to model assumptions, all methods, with the exception of CFA, assume that the test is unidimensional. CFA methods allow for DIF on more than one factor to be tested. Tests measuring more than one dimension can be problematic for other DIF detection methods because groups that do not exhibit DIF on the primary dimension of interest may have differences on a secondary dimension, which could result in an appearance of DIF. Aside from unidimensionality, assumptions for the Mantel–Haenszel test are minimal. The logistic regression method assumes that groups are equal on the c- or pseudo-guessing parameter. If this is not the case, this method may detect slope differences even when

---

[7] For the more mathematically minded, the vector of differences is multiplied by the inverse of the pooled information matrix.

there are none. The reason is that correct guessing has the effect of decreasing the relation between the total test score and the item probability. This is particularly true for lower-ability groups in which guessing can have a greater impact on scores. Under this scenario, the slope for the low-ability group will be flattened relative to the slope for the other group, which could make it look as though the item has DIF when it does not. If differences in guessing propensity are suspected, the three-parameter IRT method can be used for DIF detection. Note that CFA methods do not include a guessing parameter, so these methods should not be used if guessing is a possibility. Finally, CFA and IRT methods have strict assumptions that must be met to obtain accurate estimates of item parameters. Assumptions for the these methods were discussed in Chapters 13 and 14, so they will not be reiterated here. In short, as with most things, researchers selecting a DIF detection method must consider several criteria and the trade-offs among these. In practice, the Mantel–Haenszel procedure is probably used most widely for DIF detection. This is likely due to its relatively lower sample size requirements and its relative lack of assumptions, as well as its overall simplicity.

Purification of the Matching Variable

A final issue in DIF detection concerns the *purification* or *refinement* of the matching variable. All three of the DIF detection methods discussed in this chapter rely on some type of matching to ensure that test takers are equivalent on the construct of interest. In all methods except CFA invariance testing, items are tested for DIF one at a time. The question that arises in this context is whether items that have been found to have DIF in the analysis of a previous item should be excluded from the matching variable score in subsequent analyses. The logic behind such an exclusion is that if an item is found to have DIF, groups will, by definition, differ in their scores on that item, and this difference will be transferred into the groups' scores on the matching variable. Thus, if a DIF item were included, the groups would no longer be properly matched. For this reason, most experts recommend the exclusion of items exhibiting severe DIF (usually defined as Level C DIF, according to the ETS guidelines discussed previously) from the matching variable (Camilli & Shepard, 1994; Donoghue, Holland, & Thayer, 1993; Zwick, 2012). This exclusion procedure is known as *purification* or *refinement*. For example, if items 4 and 5 had previously been found to have DIF, these items would be excluded from the total score when examining DIF for item 6.

INTERPRETATION OF DIF AND TEST BIAS

As early as 1951, Eels and colleagues reported being unable to give any "reasonable explanation" for DIF found on intelligence test items (cited in Dorans, 2008, p. 357). Over 40 years later, Bond (1993) made the same point in a more colorful manner by relating the inability to predict which items will result in DIF to the famous Supreme Court decision in which the justice stated, "I cannot define pornography, but I know it when I see it."

With DIF, Bond pointed out, it is just the opposite. We can define DIF mathematically, but we don't necessarily know it when we see it (p. 277). By this Bond means that, although there has been much theorizing about particular item characteristics that may cause DIF, researchers have been unable to formulate general rules that can be used to predict DIF. Why has it been so difficult to determine the causes of DIF? Schmitt, Holland, and Dorans (1993, p. 281) suggest four reasons: (1) DIF is still a relatively new phenomenon, (2), theories of item difficulty are not well developed—that is, we do not really understand what makes an item difficult, (3) the focal groups studied are very heterogeneous, and (4) DIF is probably not related to just one item characteristic. In other words, it's complicated! In the context of understanding what causes DIF, Cole (1981, p. 1075) states: "We have begun to learn about small, not large, effects that are subtle, not obvious—effects that will likely have implications, when we finally understand them, for the education and testing of many individuals, whether they are members of a minority group or not." She goes on to say that, in the future, differences in scores may be found to be due to individual differences rather than group differences. In other words, item effects are so idiosyncratic, and racial and cultural groups are so heterogeneous, that individual effects are likely to be more salient than group effects.

DIF as Construct-Irrelevant Variance

According to 2014 *Standards for Educational and Psychological Testing* (referred to hereafter as the *Testing Standards*), "The detection of DIF does not always indicate bias in an item: there needs to be a suitable, substantial explanation for the DIF to justify the conclusion that the item is biased" (p. 51). What is a suitable explanation? Answers to this question vary, but most psychometricians agree that bias is a type of *construct-irrelevant variance*, as discussed in Chapter 11. Bias can therefore be seen as a validity issue or, more specifically, as a situation in which an item or test has differential validity for two or more groups. For example, the item "What color is a ruby?" used to be included in tests of general knowledge for children. However, it seems clear in hindsight that the answer to such an item would likely be more available to children who were familiar with rubies and that these children would be more likely to come from families with higher-than-average income levels. Because of this, the ruby item may measure general knowledge for higher-income children but specialized knowledge for lower-income children. Thus, although knowledge of ruby color may be construct relevant for high-income children, it may not be for lower-income children. This example illustrates the fact that in order to determine whether an item is biased, researchers must determine *why* the item shows DIF and whether the reason is relevant to the construct.

Sources of Test Bias

If the bias-inducing mechanism pervades the entire set of test items in the same way, the result would be group differences in total test scores as well as item scores. However, the item-level differences would not be detectable. The reason is that DIF detection procedures involve matching groups on total test scores, and because the total test scores would be a sum of the item-level differences, the latter differences would essentially be "covaried out" and item-level DIF would not be detected. The *Testing Standards* (pp. 54–57) suggest the following sources of test bias (some of which are also causes of DIF), although the list is by no means exhaustive.

• *Test content*: Bias can arise if the content of a test is more familiar or interesting to a particular group than to another. For example, in a review of the literature on sources of DIF, O'Neill and McPeek (1993) found that black and Hispanic examinees have consistently been found to perform better on reading passages containing content relevant to them. O'Neill and McPeek also report studies showing that test bias favoring women has often been found for content based on the humanities or on human relationships, and that bias against women is more common when the content of a test is science related. However, it has been over 20 years since these studies were conducted. It would be interesting to see if these results still hold. Another source of both test bias and DIF is content that may be offensive or disturbing to a particular group, such as reading passages or test items that refer to the Holocaust. Those using or developing tests should also guard against the use of content that depicts individuals in stereotypic roles, such as a consistent portrayal of nurses as women and doctors as men. A common issue is that in which examinees for whom English is a second language are obliged to take tests in English. In such cases, examinees may well have the requisite knowledge but answer incorrectly owing to an inability to read the question or formulate their answer in English. For this reason, language demands should be kept to a minimum unless the construct being measured is English reading, writing, or speaking ability. But if, for example, examinees' knowledge of math is being testing using word problems, care should be taken to keep the language at a level that is accessible to all examinees.

• *Test context*: Test bias can result from lack of clarity in the instructions because examinees who are test-wise will likely be better able to decipher such directions correctly. A lack of rapport with or trust for the person administering the test may also result in test bias. This is particularly true for tests that are individually administered, as the match of an examinee's race, ethnicity, gender, and cultural background to that of the test administrator has been found to affect responses.

• *Test responses*: In some cases, test bias or DIF can result from responses that were unanticipated or were arrived at using an unconventional strategy. If examinees from a particular group are more likely to provide such responses, and these responses are not accounted for in the scoring rubric, that group may be unfairly penalized for responses that are unconventional but correct. It is also important to ensure that scoring rubrics focus on the most important features of responses, rather than irrelevant features such as neatness or handwriting (unless these are the focus of the assessment).

- *Opportunities to learn*: Learning occurs both within and outside the classroom, and examinees from different groups may have more or less exposure to such learning. In education contexts, inequities in instruction may mean that students in some schools are simply not taught the material needed to answer questions on an achievement test. In other cases, such as in the ruby example, some examinees may lack the experiences or informal learning opportunities to acquire certain types of knowledge.

An example of a situation in which differential performance might not be considered bias is given by Camilli and Shepard (1994). These authors discuss a testing situation in which word problems in mathematics were found to be more difficult for black than for white examinees (Shepard, Camilli, & Williams, 1984), whereas disparities between the groups on computational problems were much smaller. Shepard and colleagues (1984) hypothesized that math content might be two dimensional, with computation and word problems measuring somewhat different aspects of the construct. However, the authors reasoned that if solving word problems were a legitimate part of math ability, the differences in test scores resulting from these problems would not be considered bias. In other words, if the ability to solve word problems was construct relevant, differences in this ability would not be considered bias. However, such a difference might prompt test developers to reconsider the mix of computational and word problems used on the test. But this would be a policy rather than a psychometric decision.

TEST FAIRNESS

As Cole (1981) points out, psychometric decisions relevant to test bias and the policy decisions relevant to the appropriateness of test makeup are separate issues. A test may be unbiased in a psychometric sense but still be used in an unfair manner. It may be appropriate to interpret a test score as a measure of intelligence, but using the test scores to select employees is a different matter and might result in unfair selection practices. *Fairness* therefore touches on a broader array of issues than does the assessment of test or item bias.

Fairness in testing has to do with the way in which test scores are used. According to Camilli (2006), "*Fairness* in testing refers to . . . the ways that scores from tests or items are interpreted in the process of evaluating test takers . . .". Fairness in testing is closely related to test validity, and the evaluation of fairness requires a broad range of evidence that includes empirical data, but may also involve legal, ethical, political, philosophical, and economic reasoning" (p. 225). According to the *Testing Standards*, the overarching standard (Standard 3.0) for fairness in testing is that "all steps in the testing process, including test design, validation, development, administration, and scoring procedures, should be designed in such a manner as to minimize construct-irrelevant variance and to promote valid score interpretations for the intended uses for all examinees in the intended population" (p. 63). One response to such calls for minimizing construct-irrelevant variance has been the development of and advocacy for *universal design* principles for testing.

Universal Design

The principles of universal design were developed to yield tests that are as accessible as possible to all test takers in the intended population. The ideal of universal design is therefore to create tests in such a way that no test taker is disadvantaged and such that sources of construct-irrelevant variance are minimized. Like all ideals, this one has not been fully realized, but it is probably safe to say that the use of universal design principles in developing and administering tests should greatly lessen test features that may result in bias. Universal design principles are based on sensitivity to all characteristics that might disadvantage test takers, including language, culture, race, and sex, but also focus on characteristics of test takers with special needs. Universal design principles include the avoidance of test characteristics that might disadvantage some test takers, such as unnecessary test speededness, wording or examples that may be unfamiliar to some test takers, or use of language that might be offensive to some groups. Universal design principles also focus on providing a range of test-taking options, such as choice of font sizes and response formats (paper and pencil, computer, or verbal). Such choices allow the test to be accessible to as many test takers as possible.

Accommodations and Modifications

Not all tests can be made accessible to all test takers, even if universal design principles are used. In such cases, *test adaptations* may be needed. Adaptations are changes to the original test that are intended to increase access to the test for certain test takers. There are two types of adaptations: *accommodations*, which preserve the comparability of scores across the adapted and original test versions, and *modifications*, which adapt the test in such a way that the construct being measured will likely change to some extent. Examples of test accommodations are the provision of time extensions, text magnification, braille formats, and English glossaries for non-native English speakers. These accommodations are designed to improve access to the test in a way that should not change the construct. Another important aspect of test accommodations is that they should not make the test easier for those receiving accommodations than for those who do not receive them. In fact, one of the defining features of a test accommodation is that it should eliminate a source of bias for those needing it but would not improve the scores of those who do not need it. For example, it is unlikely that provision of magnification or a braille format to test takers whose sight is not impaired would improve their scores. But such provisions would very likely improve the scores of those whose sight is impaired. In many cases, however, it may be difficult to determine whether, or the extent to which, an accommodation affects the interpretation of the resulting scores. For example, provision of extra time is a common testing accommodation, but it could be argued that most test takers would benefit from receiving more time. Evidence favoring this accommodation would therefore have to show that those qualifying for the accommodation perform better when given extra time, whereas those not qualifying for the accommodation do not. Such results may be difficult to obtain because many test takers perform better when given extra time. This is one reason universal design principles emphasize that tests should not be strictly timed, unless performance under strict timelines is part of the construct being measured. Eliminating time as a biasing factor eliminates the need to provide this accommodation.

Test modifications represent more significant changes to tests than do test accommodations. Modifications are usually made to provide testing opportunities for test takers for whom the test would not otherwise be accessible. For example, test takers with severe dyslexia may not be able to complete a test based on reading passages. However, these test takers may be able to answer questions on reading passages if screen readers read the text to them. If the construct being measured had been defined as the ability to decode written language, such a modification would clearly change the nature of the construct and thus the interpretation of the test score. In this case, it would not generally be appropriate to compare scores from the accommodated test to those from the nonaccommodated test. This is because such a comparison presupposes that the same inferences can be made from scores on the two tests. If the accommodation is such that the scores no longer measure the same construct, it is unlikely that inferences from the two tests will be the same. However, if the construct had been defined as text comprehension that is not necessarily written, the modification might not result in any change in score interpretations and scores from the two measures might reasonably be compared.

By definition, standardized testing procedures require standardized administration and scoring conditions, and test adaptations are essentially disruptions of these standardized conditions. Because such disruptions may compromise the validity of the resulting scores, the use of testing accommodations should be based on research showing that test scores are equally valid for accommodated and nonaccommodated groups. As stated in the *Testing Standards*, "When a test is changed to remove barriers to the accessibility of the construct being measured, test developers and/or users are responsible for obtaining and documenting evidence of the validity of score interpretations for intended uses of the changed test, when sample sizes permit" (Standard 3.11, p. 68). Claims that scores from accommodated versions of a test are comparable to those of the nonaccommodated test should be backed up by evidence in the same manner as any validity claim. The *Testing Standards* specify that modified assessments should be treated as new assessments and should adhere to the same standards of reliability, validity, and fairness as any other test (Standard 3.9, p. 67).

Construct underrepresentation is one potential threat to modified tests. For example, accommodations sometimes allow examinees to take tests under untimed conditions. But if speed of processing is part of the intended construct, such an accommodation would result in an incomplete representation of the construct. Construct irrelevance is another potential threat to construct validity for modified tests because test adaptations may result in construct-irrelevant easiness. That is, an adaptation may go beyond its purpose of allowing access to the test and instead render the test too easy. For example, suppose that calculator use were to be allowed for mathematics exams. The use of calculators may allow test takers with dyscalculia to answer but may make the test too easy for test takers without dyscalculia. As noted previously, an ideal accommodation is one that removes barriers to test access for those receiving it, without giving these test takers any unfair advantage.

In some cases, it would not be appropriate to offer testing accommodations. If the test measures essential job skills that those performing the job must be able to perform, providing accommodations that do not require those skills would not be appropriate. For example, speed is essential in some jobs, such as short-order cooks and firefighters. If performance tests for such jobs were accommodated by allowing extra time, the resulting test would not provide an adequate assessment of applicants' ability to perform the job. Finally, if testing adaptations are provided, it is important to standardize procedures, including determining who is eligible and how the adaptation should be administered. Adaptations should only be provided if the test taker has a documented need, such as an individualized education plan or documentation by a physician, psychologist, or other qualified professional (see Standard 3.10, pp. 67–68)

Need for More Research on DIF and Test Bias

As should be clear from our discussion to this point, more research is needed on the causes of DIF and test bias. Such research could use methods such as matching studies, experimental studies, or more qualitative methods such as interviews or focus groups. Matching studies could be useful for situations in which DIF or test bias is hypothesized to be due to differential patterns of course taking or to differences in reading or English-language ability. Examinees could be matched on these variables to determine if bias is reduced or eliminated after matching is done. If certain item features, such as personally relevant content or the inclusion of tables or figures, are thought to cause differential responding, these features could be manipulated in experimental studies to determine their effects. Think-aloud protocols, in which examinees are asked to verbalize their thinking as they answer items, can yield valuable information on response strategies. Examinees could also be asked directly about their strategies or about the effects of various item or test characteristics on their ability to respond. If items are given in a free response format, error analyses in which features of incorrect answers are categorized might provide useful information about misconceptions that occur for certain examinees. In addition to these analyses, which are typically conducted after test or item bias has been detected, testing organizations routinely prescreen items for possible bias. This type of screening, known as a *sensitivity review*, is the subject of the next section.

Sensitivity Reviews

Most testing organizations are quite sensitive to the possibility of item bias. As a result, items are routinely screened for content that is potentially unfair. A common practice is to convene a group of reviewers, including representatives of all groups against whom possible DIF is expected. These reviewers typically spend between a half day and a full day participating in review activities. Although procedures vary widely, a typical session begins with an orientation in which reviewers are trained in the review process. In some cases, specially selected or constructed tests that illustrate common types of biased or unfair items are used to train reviewers. For each item, reviewers may be asked to indicate whether they think there is a problem and how the item might be revised. Such judgments are by nature subjective, so the goal of training is for reviewers to come to a consensus about whether an item is problematic, whether and how it should be revised, or whether it should be deleted (Dorans & Kulick, 1983, 1986).

Following the training activities, reviewers provide judgments of actual and/or potential test items. The focus is on identifying items that exhibit stereotyping or biased representations of women or minority group members, offensive wording, or item content for which examinees may have differential levels of familiarity or instruction (Tittle, 1982). Ideally, such items will have been avoided by careful item writing during the test development stage, but typically it is not possible to avoid all types of bias during that stage. Based on the results of the sensitivity review, test developers may decide to eliminate or reword some of the test items. Tittle (1982) provides the following recommendations for sensitivity review panels:

- Include at least two representatives from each group. Writers of the items should not serve as sensitivity reviewers.
- Ask reviewers to state specific reasons for judgments of unfairness or bias.
- Provide reviewers with a rating form that delineates specific categories for types of bias (stereotypical, offensive, unfamiliar, etc.) and includes space for additional comments.

LEGAL ISSUES IN TESTING

Suppose that an organization requires applicants for employment to take a test that is clearly of dubious quality. Is this illegal in the United States? You may be surprised to learn that the answer is no, because as Sireci and Parker (2006) point out, there is no U.S. law that specifically prohibits the use of psychometrically unsound tests. These authors present an excellent overview of test-relevant legislation, and much of the discussion in this section is motivated by their article. Tests can be challenged in court if they result in different outcomes for applicants from different demographic subgroups. This is known as *disparate impact* and is prohibited by Title VI and VII of the Civil Rights Act of 1964. Tests can also be challenged in court if they violate the Equal Protection or Due Process clauses of the Fifth or Fourteenth amendments to the U.S. Constitution. Protections for test takers under these pieces of legislation have to do with the results of testing rather than tests' psychometric properties, although the latter may come into play in the argument of a specific case. Thus, tests are more often challenged in court on the basis of the results they produce than on the basis of their psychometric quality. In this section, I discuss disparate impact and the legal protections available under the Civil Rights Act and the Fifth and Fourteenth amendments, and review several important court cases that have involved the use of tests. I begin by reviewing specific provisions of the Civil Rights Act and of the Fifth and Fourteenth amendments under which testing practices may be (and have been) challenged.

Legislation under Which Tests Can Be Challenged

Title VI and VII of the Civil Rights Act of 1964 and the Fifth and Fourteenth amendments to the Constitution were designed to help prevent discrimination in a broad sense, although Title VII specifically prohibits the use of employment practices that result in "disparate impact," which includes the use of tests for hiring or promotion decisions. The Equal Protection Clause of the Fourteenth Amendment as well as the Due Process Clause of the Fifth Amendment, though not specific to testing practice, have been used to prohibit discriminatory testing practices in many important legal cases.

Title VI and VII of the Civil Rights Act of 1964

Both Title VI and Title VII of the Civil Rights Act of 1964 prohibit discrimination on the basis of "race, color, or national origin." Title VI is restricted to programs that receive funding from the federal government, including state departments of education and school districts. Title VII is somewhat broader and adds a prohibition on the use of tests that result in disparate impact. How is "disparate impact" defined? Most court cases have relied on the "4/5" rule established by the Equal Employment Opportunity Commission (EEOC) in 1978, which states that disparate impact occurs if the selection rate for a protected group is less than 80% of that for the group with the highest selection rate. Here, selection rate refers to the rate of selection for a job or promotion. For example, suppose that the use of a particular test results in 70% of male applicants being hired. According to the 4/5 rule, disparate impact is present if the selection rate of any other group is not at least 4/5 of 70%, or 56%.

Challenges under Title VI or VII can be brought against businesses alleged to be using a disputed testing practice or against the testing company that developed the test, although challenges against the former are probably more common. To make such a challenge, the plaintiff must first show that the test or testing practice has resulted in disparate impact. If disparate impact can be shown, the organization must prove that the test is job related and is necessary for the organization to conduct its business. If the organization is able to make these arguments successfully, the plaintiff can still argue that there is another test that is equally effective for accomplishing the goals of the organization and results in less disparate impact, and that the organization should use the alternative test. The court then decides on the appropriate judgment.

The Fifth and Fourteenth Amendments of the U.S. Constitution

Section 1 of the Fourteenth Amendment states, in part, that "no State shall make or enforce any law which shall abridge the privileges or immunities of citizens of the United States; nor shall any State deprive any person of life, liberty, or property, without due process of law; nor deny to any person within its jurisdiction the equal protection of the laws." Two parts of this amendment have been used to challenge tests in court: the Equal Protection Clause and the Due Process Clause. A test can be challenged under the Equal Protection Clause if it can be shown that members of a specific group of test takers have been denied employment due to use of a test that has resulted in disparate impact. In other words, members of the group have not received equal protection of their rights because of the use of the disputed test. Similar to cases brought under the Civil Rights Act, the organization using the test would then have to show that there was a "rational and compelling" reason for using the test.

Tests can be challenged in court on the basis of violations of the Due Process Clause under the Fourteenth Amendment, and such challenges do not require the plaintiff to prove disparate impact. Under due process, individuals cannot be deprived of personal or property rights by a state without due process of law. The Fifth Amendment has a similar Due Process Clause, which applies to actions of the federal government rather than the states. Because property interests have been interpreted to include licenses, certificates, and diplomas, educational tests have been challenged under this clause. Most famously, cases have been tried under the Due Process Clause in situations involving inadequate "opportunity to learn," as in the case *Debra P. v. Turlington* (1979), discussed later in this chapter.

Court Cases Relevant to Testing

In this section, I review a small number of historic cases that have involved the use of tests or testing practices in either education or employment settings. These cases are summarized in Table 16.6, in which I include several other important cases that involved the use of tests. Many of these cases have resulted in sweeping changes in the use of tests. I begin with cases involving testing in an educational context and move on to cases concerned with employment testing.

Hobson v. Hansen (1967)

In this case, tried in the District of Columbia Federal Courts, the plaintiffs were representatives of black students who questioned the practice of using scores from group-administered ability tests for tracking students into ability-based classes. The court ruled that the use of ability tests for this purpose should be prohibited on the grounds that the tests had been normed on primarily white, middle class samples and that such students had an unfair advantage on the tests because of their cultural experiences. Thorndike (2005) points out that this was the first case in which the practice of using

TABLE 16.6. Summaries of Selected Court Cases Involving Test Use

Case	Court	Defendant's claim	Outcome	Comments
Hobson v. Hansen (1967)	D.C. Federal Court	Black students were unfairly placed in low-ability track classes on the basis of a group ability test.	Court ruled use of ability tests for placement should be prohibited because the tests were normed on white samples.	First case that questioned use of ability tests for placement in special education. Also first time the courts used presence of differential numbers of black students in low-ability tracks as evidence of bias.
Diana v California State Board of Education (1970)	Settled out of court	Mexican American students were unfairly placed in low-ability track classes on the basis of ability test scores.	Out of court settlement that non-English speakers must be tested in their own language and ability tests used for placement must be appropriately constructed and normed.	Settlement formed basis for P.L. 94-142, Education for All Handicapped Children Act, now Individuals with Disabilities Education Act (IDEA).
Debra P. v Turlington (1979)	U.S. District Court Appeal heard by the Fifth Circuit Court	Black students were to be denied high school diplomas because they did not pass Florida's functional literacy test.	Court ruled the test perpetuated past inequities against minority students and prohibited use of test until 1982–1983 school year. Court also ruled that test had been implemented before students had adequate time to prepare. On appeal, Fifth Circuit affirmed that students did receive adequate time to prepare and that test did have *curricular validity* because plaintiffs had been taught the tested material.	This was the first court case in which the concepts of curricular validity and opportunity to learn were introduced. The outcome has resulted in greater attention to ensuring the intended curriculum is taught and to documentating of such coverage.

(Continued)

509

TABLE 16.6. (Continued)

Case	Court	Defendant's claim	Outcome	Comments
Larry P. v. Wilson Riles (1979)	U.S. District Court	Black students unfairly placed in low-ability track classes on the basis of ability test scores.	Court ruled the tests were biased and had a discriminatory effect on black students by placing them into low-ability track classes in disproportionate numbers.	Court enjoined the use of ability testing to place black students in special classes in California and stipulated that children (over 600) who had already been so placed must be reassessed using another method. One consequence was that black students could not be tested for placement even if their parents desired such a placement for them and requested that the student be tested. Eventually, the judge overturned this decision in a separate case in 1992.
PASE (Parents in Action on Special Education) v. Hannon (1980)	U.S. District Court	Black students unfairly placed in low-ability track classes on the basis of ability test scores.	Judge personally examined test items and concluded very few were biased. Given this conclusion and the fact that the tests were used in conjunction with other information, judge ruled that the testing procedures did not discriminate against black students.	Bersoff (1981), in a review of the PASE case, summarized the judge's procedures as "embarrassingly unsophisticated and ingenuous."
GI Forum v. Texas Education Agency (1999)	U.S. District Court	Black and Latino students were unfairly denied high school graduation because they failed the Texas high school graduation test. Plaintiffs claimed this resulted in disparate impact, as evidenced by differential passing rates for black and Latino students in comparison to rates for white students.	Court ruled test could be used because (1) the state demonstrated "educational necessity" for use of the test, (2) the plaintiffs did not identify another test that could be used, and (3) the state demonstrated curricular validity (the material on the test was taught in all state schools) and ruled that students had been provided with adequate opportunity to learn.	Outcome here differed from that in *Debra P* because the state was able to demonstrate educational necessity, equal opportunity to learn, and curricular validity. This case was discussed extensively in *Applied Measurement in Education* (2000), volume 13(4).

510

Case	Ruling body	Facts	Decision	Significance
Griggs v. Duke Power Co. (1971)	U.S. Supreme Court	Black employees of the Duke Power Company were unfairly denied promotion because they were unable to pass a required aptitude test. Plaintiffs claimed test items were unrelated to job capabilities. In addition, there was evidence of disparate impact because white employees were hired in disproportionate numbers to black employees.	Court ruled for the plaintiffs and stated that employment practices resulting in disparate impact on blacks or other racial minorities are prohibited under Title VII and EEOC guidelines unless employer can show compelling business need for test use and show the test is job-related.	First case to introduce the notion of "job-relatedness" into employment testing. Also one of the first cases in which a court indicated that there were different types of validity evidence, and that some types of evidence might be more appropriate than others for employment tests. The Court also ruled that even if employers have no intent to discriminate, they must show that a test is job-related if the test results in adverse impact.
Golden Rule Life Insurance Company v. John E. Washburn (1984)	Out-of-court settlement	Black employees of the Golden Rule Insurance Company claimed use of a licensure test for insurance agents resulted in disparate impact given that the passing rate for black candidates was 25% lower than that for white candidates.	Out-of-court settlement of the Educational Testing Service (ETS) and the Illinois Department of Insurance with the Golden Rule Insurance Company stipulated that if a test resulted in differences in the rates of correct responses between minority and majority candidates, the items with the smallest such differences should be used.	The principle of using items with smallest differences in difficulty for minority and majority group candidates was subsequently applied in several other cases. After the settlement, ETS began analyzing all tests with large enough sample sizes for DIF.

(Continued)

511

TABLE 16.6. (Continued)

Case	Court	Defendant's claim	Outcome	Comments
Albemarle Paper Co. v. Moody (1975)	U.S. Supreme Court	Black employees of the Albemarle Paper Company claimed use of an ability test for promotion decisions discriminated against them because white employees were promoted at higher rates than black employees.	Although the company presented evidence that the test was job-related, the Court rejected this evidence and stated that the company should have conducted an analysis of the skills needed to succeed in the job.	The Court ruled that the company must perform a job or task analysis, and this is now common practice in the development of employment tests. The Court went beyond *Griggs* decision by stipulating a specific form of validity evidence.
Washington v. Davis (1976)	U.S. Supreme Court	Black applicants for positions on the Washington, D.C., police force claimed they were unfairly denied jobs because they failed a written test of verbal skills. The plaintiffs claimed the use of the test was discriminatory because black applicants had failure rates much lower than white applicants.	Court ruled that claimants must show evidence of intent to discriminate; showing disparate impact was not considered sufficient to prohibit use of the test. Court also ruled that the test did not have to be validated against actual job performance.	Unlike in *Albemarle*, Court indicated that multiple ways of demonstrating the validity of testing procedures were acceptable; performing a job analysis was not the only defensible form of evidence.
Guardians Association of New York City v. Civil Service Commission (1980)	U.S. Court of Appeals	Black police officers in New York City claimed they were unfairly penalized by the use of an employment test. The officers claimed that the test resulted in disparate impact and that the city inappropriately relied on content-based evidence rather than on construct validation for the test.	Court ruled that use of the test did result in discrimination against the black officers. However, the court disagreed that use of content-based evidence was inappropriate and indicated that the crucial issue was whether the test was job-related, not what type of evidence was obtained.	Court expressed no preference for the job analysis procedures previously preferred by the U.S. Supreme Court. Court did bar the test but not on the grounds that content validation had been used. The Supreme Court refused to review the case.

a group instrument as the sole basis for placing children in special education was questioned. It was also the first time that the courts used the presence of differential numbers of black students in low-ability tracks as evidence of bias.

Debra P. v. Turlington (1979)

This case was filed in the state of Florida in the Federal District Court on behalf of 10 black students who were to be denied high school diplomas because they did not pass Florida's functional literacy test, which was a requirement for graduation. The plaintiffs charged that the test was racially biased under the Equal Protection Clause of the Fourteenth Amendment and under Title VI, as well as under the Due Process Clause of the Fourteenth Amendment. They also argued that they had not had the same opportunities as white students to learn the test content because in the schools they attended, some of the required content had not been taught. Although the court found that the test had adequate psychometric properties, it ruled in favor of the plaintiffs on the basis that the test perpetuated past inequities against minority students and had been implemented before the students had adequate time to prepare for it, thus violating due process. On appeal, however, the Fifth Circuit Court ruled that the test did have adequate *curricular validity* because the state was able to show that students had been instructed on the tested material. This was the first court case in which the concepts of curricular validity and opportunity to learn were introduced. The outcome of *Debra P.* has resulted in much greater attention being paid to ensuring that the intended curriculum is taught in all schools within an educational jurisdiction and to documenting such coverage.

I turn now to two important cases involving employment testing.

Griggs v. Duke Power Co. (1971)

This case was filed on behalf of 14 black employees of the Duke Power Company who were denied advancement opportunities because they were unable to pass a required aptitude test. The plaintiffs noted that the items on the test were unrelated to job capabilities. In addition, there was evidence of disparate impact because white employees were hired in disproportionate numbers to black employees. The company admitted that this was true but claimed it did not intend to discriminate through use of the test. The case went all the way to the U.S. Supreme Court, which noted that the EEOC (1966) guidelines required tests measuring knowledge and skills required by a job to be supported by evidence of predictive validity for that job.

According to Bersoff (1981), this was the first case to introduce the notion of job-relatedness into the employment testing lexicon. However, the Supreme Court did not specify what criteria had to be met for the test to be job-related. This was also one of the first cases in which a court indicated that there were different types of validity evidence and that some types of evidence might be more appropriate than others for employment tests. The Court also ruled that even if employers have no intent to discriminate, they must show that a test is job-related if the test results in adverse impact. The Court further ruled that employers could not use an ability test or require high school education as a condition of employment if (1) neither standard was related to job performance; (2) both requirements operated to disqualify black applicants more often than white applicants, and (3) the jobs in question had formerly been given preferentially to whites.

Washington v. Davis (1976)

In this case, also tried in the Supreme Court, black plaintiffs claimed that a personnel test used to select police recruits for the District of Columbia Police Department resulted in selection of disproportionately fewer black than white applicants. Bersoff (1981) noted that the case was tried under the Equal Protection Clause of the Fourteenth Amendment, whereas *Griggs* had been tried under Title VII. This was significant because in *Griggs* the Court had ruled that Title VII proscribed not only the deliberate use of tests for discriminatory practices, but also tests that unintentionally resulted in disparate impact. In *Washington*, the Court interpreted the Fourteenth Amendment to indicate that claimants must show evidence of intent; showing discriminatory impact was not considered sufficient. As part of its ruling against the plaintiffs, the Court ruled that the test did not have to be validated against actual job performance, thus backing away from an earlier stipulation. In *Washington*, the Court indicated that other ways of demonstrating the validity of the testing procedures were acceptable.

SUMMARY

The term *impact* describes a difference in the average scores of two groups on a test or test item. Such a difference may or may not imply that the test or item is biased because the score differences may result from true differences in the groups' construct levels. Bias can only be inferred if the groups are matched on construct level and still have unequal average test scores (test bias) or unequal probabilities of answering an item correctly (item bias). Item bias is commonly referred to as differential item functioning, or DIF in the psychometric literature.

The principles of universal design were developed in an attempt to avoid DIF through the creation of tests that are as accessible as possible to all test takers. Universal design principles include avoiding test characteristics such as unnecessary test speededness, wording, or examples that may be unfamiliar to some test takers; allowing test takers to use a larger test font; and avoiding unnecessary time limits on tests. However, even strict adherence to such principles will not render a test accessible to all test takers. Thus, it is sometimes necessary to use testing accommodations or modifications. Accommodations are adaptations of the test or testing procedures designed to improve access for test takers. A defining feature of testing accommodations is that they do not change the construct being measured and therefore preserve the comparability of scores across the adapted and original test versions. Examples of testing accommodations are the provision of time extensions, text magnification, braille formats, and English glossaries for non-native English speakers. In contrast, testing modifications often change the construct being measured, at least to some extent. Examples of modifications are allowing test takers to use calculators or to have passages from a reading comprehension test read to them.

In the context of test bias, I discussed methods of detecting intercept and slope bias using linear regression methods. Test bias is defined as a situation in which the same regression line does not predict a criterion of interest in the same way for different groups. This can be tested by entering the test score as the first variable in the regression equation, thus matching the groups on test scores. Codes for group membership and for the group by test score interaction are entered in the second and third steps of the analyses, allowing for tests of differences in the intercept and slope of the regression line, respectively.

Detection of DIF also relies on matching the groups of interest on levels of the construct. Three types of procedures are the Mantel–Haenszel (MH), logistic regression, and IRT/CFA methods. The MH method is based on contingency tables and is a variation of the chi-square test of independence. It is the simplest method computationally, and it generally requires the smallest sample size. Logistic regression methods model the log-odds of a correct answer to an item as a function of total test score, group membership, and group by test score interaction. In this sense, logistic regression methods parallel those for detecting test bias. At the item level, intercept bias, known as uniform DIF, and slope bias, known as nonuniform DIF, are detected by examining the tests of the grouping variable and interaction, respectively. IRT methods closely parallel methods for detecting measurement invariance used with CFA models. Accordingly, these methods were discussed together, with attention drawn to their similarities and differences. In both methods, DIF is tested by constraining an item parameter estimate or set of item parameter estimates to be equivalent across groups and comparing the fit of this model to one in which the estimate(s) is (are) not constrained. IRT procedures typically test the parameters of one item at a time, whereas in CFA the parameter estimates for all items are tested as a set. If the set of parameter estimates is found to differ across groups, follow-up tests are used to identify particular items for which the estimates differ.

Although procedures for detecting DIF are fairly straightforward, procedures for determining the reasons DIF occurred are not. Some causes of DIF, such as offensive or disturbing item content or wording, can be detected by sensitivity review panels prior to test use. However, it is not typically possible to identify all potentially biased items a priori. For this reason, DIF detection methods often turn up items that exhibit DIF for which it is difficult to identify any obvious reason. We are far from understanding the causes of much of the item bias that is detected by DIF procedures, and development of theories in this area is an important area of research.

Finally, legislation has been passed through which cases alleging unfair testing practices can be tried in the United States. Tests cannot be challenged in court on the basis of inadequate psychometric properties. But, they can be challenged if they are shown to result in *disparate impact* as defined in Title VI and VII of the Civil Rights Act of 1964, or if they violate the Equal Protection or Due Process clauses of the Fourteenth Amendment. Many such cases involving tests used in both education and employment settings have been tried, and these have yielded mixed results. Overall, it seems safe to say that the legal judgments resulting from these cases do not always coincide with the principles set forth in the *Standards for Educational and Psychological Testing* (2014).

EXERCISES

1. What is the difference between impact and test bias?

Indicate whether the situations in Questions 2–4 suggest (a) no test bias, (b) intercept bias, or (c) slope bias. For each question, indicate the panel of Figure 16.1 to which the situation corresponds.

2. The prediction of job performance from employment test scores is stronger for men than for women.

3. The relation between job performance and employment test scores is the same for women and men, but performance is systematically underpredicted for women and systematically overpredicted for men.

4. Predictions of job performance from test scores are the same whether the employee is a woman or a man.

5. Define DIF.

6. Why is the presence of DIF a validity issue?

Questions 7–11 refer to the data in Table 16.7 which represents numbers of test takers in three ability strata who obtained correct and incorrect answers for an item:

TABLE 16.7. Reference and Focal Group Data for Questions 7–11

	Stratum 1			Stratum 2			Stratum 3		
	Correct	Incorrect	Total	Correct	Incorrect	Total	Correct	Incorrect	Total
Reference	25	45	70	30	40	70	40	30	70
Focal	5	25	30	5	25	30	10	20	30
Total	30	70	100	35	65	100	50	50	100

7. Based only on the numbers (or proportions) of test takers in the table cells, do you think there is evidence of DIF?

8. Calculate the value of $\hat{\alpha}_{MH}$, the common odds ratio. Interpret this value.

9. Calculate the value of Δ.

10. Calculate the value of χ^2_{MH}.

    a. Is this value statistically significant? Indicate how you knew.

    b. Interpret this value.

11. According to the ETS classification system, does this item exhibit Level A, B, or C DIF? How did you know?

12. The logistic regression results in Table 16.8 were conducted to test for DIF on a test item. Do the results indicate there is DIF? If so, is the DIF uniform or nonuniform? Indicate how you knew.

TABLE 16.8. Logistic Regression Results for Question 12

Model	LL	# of Parameters Estimated	LR (–2LLdiff)	p-value
X only	–450.0	2		
X and G	–430.0	3		
X, G, and XG	–429.0	4		

13. Given the results of the CFA invariance tests in Table 16.9, are there differences in the items' loadings and/or intercepts? Indicate how you knew.

TABLE 16.9. CFA Invariance Test Results for Question 13

Model	Chi-square value	Degrees of freedom	Difference in chi-square (df)
Model 1: Configural	100	84	
Model 2: Metric	140	99	
Model 3: Scalar	150	115	

14. In what ways are CFA and IRT methods of testing for DIF similar? In what ways are they different?

15. Rory wants to conduct a DIF analysis for a test on which he suspects nonuniform DIF for some items. The sample size available is 250 per group, and there are 40 multiple-choice items on the test. Which DIF detection method should Rory use?

16. Sun-Joo wants to analyze possible DIF on a 20-item attitude scale with two factors. The items are on a 5-point Likert scale. The sample size available is 300 per group. Which DIF detection method should Sun-Joo use?

17. What is the difference between an accommodation and a modification? Give an example of each.

18. Use your research skills to find the specific legal framework on which the following cases were tried:

   a. *Debra P. v. Turlington* (1979)

   b. *Larry P. v. Wilson Riles* (1979)

   c. *Griggs v. Duke Power Co.* (1971)

17

Standard Setting

As a native of the Washington, D.C., area, I have had many opportunities to observe poor driving. During these encounters, I often ask myself the question, "How did that person ever pass the driving test?" (actually, I may have used stronger language). My conclusion is that either the driving test is very easy or the score needed to pass the test is very low. The latter issue, that of determining the score needed to pass or obtain a certain classification on a test, is the subject of this chapter. The process of setting such scores, usually termed *cut scores*, is referred to as *standard setting* in the psychometric literature. Standard setting is not strictly a statistical issue; there is no "true" cut score lurking in the atmosphere to be discovered through use of the appropriate statistical or psychometric techniques. Cut scores are tied to performance standards, which are usually brief statements of what an examinee should know and be able to do to be classified as "passing" or "proficient." These performance standards are often fleshed out in more detailed descriptions referred to as *performance-level descriptions*. As an example, I reproduce the performance-level descriptions for the National Assessment of Educational Progress (NAEP) test of 12th-grade economics in Table 17.1. The NAEP tests are national tests of what students should know and be able to do in various subject areas in grades 1–12. For each subject area test, students are classified into one of three performance levels: basic, proficient, or advanced on the basis of their scores on the test.

Whereas performance standards specify what an examinee must know or be able to do to be placed into a particular performance category such as basic, proficient, or advanced, the cut score is the numerical operationalization of the performance standard. That is, the cut scores are chosen such that examinees with scores at or above them should have the defined knowledge and skill levels. Those involved in setting cut scores must therefore determine two things: (1) the knowledge and skills that separate those in one performance category from those in another and (2) the test score that corresponds to the point at which an examinee crosses from one performance level to the next. The second determination yields the cut score. Making these two determinations

TABLE 17.1. NAEP Performance-Level Descriptions for 12th-Grade Economics

Basic
Students performing at the *Basic* level should be able to identify, recall, and recognize economic concepts such as scarcity, choices, price, supply and demand, competition, inflation, unemployment, imports and exports, and trade. They should be able to describe and explain the relationship between economic concepts. Students at the *Basic* level should be able to use data and information to identify an economic outcome.

Proficient
At the *Proficient* level, students should be able to identify, recall, and recognize economic concepts and terms such as costs and benefits in decision making, responses to incentives, the mechanics of monetary and fiscal policy, trade barriers, exchange rates, and factors that influence economic growth. They should be able to demonstrate their understanding of economic ideas and terms by explaining the relationship between a real-world economic situation and its underlying economic concepts. Students at the *Proficient* level should be able to use economic data, information, and concepts to solve problems, evaluate issues, and interpret situations.

Advanced
Students at the *Advanced* level should be able to identify, recall, and recognize economic terms such as real interest rate, elasticity, property rights, and comparative advantage and to identify, recall, and recognize concepts such as the present and future values of money, market structure, and real gross domestic product in the long run. They should be able to analyze economic data and information and to apply the economic concepts to real-world situations. Students at the *Advanced* level should be able to analyze data, determine trends, and make economic projections. They should be able to reason economically by using a variety of tools including charts and graphs, computations, and written explanations.

Note. Retrieved July 19, 2015, from *http://nces.ed.gov/nationsreportcard/economics/achieveall.aspx.*

constitutes the basis of most standard-setting procedures and, as you may imagine, is no easy task. The difficulty of these tasks is increased for some tests because, as can be seen from the NAEP Economics standards, some tests have more than just "passing" and "not passing" levels. The No Child Left Behind Act of 2001 mandated classification of students into three (or more) levels, and many state testing programs now use four levels. The names of these levels vary from state to state but are usually something along the lines of "below basic," "basic," "proficient," and "advanced."

Another area in which standard setting is common is licensure or certification testing. Such testing is common in occupations ranging from accountant to veterinarian. According to Buckendahl and Davis-Becker (2012), there are two types of credentials in the occupational realm: licensure and certification. Licensure is a "legal authorization to practice within a defined field" (p. 486) and, because of its legal nature, is a requirement for those practicing the profession. Hundreds of professions require licensure to protect the public as well as the reputation of the profession. Certification, in contrast, is not mandatory. Instead, certification provides professionals with a credential identifying them as having attained a level of knowledge or competence beyond that which is typically required for entry-level practice. For example, physicians can be board certified in areas such as plastic surgery or urology. Contrary to the common practice in state educational testing, licensure and certification examinations have only two levels: pass or fail. Thus, only one cut score is needed for these examinations.

As noted previously, standard setting is not strictly a statistical issue. This is because standards are not just numbers; they represent policies that have political, social, and economic consequences. Thus, decisions about how high (or low) to set a cut score are to some degree policy decisions. This implies that standard setting is a judgmental process because standards reflect one set of values rather than another, possibly competing, set. For example, it is in the interest of public safety to set a high cut score on medical licensure examinations. However, it is also in the public interest to have a sufficient number of doctors available. But setting stringent licensure standards, which supports the first value, will result in fewer people becoming doctors, which undermines the second value. These are the types of considerations that must be balanced in making decisions about cut scores. Those making such decisions must weigh all the consequences, good and bad, in determining the final cut score(s).

Mehrens and Cizek (2012) argue that such categorical judgments must often be made, and when this is the case it is better to base these judgments on explicit rather than implicit criteria (p. 38). Making the criteria for judgments explicit will likely result in more attention being paid to them, thus influencing curricular and training decisions. For example, making the performance standards for the NAEP and other educational examinations public will likely result in more classroom time being devoted to the knowledge and skills specified in the standards. To the extent that the standards represent desirable knowledge and skills, this can be considered a positive outcome. Similarly, making public the general content of licensure examinations can help direct candidates to develop the desired skills and knowledge.

Cut scores are typically developed by panels consisting of members of the profession or body that will make use of the results. These panelists are sometimes broadly referred to as *subject-matter experts* (SMEs). For state educational tests, SMEs are typically teachers, content specialists, special education teachers, and/or administrators from the schools in that state. For licensure or certification tests, panelists are usually practitioners of the profession and those who train them. These panelists use standard-setting procedures to develop cut scores for the test. However, this does not mean that the panelists necessarily *determine* the cut scores. Instead, the panelists' recommended cut scores are given to a policymaking board, such as the state board of education or professional board. This board considers the recommendation in light of the relevant political, social, and economic consequences and may or may not implement the recommended cut score.

In the sections that follow, I first define the elements that are common to most standard setting procedures. I then describe the specific features of several commonly used setting procedures: the Angoff, Bookmark, Contrasting Groups, Borderline Group, and Body of Work methods. These procedures have been chosen because of the prevalence of their use and consequent discussion in the standard setting literature. Many other procedures are available, however. For information on other procedures, readers should consult the references cited in this chapter. Also, although the standard-setting procedures are described here in their basic forms, in practice procedures are nearly always modified to some extent. This is done to tailor the procedure more closely to the particular situation in which it is used. Details of the standard-setting procedures as I describe them here may therefore differ somewhat in practice.

COMMON ELEMENTS OF STANDARD-SETTING PROCEDURES

Hambleton, Pitoniak, and Copella (2012; see also Cizek, Bunch, & Koons, 2004) have outlined nine steps for setting performance standards. These authors note that these steps are most relevant to standard-setting procedures in which panelists make judgments about the test items or examinees' responses to them. Such methods are sometimes referred to as "test-centered" procedures and include the Angoff, Bookmark, and Body of Work procedures. The Contrasting Groups and Borderline Groups methods are examples of standard-setting procedures that require panelists to make judgments about the examinees rather than the items. These are sometimes referred to as "examinee-centered" methods and may not require all of the steps listed here, or may require modifications of them.

The nine steps outlined by Hambleton and colleagues (2012) are as follows.

1. Select a standard-setting procedure and prepare the necessary materials for the panelists.
2. Choose the panelists.
3. Prepare descriptions of each performance category.
4. Train the panelists to use the chosen procedure.
5. Collect panelists' judgments.
6. Provide the panelists with feedback and discuss the recommended cut scores.
7. Collect a second set of judgments and use them to create a second set of recommended cut scores.
8. Conduct an evaluation of the standard-setting process.
9. Compile a technical report of the process, including validity evidence.

Step 1: Select a Standard-Setting Procedure

Currently, as many as 60 standard-setting procedures are available, according to one estimate cited by Hambleton and colleagues (2012). Of these, some are rarely used, while others are quite popular, but this does little to diminish the difficulty of selecting a procedure to use. This difficulty is exacerbated by the scant empirical research comparing different procedures. As one example, Karantonis and Sireci (2006) reviewed the literature on the popular Bookmark procedure and found only three studies that compared the procedure to other methods of standard setting. The lack of such comparative studies is understandable in light of the time-consuming and expensive nature of standard-setting applications. A typical standard setting spans two to three days, and as many as 200 panelists may participate in panels for statewide educational assessments, all of whom must usually be fed, housed, and paid. However, the lack of comparative research on standard-setting procedures is unfortunate for those with an interest in determining the best procedure for a given situation. Given the lack of empirical research, Hambleton and colleagues recommend that choices be made on the basis of practical criteria such as the type(s) of test item for which standards are being set, the time available, and the panel organizers' experience with the procedure. Of course, any empirical research that can be found regarding the efficacy and validity of the procedure should be taken into account as well.

With regard to the first criterion, the type of test item, some standard-setting procedures are appropriate only for multiple-choice items (e.g., the Nedelsky procedure). Other methods, such as the Angoff procedure, were originally developed for use with selected response items, such as multiple choice, but have been adapted for use with constructed response items, such as short-answer or essay questions. The Bookmark procedure was designed to be used with both selected and constructed response items. If the products being assessed consist of essays, performances, or hands-on activities, a holistic method such as the Body of Work procedure may be most appropriate. Hambleton and colleagues (2012) state that the choice of a method "is often a much less significant factor than the way in which the method is implemented" (p. 54). Whatever method is chosen, therefore, it should be implemented carefully.

Step 2: Choose the Panelists

Because it is the standard-setting panelists who determine the cut score recommendations, it is important to consider the composition of the panel carefully. There is no ideal composition for a standard-setting panel; much more important is a rationale for whatever choices are made. From a political point of view, the agency commissioning the standard setting must be able to justify these choices. Standard settings for statewide assessments typically include teachers at the grade level of the assessment as well as teachers one grade higher and lower, curriculum specialists, special education teachers, school administrators, and possibly school counselors. The panelists should reflect the geographical, cultural, gender, age, and ethnic diversity of the state, and they must also be sufficiently familiar with the state content standards, assessments, and students to be able to make the necessary judgments about proficiency. Usually, a standard-setting panel for one grade level and subject area will consist of 15–20 panelists, but these numbers can vary widely.

For licensure and certification tests, panelists are typically practitioners of the profession and those who train them, such as professors in the subject area or instructors from technical schools. In some cases, employers or members of the public may also be included on panels. Public members are typically included more for political reasons than for their content expertise, and they may serve more as observers or as nonvoting members. For both educational assessment and licensure/certification panels, officials from the agency commissioning the standard setting are present to observe the process.

Best practice is to convene two panels that work independently of each other. The cut scores recommended by the two can then be compared as a reliability check. Alternatively, a large panel can be broken down into several mini-panels to determine consistency across different panels. Of course, both practices add to the cost of a standard-setting panel and may therefore not be feasible. However, doing so will increase confidence in the process and allow researchers to determine the degree to which standard-setting results are likely to generalize across panel members.

Step 3: Prepare Descriptions of Each Performance Category

As noted previously, *performance-level descriptions* are statements of the knowledge, skills, and abilities that would be expected of examinees at a particular category of performance. In the past, performance-level descriptions were often prepared before the standard setting by content specialists. However, it is now a relatively common practice to have the panelists prepare these descriptions as one of their first group activities. The process of doing so helps to provide a common understanding of the performance standards and what is expected of examinees in each one. In some cases, the descriptions are not completely developed until the end of the process, with the rationale that it is not until the end of the process that panelists fully understand each standard. The level of detail of the performance-level descriptions and the timing of their development is one of the many variations in process that occur in implementing a standard setting.

Step 4: Train the Panelists to Use the Chosen Procedure

In most cases, panelists will not have participated in a standard-setting process before, so the judgments required will be new to them. For this reason, the first half day is typically devoted to training. Prior to the training, the organizers of the standard setting should have field tested all the materials to be used and checked these for accuracy. Standard settings for statewide assessments will typically consist of several panels organized according to the grade level and subject area of each assessment. For example, panels for third-, fourth-, fifth-, and sixth-grade math, science, social studies, and language arts assessment would meet separately during the standard-setting process. Each panel has a facilitator who is, in turn, part of a larger organization team. The organization teams consist of experts in assessment and measurement who specialize in the standard-setting process and who work for testing companies that contract with the agency administering the test. Prior to the standard setting, the facilitators for each panel will have been trained so that they all implement the standard-setting procedure in the same way.

On the first day of the standard setting, all panelists will typically meet in a large room for an overall orientation to the standard-setting process. Panelists then break out into smaller rooms to begin training with their facilitators. During this training, the facilitator walks panelists through the procedures they will use in determining the cut scores. Panelists often, but not always, take the actual assessment for which they will be determining cut scores to familiarize themselves with the content and difficulty level of the assessment. Another part of the training process involves discussion of how influences such as time limits, guessing, and tricky distractors on multiple choice tests can affect examinee performance. These influences may have a bearing on panelists' estimates of how examinees at different performance levels might score. As a final training activity, panelists work through a practice round in which they set preliminary cut scores for the assessment.

Step 5: Collect Panelists' Judgments

Following training, panelists begin the process of determining cut scores in earnest. For some methods, panelists work in small groups, but typically panelists determine their cut scores independently. This first round of standard setting can be quite time consuming, and it is important that panelists not be rushed. Typically, a half day is allocated to this process. Once all panelists have decided on their recommended cut scores, they are collected and collated, and descriptive statistics are calculated. These include the mean or median and standard deviation or range of the panelists' recommended cut scores, as well as a frequency distribution of the cut scores across all panel members.

Step 6: Provide Panelists with Feedback and Discuss

In the next step of the process, the facilitator shares the descriptive statistics with the group. This information can serve as a reality check for panel members whose scores are very discrepant from those of the group. The facilitator then leads the panel in a discussion of the scores and the reasons panel members chose their individual cut scores. These discussions provide an opportunity for panelists to identify any misconceptions or errors. For example, a panelist may have misunderstood the facilitator's instructions about the process to be used or misinterpreted a particular item. As a result of this discussion, some panelists may change their recommended cut scores; however, this is not required.

Another type of feedback that is sometimes provided is the distribution of actual examinee scores on the test and the difficulty level of each item, taken from a previous administration of the test. This is sometimes referred to as *impact data* because it gives panelists an idea of the percentages of students who would be classified into each performance category if the recommended cut scores were adopted. Of course, this information is available only if the test has already been administered. Provision of impact data to panelists is somewhat controversial. Some researchers feel that this type of information should not be shared because it could have too much influence on panelists' judgments. For example, suppose panelists recommend a high cut score and then realize, on the basis of examinee scores, that this cut score might result in many examinees failing or being placed in the "below-basic" category. In this case, panelists might recommend lower cut scores in the next round. Other researchers argue that impact data are exactly the kind of normative information that panelists should take into account in determining cut scores. One practical reason for providing impact data is that panelists may have difficulty determining the difference between performance in the classroom or on the job and performance on an exam. These performances can be quite different for some examinees, owing to test anxiety and other factors. Impact data can provide a reality check in such cases. Reckase and Chen (2012) note that whether such information should be provided is a policy decision. Policymakers may feel that panelists should not use such normative information to inform their choice of cut scores because such considerations touch on policy and are therefore the purview of policy boards rather than standard-setting panels.

Reckase and Chen (2012) provide the following three conclusions with regard to the provision of feedback in general:

1. Panelists' recommended cut scores become more homogeneous after feedback.

2. Panelists report higher levels of confidence in the process if impact data are provided. This makes sense because, in the absence of feedback, panelists have no way of knowing how reasonable their recommendations are.

3. Feedback does have an influence on the suggested cut scores, and the earlier it is given, the more influence it is likely to have. If feedback is given late in the process, such as after the second round of cut score recommendations, it will likely not have much influence.

Because feedback can influence the standard-setting process, Reckase and Chen (2012) suggest that the type, amount, and timing of feedback should be included as part of the planning for the standard-setting process, rather than being left to the whim of individual panel facilitators. If feedback is given, it should be accompanied by careful explanations of its meaning and of how panelists should use it. In some situations, panelists are told that the feedback is provided only for their information and that they should not change their recommendations based solely on the feedback. In other situations, panelists might be expected to take the feedback into account in their recommendations. The important point is that decisions about the use of feedback have been thought through and that everyone is on the same page regarding its use. Reckase and Chen agree with those who recommend providing at least some feedback, stating that "at the very least, there needs to be feedback that helps panelists understand their tasks. If they do not understand what they are to do, they will likely provide unreliable judgments" (p. 162).

Step 7: Collect a Second Set of Judgments and Create Recommended Cut Scores

A second round of judgments usually, though not always, follows the first. In this round, panelists may or may not take into account the feedback they were provided in the first round. This will depend on how the standard-setting process is structured, as discussed in the previous section. The second round of judgments is done in the same way as the first, but panelists may change their judgments during this round. After panelists make their individual judgments, they again participate in discussion of their recommended cut scores, and at the end of this discussion the recommended scores are collected from each participant. In some cases, a third or even a fourth round of judgments takes place, but given the expense and time commitment required, this is fairly rare. At the end of the final round of judgments, the mean or median of the panelists' cut scores is calculated. If more than one cut score is being set, as when there are multiple performance categories, the mean or median of cut scores dividing each pair of categories is calculated. If the distribution of panelists' cut scores is non-normal, or if the sample of panelists is small, the median should provide a better estimate of central tendency. The median or mean cut score(s) across all panelists is(are) taken as the final cut score recommendations.

Step 8: Conduct an Evaluation of the Standard-Setting Process

After they have submitted their final cut score recommendations and before they leave for home, panelists should complete individual evaluations of the standard-setting process. The evaluation form typically contains questions about how successful panelists felt the process was overall, as well as about specific aspects of the process such as the introduction and training exercises. Information gleaned from responses to such questions can help organizers determine whether panelists were adequately trained. Panelists may be asked to rate the adequacy of the performance-level descriptions. It is important that panelists judge the descriptions to be adequate because their recommended cut scores are tied to these descriptions. A finding that panelists did not agree with the descriptions or felt they were inadequate could therefore invalidate the resulting cut score recommendations. It is also crucial to ask panelists how well they understood the various tasks they were asked to complete. If panelists did not fully understand the tasks they completed, this too could invalidate the results of the standard setting. Panelists' perceptions of the pacing of activities (did things go too slowly or too quickly) also provide useful information. These responses can be useful in two ways. First, they help determine whether panelists might have rushed through the process without having time to think through their recommendations adequately. Second, such responses can help in planning for the next standard setting. Finally, panelists should be asked how much confidence they have that the recommended cut scores will result in appropriate classifications of examinees into performance levels. Hambleton and colleagues (2012) provide an example evaluation form (pp. 73–76; see also Cizek & Bunch, 2007, p. 62).

Step 9: Compile a Technical Report, Including Validity Evidence

After the standard setting is completed, a report should be written for the authorities who commissioned it, usually a policy board. The report should be thorough, including information on how the standard-setting procedure and panelists were selected, the qualifications of the panelists, the performance-level descriptions developed or used as part of the process, a detailed description of the procedure and how it was implemented, the types of feedback (if any) presented to panelists and when it was presented, any scripts used by the panel facilitators, summaries of the recommended cut scores from each round and how these changed over rounds, and the final recommended cut scores. Information obtained from the evaluation forms completed by panelists should be summarized and included, along with copies of all materials, such as training materials, and a copy of the evaluation form. As discussed in a subsequent section, much of the information listed here constitutes important evidence for (or possibly against) the validity of the standard-setting process. A separate section of the report should interpret this information in terms of the support (or lack of support) it provides for the validity of the process. Hambleton and colleagues (2012) provide more details on the information that should be included in the final report (pp. 65–69).

STANDARD-SETTING PROCEDURES

As noted earlier, by one estimate, there are currently over 60 standard-setting procedures, with more procedures and even more variations on these procedures being developed almost daily. In general, standard-setting procedures can be differentiated in terms of the type of information panelists consider and the type of judgment they are required to make. In some cases, panelists consider each item on a test, making a judgment about whether examinees with different proficiency levels could correctly answer each one. In other procedures, panelists consider hypothetical groups of students and make judgments about whether they fall into a particular performance level. All procedures are designed to ensure that the resulting cut score recommendations are based on high-quality data and that the recommended cut scores are systematic, objective, and defensible. As noted in a previous section, empirical research comparing different standard-setting procedures is scant. And Cizek (2012b) notes that such research has declined in recent years. This may be due to what Cizek refers to as "the end of method" or the fact that standard-setting procedures, which were never truly standardized, have been routinely adapted to fit the unique contexts and needs of individual users, be they states or districts setting standards for educational tests or professional organizations setting standards for licensure or certification tests. Although such adaptations are reasonable, they make it difficult to conduct rigorous studies of the relative efficacy of the different approaches.

Five commonly used standard-setting procedures described in the following sections are the Angoff, Bookmark, Contrasting Groups, Borderline Group, and Body of Work methods.

The Angoff Method

Although Angoff (1971) mentioned his idea for a standard-setting method in only one paragraph of a nearly 100-page book chapter, his method has become one of the most widely used methods currently in existence. Despite the growing popularity of newer methods such as the Bookmark procedure, the Angoff procedure is still commonly used in licensure and certification testing as well as in educational testing. The traditional form of the method focuses on multiple-choice tests and requires panelists to determine, for each item, the probability that a minimally competent examinee would be able to answer that item correctly. A similar judgment is made for each item on the test, and the recommended cut score is calculated by summing the item-level probabilities across all items and averaging these sums, or taking their median, across panelists. This procedure was later modified in several ways. For example, although the original procedure involved only one round of panelist judgments with no feedback provided, it was soon modified to incorporate more than one round of judgments, with feedback and discussion provided between rounds. The incorporation of at least two rounds of judgments is now standard practice for the Angoff method. Other modifications to the original procedure have become so popular that they now have their own names and are described in subsequent sections.

An important aspect of the Angoff method is the conceptualization of the minimally competent examinee. This examinee can be thought of as one who is just on the borderline between two categories, such as basic and proficient. Such an examinee might *almost* have enough knowledge to be placed into the proficient category, if the examinee were to be given the benefit of the doubt. Because this hypothetical examinee provides the basis for cut score judgments, it is crucial that panelists have the same conceptualization of what such an examinee "looks like." One of the first things that panelists in Angoff standard settings do, therefore, is discuss the characteristics of a minimally competent examinee. If there are more than two performance levels, there will be a borderline between each pair of adjacent levels, and borderline examinees for each of these must be described. At the end of these discussions, which usually take place during the training round, or before the first round of judgments, panelists should have come to an agreement about the characteristics of such examinees. As part of the discussion, panelists should consider the knowledge, skills, and abilities such an examinee would have. The panel facilitator might prompt the discussion by asking what the minimally competent examinee would and would not know or be able to do. In many cases, panelists will have firsthand knowledge of such examinees from their own classrooms or workplaces. However, panelists should not base their judgments on a particular examinee with whom they are personally familiar. Instead, the idea is to develop a generic description of such a person and to base judgments on that hypothetical person. Also, recall that the previous description of the Angoff method indicated that panelists should determine the probability that a minimally competent examinee *would* be able to answer a multiple-choice item correctly. Panelists are instructed that judgments should *not* be based on what such an examinee *should* know and be able to do, but rather on what they actually *would* know and be able to do.

Panelists use performance-level descriptions to aid them in understanding the knowledge and skills of a minimally qualified examinee. These descriptions may be developed beforehand, by a separate panel or policy body, or as part of the standard-setting process. These descriptions lay out the knowledge, skills, and abilities that the average examinee at that level (e.g., the average student who is proficient in third grade math) should have, rather than those possessed by a minimally qualified examinee. The panelists must therefore modify these descriptions to apply to minimally qualified examinees. This task is usually one of the first items on the panel's agenda. Panelists are then given an opportunity to practice making judgments based on descriptions of the knowledge and skills of the minimally qualified examinee. Next a discussion is held during which panelists can ask questions and remediate any misconceptions they may have about the process, the performance-level descriptors, or the description of the minimally qualified examinee.

Panelists then begin the first round of ratings. They are asked to estimate, for each item on the test, the probability that a minimally qualified examinee would answer correctly. If there are multiple cut scores, panelists must make such judgments for each of them. Because most people are not experienced in estimating probabilities, and even less so in estimating them for hypothetical examinees, this constitutes a very difficult task. In some cases, facilitators instruct panelists to imagine 100 such examinees and estimate the number who would answer the item correctly. However, this process is arguably no less difficult than estimating probabilities. Panelists record their estimated probabilities for each item on a form. After all panel members have generated and recorded their estimates, the forms are collected, and the facilitator or other staff member sums the estimated probabilities for each panelist to obtain their estimated cut score. The resulting cut scores are then averaged across panelists, or the median is taken, to obtain the group-level cut score estimate. The SD and range of the individual estimates is also typically obtained as an estimate of interpanelist consistency or reliability.

This descriptive information is usually (though not always) provided to the panelists, along with their own estimated cut score. Impact data may also be provided. This is followed by discussion, after which panelists provide a second round of estimates. Panelists are typically informed that they do not have to change their judgments, but if they feel they should after the feedback and discussion, they may. New cut scores are then obtained for each panelist, and a new average (or median) cut score is calculated. This may conclude the process, but sometimes a third round of judgments is obtained, following more feedback and discussion.

The Yes/No Variation of the Angoff Method

One problem with the Angoff method is that it is very difficult for panelists to make probability judgments for each item. If panelists are unable to make accurate estimates, the validity of the resulting cut scores is called into question. Impara and Plake (1997) noted that Angoff's (1971) original suggestion was for panelists to indicate whether they thought a minimally competent examinee would be likely to answer the question correctly or not, rather than to make a probability estimate for each item. In other words, instead of providing a probability estimate for each item, panelists would simply provide a "yes" or "no" answer for each. This is clearly an easier task and one that panelists might be able to complete with some degree of confidence. Aside from the fact that panelists make "yes/no" rather than probability judgments, steps in the Yes/No modification of the Angoff procedure are the same as those in the traditional version of the procedure just described. To obtain the estimated cut score for each panelist, the number of items rated "yes" is summed. The average (or median) of these sums across panelists is then obtained and used as the group-level cut score. Because the decision being made for each item is simpler, the Yes/No procedure typically requires less time than the traditional Angoff procedure. The Yes/No procedure can also be applied to constructed response or other items that are worth more than one point. For these items, panelists estimate the number of points that a minimally competent examinee would obtain on each item. The cut score for each panelist is then obtained as the sum of these points across all items. If there is a mix of multiple-choice and constructed response items, each "yes" for a multiple-choice item contributes one point to the sum.

One criticism of the Yes/No method is that, although it makes the panelists' task easier, it restricts ratings to 0 or 1 (no or yes), which could result in extreme cut scores. In explaining why this is problematic, those making this criticism assume that panelists use a criterion in which they answer "yes" if the probability of a correct response is greater than 0.5 and answer "no" if the probability of a correct response is less than 0.5. As with many assumptions, no real evidence exists that this is how panelists make such judgments, although it seems reasonable. Based on this assumption, if a test were composed of items on which a minimally competent examinee had a 30% chance of a correct answer, a panelist would rate all the items as "no." The estimated cut score would then be zero, even though a minimally competent examinee would likely obtain a score of around 30% of the total. Thus, the estimated cut score would be grossly inaccurate. A similar problem would occur if all the items had a 70% chance of being answered correctly by the minimally competent examinee. In this case, the estimated cut score would be 1. Of course, the probabilities on an actual test would not all be equal; these two examples simply show what could happen in extreme cases. Although there is no real evidence that cut scores are restricted in these ways in practice, it has been raised as a criticism (Reckase & Bay, 1999). However, studies by Impara and Plake (1997) indicate that cut scores obtained from the traditional Angoff procedure were comparable to those obtained from the Yes/No procedure, which suggests that the suggested phenomenon, if it occurs, may not be particularly problematic.

The Bookmark Procedure

The Bookmark procedure, originally introduced by Lewis, Mitzel, and Green (1996), does not require panelists to provide a probability judgment for each item, as does the Angoff procedure. The Bookmark procedure thus makes fewer cognitive demands on panelists. The procedure is versatile in the sense that it can be used with tests containing both multiple-choice and constructed response questions. Perhaps for these reasons, it has become widely used in state testing programs. To implement the Bookmark procedure, the difficulty of each test item must first be obtained using IRT methods (IRT is discussed in Chapter 14). The items are then ordered from easiest to most difficult and placed into booklets, known as *ordered item booklets*. Each item appears on a separate page of the booklet. The page shows the complete item and keyed answer along with the item's difficulty level and its item number or position in the actual test. For constructed response or other items worth more than one point, each score point has a different difficulty level because it is more difficult to earn two points than one or three points than two. Because of these differences in difficulty, each score point is placed on a different page of the booklet.

The panelist's task is to go through the booklet page by page, starting with the first page (containing the easiest item), and to consider, for each item, whether an examinee at the borderline between two performance categories (such as below-basic and basic) would be likely to answer the item correctly. For constructed response point values, panelists are instructed to determine whether the examinee would be likely to obtain a score that high or higher on the item. Panelists are usually instructed to define "likely to answer correctly" as having a probability of .67 or higher of a correct response (or a given score point). Panelists go through the booklet and place a bookmark at the first item for which they think the probability of a correct answer would be lower than .67. For example, if a panelist thinks a borderline examinee has a 70% chance of answering the item on page 10 of the booklet, but only a 50% chance of answering the item on page 11, the bookmark should be put at page 11.

Panelists may go through several rounds of setting bookmarks. If more than one cut score is needed, they will continue through the booklet after setting the first bookmark and place the next bookmark at the page where an examinee who is borderline between the next two adjacent levels will be unlikely to answer correctly. This process continues until all the necessary cut scores are completed. Each bookmarking round is followed by discussion of why panelists put the bookmark at a specific location. Following discussion, panelists may or may not change the location of their bookmarks. After the final round of bookmarking, the page numbers selected by each panelist for each cut score are recorded. These are then matched to the item on that page and to the difficulty level of that item. These difficulty levels can be translated into test scores, which are averaged (or the median is taken) for each cut score. See Cizek and colleagues (2004, pp. 38–40) for a comprehensive worked example of how page numbers are translated into test scores.

When putting together the booklets for a Bookmarking standard setting, enough items should be included to yield a uniform distribution of item difficulties. That is, there should be a sufficient number of items that large gaps in difficulty between adjacent pairs of items are avoided. If items on adjacent pages have very different difficulties, they will be associated with very different test scores. This means that if one of the items is chosen as the location of the bookmark, the difference between the cut score associated with that item and the cut score associated with the item on the next page would be very large, implying that the cut score is not very precise. For example, suppose that two adjacent items were associated with test scores of 20 and 25. Choosing one of these scores over the other could result in very different percentages of people being classified into the two performance levels created by that cut score. Lewis, Mitzel, Mercado, & Schulz (2012) recommend having at least 40 items, or 50 total scale points (assuming that some constructed response items are included).

The Contrasting Groups Method

The Angoff and Bookmark methods are sometimes referred to as "test-centered" methods because they require panelists to make judgments about test items. In contrast, examinee-centered methods require panelists to make judgments about the examinees and whether an examinee fits into a particular performance level. Two commonly used examinee-centered methods are the Contrasting Groups and the Borderline Group procedures. Some authors (e.g., Livingston & Zieky, 1982) have suggested that making judgments about examinees is easier for teachers and employers because this is something they do on a day-to-day basis. In addition, the judgment itself is about actual people who are known to panelists, as opposed to hypothetical groups of examinees, as in test-centered procedures.

To implement the Contrasting Groups procedure, one or more groups of examinees must first take the test. The scores of these examinees are used to determine the cut score for the test. However, instead of examining the test items or the examinees' answers, panelists who know the examinees and are familiar with their knowledge and ability levels assign each examinee to either a nonmaster or master performance category, based on previously defined performance-level descriptions. Panelists make these assignments only on the basis of personal knowledge of the examinees; the panelists do not know the examinees' test scores. The assignments from all panelists are then combined, and the test score of each examinee is obtained. Because examinees with different scores will be assigned to the two performance categories, there will be a distribution of scores in each category. In addition, the distributions for the two categories will have some overlap because some panelists will classify examinees with a particular score as nonmasters, and other panelists will classify those same examinees, or other examinees with the same score, as masters. Or a panelist may classify examinees with the same scores into different performance levels. Figure 17.1 shows what the two distributions might look like if graphed. In the figure, score values are shown on the horizontal axis, and the frequency of each score is shown on the vertical axis. The distribution of scores for examinees classified as nonmasters is shown on the left, with the distribution of scores for masters on the right. As can be seen from the figure, although panelists typically categorized examinees with the lowest scores as nonmasters and examinees with higher scores as masters, there was some variability among panelists with regard to the range of scores thus categorized. In addition, there is some overlap in the distributions

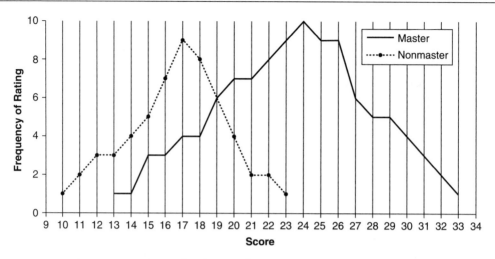

FIGURE 17.1. Score distributions for Contrasting Groups procedure.

for the two performance levels, indicating that panelists disagreed, to some extent, about the classification of some examinees.

The cut scores can be determined from the point at which the distributions for adjacent performance levels intersect. For example, the distributions of the nonmaster and master categories intersect at a score of 19, so 19 could be chosen as the cut score. Note that the points at which the lines for the two performance categories intersect are the points at which 50% of the panelists placed examinees in one category and 50% placed them in the next category. Thus, these intersections make some sense as choices for the cut point between the two.

The score distributions obtained from panelists' classifications are often jagged, as in Figure 17.1. This is because the numbers of examinees being classified is usually not large, owing to the requirement that panelists have personal knowledge of the examinees. So-called smoothing methods can be used to even out the jaggedness. Smoothing can become quite complicated mathematically, but conceptually it is usually accomplished by fitting a line in some way to the overall curve or shape of each performance-level distribution. The distributions indicated by the fitted lines or curves are then used in place of the original jagged lines in determining the cut point.

In many cases, it is difficult to determine the point of intersection visually, especially if the sample sizes for distributions are small and smoothing has not been done. In such cases, the medians (which is preferable to the mean in this case because of the small sample sizes) of the distributions can be found and the cut score taken as the midpoint between them. Using the distributions from Figure 17.1 to illustrate, the medians of the two distributions are 16 and 23, respectively, and the midpoint of these is 19.5, which is close to the value of 19 determined previously.

A more precise method for determining the cut point is logistic regression. In general, logistic regression methods are used where the dependent variable is categorical rather than continuous. These methods are used to predict the probability of being in a particular category (as opposed to another category) from one or more predictor variables. In the particular case of contrasting groups, the probability of being a master as opposed to a nonmaster is predicted from the test scores of students in the two groups. The resulting regression equation can be used to determine the score point at which the probability of being a master is .5 or greater (see Cizek & Bunch, 2007, pp. 109–112 for example calculations and computer output).

The Borderline Group Method

In the Borderline Group method developed by Zieky and Livingston (1977), the Contrasting Groups procedure is modified by instructing panelists to identify specific examinees they feel are on the borderline between mastery and nonmastery (Zieky & Perie, 2006). Although the group of examinees has already taken the test, panelists make their classifications without knowledge of the examinees' actual scores, as in the Contrasting Groups procedure. Panelists must therefore be very familiar with the examinees' knowledge and abilities, as well as with the content of the test. In addition, as in the Contrasting Groups procedure, panelists must develop a shared conceptualization of the "borderline examinee." This is typically one of the first tasks panelists complete after their initial orientation to the process, and it involves discussion of what constitutes mastery, nonmastery, and borderline knowledge. Once panelists have agreed upon these definitions, they independently identify examinees judged to be in the borderline group. The test scores for these students are then compiled, forming a distribution of scores. The median score from this distribution is taken as the cut score. Cizek and Bunch (2007, p. 113) suggest that panelists classify examinees into one of three categories: master, nonmaster, or borderline. However, because only the distribution of scores from the borderline group is used to obtain the cut score, there may be little utility in also classifying examinees into the master and nonmaster categories.

A major limitation of this method is that the borderline group may be quite small, resulting in unstable estimates of the cut score. Another limitation of both the Contrasting Groups and Borderline Group procedures is that a large group of panelists with sufficient knowledge of the skills and abilities of the examinees to make the required judgments must be obtained. Such a group may be difficult to find. Also, because the panelists must be familiar with the examinees, there is a very real threat that nontest characteristics of the examinees will influence panelists' judgments. For example, examinees' personality, work habits, sex, ethnicity, and other characteristics might influence panelists' judgments, either advertently or inadvertently.

Zieky and Perie (2006) point out that the distribution of scores from the borderline group should be fairly narrow. If the distribution is widely spread out, panelists are likely identifying examinees as borderline when they are not. This could happen because (1) panelists have difficulty in judging the abilities of some examinees, (2) panelists are basing their judgments, at least in part, on nontest characteristics, and/or (3) panelists may not share the same conceptualization of the borderline examinee or may vary widely in their standards for such judgments. To avoid the first problem, panelists should be reminded not to include any examinee in the borderline group if they do not have sufficient knowledge of the examinee's abilities. The second and third problems can be mitigated against by providing panelists with sufficient training in how judgments should be made, and by providing sufficient time for panelists to come to a shared definition of what it means to be "borderline" (Zieky & Perie, 2006).

The Body of Work Method

The Body of Work method is a variation on the Contrasting Groups procedure that requires panelists to make holistic judgments about a set of examinee responses. Because it requires holistic judgments, the Body of Work procedure is most appropriate for assessments based on essays, performances, and other work requiring extended answers. As noted previously, researchers have found that procedures such as the Angoff method, in which panelists must make probability judgments at the item level, are very difficult for panelists. One argument in favor of the Body of Work procedure is that it requires panelists to make judgments about examinees based on the examinee's complete set of test responses. This is thought to be the type of judgment that teachers are experienced in making in their classrooms on a day-to-day basis.

In the Body of Work method, panelists review the complete set of test responses for each examinee and make holistic judgments about the examinee's performance level. The set of test responses can contain answers to different types of items such as essay and multiple choice, or they may consist of longer essays or work products. The method is therefore quite flexible in accommodating different types of assessments. The Body of Work method was developed by Kahl, Crockett, DePascale, and Rindfleisch (1994) and has been used in several state testing programs. One drawback of this method is that it requires quite a lot of work to be done before the standard-setting panel meets. First, the number and nature of the performance levels must be decided upon, and descriptions of the types of performance expected for each level must be developed. These performance-level descriptors are usually developed by content specialists before the panel meets. Following the development of the performance levels and descriptors, examples of scored student papers that would fall into each of the performance levels are chosen. These samples should include multiple test papers, with varying test scores, at each performance level. The papers chosen should have been scored by at least two raters, and papers on which raters disagree or that have odd response patterns (e.g., high scores on difficult tasks combined with low scores on easy tasks) are eliminated (Cizek & Bunch, 2007). The chosen papers are grouped according to their scores, and papers with similar scores are placed in the same folder. Several such folders are created, one for each score range. For example, one folder might contain papers scored 5–10, another 11–15, and so on. The folders are ordered by score range, with folders containing low scores at the bottom and folders with the highest scores at the top. This organization scheme makes it easier for panelists to subsequently assign papers to the performance levels.

As with other standard-setting procedures, panelists first participate in a training round in which they examine only a few papers, chosen to span the range of performance levels. Kingston and Tiemann (2012) recommend that panelists also take the test and score their responses as part of their training, although this step is not always included. In the training phase, panelists independently assign the training papers to performance levels. This is done without any knowledge of the actual scores of these papers. Results are then shared and discussed. At this time, the scores of the papers may be shared with panelists, although Zieky and Perie (2006) suggest that the scores not be shared until the end of the standard-setting process.

Following training exercises, panelists are given 30–40 (the actual number can vary quite a bit) papers that are arranged in folders according to scores, as described previously. Panelists examine the folders in order, beginning with the folder containing the lowest-scored papers, and complete holistic judgments of the performance levels of each paper in one folder before moving to the next. This step is followed by more discussion, during which panelists may or may not change their judgments. Based on the reported judgments of all panelists, a preliminary set of cut scores is computed. At this point, there will likely be some papers that are so far below the lowest cut score or so far above the highest cut score that all panelists agree on the performance level to which they should be assigned. These papers can be eliminated from further judgment because they are, by definition, not at the cut score. Papers at the cut scores are those assigned to one level by some raters and the next lower or higher level by other panelists. For example, if the cut score for the lowest performance level was set preliminarily at 15, and all panelists agreed that some papers with scores of 5 were below the cut score, these papers could be eliminated from further rounds of judgments. Papers on which there is considerable disagreement among panelists as to performance level may also be eliminated. This first round of judgments (after the training round) is sometimes referred to as the *range-finding* round.

The next round of judgments is sometimes referred to as *pin pointing* because its purpose is to fine tune the preliminary cut scores. To this end, additional papers with scores near the preliminary cut scores are selected and added into the mix to replace those eliminated in the first round. As before, papers are placed in folders that are ordered from the lowest to the highest ranges of scores. The folders are given to panelists, who independently work through them in score order as before, assigning each paper to a performance level. This may be followed by a third round in which the cut scores are further fine-tuned. Given the time-consuming nature of the Body of Work procedure, however, inclusion of a third round is rare. At the end of all rounds, the panelists will have assigned each paper to one of the performance levels. Across all the panelists, there will be multiple papers in each performance category, and the scores of these papers will form a distribution for each category. These distributions are usually plotted as illustrated in Figure 17.2, which shows hypothetical distributions of scores for four performance levels: below basic, basic, proficient, and advanced. In the figure, scores are shown on the horizontal axis, and the frequency with which papers with a given score were assigned to a given level is shown on the vertical axis.

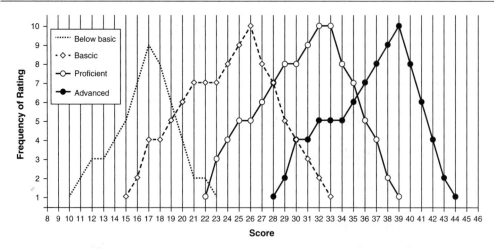

FIGURE 17.2. Score distributions for Body of Work procedure.

One method of determining cut scores is to place them where the lines for two adjacent performance categories intersect, as in the Contrasting Groups method. For example, the lines for the below-basic and basic levels intersect at a point closest to a score of 19, so 19 could be chosen as the cut score. The lines for basic and proficient intersect at a score of 28, and the lines for proficient and advanced interest intersect nearest to a score of 35, so these scores could be chosen as the other two cut points.

Although graphical methods such as these are intuitive, they can be inexact. The cut score between the below-basic and basic levels is somewhere between 19 and 20 but is closest to 19, so I chose that score. However, the closest integer score may not be clear from the graph. As with the Contrasting Groups procedure, logistic regression can be used to obtain more exact cut scores. In this form of regression, the test scores are used to predict the point at which the probability of being in a particular category or above, such as being classified as basic or above, is 0.5 or greater (see Cizek & Bunch, 2007, pp. 132–138, for example calculations and computer output).

One problem with the Body of Work procedure is that it is quite time consuming for panelists. Typically, one round of standard setting using this method takes at least half a day and may take an entire day. And because panelists are usually paid, the number of panelists that can be included is limited. This is problematic because, all else being equal, having more panelists should result in more reliable ratings. This is similar to the manner in which internal consistency reliability increases with the number of items on the test, as discussed in Chapter 8. Kingston and Tiemann (2012) considered using fewer rounds of judgments but including more panelists in a round. They found that this approach would result in somewhat greater overall efficiency. In their study, efficiency was defined as a reduction in the standard error of the cut score, calculated as the *SD* of ratings across panelists, divided by the square root of the number of panelists. However, Sweeney and Ferdous (2007), in a similar study, found only a small reduction in precision.

VALIDITY EVIDENCE FOR STANDARD SETTING

The validity claim being made when setting cut scores is that the differences among the examinees assigned to each performance level are relevant to the decisions these cut scores will be used to make. For example, suppose that those who pass a test will be allowed to take an advanced class, while those who do not pass will have to take a remedial class. Validity evidence for the cut score could be obtained by determining whether those who score above the cut score do well in the advanced class and that those who score below the cut score do not do well. However, you can probably see the inherent problem with this method: those who do not pass would not be allowed into the advanced class, so we would have no way of knowing whether they would have done well. Kane (2001) addresses the difficulty of external criteria in standard setting when he states: "To set a standard is to develop a policy, and policy decisions are not right or wrong. They can be wise or unwise, effective or ineffective, but they cannot be validated by comparing them to some external criterion. The argument for the validity, or appropriateness of a standard is necessarily extended, complex, and circumstantial" (p. 54). Validation in standard-setting contexts is complex in part because standard setting involves two distinct tasks: defining the performance levels and estimating the cut scores that correspond to these. Validation in standard setting must consider both tasks, in the sense of showing that both have been accomplished in a reasonable manner.

In Kane's (2001) view, validating the performance standard and associated cut score involves validating the interpretive argument underlying both. The interpretive argument is the chain of inferences that leads from the standard and cut score to the interpretation we wish to make. In the case of cut scores, the desired interpretation is that a person classified into a certain performance level on the basis of a cut score has the skills and knowledge associated with that level but not those of any higher level. This interpretation must be made in the context in which the score will be used. In other words, is the performance standard appropriate in light of the use we will make of it? The answer to this question depends on the likely consequences of both passing someone who does not meet the standard and of failing someone who does. In the previous example, the consequences of failing a student who could benefit from taking the advanced course and of passing a student who is not ready to take the course should both be considered. It is likely that one of these consequences would be considered less problematic than the other. For instance, suppose that some students scored above the cut score but were not ready to take the course. They may simply realize this early on, drop the course, and register for another. Although somewhat bothersome for all involved, the consequences would not be too onerous. Suppose instead that some students scored below the cut score but had the ability to do well in the course. These students would have to take a remedial course they did not need and would therefore take longer to graduate. This consequence may be considered a more serious one. In such circumstances, an argument could be made for lowering the passing score because the consequences of failing students who could have done well are more serious than those of passing students who later dropped out of the course.

Kane (2001) discusses two assumptions associated with the appropriateness of a cut score. First, the *policy assumption* is the assumption that the performance standards are appropriate for the type of decision to be made. This assumption concerns how high the standard ought to be. Second, the *descriptive assumption* is the assumption that examinees with scores above the cut score have the knowledge and skills necessary to meet the standard and that those with scores below the cut score do not. This assumption is about the degree to which the performance levels implied by the cut score are congruent with the performance standards. It would be met if it could be shown that examinees classified into a performance category have the knowledge, skills, and abilities associated with that category. The validity of the entire standard-setting enterprise also assumes that the standard-setting method chosen is consistent with the type of assessment used. For example, if a complex performance assessment is used, the Body of Work procedure would be more appropriate than the Angoff procedure. Consistency among purpose of the test, type of achievement being assessed, method of assessment, and standard-setting procedure is necessary for the process to have validity but is not sufficient to establish validity.

Kane (2001) discusses three broad categories of evidence to support the validity of standard-setting decisions: procedural, internal consistency, and external.

Procedural Evidence

Procedural evidence, as the name implies, is evidence that the procedures involved in the standard-setting method have been clearly defined, are appropriate, and have been carried out conscientiously. This evidence can be obtained from the final report in which the details of the standard-setting process are laid out. Panelists' evaluations of the process also contribute to procedural evidence, as they can provide important information on the degree to which panelists understood their tasks and had faith in the process and results. Documentation of the selection and qualifications of the panelists is also relevant procedural evidence. Kane (2001) lists five aspects of procedural evidence: (1) definition of goals, (2) selection of participants, (3) training of participants, (4) definition of performance standards, and (5) data collection.

Definition of goals, or the reason for the standard setting, is crucial because it guides all other aspects of the process. Setting cut scores for the purpose of determining whether a candidate has the knowledge and skills to be an airline pilot and setting cut scores to determine whether a student should receive remediation have different consequences and would likely imply differences in the standard-setting process. As indicated previously, participant selection and training are fundamental to the standard-setting process because it is their judgments that form the cut-score recommendations. Developing clear and agreed upon definitions of the performance standards is also crucial because the meaning of the cut scores will be tied back to these standards. With regard to data collection, Kane recommends that more than one round of judgments be included and that data on the degree to which panelists' cut scores became more (or less) divergent across rounds be collected. Interpanelist consistency, or consistency in suggested cut scores across panelists, is important because it implies that panelists had a shared understanding of the performance standards and the meaning of such abstract notions as the "borderline examinee."

Kane (2001) also recommends that panelists be provided with impact data, where appropriate, arguing that it is important for panelists to have information on the consequences of their decisions. Although evidence of appropriate procedures, properly followed, cannot establish the validity of a standard-setting process, evidence of poor implementation or failure to follow procedures can certainly cast doubt on the results. In this sense, establishment of procedural evidence plays more of a disconfirmatory than a confirmatory role in the validation of standard setting.

Internal Evidence

Internal validity evidence refers to the consistency of the standard-setting process and its results and can include (1) evidence that the same cut scores would be obtained if the study were repeated, (2) evidence that panelists are relatively consistent in their judgments (interpanelist consistency), and (3) intrapanelist consistency, usually assessed as the degree to which a panelist's judgments change across rounds of standard setting (Hambleton et al., 2012; Kane, 2001). Kane (2001) notes that internal validity evidence provides a check on the descriptive assumption of whether panelists are appropriately translating the performance standards into the cut scores. This is because, if panelists are bringing extra-test information, such as knowledge of examinees' work habits or personality characteristics to bear on their judgments, they will likely be inconsistent in their recommended cut scores. Although panelists are unlikely to reach perfect agreement, they should have reasonably high interpanelist consistency. This consistency can be assessed by calculating the *SD* of recommended cut scores across panelists. This *SD* could be transformed into a standard error for each cut score by dividing by the square root of the number of panelists. Another advantage of assessing interpanelist consistency is that panelists with outlying judgments can be identified. The inclusion of such judgments could invalidate the process, and for this reason outlying scores should probably be removed and the offending panelist retrained. Intrapanelist consistency can be calculated as the range or *SD* of each panelist's judgments across rounds. Although panelists may, and often do, change their suggested cut scores across rounds, wild fluctuations across rounds would cause one to question whether the panelist understood the procedures or was unduly influenced by the feedback provided.

One check on consistency that can be implemented when the Borderline Group procedure is used is to determine whether the performance of those classified as borderline is in line with expectations. For example, if all panelists felt that the borderline examinees would be unable to answer question 10, but few borderline examinees actually are able to answer that question, this would cast doubt on the process by which panelists are evaluating the examinees, the items, or both. Hambleton and colleagues (2012) also include evidence of consistency within method as a type of internal validity evidence. Such evidence could be obtained by convening two panels, either at the same time or close together in time, and implementing the same standard-setting procedures. The consistency of the two sets of cut scores could then be determined. This is rarely done, however, because of the obvious increase in time and expense involved in convening an extra panel. A less expensive strategy is to divide a large panel into two or more "mini-panels" that meet simultaneously and to assess the similarity of the resulting cut scores.

External Evidence

One way to investigate the validity of decisions made on the basis of cut scores is to compare these decisions to those made on the basis of other criteria. In educational or employment settings, for example, decisions based on the cut scores could be compared to decisions based on teachers' or employers' judgments about the examinees' performance category. This would, of course, require teachers or employers to make such judgments, which could be quite time consuming, and they would have to make these judgments without knowing the examinees' scores on the test. If the scores are known to those making the judgments, this information could influence judgments in the manner described for *criterion contamination* in Chapter 11. That is, an examinee might be judged to be in the mastery category simply because the judge knew the examinee's score was in that category.

Another strategy is to compare decisions based on cut scores from one test to decisions based on cut scores from another, similar test. In this case, the comparison test would have to be sufficiently similar in content and difficulty level that the comparison would make sense. An additional issue is that the cut scores from the comparison test would have to be previously validated. Otherwise, such an effort would simply lead to a situation in which one set of possibly invalid cut scores would be used to validate another set of possibly invalid cut scores. Finally, if the comparison cut scores are known to be valid and the two tests are similar in content and difficulty, one might well ask why the comparison test is not used instead of the test being validated.

These issues illustrate the difficulty of using external validity evidence for cut scores. The ideal evidence would be that obtained by giving the test to all examinees and then allowing all of them to engage in whatever activity a passing score allowed. Examinees' performances could then be assessed to determine whether those with scores above the cut score performed at a level commensurate with the standard implied by that cut score and that those with scores below the cut score performed at a lower level than that associated with the cut score. In the previous example of readiness to take an advanced course, all students could be admitted to the course to see whether students with scores above the cut score would pass and students with scores below the cut score would fail. This is rarely done, however, because of the practical and, in some cases, the ethical issues it presents. These issues are particularly salient for licensure exams. It would clearly be unwise to let everyone interested in becoming an airline pilot try flying a plane to determine whether those classified as passing the licensure test were better pilots than those who failed. Another problem is that a cut score on the criterion would have to be defined. In the case of the advanced course, course grades might reasonably be used, but straightforward criteria for other cut scores may not be available. For that matter, finding a reasonable criterion might be problematic in some situations.

Another possibility is to compare cut scores obtained from using two different standard-setting procedures for the same test. To the extent that the obtained cut scores were similar, this would support their reasonableness. Such an undertaking would likely be prohibitively expensive, however. Also, because standard-setting procedures can be quite different, they might well yield different cut scores. Jaeger (1989) reviewed studies comparing standard-setting procedures and noted that different procedures almost always resulted in somewhat different cut scores. If different cut scores were to be obtained, it would not be clear which set, if either, was "right." A final possibility is to conduct a form of the known groups study, in which classifications from populations in which the pass rates are either known or expected to be very high and very low are compared. For example, the pass rates on a licensure examination for those with substantial years of experience and training could be compared to the pass rates for those with little experience and training. If the pass rates for the experienced group were much higher than the pass rates for the inexperienced group, this finding would constitute evidence in support of the cut score. As with other methods, positive findings would not prove the cut score to be valid, but negative findings would certainly call its validity into question. Such findings are therefore useful as a "reality check," as Kane (2001) puts it. Although no one piece of evidence is sufficient to establish the validity of a cut score, a pattern of positive findings across a variety of studies can support the reasonableness of the cut scores, or at least detect major problems with them. For this reason, multiple sources of validity evidence should be obtained and compared, just as in the validation of any assessment procedure.

Validation of cut scores is so difficult in part because setting cut scores is to some degree a policy decision. The resulting cut scores are therefore arbitrary to the extent that they reflect a certain set of values rather than another, possibly competing set. For example, it is in the public interest for psychologists to be licensed to ensure that they have the knowledge and skills needed to help their clients. However, it is also in the interest of the public that psychologists have a wide variety of backgrounds. This would make it more likely that those in all segments of society could find a psychologist who would understand their problems. Setting stringent licensure standards would support the first value but could result in an inequitable distribution of psychologists across ethnic, racial, and social class backgrounds, thus failing to support the second value. Kane (2001) notes that it is the policy assumption rather than the descriptive assumption that produces arbitrary performance standards (p. 83). The descriptive assumption that the cut scores result in the levels of knowledge and skill reflected in the performance standards can be validated empirically, at least as much as any test score can be validated.

SUMMARY

Performance standards specify the level of knowledge, skill, and/or ability an examinee must have to be classified at a particular level of performance, such as pass or fail, or below basic, basic, or proficient. These classifications are usually based on cut scores, which are the scores on a test that differentiate those in one performance level from those in another. Cut scores can therefore be conceptualized as the score at which an examinee changes from being in one performance category to being in the adjacent performance category. Standard setting is the process by which the performance standards and their accompanying cut scores are determined. This process is not simply a matter of statistically estimating the optimal cut scores. Although statistics do come into play in most standard-setting procedures, the setting of cut scores is largely a policy decision and is therefore informed by practical and political concerns in addition to psychometric concerns. This is because setting performance standards and cut scores is tantamount to answering the question, "How much knowledge is enough?" Such questions fall more into the realm of judgment than statistics.

Standard setting is commonly used in education and in licensure and certification testing. In education, standards are established to help make decisions such as which students are ready to take more advanced coursework, which students should be recommended for remediation, and which students should graduate from high school. Standard setting is also common in tests used to license professionals to practice an occupation, such as nursing or tax preparation, or to certify professionals as having expertise in a specialty area of their profession. Such licensure and certification tests typically have only two levels: pass or fail. Standard-setting panels are usually composed of subject-matter experts. In educational testing, panels are composed of teachers, content specialists, and school administrators, whereas in licensure and certification testing panels are typically made up of those with experience in the profession, along with those who train these professionals. The standard-setting panels determine cut scores, which are then provided as recommendations to the policy board governing such decisions. The policy board may adopt the recommended cut scores or may adjust them for political, social, or economic reasons.

In this chapter, I have discussed some of the more widely used and researched methods of standard setting: the Angoff, Bookmark, Contrasting Groups, Borderline Group, and Body of Work methods. Although I describe basic versions of these procedures, it is important to note that the procedures are nearly always modified in some way to suit the particular situation in which they are used. There are also many more procedures available, and I encourage those interested in learning more to consult the references cited in this chapter. Regardless of the particular procedure used, nearly all standard settings follow the same basic steps, as described by Hambleton and colleagues (2012): (1) select a standard-setting procedure and prepare the necessary materials; (2) choose the panelists; (3) prepare the performance-level descriptions; (4) train the panelists; (5) collect panelists' judgments; (6) provide the panelists with feedback and discuss the recommended cut scores; (7) collect a second set of judgments and recommended cut scores; (8) evaluate the standard-setting process; and (9) write a technical report, including validity evidence.

Several types of validity evidence are relevant to standard setting. Procedural evidence is evidence that the standard-setting procedures were clearly stated, appropriate, and carried out conscientiously. One source of such evidence is the evaluation forms completed by panelists, in which they report on their understanding of the process and their confidence in the recommended cut scores. Internal evidence is evidence about the consistency of the standard-setting process and its results. It can include (1) evidence that the same cut scores would be obtained if the study were repeated, (2) evidence that panelists are relatively consistent in their judgments (interpanelist consistency), and (3) evidence that individual panelists are reasonably consistent in their judgments from one round to the next (intrapanelist consistency). A final form of evidence, known as external evidence, is that in which decisions made on the basis of the recommended cut scores are compared to decisions made on the bases of other criteria. Such evidence might take the form of comparing decisions based on cut scores to teachers' or employers' judgments of the examinees. Another form of external evidence is that in which the pass rates of those known to be at particular performance levels, such as masters and nonmasters, are compared. For example, the pass rates on a licensure test of those with years of experience in the profession and those with little or no experience could be compared. If the pass rates of the experienced professionals were considerably higher than those of the group with no experience, this would constitute evidence in favor of the cut scores.

EXERCISES

1. What is the difference between a cut score on a test and a performance standard?

2. What is the difference between licensure and certification?

3. Courtney is developing a licensure test for plumbers. What types of people should she choose for the standard-setting panel?

4. What is impact data? Provide a reason for and a reason against providing impact data to panelists.

5. The concept of a "minimally competent examinee" is important in using the Angoff method of standard setting. What is the minimally competent examinee, and how should panel members conceptualize this examinee?

6. Describe the yes/no variation of the Angoff method.

7. What is the difference between test-centered and examinee-centered standard-setting procedures? Give an example of each.

8. Madison has been asked to organize a standard setting for a visual arts program. The assessments on which the standard will be based consist of portfolios of students' artistic creations.

a. Which standard-setting method would be best suited to this situation? Explain.

b. What is one drawback of this method of standard setting?

9. Jerusha has been asked to organize a standard setting for a test of students' knowledge of ethical reasoning given at her university. The test to be used will assess students' understanding of a framework for making ethical decisions. The test consists of 20 multiple-choice questions but has not yet been administered to students. Officials at the university would like to establish three proficiency levels: developing, proficient, and advanced.

a. Which method of standard setting would be best suited to this situation? Explain.

b. What is one drawback of this method of standard setting?

10. For the standard setting in Question 8, what is one type of procedural evidence of the validity of the standard-setting results that could be collected?

11. For the standard setting in Question 9, what is one type of internal evidence of the validity of the standard-setting results that could be collected?

12. For the standard setting on the licensure test for plumbers in Question 3, describe one type of external evidence of the validity of the standard-setting results that could be collected.

18

Test Equating

When I took the SAT test in high school, I struggled with one item I thought was particularly confusing. After the test, I could not wait to ask one of my friends what answer she had given. To my dismay, she did not seem to remember ever seeing the item. I was convinced she just did not want to tell me her answer, but years later I learned there are actually many different versions or forms of the SAT. It was only then I realized my friend probably took a different form of the test and was therefore telling the truth when she said that she did not see the item in question. As I learned more about testing and how tests are constructed, I found out that many tests used to measure achievement or aptitude, as well as tests used for certification, licensure, and hiring decisions, have multiple forms.

Different forms are needed for two basic reasons. First, the use of multiple test forms within a classroom, school, or employment testing setting helps to prevent cheating. If the person sitting next to you is taking a different version of the test, copying her answers would clearly not be a good test-taking strategy. A related issue is that, if a test is used on many different occasions, items will eventually become known to potential test takers. Those taking the test will remember some of the items and are likely to discuss them with others, as I tried (unsuccessfully) to do. This has validity consequences because instead of measuring examinees' knowledge or reasoning abilities, the test becomes more a measure of memory or of access to those who have previously taken the test. The second situation that necessitates multiple test forms is that in which examinees are allowed to take a test multiple times, as is common in college admissions, licensure, and certification testing. If those retaking a test were to receive the same version taken previously, they would likely remember some of the questions and would therefore have an advantage over those who had never seen the questions.

Although multiple test forms are useful in preventing such problems, multiple forms may also complicate the test development process. The idea behind the use of multiple forms is that they are all measuring the same content, with the same level of difficulty and the same reliability. If one test form is more difficult than another, those receiving that form would be disadvantaged because their scores would likely be lower than if

547

they had taken a different form. For this reason, when multiple test forms are used, it is important that they are interchangeable, in the sense that examinees would receive the same score regardless of which form was taken. Developing multiple test forms therefore requires the forms to be based on exactly the same table of specifications or test blueprint (see Chapter 3), and to be carefully matched in difficulty. However, even the most meticulous attention to matching tests on content and difficulty specifications will not guarantee that the forms are interchangeable. Seemingly inconsequential details such as differences in item wording, use of different examples, graphs, or figures, or differences in item order can cause tests to differ in difficulty. Special procedures, known as *test-equating* procedures, are therefore used to ensure that scores on different test forms are truly interchangeable.

In this chapter, I describe some of the more commonly used methods of test equating. I begin by defining test equating and distinguishing it from two similar procedures: *vertical scaling* and *test linking*. I then describe equating designs, or methods of data collection that allow tests to be equated, followed by presentation of three methods of equating known as *mean*, *linear*, and *equipercentile equating*. These three methods can be mixed and matched with the different equating designs, but the mathematics underlying the equating methods change somewhat when they are used with different equating designs. I therefore describe the equating methods in some detail, noting some of the differences in their formulations that are entailed by different equating designs. Finally, I discuss some of the practical aspects of test equating, such as the sample sizes needed for different equating methods.

EQUATING DEFINED

Equating is a statistical process in which scores from different test forms are adjusted so that they can be used interchangeably. It is important to realize that the test forms being equated are assumed to measure the same content with the same level of difficulty and that these similarities must be built into the forms during their development. Two test forms that measure different content or have vastly different levels of difficulty cannot be equated because there is no statistical adjustment that can make such scores interchangeable. Thus, equating methods are designed to adjust for relatively minor differences in difficulty across test forms. Dorans (1990) describes four conditions, or properties, necessary for equating to be considered successful. First, the test forms that are being equated must measure the same construct and must be built to the same content specifications. If the construct being measured contains different subdimensions, the test forms being equated must have the same proportions of items within each subdimension. The forms must also be built to the same statistical specifications. That is, they should have the same levels of difficulty, discrimination, and reliability. Overall, then, the forms should be parallel, in the sense described in Chapter 7. However, even the most accomplished test developers will not be able to create exactly parallel versions of test forms, which is why equating is needed.

A second property of a good equating process is that of *equity*. If this property holds, it should not matter which test form is taken: examinees should receive the same score on any equated version of the test. To put it more formally, examinees with the same true score should receive the same mean observed score on any equated test form (this is the so-called *first-order* or *weak equity property*).

A third property of equating is that the equating transformation, or adjustment to scores, must be symmetric. That is, the transformation used to equate scores on form X to scores on form Y must be the inverse of the transformation used to equate Y to X. Note that this principle implies that scores cannot be equated by predicting scores on Y from scores on X using regression methods, because regression methods are not, in general, symmetric (recall that predicting Y from X is not the same as predicting X from Y).

The fourth and last property is the *group invariance property*, which states that the transformation used to equate test scores should work equally well in all subpopulations of interest. Dorans (1990) notes that this property will be violated if, for example, the construct being measured is not the same in different groups.

The group invariance property introduces the important point that equating adjusts scores for *groups* of people, not for individual examinees. This means that equating cannot provide equally accurate score adjustments for all examinees because examinees will find different questions easy or difficult, at least to some extent. For this reason, a person may obtain different scores on tests that have been equated, although these score differences should be fairly small. Even at the group level, it may be the case that the teachers of students in group A emphasized different topics than the teachers for students in group B, resulting in differences in the relative difficulty of those topics across groups (Livingston, 2014). Even so, equating should make test scores *more* equivalent across test forms than if no equating is done.

How does equating work? Here, I present a basic example to get the ball rolling. In later sections, I introduce the details associated with the various equating methods. Suppose two forms of a test are to be equated.[1] A new test form (X) is to be equated to the original test form (Y). First, raw scores on a new test form (X) are equated to raw scores on the old test form (Y, sometimes referred to as the *base form*) based on the raw (number correct or total scores). In this example, raw scores on Y have been converted to *T*-scores for ease of interpretation (recall that *T*-scores have a mean of 50 and a standard deviation of 10). Table 18.1 shows selected raw scores for X and Y, along with the *T*-score equivalents for Y. For example, a Y raw score of 24 converts to a *T*-score of 40. Suppose that we know from an equating procedure that form X is 1 point easier than form Y. Thus, an examinee with a score of 25 on form X would likely get a lower score of 24 on form Y because form Y is more difficult. The Y score equivalents of the other X scores could be obtained in the same way. We would then say that a score of 25 on form

---

[1] Here and throughout the chapter, for simplicity I use examples based on only two test forms. In reality, multiple test forms are often equated. The procedures I describe can, of course, be used with multiple test forms, although with the usual caveat that this makes things more complicated.

TABLE 18.1. Example of a Simple Equating Process

T-scores (based on Y)	Y raw scores	X raw scores
40	24	25
41	25	26
42	26	27
43	27	28
44	28	29
45	29	30

X equates to a score of 24 on form Y. The equating function in this case is quite simple: just subtract 1 point from each score on form X to obtain the form Y equivalent. Furthermore, because an X score of 25 is equivalent to a Y score of 24 and a form Y score of 24 is equivalent to a T-score of 40, an X score of 25 is also equivalent to a T-score of 40 on the Y form scale. T-scores for the other X scores could be obtained in the same way. For example, the T-score for an X score of 29 would be 44.

Alternatives to Equating

As noted in the previous section, equating cannot be used to make scores interchangeable if they do not measure the same content. This would be similar to equating apples and oranges, and there is no statistical (or any other) method to do that. There are, however, two equating-like processes that can be used in specific situations in which the content of tests is not strictly the same. Although these procedures are often based on the same data collection designs and statistical procedures as equating procedures, they are not true equating procedures and therefore have different names. The first of these procedures is known as *vertical scaling* and is used for situations in which tests differ in content but are intended to measure the same or similar constructs. Vertical scaling is often used with achievement tests that are administered to different grade levels to measure changes in knowledge or achievement across grades. If scores are to be compared across grades, however, it is necessary to put them on a common scale. Because the content of the tests is different and the difficulty increases with grade level, it is not possible to equate the tests in the sense of making the test forms for different grades interchangeable. But they can be put on a common scale using methods of vertical scaling. These methods allow for developmental scores, such as grade equivalent scores, to be developed.

Another equating-like process is known as *linking*. This procedure is used to relate tests that are intended to measure the same basic construct but that differ in content and/or difficulty. Linking provides a rough approximation of what a score on one test would be equivalent to if expressed as a score on another test. The extent to which this comparison is meaningful depends on the similarity of the constructs being measured by the two tests. A common example is the linking of scores on the SAT and the analogous college admissions test published by ACT. *Concordance tables* such as those found at *https:// research.collegeboard.org/sites/default/files/publications/2012/7/researchnote-2009-40-act-sat-concordance-tables.pdf* indicate that a combined SAT score of 1,560 roughly translates to an ACT score of 35. This information can be useful as long as it is taken for what it is: an approximation or estimate.

EQUATING DESIGNS

Once it has been determined that test forms are sufficiently similar in content and difficulty that equating can be done, the researcher must choose an equating design and a method of equating. An equating design is essentially a design for administering the two (or more) test forms that are to be equated in such a way that differences in test difficulty can be parsed out from any possible differences in the knowledge or ability of the samples taking the forms. In this section, I discuss three equating designs: the single-group counterbalanced design, the random-groups design, and the common-item nonequivalent groups design. I discuss methods of equating in a subsequent section.

Single-Group Design

As you might imagine, the most obvious way to ensure that differences in form difficulty are not due to differences in the samples taking the forms is to give both forms to the same sample. This is known as the *single-group design* and has the clear advantage that any differences in scores on the two tests cannot be attributed to differences in the samples taking them. Although the single-group design is powerful, it is not without its drawbacks. First, it requires examinees to take two tests, which increases testing time and therefore the possibility of fatigue and/or practice effects. Examinees may obtain lower scores on the second test because they are worn out from taking the first. Alternatively, examinees may score higher on the second test because they have had an opportunity to practice on the first. The second test might therefore appear to be easier than the first, even though it really is not. One would think that the fatigue and practice effects might balance out and could therefore be safely ignored. This view is overly optimistic, however, because there is no guarantee that this would be the case. A safer way to get around this potential problem is to *counterbalance* the order of the two test forms by splitting the group of test takers in two. In one group, the new test form is taken first and the base form second, whereas in the other group the order of the two forms is switched. This design is known as the *single-group counterbalanced design*. The idea is that any differences due to practice effects or fatigue will balance out across the two groups. The groups should take the tests as close together in time as possible, so that test takers' levels of the construct do not change.

Random-Groups Design

In this design, different groups take different test forms, but the groups are assumed to be "randomly" equivalent. To accomplish such random equivalence, the test forms are typically *spiraled* by creating stacks of tests in which the two (or more) forms are alternated (e.g., X, Y, X, Y, X, Y). This ensures that the tests are then passed out to examinees in alternating order at the testing session and should result in randomly equivalent groups of examinees taking each test. If the testing group is considered to be a sample from a larger examinee population of interest (as is usually the case), it is only necessary to assume that the relationship between the two forms (known as the *equating relationship*) in each sample is the same as that in the target population. Note that this does not require that the two randomly equivalent samples mirror the target population in terms of the ability being measured. The samples can have higher or lower levels of ability, as long as the two test scores from each sample differ from the target population in the same way (both higher or both lower) and to the same degree.

One clear advantage of this design is that examinees do not have to take two test forms. Because the groups are randomly equivalent, differences in average scores on the two forms can be taken as indications of differences in test difficulty. This makes the equating process fairly straightforward because there is no need to disentangle differences in ability from differences in form difficulty. Also, the design is easy to administer; if forms are spiraled, the tests can simply be given out as usual. The disadvantage of the design is that it requires a large number of test takers because the group is being split in half. According to Livingston (2014), the random-groups design can require 5 – 15 times as many examinees as the single-group counterbalanced design to yield the same level of equating accuracy.

Common Item Nonequivalent Groups Design

In many cases, new forms of a test are developed and administered some time after the base form of the test was administered. In such cases, it is clearly not possible to randomly split those taking the two forms into groups. Instead, the groups are formed by those who take the test at each of the different administrations. When this is the case, it may not make sense to assume that the relationship between the two forms in each group is the same as it is in the target population (the assumption made in the random-groups design) because the groups may differ in ability or other characteristics. Because it cannot be assumed that the groups taking the two tests are equivalent in terms of ability, we need some way of parsing out any differences in the ability levels of the two samples from differences in the difficulty levels of the two tests. For nonequivalent groups, this is accomplished by including a set of *common items* (sometimes called *anchor* or *linking items*). These common items are, as the name implies, included on both test forms and are used to provide information about group differences on the construct being measured. For example, if the group taking the new test obtains a score of 15 on the common items and the group taking the base test obtains a score of 12 on the common items, this implies that the group taking the new test is higher in ability. This information can then be used to determine whether any score differences on the two test forms are due to ability differences in the two groups or to differences in difficulty across the two test forms. Although the groups may differ in ability, they should not be too different; otherwise the equating process will not be able to completely adjust for differences across forms. This is one of the drawbacks of the common-item nonequivalent groups design.

As can be seen from this example, the ability to interpret score differences in the common-item nonequivalent groups design depends heavily on the common-item set. It is therefore critical that this set of items accurately reflects the composition of the forms to be equated. The common items must be representative of the overall test in terms of content and psychometric properties, such as the difficulty and discrimination levels of the items. In addition, if the forms being equating are composed of different subdimensions of content, the common items should proportionally reflect them. In general, experts in test equating recommend that the number of items in the common-item set should be about 20% of the number on the full test, or at least 20 items. However, if the test content is very heterogeneous, more common items may be needed to cover the various content areas. The common items should be in the same or very similar locations on both tests because the order in which items are presented can affect their level of difficulty. Common items should be disbursed throughout the test, rather than included in a separate block. The assumption that common items function equivalently across tests can be tested by comparing the item statistics for the common items across tests. Items that exhibit differences can be dropped from the common item set before equating is done. It is therefore good practice to have enough common items available that there will still be a sufficient number available for use even if some must be dropped.

The common-item set can be either *internal* or *external*, referred to as *internal* and *external anchors*. The difference between the two is that items on an internal anchor are counted toward the examinee's total test scores, whereas items on an external anchor are not. Even if the anchor is external, the anchor items are usually dispersed among the scored items rather than included in a separate section at the end of the test. This is done so that examinees will not know which items are scored and so that fatigue or learning will not influence the anchor items more than the other items.

Livingston (2014) used the term *external anchor* in a somewhat different sense to refer to a separate test that can be used to compare the groups taking the two forms on the construct being measured. This type of anchor is often used if the test is not long enough to include anchor items, such as tests consisting of performances or writing samples. As with any common-item design, the key assumption is that the two groups will differ in the same way on the external anchor as on the test of interest. As readers might imagine, the main problem with using this type of external anchor is finding a good anchor measure, as the external anchor test must measure the same construct as the tests being equated.

METHODS OF EQUATING

Technically, *mean*, *linear*, and *equipercentile* methods can be used with any of the three equating designs from the previous section, although some combinations are much more common than others. However, as you will see in a later section, the equating process becomes more complicated when the common-item nonequivalent groups design is used because the task of separating out differences due to form and differences due to group is more difficult with this design.

Mean Equating

Mean equating is the simplest method of equating because it assumes that difficulty differences between the two forms are the same across the entire score range. This type of relationship was illustrated in Table 18.1, in which you can see that raw scores on form X are one point higher than raw scores on Y, and that this is true for every score point. This makes equating quite easy because scores on X can be transformed to scores on Y through the simple expedient of subtracting one point from each X score. The only thing that has to be ascertained is the number of points that should be subtracted (or added) to scores on the new form. Because this number of points is the same for all scores, the simplest way to determine it is to subtract the mean of the X scores from the mean of the Y scores (assuming X is being equated to Y). For the equation-minded, the transformation of scores on form X to scores on form Y takes the following form:

$$Y(x) = x + \left[\hat{\mu}(Y) - \hat{\mu}(X) \right]$$ (18.1)

where $Y(x)$ indicates the equating of a score on X to a score on Y (the Y score equivalent of a score on X) and $\hat{\mu}(X)$ and $\hat{\mu}(Y)$ are the estimated (sample) means of X and Y. As an example, consider the data in Table 18.2. The first two rows of the table show the means, SDs, skewness, and kurtosis values for two test scores, labeled X and Y. Scores on form Y are 0.4 points higher, on average, than scores on form X, indicating that form Y is easier than form X. To equate form X to form Y, I therefore add 0.4 to each form X score to obtain $Y(x)$, the Y equivalent of a form X score. The third row of Table 18.2 shows the descriptive statistics for the resulting scores. Note that the mean of $Y(x)$ is the same as that of Y; that is, the equated X scores have the same mean as scores on Y. Values of the SD, skewness, and kurtosis for X have not changed, however.

   Although mean equating has the advantage of simplicity, the assumption that scores in the two groups differ by a constant amount across the entire score range may not be tenable. Of course, this assumption can be checked because all three of the data

TABLE 18.2. Descriptive Statistics for Test Forms X and Y

Test Form	Mean	SD	Skewness	Kurtosis
X	35.4	10.0	−0.64	−0.42
Y	35.8	10.7	−0.51	−0.68
Y(x)-mean equating	35.8	10.0	−0.64	−0.42
Y(x)-linear equating	35.8	10.7	−0.64	−0.42

collection designs discussed previously result in scores on both X and Y. If the two score distributions differ in standard deviations, skewness, and/or kurtosis, mean equating will not be as accurate as other methods. From Table 18.2 you can see that these quantities are slightly different across the two forms, so another equating method might yield slightly more accuracy in equating. It is to these methods that I now turn.

Linear Equating

In mean equating, scores on X and Y are assumed to differ by a constant amount for all scores, which implies that the two test forms differ only in their means. In mean equating, therefore, any differences in the tests' SDs or distributional shapes are not taken into account, as these are assumed to be the same for the two tests. But what if the tests differ on more than just mean level? In such cases, other forms of equating are more appropriate. *Linear equating* accommodates differences in both means and SDs. The shape of the distribution is still assumed to be the same for the two test forms, however. For the single-group and random-groups designs, scores can be linearly equated by converting scores on each test form to z-scores based on each form's mean and SD. Scores are then equated by matching z-scores on form X (the form being equated) to the same z-score on form Y (the base form). Setting the z-scores of X and Y to be equal results in the equating function shown in Equation 18.2 (math-oriented readers can work out the equality as an exercise):

$$Y(x) = \frac{\hat{\sigma}(Y)}{\hat{\sigma}(X)}\left[x - \hat{\mu}(X)\right] + \hat{\mu}(Y) \qquad (18.2)$$

Here $\hat{\sigma}(Y)$ and $\hat{\sigma}(X)$ are the estimated SDs of the two tests, and all other quantities are the same as in Equation 18.1. Note that this is similar to the formula for mean equating in Equation 18.1. Although the means of X and Y are in reverse order from that in Equation 18.2, the end result is the same. The main difference is, of course, the multiplication by the ratio of estimated SDs from the two tests. It is the multiplication by this ratio that adjusts for any difference in the standard deviations.

For the data in Table 18.2, applying Equation 18.2 results in

$$Y(x) = \frac{10.7}{10.0}\left[x - 35.4\right] + 35.8$$

Applying this equation to each x score yields the descriptive statistics in the last row of Table 18.2, which show that the linearly equated x scores have the same standard deviation as the y scores, as well as the same mean.

Linear Equating with the Single-Group Counterbalanced Design

Equation 18.2 shows the basic linear equating function for equating scores on X to scores on Y. However, recall that in the single-group counterbalanced design, we have scores on both X and Y for two groups: the group taking first X and then Y, and the group taking Y and then X. It would be wasteful not to use all of this information, so the estimates for the means and standard deviations of the two tests are pooled across the two groups. The pooled estimates of these quantities are then used in Equation 18.2. The pooled means can be obtained as

$$\hat{\mu}(X) = \frac{\hat{\mu}_{X_1} + \hat{\mu}_{X_2}}{2} \text{ and } \hat{\mu}(Y) = \frac{\hat{\mu}_{Y_1} + \hat{\mu}_{Y_2}}{2} \tag{18.3}$$

The pooled standard deviation is equal to

$$\frac{\hat{\sigma}(Y)}{\hat{\sigma}(X)} = \sqrt{\frac{\hat{\sigma}_{Y_1}^2 + \hat{\sigma}_{Y_2}^2}{\hat{\sigma}_{X_1}^2 + \hat{\sigma}_{X_2}^2}} \tag{18.4}$$

In these equations, X_1 refers to form X taken at time 1, and other subscripts have analogous interpretations.

Linear Equating with the Common-Item Nonequivalent Groups Design

Linear equating with the common-item nonequivalent groups design introduces a further wrinkle into the process. Recall that in this design one group takes form X and another group takes form Y. Throughout the rest of this chapter, I will assume that group 1 took form X and group 2 took form Y. The important point is that the groups taking forms X and Y are not assumed to be strictly equivalent. This complicates the equating process because we cannot assume that score differences on the two tests necessarily reflect differences in test form difficulty. It is always possible, with this design, that score differences might reflect differences in ability for the two groups. What we would really like is the answer to the question, "If both groups took both tests, what would the average scores for the two groups on the two tests have been?" Because we do not have these scores in the common-item design, we must use the scores we do have to estimate them. This is done by weighting the means and *SDs* from the two groups and combining them to yield estimates of the means and *SDs* for an imaginary group known as the synthetic population. The term *synthetic population* sounds quite futuristic, and possibly even alarming to some, but it is simply a designation used for some combination of the information on X and Y. Generally speaking, the synthetic population's means and *SDs* for X and Y are obtained by weighting the means and *SDs* from groups 1 and 2 in some way and then combining them. Once the synthetic population means and SDs are obtained, Equation 18.2 can be used to equate scores on X to scores on Y. The only difference is that in Equation 18.2 the estimated X and Y means and standard deviations for the synthetic population are substituted for the actual means and SDs of X and Y. The modified equation is:

$$Y(x) = \frac{\hat{\sigma}_s(Y)}{\hat{\sigma}_s(X)}\left[x - \hat{\mu}_s(X)\right] + \hat{\mu}_s(Y) \tag{18.5}$$

Here, the subscript s indicates the synthetic population. So, $\hat{\sigma}_s(Y)$ indicates the estimated SD of the synthetic population on Y, $\hat{\mu}_s(X)$ indicates the estimated mean of the synthetic population on X, and so on.

Of course, the synthetic parameter estimates are not observed because the synthetic population is based on values that do not actually exist. But because both groups take a set of common items, these items can be used to estimate what group 1's scores on Y and group 2's scores on X would have been, had they been obtained. Doing so requires assumptions about the relationships between the common items and the other items on the form, however. It is these assumptions that distinguish among the varieties of common-item nonequivalent form equating. Two such methods are the Tucker and Levine methods.

The Tucker Method of Linear Equating

The Tucker method is based on two assumptions. The first is that the slopes and intercepts that would be obtained from regressing form X or Y on scores from the common items (which I will refer to as C) are the same in group 1 as in group 2.[2] The second assumption is that the amount of variation in scores on X and Y at each score point on C is the same in groups 1 and 2. That is, whatever the variance of X or Y at a particular point on C, it is the same in groups 1 and 2. Given these assumptions, the synthetic population means and SDs of X and Y needed for Equation 18.5 can be estimated from the following equations, which hold for either an internal or external common-item set:

$$\hat{\mu}_s(X) = \hat{\mu}_1(X) - w_2\hat{\gamma}_1\left[\hat{\mu}_1(C) - \hat{\mu}_2(C)\right] \tag{18.6}$$

$$\hat{\mu}_s(Y) = \hat{\mu}_2(Y) + w_1\hat{\gamma}_2\left[\hat{\mu}_1(C) - \hat{\mu}_2(C)\right] \tag{18.7}$$

$$\hat{\sigma}_s^2(X) = \hat{\sigma}_1^2(X) - w_2\hat{\gamma}_1^2\left[\hat{\sigma}_1^2(C) - \hat{\sigma}_2^2(C)\right] + w_1w_2\hat{\gamma}_1^2\left[\hat{\mu}_1(C) - \hat{\mu}_2(C)\right]^2 \tag{18.8}$$

$$\hat{\sigma}_s^2(Y) = \hat{\sigma}_2^2(Y) - w_1\hat{\gamma}_2^2\left[\hat{\sigma}_1^2(C) - \hat{\sigma}_2^2(C)\right] + w_1w_2\hat{\gamma}_2^2\left[\hat{\mu}_1(C) - \hat{\mu}_2(C)\right]^2 \tag{18.9}$$

Although these equations may appear quite complicated, note that values of the synthetic means and SDs for Tucker equating are simply weighted functions of the observed

[2] Here I refer to assumptions as referring to the two groups. Strictly speaking, however, they refer to the populations these groups are assumed to represent.

sample means and *SDs* of X and Y from groups 1 and 2, adjusted by some function of the differences in means and *SDs* on the common items. Basically, these equations adjust for any differences in the X and Y means and variances by an amount based on the relation between X or Y with the common-item score, C. These relations are measured by the γ terms in Equations 18.6–18.9. If the means and variances on X and Y do not differ, or if X or Y is not related to C, no adjustment occurs. In the latter case (no relationship with C), as can be seen from Equations 18.6–18.9, the synthetic means and *SDs* will be set equal to the observed means and standard deviations for groups 1 and 2, making the implicit assumption that the groups are equivalent (whether they are or not). In the more usual (and desirable) case in which X and Y are related to C, the accuracy of the adjustment, and therefore of the equating process, will increase with the strength of the X/C and Y/C relations.

The γ and *w* terms in Equations 18.6–18.9 deserve some comment as well. As noted previously, the γ terms are measures of the relations of X and Y with C. These terms play an important role in linear equating with the common-item design because the different methods for linear equating in this design are distinguished by their differences in γ terms. For the Tucker method, the γ terms are

$$\hat{\gamma}_1 = \frac{cov_{XC}}{\hat{\sigma}_C^2} \tag{18.10}$$

$$\hat{\gamma}_2 = \frac{cov_{YC}}{\hat{\sigma}_C^2} \tag{18.11}$$

You may recognize these as equations for *b*-values in linear regression, which is exactly what they are. The *w* terms are weights that determine the relative contributions of quantities from groups 1 and 2 to the synthetic means and standard deviations. Kolen and Brennan (2014, p. 128) state that selection of weights "seldom makes much difference in the Form Y equivalents." Accordingly, it is often easiest to set $w_1 = 1$ and $w_2 = 0$. This has the effects of making the mean and *SD* of the new test form (X) in group 1 equal to the synthetic mean and *SD* for this test. As Kolen and Brennan point out, group 1 is usually the only group that will take the new form anyway because group 2 has already taken the base form (Y). Ultimately, though, deciding how to set the weights will depend on the research situation and on what the researcher thinks is most appropriate. Other common options are to set the two weights equal, making each 0.5, or to make them proportional to sample size. The only strict requirement is that they must sum to 1. Using weights of 1 and 0 does simplify Equations 18.6–18.9 because it causes some terms to drop out. I have rewritten the four equations, using these weights.

$$\hat{\mu}_s(X) = \hat{\mu}_1(X) \tag{18.12}$$

$$\hat{\mu}_s(Y) = \hat{\mu}_2(Y) + \hat{\gamma}_2\left[\hat{\mu}_1(C) - \hat{\mu}_2(C)\right] \tag{18.13}$$

$$\hat{\sigma}_s^2(X) = \hat{\sigma}_1^2(X) \qquad (18.14)$$

$$\hat{\sigma}_s^2(Y) = \hat{\sigma}_2^2(Y) - \hat{\gamma}_2^2\left[\hat{\sigma}_1^2(C) - \hat{\sigma}_2^2(C)\right] \qquad (18.15)$$

The Levine Observed Score Method

One reason that the common items may have a weak relation with X and/or Y is that X, Y, and/or C may not be measured reliably. Put more forcefully, it is unlikely that these test scores are perfectly reliable, and to the extent they are not the relations with C will be attenuated. The motivation behind the Levine observed score method is therefore to correct the X, Y, and C scores for any lack of reliability. The Levine observed score method is based on the following assumptions.

- The slopes and intercepts that would be obtained from regressing *true scores* on X or Y on *true scores* on C are the same in group 1 as in group 2.
- The true scores of X, Y, and C are perfectly correlated (this assumption may appear extreme, but it follows from the fact that these are parallel tests).
- The measurement error variances of X, Y, and C are the same in group 1 as in group 2.[3]

Note that the first of these assumptions is similar to that made for Tucker equating. The difference is that in Tucker equating the assumption refers to observed scores, whereas in Levine observed score equating it refers to true scores. The Levine method is similar to Tucker equating in a more direct way as well. Equations 18.6–18.9 for the synthetic population parameters are the same in Levine observed score equating as in Tucker equating. The only difference is in the definition of the γ parameters. In Levine observed score equating, these are defined as

$$\hat{\gamma}_1 = \frac{\hat{\sigma}_1(X)\sqrt{\hat{\rho}_1(X,X')}}{\hat{\sigma}_1(C)\sqrt{\hat{\rho}_1(C,C')}} \qquad (18.16)$$

$$\hat{\gamma}_2 = \frac{\hat{\sigma}_2(Y)\sqrt{\hat{\rho}_1(Y,Y')}}{\hat{\sigma}_2(C)\sqrt{\hat{\rho}_2(C,C')}} \qquad (18.17)$$

Here $\hat{\sigma}_1(X)$ refers to the estimated standard deviation of scores on X in group 1, and the other standard deviations can be interpreted in an analogous manner. $\hat{\rho}_1(X,X')$ refers to the estimated reliability of scores on X in group 1, and other reliabilities are analogous. Theoretically, any type of reliability estimate could be used in Equations 18.16 and 18.17, but different choices have somewhat different computational consequences for internal and external common item sets, making the actual computations somewhat

---

[3] As I noted under Tucker equating, strictly speaking, these assumptions refer to the populations these groups are assumed to represent rather than to the specific groups available.

complex. Those who would like more detail should consult Kolen and Brennan's comprehensive treatment in Chapter 4 of their 2014 text.

Equipercentile Equating

Recall that in linear equating, the basic idea is to match scores on forms X and Y that have the same z-score. Although this adjusts for differences in the test means and standard deviations, it assumes that the overall distributions of the tests are the same. But what happens when the distributions of the tests are not the same? In this case, linear equating will not be accurate because it assumes that score differences between the two forms are constant across the entire range of scores. When test distributions are different, however, differences in scores are not the same at all score points. Scores on the two tests may be closer together at some score points than at others. A very high or low score on the new form may even equate to a score that is outside the range of base form scores. *Equipercentile equating* can get around these problems. In this form of equating, scores on different forms are equated based on their percentile ranks. In Chapter 2, I defined percentile ranks as the percentage of scores below a certain score point. For example, if a score of 27 has a percentile rank of 50, 50% of the scores in the distribution fall below a score of 27. In its simplest form, equipercentile equating works as follows: Find the percentile ranks of scores from both test forms. Then, for each score on the new form, find the score on the base form that has the same percentile rank. This base form score is the score to which the reference form score equates. This process is illustrated in Figure 18.1, which shows the scores on forms X and Y, plotted against their percentile ranks. This graph shows that a score of 45 on form X has a percentile rank of about 85, whereas on form Y a score of about 46 has a percentile rank of 85. An X score of 45 would therefore equate to a Y score of 46.

Equipercentile equating results in equal means and *SD*s for the two sets of test scores, as does linear equating. In addition, equipercentile equating will make the two test score distributions more similar. Because it may not be possible to find an exact match between the percentile ranks from the two score distributions, the equated scores on X may not have exactly the same distribution as the scores on Y, but the two distributions will be as close as possible. Also, all the equated X scores will be within the range of scores on Y. This is not necessarily the case with other forms of equating. Note that equipercentile equating makes a nonlinear adjustment to scores on the new test, making it possible for the adjustment to work equally well for scores at all score ranges, even when the two test score distributions are not the same.

Smoothing

One problem with equipercentile equating is that distributions for most reasonably sized samples will be irregular. This can be seen from Figure 18.2, in which I have superimposed a normal curve over the histogram of scores from Test X in the example. These irregularities can be overcome by a process known as *smoothing*, which does just what its name implies. Smoothing procedures remove the irregularities from either the score

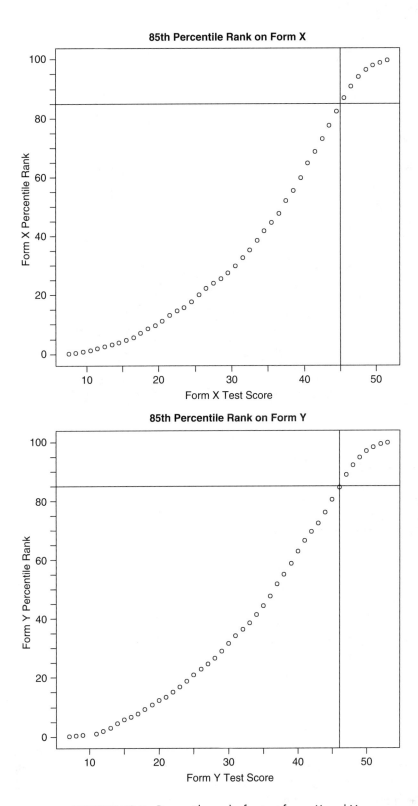

FIGURE 18.1. Percentile ranks for test forms X and Y.

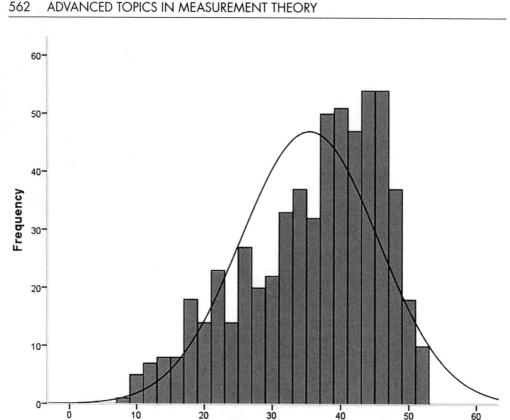

FIGURE 18.2. Histogram of scores on form X with superimposed normal curve.

distribution itself (known as *presmoothing*) or the scores obtained from the equipercentile equating process (*postsmoothing*). This is done because the irregularities are thought
to be due to the fact that only a sample from the population of interest is available for
equating. If the entire population were available, the reasoning goes, the distribution of
scores would be much smoother. In this sense, then, smoothing is done in an attempt
to obtain a distribution of scores that more closely resembles that of the population. If
successful, use of smoothing should therefore result in more accurate equated scores.

At a basic level, smoothing is accomplished by fitting a curve, such as a polynomial,
to the score distribution. This fitted function is then used to predict a new score distribution that essentially replaces the original distribution (presmoothing) or the distribution of equated scores (postsmoothing). In general, smoothing preserves the mean, *SD*,
and general shape of a distribution but removes the irregularities. This is particularly
useful for distributions based on small samples, as these tend to be the most irregular.

Smoothing also overcomes another problem with equipercentile equating, which
is that there may be scores in the distribution that are not observed. For example, note
from Figure 18.2 that no one obtained a score lower than 9 on form X. As a result, scores
below 9 cannot be equated. But if the distribution is smoothed, every score will be

obtained, whether it is observed or not, just as in regression every X has a predicted Y whether or not that X was actually observed. Thus, smoothing can overcome the problem of "holes" in the score distribution. This is particularly relevant for very low and very high scores, which are more often missing, but scores can be unobserved at any point in the score range. Again, however, if scores are smoothed, the presence of unobserved scores will not be an issue because the smoothing process will result in values across the entire distribution of possible scores. If you are familiar with the concept of extrapolation or predicting beyond the range of the data, you will realize that such smoothing may result in inaccuracies. This is because smoothing is based on fitting a curve to the observed data. For unobserved data, the curve is assumed to follow the same pattern as the observed data, but we do not really know that it would. So, we are making an educated guess, which could be wrong. Note that the problem is not as serious if the missing score is between two scores that are observed because those scores provide more of a picture of what the data in that region of the distribution look like. For data at the extremes of the distribution, however, such information is not available, so such extrapolation is riskier and introduces more error into the equating process. Finally, although smoothing is useful, it also introduces an additional source of error. This is because sampling error is inherent in the curve-fitting process on which smoothing is based. If a curve that provides a good match to the shape of the observed score distribution cannot be found, it may be better not to smooth at all. This is because use of a poorly fitting curve may introduce more equating error than it eliminates.

Equipercentile Equating with the Common-Item Nonequivalent Groups Design

The basic equipercentile equating process just described is sufficient for use with the single-group or random-groups designs. With these designs, it is reasonable to assume that the groups taking the two tests are equivalent in ability, so that any differences in difficulty can be attributed to differences in the test forms rather than to differences in examinee ability. In the common-item nonequivalent groups design, however, this is not a safe assumption. When this design is used, the common items must be used to parse out differences in ability from differences in form. As with linear equating, this makes the equating process more complex. The two main methods for equipercentile equating with the common item design are *chained equipercentile equating* and *frequency estimation* (sometimes referred to as *poststratification* or *conditioning on the anchor*). In the sections that follow, I discuss both methods in general terms. For more computational details, interested readers can consult Kolen and Brennan (2014, ch. 5).

Chained Equipercentile Equating

Chained equating is so called because scores on the common items serve as a link between scores on X and Y, thus creating a "chain" in which scores on X are equated to scores on C, scores on C are equated to scores on Y, and scores on X can then be equated to scores on Y through their common link, C. For example, if an X score of 11 had a percentile rank of 25 and a C score of 4 had a percentile rank of 25, an X score of 11 would be equated to a C score of 4. Then, if a Y score of 13 had the same percentile rank as a C score of 4, an X score of 11 would be equated to a Y score of 13.

Specifically, the following procedure is used:

1. In group 1, find the score on X that has the same percentile rank as a score on C. (In our example, these scores were X = 11 and C = 4). Assume this relation is the same in the population of interest as in the sample.

2. In group 2, find the score on C from step 1 that has the same percentile rank as a score on Y. (In our example, these scores are C = 4 and Y = 13.) Assume this relation is the same in the population as in the sample.

3. Equate the scores from steps 1 and 2 that have the same percentile ranks on C.

4. Do this for all scores on X.

Chained equating does not require a synthetic population, as does the frequency estimation method (discussed in the next section). Recall from the section on linear equating with the common-item nonequivalent groups design that the synthetic population represents an attempt to estimate how examinees in each group would have scored had they taken both exams. In chained equating, this information is not needed; all that is needed is examinees' scores on either X and C or Y and C. The common items do the heavy lifting of adjusting for any differences in ability between groups 1 and 2. Chained equating is not without its critics, however. The main criticism is that it requires that a longer form (X or Y) be equated to a shorter form (C). Critics argue that this does not really make sense if we think of equating as creating interchangeable scores because how can a score on a longer test mean the same thing as a score on a shorter test?

Frequency Estimation[4]

In this method of equipercentile equating, the idea is to estimate what the Y distribution in population 1 and the X distribution in population 2 would have been had examinees taken both exams. These estimates are based on the common items in C, which are used to create a synthetic population that combines the two populations. An assumption underlying the frequency estimation method is that, for both forms, the conditional distribution of scores on X or Y, given C, is the same in the populations represented by the two groups. This means that, for a given score on C, the distribution of X scores is the same in population 1 as in population 2, and that this holds for all scores on C. The same is true for the distribution of Y. Another way of saying this is that, if someone gets a particular score c on C, the probability that they will also get a particular score x on X (or y on Y) is the same in both populations. This allows us to obtain by assumption what we do not know empirically (the distributions of Y scores for population 1 and of X scores for population 2). This assumption cannot be tested (to do so, we would have to have data on

---

[4] This section can be omitted without loss of continuity.

X in population 2 and Y in population 1, the absence of which is the reason for making the assumption in the first place). However, we can take heart in the fact that the assumption is more likely to hold when the distributions of the two groups are most similar—that is, when the distributions of X and Y are similar and when the distributions of C in each group are similar. This information, at least, is available and should be examined.

I illustrate the frequency estimation process using a simple example in which there are only two common items and four items on the X and Y tests, yielding scores of 0–2 for C and of 0–4 for X and Y. This example is admittedly contrived, as there would normally be many more items on a test, but it serves for the purposes of illustration. The first step is to obtain the joint distributions of C and X and of C and Y. Tables 18.3 and 18.4 show these joint distributions. Each cell represents the proportion of examinees who received that combination of scores on C and X (or C and Y). For example, it can be seen from Table 18.3 that 0.07, or 7%, of the examinees obtained scores of 0 on both C and X. The labels $P_1(x)$ and $P_1(c)$ refer to the overall proportions of examinees in group 1 who obtained each X or C score. For example, 0.20 of examinees obtained scores of 0 on C, and 0.10 received scores of 0 on X. The label $CP_1(x)$ refers to the cumulative proportion of scores on X. For example, 0.70 of the total number of examinees obtained x scores of 2 or less. Table 18.4 shows analogous quantities for scores on C and Y.

The next step is to combine these distributions to estimate the distribution for the synthetic population. Recall from the earlier section on linear equating with the common-item nonequivalent groups design that the synthetic population is obtained by weighting the means and standard deviations of the two groups together in a particular way. For equipercentile equating, it is not the means and standard deviations that are combined, but the probability distributions of X and Y. You may also recall that weights of 1 for population 1 and 0 for population 2 are often used. Adopting this convention results in the following probability distributions for X and Y:

$$P_s(x) = P_1(x) \text{ and } P_s(y) = \sum_c P_2(y \mid c) P_1(c) \tag{18.18}$$

The subscripts 1 and 2 in these expressions refer to populations 1 and 2. (As before, although I refer to populations, the estimates are based on data from the two groups

TABLE 18.3. Joint Proportions of Scores on C and X for Hypothetical Frequency Estimation Example

x	c 0	1	2	$P_1(x)$	$CP_1(x)$
0	0.07	0.02	0.01	0.10	0.10
1	0.04	0.10	0.06	0.20	0.30
2	0.06	0.24	0.10	0.40	0.70
3	0.02	0.10	0.08	0.20	0.90
4	0.01	0.04	0.05	0.10	1.00
$P_1(c)$	0.20	0.50	0.30	1.00	

TABLE 18.4. Joint Proportions of Scores on C and Y for Hypothetical Frequency Estimation Example

y	c 0	c 1	c 2	$P_2(y)$	$CP_2(y)$
0	0.10	0.01	0.01	0.12	0.12
1	0.10	0.07	0.03	0.20	0.32
2	0.03	0.24	0.08	0.35	0.67
3	0.01	0.12	0.10	0.23	0.90
4	0.01	0.01	0.08	0.10	1.00
$P_2(C)$	0.25	0.45	0.30	1.00	

available.) As noted previously, a weight of 1 for population 1 and 0 for population 2 is used here. This results in the probability distribution of X for the synthetic population being set equal to that of X in group 1. This simplifies the calculations for X because it obviates the need to estimate what the probabilities $x|c$ would have been in population 2.

For Y, however, things are not so simple. The expression for $P_s(y)$ in Equation 18.19 is an estimate of what the $y|c$ distribution would have been for population 1. This expression is based on the conditional probabilities $P_2(y|c)$, which are the proportions of examinees from group 2 who obtained each value of y, collapsed across each value of c. The first step in obtaining the distribution of $P_s(y)$ is therefore to obtain these conditional probabilities. These are calculated from the group 2 data by dividing the joint probabilities ($P_2(y \ and \ c)$) in Table 18.4 by the marginal probabilities of c ($P_2(c)$) in Table 18.4, as shown in Equation 18.19:

$$P_2(y \mid c) = \frac{P_2(y \ and \ c)}{P_2(c)}$$

(18.19)

The calculations are illustrated in Table 18.5.

The joint probabilities $p(y \ and \ c)$ are simply those in the body of Table 18.4, and the marginal probabilities are those shown in the bottom row of Table 18.4 (0.25, 0.45,

TABLE 18.5. Conditional Probabilities $P_2(y|c)$ for Hypothetical Frequency Estimation Example

y	c 0	c 1	c 2
0	0.40	0.02	0.03
1	0.40	0.16	0.10
2	0.12	0.53	0.27
3	0.04	0.27	0.33
4	0.04	0.02	0.27

and 0.30). For example, the value of 0.40 in the first cell of Table 18.5 is equal to 0.10/0.25, and the value of 0.27 for the conditional probability ($c = 2$ and $y = 4$) is equal to 0.08/0.30. These conditional probabilities are the proportion of examinees who obtained each score on Y, *given that* they also obtained a particular score on C. From Table 18.5, of those who obtained a score of 0 on C, 0.40 also obtained scores of 0 on Y, 0.40 obtained scores of 1 on Y, 0.12 obtained scores of 2 on Y, and Y scores of 3 and 4 were each obtained by only 0.04 of the group.

These values of Y have been estimated from group 2 data. However, recall that to obtain the Y values for the synthetic population, what we really want are estimates of what the Y values would have been for population 1. To obtain these values, we multiply the values in Table 18.5 by the estimated probabilities of C in group 1. Note that this gives us the quantity $P_s(y)$ specified in Equation 18.18. Where do we get the estimated probabilities of C for group 1? From Table 18.3, which shows the marginal (overall) values of C for that group. The next step in the frequency estimation process (don't worry; we're almost finished) is therefore to multiply each of the values in Table 18.5 by the marginal values of C from Table 18.3 (0.20, 0.50, and 0.30). The resulting values are shown in Table 18.6.

The first three columns of Table 18.6 show the estimated values of $P_s(y)$ at each value of c. As indicated previously, these were calculated by multiplying the values in Table 18.5 by the marginal probabilities of c in Table 18.3. For example, the value of 0.08 in Table 18.6 for the cell in which $c = 0$ and $y = 0$ is calculated as 0.40 (from Table 18.5 with $c = 0$ and $y = 0$) times 0.20 (from the marginal value for $c = 0$ in Table 18.3). This represents the estimated proportion of examinees in group 1 who would have obtained scores of 0 on both Y and C, had they taken form Y. Note that the c-values in each column of Table 18.6 sum to the marginal values of c for group 1 shown in Table 18.3. This is because the c probabilities from Table 18.3 have been "superimposed" on the Y data from group 2. The next-to-last column of Table 18.6 shows the estimated probabilities of each y-value for population 1. I obtained these by simply summing the probabilities for each y score across the three values of c in each row of Table 18.6. Finally, the last column of Table 18.6 contains the cumulative probabilities at each y-value, which I obtained by summing the values of $P_s(y)$. These cumulative probabilities will be useful in the next steps, in which we will (finally) calculate the percentiles for the synthetic distributions on which the equipercentile equating is based.

TABLE 18.6. Estimated Probabilities *Ps(y)* for Hypothetical Frequency Estimation Example

	c				
y	0	1	2	$P_s(y)$	$CP_s(y)$
0	0.08	0.01	0.01	0.10	0.10
1	0.08	0.08	0.03	0.19	0.29
2	0.02	0.27	0.08	0.37	0.66
3	0.01	0.13	0.10	0.24	0.90
4	0.01	0.01	0.08	0.10	1.00
$P_1(c)$	0.20	0.50	0.30		

TABLE 18.7. Percentile Ranks and Equated X Scores for Hypothetical Frequency Estimation Example

x	$P_1(x)$	$CP_1(x)$	$F_1(x)$	$CF_1(x)$	$PR_1(x)$	y	$P_s(y)$	$CP_s(y)$	$F_s(y)$	$CF_s(y)$	$PR_s(y)$	$Y_{s(x)}$
0	10.0	10.0	10.0	10.0	5.0	0	10.1	10.1	10.1	10.1	5.06	−0.01
1	20.0	30.0	20.0	30.0	20.0	1	18.8	28.9	18.8	28.9	19.50	1.03
2	40.0	70.0	40.0	70.0	50.0	2	37.1	66.0	37.1	66.0	47.42	2.07
3	20.0	90.0	20.0	90.0	80.0	3	24.1	90.1	24.1	90.1	78.02	3.08
4	10.0	100.0	10.0	100.0	95.0	4	9.9	100.0	9.9	100.0	95.04	4.00

In this final step, I use the information in Tables 18.3 and 18.6 to obtain the percentile ranks for each *x* and *y* score. I then use these percentile ranks to equate scores on form X to the scale of form Y. Table 18.7 shows the relevant information from Tables 18.3 and 18.6, along with the calculated percentile ranks and the equated scores on X. The percentile ranks were calculated using Equation 2.1 from Chapter 2. To make the computations slightly easier for those who want to practice them, I express the probabilities in Table 18.6 as percentages (simply multiplying the proportions by 100) to make the calculations more similar to those in Chapter 2. I obtained the frequencies in Table 18.7 (shown as $F_1(x)$ and $F_s(y)$ in the table) by assuming a sample size of 100 and multiplying the proportion of examinees who obtained each *x* or *y* score by 100.

To obtain the form Y equivalents of the form X scores, I used the following procedure. First, I found the percentile rank for each *x*. Then I calculated the *y* score with the same percentile rank, using Equation 2.2 from Chapter 2. I illustrate these steps below for an *x* score of 2, using the data in Table 18.7. The first step is to find the percentile rank of an *x*-value of 2. To do this I use Equation 2.1 from Chapter 2:

$$PR = \frac{cf_l + 0.5 * f}{n} * 100 = \frac{30 + 0.5 * 40}{100} * 100 = \frac{50}{100} * 100 = 50$$

The percentile rank of an *x* score of 2 is 50, as shown in the sixth column of Table 18.7. To find the *y* score with a percentile rank of 50, I use Equation 2.2 from Chapter 2. A percentile rank of 50 would fall in the interval for a *y* score of 2 because the cumulative percentage of that interval goes up to 66%. The calculations are

$$P = x_{ll} + \frac{\text{Width}}{\text{Interval\%}}(P - CP\%) = 1.5 + \frac{1}{37.1}(50 - 28.9) = 1.5 + 0.02695 * 21.1 = 1.5 + 0.57 = 2.07$$

An *x* score of 2 therefore equates to a *y* score of 2.07 (the value of 2.07, as well as the other percentile values for Y, are shown in the last column of Table 18.7). You may wish to compute the other *x* to *y* conversions as an exercise.

One problem with the frequency estimation method occurs if examinees in one group obtain a certain score on *c*, but no one in the other group obtains the same *c* score. This is problematic because the probabilities for each *c* score in each group are needed to obtain the probabilities for the synthetic population. To get around this problem, Kolen and Brennan (2014) recommend either substituting the probability of the score closest to the missing *c* score, or using the smoothing methods described previously. Recall from the earlier discussion of smoothing methods that these are based on regression methods. In the current situation, values of the missing *c*-values could be predicted from the nonmissing *c*-values, and frequency estimation could then proceed as usual.

Choosing between Chained Equipercentile and Frequency Estimation Equating Methods

From the previous discussion of chained equipercentile and frequency estimation equating, it may be apparent that the two procedures are fairly different. Because of this difference, they do not generally yield the same results. This begs the question of how to choose between the two methods. Chained equipercentile equating does not require the populations represented by the two groups to be similar, so it may be best to use this method if the groups are somewhat different. If the two populations are equivalent, or if the common-item scores are perfectly correlated with the X and Y scores, the two methods will yield the same results. However, it is unlikely that either condition will be met in practice. If there are group differences, frequency estimation will be less accurate than chained equipercentile equating but will have a smaller standard error of equating. That is, frequency estimation will be more precise but less accurate (Wang et al., 2008). This makes conceptual sense when we consider that the frequency estimation method is much more computationally complex than the chained equating method. Although its greater complexity results in greater precision, it also opens the door to more estimation error because more quantities must be estimated (think back to all of the probabilities, percentile ranks, and percentiles that were estimated for even our small example). Each of these estimations will engender some amount of error, resulting in less accuracy overall. This trade-off between accuracy and precision is a common dilemma in statistical methods.

IRT Equating Methods

IRT methods were introduced in Chapter 14. To briefly review, IRT models were developed in the context of dichotomously scored (0, 1) data such as that obtained from multiple-choice or other achievement tests in which answers are scored as right/wrong. Since the time of their original development, IRT models have been expanded to accommodate polytomously scored items (i.e., items scored into more than two categories), including Likert-type items, performance ratings, and essay questions. Although basic IRT models require the data to be unidimensional, multidimensional models are also possible (but, of course, more complex). The mathematical function underlying IRT models relates an examinee's probability of a correct response to the underlying level of the construct, commonly termed *theta* (θ) in the IRT literature. Although theta is often referred to as "ability," it could represent any construct capable of being modeled in terms of response probabilities. Thus, IRT models are not limited to educational applications but can be used with any type of latent construct. Different IRT models are distinguished by the parameters used to model the relation between theta and the response probability. The *one-parameter model* includes only a difficulty parameter, usually symbolized as *b*. The *two-parameter model* adds a discrimination parameter, *a*. In the one-parameter model, the *a*-parameters for all items are considered to be equal, so this term essentially drops out of the model. Finally, the *three-parameter model* adds a pseudo-guessing parameter, *c*. This parameter adjusts the model to allow for the possibility that an examinee might obtain the correct answer by guessing or other construct-irrelevant behavior. Thus, even an examinee with very low ability could have a probability greater than zero of obtaining the correct answer. The formulation of the three-parameter model is

$$p_{ij}\left(\theta_i;a_j,b_j,c_j\right)=c_j+\left(1-c_j\right)\frac{\exp\left[Da_j\left(\theta_i-b_j\right)\right]}{1+\exp\left[Da_j\left(\theta_i-b_j\right)\right]} \tag{18.20}$$

Equation 18.20 specifies that the probability of a correct response for examinee i on item j is a function of the examinee's ability (θ_i), the item's level of difficulty (b_j), the item's level of discrimination (a_j), and the probability that the item could be answered by guessing (c_j). D is simply a scaling constant (usually 1.7) that is used to put IRT models based on different functions onto the same metric (see Chapter 14 for more detail).

IRT methods offer an attractive option for equating test forms because many large-scale tests with multiple forms are developed using these methods. Thus, the use of IRT equating is relatively straightforward as it can be seen as an extension of the basic IRT model. It should be noted, however, that IRT models are based on strict assumptions, such as unidimensionality of the test items (for unidimensional models) and adequate fit of the IRT model used. The latter assumption requires that the IRT model fit the data in the sense that it is able to account for the observed response probabilities. If the model's assumptions are not met, the accuracy of the equating will suffer.

IRT equating involves the following steps (Cook & Eignor, 1991). Note that, depending on the data collection design and other considerations, not all of these steps will be needed.

1. Choose and implement a data collection design. The same three designs discussed previously in this chapter (the single-group, random-groups, or common-item nonequivalent groups designs) are used in IRT equating. However, the common-item design is used most often, and data collection is implemented in the same way as described for the other equating methods.

2. Put item parameters on the same scale. In IRT estimation, it is necessary to set a scale, or metric, for ability (θ). This is because θ represents a latent construct that has no inherent metric (see Chapter 13 for a discussion of this issue in the context of CFA). In IRT, as in CFA, the scale is usually set by fixing the mean and SD of the ability scale to be 0 and 1, respectively. However, if the groups taking forms X and Y are not equivalent in terms of ability, they are likely to have different means and SDs, and setting these to 0 and 1 in both groups would incorrectly equate these values across groups. In such cases, the item and ability parameters in one group must be re-scaled to those in the other group. This can be done through transformations of the X scale using methods similar to those for mean or linear equating discussed previously.

Note that this step is not always necessary. One reason is that IRT allows for the *concurrent calibration* of items from the different test forms. In IRT, *calibration* refers to the process of putting parameter estimates onto a particular scale. In concurrent calibration, the items from both test forms (including the common items) are estimated simultaneously instead of being estimated in separate analyses. When concurrent calibration is used, parameters from the two forms are automatically placed on the same scale, so step 2 is not needed.

3. Transform the equated scores to a new metric, if needed. In most cases, scores are not reported to examinees or to the public on the IRT ability (θ) metric. This is because the θ metric is analogous to a z-score metric and therefore yields scores that are negative or zero. In IRT an additional issue is that two examinees may have the same θ value even though they have different patterns of correct answers. This is because, in IRT scoring, scores are based not only on the *number* of items correctly answered but also on the *item parameters*. This means that two examinees may have different estimated θ values even though they have the same number of correct answers. For example, if two examinees have the same number of correct items, but the correctly answered items for one of the examinees are more discriminating, that examinee will have a higher estimated θ value. Although this is perfectly reasonable to those who understand IRT, it is difficult to explain to test takers. For these reasons, once scores are equated using IRT methods, they are typically transformed into some other metric. A common example is the SAT (mean of 500 and standard deviation of 100) scale.

In the following sections, I provide more detail about the IRT equating process. To keep things manageable, I restrict the discussion to the three-parameter IRT model with the common-item nonequivalent groups design. I choose the common-item design because it is widely used in IRT equating. I use the three-parameter model because this is the most complex model, and the process for the one- and two-parameter models are simplifications of that for the three-parameter model.

IRT equating involves transforming the item parameter and ability estimates from one test form in such a way that they will yield the same scores as would be obtained on the other test form. That is, the parameters are transformed such that scores on the two forms are interchangeable. Note that this same definition of equating is used in mean, linear, and equipercentile equating. Because scores in IRT are functions of the item and ability parameters (a, b, c, and θ in the three-parameter model), appropriate transformations of these parameters will result in such score equivalence across forms. Recall from the discussion under step 2 that the mean and *SD* of θ can differ across the two groups. Because in IRT the θ means and *SD*s are functions of the item parameters, transformations can be based either on θ or on the item parameters. Also note that such transformations are only necessary for the common-item nonequivalent groups design because equivalence of the ability distributions (and item parameter values) obtained from the single and random groups design is assumed.

For the common-item design, two transformations are typically used: the mean/mean (Loyd & Hoover, 1980) and the mean/sigma (Marco, 1977) methods. Both are forms of linear equating. Recall that in linear equating, scores on one form are equated to scores on another form using equations involving the means and *SD*s of the two test forms. The mean/mean and mean/sigma methods are based on a similar process, but instead of using the means and *SD*s of the two test forms as in linear equating, the transformations are based on constants obtained from the means and *SD*s of the item parameter estimates (a and b values) from the two test forms. These means and *SD*s are based on the parameter estimates from the common items *only*, although the transformations are performed for all items. Specifically, the item parameters from form X are transformed to the scale of form Y using the following equations for the discrimination (*a*), difficulty (*b*), and pseudo-guessing (*c*) parameters:

$$a_{Y'j} = \frac{a_{Xj}}{A} \tag{18.21}$$

$$b_{Y'j} = Ab_{Xj} + B \tag{18.22}$$

$$c_{Y'j} = c_{Xj} \tag{18.23}$$

Here, I use the notation Y'_j to indicate the parameter for item j from form X transformed to the scale of form Y. For example, $a_{Y'j}$ is the *a*-parameter for item j from form X, transformed to the scale of form Y. The constants A and B are obtained from the means and standard deviations of the common item parameters. Equations 18.21–18.23 are used with both the mean/mean and mean/sigma methods, but the formulas for the constants A and B differ for the two methods. For the mean/sigma method, these are

$$A = \frac{\sigma(b_Y)}{\sigma(b_X)} \tag{18.24}$$

$$B = \mu(b_Y) - A\mu(b_X) \tag{18.25}$$

For the mean/mean method they are

$$A = \frac{\mu(a_X)}{\mu(a_Y)} \tag{18.26}$$

$$B = \mu(b_Y) - A\mu(b_X) \tag{18.27}$$

In Equations 18.21–18.27, $\sigma(a_Y)$ and $\mu(a_Y)$ represent the standard deviation and mean of the discrimination (*a*) parameter values of the common items from form Y. (Note that, although the common items are, of course, the same on both forms, the estimates of their item parameters can still differ, as the two forms are taken by two nonequivalent groups.) The other symbols can be interpreted in an analogous fashion. For both sets of equations, only the estimates of *a* and *b* from the common items are used. The *c*-parameters are not transformed, and the constants do not involve this parameter. As you can see from Equations 18.24–18.27, the mean/sigma method is so-named because the *A* constant for this method is based on *SD*s (sigmas) and the *B* constant is based on means. In contrast, the *A* and *B* constants for the mean/mean method are both based on means (although these are means of different item parameters).

I illustrate both the mean/sigma and mean/mean methods with a small example adapted from that in Kolen and Brennan (2014, p. 187). Hypothetical item parameter values for three common items from two test forms are shown in the top half of Table 18.8. In a real testing situation, we would, of course, have many more common items, but the data in Table 18.8 will serve for the purposes of illustration. I have calculated the

TABLE 18.8. Mean/Sigma and Mean/Mean Transformations for Hypothetical Forms X and Y

Item	Form X			Form Y		
	a	b	c	a	b	c
1	0.5	−1.2	0.2	0.6	−1.5	0.2
2	1.2	0.5	0.3	1.4	0.3	0.3
3	1.6	2.2	0.1	1.6	2.1	0.1
Mean	1.1	0.5	0.2	1.2	0.3	0.2
SD	0.455	1.388	0.082	0.432	1.470	0.082

Scaling constants

Mean/sigma method	Mean/mean method
$A = 1.470/1.388 = 1.059$	$A = 1.1/1.2 = 0.917$
$B = 0.3 - 1.059(0.5) = -0.229$	$B = 0.3 - 0.917(0.5) = -0.158$

Item	Mean/sigma conversion for X to Y			Mean/mean conversion for X to Y		
	a	b	c	a	b	c
1	0.47	−1.5	0.2	0.55	−1.26	0.2
2	1.13	0.3	0.3	1.31	0.3	0.3
3	1.51	2.1	0.1	1.74	1.86	0.1
Mean	1.04	0.3	0.2	1.2	0.3	0.2
SD	0.429	1.470	0.082	0.496	1.272	0.082

means and SDs for the a- and b-parameter values of the three items for both forms and used these to obtain the scaling constants A and B using Equations 18.24–18.27. I then used these scaling constants to transform the a- and b-parameter estimates (remember that the c-parameters are not changed) from form X to the scale of form Y using both the mean/sigma and mean/mean methods using Equations 18.21–18.22.

The transformed parameters are shown in the bottom of Table 18.8. As an example, to transform the a-parameter for item 1 from form X (0.5) to the scale of form Y using the mean/sigma method, I divide it by 1.059 to obtain 0.47. The b-parameter for item 1 from form X is transformed by taking $-0.229 + 1.059(-1.2) = -1.5$. Note that, after the mean/sigma transformation, the mean and SD of the transformed b-parameters are equal to those from form Y (0.3 and 1.470, respectively). Similarly, after implementing the mean/mean transformation, the means (but not the SDs) of both the a- and b-parameters are equal to those from form Y.

In Table 18.8, I have shown only the transformations of item parameters for the three common items. In practice, all of the items (common and noncommon) on form X would be transformed using the same equations. Ability estimates from form X can also be transformed to the scale of form Y using an equation similar to Equation 18.22:

$$\theta_{Y'i} = A\theta_{Xi} + B \tag{18.28}$$

Transformations of ability estimates can be based on either the mean/sigma or mean/mean method, and the constants A and B are the same as those in Equations 18.24–18.27. Using Equation 18.28, the ability level of each examinee taking form X could be equated to ability levels on form Y. Note the similarity of this process to that of linear equating.

Although the mean/sigma and mean/mean methods are fairly straightforward (once you get used to them), their use introduces a technical glitch that is of concern to those who worry about such things: different values of a, b, and c could result in very similar item characteristic curves. That is, the item parameters operate jointly to determine these curves, such that different combinations of parameter values could result in similar curves. This is problematic because it implies that an examinee's probability of success could be the same on items with very different item parameter values. Because the constants A and B used in the mean/sigma and mean/mean methods are based on these parameters, differences in these parameter values could affect the results of these methods in such a way that the transformed ability estimates differ, even though the corresponding probabilities of correctly responding (represented by the item characteristic curves) do not. This happens because calculation of the constants used in the mean/sigma and mean/mean methods does not take all of the item parameters into account simultaneously, whereas calculation of the response probabilities and item characteristic curves does.

The solution to this dilemma is to obtain values of A and B that are based on all of the item parameters simultaneously. Item response functions do just this, which is why *response function methods* for IRT equating were developed. In the interest of space, I do not provide a full description of these methods (but see Kolen & Brennan, 2014, pp. 184–186, for more detail). The basic concept, however, is to compare the IRFs of the common items on two test forms to be equated. The difference between the IRFs for each pair (form X and form Y) of common items is computed. In Haebara's (1980) approach, these differences are then squared and summed across the common items. A variant of this procedure, introduced by Stocking and Lord (1983), is to sum the differences and then square the sum. In both the Haebara and the Stocking and Lord procedures, the constants A and B are found through a minimization process. Specifically, values of A and B are found that result in the smallest possible difference between the IRFs from form X and Y (this is the same idea as the least squares criterion in regression). Use of these constants will result in transformed values of the item parameters (a, b, and c) that should yield equated X scores that are as close as possible to the corresponding Y scores.

The final step in the IRT equating process is to transform the equated scores to a new metric. Recall that transformation is often desirable to avoid the possibility of negative or zero scores that are inherent in most IRT ability metrics. One way to accomplish such a transformation is through *true-score equating*, in which two scores with the same theta values are assumed to be equivalent. Again, I leave the details to Kolen and Brennan (2014, pp. 191–200), but the basic process is reminiscent of equipercentile equating in the common-item design. Specifically, the steps are:

1. Find the theta value for each score on X (this is not as simple as it may sound, because it involves using an iterative process to solve a nonlinear equation in a, b, c, and theta).

2. Find the true scores on Y that correspond to each of these theta values.

3. Equate each X true score to the Y true score with the same theta value (theta values for Y are taken from step 2).

PRACTICAL CONSIDERATIONS IN EQUATING

The common-item nonequivalent group design is popular in practice and is therefore a design that readers are likely to encounter. Accordingly, I will spend some time on guidelines for choosing items for the common-item set, drawing on Livingston's (2014) excellent discussion. I will then discuss error in equating and how this is measured, and will end with some ideas on how to choose an equating method.

Guidelines for Choosing Common Items

When using a common-item design, the accuracy of results hinges on the quality of the common-item set. It is crucial that the common items reflect the range of both content and difficulty in the full tests, such that the common items represent a mini-version of the full test. A common question with this design is how many common items are needed. In general, inclusion of more common items will result in more accurate results. Having said this, practical considerations will limit the number of common items because increasing the number of common items will also increase the total testing time.

Given that concerns over testing time constitute one of the main reasons for using a common-item design instead of a random-groups design in the first place, it would not make sense to have an inordinately long common-item set. Kolen and Brennan (2014) suggest that the common-item set should contain at least 20% as many items as the full test. However, if the test content is very heterogeneous, more common items may be needed to cover the various content areas. It is important that the common items function in the same way on both tests. Common items should therefore be placed in approximately the same positions on the two tests to be equated. For multiple-choice tests, the response options for the common items should also be the same (and in the same order) on both tests. In choosing a common-item set, item statistics for the common items can be compared across the two tests to determine if they are functioning equivalently. Items that function differently can be dropped from the common-item set before equating is done and can be replaced with other items. If there is a set of items that refer to the same reading passage, graph, map, or other stimulus material, it is not necessary to include each of these items in the common-item set, but the whole set should be included on the full test (see Livingston, 2014, p. 36).

Although not related to the choice of common items per se, Livingston (2014) recommends that the data used in this design be screened for outliers, defined as cases for which responses to the common items and the items on the full test seem incompatible. If an examinee obtains very different scores on the common and full test items, one (or both) of the scores must be an invalid indicator of his or her ability. The problem is that there is no way to know which (if either) score is valid without further investigation. For example, an examinee with a high score on the common-item set and a low score on the full test may have run out of time on the full test or may have somehow known the content of the common-item set. To determine such outliers, scores on the common items and the full test can be converted to z-scores. If the difference between the two z-scores is large, Livingston recommends removing the case from the dataset prior to conducting the equating.

Error in Equating

Recall from the earlier discussion of equating that the groups of examinees taking tests X and Y are assumed to be representative of their respective populations of interest. The data from these samples are used to estimate the various means, standard deviations, percentile ranks, and/or proportions that are needed to conduct the equating procedure. Because these estimates are based on samples, they engender a certain amount of sampling error. The standard error of equating (SEE) is a measure of the degree to which equating results would vary from sample to sample. Specifically, suppose the form Y equivalent of a form X score of 35 were found using a particular equating design and method. Then suppose that this process was repeated over and over, using different samples of examinees each time. This would result in a distribution of form Y equivalents of a form X score of 35. The *SD* of this distribution of scores would be the standard error of equating for a form X score of 35 for the equating design and method used.

Note two things about this definition. One is that there is a different SEE at each score point because each score has its own distribution of equated values. So, the SEE differs across different scores. SEEs are typically smaller for scores in the middle of a distribution and larger for scores in the tails. This is because there are typically more scores in the middle of the distribution, and thus more information on which to base estimates. Thus, equated scores in the middle of the distribution can generally be estimated more precisely than scores in the tails, for which there is often less information available. This is particularly problematic for equipercentile and linear equating. Recall that for these methods, if no examinees obtain a particular score, the missing scores are predicted from the data that are available. Such predictions introduce additional error into the calculations, especially if predictions must be made beyond the range of the observed data (a process known as *extrapolation*).

The second point is that the SEE differs across the various methods of equating and equating designs because it is defined on the basis of the equated scores obtained from a particular method/design combination. As noted previously, equating methods vary widely in the number of quantities that must be estimated. For example, mean equating only requires the estimation of two means. Frequency estimation, in contrast, requires the estimation of a plethora of probabilities, percentiles, and percentile ranks. Another important influence on the SEE is the equating design used. This makes the calculation of SEEs quite complex because different formulas are needed for each combination of equating design and method. Presentation of all the formulations is beyond the scope of this chapter, but Kolen and Brennan (2014, ch. 7) provide a comprehensive treatment. Calculation of SEEs for many design/method combinations is difficult and generally relies on either an approximation method known as the *delta method* or on bootstrapping, or resampling techniques. Kolen and Brennan (ch. 7) provide details on these methods and present equations for some of the simpler equating methods and designs. In the next two sections, I discuss only the overall effects of design and method on the SEE. In general, mean equating results in the least error, followed by linear and equipercentile equating, in that order. This follows from the fact that mean equating requires estimation of fewer quantities, whereas equipercentile necessitates estimation of many more. It also implies that larger sample sizes are needed for linear and equipercentile equating, in comparison to mean equating. Having brought up sample-size requirements, I make a brief digression to discuss that topic before returning to choosing among equating methods.

Sample-Size Requirements

At this point, you may be wondering exactly how large a sample size is needed for equating. Unfortunately, this question is difficult to answer because of the SEE's dependency on the equating design and method of equating. Kolen and Brennan (2014, pp. 274–275) provide equations to estimate sample sizes for some of the more commonly used designs. These equations require specification of the maximum amount of error that can be tolerated, expressed as a proportion of the *SD* of scores on the full test. The *z*-score corresponding to the score of interest is also needed because the SEE is calculated at each score point. For the random-groups design with linear equating, the formula is

$$N_{total} = \frac{2}{u^2}\left(2 + z^2\right) \tag{18.29}$$

In this equation, N_{total} is the total sample size (across both groups) needed, u is the maximum error that can be tolerated (expressed as a proportion of the full test *SD*), and z is the score of interest, expressed as a *z*-score. For example, suppose that we were willing to tolerate a maximum amount of error that was 0.1 of the *SD* of the test. If the test had a *SD* of 10, this would be an equating error of 1 point. I show the calculations below for *z*-scores of 0, 1, and 2. It should be clear from these calculations that a much greater sample size is needed to obtain precise estimates for scores that are more extreme than for scores near the middle of the distribution. For this scenario, a total of 400 examinees (200 in each group for our random-groups design) is needed for scores of 0 (the mean of the score distribution), but this increases to 1,200 (600 per group) for more extreme scores of 2 (the same would hold for scores of –2). These calculations are based on the assumption that scores are normally distributed and so are best treated as approximations.

$$z = 0 : N_{total} = \frac{2}{0.1^2}(2 + 0^2) = 200(2) = 400$$

$$z = 1 : N_{total} = \frac{2}{0.1^2}(2 + 1^2) = 200(3) = 600$$

$$z = 2 : N_{total} = \frac{2}{0.1^2}(2 + 2^2) = 200(6) = 1,200$$

These calculations are based on linear equating with a random-groups design. With a single-group design, the same level of precision can be obtained with fewer examinees. This is because in the single-group design the examinees taking forms X and Y are perfectly matched (being the same people), and this eliminates a source of sampling error. Kolen and Brennan (2014, pp. 272–273) show that linear equating with a random-groups design will typically require 4 to 20 times as many examinees as linear equating with a single-group design.

For the common-item design, even greater sample sizes are needed because estimates for the common items in addition to estimates for X and Y must be computed, thus increasing the amount of sampling error. In addition, in the common-item design, we cannot assume that the two groups are equivalent in ability and have to use the common items to adjust for any differences. The precision of these adjustments will depend on the correlation between scores on the common items and the forms being equated. Specifically, the SEE will decrease as these correlations increase. These guidelines apply only to linear equating. With equipercentile equating, larger sample sizes are needed. According to Kolen and Brennan, equipercentile equating requires sample sizes of about 1.5 times those for linear equating to achieve the same precision for scores at the mean of a distribution (recall that estimation is most stable at this point). At score points farther from the mean, the sample size for equipercentile equating would have to be increased to as much as 2.5 to 12 times that of linear equating to obtain the same precision (see Kolen & Brennan, 2014, p. 271). The farther the score is from the mean, the larger the sample size needed to obtain precise estimates.

Systematic Equating Error

In addition to random error, equating results are also affected by systematic error resulting from violations of the assumptions underlying the equating method or design. These include such errors as failing to adequately control for order effects in the counterbalanced design or failing to assign forms randomly to groups in the random-groups design. Over time, both random and systematic error can accumulate as more forms are equated. Although I have focused on equating two forms of a test, large-scale achievement, certification, and licensure tests often have many forms that are given each year. In such cases, forms are often equated in *chains* (although, confusingly, the word *chain* here is used in a somewhat different way than in the chained equipercentile equating method discussed previously). For example, suppose there are five forms, A, B, C, D, and E. If A is the base form, scores might be equated back to form A by equating scores on form E to scores on form D, D to C, C to B, and B to A. Thus, scores on forms C, D, and E are not equated directly to scores on form A but are equated in an indirect way, through scores on the other test forms. Some error (both random and systematic) will be introduced for each equating, and this error will accumulate across the pairs of test forms. Consequently, scores on form E may not ultimately be comparable to scores on form A. This is known as *scale drift* and can be assessed by equating the last form in an equating chain directly to the base form. If the results are not the same as those obtained from the original equating (e.g., if the results of equating form E to form A are not the same as those from equating E to A through B, C, and D), scale drift has occurred.

If forms are administered and equated fairly close together in time, drift may not occur. But sometimes there are two *equating strains* in which different chains of forms are equated back to the same base form. For example, one strain may consist of forms B, C, D, and E and another chain of forms F, G, H, and I. Forms in both equating strains are equated back to form A using the chaining process just described. In this situation, forms in the two strains may drift differently, and even in opposite directions, so that, across strains, forms may not be comparable. To prevent this problem, a final test form (J) can be directly equated to previous forms in both strains. If the equatings to forms A and J yield the same results, one form can be chosen to continue the chain, or results from the two can be averaged. If the two equatings differ by a substantial amount, the researcher would have to trace back through the equating chain to find the reason. The reason may be that the sample for one equating was unusual, that test items have been compromised, or that the curriculum has changed so that certain topics on the test are emphasized more in certain classrooms.

In some cases, there may be so much equating error that it is better not to equate at all. This can occur if the sample size is too small, if the equating design is implemented poorly, or if the assumptions for the equating method are not met. If test forms are to be equated, this should be recognized when tests are being constructed, so that all forms can be constructed carefully using the same table of specifications and items for the test forms can be matched in terms of difficulty and other psychometric characteristics. If tests are used over a number of years, the test specifications may change so much that tests can no longer be equated because they are no longer measuring the same construct.

Choice of Equating Method

Different equating methods are based on different assumptions, and if these assumptions cannot be met, the method should not be used. For example, if scores on two test forms have different distributional shapes, mean or linear equating should not be used, and equipercentile equating should be used instead. Of course, equipercentile equating requires larger sample sizes than mean or linear equating, so this factor should also be taken into consideration. A method that requires a large sample size (such as frequency estimation or IRT equating) should not be used if a sufficient sample size is not available. The accuracy and precision of the method should also be considered. However, these two characteristics are often at odds. As noted previously, the chained equipercentile equating is more accurate than the frequency estimation method, but at the cost of more equating error. Overall, there is no simple answer to the question of which method of equating is "best." It depends on the available sample and the characteristics of the data. Researchers often try out two or more methods and compare them in terms of which yields the most reasonable results based on their knowledge of the test forms and the population of examinees. This decision clearly requires judgment as well as extensive knowledge of the testing situation. However, Kolen and Brennan (2014, ch. 8) discuss more objective methods of choosing among the results from different equating methods.

SUMMARY

Equating is defined here as a statistical process in which scores from different test forms are adjusted so that they can be used interchangeably. Equating assumes that the forms being equated measure the same construct. Also described here are two methods that are similar to equating: vertical scaling and linking. Vertical scaling is often used with achievement tests in which the construct being measured is not quite the same across grades, but researchers and school officials need some way to compare test scores across grades. Vertical scaling puts scores for different grade levels onto a common scale so that such comparisons can be made. Linking is used to relate tests that are intended to measure the same basic construct but do so differently. Linking provides a rough approximation of what a score on one test would be if it was expressed as a score on another test. Such linkages are often reported in concordance tables showing how scores on the two tests are related.

Equating requires the specification of both an equating design and a method of equating. I discussed three designs: the single-group design, the random-groups design, and the common-item nonequivalent groups design. In the first of these designs, the same group takes both forms of the test, either back to back or as close together in time as possible. As a result, fatigue and practice effects are often problematic. These concerns are alleviated by counterbalancing the order of the tests such that half of the group takes form X first and then form Y, and the order is reversed for the other group. In the random-groups design, the overall group is typically split in half, with one half taking form X and the other form Y. This reduces testing time for examinees, as only one test form is taken. However, it requires larger sample sizes than the single-group design. In the common-item nonequivalent groups design, groups are not assumed to be randomly equivalent, as in the random-groups design, although they should not differ too much in ability. In this design, different groups take forms X and Y, but both forms contain a set of common items. The common-item set is used to disentangle any differences in the groups' ability levels from differences in the difficulty of the two test forms. The success of this venture depends on the representativeness of the common-item set, which should be a mini-version of the full test forms in terms of both content and difficulty level. If it is, scores on the common items should be highly correlated with scores on X and Y. The higher this correlation, the more accurate the equating process will be.

I discussed three equating methods: mean, linear, and equipercentile equating. These methods are based on different assumptions about differences in the score distributions of the tests being equated. Mean equating assumes that scores on the two test forms differ only in their means. This implies that scores differ by a constant amount across the entire score range and that equating can be accomplished by simply adding or subtracting a constant from one set of score values. In linear equating, score distributions differ in both mean and *SD*. As the name implies, linear equating is based on a linear function that results from setting *z*-scores from the two score distributions equal. If score distributions differ in shape as well as in means and *SD*s, equipercentile equating should be used. In this form of equating, scores that have the same percentile rank are considered to be equivalent. Although fairly simple to calculate for the single- and random-groups designs, linear and equipercentile equating become much more complex with the common-item design.

The amount of error in equating, indexed by the SEE, varies according to the equating design and method. As with any standard error, the SEE decreases as sample size increases. The SEE also varies across the range of scores, with each score point having a different SEE. Scores in the middle of the distribution typically have less equating error than scores at the extremes of the score range. The single-group design results in the lowest amount of equating error; the random-groups design typically results in the largest amount of equating error; and the common-item nonequivalent groups design is somewhere in between, as long as scores on the common items are highly correlated with scores on the full test. Equating methods that require estimation of the fewest quantities generally result in the least equating error. Thus, mean, linear, and equipercentile equating result in progressively increasing amounts of equating error. Equating error is an index of the precision of estimates, however, which is sometimes at odds with the accuracy of estimates. When accuracy is the criterion, more complex methods often trump less complex methods, resulting in the commonly encountered trade-off between accuracy and precision. Overall, there is no simple answer to the question of which method of equating to choose. It is perfectly acceptable to try out different methods and compare them in terms of the reasonableness of their results.

EXERCISES

1. What is the difference between test equating and

   a. vertical scaling?

   b. linking?

2. Could the following pairs of tests be equated? Why or why not?

   a. Two parallel versions of a reading comprehension test

   b. Two personality tests that are based on different theories of personality

   c. Two tests of motor development, one for children up to 6 months of age and one for children aged 3 to 3 ½

3. State one advantage and one disadvantage of the following equating designs:

    a. Single-group design

    b. Random-groups design

    c. Common-item nonequivalent groups design

4. Use the data in Table 18.9 to equate an X score of 55 to the Y score scale using:

    a. mean equating

    b. linear equating

TABLE 18.9. Equating Data for Questions 4 and 5

	Mean	SD	Skewness	Kurtosis
Test X ($n = 4,000$)	50.40	8.35	−1.25	1.75
Test Y ($n = 3,800$)	52.50	6.25	0.61	1.05

5. For the data in Question 4, which method of equating (mean, linear, or equipercentile) would be most accurate?

6. What is the "synthetic population" used in the common-item nonequivalent groups equating design? Why is the synthetic population needed?

7. What are the assumptions underlying the Tucker method of linear equating for the common-item nonequivalent groups design?

8. What is the motivation underlying the Levine observed score method of linear equating for the common-item nonequivalent groups design?

The data in Table 18.10 are IRT item parameters from two hypothetical three-item tests. Use these data to answer Questions 9–12.

TABLE 18.10. IRT Parameters for Questions 9–12

	Form X			Form Y		
Item	a	b	c	a	b	c
1	0.4	−1.0	0.15	0.7	−1.3	0.2
2	1.0	0.5	0.20	1.2	0.6	0.3
3	1.3	2.0	0.11	1.4	2.2	0.1
Mean	0.9	0.5	0.15	1.1	0.5	0.2
SD	0.37	1.22	0.04	0.29	1.43	0.082

9. Compute the scaling constants for the following IRT equating methods:

    a. The mean/mean method

    b. The mean/sigma method

10. Transform the *a*- and *b*-parameters for form X into the scale of form Y using:

    a. The mean/mean method

    b. The mean/sigma method

11. For the mean/sigma method, the mean and *SD* of the transformed *b*-parameters should be equal to which quantities in the table? Check your work to be sure this is the case.

12. For the mean/mean method, the means of the transformed *a*- and *b*-parameters should be equal to what quantities in the table? Check your work to be sure this is the case.

13. What is the standard error of equating?

14. Rank-order the following methods of equating by the sample size required: equipercentile, linear, mean.

15. Suppose that Feiming is equating data from two test forms. The data have fairly different distributional shapes, but Feiming feels the sample sizes available are not quite large enough to carry out equipercentile equating. What would you recommend Feiming do?

Answers to Exercises

CHAPTER 1

1.
   a. A test is a procedure for obtaining a sample of behavior for the purpose of measuring a construct of interest. The sample of behavior could consist of answers to test questions, behavioral observations, verbal responses to interview questions, or any other way of eliciting the behavior.

   b. A construct is a theoretical entity hypothesized to account for certain characteristics or behaviors.

2. Social science measures are based on limited samples of behavior because we cannot ask all possible questions or observe all instances of a behavior. There are usually multiple ways of measuring a construct, and none of these is necessarily "right." Different methods have different strengths and limitations. Finally, nearly all measurement in the social sciences contains some error, so our measures are, to some degree, approximations of the "true" level of the construct.

3.
   a. This is at the ordinal level of measurement because we cannot be sure the difference between "sometimes recycle" and "usually recycle" is the same as that between "usually recycle" and "always recycle." It does seem safe to say that the categories are ordered in terms of frequency of recycling, however, making this more than nominal measurement.

   b. This is at the nominal level of measurement because the numbers are serving only as labels for the different types of housing units.

c. Distance is at the ratio level of measurement because it has equal intervals *and* has an absolute zero point. Zero distance traveled to work is an absolute lack of any distance traveled.

4.

a. According to Stevens, this does constitute measurement because it assigns numbers (1, 2, 3) to objects (urban, suburban, and rural) according to rules (1 = urban, 2 = suburban, 3 = rural).

b. According to Michell's definition, this does not constitute measurement because (1) it is not quantitative as the numbers do not have additive or ratio relations and (2) even if they did, the measurement system does not provide a method of testing the quantitative properties of the measure.

5. Testing in ancient China was conducted for the purpose of selecting and promoting civil service officials. Test content was based on subjects such officials would need to know, such as military affairs, geography, and agriculture. Tests were written, and testing and scoring procedures were highly standardized. In ancient Greece, testing was performance based rather than written, and the purpose of testing was to determine if men were qualified for Greek citizenship. As in China, however, scoring procedures for physical tasks were highly standardized. Ancient Greek testing did include some mental tasks, but scoring procedures for these tasks were much less standardized than those for physical tasks.

6. Because psychology was quite a new science in the early 1800s, many of those studying psychology had been originally trained in "harder" sciences, in which physical measurements were, of course, the norm. It was therefore natural for these scientists to adapt the physical measures with which they were familiar for use in the new science of psychology. However, when scientists began to study the correlations of these mental tests with each other as well as with external criteria such as grades in school, results were quite disappointing. This was one factor leading to the eventual displacement of anthropometric measures in favor of measures of mental processes such as problem solving.

7. Binet had been interested for some time in measuring higher mental abilities such as reasoning and problem-solving ability and the ability to adapt to new conditions. During the first decade of the 1900s, Binet served as president of an organization seeking to determine the best way to educate what were then called "mentally retarded" children. The group realized that their first task was to develop a means of identifying such children, and Binet, with his colleague Simon, developed the first intelligence scale in answer to this need.

8. Robert Yerkes, as president of the American Psychological Association, led a committee to develop tests for army recruits. He chose Terman as a member of the committee and Terman introduced the testing materials developed by his student Arthur Otis. Otis's test was the first objectively scored test and included an early prototype of the multiple-choice item. Items from this test were used on the Army Alpha.

CHAPTER 2

1. Standardized scores are obtained by applying a linear transformation based on the mean and standard deviation of the norm group to the raw scores. The resulting distribution of scores will have the same distributional shape as that of the raw scores.

   Normalized scores are obtained by applying a nonlinear transformation to the raw scores that transforms the original distribution of scores to one that is normally distributed.

2. Raw scores are not independently interpretable. To interpret scores we need to know either how others performed (norm referencing) or what score(s) is(are) considered to represent different levels of performance (criterion referencing). Taken on its own, a raw score does not provide any information about relative or absolute performance.

3. The most relevant issues here are:

   a. The median GE for fourth graders is 4.0. This means that half of the fourth graders who took these tests scored below a GE of 4.0. So, a score below 4.0 is not unusual for fourth graders.

   b. A score of 3.0 or of 2.5 does not mean her son is "performing at the third- (or second-) grade level." Students in the fourth grade do not take the tests for second or third graders. A GE lower than grade level only means that the student performed in the lower half of students in that grade.

   c. GEs are obtained by interpolation, or estimation, based on scores at two or three points during the school year. For this reason, they are somewhat inaccurate and should be taken as approximations.

4. No, this is a common but incorrect interpretation. Students in each grade only take the test for their grade. Because of this, a GE of 9.8 for a fourth-grade student indicates that the student performed very well in comparison to other fourth graders. Although the student knows the fourth-grade content very well, this is not an indication that the student knows ninth-grade material, as he was not tested on that material.

5.
   a. Norm referenced

   b. Criterion referenced

   c. Criterion referenced

   d. Norm referenced

   e. Criterion referenced

6, 8, and 9.

Score	f	cf	%	$c\%$	PR	z-score	T-score
18	4	50	8	100	96	1.54	65.38
17	5	46	10	92	87	1.15	61.54
16	6	41	12	82	76	0.77	57.69
15	9	35	18	70	61	0.38	53.85
14	8	26	16	52	44	0.00	50.00
13	7	18	14	36	29	−0.38	46.15
12	4	11	8	22	18	−0.77	42.31
10	3	7	6	14	11	−1.54	34.62
9	2	4	4	8	6	−1.92	30.77
8	2	2	4	4	2	−2.31	26.92

7. The cumulative percentage is the percentage of scores in the score interval or below, whereas the percentile rank is the percentage of scores below the interval. In calculating the percentile rank, only half of the scores in the interval are included in the calculation.

10. There are two incorrect aspects of this statement. First, because percentile ranks are not on an interval scale, it is not appropriate to average them. Second, percentile ranks are not evenly spread across the score scale. This means that a percentile rank change at one point on the scale is associated with a different amount of change in scores than the same percentile rank change at another point on the scale. It is therefore inappropriate to compare percentile rank gains at different scale points.

11.

a. Normalized z- or T-scores, stanines, or normal curve equivalents (NCEs) could be used.

b. One justification for the use of a normalizing function is that the population distribution is normal but that a non-normal sample distribution was obtained due to the vagaries of sampling. In this case, however, the sample of employees was obtained through nonrandom selection methods and would be expected to yield a negatively skewed distribution of scores. The sample is therefore not representative of the broader population of employees, making the "sampling vagaries" justification inapplicable.

12.

a. Skewed; transformation to z-scores does not change the underlying distribution.

b. Skewed; transformation to T-scores does not change the underlying distribution.

c. Normal; transformation to stanines is a normalizing function.

d. Normal; transformation to NCEs is a normalizing function.

13.

 a. No. *PRs* associated with scores in the middle of the distribution increase more quickly from one score to another than do *PRs* for scores in the extremes of the distribution.

 b. No. The fact that *PRs* in the middle of the distribution change more rapidly than *PRs* in the extremes of the distribution means that the number of score points associated with a PR change from 50 to 57 will be associated with a *smaller* gain in scores points than a *PR* change from 90 to 97 (see Figure 2.1).

CHAPTER 3

1. In determining an appropriate item format, researchers must take into account the developmental and reading levels of the intended respondents as well as the degree to which the item format will tap into the construct being measured. Although essay items would be well suited for explaining number concepts, first-grade children are unlikely to have the writing skills needed. One possibility would be to use a performance assessment in which the children demonstrated number concepts using manipulable objects or drawings. If performance assessments are too time consuming, a series of true–false questions that increase in complexity of understanding could be devised. Children could be asked the questions in order of complexity, and a rough estimate of their levels of understanding could be based on the highest-level question they were able to answer.

2. There are an inordinate number of items at the synthesis and evaluation levels. Although first-grade students could likely evaluate different sandwich-making methods verbally, writing out answers to such items would probably tax their writing skills. Also, if the objective of the lesson is to teach students how to actually make a sandwich, there should be items at the application level.

3.

 a. Application

 b. Knowledge

 c. Comprehension

 d. Evaluation

4.

 a. Inference

 b. Recall

 c. Recall

 d. Evaluation

5.

 a. Commitment

 b. Receiving

   c. Responding

   d. Characterization

6. Rochelle could conduct focus groups in which students were asked how they felt about bullying. The advantage of this method is that the researcher could use the students' own words in developing the items. This would help to ensure that students would understand and relate to the items. One disadvantage would be that students with attitudes that differed from the group might be reluctant to speak up, and this could restrict the range of attitudes represented.

   A related method would be to conduct individual interviews with students. This method would avoid the "groupthink" that might result from a focus group. However, it would also be more time consuming.

   Rochelle could also search the literature for studies on bullying in middle schools and create items based on the findings of these studies. If this were done, she should make sure that the wording of the items reflected the language used by middle schoolers. This would entail an extra step in which middle school students are asked to comment on the items. This method would have the advantage of yielding a comprehensive view of bullying attitudes, assuming a comprehensive review of the literature were conducted. Ideally, more than one method would be used.

7.

   a. Increasing the sample size should result in more sampling stability.

   b. Increasing the sample size should result in a more representative sample, assuming the sampling is not conducted in a biased manner. However, there is a point of diminishing returns at which including more people in the sample will not increase representativeness.

8. On a pure speed test, the speed limit is so strict that examinees are not expected to finish all the items. On this type of test, the items are relatively easy, so the test is designed to measure fluency or speed of performance.

   On a pure power test, examinees are given as much time to answer as needed, but items are more difficult. This type of test is designed to measure the limits and depth of an examinee's knowledge or ability.

   One disadvantage of speed tests is that they can result in a great deal of guessing and/or careless responding.

CHAPTER 4

1.

   a. True. Taking test items verbatim from the text encourages memorization.

   b. False. The students are learning to memorize, not to think critically.

   c. False. The professor can only learn whether students can memorize facts or statements from the book. Because true–false items are used, the professor does not obtain feedback about *why* students answered as they did.

2. Selection-type items are those in which a set of possible answers that includes the correct answer is provided and the respondent must choose which is correct. An example is the multiple-choice item.

    Supply-type items are those in which the respondent must provide or fill in an answer. An example is a fill-in-the-blank item.

3. A set of matching items would be well suited to this type of material, in which factual associations (between composers and musical works) are tested. Although other formats could be used, matching items would be most efficient.

4.

   a. There are two flaws: option B, the correct answer, is longer than the other options and this may clue test-wise respondents that it is correct. Also, option D is not plausible.

   b. There are two flaws: option B, the correct answer, uses the same words ("specify" and "table") as the stem, thus cluing test-wise respondents that it is correct. Also, option C contains a grammatical clue that cannot be correct. It specifies two reasons, but the stem only asks for one.

5.

   a. Items should be phrased positively. If words such as *no* or *not* are used, they should be bolded or otherwise emphasized.

   b. This item is so vague and wishy-washy that it could hardly be false.

   c. Absolutes such as *never* and *always* should be avoided.

6.

   a. The item does not direct the respondent to the type of answer desired. Given the vagueness of the item, many different responses could be correct.

   b. The word *best* is somewhat vague. Does it refer to most accurate or most efficient (or both)?

7. An extended-essay question would be most appropriate because it would allow students more freedom to select supporting materials. The professor's interest is in assessing students' ability to make such choices. Thus, it would probably be best to put as few restrictions as possible on the answers.

8.

   a. A simulated task would be best, at least at the beginning stages of instruction. Using actual patients in this type of assessment would likely raise ethical concerns. However, this does not mean that real people could not be used. Other students or faculty could pose as patients for the assessment.

   b. Assuming that students' explanations should be correct and should be tailored to the level of the patient, correctness and ability to explain the procedure to patients at different levels would be important scoring criteria. Other criteria could include making sure the student gave the "patient" time to ask questions and asked if the "patient" understood.

591

CHAPTER 5

1. To answer this question, we must determine whether the researcher is interested in assessing a person's usual level of aesthetic appreciation, or in assessing the highest level of aesthetic appreciation a person has ever experienced. Most likely it is the former, and the researcher would be interested in assessing typical performance. However, it is possible the researcher is interested in assessing how much capacity a person has for aesthetic appreciation, or the highest level of appreciation of which a person is capable. In this case, the researcher would be interested in maximum performance.

2. Judges are asked to sort the set of items into categories (usually 11). The median rating category across judges is taken as the scale value for each item.

3. Likert felt that Thurstone's method was too "laborious" or time consuming. Likert did not obtain scale values from judges but instead created a common response scale from which respondents could choose a scale value commensurate with their attitude.

4.
   a. Both those with positive and negative attitudes could agree with this item.

   b. Factual.

   c. Too long, complicated, and difficult to understand.

   d. Refers to the past.

   e. Use of absolutes such as *never* and *always* should be avoided.

5. Probably not, because it would be difficult to arrange the items into a hierarchy from least to most favorable. For example, would those with favorable attitudes toward diversity feel it is more important to interact with other cultures or to know another language? The last item is most problematic as it is likely that many respondents who are ambivalent to diversity issues nevertheless enjoy eating foreign foods. Finally, the hierarchy should be such that those who agree with items at the top should agree with those below. If the first two items were at the top (although the order of these two is not clear), where would the third item fit in? Those agreeing with the first two items may not agree that everyone in the United States should learn English. The item would therefore not fit in the hierarchy.

6.
   a. Optimizing. The respondent has made an effort to obtain the relevant information from memory, even though this effort may not have been exhaustive.

   b. Satisficing. Although the respondent has put in some minimal effort, there has been no effort to remember his or her own hospitalizations.

   c. Optimizing. The respondent has accessed the relevant memories, even though he or she has not been able to remember completely accurately.

   d. Satisficing. The respondent has made no effort to remember his or her own behaviors.

7.

    a. Response editing

    b. Interpretation

    c. Response formatting and reporting

    d. Response generation

8. The maxim of quantity suggests that superfluous information should not be provided. Respondents may therefore assume that if information is provided, it is meant to be used. The maxim of relevance suggests that all information provided is relevant to the "conversation." Thus, respondents may assume that even information that does not seem necessary must be relevant in some way to obtaining the answer.

9.

    a. A tendency to agreement (or disagreement), regardless of item content.

    b. A tendency to choose the highest or lowest response option.

    c. A tendency to choose response options in the middle of the response scale.

    d. Deliberately representing oneself as more ill, disturbed, or pathological than is the case.

10. Labels clarify the meaning of the numbers on a response scale and should therefore yield more accurate responses. Also, respondents tend to be drawn to scale points that are labeled, so labeling only a few may bias responses.

11. Inclusion of a neutral option makes sense for situations in which respondents are likely to be truly neutral. Issues of on-campus parking, however, rarely evoke neutral responses, so the researcher could probably omit the neutral option from this scale.

CHAPTER 6

1. (a) Achievement tends to be normally distributed, so most scores on achievement tests would be in the middle of the score range. Difficulty values between 0.3 and 0.7 are also in the middle range, so items with these difficulty values would best match the achievement levels of most students. (b) Difficulty values of 0.5 yield the greatest variability in scores, and variability decreases as difficulties become higher or lower than 0.5. So, keeping the difficulty values in the middle range results in a test with optimal variability in scores.

2. (a) All incorrect answers are the result of guessing. (b) All guessing is random.

3. **Item 1**

$P = 4/36 = 0.11$

$D = 0/18 - 4/18 = -0.22$

Item 2

$P = 11/36 = 0.31$

$D = 6/18 - 5/18 = 0.06$

Item 3

$P = 30/36 = 0.83$

$D = 18/18 - 12/18 = 0.33$

Item 4

$P = 11/36 = 0.31$

$D = 8/18 - 3/18 = 0.28$

Item 5

$P = 7/36 = 0.19$

$D = 2/18 - 5/18 = -0.17$

4. Distractor D is negatively discriminating, attracting more students in the high group than the low group. Distractors A and C are working well, attracting students from the low group but not the high group.

5. **Item 1:** This item may be miskeyed (B may be the correct answer). This is because B is attracting more students from the high than from the low group and because many students from both groups are choosing this answer.

   Item 2: This is a difficult item. Approximately equal numbers of students in both groups are choosing the various response options. This indicates that respondents may be guessing.

   Item 3: The distractors are not attracting too many respondents, making this an easy item. This is not a problem if it was meant to be easy. If not, the distractors are not working well and should be rewritten.

   Item 4: Distractor C is negatively discriminating, with more students from the high than the low group choosing it. This item may have two correct answers (A and C) or may be miskeyed. However, because many students in the low group as well as in the high group have chosen C, it may simply be a very plausible, but incorrect, distractor.

   Item 5: This item may be miskeyed, with D as the actual correct answer. This item is more likely than item 4 to be miskeyed because most students in the high but not the low group are choosing D.

6. Both items 1 and 5 are negatively discriminating, which is the worst possible outcome in cognitive item analysis. Although both items are poor, item 1 is probably worst, as it is a little more negatively discriminating than item 5.

7. Items 8, 9, and 10 are the worst items on the scale (in order from worst to third worst).

   Item 8 has a very low and negative (−0.011) item–total correlation, indicating that it has an overall negative correlation with the other items on the scale (and perhaps should not have been reverse coded). If this item were deleted from the scale, coefficient alpha would increase to 0.889.

Item 9 has a very low (0.086) item–total correlation, indicating it is not related to the other items on the scale. If this item were deleted from the scale, coefficient alpha would increase to .873.

Item 10 has a low (0.208) item–total correlation, and coefficient alpha would increase to 0.866 if it were to be deleted from the scale.

8. **Item 8:** The wording of this item is "Same-sex marriage should not be legalized, but civil unions that provide tax benefits should be allowed in order to be fair." This item is somewhat double-barreled. It is against same-sex marriage but provides an "out" in the form of civil unions, and it even includes tax benefits. The main problem with the wording is that people who agree with same-sex marriage would disagree with this item, but so might people who are against same-sex marriage because some of those people would probably not like the idea of civil unions (especially with tax benefits) either. Thus, this item likely does not differentiate those with positive and negative attitudes.

   Item 9: Looking at the item's wording ("There is more support for same-sex civil unions in today's society then there was 30 years ago.") reveals the problem. This item refers to the past, which is a no-no in item writing, as most respondents will likely not know what people thought 30 years ago. If respondents do know, the item becomes a factual item about how much support there was 30 years ago, not about whether they personally support same-sex marriage.

   Item 10: The wording of this item ("Many people disapprove of same-sex marriages.") reveals a clear problem: it is not about one's own attitude; it is a factual statement about what other people think. Both those with positive and negative attitudes could therefore agree (or disagree), resulting in an item that does not discriminate.

9. **Item 8:** A large proportion (29, or 30.9%) of respondents chose the neutral option, and one person did not answer. This suggests that the item is confusing, which is supported by its wording.

   Item 9: Eighty percent of respondents agreed with this item (remember that the item is reverse coded, so response options 1 and 2 are really 5 and 4). It is therefore not surprising that the item is not a good discriminator.

   Item 10: Eighty-eight percent of respondents agreed with this item (it is reverse coded), resulting in poor discrimination.

10. Yes, nearly 35% of respondents chose the neutral option for item 7. Also, six respondents did not answer. Taken together, these findings suggest that the item is either confusing or difficult to answer.

    Items 8 (~31%) and 6 (~22%) also have relatively high percentages of neutral responses.

11.

    a. A negative kurtosis value indicates a distribution that is flatter than the normal distribution (known as a platykurtic distribution). A kurtosis value of –2.0 indicates a rectangular distribution in which each response option is chosen by the same number of respondents.

b. No, because in distributions with negative kurtosis responses are more spread out than in distributions with positive kurtosis (leptokurtic distributions), and a good spread of responses is generally desirable for affective items.

CHAPTER 7

1. X is the observed or actual score.

   T is a person's true score. This is a theoretical quantity but can be thought of as the score a person would obtain if the measurement were not affected by any type of error. In other words, it is a "pure" measure of a person's level of the construct.

   E is the random error score.

   X, T, and E are related as $X = T + E$. This equation indicates that a person's score is a simple additive function of their true and error scores.

2.
   a. The correlation between T and X should equal 1.0 if a test is perfectly reliable. In this case, there is no error component to a score, so $T = X$.

   b. In most cases, the variance of X will be larger than the variance of T. This is because the variance of X includes variance due to true scores and due to error scores. However, if the test is perfectly reliable, there is no error, so the variances of X and T will be equal.

3.
   a. The reliability index ρ_{xt} cannot be calculated from real data because we do not have the true scores; these are theoretical quantities.

   b. The reliability index is a measure of the degree to which true scores are consistent with, or related to, observed scores. Because reliability can be thought of as consistency (across items, occasions, raters, or test forms), the correlation between true and observed scores is a reasonable measure of reliability.

4. The logic is that the two observed scores are both made up of a true score and an error score. Because the error scores are assumed to be random, they cannot correlate with anything. So, if the observed scores correlate, it must be because their true scores are correlated.

5. Which of the following is a correct interpretation of a reliability coefficient (as defined in Equation 7.20) of 0.80? (choose all that are true)

   a. true

   b. false; the reliability coefficient is defined on a group of people; making statements about an individual's scores in this way is not justified.

   c. true

6. The items have different means and different variances and so cannot be parallel. Tau-equivalent items may have different variances but have equal means, so the items cannot be tau-equivalent. Congeneric items are the only type in which both means and variances can vary, so the items must be congeneric.

7. The means of tau-equivalent measures are equal; the means of essentially tau-equivalent items can differ by a constant amount.

8. c: parallel

9. c: underestimated

CHAPTER 8

1. Dataset 2 should have a higher value of coefficient alpha. In Dataset 1, there is no discernible pattern of responses across the six items. In Dataset 2, there is a relatively consistent pattern in which peoples' answers tend to be lower for the first few items than for the last few. This consistency in response patterns should yield a high value of coefficient alpha for Dataset 2.

2. Dataset 1 calculations:

$$r_{xx'} = \frac{k}{(k-1)}\left(1 - \frac{\sum\sigma_i^2}{\sigma_c^2}\right) = \frac{6}{5}\left(1 - \frac{(.77+1.21+1.38+2.67+1.61+.84)}{10.72}\right)$$

$$= \frac{6}{5}\left(1 - \frac{8.48}{10.72}\right) = \frac{6}{5}(.2089) = .25$$

Dataset 2 calculations:

$$r_{xx'} = \frac{k}{(k-1)}\left(1 - \frac{\sum\sigma_i^2}{\sigma_c^2}\right) = \frac{6}{5}\left(1 - \frac{(1.07+1.17+1.61+2.62+.90+.93)}{40.23}\right)$$

$$= \frac{6}{5}\left(1 - \frac{8.3}{40.23}\right) = \frac{6}{5}(.7937) = .95$$

3.
   a. Inconsistencies across responses to different items
   b. Inconsistencies across responses at different time periods
   c. Inconsistencies across responses to different forms

4. Both are measures of internal consistency reliability and are affected by inconsistencies across item responses. However, calculation of coefficient alpha is based on responses to all the items on the test and assumes that items are at least essentially tau-equivalent. Calculation of adjusted split-half reliability coefficients is based on only half the test items, and these items are assumed to be parallel.

5. Scores from a standardized achievement test should yield higher values for reliability because, by definition, these scores are obtained under highly standardized instructions, time limits, and other testing conditions. This type of standardization should decrease inconsistencies owing to differences in these conditions, which would otherwise contribute to measurement error. Classroom tests are typically administered under less standardized conditions, and fluctuations in time limits, instructions, and other conditions would therefore be more likely, resulting in more error.

6. A test of medium difficulty would result in more variability in test scores than a test with very low difficulty, and this should lead to higher values of internal consistency coefficients. Of course, this assumes that the increase in variability was due to true score rather than error variance.

7. A one-hour time interval may not be appropriate because it is likely that some test takers would benefit from practice on the first test and/or would remember the questions from the first testing. Also, such a short time interval would not provide much time for rest or recovery and could result in fatigue for some test takers. Any or all of these factors could affect the value of the reliability coefficient.

8. Alternate forms reliability is appropriate here because there are two forms of the test that are designed to measure the same thing. The best procedure would be to administer both tests to the same group of examinees. The order of the forms should be counterbalanced, with one group of examinees taking test A and then test B, and another group taking test B and then test A.

9. The fact that the social workers had very high altruism scores, on average, indicates that the range of these scores is restricted in this sample. Samples with restricted score ranges typically yield lower values of coefficient alpha than would be obtained from a less restricted score range because restriction of range results in lower score variability.

10. Because the officials are using the study skills scores to make decisions about placement and these decisions are made some time after the scores are obtained, it is important to know whether test scores are stable over this length of time. If they are not, the students may be incorrectly placed. This is particularly important for this situation because the placement decisions are somewhat consequential. If students obtain high enough scores, they are exempted from taking (and paying for) the study skills class.

11. The low ceiling for this test indicates that the range, or variability, of scores was restricted. As with the situation described in Question 7, such a restriction of range usually results in lower values for reliability coefficients.

12.
    a. The most likely reason is that students' actual levels of self-efficacy increased as a result of taking the course. The course can be thought of as a "treatment" that changed students' scores. However, some students likely changed more than others, resulting in inconsistent patterns of scores across the two time points.

    b. No, if the construct being measured is likely to change across the time interval of interest, test–retest reliability is inappropriate.

13. When the scores are highly correlated, people tend to change in the same direction and by the same amount. This means that everyone's change score is about the same. In this situation, it is difficult to differentiate people by their amount of change because these amounts are so similar across people. When scores have lower correlations, the amount (and possibly the direction) of change differs across people, so it is easier to differentiate people by their amount of change.

14. The 95% confidence interval is 55 +/– 5 * 1.96, or 45.2 – 64.8

15. No, the standard error of measurement is based on the tests' standard deviations as well as their reliability values. Unless we know the tests' standard deviations, we cannot determine their differences in reliability from their SEMs.

16.

a. *new reliability* $= \dfrac{2(0.8)}{1+(2-1)0.8} = 0.89$

b. *new reliability* $= \dfrac{3(0.8)}{1+(3-1)0.8} = 0.92$

c. *new reliability* $= \dfrac{0.5(0.8)}{1+(0.5-1)0.8} = 0.67$

Note that the increase in the reliability value for a 30-item test is not much more than that for a 20-item test, illustrating that there is a point of diminishing returns when adding items to a test (especially if the test is already fairly reliable).

CHAPTER 9

1. Interrater agreement indices measure the degree to which different raters provide the same rating, whereas indices of interrater reliability measure the degree to which raters' ratings result in the same rank order of people.

2. For each of the following situations, indicate whether interrater reliability or interrater agreement is most appropriate.

   a. Interrater reliability, because interest is in similarity of rank ordering.

   b. Interrater agreement, because interest is in whether the trainees provide the same ratings as (or are in agreement with) the experts.

   c. Interrater reliability, because it does not matter if the raters provide the same ratings as long as they rank-order the employees in the same way.

3. $P_0 = \dfrac{1}{N} \sum_{i=1}^{c} n_{ii} = \dfrac{1}{40} \sum_{i=1}^{c} (5+14+8+7) = 0.85$

4. First, calculate the chance agreement as

$$P_c = \frac{1}{N^2} \sum_{i-1}^{c} (n_{i+})(n_{+i}) = \frac{1}{40^2} (8*7)+(19*18)+(13*15)+(10*10)$$

$$= \frac{1}{1600} (56+342+195+100) = \frac{693}{1600} = 0.43$$

Then calculate kappa as

$\kappa = \dfrac{P_0 - P_c}{1-P_c} = \dfrac{0.85-0.43}{1-0.43} = \dfrac{0.42}{0.57} = 0.74$ (remember that P_0 is 0.85, from the previous question).

599

5. Nominal agreement will be higher than kappa to the extent that chance agreement (P_C) is greater than zero. This is because kappa corrects for chance agreement, which will always make the value of kappa smaller (unless chance agreement is zero).

6. This is referred to as a halo effect, in which a rater tends to give higher ratings to those who have done well in the past.

7. A criterion-related agreement is a type of agreement measure in which ratings are compared to those of an expert or to some external standard. This type of agreement is often of interest in training situations, in which ratings of trainees are compared to those of an expert rater to determine whether the trainees are rating correctly.

8. Coefficient alpha can be obtained from rating data by treating the raters as items and calculating alpha as usual. This procedure will yield the same value as the intraclass correlation for consistency in the two-way random design.

9.

   a. Raters are crossed with employees because each rater rates each employee. Raters could be considered random because the raters used every six months are a random subset of the possible raters.

   b. Parents only rate their own child, so raters (parents) are nested within children. Raters are fixed because children will always be rated by the same parents (their own).

   c. Raters are nested within teachers because a different pair of raters rates each teacher.

10.

   a. Absolute ICC for a two-way random design, single rating is

   $$\frac{MS_B - MS_E}{MS_B + (k-1)MS_E + \frac{k}{n}(MS_R - MS_E)} = \frac{6.00 - 0.50}{6.00 + (4-1)0.50 + \frac{4}{15}(8 - 0.50)}$$

   $$= \frac{5.50}{6.00 + 1.50 + 2.00} = 0.58$$

   b. Absolute ICC of a two-way random design, average rating is

   $$\frac{MS_B - MS_E}{MS_B + \frac{(MS_R - MS_E)}{n}} = \frac{6.00 - 0.50}{6.00 + \frac{(8.00 - 0.50)}{15}} = \frac{5.50}{6.00 + 0.50} = 0.85$$

11. The ICCs for average ratings should be higher than those for single ratings. This is because an average rating is based on several ratings and will therefore be more stable than a single rating.

12. ICCs for a consistency decision should be higher than those for an absolute decision. This is because raters are not considered to be a source of error for consistency decisions, so the denominator of the ICC formula is smaller and the ICC value larger than for absolute decisions.

CHAPTER 10

1. The applicants are the objects of measurement.

2. There are two facets: elements (with three levels) and raters (with four levels).

3. All applicants complete each element and each element is rated by each rater, so the design is completely crossed.

4. This is not completely clear from the information provided. The three elements used may be the only three elements that are either possible or of interest. If so, elements is a fixed facet. However, if there are other elements candidates could have been asked to complete, and the three chosen are a subset of this broader set of elements, elements is a random facet. Raters are probably random, as it is unlikely that the four raters used are the only ones that would ever be used. If they were, however, raters would be fixed.

5. The sources of variance are:

   - Variance due to applicants, or universe score variance. This is a measure of the amount of score variability across applicants.

   - Variance due to elements. This is a measure of the amount of variability across elements, or the degree to which scores vary across elements, on average.

   - Variance due to raters. This is a measure of the amount of variability across raters, or the degree to which scores vary across raters, on average.

   - Variance due to the applicant by element interaction. This is a measure of the degree to which applicants score differentially across elements. For example, some applicants may score highest on the written essay and others on the elevator pitch.

   - Variance due to the applicant by rater interaction. This is a measure of the degree to which raters rate applicants differentially. For example, Raters A and B may give their highest ratings to different applicants, resulting in differential ratings of these applicants across raters.

   - Variance due to the element by rater interaction. This is a measure of the degree to which raters rate the elements differentially. For example, Rater A may tend to rate the essay most highly, whereas Rater B tends to rate the presentation most highly.

   - Variance due to the three-way interaction of applicants, elements, and raters. This is a measure of the degree to which applicants are rated differentially across both elements and raters. This is the highest order interaction in the design, so it is combined with the residual variance.

6. A relative decision is one in which comparisons of a person's score to the scores of others is of interest, whereas in an absolute decision, interest is in comparing a person's score to a standard of performance, such as a mastery cutoff score. For relative decisions, only interactions of persons with facets are considered error. For absolute decisions, all sources of variation except variation due to persons are considered error.

7. The purpose of a G study is to estimate the amount of variation that is likely to be contributed by each facet (and by persons). In a D study, this information is used to determine how many levels of each facet are needed to obtain adequate levels of dependability. In the D study, designs with different levels of the facets can be "tried out" to determine the combination that will yield the highest level of dependability, given the resources available.

8.

	G study		D studies		
$n'_r =$	1	3	3	5
Source of variation	$n'_t =$	1	3	4	5
Persons (p)		1.03	1.03	1.03	1.03
Raters (r)		0	0	0	0
Tasks (t)		0.06	0.02	0.02	0.01
Pr		0.47	0.16	0.16	0.09
Pt		0.12	0.04	0.03	0.02
Rt		0.01	0.00	0.00	0.00
(prt,e)		0.64	0.07	0.05	0.03
Relative error variance $(\hat{\sigma}^2_{ABS})$		1.23	0.27	0.24	0.14
Absolute error variance $(\hat{\sigma}^2_{REL})$		1.30	0.29	0.26	0.15
G		0.46	0.79	0.81	0.88
ϕ		0.44	0.78	0.80	0.87

Calculations for three raters and three tasks are:

a. $\hat{\sigma}^2_{REL} = \dfrac{\hat{\sigma}^2_{pr}}{n_r} = \dfrac{\hat{\sigma}^2_{pt}}{n_t} + \dfrac{\hat{\sigma}^2_{prt,e}}{n_r n_t} = \dfrac{0.471}{3} + \dfrac{0.119}{3} + \dfrac{0.641}{3(3)} = 0.157 + 0.040 + 0.071 = 0.268$

$G = \dfrac{\hat{\sigma}^2_p}{\hat{\sigma}^2_p + \hat{\sigma}^2_{REL}} = \dfrac{1.03}{1.03 + .268} = 0.79$

$\hat{\sigma}^2_{ABS} = \dfrac{\hat{\sigma}^2_r}{n_r} + \dfrac{\hat{\sigma}^2_t}{n_t} + \dfrac{\hat{\sigma}^2_{pr}}{n_r} + \dfrac{\hat{\sigma}^2_{pt}}{n_t} + \dfrac{\hat{\sigma}^2_{rt}}{n_r n_t} \dfrac{\hat{\sigma}^2_{prt,e}}{n_r n_t} = \dfrac{0}{3} + \dfrac{0.061}{3} + \dfrac{0.471}{3} + \dfrac{0.119}{3} + \dfrac{0.012}{9} + \dfrac{0.641}{3(3)}$

$= 0 + 0.020 + 0.157 + 0.040 + 0.001 + 0.071 = 0.289$

$\phi = \dfrac{\hat{\sigma}^2_p}{\hat{\sigma}^2_p + \hat{\sigma}^2_{ABS}} = \dfrac{1.03}{1.03 + 0.289} = 0.78$

9. If tasks had been nested within raters, it would not be possible to estimate the variance due to tasks separately from the task by rater interaction variance. Thus, although it would be possible

to determine how an increase in the number of tasks would change the G and phi coefficients, it would not be possible to determine whether these changes were due to decreases in the variance due to tasks or in the variance due to the task by rater interaction (or both).

10. If tasks had been a fixed facet, the variance component due to tasks would not be estimable. Any variance components due to interactions of tasks with persons or with any other facet would also be inestimable.

CHAPTER 11

1. The fact that a test measures what it's supposed to measure does not guarantee that the test will be useful for any purpose. Tests are typically designed with some purpose in mind, and this is why current definitions of validity include the degree to which a test is useful for the intended purpose. Another problem with the definition given is that it is often difficult to determine if a test is measuring what it's supposed to measure. This is because most constructs being measured in the social sciences are difficult to define, making validity issues more complex than the simple determination of whether or not a construct is measured by a test.

2. The traditional "types" of validity—content, criterion-related, and construct—have been termed, somewhat facetiously, the "tripartite" view of validity. According to this view, these three types of validity were appropriate in different situations, depending on what was being measured. Theorists such as Loevinger and Messick argued against this conceptualization on the grounds that all "types" of validity inform the meaning and use of test scores and that dividing these into different "types" appropriate for different situations introduced an artificial trichotomy. Instead, they argued, different types of validity evidence provide complementary information relevant to score use and interpretation. A more pragmatic argument against the tripartite view is that the separation of validity into three different "types" led researchers to obtain the three types of evidence without giving much, if any, thought about how these might inform our understanding of the meaning and use of scores.

3. It does seem possible that construct-irrelevant variance could undermine the validity of score interpretations for this test. For example, those who are quick thinkers, or simply fast writers, would likely obtain high scores on the "number of ideas" scale. However, these high scores may not necessarily indicate high levels of problem-solving imagination (PSI).

   The choice of scenarios to which test takers respond could also result in some construct-irrelevant variance. This could occur if some test takers were more familiar with a particular scenario, or set of scenarios, than other test takers. Suppose that some test takers had just had a class in current events in which they had studied similar problems to those posed in the PSI scenarios. These test takers would presumably be able to generate more and better ideas. However, would these ideas indicate more problem-solving imagination or simply more knowledge about the content in these scenarios?

4. To some extent, the answer to this question depends on the test developer's definition of problem-solving imagination. If an important aspect of that definition were not covered by the PSI material, construct underrepresentation would be likely. Without having a more detailed definition, we cannot really tell whether this is the case. However, an argument could be made that the choice of scenario could impact construct representation. For example, suppose that all the scenarios used related to problems of pollution. Although

certainly an important problem, pollution is not the only problem in need of solution. Of course, time constraints would preclude the inclusion of every possible problem, but an effort should be made to include a representative set of problems. If this is not done, construct underrepresentation could undermine the validity of scale scores.

5. We do not know the test developer's specific theories about why and to what extent creativity, problem solving, and imagination should be related to PSI scores. This makes it difficult to judge the persuasiveness of the evidence given. Ideally, the developer of the PSI would have clearly laid out his theories about how high the correlations should be and why. Lacking this (as is, unfortunately, common in most validity evidence), we can only say that positive correlations of PSI scores with creativity, problem solving, and imagination are reasonable to expect, based on previous research on these constructs. The magnitude of the correlations is more difficult to judge. The correlation of PSI scores with scores on a problem-solving scale seem somewhat low, given that both involve problem solving. However, the PSI measures problem-solving *imagination*, whereas the problem-solving scale with which it was correlated may measure problem-solving *ability* or problem solving in a broader context. If so, the lower correlation seems reasonable.

It would be also be useful to have information on the makeup and size of the samples from which these correlations were obtained. Restriction of range, nonrepresentative samples, and small sample sizes may all have affected the results.

6. Evidence based on response processes provides an indication of the degree to which test items elicit the intended responses and do not elicit unintended responses. For the PSI, we may want to know that test takers understood the tasks and scoring criteria. For example, it would be important to know that test takers understood they would have a limited amount of time to answer and that their scores would be based, in part, on the number of ideas they provided. Ideally, the test developer would have developed a cognitive model of the mental processes involved in generating ideas. This model could be tested by experimentally varying features of the scenarios thought to affect these mental processes. For example, the test developer might hypothesize that longer scenarios would engender more ideas because longer scenarios suggest more idea possibilities. But the test developer might also hypothesize that those ideas would have lower likelihoods of success because longer scenarios would likely be more complicated and thus more difficult to solve. It would also be more difficult for test takers to keep the relevant details of longer scenarios in memory. These hypotheses could be tested by manipulating scenario length in an experimental study.

7.

a. In judging evidence based on internal structure (or any evidence for validity, for that matter), it is important to know what type of results the test developer expected, based on theory. Ideally, the test developer would have stated those expectations clearly, and results could then be judged on the basis of how closely they match expectations. As with most real-life descriptions of validity evidence, however, we do not have that information. So, we can only make general statements about the magnitude of these correlations and possible reasons for them.

One thing to note is that the interrater agreement coefficients for the Creativity and Success scales are fairly low. This is not surprising, as these aspects are likely difficult to score. However, the low agreement values will attenuate the correlations of scores on these two scales to some extent.

The correlation between Number and Creativity is by far the highest, at .68. It may be that both scores are, to some degree, measures of creativity. That is, those high in creativity may well generate many ideas, and these ideas would likely be creative. Without knowing more about the theory underlying the scale, however, we cannot say much more.

b. Again, we are hampered by lack of knowledge of the test developer's theory. However, as noted earlier, correlations involving the Creativity and Success scales are likely attenuated owing to their low interrater agreement. The correlation between Number and Success may be low because, in their effort to generate many ideas, test takers include ideas that are simply not reasonable. (As an aside, this could reveal a flaw in the Number scale.) One possible reason for the low correlation between the Creativity and Success scales is that, if ideas are too creative, they may not be successful. For example, in response to a scenario involving how to cut down on pollution, a test taker might suggest the following idea: *Trees are known to absorb air pollutants, but the ground can only hold so many trees. However, if trees could simply float in the air, innumerable trees could be "planted," and these trees could absorb a large amount of pollutants.* Although this idea is intriguing and quite creative, you may have noted some logistical issues that may curtail its success. First, although aeroponic growing systems are possible, these require some means of supporting the plants being grown. Free-floating systems have yet to be invented, to my knowledge. Second, floating trees would very likely infringe on the air space of many other objects, such as airplanes.

8. The test developer specifically stated that the PSI is to be used for research purposes and *not* for purposes of selection or classification. Given this purpose, evidence that the PSI is predictive of a particular outcome is probably not crucial. Even so, if the test developer's theory suggests that PSI scores should be predictive of scores on another scale, or should differentiate among particular groups, evidence of such relations would inform our understanding of PSI score meaning and would therefore be useful. For example, suppose the test developer hypothesized that scientists would have higher PSI scores than accountants. Evidence for this hypothesis would provide more information on the meaning of PSI scores.

9. The PSI is not a high-stakes test with consequences for any given individual. However, the test developer does recommend its use in research. If the PSI is used in research and PSI scores are not truly indicative of problem-solving imagination, results from the research could be misleading. This would have a negative effect on scientific inquiry in this area, possibly setting research back many years and wasting research dollars. On the positive side, if the PSI yields valid scores of problem-solving imagination, research in this area would be enhanced by its use. Researchers may use the PSI in studies to increase people's problem-solving imagination, ultimately resulting in more problems being solved.

10. In this case, the possible consequences are more serious for individuals. Gaining admittance to a gifted program typically results in more educational opportunities and may ultimately lead to better career choices. Thus, admission to such a program can have very positive consequences for some. On the flip side, some students would not be admitted, producing a negative consequence. On a broader level, it could be argued that society benefits when greater opportunities are provided to students, especially if these students have the capacity to benefit from these opportunities and ultimately use the skills and knowledge obtained to benefit society. This is clearly a positive consequence. However, a

possible negative consequence is that those who are not admitted to the gifted program may have had the capacity to provide just as much (or even more) benefit to society but were unable to do so because of lack of training opportunities.

CHAPTER 12

1. EFA is useful for investigating the hypothesized dimensionality of a scale or set of variables, for generating theories about the reasons for variable intercorrelations, and for verifying theories about dimensionality. EFA can be used to answer questions about how many dimensions, or factors, there are and which variables are associated with each factor.

2. The u term represents the unique or unshared variance of each variable. It contains a mixture of random error, or unreliability, and specific variance owing to the fact that each variable is tapping into an aspect of the construct that is somewhat different from the other variables.

3. There would likely be three factors because there are three sets of variables (X_1–X_3, X_4–X_6, and X_7–X_9) that are highly correlated among themselves but not highly correlated across sets.

4. Even though the correlations across variables in the three sets (X_1–X_3, X_4–X_6, and X_7–X_9) are relatively small, correlated factors would provide the best fitting factor model. This is because in an uncorrelated factor model the correlations across sets would be assumed to be zero.

5. The Path diagram is shown below.

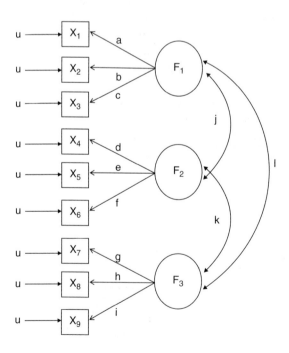

Squares indicate observed variables; circles indicate latent variables.

Single-headed arrows indicate directional paths; double headed arrows indicate nondirectional paths.

The u's are the uniquenesses.

6. a. $a * c$

    b. $c * j * f^1$

    c. $e * k * h$

7. In PAF, the reduced correlation matrix is analyzed. The reduced matrix is one in which the 1's on the diagonal are replaced with communality estimates. Because the reduced matrix is analyzed, only the shared variance among variables is included in the analysis. In PCA the full correlation matrix with 1's on the diagonal is analyzed. Because the full matrix is analyzed, both the shared and unshared variances are analyzed. These differences between the two analyses results in higher loading coefficients, eigenvalues, and explained variance for PCA than for PAF.

8. The percentage of explained variance is calculated as the factor's eigenvalue divided by the number of variables, and multiplied by 100, or 5.399/10 * 100 = 53.99%. This value indicates that Factor 1 accounts for about 54% of the variance in the variables.

9. Even though this is a PAF analysis, the percentages of variance under "initial eigenvalues" are calculated from the full correlation matrix, with 1's on the diagonal. The percentages of variance under "extraction sums of squared loadings" are calculated by summing the squared loadings for each variable across all the extracted factors, dividing by the number of variables and multiplying by 100. This is done because the quantities under "extraction sums of squared loadings" are based on the reduced correlation matrix and the eigenvalues of the reduced matrix do not have to be positive. To avoid the problem of negative eigenvalues, the sums of squared loadings from the extracted factors are used in place of the eigenvalues. Because these values are based on the reduced matrix and the quantities under "initial eigenvalues" are based on the full matrix, the former are smaller than the latter.

10. Two factors would be extracted because two of the initial eigenvalues are greater than 1.0.

11. The number of factors associated with the highest Hull test value (referred to as the Scree test value in the results shown) is chosen. For these data, one factor is suggested.

12. An argument could be made for either one or two factors. A fairly straight line could be drawn from the second point through the rest of the points, suggesting one factor. However, an even straighter line could be drawn from the third point through the last point, suggesting two factors. The points after the third fall in a fairly straight line, so no more than two factors are suggested.

13. Because the K1 criterion is least accurate, based on simulation studies, and the Hull method and scree plot (when interpreted correctly) are more accurate, I would put more weight

---

[1] Although not covered in Chapter 12, another of Wright's tracing rules is that only one double-headed arrow is allowed per path. This means that we cannot trace from X_3 to X_6 using the paths c*l*k*f. The same rule holds for (c).

on the latter two methods. Hull suggests one factor and the scree plot suggests either one or two, so I would choose one factor but would also obtain a two-factor model. I would compare the results of the one- and two-factor models in terms of fit with theoretical expectations and evidence of under- or overfactoring, and choose the model that seemed most reasonable based on these criteria.

14. An orthogonal solution forces the factors to be uncorrelated, whereas an oblique solution allows the factors to be correlated but does not force them to be. That is, if the factors are truly uncorrelated, an oblique rotation will yield factors with a correlation of zero (or close to zero).

15. From the pattern matrix, it is clear that items 1, 2, 4, 6, and 7 load on Factor 1 and 3, 5, 8, 9, and 10 load on Factor 2. The set of variables loading on Factor 1 are all positively oriented, and the set of variables loading on Factor 2 are all negatively oriented. This solution is therefore a perfect illustration of a method effect, in which positively and negatively oriented items form separate factors that appear to reflect the items' orientations rather than their content. The solution is somewhat confusing because the positively oriented items have negative loadings and the negatively loading items have positive loadings. However the loading signs are arbitrary.

16. When an oblique rotation is used, as in this example, two coefficient matrices are obtained: a pattern and a structure matrix. The coefficients in the pattern matrix are measures of the correlation between the variable and the factor, with the effects of any other factors partialed out. For example, the value of -0.908 for item 2 on Factor 1 indicates that item 2 and Factor 1 are correlated at -0.908, partialing out Factor 2. The coefficients in the structure matrix are measures of the correlation between the variable and the factor (not partialing out the other factors).

The more highly correlated the factors, the more difference there will be between the pattern and structure coefficient values. In the extreme case, when the factors are uncorrelated, the pattern and structure coefficient values are the same (which is why only one coefficient matrix is obtained for orthogonal solutions).

CHAPTER 13

1.

   a. δ represents a measurement error.

   b. ξ represents a latent factor.

   c. λ represents a factor loading (pattern) coefficient.

2.

   a. $\lambda_{21}*\phi_{11}*\lambda_{31}$ $X_2 X_3$ covariance

   b. $\lambda_{42}*\phi_{32}*\lambda_{93}$ $X_4 X_9$ covariance

   c. $\lambda^2_{52}*\phi_{22} + \theta_{\delta5}$ X_5 variance

3. Model-Implied Loadings

Variable	F1	F2	F3
X_1	λ_{11}	0	0
X_2	λ_{21}	0	0
X_3	λ_{31}	0	0
X_4	0	λ_{42}	0
X_5	0	λ_{52}	0
X_6	0	λ_{62}	0
X_7	0	0	λ_{73}
X_8	0	0	λ_{83}
X_9	0	0	λ_{93}

4. It is diagonal because no measurement error covariances (which would be indicated by curved arrows between pairs of measurement errors) are shown in the path diagram.

5. According to Bollen (1989), a CFA model is identified if (1) it has at least three indicators per factor, (2) each variable loads on only one factor (e.g., there are no cross-loadings), and (3) there are no measurement error covariances. All three conditions are met, so the CFA model is identified.

6. Model degrees of freedom are equal to the number of covariances among the observed variables minus the number of parameters to be estimated. With nine variables, there are 9(10)/2, or 45 covariance elements. The parameters to be estimated are:

   - nine loadings
   - nine measurement error variances
   - three factor covariances (actually these are correlations because factor variances are set to 1.0)

   This makes a total of 21 parameters to be estimated. Degrees of freedom are therefore 45–21 or 24.

7. This does not change the degrees of freedom; now the three factor variances are estimated, but three loadings are not estimated, so the number of parameters to be estimated remains the same. The number of covariances is also the same, as the number of variables has not been changed, so the degrees of freedom are still 24.

8.
   a. The reproduced covariance matrix $\Sigma(\hat{\theta})$
   b. The identity matrix (or no weight matrix)
   c. The observed variable covariance matrix S
   d. The asymptotic covariance matrix (ACM) which adjusts for variable non-normality by including information about the kurtoses of the variables

9. Satorra–Bentler adjustments adjust the chi-square goodness-of-fit statistic and the standard errors of model parameter estimates for the effects of non-normality.

609

10. Yes, all are statistically significant as indicated by the p-values in the last column. These are all .000, meaning that the values are significantly different from 0 at less than the .001 level of significance.

11. The R^2 values for each item are not shown but can be obtained by a simple calculation.

    a. $(-0.683)^2 = 0.466$

    b. R^2 is the percentage of variance in the variable that is explained by the factor. For X_3 this is about 47%.

12. No, the only fix index value that suggests at least an adequate fit is the SRMR, based on commonly used guidelines. The SRMR value is the average of the standardized residuals, and values less than 0.08 are often taken to indicate an adequate model–data fit, although values less than 0.05 indicate a good fit.

    The chi-square value is statistically significant, as evidenced by the low p-value. This indicates that the observed and reproduced covariance matrices are significantly different. The comparative fit index compares the fit of the model to that of a null or baseline model. A commonly used cutoff value is 0.95, and the obtained value of 0.872 falls well below this, indicating a poor fit.
    The RMSEA is an estimate of the model lack of fit in the population. This index includes an adjustment for parsimony or for the fact that a model can be made to fit better by estimating more model parameters. Often used heuristics are that an RMSEA value less than 0.05 or 0.06 is an indication of good fit. The obtained value of .134 is well above these values, indicating a poor fit. Taken together, the fit index values do not indicate a good, or even an adequate, fit of the model. Although the SRMSR indicates adequate fit, this must be interpreted in the context of other fit indices, which clearly indicate a lack of fit. Researchers should also consider the possible reasons for the lack of fit.

13. Model residuals are the differences between elements of the observed and reproduced covariance matrices. A positive residual indicates that the observed covariance was higher than the reproduced covariance, or that the observed covariance was underpredicted by the model. A negative residual indicates that the observed covariance was lower than the reproduced covariance or was overpredicted. Standardized residuals are residuals that have been transformed to a z-score metric to make them easier to interpret. The fact that standardized residuals are all positive means that the covariances for the pairs of variables shown have all been underpredicted.

14. These residuals are all for pairs of positively oriented (R1, R2; R2, R4) or negatively oriented (R9, R10) items. They therefore appear to be due to positive/negative wording or method effects.

15. An EPC is an expected parameter change statistic. These values are estimates of what the parameter value would be if the parameter were added to the model. EPCs are in the metric of the original variables, whereas completely standardized EPC values are obtained by standardizing both the observed and latent variables.

16. MIs (modification indices) and residuals will not usually result in similar rank ordering of variable pairs but will often flag the same variables or variable pairs as problematic. One reason is that the completely standardized residuals are affected by the variable standard deviations as well as the discrepancies between the observed and reproduced covariance elements.

17. Adding parameters to a model on the basis of residuals and MIs capitalizes on chance because it amounts to "data peeking," or changing one's hypotheses (represented by the model) after looking at the data. Another problem with MIs is that simulation studies have shown they do not necessarily suggest adding the parameters that are causing the problem, unless the sample size is very large. A related problem is that a misspecification may be due to more than one variable, which is difficult to detect from MIs and residuals.

CHAPTER 14

1. a is the discrimination or slope parameter; b is the difficulty parameter, and c is the lower asymptote or guessing parameter

2. The IRF is usually S-shaped because the probability of a correct answer does not increase linearly with ability. The probability of a correct answer is low for examinees below the requisite ability level, increases sharply at the point where item difficulty matches examinee ability, and then levels off for examinees with more than the requisite amount of ability.

3.
   a. Dataset C

   b. Dataset A

   c. Dataset B

4. Item 5 has the highest difficulty (about 1.5); to have a probability of 0.50 of answering this item, examinees must have an ability of about 1.5, which is higher than that of any other item.

5. Item 3 is the most discriminating as it has the steepest slope.

6. Approximately 0.55 to 0.60 (the exact value is 0.575).

7. A score of 1 is most likely as it has the highest probability at $\theta = -0.5$.

8. In the PC model, values of the discrimination parameter are equal across items, whereas in the GPC the discrimination parameters can vary across items.

9. The ML estimate of θ is approximately 0.9 because the likelihood function is highest at this point.

10. The MAP estimate of θ would be lower than the ML estimate for this examinee. This is because the MAP estimate is pulled toward the mean of the prior distribution of 0. Because the ML estimate of 0.9 is above the mean of the prior distribution, it would be pulled downward toward the prior distribution mean of 0. If the MAP estimate had been below the prior distribution mean, it would have been pulled upward.

11. The test information is highest at approximately $\theta = 1$, so the standard error of measurement is lowest at that point.

12. The test would be best suited for classifying students as passing or failing based on a cut score of 1 because information is highest at that point. Note that information is quite low at some points on the ability range, so accurate scores would not be obtained at all θ points.

13. Test developers could increase the information for low-ability examinees by adding some easier items. This is because easier items would more closely match the examinees' abilities and would therefore provide more information for them.

14. Tests with more information yield more reliable scores. But whereas reliability is estimated at the group level, test information varies across levels of θ.

15.
 a. Correct dimensionality means that the model used is one that corresponds to the dimensionality of the data. If the data are unidimensional, a unidimensional IRT model can be used. If not, a multidimensional IRT model should be used.

 b. Local independence means that the items are independent of each other, conditional on (or controlling for) θ.

 c. Functional form means that the correct model is being applied to the data. For example, if item discrimination parameters are not equal, the 1PL/Rasch model should not be used.

16.
 a. Both correct dimensionality and local independence are violated here. The test data are multidimensional, and so they should not be modeled as unidimensional. The violation of correct dimensionality also means that items will not be locally independent after controlling for θ because a dimension other than θ can cause them to correlate.

 b. Functional form is violated because a model that accommodates guessing should be used.

 c. Strictly speaking, correct dimensionality and local independence are violated, but if the general factor is much stronger than the minor factors, this violation may not be very consequential.

CHAPTER 15

1.

Model	Observed response variable type	Latent predictor variable type
Factor analysis	Continuous	Continuous
IRT	Categorical (binary usually)	Continuous
DCM	Categorical (binary usually)	Categorical (binary usually)

2. First, that the attributes are defined prior to analysis (i.e., the latent classes are defined prior to analysis). This includes defining how many attributes and operationalizing each attribute. Second, which attribute(s) are measured by each item is defined prior to analysis (i.e., the Q-matrix is specified before analysis).

3. This means the model predicts that it is more likely for examinees who have mastered neither of the required attributes to correctly answer item 1 than to correctly answer item 2. In other words, it is easier for nonmasters of the required attributes to guess the correct answer on item 1 than on item 2.

4. Yes, if the intercept is too large, there is a high probability that even if the examinees have not mastered the required attributes, they will answer the item correctly. For example, an intercept of 0 indicates that nonmasters of the required attributes still have a 50% chance of answering the item correctly. This would be inconsistent with the theory behind the model: examinees who do not have the required attributes are not expected to answer the item correctly.

5. Yes, if the main effect is near zero, the item is not measuring the attribute as it was intended to do. In other words, mastering the attribute does not impact the item response.

6. Only a master of Attribute 2, because the main effect for Attribute 2 is greater than the main effect of Attribute 1.

7. $$P\left(X_{e1}=1\,|\,\alpha_e\right)=\frac{\exp(\lambda_{i0}+\lambda_{i1(1)}(\alpha_{e1})+\lambda_{i1(2)}\left(\alpha_{e2}\right)+\lambda_{i2(1,2)}(\alpha_{e1}\alpha_{e2}))}{1+\exp(\lambda_{i0}+\lambda_{i1(1)}(\alpha_{e1})+\lambda_{i1(2)}(\alpha_{e2})+\lambda_{i2(1,2)}(\alpha_{e1}\alpha_{e2})}$$

Solution with numerical values for coefficients:

$$P\left(X_{e1}=1\,|\,\alpha_e\right)=\frac{\exp(-2+1(\alpha_{e1})+3\left(\alpha_{e2}\right)+2(\alpha_{e1}\alpha_{e2}))}{1+\exp(-2+1(\alpha_{e1})+3(\alpha_{e2})+2(\alpha_{e1}\alpha_{e2})}$$

8. The log-odds equals $-1 + 2 = 1$. The probability is equal to $e^1/1+e^1 = 0.731$.

9. The log-odds of an incorrect response is the negative of the log-odds of a correct response, so it is -1. You can check this answer by showing that $e^{-1}/1+e^{-1} = 0.269$, which is 1 minus the probability of a correct response found in part (c) (i.e., $1 - 0.731$). Also, Figure 15.1 shows that a probability of $1 - 0.731$, or of 0.269, corresponds to a log-odds of -1.

10. Item 4, because it has the largest intercept

11. $2^3 = 8$ attribute patterns

12. 2^A attribute patterns

13. Four: one for nonmasters of Attribute 1 and 2; one for masters of only Attribute 1; one for masters of only Attribute 2; and one for masters of both Attribute 1 and 2

14. Eight: one for each possible attribute pattern

15. Item 4 because the log-odds of a correct response for patterns that have one or more of the required attributes (i.e., patterns [1.0], [0.1], and [1.1]) are all equal to each other. (They are all equal to 1.5.) You can also tell because the main effects and interaction term all have the same value, with the interaction value being the negative of the main effect value.

16. [0.0], [1.0]. and [0.1] all have the same item response probability because they all have the same log-odds value of -0.5. The only pattern with a different item response probability is [1.1], the pattern in which examinees are masters of both Attributes 1 and 3. This item is a DINA-like item because all patterns that lack one or more of the required attributes have the same item response probability.

CHAPTER 16

1. Impact refers to any average difference in scores between two or more groups. Impact may or may not be due to unfairness or bias in the test or test items. Test bias is the systematic difference between the scores of two or more groups that have been matched on the construct being measured.

2. Slope bias because the relation, or slope, for the prediction of job performance from employment test scores is not the same for men and women. (Intercept bias may also exist, but there insufficient information is given in the item to determine this bias). This corresponds to the situation in either Panel 3 or Panel 4 of Figure 16.1.

3. Intercept bias; the fact that the relation between job performance and employment test scores is the same for women and men indicates that the prediction slopes are the same. However, performance is systematically underpredicted for women and systematically overpredicted for men, so the intercept for women must be higher than that for men. This corresponds to the situation depicted in Figure 16.1, Panel 2.

4. No test bias; if predictions are the same regardless of gender, there is no slope or intercept bias. This corresponds to the situation depicted in Figure 16.1, Panel 1.

5. DIF is a systematic difference in the probability of a correct response to an item for two (or more) groups that have been matched on ability.

6. The presence of DIF is a validity issue because it suggests that the item is measuring different things in the groups being compared. This is because the groups have been matched on ability, so differences in the groups' probabilities of a correct answer must be due to something other than the ability being measured.

7. Yes, because in each stratum the proportion of test takers obtaining a correct answer is much higher for the reference than for the focal group (36% and 17% for the reference and focal groups in Stratum 1, 43% and 17% in Stratum 2, and 57% and 33% in Stratum 3). Because dividing the test takers into strata based on ability essentially matches them on ability, these differences are evidence of DIF or item bias.

8. Intermediate calculations are shown in the table below.

	Stratum 1			Stratum 2			Stratum 3		
	Correct	Incorrect	Total	Correct	Incorrect	Total	Correct	Incorrect	Total
Reference	25	45	70	30	40	70	40	30	70
Focal	5	25	30	5	25	30	10	20	30
Total	30	70	100	35	65	100	50	50	100
ad/n	6.25			7.5			8		
bc/n	2.25			2			3		

$$\hat{\alpha}_{MH} = \frac{\sum_s a_s d_s / N_s}{\sum_s b_s c_s / N_s} = \frac{6.25 + 7.5 + 8}{2.25 + 2 + 3} = \frac{21.75}{7.25} = 3.0$$

This means that the odds of answering the item correctly for those in the reference group is 3 times the odds of those in the focal group.

9. $\Delta = -2.35 * ln\ (3.0) = -2.58$.

10. Intermediate calculations are shown in the table below.

	Stratum 1			Stratum 2			Stratum 3		
	Correct	Incorrect	Total	Correct	Incorrect	Total	Correct	Incorrect	Total
Reference	25	45	70	30	40	70	40	30	70
Focal	5	25	30	5	25	30	10	20	30
Total	30	70	100	35	65	100	50	50	100
E(a)	21			24.5			35		
Var(a)	4.45			4.83			5.30		

$$\chi^2_{MH} = \frac{\left[\left|\sum_s a_s - \sum_s E(a_s)\right| - 0.5\right]^2}{\sum_s Var(a_s)} = \frac{\left[|(25+30+40)-(21+24.5+35)|-0.5\right]^2}{(4.45+4.83+5.30)}$$

$$= \frac{[(95-80.5)-0.5]^2}{14.58} = \frac{14^2}{14.58} = 13.44$$

a. Yes, this is a chi-square value of 13.44 with one degree of freedom. The critical value at the 0.05 level of significance is 3.84, and the obtained value of 13.44 is above this (the actual p-value is 0.00025).

b. The significant chi-square value indicates that the proportion of test takers obtaining a correct answer is significantly different for the two groups after matching on ability level. Thus, there is statistically significant DIF for this item.

11. Level C DIF: | ΔMH | is 2.58, greater than 1.5, and χ^2_{MH} is statistically significant.

12. The LR tests in the table indicate that the groups differ on intercepts (difficulty) (LR test value comparing a model with X only to a model with X and G is 40 with 1 df, $p < 0.0001$) but not in slopes (discrimination) (LR test value comparing a model with X and G to a model with X, G, and XG is 2 with 1 df, $p = 0.1573$). This means that there is uniform DIF but no nonuniform DIF for this item.

13. Comparing the χ^2 value for configural invariance to the χ^2 value for metric invariance yields a difference χ^2 of 40 with 15 df. The p-value is 0.00045. This result indicates that (at least one) item loadings differ significantly across groups. Comparing the χ^2 value for metric

invariance to that for scalar invariance yields a difference χ^2 of 10 with 15 df. The p-value is 0.8197. This result indicates that item intercepts do not differ significantly across groups.

14. CFA and IRT methods are based on a similar conceptual framework in which sets of item parameter estimates are compared across groups. These comparisons are done by constraining parameter estimates to be the same across groups in a series of nested models. Chi-square (CFA) or G^2 (IRT) tests are obtained for each of the nested models. Comparisons of chi-square or G^2 values for models with and without parameter constraints provide tests of the invariance or noninvariance of parameter estimate values across groups. If parameter estimates are noninvariant, DIF is indicated. Both methods test for differences in item intercepts (CFA) or difficulties (IRT) and in item loadings (CFA) or discrimination parameters (IRT) by comparing nested models. Only IRT methods allow for testing a pseudo-guessing (c) parameter. Both methods match groups by scaling theta or the construct being measured in the same way across groups.

The methods differ in the way constraints are applied. In the CFA method, particular parameter estimates for all items are constrained. In the IRT method, parameter constraints for one item at a time are imposed. The methods also differ in the method of estimation used. This is because CFA is typically used with items on a continuous or Likert scale and use normal theory estimation methods appropriate for such data. IRT is typically used with dichotomously scored items and uses estimation methods that can accommodate such data.

15. The best method for Rory to use is probably the logistic regression method. The Mantel–Haenszel method can only detect uniform DIF, and Rory suspects nonuniform DIF. CFA methods could accommodate the dichotomous nature of the multiple-choice test data if the correct estimation method were used, but the sample size may be somewhat small. Also, CFA methods do not have a c-parameter. With a multiple-choice test, there is likely to be guessing, so the c-parameter would be needed. IRT methods would be appropriate for this type of data in general, but the sample size is too small, especially for a three-parameter model. Given these considerations, logistic regression methods may be his best option. However, he should be aware that if values of the c-parameter are not the same across groups, this method could indicate slope differences even when there are none.

16. If Sun-Joo is willing to treat the Likert scale as a continuous scale, the best method would probably be CFA invariance testing. Treating these items as continuous should not be problematic as long as the item distributions are fairly normal. With 20 items and 300 per group, her sample size should be large enough. Another advantage of this method is that it could accommodate the two factors. The Mantel–Haenszel method could handle the 5-point Likert items, but there would likely be many empty cells in the table as responses would be spread across five categories rather than two. IRT could accommodate the 5-point scale but would have the same problem with empty cells and would likely require a larger sample size than the 600 available. If IRT were used, a multidimensional model would be needed because there are two factors, and this would require an even larger sample size. Logistic regression

could be used but would be difficult with the 5-point scale. Also, items for the two factors would have to be modeled using scores on their respective factors as the "X" variable.

17. Accommodations are adaptations to tests or test items that preserve the comparability of scores across the adapted and original test versions. Modifications are adaptations that will likely change the construct being measured, at least to some extent. Examples of accommodations are allowing extra time, allowing use of dictionaries or glossaries for non-native English speakers, and allowing use of Braille readers or magnifying devices. Examples of modifications are providing scribes to write an examinee's answers or providing readers for examinees with dyslexia.

18.
   a. *Debra P. v Turlington* (1979): Equal Protection and Due Process Clauses of Fourteenth Amendment; Title VI

   b. *Larry P. v. Wilson Riles* (1979): Equal Protection Clause of the Fourteenth Amendment; Title VI

   c. *Griggs v. Duke Power Co.* (1971): Title VII

CHAPTER 17

1. A performance standard specifies the knowledge and skills an examinee must have to be classified into a particular performance category. A cut score operationalizes the performance standard, such that examinees with scores at the cut score or higher should have the specified knowledge and skills.

2. Licensure is a legal authorization to practice a particular profession. If licensure is required for a profession, those practicing that profession must be licensed or they will be in violation of the law. Certification is not legally mandated but is an additional credential professionals in an occupation can obtain to show that they have attained some extra level of competence.

3. Standard settings for licensure exams typically use as panelists those practicing the profession and those who train them as panelists. Practicing plumbers on the panel should be licensed. Licensed plumbers will have taken the licensing exam and so will have an understanding of the exam and what it requires. In addition, because they will have passed the exam, they will have a good idea of the level of knowledge and skill required to pass. Finally, licensed plumbers will likely have more experience, which will also have provided them with an understanding of the knowledge and skills plumbers should have. The officials commissioning the standard setting might still want to include at least one unlicensed plumber, or one with less experience. This person could provide the viewpoint of those likely to be taking the exam and could provide a reality check if the expectations of the more experienced panel members were unrealistic.

Those who train plumbers, such as instructors at trade schools and community colleges, and training programs sponsored by plumber's unions should also be included on the panel.

4. Impact data are data on the actual test scores of test takers. These data can be useful to panelists by providing empirical information on the obtained difficulty levels of items, distributions of test scores, and percentages of test takers who will fall into the different proficiency levels if the suggested cut scores were to be adopted. Panelists may have difficulty determining whether their expectations are reasonable in practice, and impact data can provide a reality check for expectations that are too high. Some experts worry that panelists will rely too much on the impact data. For example, some panelists may lower their cut scores if impact data indicate that too many test takers would fail, or they may suggest higher cut scores if impact data indicate a passing rate they consider to be too high.

5. The minimally competent examinee is one whose level of knowledge and skills just barely qualifies her or his placement into a particular proficiency category. Thus, the minimally competent examinee is on the cusp between two proficiency categories, and, if given the benefit of the doubt, could be classified into the higher category. In developing a common understanding of the minimally competent examinees, panelists should discuss what such an examinee would and would not be able to do. The minimally competent examinee is hypothetical and should represent a generic understanding of such a person rather than a specific student with whom a panelist is familiar.

6. In the original Angoff method, panelists had to determine, for each test item, the probability that a minimally competent examinee would get the item right. The yes/no variation of this method was introduced to make the judgments easier for panelists. In the yes/no variation, panelists need only indicate whether a minimally competent examinee would or would not get the item right.

7. In test-centered methods, panelists make judgments about the test items and how difficult they might be for examinees. The Angoff and Bookmark methods are examples of these methods. In examinee-centered methods, panelists make judgments about the examinees and whether they qualify for a particular performance level. The Contrasting Groups and Borderline Group procedures are examinee centered.

8.
   a. The Body of Work method would be best suited to this situation because it is the only method specifically designed to accommodate performance and extended-answer assessments. Test-centered methods could not be used in this situation because these are based on the concept of item difficulty, which may not be relevant in this situation.

   b. The Body of Work method requires a great deal of upfront work to decide on the number, nature, and descriptions of the performance levels and to organize the papers or performances into groups according to these levels. This method is also quite time consuming for panelists, which may limit the number of panelists that can be used.

9.

    a. Because the items are multiple choice, either the Angoff or Bookmark methods could be used here. However, there are only 20 items on the test, which may not be sufficient for the Bookmark method, for which 40 questions are recommended. Examinee-centered methods such as the Contrasting Groups or Borderline methods could not be used because the test has not yet been given. Thus, the necessary test score data for examinee-centered methods would not be available.

    b. One drawback of the Angoff method is that the task of making probability judgments is typically quite difficult for panelists. Jerush could use the yes/no variation of the method if she felt the original method would be too difficult.

10. Evidence that the panelists had been appropriately selected and trained and that they understood their tasks; evidence that the performance standards were clear to panelists and that panelists agreed on them; and documentation of all standard-setting activities in the final report or elsewhere are all relevant.

11. Evidence of interpanelist (across panelists) and intrapanelist (within panelists) consistency; and evidence that the same (or similar) cut scores would be obtained if the standard-setting process were repeated would be relevant. It may not be feasible to obtain the latter type of evidence, as this would require the standard setting to be repeated with a new panel. However, it may be possible to obtain a large panel and split this into two or more smaller panels to check for consistency.

12. This is a licensure test for which the validity claim is that those who pass the test have the knowledge and skills needed to be successful plumbers and those who fail the test do not. A reasonable source of evidence in this situation would be a comparison of scores from very experienced plumbers who had passed the licensure tests and less experienced or apprentice plumbers who had not passed the test. Scores of the former group should be much higher than the cut score, and scores from the latter group should be much lower.

CHAPTER 18

1.

    a. In vertical scaling, the two tests are given to examinees of different school grades or ages. The tests therefore do not cover the same content and cannot be used interchangeably. Vertical scaling is used to put the tests onto the same scale so that growth or change across years can be approximated.

    b. Linking refers to a situation in which different tests that measure the same construct, broadly speaking, can be related. Because the tests differ in content and/or difficulty, they cannot be equated, but linking can provide a rough estimate of how scores on one translate to scores on the other.

2.

  a. Yes, the tests are parallel versions, or forms, and should measure the same content with the same level of difficulty, so equating would be appropriate.

  b. No, because the two tests are based on different theories, they likely differ in content, so equating would not be appropriate.

  c. No, tests of motor development for these two age groups would likely contain different items and have different difficulties. This is a situation in which vertical scaling might be used to put the two tests on the same scale.

3.

  a. The single-group design is powerful because examinees take both tests. Thus, differences in scores must be due to differences in test forms rather than differences in examinee ability. However, this design requires examinees to take two tests, which increases testing time and introduces the possibility of fatigue or practice effects.

  b. The random-groups design has the advantage of reducing testing time because examinees take only one test. However, it requires a larger number of examinees than the single-group design. Also, examinees taking the two test forms must not be too different in ability.

  c. The common-item nonequivalent groups design does not require the groups taking the two test forms to be equal on ability, which is an advantage. However, the common items used must be carefully chosen to represent a mini-test that reflects the properties of the complete test form. Also, if groups do differ in ability, this design cannot completely adjust for this.

4.

  a. Mean equating: Scores on Y are 2.1 points higher than scores on X, so add 2.1 to each X score to obtain the equated Y score. $55 + 2.1 = 57.1$.

  b. Linear equating: Using the equation $Y(x) = \frac{\hat{\sigma}(Y)}{\hat{\sigma}(X)}\left[x - \hat{\mu}(X)\right] + \hat{\mu}(Y)$,

  $$Y(x) = \frac{6.25}{8.35}\left[55 - 50.40\right] + 52.50 = 0.75(4.6) + 52.50 = 55.95$$

5. Data from the two test forms differ in distributional shape, given the differences in skewness and kurtosis values. Thus, equipercentile equating would be most accurate. Also note that the sample sizes are quite large and should be adequate for equipercentile equating.

6. The synthetic population is a hypothetical population whose parameter values are obtained as a weighted combination of the parameters from the groups taking forms X and Y. The synthetic population is needed because equating in the common items design requires information we do not have: each group's scores on the test form they did not take. The synthetic population is used to approximate this information, given each group's scores on the common items.

7. The assumptions underlying the Tucker method of linear equating for the common-item nonequivalent groups design are: (1) the slopes and intercepts that have been obtained from regressing form X or Y on scores from the common items are the same in the two groups, and (2) the amount of variability in X and Y scores at each score point on C is the same in the two groups.

8. The Levine observed score method of linear equating for the common-item nonequivalent groups design was developed to adjust for the fact that scores on X, Y, and C are not perfectly reliable, leading to attenuation of the relations among these if no adjustment is applied.

9.

a. For the mean/mean method, use the equations

$$A = \frac{\mu(a_X)}{\mu(a_Y)} \text{ and } B = \mu(b_Y) - A\mu(b_X).$$

$$A = \frac{0.9}{1.1} = 0.82; \ B = 0.5 - 0.82(0.5) = 0.09$$

b. For the mean/sigma method, use the equations

$$A = \frac{\sigma(b_Y)}{\sigma(b_X)} \text{ and } B = \mu(b_Y) - A\mu(b_X).$$

$$A = \frac{1.43}{1.22} = 1.17; \ B = 0.5 - 1.17(0.5) = -0.085$$

10.

a. For both methods, divide each a-value by A and transform each b-value by multiplying it by A and adding B. For the mean/mean method, A = 0.82 and B = 0.09 (from Question 9).

Item Parameters Transformed Using the Mean/Mean Method

Item	a	b	c
1	0.49	−0.73	0.15
2	1.22	0.50	0.20
3	1.59	1.73	0.10
Mean	1.10	0.50	0.15
SD	0.46	1.00	0.04

621

b. For the mean/sigma method, A = 1.17 and add B = −0.085.

**Item Parameters Transformed
Using the Mean/Sigma Method**

Item	a	b	c
1	0.34	−1.25	0.15
2	0.85	0.50	0.20
3	1.11	2.25	0.10
Mean	0.77	0.50	0.15
SD	0.46	1.43	0.04

11. For the mean/sigma method, the mean and standard deviation of the transformed *b*-parameters should be equal to the mean and standard deviation of *b*-values from form Y, which they are (0.5 and 1.43).

12. For the mean/mean method, the means of the transformed *a*- and *b*-parameters should be equal to the means of the form Y *a*- and *b*-parameter values, which they are (1.1 and 0.5).

13. The standard error of equating is an estimate of the average error in equating, defined as the standard deviation of the theoretical distribution of equated values at a particular score point, obtained using a particular method of equating and equating design. Thus, the SEE varies across score points and across equating methods and designs.

14. In general, mean equating requires the smallest sample size, followed by linear equating. Equipercentile equating requires the largest sample size.

15. If the test score distributions are quite different and the sample sizes are close to those required, Feiming would likely be better off using equipercentile equating. The results from this method should be more accurate than those from mean or linear equating, although the precision would be somewhat lower, leading to larger standard errors of equating. Feiming could also compare the results of the different equating methods and choose the method yielding the most reasonable results.

References

Adelson, J. L., & McCoach, D. B. (2011). Development and psychometric properties of the Math and Me Survey: Measuring third through sixth graders' attitudes toward mathematics. *Measurement and Evaluation in Counseling and Devlopment, 44,* 225–247.

Agresti, A. (2002). *Categorical data analysis* (2nd ed.). Hoboken, NJ: Wiley.

Ahlawat, K. S. (1985). On the negative valence items in self-report measures. *Journal of General Psychology, 112,* 89–99.

Aiken, L. S., West, S. G., & Millsap, R. E. (2008). Doctoral training in statistics, measurement, and methodology in psychology: Replication and extension of Aiken, West, Sechrest, and Reno's (1990) survey of PhD programs in North America. *American Psychologist, 63,* 32–50.

Akaike, H. (1987). Factor analysis and AIC. *Psychometrika, 52,* 317–332.

Albermarle Paper Co. v. Moody, 422 U.S. 405 (1975).

Almond, R., Mislevy, R. J., Steinberg, L. S., Yan, D., & Williamson, D. M., (2015). *Bayesian networks in educational assessment.* New York: Springer.

American Educational Research Association, American Psychological Association, & National Council on Measurement in Education (2014). *Standards for educational and psychological testing:* Washington, DC: American Educational Research Association.

American Psychiatric Association. (2013). *Diagnostic and statistical manual of mental disorders* (5th ed.). Arlington, VA: American Psychiatric Association Publishing.

American Psychological Association, Committee on Test Standards. (1954). Technical recommendations for psychological tests and diagnostic techniques. *Psychological Bulletin, 52*(2, Suppl.).

Anastasi, A. (1986). Evolving concepts of test validation. *Annual Review of Psychology, 37,* 1–15.

Anastasi, A., & Urbina, S. (1997). *Psychological testing* (7th ed.), Upper Saddle River, NJ: Prentice-Hall.

Angoff, W. H. (1971). Norms, scales, and equivalent scores. In R. L. Thorndike (Ed.), *Educational measurement* (2nd ed., pp. 508–600). Washington, DC: American Council on Education.

Angoff, W. H. (1988). Validity: An evolving concept. In H. Wainer & H. I. Braun (Eds.), *Test validity* (pp. 19–32). Hillsdale, NJ: Erlbaum.

Angoff, W. H. (1993). Perspectives on differential item functioning methodology. In P. W. Holland & H. Wainer (Eds.), *Differential item functioning* (pp. 3–23). Hillsdale, NJ: Erlbaum.

Anthony, M. M., Orsillo, S. M., & Roemer, L. (Eds). (2001). *Practitioner's guide to empirically based measures of anxiety.* New York: Kluwer Academic.

Attali, Y. (2005). Reliability of speeded number-right multiple-choice tests. *Applied Psychological Measurement, 29,* 357–368.

Baker, F. B., & Kim, S.-H. (2004). *Item response theory: Parameter estimation techniques* (2nd ed.). New York: Marcel Dekker.

Bandalos, D. L. (2014). Relative performance of categorical diagonally weighted least squares and robust maximum likelihood estimation. *Structural Equation Modeling: A Multidisciplinary Journal, 21,* 102–116.

Bandalos, D. L., & Enders, C. K. (1996). The effects of nonnormality and number of response categories on reliability. *Applied Measurement in Education, 9,* 151–160.

Bandalos, D. L., & Finney, S. J. (2010). Factor analysis: Exploratory and confirmatory. In G. R. Hancock & R. O. Mueller (Eds.), *The reviewer's guide to quantitative methods in the social sciences* (pp. 93–114). New York: Routledge.

Bandalos, D. L., & Kopp, J. P. (2012). Teaching introductory measurement: Suggestions for what to include and how to motivate students. *Educational Measurement: Issues and Practice, 31*(2), 8–13.

Barnette, J. (2000). Effects of stem and Likert response option reversals on survey internal consistency: If you feel the need, there is a better alternative to using those negatively worded stems. *Educational and Psychological Measurement, 60,* 361–370.

Bearden, W. O., Netemeyer, R. G., & Haws, K. L. (Eds.). (2010). *Handbook of marketing scales: Multi-item measures for marketing and consumer behavior research* (3rd ed.). Thousand Oaks, CA: Sage.

Belson, W. A. (1986). *Validity in survey research.* Brookfield, VT: Gower.

Benson, J. (1998). Developing a strong program of construct validation: A test anxiety example. *Educational Measurement: Issues and Practice, 17,* 10–17.

Benson, J., & Clark, F. (1982). A guide for instrument development and validation. *American Journal of Occupational Therapy, 36,* 789–800.

Bentler, P. M. (1990). Comparative fit indices in structural equation models. *Psychological Bulletin, 107,* 238–246.

Bentler, P. M. (2004). *EQS for Windows* (Version 6.1) [Computer software]. Encinco, CA: Multivariate Software.

Berk, R. A. (1980). *Criterion-referenced measurement: The state of the art.* Baltimore: Johns Hopkins University Press.

Bernstein, I. H., & Teng, G. (1989). Factoring items and factoring scales are different: Spurious evidence for multidimensionality due to item categorization. *Psychological Bulletin, 105,* 467–477.

Bersoff, D. N. (1981). Testing and the law. *American Psychologist, 36,* 1047–1056.

Beuchert, A. K., & Mendoza, J. L. (1979). A Monte Carlo comparison of ten item discrimination indices. *Journal of Educational Measurement, 16,* 109–117.

Black, P., & Wiliam, D. (1998). Assessment and classroom learning. *Assessment in Education, 5,* 7–73.

Bloom, B. S. (Ed.). (1956). *Taxonomy of educational objectives: Handbook I. Cognitive domain.* New York: Longmans, Green.

Bollen, K. A. (1989). *Structural equations with latent variables.* New York: Wiley.

Bond, L. (1993). Comments on the O'Neill & McPeek paper. In P. W. Holland & H. Wainer (Eds.), *Differential item functioning* (pp. 277–279). Hillsdale, NJ: Erlbaum.

Boring, E. G. (1923, June). Intelligence as the tests test it. *The New Republic, 35,* 35–37.

Borsboom, D., Cramer, A. O. J., Kievit, R. A., Scholten, A. Z., & Franić, S. (2009). The end of construct validity. In R. W. Lissitz (Ed.), *The concept of validity* (pp. 135–170). Charlotte, NC: Information Age.

Borsboom, D., Mellenbergh, G. J., & van Heerden, J. (2004). The concept of validity. *Psychological Review, 110,* 203–219.

Bowman, M. L. (1989). Testing individual differences in ancient China. *American Psychologist, 44,* 576–578.

Bozard, J. L. (2010). *Invariance testing in diagnostic classification models.* Unpublished doctoral dissertation, University of Georgia, Athens, GA.

Bradburn, N. M. (1992). Response effects. In N. Schwarz & S. Sudman (Eds.), *Context effects in social and psychological research.* New York: Springer-Verlag.

Bradshaw, L. (2017). Diagnostic classification models. In A. A. Rupp & J. P. Leighton (Eds.), *The handbook of cognition and assessment* (pp. 297–327). Chichester, UK: Wiley.

Bradshaw, L., & Cohen, A. (2010, May). Accuracy of multidimensional item response model parameters estimated under small sample sizes. In A. Izsák (Chair), *Using cognitive attributes to develop mathematics assessments, opportunities, and challenges*. Symposium conducted at the annual meeting of the American Educational Research Association, Denver, CO.

Bradshaw, L., Izsák, A., Templin, J., & Jacobson, E. (2014). Diagnosing teachers' understandings of rational number: Building a multidimensional test within the diagnostic classification model framework. *Educational Measurement: Issues and Practice, 33*(1), 2–14.

Brennan, R. L. (1992). Generalizability theory. *Educational Measurement: Issues and Practice, 11*, 27–34.

Bridgeman, B., McCamley-Jenkins, L., & Ervin, N. (2000). *Predictions of freshman grade-point average from the revised and recentered SAT I: Reasoning Test* (College Board Research Report No. 2000-1). New York: The College Board.

Briggs, N. E., & MacCallum, R. C. (2003). Recovery of weak common factors by maximum likelihood and ordinary least squares estimation. *Multivariate Behavioral Research, 38*, 25–56.

Brown, C. (2013). *Modification indices for diagnostic classification models*. Unpublished doctoral dissertation, University of Georgia, Athens, GA.

Brown, T. A. (2006). *Confirmatory factor analysis for applied research*. New York: Guilford Press.

Brown, J. S., & Burton, R. (1978). Diagnostic models for procedural bugs in basic mathematical skills. *Cognitive Science, 2*, 155–192.

Browne, M. W. (1984). Asymptotically distribution-free methods for the analysis of covariance structures. *British Journal of Mathematical and Statistical Psychology, 37*, 62–83.

Browne, M. W. (2001). An overview of analytic rotation in exploratory factor analysis. *Multivariate Behavioral Research, 36*, 111–150.

Browne, M. W., & Cudeck, R. (1993). Alternative ways of assessing model fit. In K. A. Bollen & J. S. Long (Eds.), *Testing structural equation models* (pp. 136–162). Newbury Park, CA: Sage.

Browne, M. W., Cudeck, R., Tateneni, K., & Mels, G. (2008). CEFA: Comprehensive Exploratory Factor Analysis, Version 3.03 [Computer software and manual]. Retrieved from *http://faculty.psy. ohio-state.edu/browne/*.

Buck, G., & Tatsuoka, K. K. (1998). Application of the rule-space procedure to language testing: Examining attributes of a free response listening test. *Language Testing, 15*, 119–157.

Buckendahl, C. W., & Davis-Becker, S. L. (2012). Setting passing standards for credentialing programs. In G. J. Cizek (Ed.), *Setting performance standards: Foundations, methods, and innovations* (2nd ed., pp. 485–501). New York: Routledge.

Butcher, J. N., Dahlstrom, W. G., Graham, J. R., Tellegen, A., & Kaemmer, B. (1989). *Development and use of the MMPI-2 content scales*. Minneapolis: University of Minnesota Press.

Byrne, B. M. (2011). *Structural equation modeling with Mplus: Basic concepts, applications, and programming*. New York: Routledge.

Cacioppo, J. T., & Petty, R. E. (1982). The need for cognition. *Journal of Personality and Social Psychology, 42*, 116–131.

Cacioppo, J. T., & Petty, R. E. (1984). The need for cognition: Relationship to attitudinal processes. In R. P. McGlynn, J. E. Maddux, C. D. Stoltenberg, & J. H. Harvey (Eds.), *Social perception in clinical and counseling psychology* (pp. 91–119). Lubbock: Texas Tech Press.

Camilli, G. (2006). Test fairness. In R. L. Brennan (Ed.), *Educational measurement* (4th ed., pp. 221–256). Westport, CT: Praeger.

Camilli, G., & Shepard, L. A. (1994). *Methods for identifying biased test items*. Thousand Oaks, CA: Sage.

Campbell, D. T., & Fiske, D. W. (1959). Convergent and discriminant validation by the multitrait–multimethod matrix. *Psychological Bulletin, 56*, 81–105.

Carpenter, P. A., Just, M. A., & Shell, P. (1990). What one intelligence test measures: A theoretical account of processing in Raven's Progressive Matrices Test. *Psychological Review, 97*, 404–431.

Cattell, R. B. (1966). The scree test for the number of factors. *Multivariate Behavioral Research, 1*, 245–276.

Cattell, R. B., & Tsujioka, B. (1964). The importance of factor-trueness and validity, versus homogeneity and orthogonality in test scales. *Educational and Psychological Measurement, 24*, 3–30.

Chase, W. G., & Simon, H. A. (1973). Perception in chess. *Cognitive Psychology, 1,* 33–81.

Chen, J., Torre, J., & Zhang, Z. (2013). Relative and absolute fit evaluation in cognitive diagnosis modeling. *Journal of Educational Measurement, 50,* 123–140.

Chen, W.-H., & Thissen, D. (1997). Local dependence indexes for item pairs using item response theory. *Journal of Educational and Behavioral Statistics, 22,* 265–289.

Chi, M. T. H., Feltovich, P. J., & Glaser, R. (1981). Categorization and representation of physics problems by experts and novices. *Cognitive Science, 5,* 121–152.

Chi, M. T. H., Glaser, R., & Rees, E. (1982). Expertise in problem-solving. In R. J. Sternberg (Ed.), *Advances in the psychology of human intelligence* (Vol. 1). Hillsdale, NJ: Erlbaum.

Chi, M. T. H., & Van Lehn, K. (1991). The content of physics self-explanations. *Journal of the Learning Sciences, 1,* 69–106.

Chiu, C.-Y. (2013). Statistical refinement of the Q-matrix in cognitive diagnosis. *Applied Psychological Measurement, 37,* 598–618.

Chiu, C.-Y., Douglas, J., & Li, X. (2009). Cluster analysis for cognitive diagnosis: Theory and applications. *Psychometrika, 74,* 633–665.

Cho, S., Li, G., & Bandalos, D. (2009). Accuracy of the parallel analysis procedure with polychoric correlations. *Educational and Psychological Measurement, 69*(5), 748–759.

Chou, C., & Bentler, P. M. (1995). Estimates and tests in structural equation modeling. In R. H. Hoyle (Ed.), *Structural equation modeling: Concepts, issues, and applications* (pp. 37–55). Thousand Oaks, CA: Sage.

Chou, C., Bentler, P. M., & Satorra, A. (1991). Scaled test statistics and robust standard errors for nonnormal data in covariance structure analysis: A monte carlo study. *British Journal of Mathematical and Statistical Psychology, 44,* 347–357.

Cizek, G. J. (2012a). Defining and distinguishing validity: Interpretations of score meaning and justifications of test use. *Psychological Methods, 17,* 31–43.

Cizek, G. J. (2012b). An introduction to contemporary standard setting: Concepts, characteristics, and contexts. In G. J. Cizek (Ed.), *Setting performance standards: Foundations, methods, and innovations* (2nd ed., pp. 3–14). New York: Routledge.

Cizek, G. J., & Bunch, M. B. (2007). *Standard setting.* Thousand Oaks, CA: Sage.

Cizek, G. J., Bunch, M. B., & Koons, H. (2004). Setting performance standards: Contemporary methods. *Educational Measurement: Issues and Practice, 23*(4), 31–50.

Clark, L. A., & Watson, D. (1995). Constructing validity: Basic issues in objective scale development. *Psychological Assessment, 7,* 309–319.

Clauser, B. E., & Mazor, K. M. (1998). Using statistical procedures to identify differentially functioning test items. *Educational Measurement: Issues and Practice, 17,* 31–44.

Cleary, A. (1968). Test bias: Prediction of grades of Negro and white students in integrated colleges. *Journal of Educational Measurement, 5,* 115–124.

Cliff, N. (1989). Strong inferences and weak data: Covariance structure analysis and its use. In J. A. Keats, R. Taft, R. A. Heath, & S. H. Lovibond (Eds.). *Mathematical and theoretical systems* (pp. 69–77). Amsterdam: Elsevier.

Cohen, J. A. (1960). A coefficient of agreement for nominal scales. *Educational and Psychological Measurement, 20,* 37–46.

Cohen, J., Cohen, P., West, S. G., & Aiken, L. S. (2003). *Applied multiple regression/correlation analysis for the behavioral sciences* (3rd ed.). Mahwah, NJ: Erlbaum.

Cole, D. A., Ciesla, J. A., & Steiger, J. H. (2007). The insidious effects of failing to include design-driven correlated residuals in latent-variable covariance structure analysis. *Psychological Methods, 12,* 381–398.

Cole, N. S., (1981). Bias in testing. *American Psychologist, 36,* 1067–1077.

Cole, N. S., & Zieky, M. J. (2001). The new faces of fairness. *Journal of Educational Measurement, 38,* 369–382.

Comrey, A. L., & Lee, H. B. (1992). *A first course in factor analysis* (2nd ed.). Hillsdale, NJ: Erlbaum.

Conger, A. J. (1980). Integration and generalization of kappas for multiple raters. *Psychological Bulletin, 88,* 322–328.

Cook, L. L., & Eignor, D. R. (1991). AN NCMF instructional module on IRT equating methods. *Educational Measurement: Issues and Practice, 10*, 37–45.

Cordery, J., & Sevastos, P. (1993). Responses to the original and revised Job Diagnostic Survey: Is education a factor in responses to negatively worded items? *Journal of Applied Psychology, 78*, 141–143.

Crocker, L., & Algina, J. (1986). *Introduction to classical and modern test theory*. New York: Holt, Rinehart & Winston.

Cronbach, L. (1946). Response sets and test validity. *Educational and Psychological Measurement, 6*, 475–494.

Cronbach, L. J. (1951). Coefficient alpha and the internal structure of tests. *Psychometrika, 16*, 297–334.

Cronbach, L. J. (1971). Test validation. In R. L. Thorndike (Ed.), *Educational measurement* (2nd ed., pp. 443–507). Washington, DC: American Council on Education.

Cronbach, L. J. (1988). Five perspectives on the validity argument. In H. Wainer & H. I. Braun (Eds.), *Test validity* (pp. 3–17). Hillsdale, NJ: Erlbaum.

Cronbach, L. J., Gleser, G. C., Nanda, H., & Rajaratnam. N. (1972). *The dependability of behavioral measurements: Theory of generalizability for scores and profiles*. New York: Wiley.

Cronbach, L. J., & Meehl, P. E. (1955). Construct validity in psychological tests, *Psychological Bulletin, 52*, 281–302.

Cronbach, L. J., & Shavelson, R. J. (2004). My current thoughts on Coefficient Alpha and successor procedures. *Educational and Psychological Measurement, 64*, 391–418.

Crooks, T. J. (1988). The influence of classroom evaluation practices on students. *Review of Educational Research, 58*, 438–481.

Crowne, D., & Marlowe, D. (1960). A new scale of social desirability independent of psychopathology. *Journal of Consulting Psychology, 24*, 349–354.

Curran, P. J., West, S. G., & Finch, J. F. (1996). The robustness of test statistics to nonnormality and specification error in confirmatory factor analysis. *Psychological Methods, 1*, 16–29.

de Ayala, R. J. (2009). *The theory and practice of item response theory*. New York: Guilford Press.

de la Torre, J. (2009). The generalized DINA model framework. *Psychometrika, 76*(2), 179–199.

de la Torre, J., & Chiu, C.-Y. (2016). A general method of empirical Q-matrix validation. *Psychometrika, 81*, 253–273.

de la Torre, J., & Douglas, J. A. (2004). Higher-order latent trait models for cognitive diagnosis. *Psychometrika, 69*, 333–353.

Debra P. v. Turlington, 474 F. Supp. 244 (M.D. Fla. 1979), *aff'd in part, rev'd in part*, 644 F.2nd 397 (5th Cir.1981); *on remand*, 564 F. Supp. 177 (M.D. Fla. 1983), *aff'd*, 730 F.2nd 1405 (11th Cir. 1984).

DeCarlo, L. T. (1997). On the meaning and use of kurtosis. *Psychological Methods, 2*(3), 292–307.

DeCarlo, L. T. (2011). On the analysis of fraction subtraction data: The DINA model, classification, latent class sizes, and the Q-matrix. *Applied Psychological Measurement, 35*, 8–26.

DeVellis, R. F. (2003). *Scale development: Theory and applications* (2nd ed.). Thousand Oaks, CA: Sage.

Diana v. State Board of Education, Civ. Act. No. C-70-37 (N.D. Cal., 1970, further order, 1973).

DiBello, L. V., Roussos, L. A., & Stout, W. (2007). Review of cognitively diagnostic assessment and a summary of psychometric models. In C. R. Rao & S. Sinharay (Eds.), *Handbook of statistics: Vol. 26. Psychometrics* (pp. 979–1030). Amsterdam: North Holland.

Dilchert, S., Ones, D. S., Viswesvaran, C., & Deller, J. (2006). Response distortion in personality measurement: Born to deceive, yet capable of providing valid self-assessments? *Psychology Science, 48*, 209–225.

DiMaio, T. J. (1984). Social desirability and survey measurement: A review. In C.F. Turner & E. Martin (Eds.), *Surveying subjective phenomena* (Vol. 2, pp. 257–281). New York: Russell Sage Foundation.

DiStefano, C. (2002). The impact of categorization with confirmatory factor analysis. *Structural Equation Modeling: A Multidisciplinary Journal, 9*, 327–346.

DiStefano, C., Morgan, G., & Motl, R. (2012). An examination of personality characteristics related to acquiescence. *Journal of Applied Measurement, 13*, 41–56.

DiStefano, C., & Motl, R. (2006). Further investigating method effects associated with negatively worded items on self-report surveys. *Structural Equation Modeling, 13*, 440–464.

Dolan, C. V. (1994). Factor analysis of variables with 2, 3, 5, and 7 response categories: A comparison of categorical variable estimators using simulated data. *British Journal of Mathematical and Statistical Psychology, 47*, 309–326.

Donoghue, J. R., Holland, P. W., & Thayer, D. T. (1993). A Monte Carlo study of factors that affect the Mantel-Haenszel and standardization measures of differential item functioning. In P. W. Holland & H. Wainer (Eds.). *Differential item functioning* (pp. 137–166). Hillsdale, NJ: Erlbaum.

Dorans, N. J. (1990). Equating methods and sampling designs. *Applied Measurement in Education, 3*, 3–17.

Dorans, N. J. (2008, February). *Three faces of fairness*. Paper presented at the annual meeting of the National Council on Measurement in Education, New York.

Dorans, N. J., & Holland, P. W. (1993). DIF detection and description: Mantel-Haenszel and standardization. In P. W. Holland & H. Wainer (Eds.), *Differential item functioning* (pp. 35–66). Hillsdale, NJ: Erlbaum.

Dorans, N. J., & Kulick, E. (1983). *Assessing unexpected differential item performance of female candidates on SAT and TSWE forms administered in December, 1977: An application of the standardization approach* (Research Report No. 83-9). Princeton, NJ: Educational Testing Service.

Dorans, N. J., & Kulick, E. (1986). Demonstrating the utility of the standardization approach to assessing unexpected differential item performance on the Scholastic Aptitude Test. *Journal of Educational Measurement, 23*, 355–368.

Doyle, K. O. (1974). Theory and practice of ability testing in ancient Greece. *Journal of the History of the Behavioral Sciences, 10*, 202–212.

Drasgow, F. (1989). An evaluation of marginal maximum likelihood estimation for the two-parameter logistic model. *Applied Psychological Measurement, 13*, 77–90.

DuBois, P. H. (1970). A history of psychological testing. Boston: Allyn and Bacon.

DuPaul, G. J., Power, T. J., Anastopoulos, A. D., & Reid, R. (1998). *ADHD Rating Scale–IV: Checklists, norms, and clinical interpretation*. New York: Guilford Press.

Edwards, A. L. (1957). *Techniques of attitude scale construction*. New York: Appleton.

Eels, K., Havighurst, R. J., Herrick, V. E., & Tyler, R. W. (1951). *Intelligence and cultural differences*. Chicago: University of Chicago Press.

Elliot, A., & McGregor, H. A. (1999). Test anxiety and the hierarchical model of approach and avoidance achievement motivation. *Journal of Personality and Social Psychology, 76*, 628–644.

Elliot, A., & McGregor, H. A. (2001). A 2 × 2 achievement goal framework. *Journal of Personality and Social Psychology, 80*, 501–519.

Embretson, S. E. (1983). Construct validity: Construct representation versus nomothetic span. *Psychological Bulletin, 93*, 179–197.

Embretson, S. E. (1998). A cognitive design system approach to generating valid tests: Application to abstract reasoning. *Psychological Methods, 3*, 380–396.

Embretson, S. E., & Gorin, J. S. (2001). Improving construct validity with cognitive psychology principles. *Journal of Educational Measurement, 38*, 343–368.

Enders, C. K. (2005). Estimation by maximum likelihood. In B. Everitt & D. C. Howell (Eds.), *Encyclopedia of behavioral statistics*. West Sussex, UK: Wiley.

Enders, C. K. (2010). *Applied missing data analysis*. New York: Guilford Press.

Engelhart, M. D. (1965). A comparison of several item discrimination indices. *Journal of Educational Measurement, 2*, 69–76.

Ericsson, K. A., & Simon, H. A. (1984). *Protocol analysis: Verbal reports as data*. Cambridge, MA: MIT Press.

Factor 9.3 [Computer software]. Available at *http://psico.fcep.urv.es/utilitats/factor/Download.html*.

Fan, X., & Sivo, S. (2005). Sensitivity of fit indices to misspecified structural or measurement model components: Rationale of two-index strategy revisited. *Structural Equation Modeling, 12*, 343–367.

Fan, X., & Sivo, S. (2007). Sensitivity of fit indices to model misspecification and model types. *Multivariate Behavioral Research, 42*(3), 509–529.

Fazio, R. H., & Olson, M. A. (2003). Implicit measures in social cognition research: Their meaning and use. *American Review of Psychology, 54*, 297–327.

Feldt, L. S., & Brennan, R. L. (1989). Reliability. In R. L. Linn (Ed.), *Educational measurement* (3rd ed., pp. 105–146). Phoenix, AZ: Oryx Press.

Finney, S. J., & DiStefano, C. (2013). Nonnormal and categorical data in structural equation modeling. In G. R. Hancock & R. O. Mueller (Eds.). *A second course in structural equation modeling* (2nd ed., pp. 439–492). Charlotte, NC: Information Age.

Finney, S. J., DiStefano, C., & Kopp, J. P. (2016). Overview of estimation methods and preconditions for their application with structural equation modeling. In K. Schweizer & C. DiStefano (Eds.), *Principles and methods of test construction: Standards and recent advancements* (pp. 135–165). Boston: Hogrefe.

Finney, S. J., Pieper, S. L., & Barron, K. E. (2004). Examining the psychometric properties of the Achievement Goal Questionnaire in a general academic context. *Educational and Psychological Measurement, 64*(2), 365–382.

Fisher, R. C., Gerstner, J. J., & Bandalos, D. L. (2013, May). *A review and analysis of scale development procedures in psychology and education.* Poster presented at the annual meeting of the Association for Psychological Science, Washington DC.

Flanagan, J. C. (1949). Critical requirements: A new approach to employee evaluation. *Personnel Psychology, 2*, 419–425.

Flanagan, J. C. (1954). The critical incident technique. *Psychological Bulletin, 51*, 327–358.

Fleishman, J., & Benson, J. (1987). Using Lisrel to evaluate measurement models and scale reliability. *Educational and Psychological Measurement, 47*, 925–939.

Fleiss, J. L. (1971). Measuring nominal agreement among many raters. *Psychological Bulletin, 76*, 378–382.

Flora, D. B., & Curran, P. J. (2004). An empirical evaluation of alternative methods of estimation for confirmatory factor analysis with ordinal data. *Psychological Methods, 9*, 466–491.

Floyd, F. J. & Widaman, K. F. (1995). Factor analysis in the development and refinement of clinical assessment instruments. *Psychological Assessment, 7*(3), 286–299.

Foss, T., Jöreskog, K. G., & Olsson, U. H. (2011). Testing structural equation models: The effect of kurtosis. *Computational Statistics and Data Analysis, 55*, 2263–2275.

Frary, R. B. (1988). Formula scoring of multiple-choice tests (correction for guessing). *Educational Measurement: Issues and Practice, 7*, 33–38.

Frick, T., & Semmel, M. I. (1978). Observer agreement and reliabilities of classroom observational measures. *Review of Educational Research, 48*, 157–184.

Fu, J., & Li, Y. (2007, April). *An integrated review of cognitively diagnostic psychometric models.* Paper presented at the annual meeting of the National Council on Measurement in Education, Chicago.

Gardner, H. (1983) *Frames of mind: The theory of multiple intelligences.* New York: Basic Books.

Garrett, H. E. (1939). *Statistics in psychology and education.* New York: Longmans, Green.

GI Forum et al. v. Texas Education Agency, et al., No. SA 97-CA-1278, 1999, U.S. District Court, W.D. Tex., San Antonio, TX.

Gierl, M. J., Leighton, J. P., & Hunka, S. M. (2007). Using the attribute hierarchy method to make diagnostic inferences about respondents' cognitive skills. In J. P. Leighton & M. J. Gierl (Eds.), *Cognitive diagnostic assessment for education: Theory and applications* (pp. 242–274). Cambridge, UK: Cambridge University Press.

Gilljam, M., & Granberg, D. (1993). Should we take don't know for an answer? *Public Opinion Quarterly, 57*, 348–357.

Glorfeld, L. W. (1995). An improvement on Horn's Parallel Analysis methodology for selecting the correct number of factors to retain. *Educational and Psychological Measurement, 55*, 377–393.

Golden Rule Insurance Co. et al. v. Washburn et al., No. 419-76 (Ill. 7th Jud. Cir. 1984).

Gonzalez, R., & Griffin, D. (2001). Testing parameters in structural equation modeling: Every "one" matters. *Psychological Methods, 6*(3), 258–269.

Goodenough, F. L. (1949). *Mental testing: Its history, principles, and applications.* New York: Rinehart.

Gorin, J. S. (2005). Manipulating processing difficulty of reading comprehension questions: The feasibility of item generation. *Journal of Educational Measurement, 42*, 351–373.

Gorin, J. S. (2006). Test design with cognition in mind. *Educational Measurement: Issues and Practice, 25*, 21–35.

Gorin, J. S. (2007). Reconsidering issues in validity theory. *Educational Researcher, 36*, 456–462.

Gorin, J. S., & Embretson, S. E. (2006). Item difficulty modeling of paragraph comprehension models. *Applied Psychological Measurement, 30*, 394–411.

Gorsuch, R. L. (1983). *Factor analysis* (2nd ed.). Hillsdale, NJ: Erlbaum.

Graham, J. M., Guthrie, A. C., & Thompson, B. (2003). Consequences of not interpreting structure coefficients in published CFA research: A reminder. *Structural Equation Modeling: An Interdisciplinary Journal, 10*, 142–153.

Green, B. F., Bock, R. D., Humphreys, L. G., Linn, R. B., & Reckase, M. D. (1984). Technical guidelines for assessing computerized adaptive tests. *Journal of Educational Measurement, 21*, 347–360.

Green, S. B., & Hershberger, S. L. (2000). Correlated errors in true score models and their effect on coefficient alpha. *Structural Equation Modeling, 7*(2), 251–270.

Green, S. B., Lissitz, R. W., & Mulaik, S. A. (1977). Limitations of coefficient alpha as an index of test unidimensionality. *Educational and Psychological Measurement, 37*, 827–838.

Green, S. B., & Yang, Y. (2009). Reliability of summed item scores using structural equation modeling: An alternative to coefficient alpha. *Psychometrika, 74*(1), 155–167.

Grice, H. (1975). Logic and conversation. In P. Cole & T. Morgan (Eds.), *Syntax and semantics: Vol. 3. Speech acts* (pp. 41–58). New York: Seminar Press.

Grice, J. W. (2001). Computing and evaluating factor scores. *Psychological Methods, 6*(4), 430–450.

Griffin, S., & Case, R. (2007). Re-thinking the primary school math curriculum: An approach based on cognitive science. *Issues in Education, 3*, 1–65.

Griggs v. Duke Power Co., 401 U.S. 424 (1971).

Gu, F., Little, T. D., & Kingston, N. M. (2013). Mis-estimation of reliability using coefficient alpha and structural equation modeling when assumptions of tau-equivalence and uncorrelated errors are violated. *Methodology: European Journal of Research Methods for the Behavioral and Social Sciences, 9*(1), 30.

Guardians Ass'n of New York City v. Civil Serv. Comm'n, 630 F. 2nd 79 (2nd Cir. 1980), *cert. denied*, 49 U.S.L.W. 3932 (June 15, 1981).

Guilford, J. P. (1946). New standards for test evaluation. *Educational and Psychological Measurement, 6*, 427–439.

Guttman, L. (1941). The quantification of class attributes: A theory and method of scale construction. In P. Horst et al. (Eds), *The prediction of personal adjustment*. New York: Social Science Research Council.

Guttman, L. (1945). A basis for analyzing test–retest reliability. *Psychometrika, 10*, 255–282.

Guttman, L. (1950). The basis for scalogram analysis. In S. A. Stouffer, L. Guttman, E. A. Suchman, P. F. Lazarsfeld, S. A. Star, & J. A. Clausen (Eds.), *Measurement and prediction, Vol. 4*. pp. 66–90. Princeton, NJ: Princeton University Press.

Guttman, L. (1954). Some necessary conditions for common-factor analysis. *Psychometrika, 19*, 149–161.

Haebara, T. (1980). Equating logistic ability scales by a weighted least squares method. *Japanese Psychological Research, 22*, 144–149.

Haertel, E. H. (1985). Construct validity and criterion-referenced testing. *Review of Educational Research, 55*, 23–46.

Haertel, E. H. (1989). Using restricted latent class models to map the skill structure of achievement items. *Journal of Educational Measurement, 26*, 333–352.

Haertel, E. H. (2013). Getting the help we need. *Journal of Educational Measurement, 50*, 84–90.

Haig, B. D. (2005). Exploratory factor analysis, theory generation, and scientific method. *Multivariate Behavioral Research, 40*, 303–329.

Hambleton, R. K., Pitoniak, M. J., & Copella, J. M. (2012). Essential steps in setting performance standards on educational tests and strategies for assessing the reliability of results. In G. J. Cizek (Ed.), *Setting performance standards: Foundations, methods, and innovations* (2nd ed., pp. 47–76). New York: Routledge.

Hambleton, R. K., Swaminathan, H., & Rogers, H. J. (1991). *Fundamentals of item response theory.* Newbury Park, CA: Sage.

Hartz, S. M. (2002). *A Bayesian framework for the unified model for assessing cognitive abilities: Blending theory with practicality.* Unpublished doctoral dissertation, University of Illinois at Urbana–Champaign, Urbana–Champaign, IL.

Harwell, M. R., & Janosky, J. E. (1991). An empirical study of the effects of small datasets and varying prior variances on item parameter estimation in BILOG. *Applied Psychological Measurement, 15,* 279–291.

Hayduk, L. A. (1987). *Structural equation modeling with LISREL: Essentials and advances.* Baltimore, MD: Johns Hopkins University Press.

Henson, R. & Templin, J. (2005). *Hierarchical log-linear modeling of the joint skill distribution.* Unpublished manuscript, External Diagnostic Research Group, Champaign, IL.

Henson, R., & Templin, J. (2007, April). *Large-scale language assessment using cognitive diagnosis models.* Paper presented at the annual meeting of the National Council for Measurement in Education, Chicago.

Henson, R., Templin, J., & Willse, J. (2009). Defining a family of cognitive diagnosis models using log-linear models with latent variables. *Psychometrika, 74,* 191–210.

Hertzog, M. A. (2008). Considerations in determining sample size for pilot studies. *Research in Nursing and Health, 31,* 180–191.

Hobson v. Hansen, 269 F. Supp. 401 (D. D.C. 1967), *aff'd sub nom. Schmuck v. Hansen,* 408 F.2nd 175 (D.C. Cir. 1969).

Hofman, W., Gawronski, B., Gschwender, T., Le, H., & Schmitt, M. (2005). A meta-analysis on the correlation between the Implicit Association Test and explicit self-report measures. *Personality and Social Psychology Bulletin, 31,* 1369–1385.

Hogarty, K. Y., Hines, C. V., Kromrey, J. D., Ferron, J. M., & Mumford, K. R. (2005). The quality of factor solutions in exploratory factor analysis: The influence of sample size, communality, and overdetermination. *Educational and Psychological Measurement, 65,* 202–226.

Horan, P., DiStefano, C., & Motl, R. (2003). Wording effects in self-esteem scales: Methodological artifact or response style? *Structural Equation Modeling, 10,* 435–455.

Horn, J. L. (1965). A rationale and test for the number of factors in factor analysis. *Psychometrika, 32,* 179–185.

Horn, J. L., & Cattell, R. B. (1967). Age differences in fluid and crystallized intelligence. *Acta Psychologica, 26,* 107–129.

Hu, L. T., & Bentler, P. (1998). Fit indices in covariance structure modeling: Sensitivity to overparameterized model misspecification. *Psychological Methods, 3,* 424–453.

Hu, L. T, & Bentler, P. (1999). Cutoff criteria for fit indices in covariance structure analysis: Conventional criteria versus new alternatives. *Structural Equation Modeling, 6*(1), 1–55.

Hu, L., Bentler, P. M., & Kano, Y. (1992). Can test statistics in covariance structure analysis be trusted? *Psychological Bulletin, 112,* 351–362.

Huff, K., & Goodman, D. P. (2007). The demand for cognitive diagnostic assessment. In J. P. Leighton & M. J. Gierl (Eds.), *Cognitive diagnostic assessment for education: Theory and applications* (pp. 19–60). Cambridge, UK: Cambridge University Press.

Humphreys, L. G. & Montanelli, R. G. (1975). An investigation of the parallel analysis criterion for determining the number of common factors. *Multivariate Behavioral Research, 10,* 193–206.

Hunter, J. E., Schmidt, F. L., & Hunter, R. (1979). Differential validity of employment tests by race: A comprehensive review and analysis. *Psychological Bulletin, 86,* 721–735.

Hutchinson, S. R. (1998). The stability of post hoc model modifications in confirmatory factor analysis models. *Journal of Experimental Education, 66,* 361–380.

Impara, J. C., & Plake, B. S. (1997). Standard setting: An alternative approach. *Journal of Educational Measurement, 34,* 353–366.

Jacobson, E., Remillard, J. T., Hoover, M., & Aaron, W. (2016). The interaction between measure design and construct development: Building validity arguments. In A. Izsák, J. T. Remillard, & J. Templin (Eds.), *Psychometric methods in mathematics education: Opportunities, challenges, and interdisciplinary collaborations* (pp. 155–173). *Journal for Research in Mathematics Education Monograph Series No. 15.* Reston, VA: National Council of Teachers of Mathematics.

Jaeger, R. M. (1989). Certification of student competence. In R. L. Linn (Ed.), *Educational measurement* (3rd ed., pp. 485–514). New York: American Council on Education and Macmillan.

James, L. R., & McIntyre, M. D. (2000). *Conditional Reasoning Test of Aggression Test manual.* Knoxville, TN: Innovative Assessment Technology.

Jang, E. E. (2005). *A validity narrative: Effects of reading skills diagnosis on teaching and learning in the context of NG TOEFL.* Unpublished doctoral dissertation, University of Illinois at Urbana–Champaign, Champaign, IL.

Jenkins, J. G. (1946). Validity for what? *Journal of Consulting Psychology, 10,* 93–98.

Johnson, D. R., & Creech, J. C. (1983). Ordinal measures in multiple indicator models: A simulation study of categorization error. *American Sociological Review, 48,* 398–407.

Johanson, G. A., & Brooks, G. P. (2010). Initial scale development: Sample size for pilot studies. *Educational and Psychological Measurement, 70,* 394–400.

Jöreskog, K., & Sörbom, D. (2006). *LISREL 8.80 for Windows [Computer Software].* Lincolnwood, IL: Scientific Software International.

Junker, B. W., & Sijtsma, K. (2001). Cognitive assessment models with few assumptions, and connections with nonparametric item response theory. *Applied Psychological Measurement, 25,* 258–272.

Kahl, S. R., Crockett, T. J., DePascale, C. A., & Rindfleisch, S. L. (1994, June). *Using actual student work to determine cutscores for proficiency levels: New methods for new tests.* Paper presented at the National Conference on Large-Scale Assessment, Albuquerque, NM.

Kaiser, H. F. (1958). The varimax criterion for analytic rotation in factor analysis. *Psychometrika, 23,* 187–200.

Kaiser, H. F. (1960). The application of electronic computers to factor analysis. *Educational and Psychological Measurement, 20,* 141–151.

Kaiser, H. F. (1974). An index of factorial simplicity. *Psychometrika, 39,* 31–36.

Kamata, A., & Bauer, D. J. (2008) A note on the relation between factor analytic and item response theory models. *Structural Equation Modeling: A Multidisciplinary Journal, 15,* 136–153.

Kane, M. T. (1992). An argument-based approach to validity. *Psychological Bulletin, 112,* 527–535.

Kane, M. T. (2001). So much remains the same: Conception and status of validation in standard setting methods. In G. J. Cizek (Ed.), *Setting performance standards: Concepts, methods, and perspectives* (pp. 53–88). Mahwah, NJ: Erlbaum.

Kane, M. T. (2013). Validating the interpretations and uses of test scores. *Journal of Educational Measurement, 50,* 1–73.

Kaplan, D. (1990) Evaluating and modifying covariance structure models: A review and recommendation. *Multivariate Behavioral Research, 25*(2), 137–155.

Kaplan, D., & Wenger, R. N. (1993). Asymptotic independence and separability in covariance structure models: Implications for specification error, power, and model modification. *Multivariate Behavioral Research, 28*(4), 467–482.

Kaplan, R. M., & Sarcuzzo, D. P. (2001). *Psychological testing: Principles, applications, and issues.* Belmont, CA: Wadsworth.

Karantonis, A., & Sireci, S. G. (2006). The Bookmark standard setting method: A literature review. *Educational Measurement: Issues and Practice, 25*(1), 4–12.

Kelley, T. L. (1927). *Interpretation of educational measurements.* Yonkers-on-Hudson, NY: World Book.

Kelley, T. L. (1939). Selection of upper and lower groups for the validation of test items. *Journal of Educational Psychology, 30,* 17–24.

Kim, S.-H., & Cohen, A. S. (2007, July). *A brief history of testing in the ancient world and its implications today.* Paper presented at the International Meeting of the Psychometric Society, Tokyo, Japan.

Kingston, N. M., & Tiemann, G. C. (2012). Setting performance standards on complex assessments: The Body of Work methods. In G. J. Cizek (Ed.), *Setting performance standards: Foundations, methods, and innovations* (2nd ed., pp. 201–223). New York: Routledge.

Kline, R. B. (2011). *Principles and practice of structural equation modeling* (3rd ed.). New York: Guilford Press.

Knowles, E. S. (1988). Item context effects on personality scales: Measuring changes the measure. *Journal of Personality and Social Psychology, 55*, 312–320.

Kolen, M. J., & Brennan, R. L. (2014). *Test equating, scaling, and linking* (3rd ed.). New York: Springer.

Komaroff, E. (1997). Effect of simultaneous violations of essential τ-equivalence and uncorrelated error on coefficient α. *Applied Psychological Measurement, 21*(4), 337–348.

Kormorita, S. S., & Graham, W. K. (1965). Number of scale points and the reliability of scales. *Educational and Psychological Measurement, 25*, 987–995.

Krathwohl, D. R., Bloom, B. S., & Masia, B. (1964). *Taxonomy of educational objectives: Handbook II. The affective domain.* New York: McKay.

Krosnick, J. (1991). Response strategies for coping with the cognitive demands of attitude measures in surveys. *Applied Cognitive Psychology, 5*, 213–236.

Krosnick, J. A., & Berent, M. K. (1993). Comparison of party identification and policy preferences: The impact of survey question format. *American Journal of Political Science, 37*(3), 941–964.

Krosnick, J. A., Narayan, S., & Smith, W. R. (1996). Satisficing in surveys: Initial evidence. *New Directions for Evaluation, 70*, 29–44.

Küder, G. F., & Richardson, M. W. (1937). The theory of the estimation of test reliability. *Psychometrika, 2*, 151–160.

Kunina-Habenicht, O., Rupp, A. A., & Wilhelm, O. (2009). A practical illustration of multidimensional diagnostic skills profiling: Comparing results from confirmatory factor analysis and diagnostic classification models. *Studies in Educational Evaluation, 35*(2), 64–70.

Kunina-Habenicht, O., Rupp, A. A., & Wilhem, O. (2012). The impact of model misspecification on parameter estimation and item-fit assessment in log-linear diagnostic classification models. *Journal of Educational Measurement, 49*, 59–81.

Lai, J. (1994). Differential predictive power of the positively versus the negatively worded items of the Life Orientation Test. *Psychological Reports, 75*, 1507–1515.

Lane, K. A., Banaji, M. R., Nosek, B. A., & Greenwald, A. G. (2007). Understanding and using the Implicit Association Test: IV: What we know (so far) about the method. In B. Wittenbrink & N. Schwarz (Eds.), *Implicit measures of attitudes* (pp. 59–102). New York: Guilford Press.

Langer, G. (1989). Polling on prejudice: Questionable questions. *Public Opinion, 12*, 18–19.

Larry P. Riles, 495 F. Supp. 926 (N.D. Cal. 1979, decision on merits), *aff'd* No. 80-427 (9th Cir. Jan. 23, 1984), No. C-71-2270 R.F.P. (September 25, 1986, order modifying judgment).

Lazarsfeld, P. F., & Henry, N. W. (1968). *Latent structure analysis.* Boston: Houghton Mifflin.

LeBreton, J. M., & Senter, J. L. (2008). Answers to 20 questions about interrater reliability and interrater agreement. *Organizational Research Methods, 11*, 815–852.

Lee, Y.-S., Park, Y. S., & Taylon, D. (2011). A cognitive diagnostic modeling of attribute mastery in Massachusetts, Minnesota, and the U.S. national sample using the TIMSS 2007. *International Journal of Testing, 11*(2), 144–177.

Leighton, J. (2004). Avoiding misconception, misuse, and missed opportunities: The collection of verbal reports in educational achievement testing. *Educational Measurement: Issues and Practice, 23*(4), 6–15.

Leighton, J. P., & Gierl, M. J. (Eds.) (2007a). *Cognitive diagnostic assessment for education: Theory and practices.* New York: Cambridge University Press.

Leighton, J. P., & Gierl, M. J. (2007b). Why cognitive diagnostic assessment? In J. P. Leighton & M. J. Gierl (Eds.), *Cognitive diagnostic assessment for education: Theory and applications* (pp. 242–274). Cambridge, UK: Cambridge University Press.

Leighton, J. P., Gierl, M. J., & Hunka, S. M. (2004). The attribute hierarchy model for cognitive assessment: a variation on Tatsuoka's rule-space approach. *Journal of Educational Measurement, 41*, 205–237.

Lewis, D. M., Mitzel, H. C., Mercado, R. L., & Schulz, E. M. (2012). The Bookmark standard setting procedure. In G. J. Cizek (Ed.), *Setting performance standards: Foundations, methods, and innovations* (2nd ed., pp. 225–253). New York: Routledge.

Lewis, D. M., Mitzel, H. C., & Green, D. R. (1996, June). *Standard setting: A bookmark approach.* Symposium presented at the Council of Chief State School Officers National Conference on Large-Scale Assessment, Phoenix, AZ.

Light, R. L. (1971). Measures of response agreement for qualitative data: Some generalizations and alternatives. *Psychological Bulletin, 76*, 365–377.

Likert, R. (1932). A technique for the measurement of attitudes. *Archives of Psychology, 22* (140), 55.

Lindsay, B., Clogg, C.C., & Grego, J. (1991). Semiparametric estimation in the Rasch model and related exponential response models, including a simple latent class model for item analysis. *Journal of the American Statistical Association, 86*, 96–107.

Linn, R., L., Baker, E. L., & Dunbar, S. B. (1991). Complex, performance-based assessment: Expectations and validation criteria. *Educational Researcher, 20*(8), 15–21.

Linn, R. L., & Gronlund, N. E. (2000). *Measurement and assessment in teaching* (8th ed.). Upper Saddle River, NJ: Merrill.

Liu, J., Xu, G., & Ying, Z. (2012). Data-driven learning of Q-matrix. *Applied Psychological Measurement, 36*, 548–564.

Lissitz, R. W., & Green, S. B. (1975). Effect of the number of scale points on reliability: A Monte Carlo approach. *Journal of Applied Psychology, 60*, 10.

Lissitz, R. W., & Samuelsen, K. (2007). A suggested change in terminology and emphasis regarding validity and education. *Educational Researcher, 36*, 437–448.

Livingston, S. A. (2014). *Equating test scores (without IRT)* (2nd ed.). Princeton, NJ: Educational Testing Service.

Livingston, S. A., & Zieky, M. J. (1982). *Passing scores: A manual for setting standards of performance on educational and occupational tests.* Princeton, NJ: Educational Testing Service.

Loevinger, J. (1954). The attenuation paradox in test theory. *Psychological Bulletin, 31*, 493–504.

Loevinger, J. (1957). Objective tests as instruments of psychological theory. *Psychological Reports, 3*, 635–694.

Lord, F. M. (1953). On the statistical treatment of football numbers. *American Psychologist, 8*, 750–751.

Lord, F. M. (1980). *Applications of item response theory to practical testing problems.* Hillsdale, NJ: Erlbaum.

Lord, F. M., & Novick, M. R. (1968). *Statistical theories of mental test scores, with contributions by Alan Birnbaum.* Reading, MA: Addison-Wesley.

Lorenzo-Seva, U., Timmerman, M. E., & Kiers, H. A. L. (2011). The Hull method for selecting the number of common factors. *Multivariate Behavioral Research, 46*(2), 340–364.

Loyd, B. H., & Hoover, H. D. (1980). Vertical equating using the Rasch Model. *Journal of Educational Measurement, 17*, 179–193.

Luce, R. D., Krantz, D. H., Suppes, P., & Tversky, A. (1990). *Foundations of measurement* (Vol. 3). San Diego, CA: Academic Press.

Luce, R. D., & Tukey, J. W. (1964). Simultaneous conjoint measurement: A new type of fundamental measurement. *Journal of Mathematical Psychology, 1*, 1–27.

MacCallum, R. C. (1986). Specification searches in covariance structure modeling. *Psychological Bulletin, 100*(1), 107–120.

MacCallum, R. C. (1990). The need for alternative measures of fit in covariance structure modeling. *Multivariate Behavioral Research, 25*, 157–162.

MacCallum, R. C. (2009). Factor analysis. In R. E. Millsap & A. Maydeu-Olivares (Eds.), *The Sage handbook of quantitative methods in psychology* (pp. 123–147). Los Angeles: Sage.

MacCallum, R. C., Roznowski, M., & Necowitz, L. B. (1992). Model modifications in covariance structure analysis: The problem of capitalization on chance. *Psychological Bulletin, 111*(3), 490–504.

MacCallum, R. C., Widaman, K. F., Preacher, K. J., & Hong, S. (2001). Sample size in factor analysis: The role of model error. *Multivariate Behavioral Research, 36*, 611–637.

MacCallum, R. C., Widaman, K. F., Zhang, S., & Hong, S. (1999). Sample size in factor analysis. *Psychological Methods, 4*, 84–99.

Macready, G. B., & Dayton, C. M. (1977). The use of probabilistic models in the assessment of mastery. *Journal of Educational Statistics, 2*, 99–120.

Madison, M., & Bradshaw, L. (2015). The effects of Q-matrix design on classification accuracy in the LCDM. *Educational and Psychological Measurement, 75*, 491–511.

Madison, M., Bradshaw. L., & Hollingsworth, W. (2014). Q*Power: A web-based program for designing diagnostic assessments (Version 1.0) [Computer software]. Available from *www.lainebradshaw.com/qpower*.

Mantel, N., & Haenszel, W. (1959). Statistical aspects of the analysis of data from retrospective studies of disease. *Journal of the National Cancer Institute, 22*, 719–748.

Marco, G. L. (1977). Item characteristic curve solutions to three intractable testing problems. *Journal of Educational Measurement, 14*, 139–160.

Maris, E. (1999). Estimating multiple classification latent class models. *Psychometrika, 60*, 523–547.

Markus, K. A. (2014, April). *Problems and pseudo-problems in test validity theory: What is the best way to use the term 'validity'?* Symposium organized by Paul E. Newton, National Council on Measurement in Education, Philadelphia.

Marsh, H. (1986). Negative item bias in ratings scales for preadolescent children: A cognitive-developmental phenomenon. *Developmental Psychology, 22*, 37–49.

Martone, A., & Sireci, S. G. (2009). Evaluating alignment between curriculum, assessment, and instruction. *Review of Educational Research, 79*(4), 1332–1361.

Masters, G. N. (1982). A Rasch model for partial credit scoring. *Psychometrika, 47*, 149–174.

Mattern, K. D., Patterson, B. F., Shaw, E. J., Kobrin, J. L., & Barbuti, S. M. (2008). *Diffferential validity and prediction of the SAT* (College Board Research Report No. 2008-4). New York: The College Board.

McCall, W. A. (1922). *How to measure in education.* New York: Macmillan.

McCall, W. A. (1939). *Measurement.* New York: Macmillan.

McCormick, E. J. (1979). *Job analysis: Methods and applications.* New York: AMACOM Books.

McCormick, E. J. (1983). Job and task analysis. In M. D. Dunnette (Ed.), *Handbook of industrial and organizational psychology* (pp. 651–696). New York: Wiley.

McDonald, R. P. (1999). *Test theory: A unified treatment.* Mahwah, NJ: Erlbaum.

McDonald, R. P., & Ahlawat, K. S. (1974). Difficulty factors in binary data. *British Journal of Mathematical and Statistical Psychology, 27*, 82–99.

McGraw, K. O., & Wong, S. P. (1996). Forming inferences about some intraclass correlation coefficients. *Psychological Methods, 1*, 30–46.

McGrew, K. S., & Woodock, R. W. (2001). *Technical manual: Woodcock-Johnson III.* Itasca, IL: Riverside Publishing.

McHugh, R. K., & Behar, E. (2009). Readability of self-report measures of depression and anxiety. *Journal of Consulting and Clinical Psychology, 77*(6), 1100–1112.

Mehrens, W. A. (1997). The consequences of consequential validity. *Educational Measurement: Issues and Practice, 16*, 16–18.

Mehrens, W. A., & Cizek, G. J. (2012). Standard setting for decision making: Classifications, consequences, and the common good. In G. J. Cizek (Ed.), *Setting performance standards: Foundations, methods, and innovations* (2nd ed., pp. 33–46). New York: Routledge.

Melnick, S., & Gable, R. (1990). The use of negative item stems: A cautionary note. *Educational Research Quarterly, 14*, 31–36.

Messick, S. (1965). Personality measurement and the ethics of assessment. *American Psychologist, 20*, 136–142.

Messick, S. (1975). The standard problem: Meaning and values in measurement and evaluation. *American Psychologist, 30*, 955–966.

Messick, S. (1980). Test validity and the ethics of assessment. *American Psychologist, 35*, 1012–1027.

Messick, S. (1981). Constructs and their vicissitudes in educational and psychological measurement. *Psychological Bulletin, 89*, 575–588.

Messick, S. (1988). The once and future issues of validity: Assessing the meaning and consequences of measurement. In H. Wainer, & H. I. Braun (Eds.), *Test validity* (pp. 33–45). Hillsdale, NJ: Erlbaum.

Messick, S. (1989). Validity. In R. L. Linn (Ed.), *Educational measurement* (3rd ed., pp. 13–103). Washington, DC: American Council on Education.

Messick, S. (1995). Validation of inferences from persons' responses and performances as scientific inquiry into score meaning. *American Psychologist, 50*, 741–749.

Michell, J. (1986). Measurement scales and statistics: A clash of paradigms. *Psychological Bulletin, 100*, 398–407.

Michell, J. (1997). Quantitative science and the definition of *measurement* in psychology. *British Journal of Psychology, 88,* 355–383.

Mislevy, R. J. (1994). Evidence and inference in educational assessment. *Psychometrika, 59,* 439–483.

Mislevy, R. J. (1996). Test theory reconceived. *Journal of Educational Measurement, 33,* 379–416.

Mislevy, R. J., Beaton, A. E., Kaplan, B., & Sheehan, K. M. (1992). Estimating population characteristics from sparse matrix samples of item responses. *Journal of Educational Measurement, 29,* 133–161.

Mislevy, R. J., Steinberg, L. S., & Almond, R. G. (2003). On the structure of educational assessments. *Measurement: Interdisciplinary Research and Perspectives, 1,* 3–62.

Mislevy, R. J., Steinberg, L. S., Breyer, F. J., Almond, R. G., & Johnson, L. (2002). Making sense of data from complex assessment. *Applied Measurement in Education, 15,* 363–389.

Moss, P. A. (1992). Shifting conceptions of validity in educational measurement: Implications for performance assessment. *Review of Educational Research, 62,* 229–258.

Motl, R., Conroy, D., & Horan, P. (2000). The Social Physique Anxiety Scale: An example of the potential consequence of negatively worded items in factorial validity studies. *Journal of Applied Measurement, 1,* 327–345.

Mulaik, S. A. (2010). *Foundations of factor analysis* (2nd ed.). Boca Raton, FL: Taylor & Francis.

Muraki, E. (1992). A generalized partial credit model: Application of an EM algorithm. *Applied Psychological Measurement, 16,* 159–176.

Muthén, B. O., & Kaplan, D. (1985). A comparison of some methodologies for the factor analysis of non-normal Likert variables. *British Journal of Mathematical and Statistical Psychology, 38,* 171–189.

Muthén, B. O., & Muthén, L. K. (1998–2010). *Mplus user's guide.* Los Angeles: Muthén & Muthén.

National Research Council. (2001). *Knowing what students know: The science and design of educational assessment* (Committee on the Foundations of Assessment, J. Pellegrino, N. Chodowsky, & R. Glaser, Eds.). Washington, DC: National Academy Press.

Newton, P. E., & Shaw, S. D. (2013). Standards for talking and thinking about validity. *Psychological Methods, 18,* 301–319.

Nezu, A. M., Ronan, G. F., Meadows, E. A., & McClure, K. S. (Eds.). (2000). *Practitioner's guide to empirically based measures of depression.* New York: Kluwer Academic.

Nichols, P. D. (1994). A framework for developing cognitively diagnostic assessments. *Review of Educational Research, 64,* 575–603.

Nickerson, R. S. (1998). Confirmation bias: A ubiquitous phenomenon in many guises. *Review of General Psychology, 2,* 175.

Nixon, C., Ferster, A., Alagoz, C., & Templin, J. (2012, April). *A multilevel diagnostic model for GKIDS performance ratings.* Poster presented at the annual meeting of the National Council on Measurement in Education, Vancouver, BC: Canada.

Nunnally, J. C. (1978). *Psychometric theory* (2nd ed.). New York: McGraw-Hill.

Nunnally, J. C., & Bernstein, I. H. (1994). *Psychometric theory* (3rd ed.). New York: McGraw-Hill.

O'Connor, B. P. (2000). SPSS and SAS programs for determining the number of components using parallel analysis and Velicer's MAP test. *Behavior Research Methods, Instrumentation, and Computers, 32,* 396–402.

Olsson, U. H., Foss, T., & Troye, S. V. (2003).

Olsson, U. H., Foss, T., Troye, S. V., & Howell, R. D. (2000). The performance of ML, GLS, and WLS estimation in structural equation modeling under conditions of misspecification and nonnormality. *Structural Equation Modeling: A Multidisciplinary Journal, 7,* 557–595.

Olsson, U. H., Troye, S. V., & Howell, R. D. (1999). Theoretic fit and empirical fit: The performance of maximum likelihood versus generalized least squares estimation in structural equation models. *Multivariate Behavioral Research, 34,* 31–58.

O'Neill, K. A., & McPeek, W. M. (1993). Item and test characteristics that are associated with differential item functioning. In P. W. Holland & H. Wainer (Eds.), *Differential item functioning* (pp. 255–276). Hillsdale, NJ: Erlbaum.

Ones, D. S., Viswesvaran, C., & Reiss, A. D. (1996). Role of social desirability in personality testing for personnel selection: The red herring. *Journal of Applied Psychology, 81,* 660–679.

Oosterhof, A. C. (1976). Similarity of various item discrimination indices. *Journal of Educational Measurement, 13,* 145–150.

Orlando, M., & Thissen, D. (2000). Likelihood-based item-fit indices for dichotomous item response theory models. *Applied Psychological Measurement, 24,* 50–64.

Paek, I. (2010). Conservativeness in rejection of the null hypothesis when using the continuity correction in the MH chi-square test in DIF applications. *Applied Psychological Measurement, 34,* 539–548.

Parducci, A. (1965). Category judgment: A range-frequency model. *Psychological Review, 72,* 407–418.

Parents in Action on Special Education v. Joseph P. Hannon, No. 74C 3586 (N.D. Ill.) (1980).

Parks, A. (2010). *Metaphors of hierarchy in mathematics education discourse: The narrow path. Journal of Curriculum Studies, 42,* 79–97.

Paulhus, D. L. (1984). Two-component models of socially desirable responding. *Journal of Personality and Social Psychology, 46*(3), 598–609.

Paulhus, D. L. (1988). *Assessing self deception and impression management in self-reports: The Balanced Inventory of Desirable Responding.* Manual available from the author.

Paulhus, D. L. (1991). *Measurement and control of response bias.* In J. P. Robinson, P. R., Shaver, & L.S. Wrightsman (Eds)., *Measures of personality and social psychological attitudes* (pp. 17–59). San Diego, CA: Academic Press.

Paulhus, D. L. (2002). *Socially desirable responding: The evolution of a construct.* In H. I. Braun, D. N. Jackson, & D. E. Wiley (Eds)., *The role of constructs in psychological and educational measurement* (pp. 49–69). Mahwah, NJ: Erlbaum.

Pedhazur, E. J. (1997). *Multiple regression in behavioral research* (3rd ed.). Fort Worth, TX: Holt, Rinehart & Winston.

Perie, M., Marion, S., Gong, B., & Wurtzel, J. (2007). *The role of interim assessments in a comprehensive assessment system: A policy brief.* Washington, DC: Aspen Institute.

Peterson, C., & Peterson, J. (1976). Linguistic determinants of the difficulty of true–false test items. *Educational and Psychological Measurement, 36,* 161–164.

Pilotte, W., & Gable, R. (1990). The impact of positive and negative item stems on the validity of a computer anxiety scale. *Educational and Psychological Measurement, 50,* 603–610.

Plake, B. S., Impara, J. C., & Fagen, J. J. (1993). Assessment competencies of teachers: A national survey. *Educational Measurement: Issues and Practice, 12*(4), 10–12.

Popham, W. J. (1978). *Criterion-referenced measurement.* Englewood Cliffs, NJ: Prentice-Hall.

Preacher, K. J., & MacCallum, R. C. (2003). Repairing Tom Swift's electric factor analysis machine. *Understanding Statistics, 2,* 13–43.

Primoff, E. S., & Eyde, L. D. (1988). Job element analysis. In S. Gael (Ed.), *The job analysis handbook for business, industry, and government* (Vol. 2, pp. 807–824). New York: Wiley.

Quellmalz, E. S. (1985). Developing reasoning skills. In J. R. Baron & R. Sternberg (Eds.), *Teaching thinking skills: Theory and practice* (pp. 86–105). New York: Freeman.

Rasch, G. (1980). *Probabilistic models for some intelligence and attainment tests* (Exp. ed.). Chicago: University of Chicago Press. (Original work published 1960)

Raven, J. C., Court, J. H., & Raven, J. (1992). *Manual for Raven's Progressive Matrices and vocabulary scale.* San Antonio, TX: Psychological Corporation.

Raykov, T. (1997). Estimation of composite reliability for congeneric measures. *Applied Psychological Measurement, 21*(2), 173–184.

Raykov, T. (2001). Bias of Coefficient α for fixed congeneric measures with correlated errors. *Applied Psychological Measurement, 25*(1), 69–76.

Raykov, T. (2007). Reliability if deleted, not "alpha if deleted": Evaluation of scale reliability following component deletion. *British Journal of Mathematical and Statistical Psychology, 60,* 201–216.

Raykov, T., & Marcoulides, G. A. (2011). *Introduction to psychometric theory.* New York: Routledge.

Raykov, T., & Shrout, P. E. (2002). Reliability of scales with general structure: Point and interval estimation using a structural equation modeling approach. *Structural Equation Modeling, 9*(2), 195–212.

Reckase, M. D. (2009). *Multidimensional item response theory.* New York: Springer.

Reckase, M. D., & Bay, L. (1999, April). *Comparing two methods for collecting test-based judgments.*

Paper presented at the annual meeting of the National Council on Measurement in Education, Montreal, Canada.

Reckase, M. D., & Chen, J. (2012). The role, format, and impact of feedback to standard setting panelists. In G. J. Cizek (Ed.), *Setting performance standards: Foundations, methods, and innovations* (2nd ed., pp. 149–164). New York: Routledge.

Revelle, W., & Zinbarg, R. E. (2009). Coefficients alpha, beta, omega, and the glb: Comments on Sijtsma. *Psychometrika, 74*(1), 145–154.

Reynolds, C. R., & Kamphaus, R. W. (1992 – 2004). *Behavior assessment scale for children* (2nd Ed.). San Antonio, TX: Pearson.

Rhemtulla, M., Brosseau-Liard, P., & Savalei, V. (2012). When can categorical variables be treated as continuous? A comparison of robust continuous and categorical SEM estimation methods under suboptimal conditions. *Psychological Methods, 17*, 354–373.

Rigdon, E. E., & Ferguson, C. E. (1991). The performance of the polychoric correlation coefficient and selected fitting functions in confirmatory factor analysis with ordinal data. *Journal of Marketing Research, 28*, 491–497.

Roberts, R., Lewinsohn, P., & Seeley, J. (1993). A brief measure of loneliness suitable for use with adolescents. *Psychological Reports, 72*, 1379–1391.

Robinson, J. P., Shaver, P. R., & Wrightsman, L. S. (Eds.). (1991). *Measures of personality and social psychological attitudes*. San Diego, CA: Academic Press.

Robinson, J. P., Shaver, P. R., & Wrightsman, L. S. (Eds.). (1999). *Measures of political attitudes*. San Diego, CA: Academic Press.

Rogosa, D. R., Brandt, D., & Zimowski, M. (1982). A growth curve approach to the measurement of change. *Psychological Bulletin, 90*, 726–748.

Rogosa, D. R., & Willett, J. B. (1983). Demonstrating the reliability of a difference score in the measurement of change. *Journal of Educational Measurement, 20*, 335–343.

Rosenberg, M (1989). *Society and the Adolescent Self-Image* (Rev. ed.). Middletown, CT: Wesleyan University Press.

Rozeboom, W. W. (1966). *Foundations of the theory of prediction*. Homewood, IL: Dorsey Press.

Rubin, R. B., Palmgreen, P., & Sypher, H. E. (Eds.) (2009). *Communication research measures: A sourcebook*. New York: Routledge.

Rubin, R. B., Rubin, A. M., Graham, E. E., Perse, E. M., & Seibold, D. R. (2009). *Communication research measures II: A sourcebook*. New York: Routledge.

Rulon, P. J. (1946). On the validity of educational tests. *Harvard Educational Review, 16*, 290–296.

Rupp, A. A. (2007). The answer is in the question: A guide for describing and investigating the conceptual foundations and statistical properties of cognitive psychometric models. *International Journal of Testing, 7*, 95–125.

Rupp, A. A., Levy, R., Dicerbo, K. E., Sweet, S. J., Crawford, A. V., Calico, T., et al, (2012). Putting ECD into practice: The interplay of theory and data in evidence models within a digital learning environment. *Journal of Educational Data Mining, 4*(1), 49–110.

Rupp, A. A., & Templin, J. (2008a). Effects of Q-matrix misspecification on parameter estimates and misclassification rates in the DINA model. *Educational and Psychological Measurement, 68*, 78–98.

Rupp, A. A., & Templin, J. (2008b). Unique characteristics of cognitive diagnosis models: A comprehensive review of the current state-of-the-art. *Measurement: Interdisciplinary Research and Perspectives, 6*, 219–262.

Rupp, A. A., Templin, J., & Henson, R. A. (2010). *Diagnostic measurement: Theory, methods, and applications*. New York: Guilford Press.

Samejima, F. (1969). Estimation of latent ability using a response pattern of graded scores. *Psychometrika Monograph Supplements, 17*.

Santa Ana, O. (1999) "Like an animal I was treated": anti-immigrant metaphor in US public discourse. *Discourse and Society, 10*, 191–224.

Sarason, I. (1984). Stress, anxiety, and cognitive interference: Reactions to tests. *Journal of Personality and Social Psychology, 46*, 929–938.

Sass, D. A. & Schmitt, T. A. (2010). A comparative investigation of rotation criteria within exploratory factor analysis. *Multivariate Behavioral Research, 45*, 73–103.

Satorra, A., & Bentler, P. M. (1988). Scaling corrections for chi-square statistics in covariance structure analysis. *Proceedings of the Business and Economic Statistics Section of the American Statistical Association*, 308–313.

Schaefer, W. D. & Lissitz, R. W. (1987). Measurement training for school personnel: Recommendations and reality. *Journal of Teacher Education, 38*(3), 57–63.

Schmitt, A. P., Holland, P. W., & Dorans, N. J. (1993). Evaluating hypotheses about differential item functioning. In P. W. Holland & H. Wainer (Eds.), *Differential item functioning* (pp. 281–315). Hillsdale, NJ: Erlbaum.

Schmitt, N., & Stults, D. (1985). Factors defined by negatively keyed items: The result of careless respondents? *Applied Psychological Measurement, 9*, 367–373.

Schriesheim, C., & Hill, K. (1981). Controlling acquiescence response bias by item reversals: The effect on questionnaire validity. *Educational and Psychological Measurement, 41*, 1101–1114.

Schuman, H., & Presser, S. (1996). *Questions and answers in attitude surveys: Experiments on question form, wording, and context*. Thousand Oaks, CA: Sage.

Schwarz, G. (1978). Estimating the dimension of a model. *Annals of Statistics, 6*, 461–464.

Schwarz, N. (1990). Judgment in social context: Biases, shortcomings, and the logic of conversation. In M. Zanna (Ed.), *Advances in experimental social psychology* (Vol. 26, pp. 123–162). San Diego, CA: Academic Press.

Schwarz, N., Bless, H., Bohner, G., Harlacher, U., & Kellenbenz, M. (1991). Response scales as frames of reference: The impact of frequency range on diagnostic judgment. *Applied Cognitive Psychology, 5*, 37–50.

Schwarz, N., Hippler, H.-J., Deutsch, B., & Strack, F. (1985). Response scales: Effects of category range on reported behavior and comparative judgments. *Public Opinion Quarterly, 49*, 388–395.

Schwarz, N., Strack, F., Müller, G., & Chassein, B. (1988). The range of response alternatives may determine the meaning of the question: Further evidence of informative functions of response alternatives. *Social Cognition, 6*, 107–117.

Schwarz, N., & Sudman, S. (Eds.). (1996). *Answering questions: Methodology for determining cognitive and communication processes in survey research*. San Francisco: Jossey-Bass.

Shadish, W. R., Cook, T. D., & Campbell, D. T. (2002). *Experimental and quasi-experimental designs for generalized causal inference*. Boston: Houghton Mifflin.

Shavelson, R. J., & Webb, N. M. (1991). *Generalizability theory: A primer*. Newbury Park, CA: Sage.

Shaw, M. E., & Wright, J. M. (1967). *Scales for the Measurement of Attitudes*. New York: McGraw-Hill.

Shepard, L. A. (1993). Evaluating test validity. In L. Darling-Hammond (Ed.), *Review of research in education* (pp. 405–450). Washington, DC: American Educational Research Association.

Shepard, L. A. (1997). The centrality of test use and consequences for test validity. *Educational Measurement: Issues and Practice, 16*(2), 5–24.

Shepard, L. A., Camilli, G., & Williams, D. M. (1984). Accounting for statistical artifacts in item bias research. *Journal of Educational Statistics, 9*, 93–128.

Sherman, M. (1973). Bound to be easier?: The negative prefix and sentence comprehension. *Journal of Verbal Learning and Verbal Behavior, 12*, 73–84.

Sherman, M. (1976). Adjectival negation and the comprehension of multiply negated sentences. *Journal of Verbal Learning and Verbal Behavior, 15*, 143–157.

Shrout, P. E., & Fleiss, J. L. (1979). Intraclass correlations: Uses in assessing rater reliability. *Psychological Bulletin, 86*, 420–428.

Shrout, P. E., & Lane, S. P. (2012). In H. Cooper (Ed.), *APA handbook of research methods in psychology: Vol. 1. Foundations, measures, and psychometrics* (pp. 643–660). Washington, DC: American Psychological Association.

Sijtsma, K. (2009). On the use, the misuse, and the very limited usefulness of Cronbach's alpha. *Psychometrika, 74*(1), 107–120.

Silvia, E. S. M., & MacCallum, R. C. (1988). Some factors affecting the success of specification searches in covariance structure modeling. *Multivariate Behavioral Research, 23*, 297–326.

Sim. J., & Wright, C. C. (2005). The kappa statistic in reliability studies: Use, interpretation, and sample size requirements. *Physical Therapy, 85,* 257–268.

Simon, H. A. (1978). Information processing theory of human problem solving. In W. K. Estes (Ed.), *Human information processing* (5th ed., pp. 271–295). New York: Psychology Press.

Sinharay, S., & Almond, R. G. (2007). Assessing fit of cognitive diagnostic models A case study. *Educational and Psychological Measurement, 67*(2), 239–257.

Sinharay, S., Haberman, S. J., & Punhan, G. (2007). Subscores based on classical test theory: To report or not to report. *Educational Measurement: Issues and Practice, 26*(4), 21–28.

Sireci, S. G. (2009). Packing and unpacking sources of validity evidence: History repeats itself again. In R.W. Lissitz (Ed.), *The concept of validity* (pp.19–37). Charlotte, NC: Information Age.

Sireci, S. G., & Parker, P. (2006). Validity on trial: Psychometric and legal conceptualizations of validity. *Educational Measurement: Issues and Practice, 25,* 27–34.

Sireci, S. G., Thissen, D., & Wainer, H. (1991). On the reliability of testlet-based tests. *Journal of Educational Measurement, 28,* 237–247.

Sivo, S., Fan, X., Witta, E. L., & Willse, J. (2006). The search for "optimal" cutoff properties: Fit index criteria in structural equation modeling. *Journal of Experimental Education, 74*(3), 267–288.

Skrondal, A., & Rabe-Hesketh, S. (2004). *Generalized latent variable modeling: Multilevel, longitudinal, and structural equation models.* Boca Raton, FL: CRC Press.

Snow, R. E., & Lohman, D. F. (1989). *Implications of cognitive psychology for educational measurement.* Washington, DC: American Council on Education.

Sokal, M. M. (1987). Introduction: Psychological testing and historical scholarship — Questions, contrasts, and context. In M. M. Sokal (Ed.), *Psychological testing and American Society, 1890–1930* (pp. 1–20). New Brunswick, NJ: Rutgers University Press.

Spearman, C. (1904). General intelligence, objectively determined and measured. *American Journal of Psychology, 15,* 201–293.

Spearman, C. (1927). *The abilities of man.* New York: Macmillan.

Spielberger, C. D. (1977–1980). *Test Anxiety Inventory.* Menlo Park, CA: Mind Garden.

Steiger, J. H. (1990). Structural model evaluation and modification: An interval estimation approach. *Multivariate Behavioral Research, 25,* 173–180.

Stemler, S. E. (2004). A comparison of consensus, consistency, and measurement approaches to estimating interrater reliability. *Practical Assessment, Research and Evaluation, 9*(4).

Stevens, S. S. (1946). On the theory of scales of measurement. *Science, 103,* 677–680.

Stocking, M. L., & Lord, F. M. (1983). Developing a common metric in item response theory. *Applied Psychological Measurement, 7,* 201–210.

Stoel, R. D., Garre, F. G., Dolan, C., & van den Wittenboer, G. (2006). On the likelihood ratio test in structural equation modeling when parameters are subject to boundary constraints. *Psychological Methods, 4,* 439–455.

Stone, C. A. (1992). Recovery of marginal maximum likelihood estimates in the two-parameter logistic response model: An evaluation of MULTILOG. *Applied Psychological Measurement, 16,* 1–16.

Stout, W. (2005). DIMTEST (Version 2.0) [Computer software]. Champaign, IL: William Stout Institute for Measurement. Available at *http://psychometrictools.measuredprogress.org/home.*

Strack, F., & Schwarz, N. (1992). Communicative influences in standardized questionnaire situations. In K. Fiedler & G. Semin (Eds.), *Language, interaction and social cognition* (pp. 173–193). Thousand Oaks, CA: Sage.

Sudman, S., Bradburn, N., & Schwarz, N. (1996). *Thinking about answers: The application of cognitive processes to survey methodology.* San Francisco: Jossey-Bass.

Sweeney, K. P., & Ferdous, A. A. (2007, April). *Variations on the "Body of Work" standard setting method.* Paper presented at the annual meeting of the American Educational Research Association, Chicago, IL.

Tatsuoka, K. K. (1983). Rule space: An approach for dealing with misconceptions based on item response theory. *Journal of Educational Measurement, 20,* 345–354.

Tatsuoka, K. K. (1990). Toward an integration of item-response theory and cognitive error diagnosis. In N. Frederiksen, R. Glaser, A. Lesgold, & M. Safto (Eds.), *Monitoring skills and knowledge acquisition* (pp. 453–488). Hillsdale, NJ: Erlbaum.

Templin, J. (2004). *Generalized linear mixed proficiency models.* Unpublished doctoral dissertation, University of Illinois at Urbana–Champaign, Champaign, IL.

Templin, J. (2006). *CDM user's guide.* Unpublished manuscript.

Templin, J. (2009, July). *On the origin of species: The evolution of diagnostic modeling within the psychometric taxonomy.* State-of-the-art talk presented at the annual meeting of the Psychometric Society, Cambridge, UK.

Templin, J., & Bradshaw, L. (2013). Measuring the reliability of diagnostic classification model examinee estimates. *Journal of Classification, 30*(2), 251–275.

Templin, J., & Bradshaw, L. (2014). Hierarchical diagnostic classification models: A family of models for estimating and testing attribute hierarchies. *Psychometrika, 79,* 317–339.

Templin, J., Bradshaw, L., & Paek, P. (2016). A comprehensive framework for integrating innovative psychometric methodology into educational research. In A. Izsák, J. Remillard, & J. Templin, (Eds.), *Psychometric methods in mathematics education: Opportunities, challenges, and interdisciplinary collaborations* (pp. 97–117). Monograph Series No.15. Reston, VA: National Council of Teachers of Mathematics.

Templin, J. & Henson, R. (2006). Measurement of psychological disorders using cognitive diagnosis models. *Psychological Methods, 11,* 287–305.

Templin, J., Henson, R., Templin, S., & Roussos, L. (2008). Robustness of hierarchical modelling of skill association in cognitive diagnosis models. *Applied Psychological Measurement, 32,* 559–574.

Templin, J., & Hoffman, L. (2013). Obtaining diagnostic classification model estimates using Mplus. *Educational Measurement: Issues and Practice, 32,* 37–50.

Templin, J., Rupp, A., Henson, R., Jang, E., & Ahmed, M. (2008, March). *Nominal response diagnostic models.* Paper presented at the annual meeting of the National Council on Measurement in Education, New York.

Thissen, D. (2001). IRTLRDIF v.2.02b: Software for the computation of the statistics involved in item response theory likelihood-ratio tests for differential item functioning [Computer software]. Chapel Hill, NC: LL Thurstone Psychometric Laboratory.

Thissen, D., Steinberg, L., & Wainer, H. (1993). Detection of differential item functioning using the parameters of item response models. In P. W. Holland & H. Wainer (Eds.), *Differential item functioning* (pp. 67–113). Hillsdale, NJ: Erlbaum.

Thompson, B. (1997). The importance of structure coefficients in structural equation modeling confirmatory factor analysis. *Educational and Psychological Measurement, 57,* 5–19.

Thompson, M. S., & Green, S. B. (2013). Evaluating between-group differences in latent variable means. In G. R. Hancock & R. O. Mueller (Eds.), *Structural equation modeling: A second course* (2nd ed., pp. 163–218). Charlotte, NC: Information Age.

Thorndike, R. L. (2005). *Measurement and evaluation in psychology and education* (7th ed.). Upper Saddle River, NJ: Pearson Education.

Thurstone, L. L. (1947). *Multiple factor analysis.* Chicago: University of Chicago Press.

Thurstone, L. L., & Chave, E. J. (1929). *The measurement of attitude.*Chicago: University of Chicago Press.

Timmerman, M. E., & Lorenzo-Seva, U. (2011). Dimensionality assessment of ordered polytomous items with parallel analysis. *Psychological Methods, 16*(2), 209–220.

Tinsley, H. E., & Weiss, D. J. (1975). Interrater reliability and agreement of subjective judgments. *Journal of Counseling Psychology, 22,* 358–376.

Tittle, C. K. (1982). Use of judgmental methods in item bias studies. In R. A. Berk (Ed.), *Handbook for methods for detecting test bias,* (pp. 31–63). Baltimore: Johns Hopkins University Press.

Torangeau, R., & Rasinski, K. A. (1988). Cognitive processes underlying context effects in attitude measurement. *Psychological Bulletin, 103,* 299–314.

Torangeau, R., Rips, L. P., & Rasinski, K. A. (2000). *The psychology of survey response.* Cambridge, UK: Cambridge University Press.

Traub, R., & Rowley, G. (1991). NCME Instructional Module: Understanding reliability. *Educational Measurement: Issues and Practice, 10,* 37–45.

Urbina, S. (2014). *Essentials of psychological testing* (2nd ed.). Hoboken, NJ: Wiley.

van der Linden, W., J., & Adema, J. J. (1998). Simultaneous assembly of multiple test forms. *Journal of Educational Measurement, 35,* 185–198.

Velicer, W. F. (1976). Determining the number of components from the matrix of partial correlations. *Psychometrika, 41,* 321–327.

Velicer, W. F., Eaton, C. A., & Fava, J. L. (2000). Construct explication through factor or component analysis: A review and evaluation of alternative procedures for determining the number of factors or components. In R. D. Goffin & E. Helmes (Eds.), *Problems and solutions in human assessment: Honoring Douglas N. Jackson at seventy* (pp. 41–71). New York: Kluwer Academic/Plenum Press.

Velicer, W. F., & Fava, J. S. (1998). An evaluation of the effects of variable and subject sampling on factor pattern recovery. *Psychological Methods, 3,* 231–251.

Velicer, W. F., & Jackson, D. N. (1990). Component analysis versus common factor analysis: Some issues in selecting an appropriate procedure. *Multivariate Behavioral Research, 25,* 1–28.

von Davier, M. (2005). *A general diagnostic model applied to language testing data* (Research Report No. RR-05-16). Princeton, NJ: Educational Testing Service.

Wainer, H., Bradlow, E. T., & Du, Z. (2000). Testlet response theory: An analog for the 3PL model useful in testlet-based adaptive testing. In W. J. van der Linden & C. A. W. Glas (Eds.), *Computerized adaptive testing: theory and practice* (pp. 245–269). Dordrecht, Netherlands: Kluwer.

Wainer, H., & Wang, C. (2000). Using a new statistical model for testlets to score TOEFL. *Journal of Educational Measurement, 37,* 203–220.

Wang, T., Lee, W., Brennan, R.L., & Kolen, M.J. (2008). A comparison of the frequency estimation and chained equipercentile methods under the common-item non-equivalent groups design. *Applied Psychological Measurement, 33,* 118–132.

Washington v. Davis, 426 U.S. 229 (1976).

Wason, P. C. (1959). The processing of positive and negative information. *Quarterly Journal of Experimental Psychology, 11,* 92–107.

Wason, P. C. (1961). Response to the affirmative and negative binary statements. *British Journal of Psychology, 52,* 133–142.

Webb, E. J., Campbell, D. T., Schwartz, R. D., & Sechrest, L. (1966). *Unobtrusive measures: Nonreactive research in the social sciences.* Chicago: Rand McNally.

West, S. G., Finch, J. F., & Curran, P. J. (1995). Structural equation models with non-normal variables: Problems and remedies. In R. H. Hoyle (Ed.), *Structural equation modeling: Concept, issues and applications* (pp. 56–75). Newbury Park, CA: Sage.

Widaman, K. F. (1993). Common factor analysis versus principal components analysis: Differential bias in representing model parameters? *Multivariate Behavioral Research, 28,* 263–311.

Wilson, M., & Sloane, K. (2000). From principles to practice: An embedded assessment system. *Applied Measurement in Education, 13,* 181–208.

Wise, S. L., & Conoley, J. C. (Eds.). (1993). *Teacher training in measurement and assessment skills.* Lincoln, NE: Buros Institute of Mental Measurements.

Wise, S. L., & DeMars, C. E. (2009). A clarification of the effects of rapid guessing on coefficient α: A note on Attali's "Reliability of speeded number-right multiple-choice tests." *Applied Psychological Measurement, 33,* 488–490.

Woods, C. M. (2006). Careless responding to reverse-worded items: Implications for confirmatory factor analysis. *Journal of Psychopathology and Behavioral Assessment, 28,* 189–194.

Woods, C. M., Cai, L., & Wang, M. (2013). The Langer-improved Wald test for DIF testing with multiple groups: Evaluation and comparison to two-group IRT. *Educational and Psychological Measurement, 73,* 532–547.

Wöthke, W. (1993). Nonpositive definite matrices in structural equation modeling. In Bollen, K. A. & Long, J. S. (Eds.), *Testing structural equation models* (pp. 256–293). Newbury Park, CA: Sage.

Wright, S. (1921). Correlation and causation. *Journal of Agricultural Research, 20*, 557–585.

Wright, S. (1934). The method of path coefficients. *Annals of Mathematical Statistics, 5*, 161–215.

Xu, X., & von Davier, M. (2008). *Fitting the structured general diagnostic model to NAEP data* (RR-08-27). Princeton, NJ: Educational Testing Service.

Yang, Y., Harkness, J., Chin, T.-Y., & Villar, A. (2010). Response styles and culture. In J. Harkness, M. Braun, B. Edwards, T. Johnson, L. Lyberg, P. Mohler, & T. Smith (Eds.), *Survey methods in multinational, multiregional, and multinational contexts* (pp. 203–223). Hoboken, NJ: Wiley.

Yates, A. (1987). *Multivariate exploratory data analysis: A perspective on exploratory factor analysis*. Albany: State University of New York Press.

Yen, W. M. (1984). Effects of local item dependence on the fit and equating performance of the three-parameter logistic model. *Applied Psychological Measurement, 8*, 125–145.

Yen, W. M. (1993). Scaling performance assessments: Strategies for managing local item dependence. *Journal of Educational Measurement, 30*, 187–213.

Young, J. W. (2001). *Differential validity, differential prediction, and college admission testing: A comprehensive review and analysis* (College Board Research Report No. 2001-6). New York: The College Board.

Yu, C., & Muthén, B. (2002, April). *Evaluation of model fit indices for latent variable models with categorical and continuous outcomes*. Paper presented at the annual meeting of the American Educational Research Association, New Orleans.

Zenisky, A. L., & Hambleton, R. K. (2012). Developing test score reports that work: The process and best practices for effective communication. *Educational Measurement: Issues and Practice, 31*(2), 21–26.

Zieky, M. J., & Livingston, S. A. (1977). *Manual for setting standards on the Basic Skills Assessment Tests*. Princeton, NJ: Educational Testing Service.

Zieky, M. J., & Perie, M. (2006). *A primer on setting cut scores on tests of educational achievement*. Princeton, NJ: Educational Testing Service.

Zimmerman, D. W. (2009). The reliability of difference scores in populations and samples. *Journal of Educational Measurement, 46*, 19–42.

Zimmerman, D. W., Zumbo, B. D., & Lalonde, C. (1993). Coefficient alpha as an estimate of test reliability under violation of two assumptions. *Educational and Psychological Measurement, 53*, 33–49.

Zumbo, B. D. (2009). Validity as contextualized and pragmatic explanation, and its implications for validation practice. In R.W. Lissitz (Ed.), *The concept of validity* (pp. 65–82). Charlotte, NC: Information Age.

Zwick, R. (2012). *A review of ETS differential item functioning assessment procedures: Flagging rules, minimum sample size requirements, and criterion refinement* (ETS Research Report No. 12-08). Princeton, NJ: Educational Testing Service.

Zwick, W. R. & Velicer, W. F. (1986). Comparison of five rules for determining the number of factors to retain. *Psychological Bulletin, 17*, 253–269.

Author Index

Subject Index

Note. *f* or *t* following a page number indicates a figure or a table.

About the Author

Deborah L. Bandalos, PhD, is Professor and Director of the Assessment and Measurement Doctoral Program in the Department of Graduate Psychology at James Madison University, where she teaches courses in exploratory factor analysis, measurement theory, and missing data methodologies. Her research areas include structural equation modeling and the effects of item-wording changes in instrument development. Dr. Bandalos has published articles and book chapters in the areas of structural equation modeling, exploratory factor analysis, and item and scale development. She is an associate editor of *Multivariate Behavioral Research* and a past associate editor of *Structural Equation Modeling*. In addition, Dr. Bandalos serves on the editorial boards of *Psychological Methods and Applied Measurement in Education*, is on the Executive Committee of Division 5 (Quantitative and Qualitative Methods) of the American Psychological Association, and has been elected 2019 president of the Society for Multivariate Experimental Psychology.